THE BLOOD OF KINGS

Dynasty and Ritual in Maya Art

THE BLOOD OF KINGS

Dynasty and Ritual in Maya Art

Linda Schele

Mary Ellen Miller

Photographs by Justin Kerr

GEORGE BRAZILLER, INC., New York
in association with the
KIMBELL ART MUSEUM, Fort Worth

For information, address the publisher:
  George Braziller, Inc.
  60 Madison Avenue
  New York, N.Y. 10010

Library of Congress catalogue number: 86-80193

Schele, Linda.
  The blood of kings.
  Bibliography: p.
  Includes index.
  1. Mayas—Art. 2. Mayas—Social life and customs.
3. Indians of Mexico—Art. 4. Indians of Mexico—
Social life and customs. 5. Indians of Central
America—Art. 6. Indians of Central America—Social
life and customs. I. Miller, Mary Ellen. II. Kerr, Justin.
III. Kimbell Art Museum. IV. Title
F1435.3.A7S34 1986   704.9′097281   86-80193
ISBN 0-8076-1278-2

Reprinted with corrections September, 1986

All photographs © Justin Kerr, 1985 except where noted.
Figures 6, 7, III.3, V.5b, V.6, and Plate 40 © President and Fellows
  of Harvard College, 1985
Plate 66 © Paul Macapia, 1985
Figure IV.3, Plate 72 © National Geographic Society, 1975
Plates 111, 119 © Merle Greene Robertson, 1975
Plates 80, 98, courtesy of the Seattle Art Museum
Plate 91, courtesy of the Field Museum of Natural History, Chicago
Figure 11, courtesy of The Baltimore Museum of Art
Figure VI.6, The Ada Turnbull Hertle Fund, © The Art Institute of Chicago
All drawings by Linda Schele except where noted.

Drawings from the *Corpus of Maya Hieroglyphic Inscriptions* (Peabody Museum Press) reproduced courtesy of the Peabody
Museum of Archaelogy and Ethnology, Harvard University. Figures V.2, V.3; Plates 62a, 63a, 64a, 65a (1977); Figure
VI.7 (1982) © President and Fellows of Harvard College

ISBN: 0-8076-1278-2

Cover illustration: Detail, Yaxchilan Lintel 24,
Plate 62, The British Museum, London.

Printed in Japan

CONTENTS

Dedicated to Gillett G. Griffin

This publication has been aided by a generous grant from InterFirst Bank Fort Worth

This publication was issued in connection with the exhibition *The Blood of Kings: A New Interpretation of Maya Art*, shown at the Kimbell Art Museum, Fort Worth, May 17–August 24, 1986, and The Cleveland Museum of Art, October 8–December 14, 1986. All objects in the exhibition are illustrated here in color, with the exception of Fig. 11. For didactic purposes, several unexhibited works are also illustrated, in Plates 9, 10, 19, 38, 39, 45, 46, 58, 72, 90, 106, 111, 113, 119, 122. Organized by the Kimbell Art Museum, in association with The Cleveland Museum of Art, the exhibition has been made possible, in part, by grants from InterFirst Bank Fort Worth, The Anne Burnett and Charles Tandy Foundation, Fort Worth, and The National Endowment for the Arts, a federal agency. A federal indemnity was provided by the Federal Council on the Arts and Humanities.

FOREWORD

The Blood of Kings: Dynasty and Ritual in Maya Art seeks to establish a social and historical framework for the architecture and objects produced by the ancient Maya. Previously lost to the obscurity of prehistory, these remarkable people have begun to emerge as genuine historical figures—with names, dates, whole lineages, and a series of recorded actions—all thanks to the tremendous progress made since 1960 in deciphering Maya hieroglyphic script. As an orientalist by training with some familiarity with Chinese and Japanese, I can appreciate the awesome challenge of learning to read a language recorded in abstract pictographs. The imagination, reconstructive scholarship, and sheer intellectual tenacity required to crack the code of this language when the culture had no continuous history, and when informants literate in the ancient language were no longer living, is staggering to contemplate.

It is now possible to show the Maya were a real people, who lived, loved, hated, created, possessed and destroyed in a manner characteristic of human beings. A synthesis of new information about the Maya, who have been romanticized for many decades, is made possible through the combined cooperative efforts of scholars in many disciplines—archaeology, anthropology, epigraphy, comparative linguistics and art history. This new picture of the Maya inevitably raises the questions of their origin and place in the history of world culture. Superficial similarities to Asian culture, particularly that of the ancient Chinese, are apparent. For a student of Asian art, it is impossible to overlook a correspondence in important skills and uses of objects—writing, jade carving, stone sculpture in both three-dimensional and stelae form, ceramic productions in vessels and figurines, the use of mirrors—as well as fundamental ideas about the cardinal points and their association with colors, Hell, and even the reliance on ancestors to guide the living. These similarities will, no doubt, continue to inspire diffusionists who argue for an Asian source of native American Precolumbian culture. However, while the ultimate Asian origin of the people who populated the American continent is accepted, the form of Maya civilization, its concerns and its peculiar expressions, are not better understood by comparison to the Chinese. The Maya still must be taken on their own terms and in the context of their time and place in Mesoamerica to be correctly appreciated. Moreover, we will never know the Maya as well as we can know the Chinese of 100 B.C. to A.D. 900 for whom countless volumes of text and considerable material culture remains, but we may be able to know them almost as well as the Egyptians and Assyrians.

The work here of Linda Schele and Mary Ellen Miller and their colleagues has shown us the quality of mind and artistic product that mark the Maya as a great civilization. This recognition of an advanced culture in the Americas necessarily removes Precolumbian art from the historical concept of "primitive" art. Maya art, the lives of these great people, their thoughts, their tremendous powers of imagination and reflection make them, as our authors tell us, equal to the great figures of other civilizations. They were a people who had the social organization and the skills to manipulate their own world. As we continue to look back at them, we may learn why they ultimately failed; in the meantime, our respect and wonderment for all they accomplished grows.

In February 1985, I encountered a Maya ruin for the first time. At Copan in Honduras I stood at the top of Temple 11, the most sacred building there, and experienced the extraordinary thrill of a sacred site—empty, silent, even partially crumbled, yet strongly imbued with the sense of a world in another time that I could not know. That experience, shared by thousands of visitors to ruins in Mexico, Guatemala, Belize and Honduras since the end of the nineteenth century, accounts for the fascination with the Maya. Their spectacular cities of palaces and temples built of hewn blocks of stone are hardly the only attraction: stately sculpture, pottery painted with lively images, beautifully worked jade and shell ornaments, and, most of all, their mysterious hieroglyphic writing are the material remains that speak eloquently of a sophisticated, complex, highly intelligent people.

This volume is published on the occasion of an exhibition by the Kimbell Art Museum in celebration of the Texas Sesquicentennial. The museum has no plans to build a major collection of Precolumbian art and has no professional in this field on its staff. The idea for the show was presented to me by Mr. Dee Smith, a resident of Fort Worth and Maya enthusiast who had attended Professor Linda Schele's Hieroglyphic Workshop in Austin. Intrigued by the idea of an exhibition of the Maya, we invited Linda Schele to Fort Worth to explore the possibility of such an exhibition. Schele and her colleague, Mary Ellen Miller of Yale, assisted as guest curators for the show; they created the exhibition structure of eight themes that explore different aspects of the lives of Kings as portrayed in art and prepared the preliminary list of objects to be borrowed.

For the exhibition, it was decided that objects should be first and foremost of supreme aesthetic quality and historical interest to do justice to the extraordinary artistic legacy of Maya civilization. Secondly, and equally important, there was a concern that objects included in the exhibition come from the public sector. This condition, although viewed as arbitrary by some and insufficiently restrictive by others, excluded from consideration works that might have a future commercial life. In making our selection, we received advice from leading scholars throughout the world. In particular, we relied upon the counsel and good judgment of those pre-eminent authorities who agreed to serve on the Advisory Board for the organization of the exhibition:

Miss Elizabeth Benson, Institute of Andean Studies, Bethesda, Maryland

Dr. Elizabeth Boone, Dumbarton Oaks, Washington, D.C.

Miss Elizabeth Carmichael, Museum of Mankind, The British Museum, London

Professor Michael D. Coe, Department of Anthropology, Yale University

His Excellency Federico Fahsen, Former Ambassador of Guatemala to the United States

Professor David Freidel, Department of Anthropology, Southern Methodist University, Dallas

Professor Beatriz de la Fuente, Instituto de Investigaciones Esteticas, Universidad Nacional Autónoma de México

Mr. Gillett G. Griffin, Curator of Precolumbian and Primitive Collection, The Art Museum, Princeton University

Dr. George Kubler, Professor Emeritus, Department of the History of Art, Yale University

Professor Miguel León-Portilla, Instituto de Investigaciones Historicas,
Universidad Nacional Autónoma de México

Dr. Floyd Lounsbury, Professor Emeritus, Department of Anthropology, Yale University

Mrs. Merle Greene Robertson, Precolumbian Art Research Institute, San Francisco

Dr. George Stuart, National Geographic Society, Washington, D.C.

Dr. Gordon Willey, Professor Emeritus, Department of Anthropology, Harvard University

As a corollary of the exhibition, the Kimbell Art Museum undertook to publish an independent study of the Maya based upon the results of the latest scholarly research. The pioneering approach adopted by Schele and Miller led us away from the traditional format of an exhibition catalogue to a book with a broader purpose. In proposing this idea to the authors, Dr. Edmund P. Pillsbury, Director of the Kimbell, wrote to them as follows:

> I would like to see the publication developed as a book rather than as an exhibition catalogue. The book should include a substantial introduction outlining the previous literature on the subject and placing the new research into a meaningful context for a general audience. Following the introduction there should be eight long chapters, lucidly written, I trust, treating the individual themes of the exhibition. Both introduction and individual chapters could be illustrated with material that is not in the exhibition as well as the pieces that are shown, accompanied by descriptive notes. At the end of the volume there may be a glossary of technical terms, a bibliography, an index, and other relevant material.

As project director and general editor of *The Blood of Kings*, I wish to acknowledge those individuals crucial to the project: the invaluable Karen King, Curatorial Secretary, put the entire text of a four-hundred page manuscript on disk, working singlehandedly through first draft and revisions. She worked, not only under the pressure of time and massive volume, but also with characteristic grace. I am grateful for the advice of Professor Michael Coe of Yale University and Marilyn Ingram, Curator of Education at the Kimbell, who read the entire manuscript and offered many suggestions. I owe special thanks to Pat Loud, Slide Librarian, who undertook the task of reading the galleys; the staff of the museum library who fielded bibliographical questions; Registrar Peggy Buchanan, who coordinated loans and photography; Wendy Gottlieb, who so efficiently handled promotion of the exhibition and book; and Kathleen Schorn who assisted me through numerous Federal Express deadlines.

The glorious color photographs by Justin Kerr, commissioned by the Kimbell Art Museum for this publication, are a tribute to the extraordinary talents of this photographer. I wish to thank him, and his gracious wife and able assistant, Barbara, for their generous assistance to me and to the authors. The choice of Dana Levy to design the book was an ideal one, because the complexity of the text and volume of illustrations required the assurance and enormous talent that he brings to his craft. The challenging task of copyediting the long manuscript was entrusted to Letitia Burns O'Connor of Perpetua Press and her associate Sylvia Tidwell.

I deeply appreciate the efforts of Deputy Director Dr. William B. Jordan who contributed substantially to the negotiation for loans and to the promotion of the book and exhibition. I also wish to express profound thanks to Edmund Pillsbury for his unstinting support of the project. Dr. Pillsbury recognized the great contribution to be made to the advancement of scholarship and fully committed the museum to a high standard in both the exhibition and the book. Without his vision and sympathetic concern, this project could not have been possible. Finally, to Linda and Mary I wish to say thank you for countless hours of work under the heavy pressures of full-time academic schedules, for the use of their drawings and photographs, for their enduring patience through crises, large and small, and for the contribution of an enthusiastic manuscript that brings the ancient Maya to life. Initially entranced by the lively intelligence of these two women, I have also come to admire and respect them for their remarkable strength of character and generosity of spirit.

Emily J. Sano
Kimbell Art Museum

Preface

"Blood was the mortar of ancient Maya life," as the authors of this unique volume assure us. Such a statement, based upon the soundest of scholarship, would have been unthinkable 25 years ago. A virtual revolution has taken place in the last quarter century in our knowledge of the New World's most advanced, sophisticated and subtle civilization, a revolution that reaches its culmination and most definitive statement in *The Blood of Kings*.

This intellectual turn-about has taken place on many fronts, but most especially in epigraphy and iconography. I well remember a day in the year 1959, when the late, great Tatiana Proskouriakoff—seated as usual in the smoking room of Harvard's Peabody Museum (she was a cigarette addict)—took me through what she called "a peculiar patterns of dates," along with associated glyphs, that she had detected on the carved stelae of Piedras Negras. I was astounded at her accomplishment. She had made the greatest single advance in the study of the ancient Maya: the Classic Maya inscriptions had become part of history, as John Lloyd Stephens had foretold in the last century, not just records of the passing of time, or of the movements of the heavenly bodies. So modest and unassuming was "Tania" that she never would have called this the beginning of a revolution, but so it was.

To continue on a personal note, in March of 1956, my wife and I, then both graduate students at Harvard and on our spring vacation, found ourselves guests in a Mérida hotel along with Tania. I had just picked up in a local bookshop a Mexican translation of a work on Maya hieroglyphic writing by a Soviet scholar reputed to have cracked the script, but otherwise unknown to most Mayanists. The author was Yuri Valentinovich Knorosov, a specialist in the comparative study of writing systems. Knorosov had had the audacity to revive the long-discredited "alphabet" written down in the sixteenth century by Bishop Landa, and had gone on to propose phonetic-syllabic readings of various glyphs in the Dresden Codex. I found many of these readings plausible, and I am convinced that Tania—to whom we lent the pamphlet—did, too, although then and subsequently she never committed herself to the Knorosov approach, probably through awe of Eric Thompson, the leading figure in twentieth-century Maya research and until his death a bitter opponent of the Knorosov school.

My bilingual wife eventually translated into English the bulk of Knorosov's work, and David H. Kelley took up the cudgel in defense of his approach. Kelley became the first to recognize the names of rulers spelled completely phonetically in the Maya inscriptions (for instance, Kakupacal, "Fiery Shield," at Chichen Itza), and made notable advances in the dynastic history of Copan and Quirigua. All subsequent research on the subject has confirmed the essential correctness of the hypothesis that the Maya could write everything they wanted to purely phonetically, but never did this in complete form because of the sacredness and prestige of the ideographs or logograms.

In fact, we know that the Maya script bears a close typological resemblance to other mixed logographic-phonetic systems of the world, such as Egyptian and Japanese. This resemblance had not been lost to Knorosov, and it probably was the stimulus behind his discoveries.

The pace of research on the dynastic inscriptions of the Classic Maya increased after 1960 (when Tania's epoch-making paper was published), as younger scholars using the historical approach entered the field. In the 1970s, another element was added to the intellectual ferment. This was iconography, a subject in which the pioneering figure was not Tania, as one might have expected from her long career as an artist, but Eric Thompson. Others may dispute this, but I think that the reasons were personal. I knew and liked and admired both of them. Tania was a dedicated atheist, and would even argue that one should not listen to the B-Minor Mass since it was religious! She consistently denied that the Maya even *had* gods. Thompson was the exact opposite, an enormously devout and conservative—in every sense of the word—Anglican of High Church persuasion. To Eric (later Sir Eric), his beloved Maya were wonderful mainly because they were so imbued with faith and piety. There are passages in his great work, *Maya Hieroglyphic Writing* (a fountainhead of insights into Maya iconography but not into the script), which suggest that he thought of the Classic Maya as Anglicans like himself, chanting antiphonal Psalms in the quiet calm of an Evensong service.

A final ingredient was the input of field archaeology. In his contribution to the Alfred Tozzer festschrift, *The Maya and their Neighbors* (1940), my old teacher Clyde Kluckhohn laid the intellectual mine that eventually destroyed the archaeological section of the Carnegie Institution of Washington, for the previous three decades the leading institution in the Maya area; parenthetically, this critique of Maya research was also the foundation of what was to become the "New Archaeology," the wave of the future. In the post-war years, all archaeological projects focusing on the Maya would have to solve far larger and more anthropologically significant problems than those to which Carnegie had previously been devoted. Among these were questions regarding settlement patterns—where and how did the Maya live, and were the great Maya sites cities or relatively empty "ceremonial centers"?—patterns of trade, and nature of Classic Maya subsistence in the Lowlands. As the reader will find from this volume, it has now been determined that the Maya *did* live in real cities, and that while they carried on milpa or slash-and-burn agriculture, as advocated in the well-known books of Sylvanus Morley and Eric Thompson, there was widespread and highly productive intensive agriculture in the swampy *bajos* that characterize the southern Lowlands.

All of these lines of inquiry came together in the conferences of the 1970s and 1980s that were held at Dumbarton Oaks, Princeton, and Palenque. Those of us who were present at the Primera Mesa Redonda de Palenque, held in December 1973, will never forget that occasion. Linguists, epigraphers, art historians, archaeologists and ethnologists came together in a remarkable collaboration that broke new ground for Maya studies. The *pièce de résistance* of the meeting was when Peter Mathews, Floyd Lounsbury, and Linda Schele worked out before our very eyes the dynastic sequence and architectural history of Palenque, including the long rule of Pacal the Great, the seventh-century king buried in the crypt of the Temple of the Inscriptions. This was my first meeting with Linda, an artist who had drifted into Palenque one day with her husband David, and who had fallen immediately in love with this beautiful site and with the Classic Maya. There is no doubt in my mind that she has become one of the great Mayanists of all time, combining just those fields of epigraphy and iconography that, to use an academic cliche, represent the "cutting edge" of Maya research.

I must admit that I have been proud of the Yale representation at this and subsequent conferences. It was at Palenque that David Joralemon, for example, first presented his groundbreaking paper of bloodletting rites among the Classic Maya elite; and the much-lamented Jeffrey Miller, who died early in his career, did the same with his extremely important study of the iconography and epigraphy of mirrors, which were manipulated and used by Classic rulers as emblems of their power, and which appear on the bodies of supernatural beings as "god-markings." Certainly the influence of Floyd Lounsbury, now Professor Emeritus at Yale, has been immense, both in his linguistic and epigraphic work (it was he who told us how to read the *mah k'ina* and *ahpo* titles of the Classic kings) and in his researches into Maya calendrics and especially astronomy. The art historian George Kubler, now also emeritus, has trained many new people in the Maya field, not the least of whom is Mary Miller, co-author of this study, whose major work on the paintings of Bonampak is a tour de force of placing art in context.

Somewhat immodestly, I will bring forth my own contribution to the new outlook on this ancient and definitely alien people. In 1971, while organizing an exhibit on Maya writing for the Grolier Club of New York, I had the opportunity to look at a large number of pictorial Maya ceramics, perhaps the largest collection of these that any scholar had been able to examine at one time. It suddenly struck me that there were certain patterns to be discerned here, not only in the scenes and *dramatis personae*, but also in the texts. I began to see imagery clearly related to the Underworld sections of the Popol Vuh, the great Quiche Maya epic written down in its present form after the Spanish Conquest. To make a very long story short, the evidence is now overwhelming that 1) Maya pictorial vessels are basically funerary in iconographic content as well as in function; 2) the myriad gods, divine heroes, beasties and hobgoblins on these ceramics can be related in large part to the Xibalba (Underworld) section of the Popol Vuh, while keeping in mind that the latter transmits to us only a tiny fragment of what must have been an immensely long "Book of the Dead"; and 3) these wonderful ceramics present the largest corpus of Classic Maya iconography available to modern scholarship.

Having said this, what is the picture of the Classic Lowland Maya so vividly presented to us in *The Blood of Kings*? First of all, these were no peaceful theocracies, as claimed by Morley and Thompson, but rival and very aggressive city-states, no one of which ever managed to dominate all of the others. Constant warfare and the taking of prominent captives (and dispatching them after lengthy degradation and torture) were the name of the game. The rulers of these petty states seemed to have dragged around some of the unfortunate victims for years, and they always boasted about them (cf. Yaxchilan's "He of the 20 Captives"). The carnage was probably only occasionally subdued by royal marriages between polities, making the Maya not so different—in this respect only—from the principalities of northern Italy during the Renaissance.

And how do we get to the statement about blood that began this Preface? These rulers were divine, descended from the most ancient of gods. The Maya equated (as we do) lineage with blood, and it was the obligation of these kings and queens to shed their own blood on important ritual occasions, undoubtedly before the assembled nobility and perhaps even in view of an awestruck populace. So significant was this act that the bloodletter, often a stingray spine, was itself deified. The magnificent stone lintels from Yaxchilan included here show the majesty and mystique of this painful ceremony, which must have confirmed the royal legitimacy. Perhaps more private were the rituals surrounding the taking of intoxicating enemas, known largely on polychrome pottery but surprisingly frequent in that medium. Some of the actions of the Maya elite were very strange, indeed.

It was not only their own blood that the kings shed, but also that of high-ranking captives, the most important of whom were themselves rulers of rival states. The sinister role that the ballgame played in this process is made apparent by Linda Schele and Mary Miller: it now seems that captives were forced to play a game in which the dice were loaded, so to speak, with decapitation the inevitable result. The Aztecs have received a very bad press for their penchant for human sacrifice, but they certainly never inflicted upon their victims the torture and mutilation that were characteristic of Maya sacrifice.

Since we now can actually read most of the Classic Maya texts, we are in a position to say something about the meaning of what we see in Maya architecture and sculpture. As the authors say, Maya buildings, beginning in the Late Preclassic, were virtual billboards, replete with stucco and stone reliefs proclaiming the oneness of the ruling elite with the gods. The stelae, lintels and panels celebrate major events in the lives of the dynasts and their predecessors (even mythological ones, as in the case of Palenque). In the close marriage of picture and text, they remind one of the reliefs of ancient Egypt, in which pharaohs smite enemies, take captives, and celebrate jubilees. As with Egypt, the Maya inscriptions are extremely parsimonious in what they say: these are the concerns of the royal persona, not of the populace as a whole.

A deep concern with death and the Underworld pervades Maya art and architecture. Ever since the epoch-making discovery of Pacal's tomb, it has become increasingly clear that most Classic temple-pyramids were built as the last resting-places of deceased kings. Here the great paradigm for the rulers was the myth of the Hero Twins, preserved for us in the Popol Vuh, which must have played a role among the Classic Maya that the *Iliad* and *Odyssey* did for the ancient Greeks. The myth states that the Twins, unlike their father (the Maize God) and uncle, were not slain by the horrible denizens of Xibalba, the Underworld, but defeated them and thus overcame death itself, rising up to become heavenly bodies.

The elite caste which ruled the Maya masses must have identified themselves with these marvelous heroes: they would never really die like ordinary mortals. Interred inside their mausoleum-pyramids, they would continue to be worshipped as divine ancestors by their descendants, nourished with the blood of their own royal lineages.

Although we can now understand much of the thousand years of art so beautifully illustrated here, there is much yet to learn. The discovery of a single bark-paper book of Classic date, or even better, ten or twenty of them, would probably change all our thinking about these strange people. We would certainly get a better idea of the role played by the scribes, who may have fulfilled many of the functions one attributes to priests in the outdated model of a "theocratic" Maya society. But, as this book exemplifies, we have come a very long way in the past quarter century in arriving at the ultimate meaning of Maya art.

MICHAEL D. COE
Yale University

ACKNOWLEDGMENTS

THIS BOOK HAS BEEN WRITTEN WITH THE HELP AND SUPPORT of many individuals, but most of all, we wish to thank Emily Sano, Assistant Director for Programs and Academic Services and the Curator of Asian Art at the Kimbell Art Museum, who read every word of the book many times and thoughtfully commented on both details and ideas in the manuscript. Through Emily's patient editing, the manuscript took shape, and without her drive, energy and encouragement, this book could not have been written.

It has been a pleasure for us to collaborate with Justin and Barbara Kerr, who took the photographs for this volume. Their images have shaped this book, and at times their insights have also helped us shape our ideas. In addition to the Kerr photographs, this book is heavily illustrated with Linda's drawings. Many were drawn from photographs, and some were redrawn from other sketches and drawings, but still others were made from the original object. We thank Ian Graham at Harvard's Peabody Museum for having made many of his drawings available to us, not only now, but throughout the years. Barbara Fash provided many drawings of Copan materials. In New York, Anna Roosevelt, formerly Curator of South and Middle American Archaeology at the Museum of the American Indian, Heye Foundation, and Gordon Eckholm, Curator Emeritus, Department of Anthropology, the American Museum of Natural History, made it possible for Linda to handle and draw complicated objects. Virginia Crawford offered assistance at The Cleveland Museum of Art, as did Yvonne Schumann of the Merseyside County Museums, Liverpool. Elizabeth Carmichael, Assistant Keeper, The Musuem of Mankind, facilitated the documentation at The British Museum, and Ted J. J. Leyenaar, Deputy Director and Curator, Latin American Department at the Rijksmuseum voor Volkenkunde, assisted in Leiden. Ricardo Agurcia, Director, Instituto Hondureño de Antropología e Historia in Tegucigalpa, supported our work at Copan, and his enthusiasm for this project has been especially gratifying.

Many other people have generously shared their ideas with us. Dee Smith was the catalyst in initiating the project, and Beverly and Gordon Smith graciously opened their home to us during the planning stages of our work. At critical moments, George and Gene Stuart offered moral support. George, in particular, understood the difficulties of such an undertaking and provided photographs, encouragement, and friendship. Milbry Polk shared her time and home with us as well. When we were launching this project, Betty Benson gave us sound advice.

Michael Coe read the entire book in draft and made many helpful suggestions. William Fash and David Freidel also read much of the manuscript and offered useful comments. David Stuart, Stephen Houston, and Karl Taube have kindly shared their unpublished work with us.

Part of the excitement of writing this book was the fun of working together. Dashing from one computer to another and exchanging ideas as fast as we could, we wrote the Introduction together in Austin. Later, at our respective homes, we learned from one another as Linda wrote the chapters on themes 1, 2, 4, 7 and 8, as well as the sections on the hieroglyphic writing system and the Maya calendar, and Mary wrote the chapters on themes 3, 5 and 6. Throughout, our generous husbands have been bulwarks, and when called upon, they repaired computers and retooled grammar. We thank them most heartily.

LINDA SCHELE
Austin

MARY MILLER
New Haven
February 1986

NOTE TO THE READER

The pronunciation of Maya words in *The Blood of Kings* presents a problem to English speakers unfamiliar with Spanish and the conventions used to record the consonants particular to Mayan languages. Mayan languages were first transcribed into a Latin alphabet by early Spanish friars, who developed special orthographies, many of them confusing to the modern reader, to record the sounds of Maya words. The vowels follow the conventions of Spanish, as follows:

a is like the *a* in "far" or "father"
e is like the *e* in "prey" or "obey"
i is like the double *e* in "see"
o is like the *o* in "hello" or "open"
u is like the double *o* in "zoo."

When *u* precedes *a, e, i,* or *o* or falls at the end of a word, it is pronounced like the English *w*, as in *ahau*, pronounced "a-haw." Each vowel in a word is an independent syllable, except for the *u* pronounced as w. El Baul is "el ba-ool."

Mayan languages have a number of consonants that do not exist in Spanish—or, for that matter, in English. For these, the Spanish friars developed a number of conventions still used today. The sound like the English *sh* was written with an *x*. The word *yax* is pronounced "yash," and Xcalumkin is "sh-ka-loom-kin." The letter *c* is always pronounced like a *k*, regardless of the vowel it preceeds. The word *cimi* is pronounced "kee-mee," and *ceh* is pronounced "kay."

Mayan languages also distinguish between consonants in plain form and those in glottalized form. Glottalized consonants are pronounced with the glottis, or "voice box," closed. Since we do not use glottalized consonants, they are hard for English speakers to hear and to pronounce; they sound like a very hard form of the regular consonant. The glottalized *k* is written with a *k*, and all other such consonants are written with an apostrophe following the letter, as in *t'*. To Maya speakers, the words *tul*, "person," and *t'ul*, "rabbit," are as different as *very* and *berry* sound to English speakers.

One other consonant in both its plain and glottalized form is difficult for English speakers, because neither form exists in English. Written as *tz* or sometimes as *dz,* the sound is somewhat like an English *z* but is pronounced with the blade of the tongue against the ridge behind the teeth. Its glottalized form is written *tz'*, as in the word for "bat," *zotz'* or in the day name Etz'nab.

The use of the Spanish letter *j* also causes problems for English speakers—even for professional archaeologists. The *h* sound in Mayan languages is very close to the *h* in English, as in "hat," or the *h* in final position, like the English exclamation "ahah." Because the Spanish *h* is very weak, many place names are spelled with *j* to approximate the Maya sound more closely. English speakers often make the mistake of pronouncing this Spanish *j* as if it were the English *j* in "jet." The place name Abaj Takalik is pronounced "a-bah ta-ka-lik," and Kaminaljuyu is "ka-mee-nal-hoo-yoo." The *j* in Maya names is never pronounced like the English *j*.

The accent in Maya words is almost always placed on the last syllable, as in the following names for rulers of the Palenque dynasty and Maya sites:

Pacal	"pak-kál"
Chan-Bahlum III	"chan bah-lóom"
Kan-Xul	"kan shóol"
Chaacal	"cha-kál"
Uaxactun	"wa-shak-tún"
Xunantunich	"shoo-nan-tun-ích"

We use the adjective Mayan to refer exclusively to the language: the people are the Maya, and the subject of this book is Maya art.

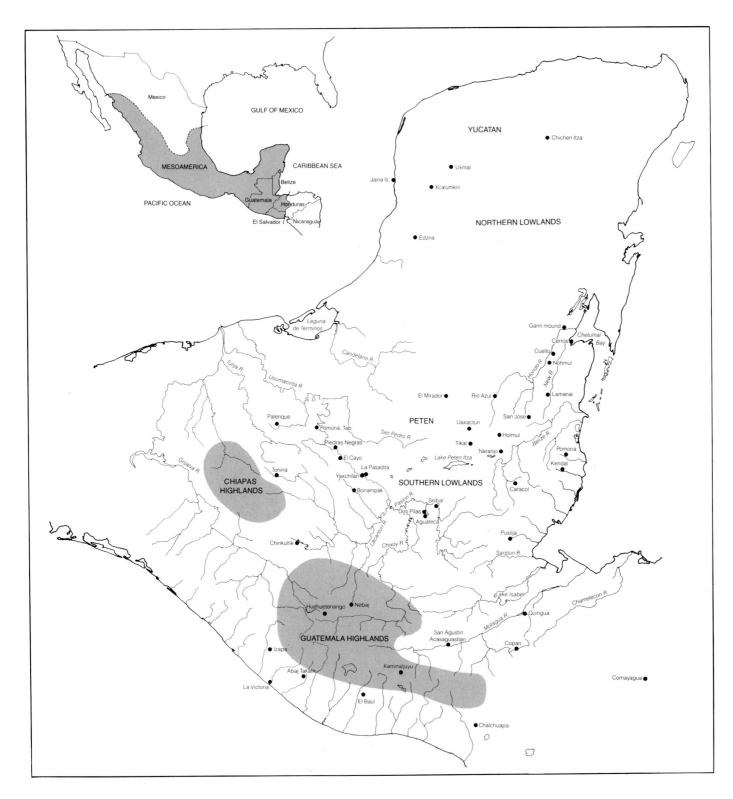

FIGURE 1

INTRODUCTION

PROLOGUE

THE GREAT PROGRAMS OF MAYA ART, INSCRIPTIONS AND ARCHITECTURE known today were commissioned by Maya kings to memorialize themselves and ensure their place in history. They would sometimes declare their actions to be reenactments of cosmic events that had occurred millions of years in the past, and by projecting dates and events forward to our time and beyond, they anticipated that they would be known and remembered for millennia. Yet for about one thousand years after the abandonment of their cities, the art and architecture of the Classic Maya were lost to the jungle, unseen and unknown.

The Maya, builders of one of the most fascinating civilizations in the history of the world, are not just an archaeological race. There are over two million people who still speak one of the more than thirty Mayan languages living today in Mexico, Guatemala, Belize and Honduras. One of the largest groups of native American peoples to survive as a coherent group, the Maya still live in traditional communities as well as in modern, integrated societies. More than just the genetic descendants of the ancient Maya, these people retain a mythology, world view, languages and beliefs that have roots in the Precolumbian civilizations of their ancient forebears. As with all native American peoples, they struggle to retain their traditional mode of living against the pressures and political realities of twentieth-century life.

The ancient Maya lived in an area that modern researchers call Mesoamerica, a term designating a cultural and historical context as well as a geographical region.[1] The societies identified as Mesoamerican share a number of features: the 260-day calendar; various elements of religion, including parts of a deity pantheon, self-inflicted bloodletting and captive sacrifice; cultivation of maize; the use of cacao as money and as a beverage; folding-screen books made from either fig-bark paper or deerskin; a ballgame played in specially built courts; pyramidal architecture; and the sense of a common cultural origin—in much the same sense that most Europeans think of themselves as the natural inheritors of Greek and Roman civilization.

The ancient Maya lived in the eastern third of Mesoamerica (Fig. 1). Maya lands, both ancient and modern, occupy the Yucatan Peninsula, whose topography varies from volcanic mountains, called the Highlands, in the south, to a porous limestone shelf, called the Lowlands, in the central and northern regions. The Lowlands extend from Copan, Honduras, in the south to northern Yucatan. The east-west axis includes Belize, most of modern Guatemala, and the Mexican state of Tabasco, where Comalcalco, the westernmost Classic-period Maya center is located. Few sites of the Classic period are located at any significant altitude. Among the highest are Caracol, Belize; Chinkultik, Chiapas; and Copan, Honduras, all of which are under 3,000 feet. The Puuc Hills, in the states of Campeche and Yucatan, the Maya Mountains of Belize and the Chiapas Mountains (as opposed to the Sierra Madre of Chiapas) are the only topographic relief completely encompassed by the Classic Maya realm. Geologically, most of the region has an undulating karst foundation, making limestone and flint the most readily available stone. Fine kaolin clays also abound, particularly along sources of water.

The limestone underlying the Lowlands creates a distinct topography and special conditions. In the southern Lowlands, where rainfall can be as high as 160 inches a year, water drains toward the Gulf and the Caribbean in great river systems. As the yearly rainfall diminishes toward the north, surface water disappears. Water is found only where the stone formations above underground rivers collapse to form water holes, called cenotes, or artificial water cisterns, called *chultuns*, that were built by the ancient Maya to collect rainwater. River systems were vital to Lowland civilization as the transport system that moved people and materials. Of the rivers that drain the southern Lowlands, the largest are the Usumacinta, with its tributaries the Lacantun, the Chixoy and the Pasión; the Grijalva River drains the Chiapas Highlands. In the eastern regions, the Rio Hondo, the New River, the Belize River and the Sarstoon empty into the Bay of Chetumal and the Caribbean. In the south, the Motagua, which runs through the Guatemalan Highlands and the Chamelecon, in the Honduran Highlands, both drain into the Caribbean.

The southern Lowlands are covered by a rain forest whose average height is around 150 feet; it is broken by savannas and swamps, or *bajos*. The drier forest of the northern Lowlands characteristically has smaller, often thorny, trees. The Highlands, defined as lands above 1,000 feet (305 meters), are covered by pine forests. The Highlands are cooler and drier than the hot and humid Lowlands, which are, for the most part, only slightly above sea level. Certain resources—obsidian, jade and other precious materials, such as cinnabar and specular hematite—could only be obtained from the volcanic Highlands, and a lively trade in these minerals developed. Maya civilization in ancient, colonial and modern times has always contrasted the societies of the Lowlands to those of the Highlands. This contrast is less apparent today because the Spanish depopulated the central Lowlands in the seventeenth and eighteenth centuries in their efforts to bring what they perceived as savages under civil and religious control. Only in the last decades has this process begun to reverse itself, as Tzotzil-, Tzeltal-, and Chol-speaking groups have begun establishing communities in the Lowlands of Chiapas; Kekchi-speaking groups have established similar communities in the Lowlands of Belize and Guatemala.

The tropical forests were rich in animal life, of which the most dangerous species to man were the jaguar, the largest spotted cat in the world; the caiman, an American crocodile with the same appetite as its Old World cousins; the bull shark;[2] and a variety of poisonous snakes, including the rattlesnake, the fer-de-lance, the bushmaster and the coral. Food animals included deer, turkeys, peccaries, tapirs, rabbits and several kinds of large rodents, such as paca and agouti. The upper canopy of the forest was inhabited by spider monkeys, loud-voiced howler monkeys and a variety of brilliantly colored birds, including parrots, macaws, motmots and, in the elevations between the Lowlands and the Highlands, the famous quetzal. Other animals consistently represented in Maya art include foxes, coatimundis, armadillos, water birds, such as the heron and cormorant, owls, harpy eagles and hummingbirds.

In the tropics, the yearly seasons are very different from the strongly contrasting winter and summer seasons of the northern latitudes. February through May (when we think of springtime and renewal) is the dry season, the hottest and most uncomfortable time of the year. The newly cut fields must be burned during this time so that they will be ready for the coming of the rains in late May or early June. Thus, not only is the dry season hot but, even today, the smoke from burning fields makes it a time of dingy, gritty skies, with no rains to wash them clean. With the coming of the rains, the earth and the forest are renewed in a contrast almost as dramatic as the rebirth of spring in the north. The smell of dead animals is washed away from fields and forests; the air is cleansed and cooled; the leaves of plants swell visibly with the water of life. The thunderstorms of summer are followed by a short, two- to three-week dry period in August, and then by the winter rains, the gentle, soaking rains that come with the storms called *nortes*. The rhythms of Maya life are built on the changes from the dry to the wet season, as the success or failure in farming and life itself depends on the timely arrival of the rains.

The principal cultigen was maize, but the Maya grew squash, beans, chili peppers, amaranth, manioc and cacao. One of the main methods of farming involved clearing the forest and burning the debris to create fields, called milpas, that were planted just before the rainy season began. Such slash-and-burn agriculture is inefficient, since any single field cannot be planted for more than two or three years before it is exhausted, and from very early times, the Maya developed intensive farming methods. Land on slopes or near gullies was often terraced, but raised-field farming, the most widespread and effective method, was practiced along slow-moving rivers and in swampy areas. Canals were cut between fields and their bottom matter placed on the prepared fields to enrich the soil. Periodically, when the canals were dredged, the bottom detritus was again used to fertilize the fields. The attributes associated with this type of farming—the chest-deep water, the water-lilies that grew in the canals, the fish that lived in them, the birds that ate both plant and fish and the caiman that ate everything—came to symbolize abúndance and the bounty of the earth.[3] Added to the yields from milpa and raised-field production were domestic gardens and husbandry of the forest. The fruit imagery incorporated into Maya art, as on the sides of Pacal's sarchophagus at Palenque, indicates that they either raised or harvested from the forest quantities of avocados, chico zapote fruit, guanavana, nancé, cacao and possibly also ramon nut or breadfruit. Other important crops included cotton, used for light cloth, and sisal, used for heavy cloth and rope.

Maya history is divided into three great phases, each with several subdivisions (Fig. 2). The Preclassic period, during which civilization emerged in many parts of Mesoamerica, begins at 1500 B.C. and continues until A.D. 200. Its subdivisions are the Early Preclassic (2000–900 B.C.), the Middle Preclassic (900–300 B.C.) and the Late Preclassic (300 B.C.–A.D. 200), the period during which Maya civilization arose. The Classic period (A.D. 200–900), considered to be the golden age of Maya civilization, is divided into two subdivisions, the Early Classic (A.D. 200–600) and the Late Classic (A.D. 600–900). The society of the Classic period collapsed around A.D. 900, which led to the final phase of Precolumbian Maya history—the Postclassic, dated from A.D. 900 to the Conquest of the Maya region by the Spanish in 1541.

For about 150 years, ever since John Lloyd Stephens and Frederick Catherwood made their famous explorations of the Maya realm and brought back romantic drawings of abandoned ruins shrouded by damp rain forests, the Western world has been fas-

THE MAYA IN WORLD HISTORY

The chronologies for Europe and Asia are based on *People and Places of the Past*, general editor, George Stuart (Washington, D.C.: National Geographic Society, 1983).

Asian History	European History	Maya Dynastic History	Cultural History of the Maya	Cultural Periods	Date
	Henry VIII rules England		Conquest of Yucatan	POST CLASSIC	1530
	Voyages of Columbus				1500
Ming Dynasty rules China / Mongol conquest of northern China	Beginnings of the Renaissance / Black Death in Europe				1400
Marco Polo's journey					1300
Khmer Empire in Southeast Asia	Mongol invasions / King John and the Magna Carta				1200
First book with moveable type in China / Song dynasty in China	European crusades begin / Norman conquest of England				1100
					1000
Gun powder used in China for fireworks		Last Classic monument erected at Tonina / Kakupacal reigns at Chichen Itza / Last ruler at Tikal / Period-ending monuments at Seibal	Last recorded date in Classic system / Temple A-1 at Seibal / Cacaxtla paintings / Last date at Palenque, Copan		900
Heian-Kyo becomes Japanese capitol	Charlemagne accedes / Viking raids in Britain	6-Cimi-Pacal rules at Palenque / war at Yaxchilan / Chan-Muan of Bonampak marries woman of Yaxchilan / Bird Jaguar accedes at Yaxchilan / Yax-Pac accedes at Copan / 18-Rabbit of Copan captured /Dos Pilas tries to establish a regional state	Bonampak paintings executed / Copan Temple 11 / Yaxchilan Temple 33 / Temples 1 and 2 at Tikal	LATE CLASSIC	800
Imperial capitol established in Nara, Japan		Chan-Bahlum at Palenque accedes 132 days after Pacal's death / Shield Jaguar of Yaxchilan and Ruler A of Tikal begin their reigns / Caracol defeats Naranjo	Group of the Cross at Palenque / Temple of Inscription at Palenque / Copan jade pebble cached		700
Imperial government established in Japan / Tang Dynasty rules China	Muslims conquer Jerusalem / Islam spreads in the Mideast / Legendary King Arthur rules Britain	Smoke Jaguar accedes at Copan / Pacal accedes at Palenque / Series 1 ruler accedes at Piedras Negras		EARLY CLASSIC	600
Buddhism introduced into Japan / Sui Dynasty rules China	Emperor Justinian builds Hagia Sophia in Constantinople	Florescence begins at Caracol / Lintel 12 event at Piedras Negras	Caracol Stela 16		500
Korean scribes hired by Yamato chiefs introduce the Chinese script into Japan	Rome sacked by vandals	Early monuments at Copan and Quirigua / Stormy Sky of Tikal accedes / Earliest dynastic records at Palenque	Rio Azul tombs / Tikal Stela 31		400
Gupta Dynasty rules India	Roman Empire divided / Christianity becomes the official religion of the Roman Empire	Curl Snout of Tikal accedes / Early kings at Yaxchilan / Jaguar Paw rules at Tikal / First Classic-period monument	Interaction with Teotihuacan begins / Kendal tomb / Leiden Plaque / Tikal Stela 29	PROTO CLASSIC	300
	Barbarian invasions of Western Europe begin	First recorded bloodletting rite	Hauberg Stela		200

FIGURE 2

Timeline Chart

Asia / China row:

- Buddhism introduced to China / Silk routes open
- Paper invented in China
- The Great Wall is finished
- Han Dynasty rules China
- Qin Shi Huangdi unifies China
- Metal working and wet-rice agriculture introduced into Japan and Korea
- Buddhism spreads from India
- Warring States in China
- Legendary Emperor Jimmu establishes state in Japan
- Confucius works in China
- Zhou dynasty in China
- Logographic script develops in China
- Shang Dynasty bronzes in China

Mediterranean / Near East row:

- Birth of Jesus
- Roman republic replaced by empire
- Julius Ceasar assassinated
- Rome defeats Carthage
- Alexander conquers the Middle East
- Peloponnesian Wars in Greece
- Parthenon is built in Athens
- Greek city-states
- Roman republic established
- Nebuchadnezzar rules Babylon and destroys Jerusalem
- Carthage founded
- Assurnasirpal rules Assyria
- Homeric epics and the sack of Troy
- King David makes Jerusalem his capital
- Akenanten and Tutankhamen rule Egypt
- First Minoan palace on Crete

Maya / Mesoamerica row:

- First recorded accession
- Writing and the Long Count Calendar spreads throughout Southeastern Mesoamerica
- Major construction of public monuments begins in the Lowlands
- Maya Lowland civilization begins
- Tombs at Copan with Olmec symbols on pottery
- Early writing develops in Oaxaca

Lowland archaeological events row:

- Pyramids of the Sun and Moon at Teotihuacan
- Cerros abandoned
- Abaj Takalik monuments
- El Baul monument
- Kaminaljuyu monuments
- Cerros Structure 5C-2nd built
- Lamanai building constructed
- Tikal and Uaxactun buildings constructed
- Izapan monuments
- El Tigre and Danta built at El Mirador
- Mass sacrifice of 26 victims at Cuello
- Early writing develops in Oaxaca
- La Venta flourishes
- San Lorenzo destroyed
- Olmec civilization flourishes on the Gulf Coast
- First Minoan palace on Crete
- Cuello temple and Swazey ceramics

Periods:

LATE PRECLASSIC	MIDDLE PRECLASSIC	EARLY PRECLASSIC	ARCHAIC

Time scale:

100 — 0 — 100 — 200 — 300 — 400 — 500 — 600 — 700 — 800 — 900 — 1200 — 1500 — 2000

cinated by the beautiful and mysterious art of the ancient Maya. Detached from the context that once gave them meaning, these works were regarded as exotic objects. The hundreds of thousands of visitors to the ruins of Maya cities have gazed at the Mayas' descendants in detached curiosity and have bought their crafts to adorn their homes.

The Classic Maya are now emerging from a dimly perceived archaeological prehistory to become a people with a written history. From 50 B.C. until A.D. 900, the Maya recorded the histories of their kings and captains on stone monuments in a script that until 1960 remained mute and unread. During the last twenty-five years, however, advances by epigraphers and scholars have pierced the mystery of that writing system, thereby providing us a window into a world that heretofore was shrouded by the mists of prehistory. Rather than anonymous priests and unnamed gods, the works depict men and women of power and renown in their own time. From stone monuments that recount their deeds and the source of their power, we reclaim not just the faces of these kings, but more important, a detailed record of their lives, their names, their ancestry and their view of the world around them. The written history of the Americas began in 50 B.C., and from that moment on, the records resound with the names and lives of individuals: Pacal of Palenque, Bird Jaguar of Yaxchilan, Yax-Pac of Copan, among many others. Now these kings and the world they constructed can take their place on the stage of world history beside such counterparts in the Old World as Rameses II, Assurnasirpal and Alexander the Great.

This study is called *The Blood of Kings* for very specific reasons. The word *king* is used instead of the Maya words for their rulers, *mah k'ina* ("great sun lord") or *ahau* ("lord"), because the Maya words have no meaning to English speakers and because the original English meaning of *king* is appropriate to the way these rulers lived. *King* is an Old English title borne by leaders of Anglo-Saxon tribes; it shares its root with the words *kin* and *kinship*, and it originally referred to rulers of petty states, not unlike those that existed among the Classic Maya.[4] There was no Maya emperor, no single Maya king who gained ascendancy over all others. Pacal of Palenque ruled at the same time as Smoke Jaguar of Copan; one hundred years later, Kuk of Palenque and Yax-Pac of Copan reigned simultaneously. We use the word *king* here in the sense that Arthur, not Henry Tudor, was king.

The *Blood* of the title refers directly to several aspects of Maya life and to Maya beliefs about their world and their kings. Blood was the mortar of ancient Maya ritual life. The Maya let blood on every important occasion in the life of the individual and in the life of the community. It was the substance offered by kings and other nobility to seal ceremonial events. Even more important, the purpose of art was to document the bloodlines of Classic Maya kings. Kingship normally passed from father to son: descent and bloodlines dominated the determination of legitimate rule. For this reason, records of parents and ancestors transferring power to their children consume a large part of Maya pictorial imagery and writing. After the birth of an heir, the king performed a blood sacrifice, drawing his own substance as an offering to his ancestors. Human sacrifice, offered to sanctify the installation of a king in office, was in some cases recorded as a vital part of accession imagery. Among the most common events recorded on Maya monuments are war and capture. Although Maya warfare fulfilled several needs, the primary ritual role was to provide the state sacrificial victims, whose blood was then drawn and offered to the gods. At death, Maya kings were placed in richly furnished tombs that often displayed the imagery of the watery Underworld, their walls painted the color of blood or in blood symbols. In the Maya view, none of these behaviors was bizarre or exotic but necessary to sustain the world. To speak of the Maya and their rulers is, therefore, to speak of *The Blood of Kings*.

The title and point of view put forth in this study are revolutionary. The heretofore popular view of the Classic Maya has never taken into account such preoccupations as blood and bloodlines, nor has it emphasized the individual rulers prominent in Maya history. As this new understanding of the Maya has emerged over the past twenty-five years, many people have been repulsed by convincing evidence of human sacrifice and blood offerings and have drawn away from such a tangible or realistic view of the Maya. In Mesoamerican studies, a propensity for gore had always been attributed to the Aztecs. In contrast, the Maya were always assumed to be a superior race, thoroughly removed in time, space and culture from such behavior. In the new view presented here, however, the Maya have fallen from their pedestal; in doing so, they become a part of the community of man, the builders of a civilization that included both the darkest and the most brilliant possibilities of human behavior.

The methodology of this study derives from the union of hieroglyphic decipherment and the interpretation of pictorial imagery, which together allow us to discover patterns inherent in Maya art. Writing loses meaning unless it follows structural rules governing word use and grammar. These patterns are so prevalent in Maya writing that twenty-five years ago, Tatiana Proskouriakoff was able to deduce the meaning of glyphs without determining the Maya words they represented.[5] Maya imagery, like their writing, has inherent patterns that can be "read" like glyphs. These patterns are the primary key to understanding Classic Maya art.

The dates the Maya recorded on many of their monuments make up one of the primary patterns that have been used to construct a history of Maya art. The assumption that the dates are generally contemporary with their images has been confirmed by archaeological data. For some time, early works have been distinguished from late works, even when their meaning remained obscure, and undated works could be ascribed to an appropriate period of manufacture, because of their stylistic similarity to dated monuments. When combined with knowledge of the origin and intent of works of art, chronological information could be used to determine the continuities and changes in style that depended on time and place.

The texts embedded in pictorial scenes or carved on the sides and backs of Maya stelae are our primary sources in working out the meaning of Maya art. Fundamentally, the imagery of Maya art portrays the text in explicit terms. A text can be cleverly configured by a superb artist or perfunctorily inscribed by a less inventive one, but it is always embedded meaningfully, and it is not to be treated lightly—it is never a gloss or an afterthought. The most important verb (or in many cases the sole verb) is illustrated by the picture, although the same verb is rarely illustrated in identical fashion twice. Through these verbs, we may identify the same action as it was recorded at different times and places; by comparing the way in which representations of the actions differ according to time and place, we can come to an understanding of Maya ritual and historical interactions. At Yaxchilan, capture may be shown actively as an ongoing event. At Piedras Negras, it may be recorded only by the display of the victims caught. When a static verbal locution is provided alongside a more diverse pictorial image, different aspects of a single event are revealed. This in turn permits us to understand what the relationship, in terms of programmatic sequence among several monuments, may have been; how the objects associated with the event were used; and how the event functioned in a ritual cycle. Furthermore, the images not only memorialize and illustrate a text but also reflect the historical circumstances elucidated by that text. A war event illustrated and recorded on one monument, for example, may reveal how the artistic style from the site of the defeated reshaped or influenced the artistic tradition of the victors.

The surviving glyphic repertory of Classic-period Maya inscriptions is limited, as is the visual imagery. Certain verbs occur again and again. Accession, bloodletting, success in battle—these are the events celebrated by Maya kings across the Lowlands for one thousand years. Other events, such as birth and burial, are not illustrated, although rituals associated with them may be. Warfare, because of its inherent sequential nature, gave rise to more varied depictions than did any other theme.

Maya writing was recorded in inscriptions on stone and wood used within architecture or in conjunction with it; on jade and shell objects; on pottery; and in folding-screen books made from the bark of the fig tree. Many of these books were placed in tombs but did not survive the destructive humidity of the tropics. Many others were deliberately destroyed by the Spanish as the work of the devil.[6] The four Maya books known today—the Dresden Codex, the Madrid Codex, the Paris Codex and the Grolier Codex[7]—record astronomical and calendric information and were very probably used to time events in the ritual life of the Maya. All four date from the Postclassic period, but there is no doubt that there were many such codices used in the Classic period as well, not only to keep track of ritual but to record fully detailed historical information—the genealogies of kings and noble lineages, as well as tribute and trade exchanges.

The hieroglyphic writing of the Maya was a fully functional writing system capable of recording every nuance of the spoken language. It is composed of a combination of different signs, some representing the value of whole words, others recording the sound of a single syllable (a consonant plus vowel). Information could be conveyed in inscriptions alone; most often, however, a text recording when, what and who is combined with pictorial information that shows action. Text was often not limited to the event pictured but linked the scene depicted to previous events as well. The inscriptions are in many ways the most important cultural remains of the Maya, since their decipherment has produced the names of their kings and precise details of their history. The texts name the actors as priests, gods, kings or military officers; without them, we would not know that a scene depicts accession, why a bloodletting rite took place or the nature of many of the other rituals.

The events recorded in the inscriptions were set in a complex and precise temporal framework. The Maya believed that the world had been created and destroyed at least three times, the last creation beginning on August 13, 3114 B.C.[8] Historical dates in Maya inscriptions are given in one of two forms—the Long Count and Calendar Round dates. Long Count dates are precise counts of elapsed time based on a 360-day year, called a tun, which was divided into 18 months of 20 days each, called a uinal. Since the Maya numbering system is based on twenty rather than on ten, they counted years in groups of twenty tuns, called a katun ("20-tun"), and twenty katuns, called a baktun ("400-tun"). A Long Count date, such as 9.13.0.0.0, simply records that nine groups of 400 tuns and thirteen groups of 20 tuns have ended since the beginning of this era, or 9x400 + 13x20 = 3,860 years of 360 days.

A Calendar Round date simply names the same day in two different calendars: the Tzolkin, composed of twenty day names and thirteen numbers combining to give 260 days, and the Haab, a year of 365 days, composed of eighteen 20-day months and a 5-day period at the end of the year. A day like 8 Ahau 8 Uo is named in both systems: it is 8 Ahau in the 260-day Tzolkin and the eighth day of the month Uo (the second month) in the 365-day Haab. It takes 18,980 days, or fifty-two 365-day years, for a day of this combined name to repeat. A combination of a Calendar Round date and the Long Count date, as in 9.13.0.0.0 8 Ahau 8 Uo, is a unique day in the history of the currently running era of creation.

In the past it has been assumed that since 13.0.0.0.0 will occur again in the Maya calendar on December 23, 2012, the Maya era, and the world with it, will end on that day. This is a misconception, however: the Maya projected events forward to October 15 and 23, 4772, and there is evidence that they perceived this creation to have a minimum cycle of slightly under 142 nonillion years.[9] A more detailed explanation of the calendar, the writing system and the process of glyphic decipherment appears at the conclusion of this book.

This study is organized into discussions on eight themes, or patterns, of Maya art; they have been chosen because they recur in Maya art time and again.[10] Through them we can understand the preoccupations of Classic-period Maya life. The first theme, "The Royal Person," is an explanation of the royal costuming and ritual objects depicted throughout Maya art.

"Kingship and the Rites of Accession," treats the single most important ritual of a king's life, his installation into office, the point at which he inherits the position of head of his lineage and leader of his city. The religious explanation that upheld the institution of kingship asserted that Maya rulers were necessary for the continuance of the universe itself.

The kings who ruled the major sites were served at home and in subsidiary sites by nobles, or *cahals*, who acted as administrators and governors. The activities of these nobles—the delivery of tribute, interaction with foreigners, marriage alliances, formal rituals of dress and courtly councils—are all shown in Maya art and, here, under the theme "Courtly Life."

Personal bloodletting, now recognized as a regular ritual of Maya life rather than an occasional penance, is the subject of the theme "Bloodletting and the Vision Quest." Through bloodletting, the Maya elite demonstrated their legitimacy and communicated with ancestors who were understood to reappear as visions. These rituals occurred under many circumstances, as part of the life events that include accession, marriage, birth and warfare. They occur with greatest regularity, however, at the completion of the twenty-year period, the katun.

In "Warfare and Captive Sacrifice," the imagery of battle that dominates certain sites is discussed. Undoubtedly some Classic Maya city-states were more belligerent than others, but few places failed to record victory in war in some way. Even during the Early Classic period, when texts were more laconic and multifigural compositions unusual, captives were shown bound under the feet of the ruler.

"The Ballgame" discusses an activity that was by no means a sport in modern terms but a ritual of kingship. Ballgame imagery—in which the Maya king is victorious at play—relates closely to that of warfare.

The final themes, "Death and the Journey through Xibalba" and "Kingship and the Maya Cosmos," are closely connected. Maya funerary imagery prepared the king for his journey into the Underworld, where he was required to defeat the Lords of Death in order to ensure his rebirth into the sky as a celestial being.

The Modern Invention of the Ancient Maya

The popular understanding of the ancient Maya has changed over time, depending on the historical perspectives of the people who have studied them. Sylvanus G. Morley's *The Ancient Maya* and J. Eric S. Thompson's *Rise and Fall of the Maya Empire* were published over thirty years ago. These two books, addressed to the public by the two most important Mayanists of their time, espoused a view that lingers today. The publications found an eager audience, for the romance of a lost civilization rediscovered in ancient pyramids and sculptures hidden deep within tropical rain forests captured the imagination of the public, just as it had at the beginning of the nineteenth century through the writings of John Lloyd Stephens. These books were different from earlier popular writings, however, for their authors were the leading scholars of the day, and their work carried the weight of professional anthropology and archaeology. Morley and Thompson, who also published articles in such popular magazines as *Life*, *National Geographic* and the *Illustrated London News*, completely dominated the information available to the layman; even today, their works are the most likely to be found in public libraries around the world.

In 1955, a reader of Morley would have found the Classic period of Maya civilization, his "Old Empire," almost like a glorious Camelot. For most of their history, the Maya occupied the Lowlands, from northern Honduras to southern Mexico, in communities surrounding great ceremonial centers. This version of Maya culture focused upon the calendar priests, who manipulated knowledge of the heavens to mystify the masses, and under their direction, the Maya created their greatest works of art and architecture, all datable by Long Count inscriptions to A.D. 300 to 900, or the Classic period. Befeathered priests were thought to have passed their lives casting complex auguries and stargazing long into the nights to fix the movements of heavenly bodies with minute precision. They were said to have commissioned texts that chronicled the relentless march of time, which was perceived to consist of burdens carried by the gods of numbers. As Thompson stated,

> These texts, to the best of our knowledge, contain no glorifications of ruler or recital of conquest, such as are customary on the monuments of other peoples. Instead, they are an impersonal record of steps in the search for truth, as the Maya saw it, that is, the whole philosophy of time with its interlocking cycles of divine influence. [11]

The calendar priests were anonymous and impersonal. A reader of Morley and Thompson was led to believe that the images on stelae were priests or gods, not kings or captains; unlike writers of inscriptions anywhere else in the world, however, the Maya calendar priests were without vanity: they did not record information about themselves.

> The Maya inscriptions treat primarily of chronology, astronomy—perhaps one might better say astrology—and religious matters. They are in no sense records of personal glorification and self-laudation like the inscriptions of Egypt, Assyria, and

Babylonia—indeed, they are so utterly impersonal, so completely non-individualistic, that it is even probable that the name glyphs of specific men and women were never recorded upon the Maya monuments.[12]

We are expected to believe that these priests did not live in cities like those of the preindustrial Old World, such as Beijing, Timbuktu or Constantinople. Rather, they were said to live in ceremonial centers, mostly vacant until the priests invited the peasantry to witness spectacle and ritual. The word *city* was even expurgated from writings on the Maya, lest it convey the notion of true habitation.[13]

The ancient Maya were described as worshipers of time, involved totally with abstractions. They were peace loving, religious, modest, conservative and clean about their persons! Nameless and faceless to modern man, the Classic Maya dwelt during a time of peace. Contact between ceremonial centers was limited to conferences on the calendar and astronomy. War did not exist; in fact, the Maya were said to adopt warlike behavior only centuries later, under the tutelage of central Mexicans.

Thompson and Morley believed that the peasantry practiced swidden, or slash-and-burn agriculture, to support the small elite of calendar priests who advised them when to plant and when to reap. Since this severe agricultural system soon diminishes the soil and requires new plots to be brought into production after three years of use, savannah eventually replaced jungle. Without metal plows to break sod, the Maya eventually found themselves without arable land in the tropical rain forest. According to the view espoused by Morley and Thompson, during the ninth century, the Maya, now desperate, began forced migrations north to the Yucatan, where the "New Empire" was founded during the Early Postclassic period. Civilization thrived there at Chichen Itza, particularly in the tenth and eleventh centuries, under central Mexican cultural dominance. During this "Mexican" florescence, the peaceful paradise known under the "Old Empire" vanished. The Maya, who were by nature kind, honest and good people, adopted bloody Mexican habits. Sacrifice, both self-inflicted and that of captives, was offered to the gods, and belligerent behavior prevailed.

The foregoing view of the Classic Maya spelled out cultural behavior known from no other civilization on earth. In fact, if we were to learn today that a highly sophisticated culture had been found in which there was no warfare, in which all intellectual activity was devoted to the chronicling of the heavens and time and in which the peasantry supported the elite merely in exchange for the knowledge of agricultural timing that any seasoned farmer has already mastered—we would register profound disbelief. This was, however, the popularly established view of the Maya, and like compelling science fiction, it was accepted.

The ideas culminating in Morley and Thompson's summary works had evolved slowly. During the nineteenth and early twentieth centuries, the Maya were styled as filling this peace-loving role as a necessary foil to the Aztecs in the New World. Customs of warfare and sacrifice, as well as of dense city living and the "crass" commercial practices of merchant warriors known as *pochteca*, were well known among the Aztecs, and these concerns were thought to be reflected in their art. When early nineteenth century explorers began to document Maya art and architecture, works of a profoundly different nature were discovered. It is perhaps not surprising, then, that by the time of Morley and Thompson, Maya art seemed to reflect a culture so different, it would appear to hardly have been part of Mesoamerica at all.

The most important nineteenth-century commentator on the Classic Maya

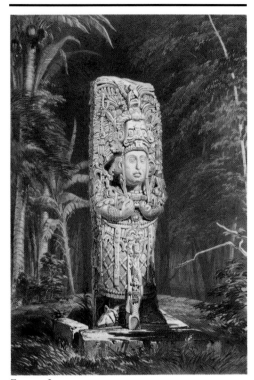

FIGURE 3
Stela A, Copan, Honduras
Late Classic period, ca. A.D. 750
Lithograph by Frederick Catherwood, 1844

was John Lloyd Stephens, who, without evidence to the contrary, thought that the Maya had been contemporaries of the Aztecs. Basing his views on their art and inscriptions, Stephens believed that Maya civilization was independent of other Mesoamerican cultures; he did assume that they shared what we would call today a cultural tradition, however.

Trained as a lawyer with a sharp eye for details, Stephens described the Maya ruins he visited with care. He believed that the acres of rubble at Copan, Honduras, were the remains of a city with a residential population and that the men carved on the monuments there were that city's rulers. When he looked at the carved inscriptions, he hazarded a guess as to their content:

> One thing I believe, that its history is graven on its monuments. No Champollion has yet brought them the energies of his inquiring mind. Who shall read them?[14]

And of Stela A at Copan, he wrote:

> The front view is a portrait. The back is entirely made up of hieroglyphics, and each tablet has two hieroglyphics joined together.... The tablets probably contain the history of the king or hero delineated, and the particular circumstances or actions which constituted his greatness.[15]

Perhaps because Stephens believed the Maya to have flourished in the same era as the Aztecs, he assumed that there had been war and sacrifice; he also noted, however, that he saw no monuments on which weapons of war were wielded, thereby inadvertently laying the seeds for later notions about the Maya and their "peaceful" behavior.

Perhaps no other work about the ancient Maya has been studied so intensely as the four volumes that Stephens published between 1841 and 1843. The books were among the great bestsellers of the nineteenth century, and these volumes remain some of the best books ever written on the Maya. The illustrations, engravings by Frederick Catherwood (Fig. 3), conveyed the romance of the subject, as well as fairly dependable information about the ruins. Stephens noted the consistent unity of the hieroglyphic writing system throughout the region where he traveled, whether the writings were recorded on stone or in book form, and he argued that the monuments were historical art. Most important for his own time, he firmly believed Maya culture to have been an indigenous civilization of the Americas, one that developed without fertilization from Egypt, India or China, the sources popularly mentioned in his day.

Over the course of the nineteenth century, many of Stephens's ideas were lost to scholars. By the end of the century, the notion of a peaceful Maya civilization had begun to grow because little progress had been made in determining the meaning of the carved monuments and inscriptions. Of the many Maya cities, little was known outside of a handful of principal temples. The first Maya art to become widely known, for example, came from Palenque and Copan, largely by means of Catherwood's engravings. The placid, courtly images of monuments at these two sites were highly readable. They emphasized human forms and placed particular emphasis on faces, especially when compared with the conventionalized human figures of Aztec art. Western observers embraced the art of the Maya, whose culture seemed to be pure and untarnished by the preoccupations of the Aztecs. Count Waldeck, a French explorer who lived for a time in the ruins of Palenque, expressed a sentiment in 1838 that conformed to the prevailing notions of the day. The Maya were, he assured his readers, a people and culture derived from Asia, perhaps from India. Even when his writings were

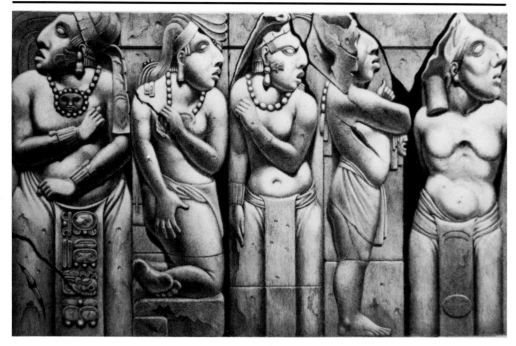

dismissed, the illustrations he made in an Egyptianizing style subtly promoted his ideas (Fig. 4). Moreover, his comments may also have promoted the notion of the peaceful Maya. When Count Waldeck looked at the stuccoed piers of the Temple of Inscriptions at Palenque, he wondered if the tender-hearted ancient Palencanos could have ever been cruel, or even rough, to one another, since he thought the adult figures on the monuments were depicted carrying children. It is now known that what Waldeck assumed were children are, in fact, supernaturals, right down to their snaky bodies and serpent feet.[16]

The still-intractable hieroglyphic writing system on the monuments further compounded the romantic ideas that Westerners had about Maya art. By the end of the nineteenth century, many breakthroughs had been made in deciphering dates, but little else; the remaining inscriptions seemed to be abstract, beautiful texts to be admired but perhaps never to be read. The dates were clear evidence of the arithmetical and calendrical skills of the Maya, and this gave rise to the idea that they were philosophers of time and numbers.

The correlation between the Christian and Maya calendars determined by J.T. Goodman in 1905 has held to the present day. By the Christian calendar, the Classic Maya were found to have erected their great Lowland monuments from the fourth to the ninth centuries A.D. The fact that in Yucatan, most monuments were of later date gave rise to the theory that the Maya had two periods of florescence, the so-called Old and New Empires. The Maya were considered the Greeks of the New World, and the Aztecs were seen as Romans—one pure, original and beautiful, the other slavish, derivative and cold. By the end of the century, these notions had begun to be systematized. Alfred P. Maudslay wrote:

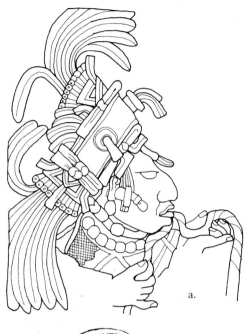

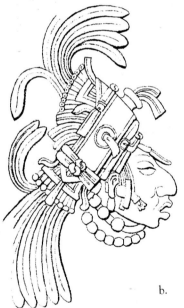

FIGURE 5
Contrasting studies of a detail from Yaxchilan Lintel 17
Late Classic period, ca. A.D. 775–770
a. Modern drawing
b. Nineteenth-century drawing by
 Annie Hunter for Alfred P. Maudslay

Judging from the sculptures and mural paintings at Chichen Itza, this change from south to north seems to have been a change from a peaceful to a warlike condition, and it therefore appears likely that the peopling of Yucatan may have taken place after the Maya had been driven by force from their peaceful southern homes, and had been compelled to cultivate the arts of war in order to save their race from extinction.[17]

Other evidence was thought to corroborate the view that the Maya had been peaceful, too preoccupied with time and their calendar to wage war. The first Classic Maya site to be explored in any detail (and it remained the only one for thirty years) was Copan. At that time, the end of the nineteenth century, excavators from the Peabody Museum found no walls such as would have been built for defense. The stelae and reliefs did not show figures readily identifiable as warriors. Burials, when found, did not suggest the mass burials one might expect from the carnage of warfare. For many years the data gathered at Copan (and just as important, the data not gathered) helped shape a view of the peaceful Classic Maya. Practices described by both the Maya and the Spanish at the time of the Conquest continued to be discounted as Postclassic inventions, atypical of the Classic Maya and inspired by central Mexicans. That, of course, returned the source of barbaric practices to the precursors of the Aztecs and stimulated the notion of a Greek-Roman dichotomy.

Yet other ancient Maya ruins, which also came to light at the turn of the century, should have challenged some of these interpretations. Maudslay, for example, visited Yaxchilan in 1882; he was so struck by the beauty of the monuments that he ordered several to be shipped to England, where they became the core of the British Museum's collection of Precolumbian antiquities. Nearly twenty years after he first saw the lintels, Maudslay published some of the Yaxchilan material without comment on the imagery. Nevertheless, the drawing that accompanied Lintel 17 is telling; in the scene—quite obviously one of self-sacrifice—the woman pulls a rope through her tongue, and the man directs a sharpened bone to his groin. In Maudslay's drawing, however, only the text and faces of the protagonists are shown. The rope was not shown being drawn through the woman's mouth, and the scene no longer held any indication of violence or blood sacrifice (Fig. 5b). Apparently, either Maudslay or Annie Hunter, his excellent draftsman, made an editorial decision.

It now seems surprising that in the first few decades of the century, no one who looked at the newly discovered Maya art of Yaxchilan and Piedras Negras noticed the clear evidence for the Maya preoccupation with battle and blood offerings. At Piedras Negras, nearly half the monuments show warriors, many of them with captives, and on some of the "niche" stelae, a single sacrificed victim is shown. At Yaxchilan, whole lintel programs were dedicated to showing assaults on captives. Despite the weight of all these images, however, the content of these monuments was not acknowledged.[18] In a series of photographs of the monuments, published between 1896 and 1911 by the Peabody Museum, it would appear that Teobert Maler made no judgments about the interpretation of the Yaxchilan and Piedras Negras material; nevertheless, unless they were on the front of the monument, glyphs were not included in his photographic documentation (Fig. 6). Not only were they not available for study, to Maler they appeared not to exist, for he did not even include them systematically among his unpublished materials. A few years later, Herbert Spinden correctly recognized ruler portraits and the violent content of the monuments photographed by Maler at Piedras Negras and Yaxchilan, but his obsession with the correlation of the Maya and Christian calendars and his position just outside of what was becoming the Mayanist mainstream prevented serious consideration of his ideas.[19] Even when the monuments of Piedras Negras were studied, as they were by the influential art critic Roger Fry in 1918 (who, ironically, advocated "a revolt against the tyranny of the Graeco-Roman tradition"), he used them as a foil to Aztec art: "In Mexico there is no doubt about the superiority, from an aesthetic point of view, of the earlier culture—the Aztecs had everything to learn from the Maya, and they never rose to the level of their predecessors."[20] Fry effectively ignored the content of Maya art and unwittingly preferred the linear, representational elements of Maya art, which more closely approximate the Graeco-Roman tradition he professed to abhor.

From its first funding in 1914 until its dissolution in 1955, the Historical Division of the Carnegie Institution of Washington dominated Maya studies in the United States. It directed, published and plotted the design of most of the Maya archaeology carried out by Americans during those years, and it influenced all other work on the Maya done elsewhere. The moving force behind the Carnegie Institution was Sylvanus G. Morley. Morley set up projects at Uaxactun, Guatemala and Chichen Itza in the Yucatan to test theories about the Maya, and he embarked on a campaign of exploration to document all Maya ruins and inscriptions, a project that eventually led to the discovery of many new sites and sculptures.[21] For this work, the most important consideration is the point of view the Carnegie Institution publications espoused.

One of the by-products of archaeology in the Maya region was familiarity with modern Maya life. For those who worked at Chichen Itza, the cycle of modern Yucatec life was compelling, and many researchers fell under its spell. Morley watched the pattern of slash-and-burn agriculture and applied it to the past, thus making the Maya an anomaly: a high civilization based on primitive agricultural methods. This conclusion, however, limited conjecture of the total population of the Classic Maya to one supportable by such techniques. To Thompson, the vacant market towns of highland Guatemala revealed that ancient ones were little more than ceremonial centers.[22] His view (and perhaps his ability to argue it) was so overpowering that despite the fact that settlement studies carried out at Uaxactun argued for a population of 50,000 or so, Tatiana Proskouriakoff's reconstruction drawings of Uaxactun (made for the Carnegie Institution) show vacant ceremonial centers isolated in the jungle, as if there had been no resident population. No other drawings of Maya architecture have been as accurate as Proskouriakoff's, but they conveyed a powerful point of view. Her drawings remain the most influential reconstructions of Maya architecture and may never be superseded in quality, yet they will continue to promote the notion that Maya cities were vacant (Fig. 7).[23]

Early in his career (and notably before his long association with Thompson), Morley adopted the view of the Maya put forth by Stephens: that mundane, historical information was borne by Maya inscriptions. Nevertheless, by the time he amassed his great five-volume corpus, *Inscriptions of Peten*, he had apparently abandoned any hope of reconstructing the historical content. Morley's treatment of inscriptions beyond calendrical data was simple: he did not draw them.[24] The assumption, one might say, was bold—if he could not decipher them, then no one could. Thompson, who espoused this negative viewpoint more energetically, may have been responsible for persuading his colleague to follow his lead. Indeed, elaborate hypotheses were invented to explain the content of Maya writing:

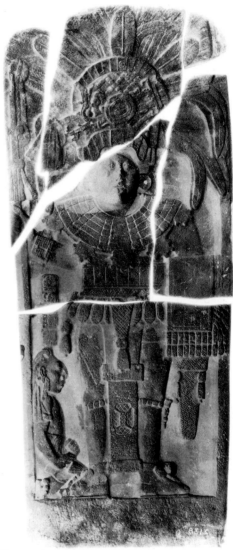

FIGURE 6
Stela 35, Piedras Negras, Guatemala
Late Classic period, ca. A.D. 662
Photo by Teobert Maler
Courtesy of the Peabody Museum of Archaeology and Ethnology, Harvard University

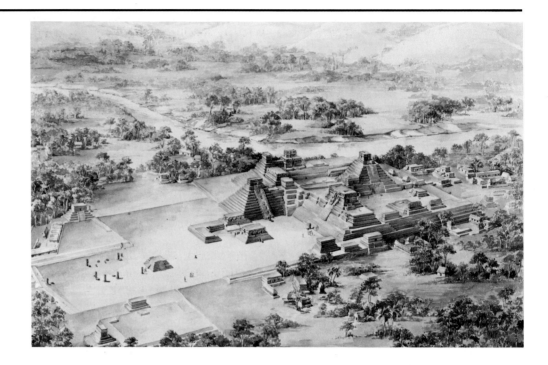

I am persuaded that inscriptions were longest around 9.13.0.0.0 (A.D. 692) because the Maya scientists were then deep in argument on two problems: the length of the solar year and how best to record lunar data. A century later, after these matters had been solved to the satisfaction of the priest-astronomers, the inscriptions on stelae were much abbreviated.[25]

The discovery in 1946 of the painted murals of Bonampak is a watershed of Maya studies, for these paintings transformed our view of the Classic Maya. In no other work of Maya art do so many figures appear, and even to the uninitiated, they look like particular individuals, and the short columns of glyphs beside them are almost undoubtedly captions. In a pageant of rulership that covered the walls of three rooms in a small temple, the murals showed a series of ceremonies, including the single greatest battle painting of the ancient New World. Thompson, who wrote about these works for a Carnegie Institution publication, forced them to conform to his own view of Maya society by calling the scene a minor raid of little historical significance. The pictures, however, spoke for themselves; the idea of the peaceful Maya was on the point of becoming a vanishing myth.[26]

The identity of the figures on Maya stelae was a subject both Morley and Thompson obscured, preferring not to mention it, although at various times they called them "gods" or "calendar priests." They were not, to Thompson or Morley, the men and women who had ruled their respective sites. To have made them tangible would have necessitated an explanation of their behavior. Instead, the image of a peaceful, theocratic and nondynastic Maya became a philosophical haven from the warlike, secular twentieth century known to these writers.

Mesoamericanists only began to see the Maya in a different light when the hieroglyphics became better understood. In 1958 Heinrich Berlin showed that certain glyphs, which he called "emblem" glyphs, were site-specific references of either lineages or places. In 1960 Tatiana Proskouriakoff published a watertight argument about the historical content of Maya glyphs and art. Although it focused on the inscriptions at Piedras Negras, her work showed beyond a doubt that similar historical information was found at all sites. In two essays on Yaxchilan, she showed the rulers Shield Jaguar and Bird Jaguar to be military leaders who memorialized themselves in image and text as great warriors. Thus, by the early 1960s in just four seminal articles, the Maya had become regionally oriented, dynastic and warlike. Their images were no longer abstract representations of calendar priests but glorifications of individual kings.

Following the dissolution of the Carnegie Institution in 1955, many Maya archaeologists chose to investigate technical and theoretical problems. Leading a worldwide trend in archaeological studies, Mayanists turned away from the study of site centers and began to concentrate on the archaeology of mundane life. The archaeologist's tools were enriched by new technical capabilities, such as radiocarbon dating, pollen studies and aerial photography. Sensitive to criticism that Mayanist studies had become "intellectual stamp collecting,"[27] they concentrated on "scientific" questions, three of which have implications here: What was the basis of Maya agriculture? Where did the Maya live? When did Classic Maya civilization emerge?

For most of the century, and because of observation of the modern Maya, the notion of small populations supported by slash-and-burn agriculture had thrived—in notable contrast to Aztec raised-field agriculture—by observation of the modern Maya. In 1972, however, Dennis Puleston and Alfred Siemens used aerial photography to document raised fields, probably of Classic-period date, in southern Campeche. Suddenly, after years of considering only the hypothetical possibility of greater agricultural yields, Maya archaeologists understood intensive agriculture to have been the rule, not the exception. This revelation admitted to denser, more urban environments. Moreover, new studies had begun to indicate that ceremonial centers were surrounded by significant populations during the Classic period. At the site of Dzibilchaltun in northern Yucatan, for example, a population of 50,000 was projected for Classic times; a similar size was subsequently calculated for Tikal.[28] One can only hazard a guess at the total population of the Maya area during the Classic period, but many archaeologists consider two million to be a reasonable estimate. Although not large by preindustrial standards—Teotihuacan in central Mexico is thought to have had a population of nearly 250,000 by A.D. 550—centers of 50,000 people were indeed cities, supporting dense residential settlements, and the Maya may have had twenty cities of this size. The image of the peaceful, pastoral Maya and its corollary theories had lasted less than a century, but at last these theories gave way before overwhelming evidence to the contrary.

Finally, the earliest date of many of the cultural elements we call Classic—long accepted to be around A.D. 300—can be attributed to the Late Preclassic period, to as early as 150 B.C. The earliest dated Maya monument (Stela 29 at Tikal, dated to A.D. 292) has traditionally been used to mark the beginning of the Classic period and, by extension, the beginning of Maya civilization. Yet evidence from excavations at El Mirador, Tikal, Uaxactun, Lamanai and Cerros makes it patently clear that, with the exception of stelae, all elements characterizing Maya civilization were thriving in the Maya Lowlands in the first century B.C., and the huge buildings at El Mirador may have been constructed a century earlier. Thus, in the truest sense of the word, "Classic" Maya civilization was in place by 100 B.C. The origins of Classic Maya civilization are now shown to conform chronologically to the rest of Mesoamerica, and are confirmed to be contemporary with developments in central Mexico and Oaxaca.

The first great phase of Mesoamerican cultural history, the Preclassic, corresponds in general to the emergence of civilization in Mesoamerica. The Early Preclassic period (2000–900 B.C.) is dominated by the Olmec, who developed into the dominant society in Mesoamerica by 1200 B.C. Their far-flung trade routes served as distribution networks, not only for material goods but for ideas. By 1000 B.C., Olmec symbolism often appears on pottery in the Copan Valley, and sites of this early date that exhibit Olmec influence are documented throughout the Chiapas and Guatemalan Highlands, especially on the Pacific side (although Olmec symbolism is, by comparison, rare in Lowland archaeology).

The Middle Preclassic period (900–300 B.C.) is a time of change, especially in the Maya region. The great Olmec city of San Lorenzo was abandoned by 900 B.C., and La Venta arose as the prominent Gulf Coast site of the Olmecs. By 600 B.C., villages were being established throughout the Maya Lowlands and Highlands, many of them specializing in trade or production.[29] The growing complexity of public ritual is in evidence at Cuello, where a new platform was dedicated around 400 B.C. with the sacrifice and dismemberment of over twenty victims.[30] Perhaps most important for the development of civilization, the Middle Preclassic period saw the beginning of intensive agriculture in raised-field systems and the development of major water management programs at sites like Edzna.[31]

The Late Preclassic period (300 B.C.–A.D. 300) was a time of transformation for the Maya; it resulted in what we see today as civilization. Both in the Highlands and the Lowlands, the Maya began building large population centers ruled by elite groups. In the Lowlands, long-resident populations replaced their villages with massive buildings, some of the largest ever built in the Precolumbian Americas. In the south, architecture was less overwhelming in size, but it was accompanied by stelae depicting the Long Count calendar, as well as images of rulers enacting important rituals. Most of the early sites in the southern area—Izapa, Abaj Takalik, El Baul, Chalchuapa—are on the Pacific side of the Continental Divide. Only Kaminaljuyu was built in the region between the northern and southern drainage system. Early sites in the Lowlands are found along the river drainages, although at least one, El Mirador, sits in swampland between the Caribbean and Gulf drainage systems. During the Late Preclassic period, the template for Maya kingship and their world view was set for the next one thousand years of civilization.

At Cerros along the coast of Belize and at El Mirador in the Peten, a dramatic change occurred that allows us to speculate on how Classic Maya civilization developed. Throughout Mesoamerica in general and the Maya region in particular, populations were growing rapidly. Long-distance trade expanded, concentrating wealth in just a few hands—probably in one clan or lineage, who exercised increasing power. The world in which the Maya of Cerros lived, for example, was no longer an egalitarian farming community. Around 50 B.C., all constructions at Cerros were razed, and new constructions—stepped pyramids dominated by huge stucco masks in a dramatic new imagery—were built; in this imagery, the primary elements of Classic Maya iconography, the sun and Venus, appeared for the first time. Great jaguar masks marked by *kin*, the Maya glyph for sun or day, were placed at the base of the lowest tiers of these pyramids. A long crocodilian snout at the top of these masks probably identifies the form as Venus. This configuration shows the prototype of the Morning Star pulling the sun in its journey across the sky. Like billboards, this cosmic imagery dotted the landscape across the Maya Lowlands at most sites in Late Preclassic times.

Meanwhile, particularly at Abaj Takalik and El Baul in the Highlands, the Maya erected slab stelae showing individuals who were probably historical rulers. On Stela 1 at El Baul, a ruler stands with his face and legs in profile and his torso frontally positioned (Fig. 8). He wears great ritual paraphernalia while holding a wavy-bladed flint knife, and he is accompanied by a Long Count date of the seventh cycle, in the year A.D. 37.[32] It is possible that the preoccupations of historical rulership were never lost in the Highlands but were maintained continuously from Olmec times. Whatever the impetus, by the Late Preclassic period, the stela format was an established method of illustrating historical records in the Highlands.

By A.D. 200 at the latest, at Tikal and Uaxactun in the central Peten region, as well as at other Maya sites there, including Rio Azul, these two critical aspects of Late Preclassic art—architecture carrying mask assemblages and stelae recording historical kingship—coalesced to forge the Early Classic. While this symbolic system had been manifested on building facades during Late Preclassic times, during the Early Classic period, Maya kings took the imagery from the architecture and *began to wear* it. The most complete early records contributing to our incomplete understanding of this transformation are stelae from Tikal dating to the third and fourth centuries; even by then, however, it is clear that the visual symbolism of kingship had been systematized and was shared by all Lowland Maya: the Maya had embarked on the civilization that would thrive through the ninth century A.D.

The Classic period saw the great flowering of Maya art and architecture and the widest dispersion of elite cultural manifestations, such as the stela cult, the iconography of kingship and hieroglyphic writing. The two main phases of the Classic period, Early Classic (A.D. 200–600) and Late Classic (A.D. 600–900), are separated by a fifty-year gap, dubbed the "hiatus" by Morley, who noted the paucity of inscriptions datable to A.D. 530–580. Ceramics, sculptural style and composition, architectural elements and the nature of imported goods all change at this boundary, although the differences are neither so marked nor so dramatic as once supposed. Even so, inscriptions discovered from the period are still limited, particularly at Tikal and Uaxactun, where the hiatus appears to have been the most profound, but at many other cities—Yaxchilan, Palenque and Caracol—it appears to be a time of expression and growth. Since most buildings constructed before the Late Classic period (and probably most other art as well) were overlaid by subsequent construction, the Early Classic forms are known only at sites that have been extensively excavated.

Most archaeological evidence for occupations of the first half of the Early Classic period have been found in the central and northeastern Peten region. Around A.D. 350, however, three occurrences of major importance to the cultural history of the Maya took place. Sites all over the area inhabited by the Maya, especially those at the periphery, such as Copan, Palenque and Tonina, begin to develop their own dynastic histories, presumably as independent states. At about the same time, most of the sites in the southern region (except Kaminaljuyu) lost vitality and thereafter did not participate in the elite manifestations of Maya culture. Finally, in both the Highlands and the

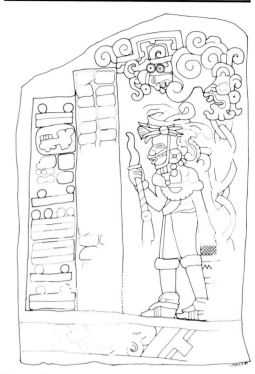

FIGURE 8
Stela 1, El Baul, Guatemala
Late Preclassic period, A.D. 37

Lowlands, substantial interaction between the Classic Maya and Teotihuacanos from the Valley of Mexico is evidenced by the appearance of alien iconography, exotic goods (such as obsidian, feathers, cotton and shells), pottery vessel forms and some sharing of architectural conventions (although it is clear that the Lowland Maya absorbed the other culture's forms far more liberally than did the Teotihuacanos).

The Late Classic period (A.D. 600–900) saw the intensification of Maya elite culture through the southern Lowlands, including the florescence of sites in the Chenes and Puuc regions of the northern Lowlands. Previously small and unimportant sites, such as Quirigua and Palenque, expanded dramatically and competed with more established neighbors. Hundreds of cities, large and small, were ruled by lineages that warred with one another, oversaw the construction of extraordinary buildings and recorded their histories in stone and plaster monuments.

Hereditary kingship flourished throughout the Maya area, at what would appear to be many city-states. These city-states battled one another frequently, and their ruling lineages intermarried, possibly to forge alliances but to draw the royal families together and reduce competition as well. Since such tactics were ineffective for the royal families of Europe, it should come as no surprise that the Maya were often at war with close kin. Kings were often polygamous, and the size of the lineage must have expanded over time.

Important members of these ruling lineages were called *ahau*, "lord," but only the king bore the title of *mah k'ina*, or "great sun." Particularly at places adjacent to Yaxchilan, Bonampak and Palenque, elite figures who are depicted with the king generally bear the title *cahal*. These underlords may have been governors (possibly military governors) of the towns that fell within the sphere of influence of the greater city. The Maya practiced primogeniture; kingship generally passed from father to son. Royal women bore elevated titles, such as lady *ahau*, or lady *cahal*, but they do not seem ever to have carried the *mah k'ina* title. Nevertheless, at least at Palenque, inscriptions show that twice a woman was the chief ruler and occupied the office normally held by the male king—in other words, women on rare occasions could become "kings." Records indicate that the political machinery was elaborate during the Late Classic period, and the visual documentation of the situations grew increasingly complex.

During the last two hundred years of this period, monuments celebrating war and conquest became gradually more numerous. By A.D. 810, people without the ethnic features—the sloping foreheads and stepped haircuts—of the Classic Maya appear on the monuments of Aguateca, Seibal and other sites within the Usumacinta drainage system, and with them came fine orange ceramics, taken by Mayanists to signal an invading people, called the Putun, from the Gulf Coast of Tabasco.[33] Around this time, Classic sites began simply to shut down—Palenque, Yaxchilan and Copan around A.D. 800; Naranjo and Quirigua by A.D. 820. The latest date at Tikal and other nearby sites is A.D. 869. Around A.D. 849, Seibal underwent a short-lived renaissance, during which these ethnically foreign rulers tried to use the traditional symbolism of Maya kingship to support their reigns; the revival did not hold, however. At Chichen Itza, Kakupacal and his family[34] (also described as foreigners in Yucatec sources) ruled, while Lord Chac sat on the throne of Uxmal: The dates of both dynasties occur between A.D. 850 and 900. The last Long Count date was recorded on an unassuming little monument at Tonina in the central part of Chiapas in A.D. 909. The glories of the Classic period were over, and Maya civilization (at least in its first manifestation) had collapsed.

The continuity and success of Maya civilization for nearly a thousand years is astonishing, and their collapse has always fascinated modern people, perhaps because the cities of the Classic landscape were abandoned. As early as Maudslay's time, it had become evident that the latest dates recorded in the Maya inscriptions were five hundred years earlier than the Conquest.[35] Morley, finding no counterevidence, based his Old and New Empires on this pattern of dates. The Old Empire, he thought, had ended in the ninth century because of overuse of the tropical rain forest. Thompson, influenced by the traumatic history of this century, assumed that there had been a popular revolution of the masses, who rose up and slaughtered their masters. The collapse has continued to be one of the great preoccupations of Maya archaeologists, who have tested many of the speculated causes, such as agricultural failure, disease, overpopulation and foreign invasion. Current evidence suggests that all of these factors contributed to or were symptoms of the decline, but no single causal factor has yet been determined.

Few investigators, however, have used the most important evidence that remains, namely, the history of the collapse as written by the Maya themselves.[36] For example, interesting changes occur in the focus of Maya political art in the eighth century. While warfare was prominent in Maya records throughout the Late Classic period, in the late eighth century, its documentation changed in scale and purpose. War became an event that served individuals rather than systems and allowed small sites and their rulers to achieve status far in excess of their historical position. As more warfare was carried out, it seems to have gained a new scale and purpose, and under the leadership of expansionist kings, some small sites and their lords furthered their status dramatically. Palenque, Copan, Naranjo and Seibal lost their kings, who were taken captive and probably sacrificed by conquering cities. At Piedras Negras, Yaxchilan and Bonampak, the last statements recorded and illustrated are of victory in warfare. Inscriptions at many sites along the Pasión and Petexbatun rivers in the southern Peten region in central Guatemala record war waged by Dos Pilas kings, who may have been attempting a unification of that area into a single "superstate."[37] We can only guess at the number of battles that went unrecorded, but it is evident that some Maya kings felt the need to establish hegemony over larger territories than they had ruled in earlier times. The movement toward centralized regional states, however successful, did not survive longer than the lifetimes of the men who forged them. No regional states or confederations arose until after the collapse, and then, only among Yucatec speakers in the north, whose rulers were invaders and thus foreigners.

Outside pressures were undoubtedly present as well. Throughout Mesoamerica in the eighth and ninth centuries, long, stable cultural traditions disappeared. The history of Maya civilization followed the pattern of the whole of Mesoamerica, in that the established mechanisms of statecraft, kingship and symbolism disappeared. Non-Mayas were probably perceived as barbarians; and their search for croplands and rights to waterways may have been an impetus to warfare. It is possible that in such warfare, the old rules of capture and sacrifice, followed by tribute without exchange of territory, no longer applied and that new conditions of warfare, particularly expansion of territory by capture, replaced them. Thus, the view of cultural reality of the Classic Maya elite, which had been carefully manipulated since the Late Preclassic period, no longer described the world in which they lived. The Classic Maya, unlike their forebears of a thousand years earlier, were not able to adjust their ideology to the new reality. Cultural

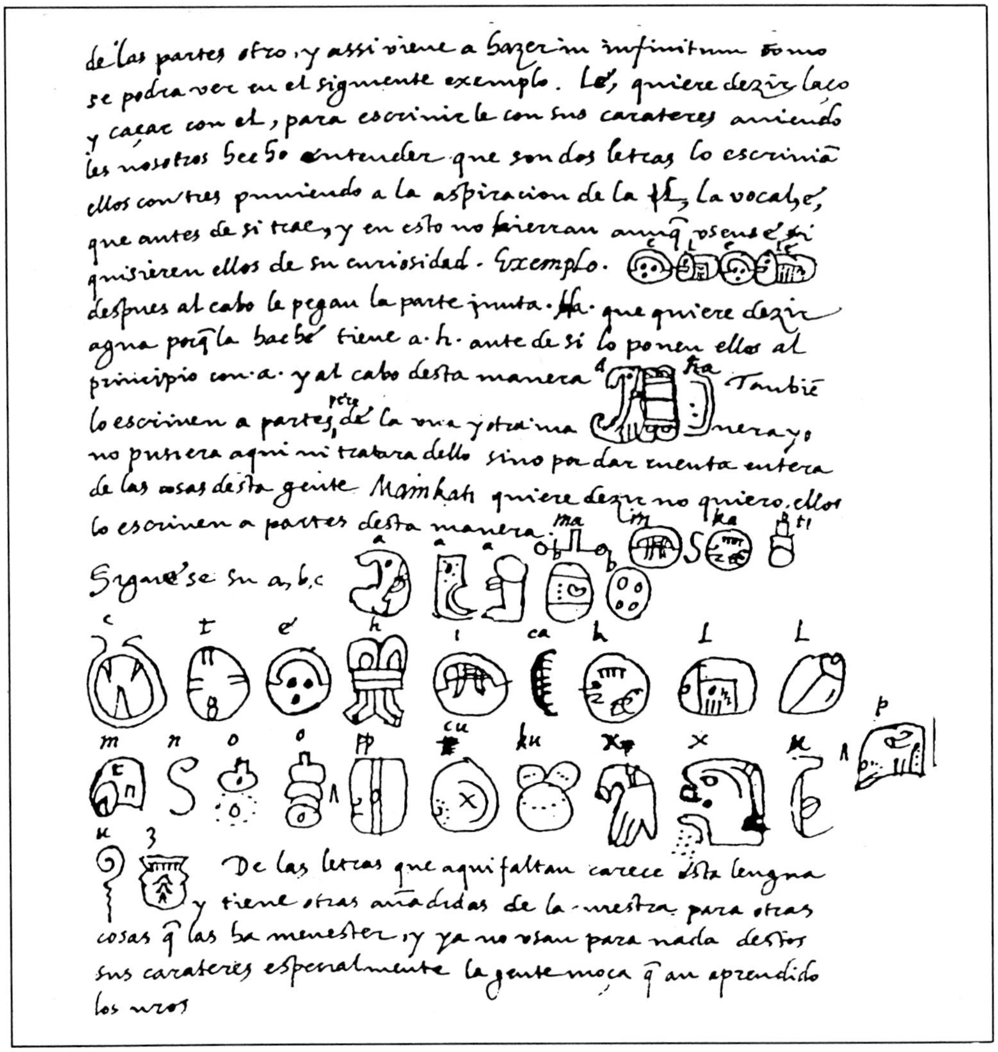

FIGURE 9
The "alphabet" recorded in Landa's *Relación de las cosas de Yucatan*

dinosaurs, the Maya elite, their cities and their art largely vanished within a few generations from the southern Maya Lowlands.

During the Postclassic period, a different kind of Maya culture thrived, even at places like Dzibilchaltun, where the collapse had little affect. New styles of architecture arose; correspondingly, given Lowland Maya patterns, a slightly altered cosmic vision of how the world worked was in place. Maya inscriptions and art were still made, but the glorification of the ruling dynasty was different in character, and the offices may have become more important than the individuals who held them.

It should be emphasized that the people and their complex society did not disappear during the Postclassic period. In Yucatan, Puuc sites, such as Uxmal, Labna, Sayil and Kabah, continued until A.D. 1100, and a series of confederations, one centered at Chichen Itza and another at Mayapan, developed; they were controlled by lineages, such as the Itza, that the Yucatecs described as foreigners.[38] In the Highlands of Guatemala, Cakchiquel and Quiche dynasties came to dominate the region, both claiming that they were inheritors of the Toltec, the legendary people of the Terminal Classic period, from whom most Postclassic peoples claim political descent. The Highlands of Chiapas were dominated by the Tzotzil; the Candelaria and lower Usumacinta rivers by the Acalan Chontal Maya.

The Spanish conquered Yucatan and established their capital at Mérida in 1542; the Quiche and Cakchiquels of the Highlands had come under the Spanish heel one year earlier, in 1541. We know far less about the people who the Spanish found in the southern Lowlands, because the conquerors did not thrive in those regions. They systematically depopulated the region by enslavement, raiding and conversion, moving what they called "wild indians" to Highland or coastal communities established for the sole purpose of keeping the Maya under control. The last Maya community of any size, the Itza stronghold on Lake Peten-Itza, fell in 1697. The tired remnants, ancestors of today's Lacandon, were left to roam the forest in small family bands.

At the time of the Conquest, elite Maya held an understanding of the Classic world that, despite major transformations, brought them closer to the past than we will ever be. Many of the same deities were worshipped, but most important, they continued to write in the same script as the Classic Maya. These deities and the customs of Maya sacrifice provoked Spanish outrage. Catholic priests began extirpating the indigenous religion; the native books and sculptures were gathered and destroyed.

Diego de Landa, the first bishop of Yucatan, was recalled to Spain in 1568 by the Inquisition for his overzealous application of their own religious laws. Landa wrote his *Relación de las cosas de Yucatan*, an account of life in Yucatan, as part of his legal defense. Although scanty when compared to the volumes written on the New World by friars in central Mexico, Landa's text is an invaluable document. He described the place, the modern towns, the Maya cyclical rituals and the calendar—even his call for native manuscripts in order to burn them. Most important for Maya archaeology, Landa described a hot afternoon when he sat with a literate Maya informant and asked of him his "letters" (Fig. 9). Landa wrote out the Spanish alphabet, and pronouncing each Spanish letter, he queried his informant for glyphic equivalents, an inappropriate but understandable attempt on the part of a man who could not imagine that a writing system worked otherwise. The confused Maya gave him back exactly what he asked for—the sound of the Spanish letters written in the syllabary system of the Maya. Exasperated at not getting single signs for single letters, Landa told the Maya to write anything he wanted. In a wry commentary on his frustration, the Maya wrote *ma in ka-ti*, or, in colloquial English, "I don't wanna." For nearly a century Landa's record baffled scholars before it was conclusively demonstrated in 1952[39] that the values he recorded provided a profound key to Maya writing, of both the Postclassic and Classic eras.

Throughout the New World in the sixteenth century, Spanish friars taught the native nobility how to read and write their own language using the roman script of Europeans. No native Maya hieroglyphic books recounting extensive mythic narrative survive; one, however, was transcribed into European script in the middle of the sixteenth century by a young Quiche noble in Guatemala. The single most important document of Maya mythology, the Popol Vuh, describes the creation of the world, the exciting adventures of the Hero Twins and the legendary origins and history of the Quiche Maya, one of the groups that dominated the Guatemalan Highlands at the time of the Conquest. The Popol Vuh stories are not illustrated word for word in the art of the Classic period, but many elements of the story line have compelling parallels in Classic imagery created seven hundred years before, and some appear to be directly illustrated, suggesting that these stories are fragments, surviving to the time of the Conquest, of very ancient myth cycles describing the universe and the origins of gods and man. Above all, the Popol Vuh expresses Maya concepts of good and evil, of defeat and victory. The discovery that the Popol Vuh had direct meaning for the Classic Maya should be no more surprising than Schliemann's discovery that Homer's works record real, historical events, couched in mythic terms.

The Popol Vuh is divided into four parts. A new translation of the text has shown that the work is conceived as a performance, an oral narrative that could have taken days to complete.[40] In Part One, great gods gather and attempt to create man three different times, each time without success. In Parts Two and Three, stories of the Hero Twins, Hunahpu and Xbalanque, are told, although not in chronological sequence. In Part Two, the Hero Twins defeat evil deities of the earth. Part Three returns to a time before the birth of the Twins, when their father and uncle were defeated by the Lords of the Underworld. The Twins were conceived when spittle from their father's severed head impregnated an Underworld goddess, who fled from the Underworld to the Middleworld to give birth. Like Hercules, the Hero Twins were demigods whose mission was to overcome divine opponents.

The Hero Twins exemplify the Maya definition of a hero, which is fundamentally different from the hero of Western oral literature. A hero need not overpower his enemy. Brute strength is no advantage, nor, as in the case of Western epics, is divine intervention from an Upperworld. There is no deus ex machina for the Maya. The Hero Twins win because they are witty and clever, not because they are purer, stronger, greater brutes or more faithful to gods or ideals. In the Underworld, for example, evil lords try to sacrifice the Twins each successive night following ballgame play, and each night the lords are unsuccessful—not because they are weak, but because they are outwitted. When the lords substitute Hunahpu's head for the ball in the final ballgame, Xbalanque in turn substitutes a rabbit, who bounds out of sight, distracting the lords and giving Xbalanque time to repair his brother's head. The ability to recognize falseness and combat it with imaginative, even amusing, solutions is the primary quality of the Maya hero.

When a Maya king died, like the Hero Twins he descended into the Underworld to enter into a contest with the evil Lords of Death. He had prepared himself mentally to combat terror with wit in order to survive the Underworld trials and be reborn as a celestial body. Thus, mental quickness regenerates Maya kingship, perpetuating a cycle from earth to Underworld to Upperworld. This sophisticated wit is still perceived by modern Maya in Honduras, Belize, Mexico and Guatemala today to be the sine qua non of a great man. Verbal quickness, repartee and humor based on punning are, for example, highly respected among the Maya.

In Part Four of the Popol Vuh, the gods successfully create man from maize. Unlike the gods' previous creations of animals and men from mud and wood, this one was successful: the maize men could praise their creators and acknowledge their debt to them. When the gods saw what they had made, however, they realized that these humans could see altogether too well. Man "understood everything perfectly," so the gods sought to limit his vision and his understanding, for it was not right for man to have the very power of divinities. The gods gathered together and said, "Now we'll take them apart just a little, that's what we need," and changed the nature of human vision. Mankind was "blinded as the face of a mirror is breathed upon. Their eyes were weakened. Now it was only when they looked nearby that things were clear. And such was the loss of the means of understanding, along with the means of knowing everything."[41]

Like those first men, our vision, too, is dimmed. We can see only what is close at hand or what is passed, not what lies ahead. Like all those who have come before us, we are bound by historical perspectives that will be clear only to our successors, and they cast a shadow over the mirror in which we look to seek the face of the Classic Maya.

THE CHARACTERISTICS OF MAYA ART

THE OBJECTS THAT WERE SELECTED TO BE THE BASIS OF *THE BLOOD OF KINGS* ARE beautiful works of art that touch our sensibilities even without knowledge of their meaning. They date from the earliest to the latest periods of the Classic Maya and were imbued with meaning by their makers. They come from palaces, temples and tombs; they were made for domestic and ritual life or to accompany the dead into the Afterlife. They are made from stone, clay and shell, for the use of the individuals who owned them, or as public propaganda by the kings who commissioned them. Their importance for us is in their beauty as objects of art and their function as carriers of cultural information. Moreover, they are imprinted with a symbolic language combining imagery and writing that was shared by the people who made them.

The experience of art in our own lives does not prepare us to encounter and understand the role of art and the artist in Maya society. The language of Maya art is alien to us: it was wrought from a different kind of social experience, its message aimed at people of another age. To experience Maya art as more than an exotic creation of curious aspect, we must learn to see in a different way and to hear a different message. The Maya artist was not concerned with creativity and originality as defined by twentieth-century critics. The content, the media and the function of art were givens, established by cultural experience, education, and tradition. The artist had little control over subject matter or iconography; individual creativity was demonstrated by the refinement of execution, in innovations of style and in the use of subtle metaphor that at times approaches visual word play.

Technologically, the Maya must be classified as Stone Age artisans, since all sculpture, architectural construction, and lapidary art were executed without the use of metal. Preferred sculptural media were the softer, more pliable stones, such as the limestone characteristic of the Maya Lowlands. To some degree stylistic development was formed by the properties of locally available stone. For example, Palenque sculptors preferred wall-mounted slabs to stelae, perhaps because their local limestone, although an excellent medium for relief, was too brittle to use for freestanding stelae. By contrast, the tuff available in the Copan Valley gave rise to a brilliant, fully volumetric sculptural style, the rival of any European tradition. Harder stones from the volcanic

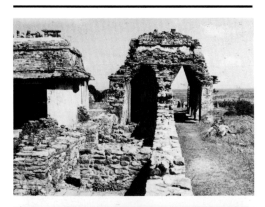

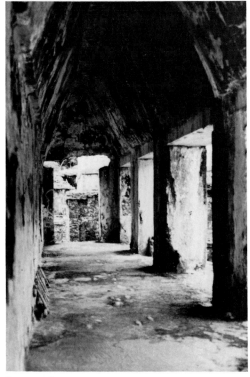

FIGURE 10
Corbel vaults
House A and the west gallery of House C, the Palace at Palenque, Chiapas.
Late Classic period, A.D. 675–750

Highlands, such as jade, fuchsite, serpentine, specular hematite and obsidian, and marine shell from the Lowlands became the preferred material for small sacred objects and jewelry. Plaster, clay and wood were also exploited, although very little wood carving has survived the ravages of a tropical environment. Weaving in cotton, palm, reed, henequen and other fibers was also a highly developed art, as were feather work and feather mosaic, but like wood, these media do not survive archaeologically. We can only reconstruct their rich development from the pictures of clothing shown in other media. Finally, although only a small portion of painting and calligraphy survives on walls, stone objects, pottery vessels, plastered objects and in fig-bark paper books, the Maya clearly established one of the great painting traditions of the world.

Maya art did not develop spontaneously. The Maya inherited artistic techniques, media and much of the imagery developed by early Mesoamerican cultural traditions. Techniques for carving hard and soft stones in relief as well as in fully volumetric styles were invented and exploited by the Olmec of the Gulf Coast in the Early Preclassic period. At the same time, in the highlands of Guerrero, sophisticated wall paintings showing Olmec iconography were executed at the caves of Oxtotitlan and Juxtlahuaca; and a tradition of architectural sculpture, also using symbols indistinguishable from those used in the Gulf Coast Olmec region, flourished at the newly discovered site at Teopantequanitla and nearby Chalcatzingo.

The stone stela, the most important sculptural format to be used by the Classic Maya, appeared at La Venta and in Guerrero by the Middle Preclassic period. By 600 B.C. many different peoples throughout Mesoamerica were using Olmec symbols in their own art and the stela was in use in the Chiapas and Guatemalan Highlands. By 100 B.C. the stela had become the dominant format among the peoples living at Izapa, Kaminaljuyu, El Baul, Abaj Takalik and Chalchuapa. By 50 B.C., Lowland Maya had experimented with the stela, adding it to their expressive repertoire as a major narrative format by the second century A.D. The Hauberg Stela (Pl. 66), the earliest known dated Lowland Maya monument, is inscribed with a date in the year A.D. 199, but eventually even earlier dates will surely emerge as archaeological investigations of Late Preclassic level continue.[42]

The indigenous artistic form of the Lowland Maya was architectural sculpture executed in plaster over stone armatures. These large works, which are on a scale with the freestanding colossal heads of the Olmec, first appeared in architecture on pyramidal terraces at Tikal, El Mirador, Lamanai, Cerros (Fig. II.1) and Uaxactun as early as 150 B.C. Earlier societies in Mesoamerica had experimented with architectural sculpture, but the medium was stone, the technique shallow relief and the impact limited. Because the first successful Maya exploitation of public art for political goals was in the form of architectural sculpture, architecture became the principal vehicle of all public art throughout subsequent Maya history. Architecture was programmed with symbolic information expressed in sculpture or painting. Substructures bore huge masks. Outer surfaces of bearing walls were often covered with relief sculpture, usually executed in plaster. The entablatures and roofcombs were sculpted in relief or volumetric imagery. Door lintels, whether wooden beams or stone slabs, could be carved with relief images. Interior benches were carved or painted, and stone slabs and plaster reliefs were applied to interior walls. Stelae were mounted in the plaza spaces between buildings, and their programming was often related to the surrounding architectural imagery.

Interior space in Maya stone architecture imitated the characteristic shape of the thatched house. Interior spans were constructed using the corbel vault—or successive courses of masonry stepped inward to a small gap bridged by a capstone (Fig. 10)—although thatch and thick, wood-reinforced plaster were used simultaneously as roofing material for residential structures and, more rarely, in ceremonial structures. The corbel technology of Maya architecture severely limited the amount of interior space that could be incorporated into a building. By functional necessity and traditional definition, access to interior spaces was limited, and the exterior plaza is the operational space in Maya architecture. Architectural sculpture and painting, as well as the stelae, face this open space. Maya buildings functioned like huge billboards manifesting religious and political propaganda for the elite who commissioned them. They were also great stage fronts for the rituals vital to the sustenance of society as a whole. Through the symbolic information carried by sculpture and painting around and within the architecture, the framework of ritual was defined in terms of the larger Maya cosmos, the history of the site and region and the personal actions, authority and ancestry of kings.[43]

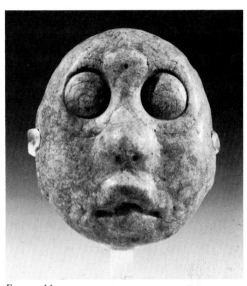

Like public art, objects made for the use of individuals and within small groups communicated information about the object and its user. Symbols on such objects could mark them as instruments of power and identify the owner in terms of name, rank, source of authority and his role in ritual. Symbolism also functioned to transform mundane objects into power instruments for use in ritual.

In Maya art, and in all great art styles, the formal properties of art—the way in which an image could be presented—were limited by tradition and technology. Each society also has its own natural way of seeing and producing images. The decisions about reality that comprise these ways of seeing are often unconsciously made, learned by children as they grow to understand their world and to create two-dimensional imagery that refers to their three-dimensional experience. We do not know the cultural source of these artistic decisions, or why the Maya considered their particular set of decisions to be the best solution. But because we too carry culturally acquired ways of seeing that are different from those of the Maya, it is helpful in deciphering Maya imagery to consider some of the ways that their visual canon differs from our own.

The Maya artist did not regard light and shadow to be significant information in two-dimensional representation. Shadow is never reproduced by change in color, tone, hue or by the application of modeled shades of gray. The Maya were simply not interested in creating the illusion of shadows—chiaroscuro in traditional art historical terminology.[44] However, using natural light sources the Maya created shadows on volumetric and relief sculptures, as in the architectural sculpture at Copan (Pls. 57, 110). Volumetric sculpture was carved to produce modeled patterns of light and shadow. Costume objects such as pectorals (Fig. 11), belt heads and headdress elements, were often manufactured in half-round forms with a flat, back plane for attachment. The outer surfaces were modeled so that light and shadow would naturally emphasize these sculpted features. In relief carving, shadow cast across relief defines the line, as seen on Yaxchilan Lintel 24 (Pl. 62), with its deeper carving, and on Yaxchilan Lintel 17 (Pl. 64), with its shallow relief.

Flat color was applied to sculpted or smooth surfaces, with variation usually achieved by diluting the pigment, as in thin washes of codex-style pottery painting (Pls. 115, 116) rather than mixing pigments. Maya color was often translucent, so overlapping strokes would cause changes in hue, seen in the paintings at Bonampak (Pl. 38a).

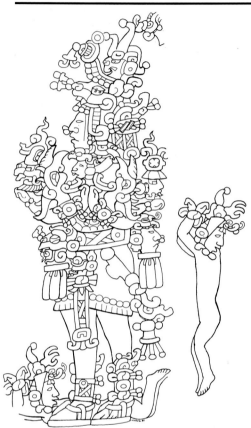

FIGURE 12
Jade plaque, the Leiden Plaque
Early Classic period, A.D. 320
See also Plate 33

The artist has drawn the figure of the captive at a smaller scale than the ruler, both to signal his lesser importance and to fit the drawing within the narrow horizontal space of the celt.

Light and shadow patterns resulting from the sculptural modulation of the surface also interact with the color patterns (Pl. 2), but color was not changed to create the illusion of shadow. Paint was often applied to fill in shapes, usually defined by the relief pattern or linear outlines. It also could be applied as line, either following sculptural line or adding detail not carved on the surface (Pl. 39). Colors were bright pigments from mineral sources, such as iron oxides, and were rarely mixed to produce different colors, with the exception of the mixing of yellow and blue to produce green. The Maya, unlike most other preindustrial people, had an unlimited source of permanent, intense blue—the attapulgite clay used today in commercial paper forms such as write-through checks[45]—whose use can be seen on the figurines in Plates 52 and 79. Color could be used naturalistically to signal the inherent color of materials, as in the clothing of a king (Pl. 2), but it also had symbolic value. Sometimes the color that appears on monuments bears no relationship to the naturalistic representation of particular objects, as in Yaxchilan Lintel 24, which appears to have been painted a solid blue (Pl. 62).

Most stela compositions included only one figure, as on the Hauberg Stela (Pl. 66), perhaps because of the verticality of the stela slab. The use of two figures began with the addition of captives, as on Dos Pilas Stela 16 (Fig. V.4), or ancestral figures, as on Yaxchilan Stela 11 (Fig. V.5a), to the visual field; and tri-figural compositions (Fig. II.7), began with the presentation of parents flanking the ruler as a statement of legitimate claim. In the Late Classic period, multifigure compositions were exploited, but usually on wall-mounted panels like Piedras Negras Lintel 2 (Pl. 40), throne backs, building walls, like the Bonampak paintings (Pl. 38), or in other formats with a dominant horizontal axis.

Spatial illusion in two-dimensional art was severely limited, and the optical devices used to imply position in space were very few. Most pictorial representations in both stone relief (Pls. 1, 40) and pottery painting (Pls. 48, 117a) used a groundline to establish the setting of a scene. People and objects were shown from only two points of view, frontal and profile, which could be combined in ingenious ways, as in the twisted back view of the captive on the middle level of Piedras Negras Stela 12 (Fig. V.8). Objects were arranged on the groundline in a logical manner. Human figures always stand on it (Pl. 48), and even when the groundline was not drawn, figures are arranged as if it were there (Fig. 13a). Overlapping, not position in picture plane or relative scale, is used to show position in space, as in the group of captives on the bottom level of Piedras Negras Stela 12. Changes in size have meaning, such as indicating relative rank (Fig. 12), but smaller size does not refer to distance. Color and value are not changed by distance. Maya art gives the impression that all the action takes place within two feet of a blank wall, an effect particularly evident in Piedras Negras Lintel 2 (Pl. 40). Any action or object that violates these rules can be taken to be supernatural; for example, the floating figures of Ixlu Stela 2 (Fig. IV.3) are gods.

The use of groundlines as the major spatial device made it easy to arrange multiple figures in horizontal compositions. This device was also used by painters who worked on pottery walls, since the horizontal axis was usually the longer one. Figures can be shown in processional sequence with minimal overlap of individuals, as on Piedras Negras Lintel 2. These long horizontal picture planes can also be broken up into different episodes, often distinguished by the direction in which the figures face (Pl. 68). However, the format of the stela is usually vertical, making compositions of multiple figures difficult to compose and, therefore, unusual. Several compositional solu-

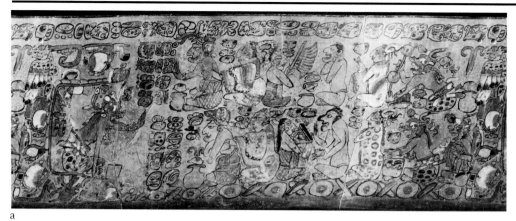
a

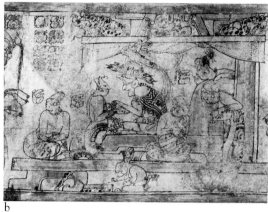
b

tions were developed, including multiple horizontal registers, as in the Bonampak murals in Room 1 (Pl. 38), but the most successful was the use of architectural terracing and interior benches (Fig. 13b) as a logical motivation for placing figures on different levels. The Kimbell wall panel (Pl. 86) uses this architectural device, but the most extraordinary examples, showing the most complex architectural configurations, are found on Piedras Negras Stela 12 (Fig. V.8) and in the compositions of murals in Room 2 (Fig. V.6) and Room 3 at Bonampak.

Particularly in the Late Classic period, relative position in space was indicated by overlap. Some Maya artists, especially at sites in the western area, were accomplished practitioners of foreshortening (Fig. 14). They became quite adept at representing bodies in twisted and other unusual postures. Particular skill was used in representing the cross-legged, seated position and the sideview of body parts, such as shoulders, as on the Kimbell panel (Fig. 15). Captives and ballplayers were subjects that permitted artistic experimentation with contorted body positions. The captive on Tonina Monument 122 (Fig. V.11) twists his upper torso, looking behind him, and the legs of the fallen ballplayer (Pl. 101) are awkwardly twisted. Apparently the conventions of drawing these secondary figures were much less rigid.

Maya art, both painting and sculpture, shows a marked sensitivity to the boundaries of the pictorial field, notably through the many innovative devices artists used to break them. Most compositions are framed by borders, some plain bands (Pl. 86), others glyphic (Pl. 1) or figural. The most accomplished and innovative artist defined these framing bands as cosmic or architectural elements, as on Piedras Negras Stela 11 (Fig. II.4). In a tour de force of spatial manipulation, the "Cookie Cutter" Master of Yaxchilan arranged the glyphs on the rear of Stela 11 (Fig. V.5a) to reproduce the stepped contour of a corbeled vault. Bird Jaguar stands inside the building; his victims kneel on the step in front of it. Many artists focus attention on these framing devices by violating them: feathers overlap them; hands hold them; supernaturals climb on them; body parts vanish behind them or overlap them. On the Art Institute of Chicago panel (Pl. 101), the foot of the fallen player overlaps the frame. At some sites, imagery in the framing bands was used to carry cosmological information separate from the narratives, such as the use of the Cosmic Monster to form the band and genealogical information about the protagonist, as on Yaxchilan Stela 11 (Fig. V.5a,b). Glyphic

FIGURE 13a
Pot depicting Chac-Xib-Chac and the Pauahtuns
Late Classic period, A.D. 650–800

The Pauahtuns and their female attendants are arranged in two registers. The upper set of figures sit in a row as if a groundline had been drawn under them.

FIGURE 13b
Detail, cylindrical vessel
The Art Museum, Princeton University
See also Plate 115

The architectural elements of a building platform and a bench are used by the artist to justify placing the figures on different vertical levels. The doorway, curtain and roof decoration of the temple function as a framing device for the scene.

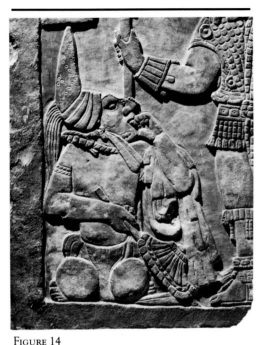

FIGURE 14
Detail, Lintel 16, Yaxchilan
See also Plate 87

The legs of the seated captive are foreshortened as he twists toward his captor, Bird Jaguar.

texts were also used as framing devices or could be set directly into the pictorial space.

Narrative was presented in a variety of compositional formats. For example, it could show a single moment characteristic of the entire sequence of action, as at Palenque; continuous series of moments that move from one to another, as in Room 1 at Bonampak (Pl. 38); contrasting episodes from different parts of the action sequence, such as bloodletting and accession (Pl. 68); or simultaneous narrative. This last form is the most difficult to understand. It presents a single moment, but it uses the features of several different stages in a sequence. For example, a captive shown at the instant of his capture could be dressed in the uniform of the sacrificial victim, which in the real episode he would not wear for hours or days after his capture, as on Yaxchilan Lintel 8 (Fig. V.3).

The Maya focused attention on three moments in the continuous sequence of ritual experience: the inceptive, the progressive and the completive. The inceptive moment is either just before or just after a sequence begins. In Bonampak Room 1 (Pl. 38), lords stand around in informal groups as the chief attendant turns his head to get last-minute instructions from his king. At Palenque, the king designate leans in anticipation toward his father, who is beginning to pass the crown to his son (Fig. II.7).

The progressive moment shows part of an ongoing action. At Yaxchilan, Lady Xoc stares at her vision (Pl. 62), or her hands are frozen mid-action as she pulls a barbed rope through her tongue (Pl. 63). The stream of blood given by Bird Jaguar is poised midway on its fall to the censer in front of his feet (Pl. 76).

The completive moment occurs when the ritual is done. On the Leiden Plaque (Pl. 33), the king who was installed is shown wearing the full regalia of kingship. The transformation process shown at its inception at Palenque is completed.

Tension was achieved by an extraordinary device developed at sites along the Usumacinta River. At Bonampak and Yaxchilan, lintels of the three doors of a single building were programmed to give one level of information in the narrative scenes and another in the text.[46] Each image shows a moment in a single ritual; together they encompass the entire ritual sequence. By contrast, the texts specify that this ritual took place at different times, and at Bonampak, with different actors.

Tension was also achieved between two-dimensional and three-dimensional imagery. Early Classic clay artists often began an image on the body of a pot with a drawing or incision but completed it in a three-dimensional extrusion from the lid. Thus, a pot lid could represent a bird, its wings, tail and body painted in line, its head emerging three-dimensionally from the surface to become the handle (Pl. 105). This tension between two-dimensional and three-dimensional imagery is also characteristic of the sculpture of Piedras Negras and Tonina, although the most successful examples are found in the zoomorphs of Quirigua and the architectural sculpture of Copan.

Line was preeminent throughout all periods of Maya art, which rivaled the Chinese and the Japanese as one of the world's great calligraphic traditions. The primary tool used in Maya writing and painting was the brush (Fig. 16). Like written Chinese, Maya script was linear and calligraphic in nature. The use of the brush as the principal writing tool profoundly affected both the graphic configuration of writing and the style of pictorial art.

No writing brushes have survived archaeologically, but brushes are depicted in painted sources. In scenes painted on pottery, scribes use paint pots made from conch shells (Pl. 44) and pointed brushes made of flexible animal hair. The clearest representation of a Maya brush now known, which was incised on a bone excavated from Burial

116 at Tikal, shows an elegant human hand emerging from the gullet of a snaggle-toothed dragon holding a brush delicately between thumb and first finger poised for a stroke (Fig. 17). The shaft of the brush is rigid and of even width. The heel of the brush is smaller in diameter than the shaft, and it swells to a broader diameter below the heel, before tapering to a fine tip. The Maya seem to have invented a brush identical in form to the Chinese brush, to fulfill the same function—as the tool for calligraphic line work in both writing and painting.

Drawings from Palenque demonstrate the dominance of line in Maya art and the use of this Chinese-style brush, and reveal rare information about how the Maya made public art. A plaster medallion, which once completely surrounded the painted limestone panel called the Oval Palace Tablet, has fallen from the wall, revealing an underlying master drawing that was used as a guide by the plasterers (Fig. 18). Parts of the master drawing for the carved reliefs on King Pacal's stone sarcophagus in the Temple of Inscriptions (Pl. 119) have also been preserved, perhaps due to the necessity of a quick burial. These drawings were painted on the stone sides before the burial chamber was built, and the relief was carved after the chamber was completed.

In both examples, a line drawing was applied in black paint by a master calligrapher. Lines in the drawing are about one-eighth of an inch thick and of relatively even width throughout. The artist pulled long, flowing strokes, some of them continuous pulls over a length of two feet or more. Only the Chinese-style brush can hold enough paint to pull such a long stroke over a porous surface like plaster or limestone while maintaining such precise control over line width and quality.

Maya drawings and paintings show a freehand execution. Producing such a long stroke while retaining a controlled line required the artist to work rapidly, sustain a light touch, and pivot his arm from his shoulder. Linear paintings in the tombs at Rio Azul and in Burial 48 at Tikal were executed so rapidly that excess paint fell from the rapidly moving brush, forming drip patterns that were retained as part of the imagery. The spontaneity and calligraphic quality of these paintings could not be achieved by tracing previously prepared master drawings.

The contents of inscriptions and pictorial compositions, as well as the relative proportions of each part of the whole composition, may have been worked out in advance. Guidelines indicating placements for glyphic blocks and pictorial elements exist in the Dresden Codex and in the wall paintings of the Rio Azul tombs. An unfinished hieroglyphic stair at Dos Pilas has glyph blocks and rectangular shapes for figures cut away from the background stone, but the next two steps in the process—adding the master drawing and carving it into the stone—were never done (Fig. 19).

Mistakes in computation, drawing and execution provide interesting information about the artist. At Palenque, Dos Pilas and elsewhere, blatant errors of mathematical computation or in the use of signs were not corrected. Either the Maya did not proofread the first drafts made by the masters, or errors were considered to be divine intervention and protected from correction.[47] The frequency of such mistakes also suggests that the process of creating the master drawing was a ritual occasion of major importance that included fasting, bloodletting and, perhaps, heavy drinking of Maya beer, called *balche*. If so, the masters were probably not at their best when they drew the master painting.

Works at Palenque suggest that a sculpted relief based on a drawing was produced by other artists, usually more than one. Examination of the Palace Tablet and the sarcophagus in the Temple of Inscriptions shows the hand of the master drawing to be

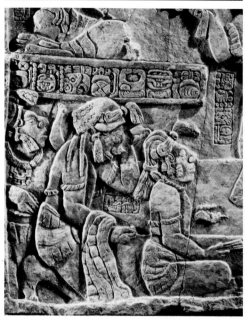

FIGURE 15
Detail, captives from a carved panel
See also Plate 86

The three captive are drawn with fluid motion, animated gestures and body positions. Overlapping is used to signal position in space. The progression of the hand from the mouth of the left figure to the forehead of the kneeling central figure to the extended gesture of the seated figure on the right suggests a sense of ongoing activity.

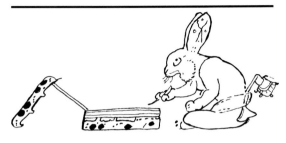

Rabbit Scribe from the Princeton Pot

FIGURE 16
Detail, the rabbit scribe from a cylindrical vessel
See also Plate 115

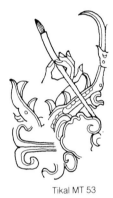

Tikal MT 53

FIGURE 17
Incised bone from Burial 116, Tikal, Guatemala
Late Classic period, A.D. 735

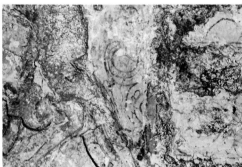

FIGURE 18
Detail, master drawing from the medallion around the Oval Palace Tablet
House E of the Palace, Palenque, Chiapas.
Late Classic period, ca. A.D. 650
Photo by Merle Greene Robertson

uniform, but the execution of the modeled relief varies in technique and skill. The most accomplished sculptors carved the figures and important parts of the inscriptions; craftsmen of lesser skill were allowed to work on less sensitive areas. Most interestingly, the craftsmen who applied the plaster and carved the relief of the two drawings described above did not follow exactly the lines of the master. Sculptors apparently exercised their own judgment in finishing the sculpture, using the master drawing only as a guide, since the sculptor was a master in his own right and finished the final surface according to his own sense of aesthetics.

Since most Maya draftsmanship was freehand drawing, accuracy, especially in delineating important symbols, was controlled by convention.[48] Certainly, an artist did not bring the king and his attendants to a prepared stone or wall to sit for their portraits. The configurations of imagery were conventions, learned very probably by rote, with training beginning in childhood. Maya artists were born into their profession, although particularly able individuals were probably absorbed into the lineage groups specializing in the scribal arts. The recently excavated residential compound of one such scribal lineage at Copan indicates that scribes and artists were high on the social ladder.[49]

Smaller objects, such as pottery and jade, appear to have been produced by only one hand. However, we do not know if the potter also painted his works, or if the lapidary artist had assistants to help block in an image. Skill levels, as with monumental art, are varied. Masters of superlative skill worked on special vessels, but workshops appear to have mass-produced pottery mediocre in construction and painting. Wealthier and more prestigious patrons probably acquired the higher-quality products.

Clay sculpture was made by both slab and coil techniques, and their surfaces were modeled, incised and painted with clay slips and mineral pigments. Plaster grounds were used as paint bases on pottery vessels, as well as on walls and in books. Plaster artisans used mold casting, additive techniques and subtractive modeling. Usually a stone armature was inserted to reinforce the interior of such sculpture, which is found in styles ranging from shallow relief to fully three-dimensional.

Although evidence is scanty, it appears that artists shared common pattern books, knew of one another's work, and even trained together. At Mul-Chic, for example, the drawing of the prominent seated warrior in the paintings resembles so closely that of Ruler Seven on the top of Piedras Negras Stela 12 that one artist seems to have copied the other. The contours of a captive displayed by Bird Jaguar on the La Pasadita lintel in Berlin is nearly identical to a captive painted in the Bonampak paintings, nearly thirty years later, but the Bonampak figure is reversed, as if an intermediate tracing had been made. We also suspect that skilled artisans accompanied royal wives into foreign tribute and may have been exchanged as tribute.

The Maya created one of the great art traditions of the world, one that stands beside the art of the ancient Egyptians or the early Chinese. Maya painting is both powerful in its imagery and execution and elegant in its line work; the fine incisions on shell and jade are precise, yet lyrical in style. Small figurines were modeled from clay with all the detail and presence of life-size stone and plaster portraits of rulers and gods. As much attention was paid to the execution and the message conveyed on a small bone handle for a fan as was spent on the huge architectural monuments that celebrated the deeds of kings and the order of the universe. Maya art communicates powerfully with people of the twentieth century, yet at the same time transmits in eloquent detail the world view, beliefs and history of the people who made it.

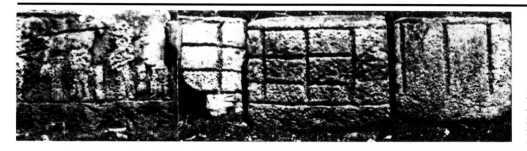

Maya Gods and Icons

Maya art was a complex symbolic language with profoundly important social functions. It was mainly commissioned by kings and other high elite to fulfill their political and social purposes. Since art communicated the message of the king to his subjects, the artist was confined to producing works that affirmed a shared reality. These constraints did not, however, inhibit the creation of an art of such sensuality and power that it has reached us across the centuries, even when its message was not understood. As we decipher the writing system and decode the imagery, we are learning to understand this message, which, since it is not addressed to us or our sensibilities, is sometimes disturbing. But by reclaiming its meaning, even in part, we will preserve it as part of the heritage of all humanity.

In many ways, Maya monumental art is best understood, not as the portrait of people, but as the portrait of ritual. The combination of writing with imagery allowed the time, location, action and actor to be described with absolute precision. Glyphic texts reinforced visual narratives recording rituals, documenting a specific ritual involving a named individual at a particular time and place. Maya narrative sculpture froze the moment of ritual in time, but since it continued to exist, this art became the means by which society was instructed in correct behavior. The historical precedent thus established was intended to guide posterity.

Since art had to communicate cultural information, it was restricted to symbolism and imagery whose meanings were shared by members of the Maya community. The visual symbol system in Maya art worked like a language, and, as with a spoken language, individual taste and creative expression had to be subordinated to the imperative of communication. Arbitrary change could not be tolerated. If, in order to express personal choice or aesthetic judgment, an artist changed the form of a temple so that it looked like a residential building; or altered the way a god was drawn so that its attributes could no longer be discerned; or invented new emblems to mark the rank of a king or lineage head, then the purpose of this art would have been lost. Because of its social function, Maya iconography was of necessity conservative.

The symbolism of Maya art identified the role of individuals in their immediate context, as well as in relationship to the larger Maya world and to the Maya cosmos. The proper order of society, the role of the king, commoners and nobles alike, was expressed in permanent and public form through art. Imagery described the cosmos, the origin of supernatural power and how to manipulate it, the reason for the existence of human beings, and their place in the cosmos. Ritual was conceived as the bridge between the supernatural and the mundane worlds, and the king was the agent of power who made the transition from the sacred to the mundane. Thus, Maya art depicts the historical action of civil kings, but those kings acted with sacred authority and supernatural power. The imagery of art was a symbolic language that depicted both the historical actions of kings and the supernatural framework of the cosmos that gave those actions sacred purpose.

The Maya Universe, in which historical action and daily life took place, was a three-leveled structure, consisting of the Overworld, the Middleworld, and the Underworld. The Underworld was entered either through a cave or through bodies of standing water, such as the ocean or a lake. The Middleworld, the world of humankind, was oriented by the four cardinal directions, each associated with a tree, bird and color. The principal direction was east, the point of the rising sun; its color was red. North, the direction of the ancestral dead, was white. West was black and associated with death and the Underworld. South was yellow and the right hand of the sun. At the center stood an *axis mundi*, or central axis, which was most often shown as a great ceiba tree with a supernatural bird at its crown. The roots of the tree were in the Underworld, its trunk in the Middleworld and its branches in the Overworld. The souls of the dead and the supernaturals of the Maya cosmos traveled from level to level via this tree.

The Overworld, also called the Upperworld, best described as the heavens, was marked by the passage of the sun across the sky. In fact, the Maya may have seen the day sky as the Overworld and the night sky as the Underworld passing over their heads daily. The Milky Way and the fixed stars formed the canopy of the night sky. The moving planets, the procession of constellations and the erratic dance of the moon were as the manifestation of the normal activity of the gods. Tracking these movements was a critical function of Maya religion, for the behavior of the gods could be either beneficial or terribly dangerous to the inhabitants of the Middleworld.

The gods of Maya myth fall into one of four categories: worldly phenomena, anthropomorphs, zoomorphs and animals. A particular god can be manifested in more than one of these forms. Some god images seem to have been immutable; others age and transform, perhaps in symbolic reference to the biological life cycle. The iconography of each deity consists of a distinct set of pictorial and glyphic attributes, and individual images display a partial or complete set of these attributes. Features are sometimes shared by more than one deity, however, and features may be borrowed from one deity by another as a signal of a role change or transformation. Thus, the boundaries between these complexes of images are not sharp. As new patterns of features are discovered and as other are found to be equivalent (or not), the known identities of these gods change.

The worldly phenomena, which symbolize sacred environments, have only recently been recognized as a special category in Maya art. The Maya believed in a living universe in which mountains, rivers, the sky, the earth, caves and other things we think of as being inanimate are alive with spiritual power. In the imagery of Maya art, these things do not behave like gods with personality who interact with humans and other beings. They are instead part of the sacred cosmos. They occur as arches above actors, as seats on which they sit, as the doors of buildings in which ritual took place or as portal leading from one kind of place to another. Human beings and supernaturals act upon them, but the worldly phenomena do not themselves act as individual beings. They are simply there to give a sacred context to the actions of others.

The anthropomorphs are primarily human in aspect, but they can carry animal features as part of their distinctive attributes. While they can be indistinguishable from living humans, they frequently have nonhuman square eyes, and their bodies have distinctive markings on the arms, legs and torsos, indicating their status as gods. The god markings—either mirrors or signs for darkness—are shown in half view, because they are wrapped around a "three-dimensional" body part (Fig. 20). The mirror signals brightness and perhaps a positive nature; darkness (*akbal* in Maya) signals an Under-world identity and perhaps an association with the night. Historical individuals who have died, have become ancestors and dwell in a supernatural realm, also bear god markings that reflect their status.

Zoomorphs may display human or animal characteristics, but their appearance is not naturalistic. Their overall form may derive from a particular animal—such as a bird, crocodile or deer—but because their features combine with those of several animals, they would never be mistaken for creatures of the natural world. Zoomorphs often have distinct head types; these include a ubiquitous head with a long nose, dragons derived from both lizards and snakes, and jaguar-based heads with comparatively short snouts. Deer, fish, snakes, crocodiles, birds and human bodies are merged with these zoomorphic heads. The Maya deliberately combined features from animals that occupy different ecological niches to confer supernatural status without ambiguity. In Maya cosmology, zoomorphs are usually actors who manifest both cause and effect in ritual and in the natural world. They can be individual beings with independent personalities, but they can also manifest the power and animate force of objects, locations and substances in the Middleworld. Because of this, there is some crossover between the categories of zoomorphs and the worldly phenomena.

Images of animals generally have bodies and physical features like animals of the natural world. However, they move and behave like human beings (as do contemporary animal cartoon characters). They participate in a variety of Underworld activities, including acting as scribes and playing instruments in Underworld musical bands. In the Underworld, animals are intelligent: they are the first generation of creatures made by the gods, and they behave like men.

In Maya thought certain points and substances in the natural world may have supernatural force that was manifested symbolically in art. These symbols represent categories of phenomena, much as we use the generic term *man* to refer to all human beings. Cave, tree, water, blood, cloud, vision, lightning bolt, maize, water-lily, body parts and emanations—all of these could be manifested as animate persona. Sometimes the properties of two objects or substances were conceived to be structurally analogous: blood is to the human body as sap is to the tree; smoke is to fire as breath is to humans; blood is to humans as water is to earth. Symbols representing structural categories with similar appearances were also freely interchangeable. For example, flame, smoke, mist, breath, flowing blood, clouds, farts, belches and new maize sprouts were all represented by the same double scroll.[50] The precise meaning of such a scroll can only be distinguished from the context, and the double entendre was probably intentional.

Inanimate objects manufactured for royal use accrued potency through their use. This accumulated power became so intense and dangerous that, in order to release it, the Maya regularly "killed" buildings by removing faces of sculptures depicting both

mirror "brightness"   akbal "darkness"

God markings

FIGURE 20

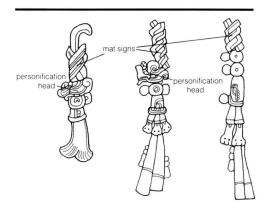

mat signs

personification head

personification head

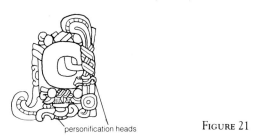

Mat in plain and personified forms

personification heads

FIGURE 21

humans and zoomorphs and drilling holes in pottery. Much of the deliberate damage done to the faces of kingly portraits and other sculpture was the result of these killing rituals. In the Maya system of imagery, this accrued power is depicted as a long-nosed personification head attached to objects (Fig. 21). The personification head carries no specific inherent meaning beyond the concept of force. When it is attached to an object—a wristlet, an earflare or a cloth sash, for example—the personification head signals that these objects have accumulated sacred power.

Individual entities that appear visually and glyphically unrelated can be the same gods. For example, the sun can appear as a young male, an aged male, an anthropomorph with jaguar features or a half-skeletal zoomorph with a sun-bowl on its forehead. These contrasting and superficially unrelated forms appear to express different aspects of the same entity—in this case the newly risen sun, the sun near sunset, the sun in the Underworld and the sun as a cosmic object. Each version is complete, and yet they are all related variations on the same subject. In any given scene, normally only one aspect will be presented.

In Maya religious thinking, all of these supernatural entities could enter human space as physical beings, and humans are depicted interacting with them in a real, physical sense. The vision quest provided one means of access to the divine, the letting of the ruler's blood another. The costumes characteristic of gods were worn by the nobility during these events. Images of these rites show humans wearing full-body costumes, including masks, to transform themselves symbolically into gods. These scenes do not appear to represent playacting but, rather, a true transformation into a divine being. However, the Maya maintained a clear distinction between images of a true god and those of a human transformed into a god, by showing a cutaway, or X-ray, view of the mask that revealed the human profile inside.

The nomenclature for Maya gods currently suffers from inconsistency. At the turn of the century, the glyphic names and pictorial images of the gods were first recognized in the Postclassic codices and given designations in an alphabetic system. The same gods, however, had also been given names based on their functions or their association with deity descriptions compiled by friars after the Conquest, or from Yucatec Maya literature, such as the Chilam Balam. The problem was further exacerbated as new deities and deity complexes were named without reference to earlier terminology. Thus, the same god may be assigned designations in more than one system of nomenclature.

This confused nomenclature is obviously imperfect. Many of the names of gods are sterile and have nothing to do with the nature of the deity or with his importance in Maya cosmology. Since Classic Maya mythology is not yet fully understood, however, invention of another set of terms at this time would only compound the problem. Therefore, this study uses the existing names but is restricted to the most common and frequently recognized names for each god. Maya mythology and painting are filled with hundreds of supernaturals. While it is not possible to catalogue them all, the most important ones are described here as a guide for the reader.

SACRED PLACES AND THINGS

The Celestial Monster
The Celestial Monster, sometimes also called the Bicephalic Monster or the Cosmic Monster, has two heads and a single body (Fig. 22). The body may be rendered as crocodilian or by a band of symbols, most commonly the skyband. The front head has a long snout, a beard and large teeth and its eye is always lidded and often includes either a Venus or a crossed-bands sign. It has the ears of a deer and often has deer hooves as well. The body of this monster belongs to the front head; it is not a fusion of two bodies.

In contrast to the front head, the rear head is usually inverted because it was carried as a burden by the crocodile. This head has a blunt snout, fleshy eyes and a skeletal lower jaw. The forehead is a deep bowl with an inverted rim fused with the glyphic sign of the sun, *kin*. Atop the bowl rest three symbols: crossed bands, a stingray spine and a shell. This four-part configuration is known as the Quadripartite Badge; in instances when the rear head appears detached from the crocodile, it is called the Quadripartite Monster.

The Celestial Monster is composed of the paired opposition of Venus and the sun. As the Morning Star, Venus leads the sun out of the Underworld and trails behind it at sunset. The Monster appears to represent the dawn with the sun following Venus; the concept of the journey and its westerly direction is also implicit in the image. When the Monster is used on architecture, it is generally placed so that the front head is on the western side of the building. In both pictorial and architectural contexts, it frames portals or creates a framing band, or it may form a throne or altar. Rarely, it can be held as a scepter by a king.

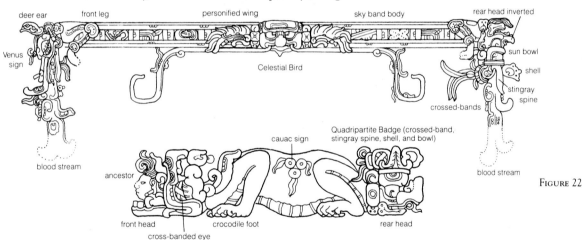

FIGURE 22

Celestial Monster from Copan Altar 41

FIGURE 23

The Cauac Monster
The Cauac Monster (Fig. 23) is always zoomorphic. Its distinguishing features are a cluster of loops that look like grapes, or three disks forming a triangle and a partial circle with a dotted perimeter. Its eyes are half closed and its forehead is indented by a stepped cleft, out of which maize may grow (Fig. 23a). The Monster generally appears as a head only, but on the roof of the Temple of the Cross at Palenque, in one of its few appearances with a body, it has reptilian legs.

The Cauac Monster is the essence of stone; like rock it is a thing of the ground. It represents openings in rock and in buildings made of rock. It is carved on huge boulders used as altars and shown in painted and carved scenes as stone altars and pedestals (Fig. 23b). When it is shown in stacks, it represents stony walls. The distinctive features of the Monster are shared by the glyph

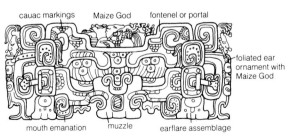

Cauac Monster from Bonampak Stela 1

for the day Cauac, a day name derived from the word for lightning bolt. Even today, Maya peoples believe that obsidian and flint are made when lightning strikes the earth (the word for ax also derives from "lightning bolt"). Images of the Cauac Monster may represent a cave, which was thought to be the physical source of lightning, or the lightning bolt itself; the Monster can also be the place where lightning strikes. It is, however, never shown as an actor.

Images of stone objects also carry *cauac* markings, but they are distinct from the Cauac Monster. For example, the glyph for stone, *cauac*, may be joined to that for tree to read "stone tree"—a stela (Fig. 23c). Images of both ritual and functional objects made of flint are also marked by *cauac* signs to signify stone (Fig. 23e). Images of the personified form of flint, however, have skeletal features and circular indentations in the contour, in imitation of the edge of chipped eccentric flints (Fig. 23d); these distinguish personified flints from the Cauac Monster proper.

FIGURE 23

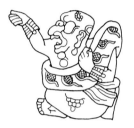

Full-figure Cauac in *te'-tun* "stone tree" from Copan Stela D

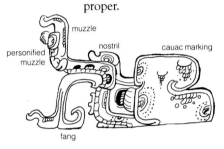
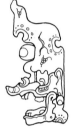

Cauac Monster from the Metropolitan Pot

Personified eccentric flint from Tablet of the Slave, Palenque

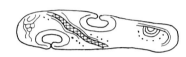

Stone ax head from Dumbarton Oaks Panel

The Water-lily Monster

In Lowland Maya languages, the words for water-lily and lake are homonyms, hence, the water-lily and its personifications are natural symbols for water. In one primary form, the water-lily is shown as a zoomorphic head, with a mirror or Kan-cross in its forehead (Fig. 24a). Rootlike projections emerge from the top and stems, and pads and blossoms rise from these root forms. In an alternative form, a water-lily pad is tied across the forehead by a stem and a blossom, and the body is rendered as a fish with another, smaller fish nibbling at its tail (Fig. 24b). This configuration represents the god of the number 13 and the personification of tun ("year") in Long Count dates. The Water-lily Monster is the symbol of standing bodies of water, such as the ocean, lakes, swamps and agricultural canals.[51] Moreover, because water-lilies were abundant in the canals used by the Maya, they became the symbol of the earth's abundance.

FIGURE 24

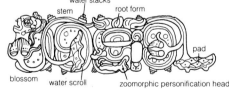

Water-lily Monster—surface of water

The Vision Serpent

The hallucinatory visions central to Maya ritual were symbolized visually by a rearing snake (Fig. 25a). Most Vision Serpents have smooth bodies, but some also show areas of flayed skin and, in some cases, feathered bodies. Serpent heads have long, sometimes bulbous snouts, and most are bearded. The persona contacted through the vision is shown emerging from a gaping mouth. In the most common representation of the Vision Serpent, the end of the tail is surmounted by a second head with completely different features. This rear head can be replaced by a flint knife or a smoking *ahau* glyph and, in one example, Yaxchilan Lintel 25, the Vision Serpent is truly double-headed (Fig. 25b). The most common rear head is the skeletal personification of blood, which indicates that the vision comes from blood. When the personified symbol of blood is absent, the Vision Serpent rears up from a blood scroll instead.

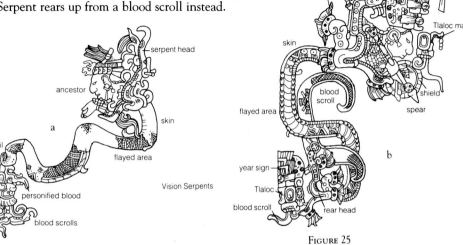

FIGURE 25

Sky

The symbol for sky is a band divided into compartments by vertical bars (Fig. 26). Each compartment is filled by the symbol for a particular star, constellation or planet, many of which are as yet undeciphered. Skybands may appear as the body of the Celestial Monster, as frames around a scene or as a bench; they are often on the borders of cloth, as though they represented the concept of an edge.

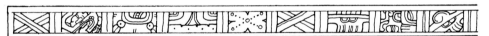

Sky-Band

FIGURE 26

Earth

The earth was represented by bands with coiled spirals characteristic of the glyph *caban*, a day sign (the word *cab* means "earth") (Fig. 27). No personified form of the earth has yet been identified.

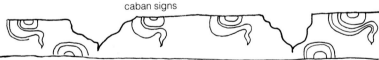

Earth Band

FIGURE 27

Water

Water was represented by a series of signs, including a shell, lines of dots (usually alternating groups of small and large dots) and a short stack of graduated rectangular shapes that by their configuration suggest a loaded canoe (Fig. 28a). These signs can be set in a line representing the surface of water, or they may be arranged within and around a thick line that is usually marked with the water-dot pattern (Fig. 28b). Images of water-lilies or their glyphic counterparts can be set among these water signs.

FIGURE 28

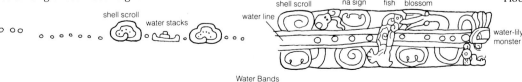

Water Bands

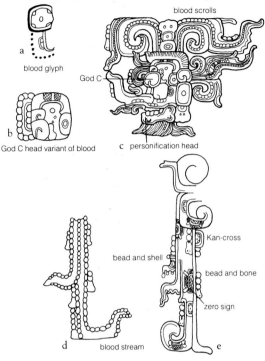

blood glyph

God C

God C head variant of blood

c personification head

blood scrolls

Kan-cross

bead and shell

bead and bone

zero sign

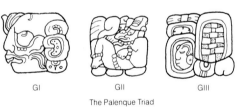

blood stream

FIGURE 29

Blood

Blood was represented in numerous ways (Fig. 29), but it is commonly indicated by a scroll-shaped form outlined with a contour of beads (Fig. 29d,e). Often the glyphs for the colors red, yellow and blue, as well as the signs (Fig. 29a,b) for precious materials, such as shell, jade and bone, are attached to or placed within the scrolls.[52] The glyphic form for blood shows drops of blood falling from one of the "precious" signs. The monkey-faced god known as God C is one personified form of blood and forms part of a more elaborate personified form, in which God C is the forehead of a larger skeletal zoomorph (Fig. 29c). Blood may also appear as a bifurcated scroll or a lazy-S scroll, with or without beaded outlines. Both kinds of scrolls may have signs of precious materials attached to their edges and set inside their borders. The zoomorphic form of blood is identified as a Square-nosed Dragon with beads around the mouth, who often emerges from a branch of the World Tree.

GODS

THE PALENQUE TRIAD

The Palenque Triad[53] is a trio of gods, GI, GII and GIII, celebrated as divine ancestors by the kings of Palenque (Fig. 30). The three gods were born eighteen days apart to parents whose births occurred before the beginning of the present era. The first- and second-born, GI ("G-one") and GIII ("G-three"), are prototypes of the Popol Vuh Hero Twins. These two gods in particular appear in several forms with different visual features and names; these manifestations are nonetheless aspects of the same deity complex.

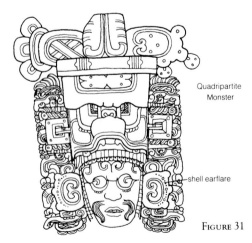

GI

GII

GIII

The Palenque Triad

FIGURE 30

GI

GI, the oldest of the Triad siblings, has the same name as his father, but the name is in the form of a portrait head, and its reading is not known (Fig. 31). One of the glyphs that appears in his name phrase may read Hun-Ahpu, matching the name of one of the Hero Twins from the Popol Vuh. He is associated with Venus, but since he also appears at Quirigua as the number 4, which is more commonly represented as the Sun God, he could also be identified with the sun. This dual identification with Venus and the sun is echoed in the Hero Twin myth; in some versions, Hunahpu becomes the Sun, but in others, he becomes Venus.[54]

GI rarely appears on painted pottery, but his image is common on Early Classic cache vessels, and the kings represented on Stela 2 at Tikal and Stela 1 at Copan wear GI masks. He has scalloped eyebrows, square eyes and a Roman nose. His front teeth are often replaced by a shark's tooth or filed into a T-shape, and he wears fishfins on his cheeks. A shell earflare and a headdress of the Quadripartite Monster, often combined with a Water Bird, complete his appearance.

Quadripartite Monster

shell earflare

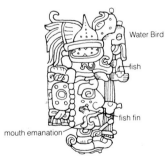

Water Bird

fish

fish fin

mouth emanation

FIGURE 31

GI as Chac-Xib-Chac

Visually, this god is almost identical to GI, except that he is usually zoomorphic (Fig. 32). In addition to the shell earflares, he wears a shell diadem, and his long hair is gathered up atop the head and falls forward in a loop. His body features are reptilian; his arms, legs and body are marked by water scrolls; and he carries both an ax and a God C disk. His form in miniature often hangs from the belts of Classic-period rulers. He is the figure fishing on the Tikal bones (Fig. 32a), and he is profoundly associated with the sacrificial death dance, both in the Underworld and in human ritual, as depicted in Room 3 at Bonampak. When he occurs in anthropomorphic form, he has a normal human eye and a shell beard, but he lacks the fishfin of the GI form discussed above. His name, as recorded on pottery, is Chac-Xib-Chac (Fig. 32c).[55]

FIGURE 32

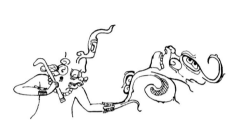

GI/Chac-Xib-Chac

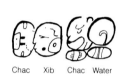

Chac   Xib   Chac   Water

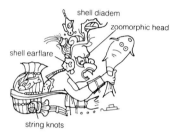

shell diadem

zoomorphic head

shell earflare

string knots

Fishing on the Tikal Bone

shell diadem   blood stone

Cauac marking   human head with shell beard

                           water body mark

string knots

ax

Ax-wielder from the Metropolitan Pot

GII (God K)

GII ("G-two") has long been recognized and as such has acquired many different names, such as God K, Bolon Dzacab, the Flare God and the Manikin Scepter. He is always zoomorphic (Fig. 33) and frequently has a serpent-headed foot. His body has reptilian features, but his hands and one foot are always human. His most characteristic feature is a forehead mirror punctured by a celt, a smoking celt, a smoking cigar, a smoking torch or a ceramic torch holder. The torch sign is a phonetic complement designating that the mirror is made from a material that sounds like the word for torch, pronounced *tah* in Mayan languages. Since obsidian is also *tah*, GII is "the obsidian mirror." A mirror can replace his head (Fig. 33d), or the mirror alone can stand for his name (Fig. 33c).

GII, the third-born of the Triad brothers, was particularly important to elite lineages and to rulers. His portrait glyph often occurs in rulers' names. He forms the scepter that appears on many different official occasions, including accession, and he is profoundly associated with sacrifice, in particular, with self-inflicted bloodletting. Throughout this work, he is called God K.

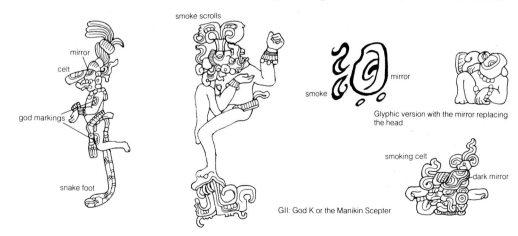

smoke scrolls

mirror

celt

god markings

snake foot

smoke   mirror

Glyphic version with the mirror replacing the head

smoking celt

dark mirror

GII: God K or the Manikin Scepter

FIGURE 33

GIII

GIII, the second-born of the Triad brothers, has the most complex glyphic and pictorial forms. In his "birth" passage on the Tablet of the Sun at Palenque, he is named in several ways: *Ahau-Kin*, or "Lord Sun"; with signs of a torch and a jaguar-covered *ahau*, or *Mah k'ina Tah Balam-Ahau*, which means "Lord Torch Jaguar Lord"; and as a sun sign preceding the decapitated body of a jaguar. Some of the same names are also found on pottery, and each is associated with a different figural representation. Since the names are associated with different sets of attributes, in the past, they were believed to be of different gods. Discrimination among these slightly varying representations (most of which have jaguarian aspects) is complicated, and the patterns presented below may prove inadequate. Each manifestation described will be assigned a simple descriptive name.

GIII as the Sun God

Ahau-Kin, or "Lord Sun," has a face with a prominent Roman nose and a square squint-eye (Fig. 34). The *kin* sign is usually placed on his cheek or forehead, sometimes on the arms or legs. He has a long, bound hank of hair that falls forward, and his front teeth are often filed into a T-shape. He is the god of the number 4 and presumably the daytime sun. He appears in both youthful and aged aspects, but it is not known if these are, in fact, the same divinity at different ages, or if they are different persona entirely.

The most important title of kings, *Mah k'ina*, could be written in a personified form as the Sun God, and the Sun God also appears as a pectoral worn by royal persons, both male and female. He rarely appears as an actor in pottery or monumental scenes.

FIGURE 34

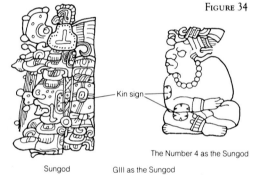

Sungod

Kin sign →

The Number 4 as the Sungod

GIII as the Sungod

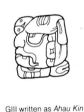

GIII-glyphic name

GIII written as *Ahau Kin*

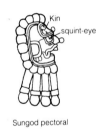

Kin

squint-eye

Sungod pectoral

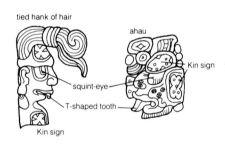

tied hank of hair

ahau

Kin sign

squint-eye

T-shaped tooth

Kin sign

GIII as the Jaguar God of the Underworld

The facial structure of the Jaguar God of the Underworld is identical to that of GI, but his features are different (Fig. 35). He has the same Roman nose, scalloped eyebrows, square eyes and pointed front tooth, and he often wears a shell beard. Sometimes his eye squints like that of the Sun God; usually, however, it is a spiral like that of GI. On the Jaguar God of the Underworld, the curl extends upward from the lower lid rather than downward from the upper lid, as on GI.

His hair is pulled into a bound knot above the forehead; he has a jaguar ear above his earflare and, most characteristic of all, he has a twisted device, called a "cruller" (named for the pastry), placed between and under his eyes. Kings wore this cruller when they impersonated GIII.

The Jaguar God of the Underworld rules the number 7. Since he is the most common image on shields, he is thought to be a patron of war. He rarely appears as an actor in narrative scenes, but he is the most frequent main head represented on Late Classic incensarios.[56] He probably represents the sun when it is in the Underworld.

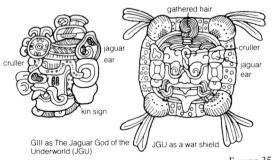

cruller

jaguar ear

kin sign

GIII as the Jaguar God of The Underworld (JGU)

gathered hair

cruller

jaguar ear

JGU as a war shield

FIGURE 35

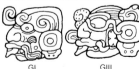

GI   GIII

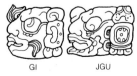

GI   JGU

GIII as the Baby Jaguar

This manifestation had particular importance during the Early Classic period in the central Peten region. It appears most often paired with Chac-Xib-Chac in scenes of the sacrificial death dance painted on pottery. His features are subject to some variation, although he is always anthropomorphic in form (Fig. 36). His feet and hands may be human or feline, but he always has a jaguar tail. His face may be the same as the glyph for "young man" (*xib*); it may be human with a cruller between the eyes; or it may have the scalloped eyebrow, prominent nose and pointed tooth of GI and the Jaguar God of the Underworld.

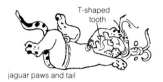

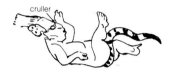

Figure 36

GIII as The Baby Jaguar

GIII as the Water-lily Jaguar

This form of GIII is entirely zoomorphic, but he walks and acts like a human. His special attribute is a water-lily blossom or leaf lying atop his head, which may be a reference to the jaguar's love of water (Fig. 37). He sometimes wears a special necklace, called a death-eye collar, but his normal attire is a wide scarf tied at the throat. His association with the GIII complex derives from the appearance of the *kin* sign on his belly and from the use of the "sun/decapitated jaguar" phrase as his name. He can be a substitute for the Baby Jaguar in the sacrificial death dance scene, and his head is worn on the belts of kings. He is a frequent character in Maya narrative scenes, in which role he is not yet fully understood.

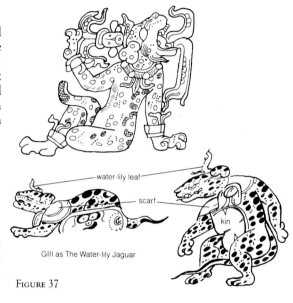

GIII as The Water-lily Jaguar

Figure 37

Twins and Oppositions

A number of Maya deities are associated as pairs or triads. The members of the Palenque Triad, for example, were triplets born at Palenque, and within this Triad, GI and GIII are twinlike, having the same facial "chassis" with slightly varied features added to differentiate them. Twins are also at the heart of the Popol Vuh. The Hero Twins are half brothers to the twins Hun-Batz and Hun-Chuen, and in the Underworld, they actively contest the paired deities One-Death and Seven-Death. Twins of various sorts are also at the heart of Classic-period Maya mythology. In some instances, twins appear to represent paired oppositions, such as light and dark. Such paired oppositions—analogous to the yin-yang concept in Chinese thought—are an important component of Maya languages and are often found in hieroglyphic inscriptions.

The Headband Twins

These twins are always anthropomorphic and are named for the elaborate knotted cloth headbands they wear (Fig. 38). Their glyphic names are Hun-Ahau and Balam (or perhaps Bolon), and they are undoubtedly the same divinities as the Hero Twins of the Popol Vuh.[57] Hun-Ahau has a single black spot on his cheek and single black spots on his body. He appears in the Dresden Codex as one of the Gods of Morning Star, and in the earlier alphabetic systems, he is God H, believed incorrectly to be a Chicchan god. The other twin, Balam, has jaguarlike spots on his lower face and patches of jaguar pelt on his arms, legs and back. He will often wear a shell on his forehead. He is the god of the number 9 and the other so-called Chicchan god in the Dresden Codex.

These twins are very active in Maya narrative scenes. They shoot blowguns; they carry the garments of the Maize God; they confront old gods and they play the ballgame.

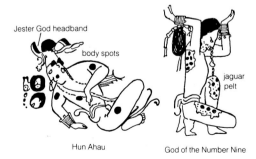

Hun Ahau

God of the Number Nine

Headband Twins

Figure 38

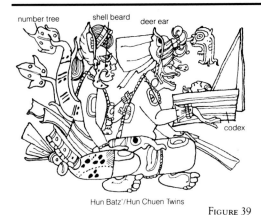

number tree   shell beard   deer ear

codex

Hun Batz'/Hun Chuen Twins

FIGURE 39

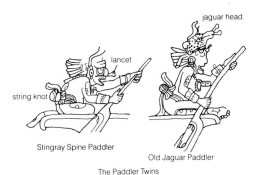

jaguar head

lancet

string knot

Stingray Spine Paddler

Old Jaguar Paddler

The Paddler Twins

FIGURE 40

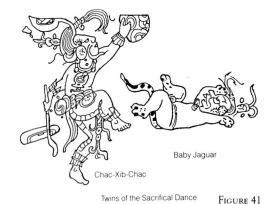

Baby Jaguar

Chac-Xib-Chac

Twins of the Sacrifical Dance   FIGURE 41

The Monkey Scribes

The Monkey Scribe twins carry paint pots, books, writing brushes, carving tools and work in progress (Fig. 39). They are the gods of writing, artists and artisans, and of calculations. They are the original model for Hun-Batz and Hun-Chuen, the older, twin brothers of the Hero Twins, who are transformed into monkeys for tormenting their younger brothers.[58]

These twins appear in several variant forms. First, both can be depicted as howler monkeys with human bodies. In this incarnation, each has a shell beard, a deer ear and a tied cloth headdress, usually in the form of a turban. This monkey version appears as the *kin* glyph for "day" in Long Count dates. Second, both twins can appear as the "Printout God," a nickname inspired by the stream of bar-and-dot numbers on the tree that emerges from under the arm. The Printout God is fully human (and quite handsome), although he wears the shell beard and the same deer ear as the monkey. The twins are frequently depicted as one monkey and one Printout God.

The Paddlers

These old gods (Fig. 40) are named for their appearance as the paddlers of the canoe of life found on the bones from Burial 116 at Tikal. As deities they have a particular association with period-ending rites and are brought into physical existence through bloodletting rites held on these days. In the Early Classic period, they appear in the mouth of the Vision Serpent; in the Late Classic period, in the mouth of the Double-headed Serpent Bar, a scepter carried by rulers. They are also the miniature gods who float in blood scrolls in scenes of scattering rites. In glyphic inscriptions, they are designated by their portrait heads or by the glyphs for night and day. Their manifestation of this basic opposition is reflected by the presence of bright, mirror god markings on one and dark markings on the other.

One Paddler, who has acquired the name of the Old Stingray Spine God, is characterized by a squint-eye and the presence of a lancet, either a stingray spine or bone awl, in the septum of his nose. He can also wear a shark head as a hat. The other Paddler, the Old Jaguar God, wears a jaguar-head hat. Both have prominent Roman noses and the sunken mouths of toothless old men, and both wear string knots on their belts. Many of the other twins described here wear the same knot.

The Twins of the Sacrificial Dance

Chac-Xib-Chac and the Baby Jaguar, the Twins of the Sacrificial Dance, have been discussed above as individuals (Fig. 41). While each can appear alone or paired with other actors, they also have a special affinity to each other. On pottery they are actors in a sacrificial death dance, in which Chac-Xib-Chac dances toward a reclining Baby Jaguar. On the stela of Xultun, they are displayed by kings as objects of power and authority.

The Uc-Ek-Kan and Bolon-Mayel Pair

This pair appears only in glyphic or emblematic form, and to date they have not been identified as actors. One emblem is composed of the number 7 and the glyphs for black and yellow; the other has the number 9 and a rare glyph for the number 20, with footprints above it (Fig. 42).[59] These forms occur most often as objects or emblems in scenes on stone stelae; in Early Classic examples, however, one or the other can be held as an object by a ruler. Although their meaning is not yet understood, their most important usage is on top of lip-to-lip cache vessels, special offering containers made from two large plates stacked together lip to lip.[60]

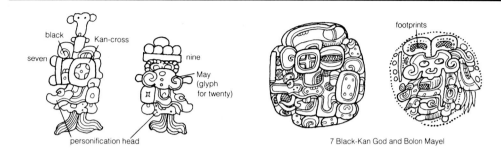

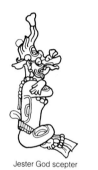

7 Black-Kan God and Bolon Mayel

FIGURE 42

OTHER GODS

The Jester God

The Jester God, named for the resemblance of his tri-pointed forehead to the cap of medieval court jesters, is an emblem of royalty rather than an actor (Fig. 43). The image is derived from the zoomorphic personification head attached to a tri-pointed headband element that served as the crown of Maya kings in the Late Preclassic period. The god can also be personified in anthropomorphic form; in full-bodied form, it was held as a scepter.

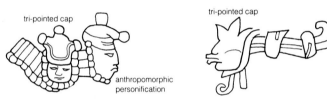

The Jester God

FIGURE 43

The Maize God

The Maize God is a handsome young man at the peak of his strength and beauty. Maize leaves and often an ear of corn spring from the top of his head (Fig. 44). In the Early Classic period, he was marked by a line-and-hook design on his cheek, and in this period the foliation often emerges from the glyph for maize instead of from the god's head itself.

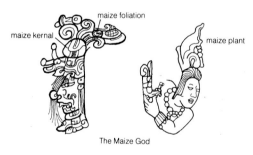

The Maize God

The Death Gods

The Maya cosmos was populated by a plethora of death gods, each with its particular name and attributes. The principal of these was designated God A (Fig. 45a). His face has skeletal features, his limbs are thin and his body is marked by a bloated stomach associated with starvation and parasitical infestation.

Death God A' (Fig. 45b) has human features, but unlike God A, his body is well fleshed, not like that of a victim of starvation. His lower jaw is skeletal, and a black stripe is painted across

FIGURE 44

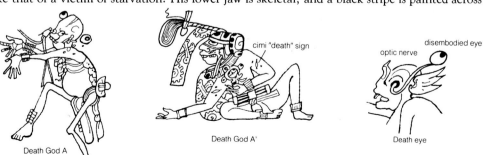

Death God A

Death God A'

Death eye

FIGURE 45

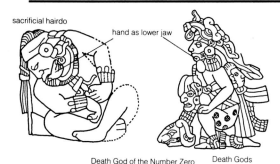

sacrificial hairdo

hand as lower jaw

Death God of the Number Zero   Death Gods

FIGURE 45

his eyes. *Akbal*, the glyph for "night and darkness," covers his forehead, marking him as a creature of the night.

The personification of the number zero is a god of sacrificial death (Fig. 45c). He is human, but a human hand grips his lower jaw, a gesture that may represent a particularly gruesome form of sacrificial death, the removal of the lower jaw from a living victim.[61] The hair of this god is bound in the long hank common to sacrificial victims, and he appears dressed as a ballplayer. He may represent sacrificial death, in contrast to other forms of death.

Death gods and other inhabitants of Xibalba, the Underworld, have a set of special attributes that distinguishes them from other creatures. The Maya, who lived in the tropics, conceived the Underworld as a place replete with disease and vile smells rather than as a condition of extreme hot or cold. One word for devil was *cizin*, which literally meant "farter." The foul odors expelled from the Xibalbans are visibly represented with foliated scrolls. Their jewelry is made not from jade but from disembodied eyes taken from the dead and dying (Fig. 45d). Their special symbol is the percent sign (%) from the day sign *cimi*.

The Old Gods

A set of toothless old gods, characterized by sunken lips and wrinkled faces, seems to have presided over Xibalba. The first, God L, wears a Muan Bird headdress and has a jaguar ear (Fig. 46). He can have either a human or a square eye. His is usually depicted sitting on a throne, and he clearly reigns as a principal god of the Underworld.

The second, God N or Pauahtun, has several forms.[62] He emerges from or wears a shell, either that of a conch or a turtle (Fig. 47b). He can also appear in full-bodied form wearing a section of shell as a pectoral, and a napkin or net headdress (Fig. 47a). His ear is often that of reptiles or is depicted as a Kan-cross with the number 7. In a third form, he is the earth bearer, wearing water-lilies, a net headdress and *cauac* signs on his body—signs that combine to indicate his name, Pauahtun (Fig. 47c). In a younger, more handsome form, he is Bacab, the sky bearer (Fig. 47d). The Old Pauahtun also overlaps with the Monkey Scribes and seems to have been the god of writing and of art.

The third god, designated God D, has the glyphic name Itzamna (Fig. 48). Like the other gods, he has an old man's face, but his eyes are always square with squint pupils. His most distinctive feature is a headband extending beyond his forehead to a shield-shaped medallion containing *akbal*, the glyph for "night and darkness," a symbol that is also part of his name glyph. He wears a shell pectoral and a cut-shell ornament on his head. This god is the only image from the Classic period that can be tied through glyphs to the name Itzamna, the so-called Lizard House of Maya religion. That concept, if it existed in the Classic period at all, was not associated with this god, however.

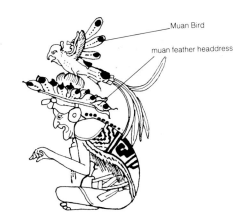

Muan Bird

muan feather headdress

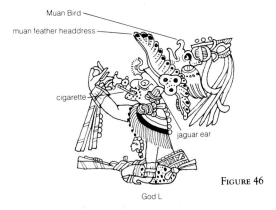

Muan Bird

muan feather headdress

cigarette

jaguar ear

FIGURE 46

God L

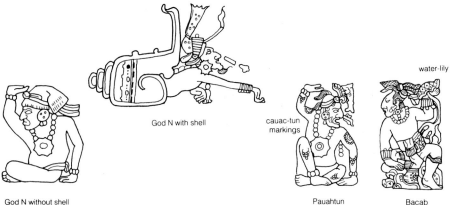

God N without shell

God N with shell

cauac-tun markings

water-lily

Pauahtun   Bacab

FIGURE 47

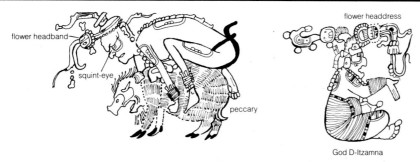

flower headband

squint-eye

peccary

flower headdress

God D-Itzamna

FIGURE 48

The Moon Goddess

The Moon Goddess is a young woman who sits in the crescent of the moon. She often holds a rabbit (Fig. 49), whose shape can be seen in the gray patterns on the surface of the moon, especially when it is full. She is the personification of the number 1. The mothers of rulers at Yaxchilan were sometimes set in moon signs, while the fathers were presented in sun signs. This usage reveals a mythology that defined the moon as female and as the wife of the sun.

The Celestial Bird

Many birds populate Maya cosmology. Chief among them is the supernatural Celestial Bird, also called the Serpent Bird and the Principal Bird Deity (Fig. 50). This Bird has long feathers like those of tropical birds, short legs with talons and a mirror device set at the base of his tail. His wing, which merges with a personification head, has led to the misnomer the Serpent Bird. His head is zoomorphic with a squint-eye and a mirror forehead, and he wears the same shell pectoral and head ornament as God D. His lower jaw is usually obscured by a disk that hangs from his mouth; it is marked by a triangle of dots and is hung with braided ribbons. This Bird resides at the top of the *axis mundi*, the World Tree of Maya cosmology.

The Muan Bird

The image of the Muan Bird is modeled on a horned owl (Fig. 51). His eyes are round and his feathers tipped black. He is the Bird that sits in the headdress of God L. His name was Oxlahun-Chaan, or 13-Sky, and he is the personification of the katun and of the sky.

The Water Bird

The Water Bird (Fig. 52) appears to symbolize the general class of aquatic birds that thrived along the canals, swamps and rivers of the Maya landscape. He has a crested head like that of a heron, with short legs and a long neck. His beak is shaped like that of a cormorant, and he is often represented holding a small fish. The Water Bird is associated especially with GI; his head is the main sign of the Palenque Emblem Glyph.

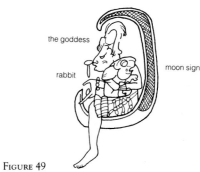

the goddess

rabbit

moon sign

FIGURE 49

The Moon Goddess

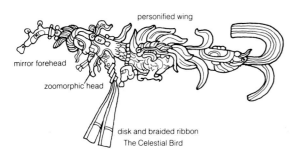

personified wing

mirror forehead

zoomorphic head

disk and braided ribbon
The Celestial Bird

FIGURE 50

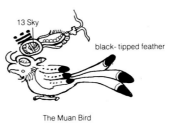

13 Sky

black-tipped feather

The Muan Bird

The Sacred Birds

FIGURE 51

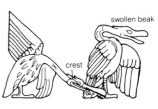

swollen beak

crest

The Water Bird

FIGURE 52

NOTES

1. The term *Mesoamerica* was proposed by Paul Kirchhoff ["Mesoamerica," *Acta Americana* 1, no. 1 (1943), pp. 92–107] to be used as both a cultural and geographic term in reference to the region bounded to the northwest by the limit of aboriginal farming, which could not extend beyond the deserts of northern Mexico, and to the southeast by the eastern extension of Mayan-speaking peoples and their cultural and economic influence.

2. J. Eric S. Thompson first identified the shark as a sign in the Maya writing system, used, he proposed, as a rebus sign for the word *count* ("The Fish as a Maya Symbol for Counting," *Theoretical Approaches to Problems*, no. 2 [Cambridge, Mass.: Carnegie Institution of Washington, Division of Historical Research, 1944]). Tom Jones ("The Xoc, the Sharke, and the Sea Dogs: An Historical Encounter," *Fifth Palenque Round Table, Vol. 7*, gen. ed. Merle Greene Robertson, vol. ed. Virginia M. Fields [San Francisco: Pre-Columbian Art Research Institute, 1985], pp. 216–217) cites documented examples of a marine shark being caught in freshwater rivers as far as 300 kilometers from the ocean. He proposed the model of the Maya Xoc Monster to be *Carcharhinus leucas*, the bull shark, whose presence has been amply recorded far up freshwater rivers in North, Central and South America. The bull shark, like the caiman, has a reputation as a man-eater. Jones presented a convincing argument that the Yucatec Maya word *xoc* is the etymological source of the English word "shark."

3. Dennis Puleston, "The People of the Cayman/Crocodile: Riparian Agriculture and the Origins of Aquatic Motifs in Ancient Maya Iconography," in *Aspects of Ancient Maya Civilization*, edited by François-Auguste de Montequin (Saint Paul, Minn.: Hamline University, 1976), pp. 1–26.

4. Early, pre-Norman kings held power over petty states. Descent among them did not follow strict rules of primogeniture, established later, but in each petty state, there was a kingly lineage. Even after the establishment of a sovereign English king, minor kings survived in Ireland and Scotland (*Compact Edition of the Oxford English Dictionary*, s.v. "king").

5. Tatiana Proskouriakoff, "Historical Implications of a Pattern of Dates at Piedras Negras, Guatemala," *American Antiquity* 25 (1960), pp. 454–475.

6. Bishop Landa said, "We found a large number of books in these characters [Maya writing] and, as they contained nothing in which there were not to be seen superstition and lies of the devil, we burned them all, which they regretted to an amazing degree, and which caused them much affliction" (Alfred M. Tozzer, ed. and trans., "Landa's Relación de las cosas de Yucatan: A Translation," *Papers of the Peabody Museum of American Archaeology and Ethnology, Harvard University* 18 [New York: Kraus Reprint Corp., 1966], p. 149).

7. The Dresden, Madrid and Paris Codices were discovered in European libraries or archives and published late in the nineteenth century. Work by early epigraphers, especially Ernst Förstermann, who worked at the Dresden library, and Eduard Seler, is the foundation of decipherment today. These scholars brilliantly worked out the Maya calendar and many of the initial readings of glyphs in the codices and the monuments. The fourth codex was lent by the Saenz Collection to a 1971 exhibition in New York, sponsored by the Grolier Club and published by Michael D. Coe in *The Maya Scribe and His World* (New York: Grolier Club, 1973). It is now in the National Museum of Anthropology in Mexico City.

8. The base date of the Maya calendar has been correlated to the Christian Gregorian calendar on the basis of many kinds of evidence. The most widely accepted is the Goodman-Martinez-Thompson correlation, which sets the beginning of the Maya calendar 584,285 days after the first day of the Julian calendar. Thompson later corrected his original correlation two days, to account for the ongoing Maya calendars still in use today in the Guatemalan Highlands. All Christian correlation dates in this study are given using the original Goodman-Martinez-Thompson correlation.

9. In the west panel of the Temple of Inscriptions, Pacal projected the eightieth Calendar Round anniversary of his accession date to eight days after the end of the first pictun (8,000 tuns), which will occur in A.D. 4772.

10. This thematic approach was developed and used by George Kubler in *Studies in Classic Maya Iconography, Memoirs of the Connecticut Academy of Arts and Sciences* 18 (1969), pp. 2–4.

11. J. Eric S. Thompson, *The Rise and Fall of the Maya Empire* (Norman: University of Oklahoma, 1956), p. 256.

12. Sylvanus G. Morley, *The Ancient Maya* (Palo Alto, Calif.: Stanford University, 1946), p. 262.

13. Mary Ellen Miller, "Sylvanus G. Morley and the Ancient Maya: The Posthumous Revisions," paper read in honor of Sylvanus G. Morley's one-hundredth birthday, July 1983, Merida, Yucatan. When George Brainerd revised Morley's *The Ancient Maya,* he systematically excised the word *city* and replaced it with *ceremonial center.*

14. John Lloyd Stephens, *Incidents of Travel in Central America, Chiapas, and Yucatan* (New York: Harper & Bros., 1841), I, pp. 159–160.

15. Ibid., p. 158.

16. Jean Frédéric Waldeck, *Voyage pittoresque et archéologique dans la province d'Yucatan* (Paris, 1838), p. 101.

17. Alfred P. Maudslay and Anne C. Maudslay, *A Glimpse at Guatemala and Some Notes on the Ancient Monuments of Central America* (London: John Murray, 1899), p. 244.

18. Teobert Maler, the discoverer of many of these carvings, correctly identified many, but his ideas were not taken seriously—he had become an enemy of the Peabody Museum, his patron, a fact that did not help his credibility. In addition, he couched such valid perceptions in a mishmash of ideas about Quetzalcoatl, a principal Postclassic deity. Given the Old Empire–New Empire thinking of the time, that deity could not have been represented on the monuments. Maler's ideas were discredited as those of a crank. See Teobert Maler, *Researches in the Central Portions of the Usumatsintla Valley, Peabody Museum Memoirs,* vol. 2 (Cambridge, Mass.: Peabody Museum of American Archaeology and Ethnology, Harvard University, 1901 – 1903).

19. In a little-known article, "Portraiture in Central American Art," which Spinden wrote for W. H. Holmes's festschrift, itself a volume of small distribution (*Holmes Anniversary Volume: Anthropological Essays* [Washington, D.C.: Smithsonian Institution, 1917], pp. 434–452).

20. Roger Fry, "American Archaeology," *The Burlington Magazine* 33, no. 188 (November 1918), p. 156.

21. The important contributions of the Carnegie Institution are too many and too varied to report in detail here—for example, at Uaxactun, archaeologists explored for the earliest Maya and made the first settlement study. They determined a ceramic sequence, correlated to the inscriptions, that survives today. Tens of sites and hundreds of monuments were documented by Morley himself, and toward the end of the Carnegie Institution's hegemony over Maya studies, the contemporaneity of Teotihuacan and Lowland Maya cultures was demonstrated.

22. A historical problem carefully examined by Marshall Becker, in "Peasants, Priests, and Ceremonial Centers: The Intellectual History of a Model," in *Maya Archaeology and Ethnohistory,* edited by N. Hammond and G. R. Willey (Austin: University of Texas Press, 1979), pp. 3–20.

23. Tatiana Proskouriakoff, *An Album of Maya Architecture* (Washington, D.C.: Carnegie Institution of Washington, 1946).

24. A pattern begun in his 1920 monograph, *Inscriptions at Copan* (Washington, D.C.: Carnegie Institution of Washington). There, however, he did not dismiss their potential dogmatically.

25. J. Eric S. Thompson, *Maya Hieroglyphic Writing,* 3rd edition (Norman: University of Oklahoma Press, 1971), p. 15.

26. Particularly to a number of Mexican scholars, among them Alfonso Caso, Salvador Toscano and Paul Westheim. Writing in 1958 (although for a book that did not appear until 1962), George Kubler commented on a "Mexican mode of behavior" in the presence of "military leaders" at Bonampak and Yaxchilan (*Art and Architecture of Ancient America* [London: Pelican, 1962], p. 170).

27. As the invited outsider at a conference to honor Alfred M. Tozzer, Clyde Kluckhohn took the opportunity to attack the Carnegie Institution, in particular, A. V. Kidder, for the lack of theoretical foundation ("The Conceptual Structure in Middle American Studies," in *The Maya and Their Neighbors* [New York: D. Appleton-Century Co., 1940], pp. 41–51).

28. The Dzibilchaltun population estimate, as well as a good history of the problem, was worked out by Edward Kurjack, in *Prehistoric Lowland Maya Community and Social Organization: A Case Study at Dzibilchaltun, Yucatan, Mexico,* Middle American Research Institute, vol. 38 (New Orleans: Middle American Research Institute, Tulane University, 1974). William Haviland has worked out various estimates of the population of Tikal. His most recent hovers near 50,000 ("A New Population Estimate for Tikal," *American Antiquity* 34 (1969), 429–433). D. B. Dickson has suggested that this number could be increased by half again ("Ancient Agriculture and Population at Tikal, Guatemala: An Application of Linear Programming to the Simulation of an Archaeological Problem," *American Antiquity* 45 [1980], 697–712).

29. Komchen, near the coast of Yucatan, was apparently established to gather salt for trade to the south, and Colha, in northern Belize, specialized in the manufacture of flint tools. Cerros, Tikal, El Mirador and other Lowland sites were settled around this time.

30. Norman Hammond, "Unearthing the Oldest Known Maya," *National Geographic,* July 1982, pp. 128, 132, 138.

31. Evidence from Pulltrouser Swamp (Robert E. Fry, "The Ceramics of the Pulltrouser Area: Settlements and Fields," in *Pulltrouser Swamp: Ancient Maya Habitat, Agriculture, and Settlement in Northern Belize,* edited by B. L. Turner II and Peter D. Harrison [Austin: University of Texas Press, 1983], pp. 194–211) suggests that the full exploitation of the raised-field system began between 400 and 300 B.C. Similar systems began to be developed at Tikal in the last part of the Middle Preclassic period (Peter Harrison, "Tikal" [a paper presented at the conference on "City-States of the Maya: Art and Architecture," Denver, January 1986]). At Edzna, the extensive hydraulic system of canals was begun in Middle Preclassic times and matured during the Late Preclassic period (Ray T. Metheny, "Northern Maya Lowland Water-Control Systems," in *Pre-Hispanic Maya Agriculture,* edited by Peter D. Harrison and B. L. Turner II [Albuquerque: University of New Mexico Press, 1978], p. 199).

32. Michael D. Coe, "Early Steps in the Evolution of Maya Writing," *Origins of Religious Art and Iconography in Preclassic Mesoamerica,* edited by H. B. Nicholson (Los Angeles: Latin American Center Publications and Ethnic Arts Council, University of California, Los Angeles, 1976), p. 113.

33. J. Eric S. Thompson (*Maya History and Religion* [Norman: University of Oklahoma Press, 1970], pp. 3–47) first used ethnohistorical and archaeological evidence to suggest that the Putun Maya existed and that they were Chontal speakers from the Tabasco Gulf Coast region. Robert Rands ("A Chronological Framework for Palenque," in the *Primera Mesa Redonda de Palenque, Part 1* [Pebble Beach, Calif.: Robert Louis Stevenson School, 1974], pp. 35–38) relates that fine paste pottery is particularly associated with the Tabasco region and with the Palenque ceramic tradition, supporting Thompson's suggestion that the origin of the invading foreigners was the Tabasco coast. Jeff Kowalski (personal communication, 1985) has found convincing evidence that iconography and glyphic patterns were shared by the Kakupacal monuments at Chichen Itza (dated between A.D. 849 and A.D. 890) and the period-ending monuments associated with Temple A-1 at Seibal (dated A.D. 849). For the iconographer and epigrapher, these late monuments at Seibal are particularly interesting, for one can trace the disintegration of the Classic Maya symbol system, which had been in place for the prior one thousand years.

34. David Kelley, *The Puuc: New Perspectives,* edited by Lawrence Mills (Pella, Iowa: Central College, 1982).

35. J. T. Goodman, "Maya Dates," *American Anthropologist* 7 (1905), 642–647.

36. An exception: David Freidel, "Political Systems in Lowland Yucatan: Dynamics and Structure in Maya Settlement," in *Prehistoric Settlement Patterns: Essays in Honor of Gordon R. Willey,* edited by Evon Z. Vogt and Richard M. Leventhal (Albuquerque and Cambridge, Mass.: University of New Mexico and Peabody Museum of American Archaeology and Ethnology, Harvard University, 1983), pp. 375–386.

37. Glyphic evidence from Dos Pilas, Naranjo, Cancuen, Aguateca, Seibal and other sites in the same region suggests that the rulers of Dos Pilas, Flint-Sky-God K, Shield-God K and his son Jeweled Head, attempted through conquest to establish a larger hegemony in the Petexbatun region. The last of these Dos Pilas kings certainly took the ruler of Seibal captive, sacrificing him seventeen years later and recording the event on a set of hieroglyphic stairs at Seibal. This "superstate" did not, however, last beyond that king's lifetime. See Stephen D. Houston and Peter Mathews, "The Dynastic Sequence of Dos Pilas, Guatemala," *Pre-Columbian Art Research Institute,* Monograph 1 (San Francisco: Pre-Columbian Art Research Institute, 1985). George Cowgill, in "Teotihuacan, Internal Militaristic Competition, and the Fall of the Classic Maya," in *Maya Archaeology and Ethnohistory,* edited by Norman Hammond and Gordon R. Willey (Austin: University of Texas Press, 1979), p. 61, has also speculated that the intensification of war-related art in the seventh and eighth centuries reflected attempts to establish empire and may have been a factor contributing to the collapse.

38. Michael D. Coe (*The Maya,* revised edition [London: Thames and Hudson, 1980], pp. 121–142) gives a readable summary of the Postclassic history of the region.

39. Yuri Knorosov, "The Ancient Script of Central America," *Sovietskaya etnografiya* 3 (1952), pp. 100–118.

40. Dennis Tedlock, *Popol Vuh: The Definitive Edition of the Mayan Book of the Dawn of Life and the Glories of Gods and Kings* (New York: Simon and Schuster, 1985).

41. Ibid., pp. 166–167.

42. Linda Schele, "The Hauberg Stela: Blood-letting and the Mythos of Maya Rulership," in *Fifth Palenque Round Table, Vol. 7*, gen. ed. Merle Greene Robertson, vol. ed. Virginia Fields (San Francisco: Pre-Columbian Art Research Institute, 1985).

43. For a detailed analysis of the symbolic functions of Maya architecture, see discussion of Cerros Structure 5C-2nd (Fig. II.1).

44. Michael D. Coe has noted the use in pottery painting of darker tones on the interior of shapes with lighter ones toward the edges, proposing this use of light and dark to be a "reversed chiaroscuro." This painting technique does not appear to be an attempt by the painter to reproduce the effect of light and shadow on three-dimensional objects; rather, it seems to be the result of the accumulation of denser pigments in the center of the shapes, perhaps deliberately sought as a tonal effect or the natural result of strokes that overlapped while the shapes were filled in. See Michael D. Coe, *Old Gods and Young Heroes: The Pearlman Collection of Maya Ceramics* (New York: American Friends of the Israel Museum, 1982), p. 14.

45. Dean E. Arnold and Bruce F. Bohor, "Attapulgite and Maya Blue: An Ancient Mine Comes to Light," *Archaeology* 28 (1975), pp. 23–29.

46. See discussion of Lintels 24,25, 26 (Pls. 62, 63 and Fig. V.2) and Lintels 15,16,17 (Pls. 64, 65, 87).

47. The kind of errors we refer to are those that should have been caught with even casual proofreading: for example, the Long Count date on Dos Pilas Stela 8 does not match the recorded Calendar Round date, although subsequent calculations on this monument are made from the correct position, rather than from the erroneous one. The inscriptions of the Group of the Cross at Palenque are particularly notable for this kind of error. The Distance Number used to establish the 819-day Count station for the Long Count date of the Temple of the Foliated Cross is correctly calculated, but it is incorrectly used in the inscription. It is likely that a master scribe calculated the correct Distance Number, then turned that information over to someone of lesser skill, who was to calculate the Calendar Round date of the 819-day Count. This secondary craftsman mistakenly added the Distance Number rather than subtracting it, as he should have. Since the 819-day Count is always earlier than the main date, the scribe should have caught the mistake with the most superficial check—he did not.

The most revealing error, however, is on the Tablet of the Cross. The first clause of the text records the birth of the mother of the Palenque Triad gods before the beginning of the current era. This important date was recorded in Long Count format, along with the Lord of the Night, the age of the moon and its 819-day Count station. Later in the text, the scribe recorded her accession 815 years later; in calculating that date, however, he made two errors: he counted the Distance Number from the 819-day Count station, rather than from the date of the birth, and, in using tables of 1.0.4.0 (twenty computing years) to find the name of the day in the Calendar Round system, he stopped one line short, obtaining the wrong month position: he wrote 0 Zac, but he wanted 0 Yax. Furthermore, we know that the scribe was aware that he had made these errors, because in the next clause he used the correct date rather than the erroneous one. Furthermore, he used very unusual syntax in that clause to call the reader's attention to the presence of the error. In other words, the scribe of the Temple of the Cross knew he had made an error; he could easily have corrected it simply by washing off the paint of the master's drawing and redrawing the correct glyphs before the text was carved in relief—yet the erroneous date and Distance Number were deliberately left in the text.

A later king, Chaacal III, used this same date on the doorjambs of Temple 18, in order to establish the date of his own accession and to sanctify that event by linking it to the accession of the Mother of the Gods. In this situation, the scribe of Temple 18 chose to use the erroneous date as it is written on the Tablet of the Cross, rather than the arithmetically correct date. If scribes allow such easily corrected errors to be retained in a text of such critical political and religious importance as the Tablet of the Cross, especially when we know they had caught the error by the time they wrote the very next sentence, then it is possible that the Maya considered such errors to be the result of divine intervention. If in sanctifying so important an event as the accession of King Chaacal by linking it to the accession of this Mother Goddess, the scribe chose to use the incorrect date instead of the corrected one, then the Maya may have considered the written record to be more important than the arithmetically correct one. History as recorded in stone became the truth, even when the Maya themselves knew it to be in error.

48. George Kubler, "Studies in Classic Maya Iconography," *Memoirs of the Connecticut Academy of Arts and Sciences* 18 (Hamden, Conn.: Archon Books, 1969), p. 6.

49. David Webster and Elliot M. Abrams, "An Elite Compound at Copan, Honduras," *Journal of Field Archaeology* 10 (1983), pp. 285–296; William L. Fash, Jr., "The Sculpture of Structure 9N-82: Content, Form, and Meaning" (paper prepared for a publication on Copan Structure 9N-82, edited by David Webster).

50. David Freidel was the first researcher to explain the use of the same scroll for these substances ("Polychrome Facades of the Lowland Maya Preclassic," in *Painted Architecture and Polychrome Monumental Sculpture,* edited by Elizabeth Boone [Washington, D.C.: Dumbarton Oaks, 1985], pp. 5–30).

51. The term "still bodies of water" refers to large bodies of water that do not have the running motion associated with swiftly moving rivers. While for modern Westerners, the ocean, being associated with motion, is not still, the Maya apparently considered it to be a super-lake, for the Yucatec word for it is *kak-naab,* and *naab* is the word for "lake" and "water-lily."

52. The words for red, yellow and blue—*chac, k'an* and *yax*—have secondary uses as superlative adjectives. *K'an* is especially appropriate as a sign of preciousness, for it was used to refer to the materials (stone and shell) from which jewelry was made. In this context, the *k'an* sign freely interchanges with representations of jewelry objects—shells, bones and jade beads, cylinders and earflares. The glyph used for the number zero (or perhaps "completion") also occurs with blood. These signs, which are painted on the walls of Tikal Burial 148 and drawn in the background of the sarcophagus at Palenque, are all members of this class; when they are used as a group, they signal blood, even in the absence of scrolls.

53. Heinrich Berlin (in "The Palenque Triad," *Journal de la Société des Américanistes* 52 [Paris, 1963], pp. 91–99) first identified the names of these gods in the inscriptions of Palenque, naming the complex the Palenque Triad and giving individual designations to GI, GII and GIII (abbreviations for God I, God II and God III). He identified GII with God K and GI with one of the Chicchan gods in the codices, arguing for the identities of the three Palenque names as gods. David Kelley (in "The Birth of the Gods at Palenque," in *Estudios de cultura Maya,* vol. 5 [Mexico City: Universidad Nacional Autónoma de México, 1965], pp. 93–134) demonstrated that their births are recorded in the left half of the Tablet of the Cross. Floyd Lounsbury, in "Some Problems in the Interpretation of the Mythological Portion of the Hieroglyphic Text of the Temple of the Cross at Palenque" (*Third Palenque Round Table, 1978, Part 2,* edited by Merle Greene Robertson [Austin: University of Texas Press, 1980], pp. 99–115), added the births of the mother and father of the Triad to their biographies. Interestingly, the order of their births is different from the order of their names in Triadic statements; moreover, the father and the firstborn child are called by the same names, as in the Popol Vuh relationship between Hun-Hunahpu and Hunahpu. The birth dates of their parents and each of the gods are as follows:

The Father	12.19.11.13.0	1 Ahau	13 Mac	June 16, 3122 B.C.
The Mother	12.19.13.3.0	8 Ahau	18 Zec	Nov. 17, 3121 B.C.
GI	1.18.5.3.2	9 Ik	15 Ceh	Oct. 21, 2360 B.C.
GII	1.18.5.3.6	13 Cimi	19 Ceh	Oct. 25, 2360 B.C.
GIII	1.18.5.4.0	1 Ahau	13 Mac	Nov. 8, 2360 B.C.

54. Thompson reports on these alternative forms in *Maya History and Religion* (Norman: University of Oklahoma Press, 1970), pp. 365–369.

55. Most earlier researchers had identified the fishing gods on the Tikal bones as Chacs because of their association with water and their long noses. More recently, these gods had been associated with GI, because of the identification of the central figure on the Dumbarton Oaks Tablet from Palenque with that god. However, David Stuart (personal communication, 1985) has confirmed the Chac-Xib-Chac identification through a glyphic name phrase on a Classic-period plate (Pl. 122). The diagnostic features of GI and Chac-Xib-Chac are interrelated, and at present, it is not clear whether these gods were considered by the Maya to have been different aspects of the same god or two distinct gods.

56. Incensarios are heavy clay tubes with flanged slabs attached to opposite sides. A conical censer was set atop the tube for burning copal, rubber, blood and other offerings. The potter attached imagery to the tube and flanges by applying modeled clay slabs, which were then painted in bright colors. At Palenque, the main head of these incensarios was most frequently rendered as the cruller-eyed Jaguar God of the Underworld. In Early Classic equivalents, GI was the favored image, and in Postclassic incensarios from the Guatemalan Highlands, GIII was most frequently attached to the bowl-shaped body of the censer.

57. Hun-Ahau is the equivalent of Hunahpu in the languages of the Maya Lowlands. The name of the

other twin is simply his portrait head, which is marked by a jaguar pelt on his chin. Balam, or Xbalam or the near-homophonous word for the number nine, *bolon*, seems the most likely reading of the glyph.

58. Michael D. Coe, "Supernatural Patrons of Maya Scribes and Artists," in *Social Process in Maya Prehistory*, edited by Norman Hammond (London: Academic Press, 1977), pp. 327–347.

59. Floyd Lounsbury has informed us that Martin Pickens made a tentative identification of this god as Bolon Mayel, based on the appearance of the numbers nine (*bolon*) and twenty (*may* in some Mayan languages) in his name. This god is mentioned in post-Conquest sources from Yucatan, but not much is known about him.

60. Lip-to-lip cache vessels were found under the floors of buildings at Tikal, Uaxactun and Colha. Composed of two large plates with flat bottoms and angled walls, they are known to have contained flint blades, decapitated heads, bloodletters of various types, and other material, such as sea fans, imported from coastal areas. Since they are almost always found in subfloor caches rather than in burials, it seems likely that they were particularly associated with rituals of building dedication and perhaps of termination, before new buildings were constructed over the old.

61. A number of gods in the Classic repertoire, including the patron of the month Pax, are shown with their lower jaw missing and huge double scrolls of blood streaming from their mouths. The God of the Number Zero is marked as a death god by the presence of *cimi* signs and the bound hair of a sacrificial victim, and his method of dying seems to be indicated by a human hand shown gripping his lower jaw. The combination of jawless, bleeding victims and the hand gripping a lower jaw suggests that one method of Maya sacrifice involved the removal of the jaw of a living victim.

62. To our knowledge, Michael D. Coe was the first epigrapher to read the name glyph of God N. In the Dresden Codex, this god's name is composed of a net bag, pronounced *pa* and *pawa* in Yucatec, over a *cauac* or a drum sign, both of which were read *tun*. These signs combine into the name Pawahtun, a god named in Postclassic Yucatec sources as one of the world bearers standing at the four corners of the earth. The Bacabs, however, are named in the same function, which suggests that there were two sets of world bearers in Classic-period cosmology — the Bacabs, who held the sky above the earth, and the Pauahtuns, who held the earth above the Underworld.

I

The Royal Person

Early in the history of Maya studies, scholars speculated that the mysterious figures portrayed in the sculpture and painting of that society depicted historical Mayas, and the partial deciphering of Maya hieroglyphs has confirmed this initial intuition. The faces carved in stone, modeled in plaster and clay and painted on walls are those of a real people, not idealized and anonymous priests who tracked the movement of time but rulers and nobles who governed cities. Maya art and inscriptions are a rich source of information about the aspirations, religious beliefs and practices, daily life and appearance of the Maya. Because Maya culture was governed by fiercely conservative traditions, the physical appearance of the nobility as represented in Maya art remains remarkably consistent over one thousand years. By examining in detail their names, portraits, headdresses, necklaces, belts, backracks and other accouterments, such as scepters and weapons, we can identify the functions of many recovered objects and arrive at a fuller understanding of their symbolism.

From the written history left in the silent ruins of Maya cities, we have recovered names and events. In the literature today, the glyphic names of these ancient kings appear, rendered variously in English, Spanish and modern Mayan languages, such as Yucatec and Chol. English words that are either descriptions or translations of name glyphs may be used; for example, when a name combines a glyph for hummingbird and one for jaguar, it yields the name Bird Jaguar. Many of these modern renditions of

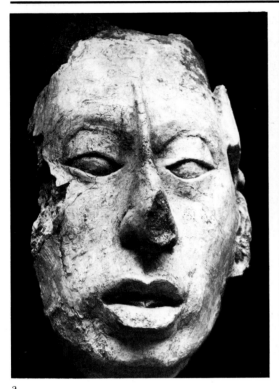
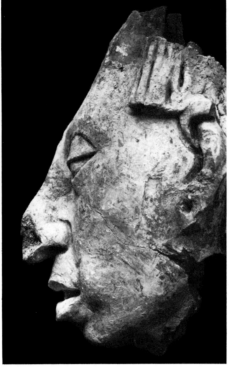
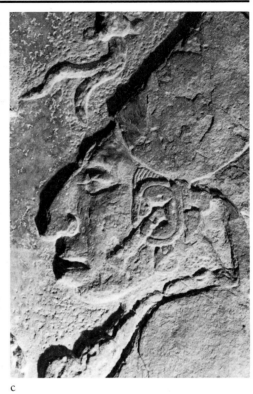

a   b   c

FIGURE I.1a,b
Stucco portrait of Chan-Bahlum
Temple 14, Palenque
Late Classic period, ca. A.D. 700

FIGURE I.1c
Portrait of Chan-Bahlum (detail of panel)
Temple of the Sun, Palenque
Late Classic Period, A.D. 672

names are only approximations of the originals, because the Maya words that corresponded to the name glyphs are not yet known. Mayan languages are also used to produce names of other rulers, such as Kakupacal, "Fire Is His Shield," or Yax-Pac, "First Dawn." Some of these are phonetic readings of the name glyphs, while others—like the English-language names—are only approximations. While this system is irregular, modern researchers respect the names established by previous scholars in order to avoid multiple designations for the same historical person. Regardless of the language used, the reconstruction of names for individual Mayas is a highly significant event that reestablishes their place in human history. Shield Jaguar (perhaps in Maya, Itzam-Balam) and Bird Jaguar (Ix-Tzunun-Balam), two kings of Yaxchilan, were the first two names to emerge from the darkness of a prehistoric past.[1] Others followed rapidly, such as Two-Legged Sky of Quirigua, 18-JOG (or 18-Rabbit) of Copan, and Pacal, Chan-Bahlum, Kan-Xul, Chac-Zutz', Chaacal and Kuk, who were all kings of Palenque.[2]

This identification of names has contributed to the recognition of portraits of these kings in sculpture and, more rarely, in painting. To modern sensibilities, the portraits from Palenque are the most lifelike, especially the three-dimensional heads modeled in plaster for use as architectural sculpture. At Palenque, the fifteen royal temples excavated to date in the sacred precinct at the center of the city constitute only a fraction of the structures at this great site. The excavated structures are all seventh- and eighth-century temples built by kings—starting with Pacal and ending with Kuk—both as mausoleums and as memorials to their reigns.

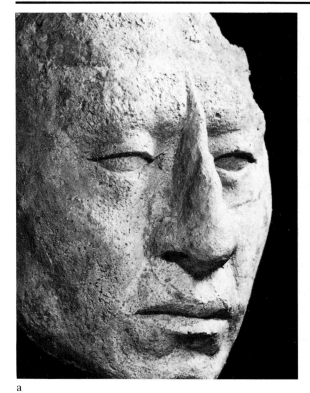

a

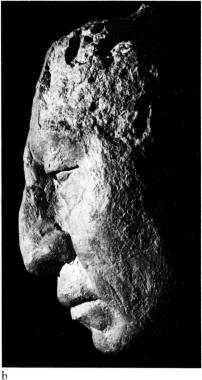

b

FIGURE I.2a,b
Plaster mask of an unknown noble
Palenque
Late Classic period, ca. A.D. 700–750
Museo Nacional de Antropologiá e Historia
Photos by Imgard Groth and Linda Schele

Among the portraits found at Palenque, the most famous is one of Pacal from his burial tomb in the Temple of Inscriptions. His eldest son, Chan-Bahlum, however, with his monumental nose and drooping lower lip, is the most readily recognizable king. Chan-Bahlum, who reigned from February 10, A.D. 684, to February 20, A.D. 702, constructed the group of temples called the Group of the Cross to house the panels that recorded his ancestral history, the divine origin of his lineage, his accession and other important rituals that took place during the first ten years of his reign. After his death, his younger brother, Kan-Xul, erected Temple 14 to contain the dangerous power that had accumulated in the Group of the Cross during his brother's lifetime.[3] One of two portraits of Chan-Bahlum found in the rubble of Temple 14 in Palenque is complete (Fig. I.1a,b). It was modeled in plaster over stone armatures attached either to the piers of the temple or to its entablature. Somber and dignified, the portrait depicts Chan-Bahlum in his prime with the intense look of a powerful ruler. His earlobe is pierced, and a square-cut lock of hair survives above his right ear. Once painted in full polychrome, this portrait reveals the artist's excellent understanding of facial anatomy and rivals Roman portraiture in its power and accuracy. Other portraits of Chan-Bahlum are found in relief carvings on stone tablets placed inside the three temples of the Group of the Cross. The profile of the head from Temple 14 is remarkably similar to those in the Group of the Cross, especially to the one in the Temple of the Sun (Fig. I.1c).

Other portraits at Palenque display a remarkable sense of humanity and realism. A handsome plaster head of a man (Fig. I.2) is remarkable for the intensity of

FIGURE I.3
Headdress styles

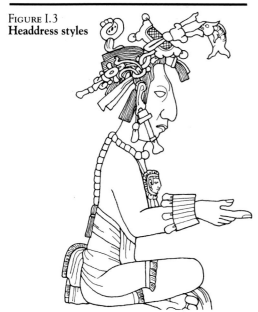

a. Pacal wearing the informal dress of Maya kings from the Palace Tablet at Palenque

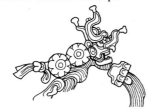

b. Jester God headband worn by Shield Jaguar on Yaxchilan Lintel 26

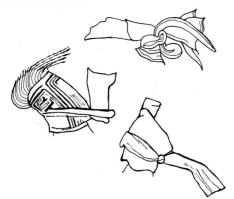

c. Cloth headdress of an *ahau* on Bonampak Sculpture Panel 1

d. and e. Cloth headdresses worn by nobles of the rank *cahal* in Room 1 of Bonampak

emotion expressed in the face. This is one of the most dramatic and insightful portraits known from Classic Maya art, but because we do not know where in Palenque it was found, we cannot identify the subject. Modeled with exacting control, the mask depicts a self-confident, serious man whose strong features are set with the dignity of his rank and responsibility. Other sculptures depict physical abnormalities of genetic origin. Lady Zac-Kuk, King Pacal's mother, is portrayed with swollen and clubbed fingers, perhaps the result of acromegaly, caused by a tumor in the pituitary gland. Her son Pacal may have had a clubfoot, and her grandson Chan-Bahlum had six toes and fingers.[4]

At other Maya sites, figures may not be immediately recognizable as portraits. It is possible that certain Palenque sculptures, particularly those of Pacal and Chan-Bahlum, were used, like death masks, to memorialize the king after death, and special attention may therefore have been paid to capturing an individual's likeness. It seems clear, however, that Maya artists did not ask kings to sit for portraits in front of stone panels. Their work was governed by strict conventions, and most drawings were never intended to be faithful, lifelike resemblances (see Fig. I.1). Instead, artists focused on prominent physical features to characterize individuals, emphasizing, for example, Chan-Bahlum's drooping lower lip or Pacal's characteristically delicate facial structure. Bird Jaguar of Yaxchilan is often depicted with large thighs and buttocks that have earned him the affectionate nickname Old Thunder Thighs among modern researchers, and Smoke Squirrel of Copan is shown with very high and prominent cheekbones that give his chiseled visage a rather dire expression.

Portraits, however, were rarely executed simply to record the likeness of an individual. Maya art depicts ritual: the critical information communicated is not *who* did something, but *what* he did. The identification of individuals is made concrete through the writing system or, more rarely, through context. Since most figures are named in glyphs, the body—its dress and accouterments—carries symbolic information about the ritual that transpired and about the supernatural sanction that gave the action meaning. Time, action, person and place are recorded in texts, and the subject of art is the depiction of the action.

Maya ritual was more than a symbolic act. It was conceived as a power process that transformed spiritual beings into corporeal existence in the human realm and allowed people and objects to become the sacred beings they represented. This transmuted state seems only to have lasted for a ritual's duration, for within a group of artworks, a single individual can be seen in the guises of many different gods.

In the imagery surrounding the king and his nobles, costume and regalia are not only symbols of rank, wealth and prestige. They are the conduits and the instruments in which sacred power is accrued. The person of the king, the clothing he wore, the symbols he hung on his body, the objects he manipulated—all these were directly connected to the Maya perception of the cosmos. Thus, to understand the temporal and supernatural reality of the Maya, we must decipher this system of symbols.

For Maya nobles, everyday clothing was made of thin cotton. The men wore it both as narrow loincloths and as larger pieces that covered the hips and buttocks (Fig. I.3a). Male nobles also wore calf-length white capes that were usually undecorated, except for the borders, and were typically worn with a necklace of large spondylus shells. Women wore a long, voluminous outer garment called a *huipil*, which was worn over a long underskirt (Pl. 1).

The *huipil* was made from long strips of cloth woven on a backstrap loom. The cloth was sewn together along the outer edges, with openings left for the arms; a slit for the head was left open during the weaving process. As among modern Maya weavers, woven cloth was not cut to make clothing. In very hot weather, the everyday dress of women could consist of the underskirt only, so that the breasts were left exposed (this is common today among older Chol and Kekchi women who live in the more remote areas). The *huipil* was worn on more formal occasions, and together the garments provided a loose-fitting, comfortable costume for Maya women in the hot Lowlands.

Both male and female clothing was worn high enough at the waist to cover the navel, a rarely exposed part of the body. Most garments were richly decorated with woven, dyed, embroidered or painted designs. Surprisingly, the king's hipcloth was often simpler than those worn by people of lesser rank. It could be decorated with a narrow design woven into the border, but if the colors of cloth depicted in the Bonampak paintings were accurate, the king's garments were often made simply of white cotton.

Cloth, especially bark cloth—a stiff, clothlike paper made from the felted bark of the fig tree—was a valued tribute item and important in sacrificial rites. For bloodletting and war rituals, strips of cloth were pulled through earlobes and tied around the hair, wrists and ankles. Cloth cut with round or T-shaped flapped holes was tied to wooden shafts or worn as part of a costume. This cut cloth is associated with captives and sacrificial victims, but on rare occasions, kings also wore it for bloodletting.

Costume for ritual occasions (Pls. 2–4) and for war were far more elaborate than everyday wear and used exotic materials imported from distant regions (Pls. 5, 6). Ornate and weighty headdresses, masks, capes of complex design, large belts, ornate loincloths, skirts of jaguar pelt, ornamented backracks, high-backed sandals, leg straps and jade and shell jewelry encased the body (Pls. 1–6). Little of this costuming has survived, since most of it was perishable, made of wood, paper, cloth and feathers. Nevertheless, much can be reconstructed from pictorial representations, and the costume parts made of shell, jade and other stones have been recovered. These costumes were a blaze of colors. They combined decorated cloth with the brilliant feathers of tropical birds—quetzals, macaws and parrots—and the sparkle and richness of polished jade, pyrite, obsidian, shell and animal pelts—especially the spotted fur of the jaguar. All this finery must have been heavy and awkward, necessitating cautious, measured movement to maintain balance and dignity in public ritual.

The black hair of the Mayas was dressed to accommodate a variety of headdresses, which ranged from simple headbands to complex assemblages towering high above the head. Both men and women wore the lock in the center of the forehead longer, often pulling it through a jade or wooden ornament (Pl. 7). Men of noble rank, particularly at Palenque, cut their bangs and sidelocks in a stepped pattern, with the hair on top of the head worn longer and often tied like a scalp lock. In battle, captives were held by this long scalp lock. Warriors deliberately wore their hair long, as if to declare their lack of fear at being taken captive. A shaved band extending from ear to ear at the back of the head, just above the nape of the neck, appears in many depictions, the hair below it cut short. In bloodletting rituals, a cloth was pulled through one earlobe, around the back of the head along this shaved area, then through the other earlobe. Woman wore their hair longer than did men and apparently did not shave the rear strip unless they held high office.

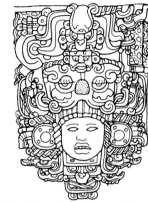

f. Flanged headdress from Copan Stela P

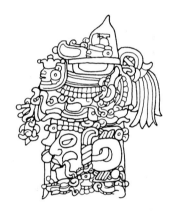

g. Flanged headdress from Tikal Stela 2

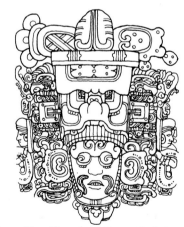

h. Flanged headdress from Copan Stela I.

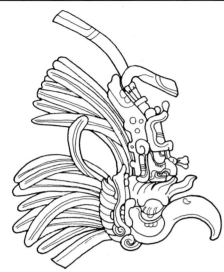

i. Headdress with a quetzal representing the name of the person depicted, Lady Zac-Kuk, from the sarcophagus from the Temple of Inscriptions at Palenque

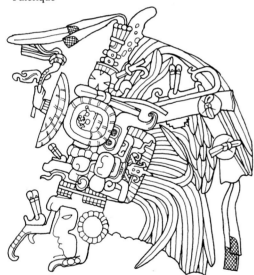

j. Chac-Xib-Chac headdress with a see-through mask from Machaquila Stela 2

Both men and women used headbands to hold their long hair away from their faces. Made of leather or cloth, these bands were often mounted with ornate carved jade plaques (Pl. 8). Kings wore an image of the Jester God on these headbands as the symbol of their rank and office (Fig. I.3b). Cloth, often richly decorated, was frequently tied around the head as a turban, encasing the hair (Fig. I.3c–e). Such wrapped headdresses took many forms and may have signaled rank, lineage affiliation or vocation. While extant images hint at such a system, it is not yet fully understood. In the Bonampak murals (Pl. 38), for example, the musicians all wear the same white woven headdress, which suggests that it is characteristic of their role in the ritual.

Ornate headdresses were constructed on wooden frames and tied under the chin with straps (Fig. I.3f–h). During the Early Classic period, headdresses of this type also had prominent wide side flanges. Side flanges always carried the same objects, an earflare, whose weight was supported by the flange, and knot or mat signs—pieces of reed or cloth either braided into a mat pattern or tied in a slipknot and used as a sign of royalty. The earflare was usually a round jade disk with a central hole; the mat signs were mounted above and below this disk. The large Pomona earflare in the British Museum (Pl. 9) was originally mounted on a Late Preclassic flanged headdress.[5] The muzzle of a zoomorph often emerged from the outer side of the disk, and the knots and mat sign, as well as the chin strap, could be personified with a blank zoomorphic head, which identified them as power symbols. When a king appeared in the guise of a particular god, such as Chac-Xib-Chac or GI, the disk earflare could be replaced by the god's characteristic shell earplugs, as is seen on Copan Stela I (Fig. I.3h). An example of these special earplugs, carved from a green stone to signal their preciousness, has also been recovered (Pl. 10).[6]

The main symbol decorating ornate headdresses was a head, usually zoomorphic, mounted directly above the face of the wearer on a cloth cap or on a headband of cylinders and beads (Fig. I.3f–j). These zoomorphic heads usually lacked a lower jaw, so that the face of the wearer appears to emerge from the mouth of the zoomorph, although in some very early representations, the chin strap doubled as the animal's lower jaw (Fig. I.3f, g). The identity of the headdress's central head depended on the ritual context. Sometimes it would refer to the name of the wearer (Fig. I.3i); at other times, especially as part of a battle costume, it represented an animal (Pl. 3); most often, however, it was a god (Fig. I.3j, k). Multiple heads were sometimes stacked one on top of the other, or small, full-figure effigies of gods were placed among the larger elements of the headdress to peer, like Maya leprechauns, at the world around them (Fig. I.3h). Kings wore Jester God headbands on the forehead in addition to complex headdresses (Fig. I.3k), or had the Jester God and his equivalent *ahau* sign mounted on the headdress (Fig. I.3i). In many examples, a stuffed jaguar tail (more rarely, the stuffed skin of a boa constrictor) was mounted at the top, along with other ornaments made of jade and cloth (Fig. I.3i–k).

Long, flowing feathers framing the head were arranged either in a continuous arc or in three groups, one on either side and one at the top. This pattern was developed during the Early Classic period and apparently arose from a conception of the headdress as a full-bodied bird. Especially when the king appeared in the guise of the god GI, the muzzle of the headdress zoomorph became the head and neck of the Water Bird holding a fish in its mouth; its wings were personified and set, usually vertically, on either side of the head (Fig. I.3g).[7] The fan of feathers at the upper back represented the bird's tail.

The headdresses of kings and warriors were shaped like domes or cylinders (Fig. I.3k). In accession scenes at Palenque, the high-cylinder type, called the "drum-major" headdress, is seen being delivered to an incumbent by his parents as a sign of his kingship (Fig. I.3l). Made of jade or shell plaques mounted on a wooden or mat armature, the headdress had long feathers on its crown and a large jade image of the Jester God mounted above the face of the king (Pl. 11). In contrast, the version worn by warriors was domed rather than flat on top and did not include a Jester God (Fig. I.3m).

Those ear ornaments not mounted on headdress flanges were smaller and exhibited greater variety. Usually made of jade, including jade mosaic, and sometimes of shell, they were most often carved to flare out to a flat surface and were pierced by a large central hole (Pls. 12, 13). Suspended from a string pulled through pierced earlobes, such ear ornaments included a thin cylinder held at a diagonal by counterweights behind and below the earlobe (Fig. I.3a, Pl. 14). The string was lengthened until the counterweight exactly balanced the jade cylinder. The counterweights found in Pacal's tomb were large, tear-shaped pearls, although jade and other stones were apparently also used. The main flare was frequently decorated with a pattern of five dots, called a quincunx, and flower shapes were also common. Although figurative imagery was rare, it is found on shell earflares and in mosaic constructions. Sometimes glyphs identifying the earflares' owners were incised, either on the earflares or on other costume elements. Depictions of earflare assemblages almost invariably show scrolls made of maize leaves above the central flare, but such scrolls have never been recovered.

The Maya nobility marked their faces in a number of ways. Nose plugs of jade, shell and perhaps wood were worn in a hole piercing the septum of the nose. Lip plugs have also been identified, although these are rarely shown pictorially. Faces were painted in patterns, such as skulls, to resemble the visages of gods or other supernaturals, and body painting in different patterns was common (Pls. 70, 82). An unusual rectangle made of pyrite mosaic was found placed around the mouth of King Pacal's skull in his tomb below the Temple of Inscriptions at Palenque;[8] the plaster figures in that tomb wear the same ornament over the mouth, as do a Dos Pilas king dressed as the Holmul Dancer and a figurine in the collection of the Kimbell Art Museum (Pl. 2).

Half masks and full masks were used regularly (see Figs. I.3, I.5), sometimes in conjunction with full body suits representing various gods—especially the jaguar gods. By a remarkable coincidence, an anthropomorphic jade mask given to the British Museum[9] in the nineteenth century (Pl. 15) is almost identical to one worn by the ruler depicted on the Hauberg Stela, dated to A.D. 199 (Pl. 66). The fact that both the mask and the stela are dated to the Late Preclassic period suggests that masks were used early, that the rituals incorporating them were widespread, and that masks of the same gods were worn at many different sites. Masks were often depicted cutaway or in X-ray view, revealing profiles of the mask as well as the face, as in Yaxchilan Stela 11 (Fig. V.5) and the Chicago Vase (Pl. 92). The Maya believed that ritual transformed its participants into the gods they portrayed, and masks and body suits contributed to this perceived transformation. Nevertheless, in their art the Maya carefully distinguished between representations of gods and depictions of historical people dressed as gods in ritual contexts. Cutaway images clearly show that a human is wearing a mask, and thus they underscore the intention of the narrative image.

The body, exclusive of the head and face, was also used to carry vital symbolic information. Ornate costuming elements were worn around the neck and on the shoul-

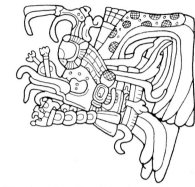

k. Headdress from Yaxchilan Lintel 14

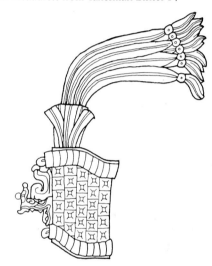

l. Drum-major headdress from the Palace Tablet at Palenque

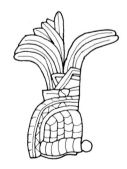

m. Domed headdress from Piedras Negras Lintel 2

ders. Belts carried arrays of symbols and served also as mounting devices for huge backracks that displayed information to viewers behind the wearer (Fig. I.5). Cuffs were tied around the wrists, ankles and knees.

The chest was an important region for symbolic display, but because the Maya preferred profile views of human figures, chest ornaments presented particular problems to the artist. To display the ornaments, the artist would turn the chest toward the viewer or would perhaps keep the chest in profile view while turning the object toward the viewer.

Capes were made of paper, cloth or feathers, but undoubtedly the most prestigious were those composed of rectangular jade pieces sewn to leather or cloth. Such capes are rare, but two of their jade rectangles (Pl. 16) have been found in a grave at Lubaantun.[10] Jade necklaces were commonly worn, even on informal occasions. In ritual costumes, necklaces were more ornate, often having multiple strands of beads. Pectorals were hung on necklaces or suspended independently on leather straps (Fig. I.3a). The heavy weight of these ornaments was counterbalanced by long strands of beads hanging down the back. Some of the earliest examples of Maya necklaces (Pl. 17) were found in a Middle Preclassic grave at Copan.[11] Discovered together with pottery carrying Olmec symbols, these necklaces document the emergence of a wealthy elite class among the Maya of the Copan Valley, who adopted the Olmec symbolic system to reify their status and rank.

Pectorals were carved from jade or wood or were mosaics assembled from thin pieces of jade (Pl. 18). Imagery included important gods and symbols of rulership—principally the jaguar, the Jester God, the Sun God and *ahau* in its anthropomorphic form. One of the few carved pectorals identified with an archaeological site (the Kendal Tomb in Belize) depicts the anthropomorphic version of *ahau* (Pl. 19); its distinguishing facial circles are drilled through the cheeks.[12] This *ahau* pectoral was worn with a shell earflare and an ax incised with the portrait of GI, all of which are Early Classic, perhaps even Protoclassic, in style. These elements reveal that the ruler buried in the Kendal tomb went to his grave dressed in the costume of the god Chac-Xib-Chac.

Also suspended from the neck were bar pectorals, both plain and carved with the images of gods. Carved bars are frequently depicted and have been found with some frequency at Copan, but their general occurrence is rare. One of the few carved bars that has been recovered was found over the chest of a skeleton in an Early Classic tomb (Pl. 20); the grave's contents suggest that the deceased was a distinguished and wealthy warrior.[13] Other bar pectorals depict skulls (Pl. 2). (Shrunken heads were also worn, especially in war and sacrificial costumes.) One of the most significant pectorals was a knot tied from groups of thin twine that ended in three loops on either end (Pl. 2), which signaled that the wearer was dressed as one of a complex of gods that included the Palenque Triad, the Paddler Gods and Chac-Xib-Chac.

Belts and skirts carried symbolic information at the waist and loin. The underclothing of males, normally a high-waisted hipcloth concealing the navel, was covered with a variety of belts. For sacrificial rituals, as depicted on Yaxchilan Lintel 24 (Pl. 62), strips of woven cloth were wrapped repeatedly around the waist, then overlaid with more elaborate belts. One common belt, made of jade cylinders sewn to a band of leather or cloth, was tied over the hip by a cloth sash.

The most important belt reserved for kings and very highly ranked nobles was composed of a wide band decorated with a thin border and crossed bands and disks mounted between the framing borders (Fig. I.4d, e). The middle area of the belt was also often decorated with skyband symbols and mat signs. A head, usually made of jade mosaic, was fixed to the front of the belt, and such heads were often placed at the sides as well. They most often depicted the human version of *ahau* (Pl. 21), but they could also represent the Water-lily Jaguar, GI, GIII or the Paddler Twins, among others. The *ahau* would often be surmounted by an arched knot, while a mat, mirror or knot symbol was placed below—a combination of images that metaphorically established the lordly status of the wearer. Because kings and nobles sat on mats in addition to wearing the ubiquitous braid we call the mat sign, they were called "lords of the mat." So important is this braided pattern as a symbol of royalty that two stone monuments—Stela J at Copan and Stela S at Quirigua—that bear this design have the glyphic text incised following the pattern of the weave.

The image of the combined *ahau* head and mirror is derived from a different metaphor. Since kings were conceived as both the reflection of the populace and as the seers of truth, they were the "mirrors of the people." They were also the holders of bundles in which the effigies of the gods, the instruments of bloodletting and the power objects of the ruling lineages were kept. Belt assemblages with this imagery simply name the wearers as Ahau-Pop, "Mat Lord," Ahau-Nen, "Mirror Lord," "Lord of the Bundle" or lord of a particular god. Three celts—thin, flat pieces of flint, limestone or, most often, jade—hung below belt heads, and olivo shells were suspended in single and double rows from the main strap of the belt. In its most ancient configuration— one that remained particularly sacred throughout the Classic period—an image of Chac-Xib-Chac was suspended from this belt. The god hung behind the ruler's knees. A chain of *yax* symbols alternating with jade spheres bears the image of Chac-Xib-Chac.

Although these belts were made largely from perishable materials, such as wood and leather, some parts have survived. The Leiden Plaque (Pl. 33) is one of the celts that once hung under a belt head; another celt from the Dumbarton Oaks collection displays a very early Maya ruler and records a period ending on the back (Pl. 22). At Palenque a belt with flint celts was found in the Early Classic tomb under Temple 18a.[14] Dated to A.D. 500, the tomb is thought to have been the burial place of either Chaacal I or Chaacal II; the Late Classic building above the tomb was built by their descendant, Chaacal III. A similar belt was laid on top of Pacal's sarcophagus just before his tomb in Palenque was sealed.[15] Perhaps the most interesting belt head (Pl. 21) was one found near Copan; it carried an inscription naming a lord from Palenque.[16] Since the mother of Yax-Pac, the last king of Copan, was from Palenque, it is very likely that she brought the belt to Copan at the time of her marriage.

Other types of belts were worn in special rituals. Bloodletting required one of two belts—a xocfish-shell combination or the Perforator God, a personified lancet used to draw blood. The xocfish head and a giant spondylus shell, along with a macrame-like net overgarment, were symbols most often worn by women; men wore these symbols only in bloodletting rituals, in order to celebrate their role as nourishers of the gods. An image of the Perforator God was also inverted and worn over the genitals (Fig. IV.1), and this image marked small bags worn on belts that probably held stingray spines (the use of these bags accounts for the frequent presence of stingray spines around the pelvic areas of excavated skeletons).

Belts were used to support the backrack, another extremely important element of ritual dress (Pl. 2a). The backrack was fashioned from a long piece of wood, which was bent into an arch as a frame, thrust downward and fixed in place through the back of the belt. Long feathers were attached to the frame to fan out behind the wearer like a huge peacock tail, which sometimes extended to the feet. This fan of feathers also highlighted an array of images attached to the center of the backrack.

These images can be divided into two main compositional types. The first, the Holmul Dancer (named from a vessel found at Holmul), shows figures wearing xocfish-shell belts and huge feathered backracks marked by a fixed program of images (Fig. I.4d, e). The set of images includes a Celestial Bird sitting on a skyband bracket rising from a monster head, usually the Cauac Monster, more rarely the Quadripartite Monster. One of four creatures sits in the opening formed by the skyband and the monster head: a jaguar named 6-Ix, a serpent-dragon named 6-Sky, a howler monkey named 6-Chuen or a human. In a second type of backrack from Tikal, a large ancestor cartouche with toothy dragons at its corners forms the main symbol, replacing the skyband-monster-bird design of the Holmul Dancer backrack. Inside the cartouche rests a zoomorphic head along with other variable symbols.

A visible serpent-fret apron is worn below the main symbolic array on the backrack. Over their cloth undergarments, Maya males wore a variety of skirts woven with symbols of ritual purpose and rank. The God C serpent-fret apron, which is also understood as a version of the World Tree, was the most common of these (Fig. I.4a–c). Although square-nosed dragons normally appear on the branches of the tree so as to form a cross, here they are bent downward to form the serpent-fret borders of stiff aprons. Together with the symbolic array on the backrack, this apron underscored the central, cosmically significant role of Maya rulership. It identified the king as the *axis mundi* of the temporal and supernatural worlds.

Costumes depicted widely on sculpture and pottery during most of Maya history functioned to establish the identity of the Classic Maya peoples, and judging from their long history, this strong tradition overcame the tendency toward divergence that must be expected in a society dispersed over a large region. Not only did the costumes of rulers incorporate symbolism, but the objects they carried and used in rituals also conveyed information about the ruler's relationship to the world and society. The objects most frequently depicted include bundles, strips and bolts of cloth; effigies of various gods (Pls. 23, 24); a variety of scepters, and weapons of war and sacrifice.

Although bundles made of cloth only rarely survived, several are known from Tikal. Pictorial representations reveal that bundles held two classes of objects—the effigies of gods and the instruments of bloodletting. These sacred objects were stored on plates with sloping walls and everted rims, then shrouded in cloth and tied with a narrow strip of cloth. Bundles were opened to display their contents during important rites, such as accession. Women are often shown holding them unopened in bloodletting rites, and bundles appear in palace scenes, placed on the floor near the rulers. Most interestingly, scenes of the Underworld or the beginning of the current era indicate that gods, like humans, used bundles.

The paucity of surviving scepters suggests that they were made of wood or other perishable materials. Pictorial sources inform us, however, that among the many different types of scepters carried by kings, two types dominate—the Double-headed Serpent Bar (Pl. 33b) and the Serpent-footed God K scepter. The Double-headed Serpent

Bar is a stiff bar mounted on each end with an open-mouthed serpent head from which a god emerges; this bar occasionally undulates like the body of a serpent. The God K scepter depicts this important icon of rulership and bloodletting in a number of ways. While the god's head can simply be mounted on a staff, he more commonly appears in a full-bodied form, one leg turning into a serpent's head. In a rare example, God K appears not as an inanimate object but as a living being who twists around as though to talk to the royal woman who holds him (Pl. 1).

Weapons were used as ceremonial objects. In addition to functional weapons, some spears and knives with blades of chipped stone too fragile for use in battle have survived; strips of stiff bark cloth were frequently tied along their shafts in a pattern of diamonds alternating with groups of three knots. Such blades were also used to draw blood in sacrificial rites.

The Maya apparently believed that flint and obsidian were created when lightning struck the earth, and so they treated these materials as sacred and presented them in personified form. The most exotic objects to modern eyes are the so-called eccentric flints, which were flaked and shaped into complex, multifaceted symbols of sacred power. Most eccentric flints are abstract shapes, but several, such as one from the Cleveland Museum of Art (Pl. 25) and another from the Metropolitan Museum of Art (Pl. 26), depict multiple human profiles with the smoking celt of God K emerging from their foreheads. At first glance, the unmistakable form of the smoking celt may lead one to think these anthropomorphic figures are indeed images of God K. Yet in every other known representation, God K appears in zoomorphic, not human, form. A combination of the God K smoking celt with a human portrait, carved on these two eccentric flints, is otherwise known only on two monumental sculptures: on the sarcophagus at Palenque, the same celt pierces the forehead of Pacal, just as it does that of 18-Rabbit on Stela 11 at Copan. Both portraits are posthumous, a common trait that may explain the significance of eccentric flints. Human profiles chipped in flint could represent dead ancestors. If this is so, the Maya worked material they thought was created by a bolt of lightning into an object that embodied and focused power emanating from the souls of the dead.

During the Classic period, ritual objects of all sorts bore coded information about their owners or their function. On one level a conch shell trumpet was a musical instrument, but when a Maya covered it with imagery, it became pregnant with the meaning of his existence. The owner could commission his portrait, recording his name on the trumpet (Pl. 27), or he could display an image of the supernatural world, implying the trumpet's capacity to call forth supernatural powers (Pl. 121). In this way the imagery on ritual objects—on the ceramic vessels that went into the Afterlife with the dead, on clothing worn in ritual and on the instruments used in bloodletting— transformed mundane objects into sacred ones. Today, those who study the remnants of Maya civilization recognize the symbolism—both written and pictorial— that marks the objects they made as a key that opens the minds of that ancient people.

NOTES

1. Tatiana Proskouriakoff gave these kings English names based on the pictorial elements in their glyphic names. See "Historical Data in the Inscriptions of Yaxchilan, Part I," in *Estudios de Cultura Maya* (Mexico City: Universidad Nacional Autónoma de México), vol. 3 (1963), pp. 149–167; and Part II, vol. 4 (1964), pp. 177–201.

2. Pacal means "Shield"; Chan-Bahlum, "Serpent Jaguar"; Kan-Xul, "Precious Animal"; Chac-Zutz', "Great Bat"; Chaacal, "Lightning"; and Kuk, "Quetzal."

3. The widespread practice of "killing" ritual objects was apparently required because of the conceptual definition of Maya ritual as the means by which supernaturals were brought into human space. Manifesting gods within an inanimate object vested them with power, which remained at least in vestigial form after the supernatural left. Since the king himself was a supernatural, the objects and the buildings he used also accrued a sacred power that was especially dangerous after his death. Objects were killed in order to release the dangerous power. Pottery was drilled with a hole to release its accumulated power; zoomorphic masks on architecture were slashed, and very often the left eye and muzzle were broken off. This last kill pattern is also found with royal portraits. Temple 14 is unusual in that it is less a kill pattern, which apparently released the accumulated power, than it was a containment pattern, which prevented the uncontrolled release of the power. The same containment pattern was used at Tikal by Ruler A, who built the last stage of Temple 33 to "cork" the North Acropolis when he shifted the ceremonial focus to the Great Plaza.

4. Merle Greene Robertson posits that these physical defects are presented consistently in the portraits of these rulers at Palenque. Although her proposed reconstruction of the marriages has since been disputed, the visual evidence remains a strong argument. The case for the clubfoot is the weakest, because the odd positioning of legs and feet is just as likely to have resulted from Maya spatial conventions. Pacal's skeleton is still untouched in the sarcophagus, however, and one day osteologists and physical anthropologists may have the opportunity to examine the skeleton for evidence of a clubfoot. Chan-Bahlum's tomb remains under the Temple of the Cross and awaits excavation. We believe the skeleton inside will prove to have six toes and fingers. See Merle Greene Robertson, Marjorie S. Rosenblum Scandizzo, and John R. Scandizzo, "Physical Deformities in the Ruling Lineage of Palenque and the Dynastic Implication," in *The Art, Iconography & Dynastic History of Palenque, Part III* (Pebble Beach, Calif.: Pre-Columbian Art Research and Robert Louis Stevenson School, 1976), pp. 59–87.

5. The Pomona earflare was discovered in 1949 when a mound was bulldozed on the Pomona citrus estate on North Stann Creek in central Belize. Alfred Kidder and Gordon Ekholm, who were in the area at the time, reported that the mound held two tombs; there is some confusion as to which one contained the flare, however (A. V. Kidder and Gordon F. Ekholm, "Some Archaeological Specimens from Pomona, British Honduras," in *Notes on Middle American Archaeology and Ethnology*, No. 102 [Washington, D.C.: Carnegie Institution of Washington, 1951], vol. 4, pp. 125–142). Using available evidence, Norman Hammond assigned the flare to Tomb I, which he dated to the end of the Late Preclassic period. In the same paper, Justeson and Norman analyze the text and propose that it consists of two sentences, one containing three glyphs, the other containing one. Although Justeson and Norman's syntactical analysis is open to further study, they have correctly identified the personages named as supernaturals and have discerned that the supernaturals are named as actors. Moreover, their suggestion about the function of the text is exactly on target: "[It makes] an association of sacred ritual, as in Classic times, with the acquisition of secular power. [It is] . . . a claim of sacred justification for the secular political activity of Lowland Maya elite." See John Justeson, William Norman, and Norman Hammond, "The Pomona Jade Flare: A Preclassic Mayan Hieroglyphic Text" (paper delivered at the Princeton Conference on the Beginnings of Maya Iconography, Princeton, N.J., October 1982 [forthcoming]).

6. Reported by H. W. Price in *Proceedings of the Society of Antiquaries* (vol. 17 [1899], pp. 339–344), this shell-shaped earflare was found along with a jade pectoral, an incised ax and other material at Kendal, Belize, twelve to fifteen miles from the mouth of the Sittee River. In 1892 Price opened a mound sixty feet long, forty feet wide, and twenty feet high. Starting a trench six or seven feet below the summit on the north slope, he immediately found a chamber four feet high, which had not been closed with a roof. The floor was made of small slabs of shale, and the height of the chamber walls followed the slant of the mound. Inside he found this jade earflare, a jade pectoral, a dark mirror about the size of a silver dollar, and several celts of polished green and pink stone. Although no bones were found, these objects clearly belonged to the costume of a Maya lord. Thomas Gann (*Maya Indians of Yucatan and British Honduras*, Smithsonian Institution, Bureau of American Ethnology, Bulletin 64 [Washington, D.C.: U.S. Government Printing Office, 1918], pp. 90–92), reports that these objects were found in the west wall in a recess half filled with earth. He also reports the discovery of six celts and notes that the mirror was made of pyrite pierced in the center. The shell-shaped earflare, the pectoral and the ax were given by Gann to the Merseyside County Museums in Liverpool, but the remaining material has disappeared.

7. These are the so-called serpent wings. To our knowledge, Nicholas Hellmuth (personal communication, 1982) was the first person to recognize that the Early Classic headdress represents a full-bodied bird.

8. Alberto Ruz Lhullier, *El Templo de las Inscripciones, Palenque*, Coleccion Cientifica Arqueología 7 (Mexico City: Instituto Nacional de Antropología e Historia, 1973), p. 161 and figs. 220, 221.

9. Records in the British Museum relate that this mask was purchased in 1860 in Hamburg, Germany, for fifteen pounds and presented to the museum in 1872. The only provenience data lists that it came from Laguna, about twenty miles from Santa Cruz.

10. These jade plaques were found at Lubaantun in a grave associated with an early phase of construction in Mound D. Found near the center of the mound at the top of a well-preserved plastered stairway, the grave contained potsherds, teeth and other skeletal fragments, a pendant and four large beads, two earflares, one round ear ornament, and two square plaques. The jades seem to have been part of the funerary costume of the deceased. T. A. Joyce, J. Cooper Clark, and J. E. S. Thompson, "Report on the British Museum Expedition to British Honduras, 1927," *Journal of the Royal Anthropological Institute* 57 (1927), p. 305.

11. Excavations by William Fash, Jr., in Plaza A of Group 9N-8, Copan, have yielded the longest occupation sequence in western Honduras. This jade necklace was found in the richest Early Preclassic burial so far discovered in the Maya region. Found in the north building of a residential complex (see n. 3, Chap. 2), this necklace was found in Burial XVIII-27, along with ceramic vessels (including the red bowl with incised flame eyebrow motif [Pl. 28]), eight polished celts, over three hundred pieces of jade or greenstone and the skull and two long bones of a young adult (William Fash, Jr., personal communication, 1985, and "A Middle Formative Cemetary from Copan, Honduras" [paper delivered at the annual meeting of the American Anthropological Association, 1982]).

12. This pectoral was found in the Kendal tomb in Belize, along with the jade shell discussed in note 5, above. H. W. Price (*Proceedings of the Society of Antiquaries*, p. 341) reports that several jade cylinders (none longer than one-half inch) and jade pendants carved in the form of alligator heads were found with the pectoral, but these were not among the material Thomas Gann gave to the Merseyside County Museums in Liverpool.

13. This bar pectoral was found in a tomb six feet under the summit of a twenty-foot-high mound, half a mile east of the site of Nohmul. The body was laid on its back, its head on the east side of the east-west burial chamber. Twenty large jade spheres were found in each of the eastern corners, and a large number of chert spearheads, two axes and two shells were found near the skull. Next to the hands were other blades, as well as two broken pots, including a polychromed fragment depicting a warrior wearing the Mosaic Monster headdress associated with the Tlaloc sacrifice complex. The bar pectoral was found atop the chest area of the body. This burial lay directly over another chamber about nine feet long and divided into three subchambers; each subchamber contained a burial and a single pot. Thomas Gann and Mary Gann, "Archaeological Investigations in the Corozal District of British Honduras," *Anthropological Papers*, No. 7; Smithsonian Institution, Bureau of American Ethnology, Bulletin 123 (Washington, D.C.: U.S. Government Printing Office, 1939), pp. 1–15, pls. 1–4.

14. Alberto Ruz Lhullier, "Exploraciones arqueológicas en Palenque, 1957," *Anales del Instituto Nacional de Antropología e Historia* 14 (Mexico City: Instituto Nacional de Antropología e Historia, 1962), pp. 62–85.

15. Alberto Ruz Lhullier, *El Templo de las Inscripciones, Palenque*, p. 152, figs. 184–186.

16. The records of The British Museum provide the provenience for this jade head as follows: "It was presented to the Museum on September 20, 1875, by Aug. W. Franks, who had bought it from F. T. Tappenden, Sutton Court, Chiswick for 12 Pounds." Additionally, the entry notes that it "was formerly in the possession of Indians of the town of Tambla, south of Comayagua, Honduras." Nothing more is known, although the head is likely to have come from a tomb at Copan or one of its subsidiary sites.

17. Although he resembles God C, this is a different god, one who appears in Early Classic glyphs associated with the four cardinal directions and special phrases that go with them—"He of the Sun" with the east; "He of Darkness" with the west; "He of the Moon" with the south; and "He of Venus" with the north. This directional complex appears on a set of obsidians found in a stela cache at Tikal and in a newly discovered tomb at Rio Azul. Moreover, the "He of the Sun" phrase appears in the name phrase of GIII at Caracol. Since the god on this jade has only recently been identified, we do not yet fully understand his meaning or function. Insofar as can be told from the available evidence, he is associated with the personification of the World Directions.

Plate 1
Panel of a woman with God K
Late Classic period, A.D. 600–800
Limestone
60.4 x 69.8 cm
The Cleveland Museum of Art
Purchase from the J. H. Wade Fund

This lintel depicts a Maya woman who may have been the ruler of her site, perhaps El Cayo. Her clothing, typical of Classic Maya women, is composed of two garments. The dress is made from a lightweight thin cotton cloth, woven with patterns that indicate her rank and perhaps her family affiliation or the ritual in which she is shown. Longer than the outer garment, the inner slip has a fringed and woven border. The outer garment, called a *huipil*, is made from long strips of cloth woven on a backstrap loom and sewn together at the outer edges; this leaves a woven opening for the head and openings for the arms. Even among the modern Maya, clothing is made in this fashion, and woven cloth is usually not cut. Quadrifoil shapes with crossbands and double scrolls decorate the *huipil*; it has a double border at the bottom, decorated by stepped-frets, T-shapes and mat symbols. Feathers are woven into this border around the arm openings.

Standing barefoot, the lady wears jade bead wrist cuffs, collar and necklace. Her ear ornaments, consisting of a disk, a diagonally hung cylinder and counterweights behind the ear, hang from her earlobes. Her elaborate headgear includes a jade disk headband and a headdress with a zoomorphic head, surrounded by a fan of cropped as well as long, windblown feathers, a stuffed jaguar tail, a capped *ahau* (now badly damaged) and spherical, bell-shaped and cylinder-shaped ornaments, perhaps made of jade or wood. Her headdress zoomorph has its own earflare assemblage, complete with a personification head below the disk and a scroll and vegetation motif above it. The personification head has eyes that are square with squint pupils; his forehead bears a mirror infix, and his muzzle is long and upturned. His headband is made of jade cylinders with floral devices attached to the front and sides. This headband and his facial features suggest that he is the Celestial Bird, who sits atop the World Tree in Maya cosmology.

In her right hand the lady holds God K, who is depicted in an unusually animated style. His serpent leg drops below her hand, while his other leg is bent up against his chest as he twists back toward the lady, as though in conversation. The artist's depiction of God K is not simply as a wooden statue; it makes the god alive and animate. The head is tilted back, and the bifurcated smoke scrolls rise above the cigar thrust through his forehead mirror. The presence of this god marks the woman as an individual of very high rank, either the mother or the wife of the king, or perhaps a ruler in her own right.

The Inscription
The Initial Series date of this monument contains an error, although it is perhaps one deliberately recorded. The Long Count 9.14.17.9.3 requires a Calendar Round date of 4 Akbal 6 Uo, but the Tzolkin recorded is 1 Ahau, three days earlier. The supplementary data, however, are in agreement with the Long Count as written; these are the third Lord of the Night and a moon age of five days after the end of the first moon of the lunar half year. Either the 1 Ahau is in error or the scribe was deliberately trying to make reference to both dates.

Two rows of glyphs were sawn off the top of the lintel when it was removed from its original location, making it impossible to determine the actor or the action for this first date. However, the surviving glyphs from the other side provide some clues. The last four glyphs record a Distance Number of 10 days and 10 uinals, and 4 Ahau 13 Ceh, with a notation that it was the end of the first five tuns of the katun. This Calendar Round occurred on such a period ending only once in this era— 9.18.5.0.0, or September 15, A.D. 795. This passage tells us that an event had taken 210 days before this period ending on 9.18.4.7.10 2 Oc 3 Uo, or February 17, A.D. 795. Since this event is almost sixty-six years after the Initial Series date, we may surmise that the earlier event was either the birth of the protagonist or some other event that happened to another person, perhaps the previous ruler.

The later event is the one shown in the scene, and it is recorded as the first whole glyph visible in the right-hand columns; the woman's name, Lady Shellfist-Quincunx (in Maya, something like Lady Kab), follows the verb. The text further records that she completed the ritual "under the auspices" or "in the territory of" a lord whose name includes a bat glyph. Her overlord is himself named to be a *cahal*, a member of the nobility below the king who administered his territory.

Plate 2
A ruler dressed as Chac-Xib-Chac and the Holmul Dancer
Late Classic period, A.D. 600–800
Ceramic with traces of red, orange, and blue pigments
23.8 x 9.9 x 9.8 cm
Kimbell Art Museum, Fort Worth

This extraordinary clay figurine depicts a Classic-period king with such presence and detail that one might expect it to be a much larger sculpture. The king is dressed in very special regalia associated with war and the ritual of bloodletting; this regalia is also identified on images of kings at Palenque and Dos Pilas. The zoomorphic headdress sits above a headband made of jade cylinders and yellow beads. Behind the red-eyed zoomorph, a huge fan of long blue feathers with red outlines forms a framing arc around the king's head. Yellow shapes rise diagonally from the upper corners of the zoomorph's head, then fall downward to round disk shapes— motifs identified with the bloodletting rite. They are disks with cloth knots attached. The zoomorph in the headdress has yellow-banded blue shells as earflares and a yellow diadem atop its head. He is Chac-Xib-Chac, a god associated with war, sacrifice, dancing and fishing scenes. The king's red-painted face is flanked by blue earflares; a rare rectangular mouthpiece, painted yellow, is suspended around his mouth. Such a mouthpiece is also depicted on the stucco figures in Pacal's tomb at Palenque and on Dos Pilas Stela 17. The actual artifact, made of thin pieces of pyrite covered with red-painted plaster, was found near Pacal's skull in the Temple of Inscriptions.

The rest of the figurine's costume is standard for Maya rulers; it is identical to costumes worn by rulers on Dos Pilas Stelae 1 and 17. Here, a large round pectoral with triple loops decorating both ends covers the king's chest. From other examples, especially the Tablet of Creation of Palenque, we know this pectoral to have been a special knot tied from groups of thin twine. When it is worn, the king always appears in the costume of one of several gods, including Chac-Xib-Chac, the Paddler Twins from the canoe scenes at Tikal or the Palenque Triad. Here, the king wears Chac-Xib-Chac in his headdress. Below the knot pectoral, he wears a second one—a bar carved in the form of a skull, with three cylinders attached to each end. This skull pectoral is normally worn when the king is dressed as a warrior and plans to take captives. The same two pectorals are worn by Shield God K, the ruler on Dos Pilas Stela 1.

The king wears a heavy, wide, double-banded blue belt that signals his kingship and rank.

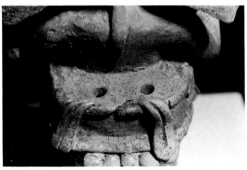

PLATE 2a

FIGURE I.4
The Meaning of the God C Apron

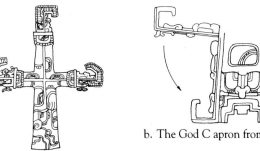

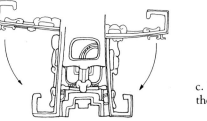

c. The God C apron from the Kimbell figurine (Pl. 2)

a. The World Tree from the sarcophagus lid at Palenque

b. The God C apron from Dos Pilas Stela 1

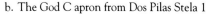

Three blue heads, each with blue celt-shaped objects hanging below them and a red knot draped above them, are mounted on the belt, and a double strand of yellow shells hangs below. This representation of the royal belt is the only one to have survived from the Classic period with its color intact.

Under the belt, the king wears a stiff, knee-length apron. The painted imagery on the front of the apron can be recognized as the standard apron design—God C with the Square-nosed Serpent fret framing each side. Here God C's tooth hangs below the bottom edge, defining the blank between the serpent frets as the mouth. This apron represents the World Tree, rendered so that its bent branches parallel the God C image on the trunk, and it symbolizes that the king is the *axis mundi*, the central axis of the Maya world.

The king's costume is completed with knee ornaments and high-backed sandals with conical ornaments tied to the front. Except for the headdress zoomorph, this king's dress is identical to Flint Sky God K on Dos Pilas Stela 17. Like that ruler, he probably once held a God K scepter in his right hand, to balance the round shield in his left. The Dos Pilas ruler wears the same mouthpiece, and the manner in which the belt extends well beyond the back is similar in both costumes. The Dos Pilas belt supports the backrack of the Holmul Dancer, which has the Water-lily Jaguar, who is often paired with Chac-Xib-Chac, sitting within a skyband. This backrack is missing on the figurine, but two holes are drilled into the top of the belt (Pl. 2a). A Holmul Dancer backrack, perhaps resplendent with real feathers, was once thrust into these holes.

The Dos Pilas monuments suggest the date of this figurine and the ritual in which the king acts. Stela 17 is dated to 9.12.10.0.0 9 Ahau 18 Zotz', or May 10, A.D. 682, and shows Flint Sky God K, while Stela 1 shows his son Shield God K

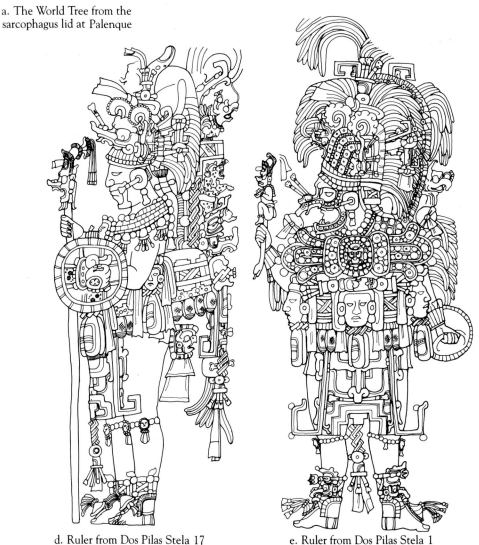

d. Ruler from Dos Pilas Stela 17

e. Ruler from Dos Pilas Stela 1

on 9.13.15.0.0 13 Ahau 18 Pax, or December 31, A.D. 706. The figurine may date from approximately this period, but evidence of costume is inconclusive support for the Dos Pilas region as its source. It is, however, indicative of a particular ritual, and since both Dos Pilas dates are period endings, the costume must be associated with ceremonies conducted on those occasions. Since some of his costume's elements occur with war scenes, we deduce that the king is dressed in his role as warrior, either in preparation for taking captives or for offering captives as sacrificial victims at the period ending rites.

Plate 3
Figurine of a seated lord
Late Classic period, A.D. 600–800
Ceramic
H. 21 cm
Munson-Williams-Proctor Institute, Utica, New York

This seated figurine of a warrior is dressed for a special kind of ritual war—associated with the Tlaloc complex—that is featured at Piedras Negras, Tikal and Copan. His movable headdress has the same arc of feathers and the hanging motif of the figurine from the Kimbell Art Museum (Pl. 2), but the main zoomorph is the Mosaic Monster, whose huge mouth gapes open to emit an animal skull with an articulated lower jaw. This skull is a mask that fits over the face of the king. Thus, the king becomes the apotheosis of this god when he goes to war.

Without the mask, the king's face proves to be fully human. He wears disk flares suspended from his ears; his hair is tied up in the fashion of warriors and captives, and he wears long cotton armor that hangs over his knees as he sits on a four-legged bench. A pectoral and four large beads are mounted on his armor; vertical cylinders hang on his cape. He wears cuffs on his wrists, and his sandals are the same high-backed type worn by the Kimbell figurine above (Pl. 2). In his right hand, he holds a folded cloth; the other hand is modeled to hold a now-missing object, perhaps a knife or spear. This ruler is prepared for actual battle, rather than for ritual preparations for battle or for the sacrificial rites following it.

Plate 4
Figurine of an enthroned ruler
Late Classic period, A.D. 600–800
Ceramic
Figure: 16.8 x 11.6 cm; Throne: 10.6 x 12.6 x 8.7 cm
Lent courtesy of The Art Museum, Princeton University

This figurine, now missing its removable headdress, sits on an elaborately carved bench covered by a jaguar pelt. The bench's upright back is carved with a seated figure, surrounded by huge volutes designated as blood by bone and bead motifs. The king sits upright with his hand spread on the bench as he gazes in concentration; his face, framed by disk and cylinder earflares, frowns in disdain. He wears a high-waisted hipcloth and a wide, feather-lined collar, whose three hanging panels cover his chest and shoulders. This three-paneled cape is the same one worn by warrior figures on Piedras Negras Lintel 2 (see Pl. 40).

Plate 5
Shell ornament
Tula, Hidalgo, Mexico
Late Classic period, A.D. 600–800
Carved shell
5.8 x 9.5 cm
Field Museum of Natural History, Chicago

The Maya used precious material of all sorts to create costume objects decorated with ritual costume imagery. This ornament uses abalone shell, which is not indigenous to the Maya region and had to be imported. The nearest source would have been the present Baja California, Mexico. Carved at least twice by the Maya, this shell pectoral was found during the nineteenth century at Tula, Hidalgo, outside the Maya region. The elegantly carved shell depicts a Maya lord, seated frontally before an upright throne back. His head turned to the side, he leans forward with his right arm extended beyond the now-broken surface of the shell. He wears disk and cylinder earflares and a bar through the septum of his nose. A pectoral hangs suspended from a bead necklace. The zoomorph in his headdress is marked by feather fans on its forehead and muzzle, which identifies it as the Vision Serpent. Long feathers emerge from the top of its head, and the king's cylinder and bead headband emerges from its open mouth.

The rear of the shell is inscribed with a diagonal row of glyphs, which are oriented to face in the direction opposite to the figure on the front surface. Like the figure on the front, these glyphs are cut by breaks on both sides of the shell. Clearly, the shell was broken at least once, and since the

orientation of the glyphs and the figural scene are opposite one another, it seems also to have been recarved.

Plate 6
Jade plaque
Late Classic period, A.D. 600–800
Jade
6 x 8 x 1.3 cm
Courtesy of the Museum of the American Indian, Heye Foundation, New York

Collected in Oaxaca, this jade plaque was carried out of the Maya area and used as a prestige item in a different cultural region. The depicted ruler, probably the plaque's original owner, is seated cross-legged upon a small pillow; long flowing feathers emerge from the rear of the jawless zoomorph in his headdress. Huge double scrolls that emerge from behind his hips surround him with the symbols of sacred blood. The position of the body—the head turned to the side, one arm held across his chest and the other on a knee—is a formal posture Maya rulers assumed when giving audience.

Plate 7
Hair ornament
Campeche, Mexico
Late Classic period, A.D. 600–800
Jade
2.2 x 1.1 cm
Courtesy of the Museum of the American Indian, Heye Foundation, New York

This highly polished, wide cylindrical hair ornament has thin walls that flare into a narrow plane, which is notched to represent a flower. The front lock of hair was pulled through this flower-shaped ornament in one of the distinctive hairstyles of Maya nobility.

Plate 8
Headband ornaments
Late Classic period, A.D. 600–800
Jade
4.3 x 4.6 x .5 cm; 4.7 x .3 cm
Courtesy of the Museum of the American Indian, Heye Foundation, New York

Carved from a richly colored green jade, these two ornaments were originally attached to a headband worn by a Maya lord. Shaped to form a four-petaled flower, each ornament had a central hole that permitted it to be attached to a leather or cloth band. On Yaxchilan Lintel 26, Shield Jaguar wears a headband made of this kind of jade plaque (Fig. V.2).

Plate 9
Earflare
Pomona, Belize
Late Preclassic period, 50 B.C.–A.D. 50
Jade
Diam. 18 cm
The Trustees of The British Museum, London

This exquisite earflare, discovered in a Late Preclassic tomb in southern Belize, is one of few recovered examples of the large type of earflare. It is incised with four texts arranged on opposite sides of the flare. On one axis, two gods—the Sun God of Number 4 and the Maize God of Number 8—are recorded with their appropriate numbers and a footprint. On the opposite axis, each text includes two glyphs, apparently a verb and its subject. One actor is the Sun God, and the other is a zoomorphic deity not yet identified. These glyphs refer to gods and apparently record the cosmic sanction that this ruler wished to invoke.

Plate 10
Shell-shaped earflare
Kendal, Belize
Early Classic period, A.D. 250–400
Greenstone
11.8 x 5.7 x 1.7 cm
Merseyside County Museums, Liverpool

This greenstone earflare, one of the most extraordinary objects known in Maya art, is carved to represent half of a bivalve shell. It was tied to the side flange of a headdress through two holes drilled on the hinge side. It is the kind of earflare worn by both God GI of the Palenque Triad and Chac-Xib-Chac. Since it was found with a jade pectoral and a stone ax incised with a portrait of GI, we can surmise that it was one of a pair of earflares of a Chac-Xib-Chac/GI costume. This earflare was recovered from a burial mound at Kendal, Belize, by H. W. Price in 1892.

    The rear surface is incised with glyphs of an early style that appear to record seven god names. The first glyph is a human holding an ax in front of his face, with phonetic signs for the sounds *ma* and *la* placed above and below it. The second glyph is also anthropomorphic and has a dark mirror sign overlaying the forehead and eye. The third glyph is an anthropomorph with a square-eye, scalloped eyebrow, pointed tooth and beard. The fish fin behind the head and at the corner of the mouth may identify it as God GI of the Palenque Triad. The fourth glyph is a zoomorphic head, identified as a bird by the feathers in the upper rear corner; a second bird with a longer beak emerges from its

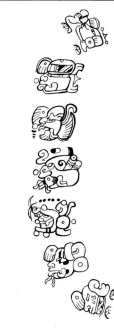

Plate 10a

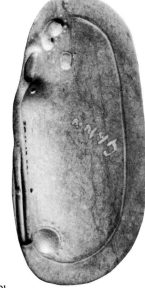

Plate 10b

mouth. The fifth glyph is a snarling jaguar with a human face deep in its open mouth. The sixth glyph is again anthropomorphic, with a dark spot on its cheek and a spotted *chicchan* marking in the upper right corner of the face. These markings combine to help identify this character as the Hun-Ahau member of the Headband Twins, perhaps the earliest example so far known. The last glyph is an unidentified anthropomorph.

Plate 11
A Jester God
Late Classic period, A.D. 600–800
Jade, traces of cinnabar
13.5 x 9 x 3.5 cm
Utah Museum of Fine Arts, Salt Lake City
Permanent Collection

The Jester God is one of the earliest symbols associated with Maya rulership. Developed during the Late Preclassic period as the personification of a three-pointed shape worn on the cloth headband of rulers, the Jester God was the crown of kings until the collapse of Classic Maya civilization in the ninth century. Numerous Jester Gods have been recovered. They are always carved from jade or some other precious green stone, and almost all are small and worn on cloth headbands. Only one example has been recovered of another, larger form, which is shown attached to the front of the Drummajor headdress in depictions at Yaxchilan and Palenque. A jade slab two inches thick was carved on both sides and drilled along the rear edge in order to mount it vertically against the headdress. In this position, the imagery could be read from both sides. This Jester God is also remarkable because it has the triangular shark teeth characteristic of the Jester Gods of Palenque. The depression below the eye may have once held an inlay, perhaps of shell or coral, representing a fish fin.

Plate 12
Flower-shaped earflares
Early Classic period, A.D. 350–600
Jade
Diam. 5.7 x 2.0 cm
Lent courtesy of The Art Museum, Princeton University

PLATE 13
Earflares carved with scroll patterns
Early Classic period, A.D. 350–600
Jade
Diam. 6.5–7.5 x 1.0 cm
Lent courtesy of The Art Museum, Princeton University

These two sets of beautifully finished earflares were carved from a finely grained, light green jade, probably during the Early Classic period. One set is carved with a deep flare and the four divisions of the flower. U-shapes were cut in each petal by a drill and string saw. The flare of the second pair is more shallow; it is marked by a pattern of four lobes that are separated from one another by incised lines. Each lobe is further emphasized by an openwork scroll penetrating through the flare. The flares were cut from one jade core, but the artisan turned one flare ninety degrees from the other when he cut the openwork scrolls. Identical scrolls are shown attached to Vision Serpents on a Late Preclassic stone vessel (Pl. 67), suggesting that these earflares date to a very early period. Presumably, each pair of earflares once had the central cylinder and the rear counterweights typical of Maya ear ornaments.

PLATE 14
Earflares with diagonal cylinder and bead
Late Classic period, A.D. 600–800
Jadeite
Diam. 8.3 cm
The Denver Art Museum

These earflares represent the type most commonly worn by Maya nobles. Often cut from one sphere of jade, such earflares include a flaring disk with a large central hole, a long, thin cylinder drilled through its long axis and a bell-shaped flare at the end of the cylinder. These earflares are unusual in that a second disk is set inside the opening of the main flare.

PLATE 15
Deity mask
Late Preclassic or Early Classic period, A.D. 50–300
Jade
23.2 x 15.6 cm
The Trustees of The British Museum, London

From its style, this stunning jade mask can be dated to the last half of the Late Preclassic period or to the very early part of the Early Classic period. The mask was not designed to be worn, for the eyes are solid, and the roughened surface of their depressions suggests that they were once inlaid, perhaps with shell. The persona depicted is not human but is, rather, an anthropomorphic god. His forehead is outset with a rectangular panel of the sort particularly characteristic of Late Preclassic architectural masks. The eyebrows are also rendered as in very early sculptural traditions (in later styles, the eyebrows become more rounded, and the bifurcated end is lost). Finally, the bifurcated emanations attached to the corners of the mouth may well represent the fish fins of God GI of the Palenque Triad; if so, however, they are in the wrong location: fish fins should emerge from the cheek line rather than from the corners of the mouth.

This jade mask is virtually identical to the one depicted on the Hauberg Stela (Pl. 66), dated to A.D. 199. Since the mask and the stela almost certainly did not come from the same site, the similarity not only dates this mask to approximately the same period but testifies to the widespread use of masks in Maya ritual and to the uniformity of Maya state religion, even at this very early time.

PLATE 16
Rectangular plaques
Lubaantun, Belize
Late Classic period, A.D. 600–800
Jade
4.2 x 3.8 cm
The Trustees of The British Museum, London

These light green jade plaques are pierced in the center for attachment to an underlying garment. Although these two were the only plaques found in the grave at Lubaantun, Belize, they are exactly the type of jade ornament used on the shoulder capes worn by both male and female Maya nobles. Aligned in horizontal rows, the plaques were sewn to leather or cloth foundations, and they were often accompanied by jade heads set in the center of the chest and on the shoulders. Although such a cape must have been enormously heavy, the garment would have made a colorful display in the ritual processions of Maya ceremony, with its brilliant display of blue green, perhaps bordered by feathers of a different color and contrasted with a richly colored feather headdress and woven cloth.

PLATE 17
Bead and claw necklaces
Burial VIII-27, Copan, Honduras
Middle Preclassic period, B.C. 800–600
Jade
Large: 84 cm; Small: 43.3 cm
Instituto Hondureño de Antropología e Historia, Tegulcigalpa, Honduras

Found in a rich burial of the Middle Preclassic period, these necklaces are one of four deposited in the grave of a Copan lord around 900 B.C. The grave was placed in the largest of four houses situated around a plaza to form an elite residential compound. The necklaces are composed of jade, probably brought from the nearby source on the Motagua River in modern Guatemala. The long strand is composed of spheres of various sizes, which alternate with longer pieces modeled in the form of jaguar claws. This lord was also buried with seven finely polished plain celts and four pottery vessels, two of which display orthodox Olmec symbolism. The longer necklace, like the pots, transmits a coded ideology: the jaguar-claw motif is also found in Olmec jade jewelry and was perhaps a way of calling upon the supernatural power of the jaguar to sanction secular activity and rank.

PLATE 18
Profile of a face
Late Classic period, A.D. 600–800
Jade
H. 7 cm
The Museum of Fine Arts, Houston
Museum Purchase

This thin jade profile was once part of a larger mosaic with a slightly convex surface; it may have been a chest pectoral or some other ornament of costume. The rear contour is cut to fit adjacent pieces that once delineated the earflare and hair; the forehead is flat to accommodate the headdress. The hard jade is subtly fashioned to emphasize surface modulations around the eyes, nostrils and mouth. Delicately incised lines delineate the eyebrows; other such lines are incised on the nose to indicate face painting. The mouth, with its relaxed and slightly open lips, is typically Maya. The chin drops sharply away from the lower lip, giving the face a chinless look; however, it is possible that another piece of jade completed the chin contour to produce a more orthodox outline. The quality of the blue-green jade and the subtly controlled modeling make this one of the finest Maya jades now known.

PLATE 19
Ahau pectoral
Kendal, Belize
Early Classic period, A.D. 250–400
Greenstone
6.8 x 6.8 x 2.5 cm
Merseyside County Museums, Liverpool

This jade pectoral, carved as an extraordinary face, was found with thin cylindrical beads and jade alligator heads, which were once suspended from the five holes drilled along its chin. There are additional drilled holes in the earlobes, perhaps for hanging ornaments made from a different material. The rear surface is concave and has a flat edge around the circumference to allow the piece to rest against the chest. Drilled through this edge are two larger holes not visible from the front, from which the pectoral hung on a leather strap.

This skillfully modeled portrait is human, almost childlike in its appearance, perhaps because the drilled eyeholes are so large in relation to the other features. The eyes may originally have been filled with some other material, perhaps even the silver-dollar-size piece of pyrite found near the pectoral. The button nose has drilled nostrils, and the open mouth is flanked by two larger holes. These circles in the cheek may once have been inlaid with another material, but they are certainly the right size and at the proper location to represent the cheek circles of the human variant of *ahau* and the Headband Twin named Hun-Ahau. Thus, this pectoral is a very early representation of the Headband Twin and of the title *ahau* and was meant to be worn by a king on his chest to declare his status and office.

The most important stylistic feature is the treatment of the forehead, with its division into three panels. A straight saw cut creates a horizontal band across the top of the central panel, above incised arcing lines that resemble the top of the *akbal* sign. A bead and pendant motif is incised in each of the three panels, and in the central one, these lines overlay the earlier incision. Such a three-paneled division of the forehead also appears on the Nohmul bar pectoral (Pl. 20); most significantly, however, it characterizes the Late Preclassic version of the Jaguar Sun God at Cerros. It is probable that the same forehead treatment was used in depictions of the Sun God's Twin, Hun-Ahau, but this particular way of drawing him did not persist long in the Classic period. Either the grave in which this pectoral was found was Late Preclassic or Protoclassic, or the pectoral was kept as an heirloom, then buried with an Early Classic ruler.

PLATE 20
Jester God bar pectoral
Nohmul, Belize
Early Classic period, A.D. 350–600
Jade
14 x 2.5 cm
The Trustees of The British Museum, London

Found on the chest of a warrior in a grave near Nohmul in Belize, this bar pectoral, drilled through the axis for suspension, depicts a deity in the hands-to-chest posture of Maya kings. The bar's four planes are carved to represent the four sides of a full-figure god. He has squint-eyes—square-shaped eyes with square-shaped pupils in the inner lower corners—a human nose and a wide mouth with emanations at the corners and a crossed-band cartouche emerging like a tongue. The god's earflare assemblages, consisting of a central disk, counterweight and scroll, are carved on each side plane. His forehead is divided into the three sections characteristic of Late Preclassic and very Early Classic styles. A band encircles his head; it supports an early *ahau* shape surmounted by three leaves. The rear surface depicts the knotted cloth that ties the *ahau* band on the head. While this motif eventually became the decorated *ahau*, in this case it is probably intended as a reference to the three-pointed head of the Jester God; thus, this pectoral is an early full-figure version of that god.

The god's hands are held in front of his chest, touching wrist to wrist, in the position Maya kings traditionally used to hold the Double-headed Serpent Bar. A shell pectoral, suspended from a bead necklace tied by cloth strips at the back of his neck, drops below his wrists. Characterized by its scalloped lower contour, this pectoral is commonly worn by Early Classic kings, such as Stormy Sky on Tikal Stela 31. The four parallel lines in the interior represent reflections on a polished surface, which signal that the pectoral is made of jade or some other bright material.

The wide belt encircling the god's waist supports fancy loincloth ornaments in both front and back, composed of spherical, bell-shaped and cylindrical jade decorations. The toes are indicated by a series of parallel lines cut on the front of a bottom ledge that represents the god's feet. Worn horizontally across the chest of a ruler, this pectoral declared the wearer's supernatural affiliation and rank as an *ahau*.

PLATE 21
Portrait head
Comayagua, Honduras
Late Classic period, A.D. 600–800
Jade
15.2 x 9.9 cm
The Trustees of The British Museum, London

This solid stone head was once mounted above three flat celts as part of a royal belt assemblage. Such belt heads were usually assembled from thin jade pieces, shell, obsidian or similar materials glued to wooden foundations. This is the only known example of a belt head carved from a single stone. It was tied to the belt by straps pulled through eye-level holes drilled near the rear edges; a third hole, begun in the top, was never completed.

The face is a beautifully modeled portrait of a male ruler or possibly the god who personifies *ahau*, the Hero Twin Hun-Ahau. His relaxed mouth is slightly open, his face calmly composed. A shallow hole is drilled in the inner corner of each eye depression; the rough texture of these depressions suggests they were once inlaid. The polish has been worn from the tip of the nose and the eyebrow ridge, a result of abrasion incurred when the belt was in use. Since heads mounted on the side of the belt are more susceptible to this kind of wear, this head was probably mounted on the side rather than on the front of the belt.

The head was collected from Comayagua, Honduras, from Indians who lived in Tambla. It

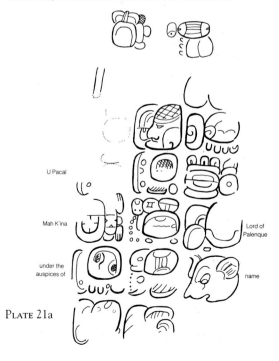

U Pacal

Mah K'ina

Lord of Palenque

under the auspices of

name

PLATE 21a

can be presumed that it rested originally in a tomb at Copan or one of the smaller Maya sites in the Copan region. However, the inscription, composed of three partially eroded columns incised on the rear, permits us to deduce more about its origin and use. The inscription (Pl. 21a) includes at least one and perhaps two sentences, but it is without a readable date. Beginning with the first legible glyph in the central column, the action is recorded with a God N verb, an undeciphered event that also appears in the Primary Standard Sequence on pottery. The next glyph is eroded, but the following phrase is a name written with the phonetic glyph *u pacal*, a title, *Mah K'ina*, and the Palenque Emblem Glyph, or "the shield of the great Sun, lord of Palenque." Many scholars have taken this Palenque passage to refer to the great ruler Pacal, but this seems not to be the case. The phonetic reference to the word Pacal is preceded by a possessive pronoun (*u*, in the language of the writing system). Furthermore, the same phrase, *u pacal*, or "his shield," occurs on a fragment from a Palenque tablet now in the Art Gallery of Notre Dame University (Fig. I.5). That text contains a nearly identical passage, reading, "*chac u pacal Mah K'ina Kan-Xul, lord of Palenque*" ("great is the shield of the great sun Kan-

Xul, lord of Palenque"). The information is the same, but the protagonist is Kan-Xul, the second of Pacal's sons. Assuming that the Copan text is related to the Notre Dame text, the passage can be construed to refer to someone from Palenque, like Kan-Xul, who had the right to name himself "the shield of."

Present knowledge of the history of Copan allows us to suggest who this person might have been. Yax-Pac, one of the last rulers of Copan, is recorded on Stela 8 as the "child of a lady of Palenque." The previous ruler of Copan, Smoke Squirrel, married a woman of Palenque, who very probably brought her own costumes and attendants with her to her new home, including this belt head. The dates surrounding her arrival support this suggestion. Smoke Squirrel acceded on December 31, A.D. 746, some sixty-four years after Pacal's death. The woman was several generations younger than Pacal but was apparently a member of his line. We can surmise that the belt head was passed on to her and then to her descendants. The Comayagua region was closely tied to the Copan Valley during the eighth century. The head may have been transferred by the looting of a Copan burial in the Postclassic period or through the gift of this piece to a Comayagua noble by a Copan ruler.

Plate 22
Celt fragment
Early Classic period, A.D. 250–400
Jadeite
11.7 x 5.4 cm
Dumbarton Oaks, Washington, D.C.

This lovely light green celt is one of three originally hung below the heads on a royal belt. Looted from a tomb in Precolumbian times, it was broken, then redrilled for horizontal suspension. The drawing of the figure is Early Classic in style, but the style of the glyphs suggests a date that is earlier, perhaps even Protoclassic.

The image of a standing king incised on the front surface of the celt (Pl. 22b) shows him holding one arm rigidly at his side, the other raised to his shoulder with a finger pointing upward. While his head is missing, the bottom detail of his earflare assemblage and what may be the bifurcated scroll of a face mask can be seen below the upper edge. A chain of bell-shaped jades hangs around his neck, and he wears beaded cuffs on his wrists. Mat and disk signs mark his belt, and a jaguar head is mounted on its front. Three celts cut with interior T-shapes hang below the Jaguar God's head. Because only the tip of a muzzle and forehead of a

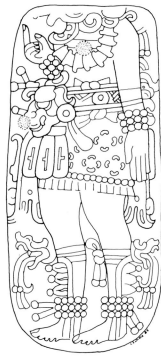

Plate 22b

rear head are visible behind his right wrist, we cannot identify the other god he wore. The skirt is made of a jaguar pelt, and the bifurcated loincloth he wears is characteristic of early royal dress. The rear and front loin apron are finished with a serpent-fret border.

The king's leg cuffs are the most unusual item of dress. A knot with an open-mouthed zoomorph is tied around each leg below the knee. This knot is connected to a panel inset with three pointed shapes that appear to wrap around his leg. At the base of the panels are beaded cuffs, and a panel covers his ankles. The rendering of the toes as a scalloped line is unusual.

The Inscription
The celt inscription (Pl. 22c) begins with four glyphs that record a period ending in a most unusual form. The first two glyphs are partially obliterated by the break, but it can be reconstructed as "8 or 9 baktuns were completed." The next two appear to record that "4 katuns were completed," although both the katun glyph and the number are very unusual. Many of the remaining glyphs cannot be read, but B4 is a "kin-in-hand" glyph that appears repeatedly in Protoclassic texts, but not later. A6 is also a

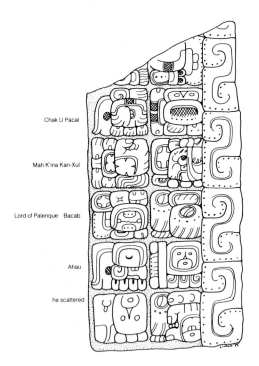

Chak U Pacal

Mah K'ina Kan-Xul

Lord of Palenque Bacab

Ahau

he scattered

Figure I.5

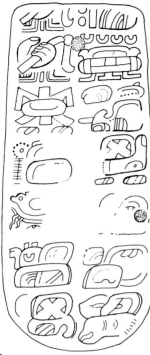

PLATE 22c

very early form of the *ahau* title. The final sign is the earliest known example of a title prominent in royal names of the Classic period: the main sign here is a penis. Although this text is not fully deciphered, it still provides considerable information. The last four (or perhaps six) glyphs name the ruler pictured on the opposite side. The ritual shown is probably a period-ending rite, and the early form of the glyphs supports the earlier position of the period-ending notation. If the baktun coefficient is 8, then the date is 8.4.0.0.0, or July 15, A.D. 120. The later position, 9.4.0.0.0, places the celt in the year A.D. 514, which seems to be too late for the style of drawing and glyphs.

PLATE 23
Deity plaque
Pusilha, Belize
Late Classic period, A.D. 600–800
Jade
5.7 x 3.2 cm
The Trustees of The British Museum, London

The artist who worked this light green jade flattened the stone surface carefully before cutting the contour. Since it has no holes for suspension, this jade may have been used simply as a ritual object, or

it may have been glued to a wooden surface. The image depicts a god seated in profile with his shoulders turned toward the viewer. His arms are held in front of his chest; his hand is turned downward, the thumb across his fingers. A beaded belt encircles the god's waist and neck. His head is surrounded by three smokelike shapes, and facial features include a squint-eye, a forehead panel, a mirror at the rear of the head and a single curved line representing the mouth. Here his image was incised on a jade ornament as a supernatural sanction of the secular authority of the king or as a power object to be used in ritual.

PLATE 24
Costume ornament
Late Classic period, A.D. 600–800
Carved shell
7.7 x 7.1 cm
The Art Museum, Princeton University
Gift of Gillett G. Griffin

This shell exemplifies the silhouette style of carving that employs cutout latticework for the main contours of the image. Here the image is a day-sign cartouche and, occupying the interior shape, a human personification. Incised lines are used for his features and for the interior details of the cartouche. At one time the headdress was highlighted by mosaic pieces glued to the shell surface. The whiter shapes of this mosaic are still discernible above and behind the head. The drawing reverses the standard reading direction, with the head facing right. This personification has the small dot of the *ahau* head on the cheek but has the dotted circle of the *cauac* sign on the shoulder. It is not known which day sign was intended, but since *cauac* very rarely appears in human form, the sign is likely to represent *ahau* in its manifestation as Hun-Ahau, one of the Classic-period Hero Twins.

PLATE 25
Eccentric flint
Late Classic period, A.D. 600–800
Flint
34.5 x 19.2 cm
The Cleveland Museum of Art
John L. Severance Fund

This dark brown flint was chipped into a silhouette with five heads extruding from the main shaft. The central profile is human in its features; God K's smoking celt penetrates his forehead, and feathers fan out behind his head. These feathers flow downward in an arc that rises to form another profile head, which also is embedded with a smoking celt.

A third head emerges from the shaft where the first figure's arm should appear; he looks upward toward the celt of that figure's head. Below it a fourth head faces outward, balanced by a pointed shape on the opposite side of the shaft. The lower end of the flint curves into a hook, now partially broken.

PLATE 26
Eccentric flint
Late Classic period, A.D. 600–800
Flint
H. 34.5 cm
Lent by The Metropolitan Museum of Art
The Michael C. Rockefeller Collection, Purchase,
Nelson A. Rockefeller Gift, 1967

This flint has two profiles and various protrusions from its shaft. The main head at the top of the shaft has puckered lips and God K's smoking celt in its forehead. A tall headdress terminates in a feather fan with the shape of a hook above it. At shoulder level behind this head, another protrusion emerges at an angle to terminate in a profile looking upward. This head also wears a feather fan. The remaining protrusions do not appear to refer to recognizable shapes.

PLATE 27
Incised conch shell
Early Classic period, A.D. 250–400
Shell with cinnabar tracings
29.3 x 13.4 cm
Kimbell Art Museum, Fort Worth

The artist worked this medium-size conch shell into a trumpet by cutting off the tip of the spire to make a mouthpiece and drilling holes into the shell wall. A hole drilled on the opposite end provided a means of suspending the trumpet from the trumpeter's neck during ritual performances and of storing it when not in use.
The face of a king incised on the surface is subtly modeled to follow the highly irregular shape of the shell. On the left, a vertical line of glyphs leads into the image (Pl. 27a). The first two glyphs record a possessed noun. The second of these, the quincunx sign—a pattern of five dots regularly arranged—is known to have the phonetic value *be* or *bi*. The noun should then be a word ending with the consonant *b*. Since objects like this shell are sometimes tagged with the names of their owners, this possessed noun may record "his conch-trumpet," or *u hub*, in Yucatec Maya. The remaining glyphs record a name, with the title *ahau*, in the

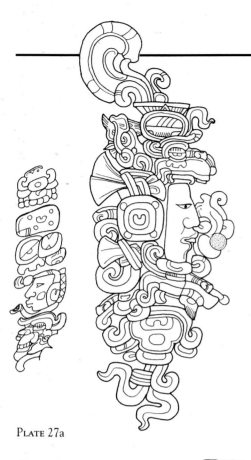

PLATE 27a

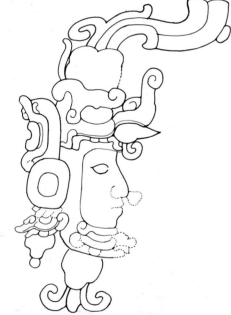

PLATE 27b

fourth glyph and the personal name of the owner in the fifth.

The image shows a person wearing the flanged headdress of Early Classic kings and looking to the right. The surface of the shell was subtly modeled to make the ground drop away from the contour of his face. The eye, nostrils and lips are delineated in a fine line, and the teeth dropping from his upper lip suggest a rather severe overbite. The headdress has a large earflare, and a knot is mounted above and below the disk, a personification head attached to each. The chin strap is also personified and has an inverted smoking *ahau* dropping from it. The main zoomorphic head is the Water-lily Jaguar, a head that appears to match the personal name written as the last glyph in the text. The "smoking *ahau*" attached to the chin strap may be the key to the meaning of this portrait image. On Early Classic stelae at Tikal, various images are shown floating in the top portion of these monuments, above the heads of the rulers portrayed. On Stela 31, a monument of the ruler Stormy Sky, this floating image wears as its headdress the name of Curl Snout, the previous ruler of Tikal. In the rear text of Stela 31, Curl Snout is named as the father of Stormy Sky; the floating image, therefore, is the manifestation of the dead father. On Stela 4, the accession monument of Curl Snout himself, this floating image is God K, the deity particularly associated with ancestral bloodletting rites. These floating images throughout Classic Maya history are either portraits of ancestors or realizations of the ancestors recalled to earth by means of the bloodletting rite. On Stela 29, the earliest dated monument at Tikal, the floating figure is human in form, but it has the same "smoking *ahau*" attached to its chin strap as the portrait on our trumpet (Fig. I.6). The occurrence of this symbol with both images suggests that the portrait on the Kimbell trumpet is the ancestor who was to be recalled by the bloodletting rite in which the trumpet was used (see Chap. VIII).

PLATE 1. Panel of a woman with God K

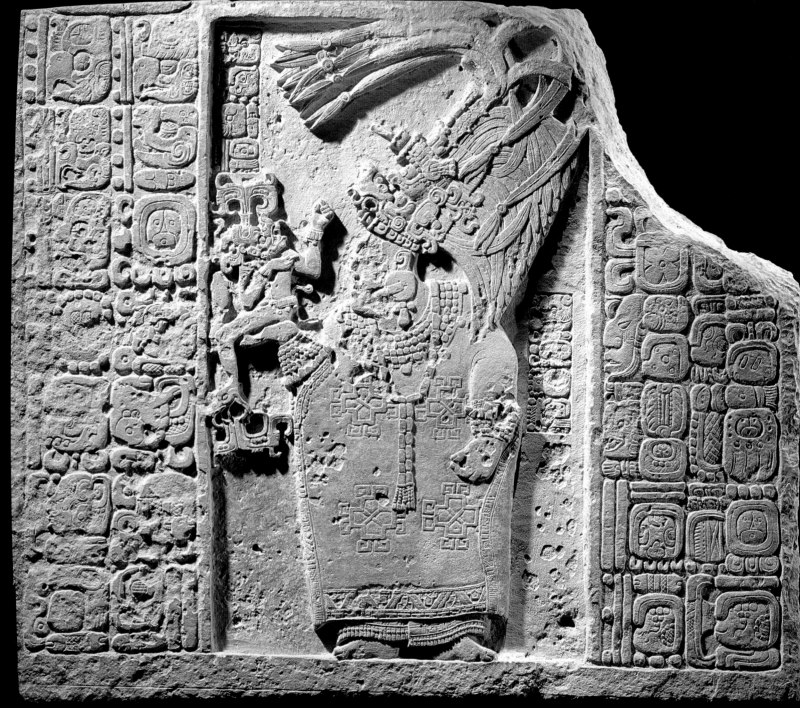

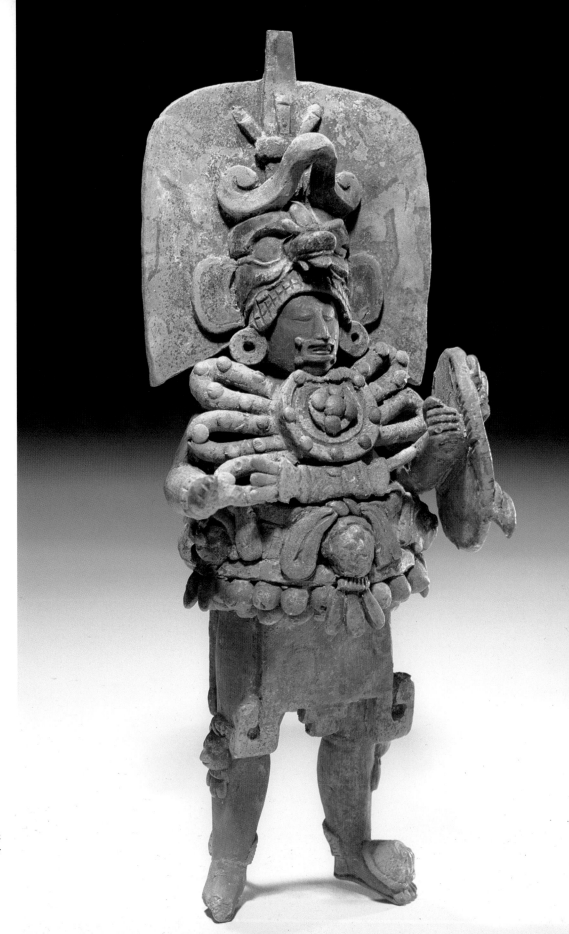

PLATE 2. A Ruler dressed as Chac-Xib-Chac
and the Holmul Dancer

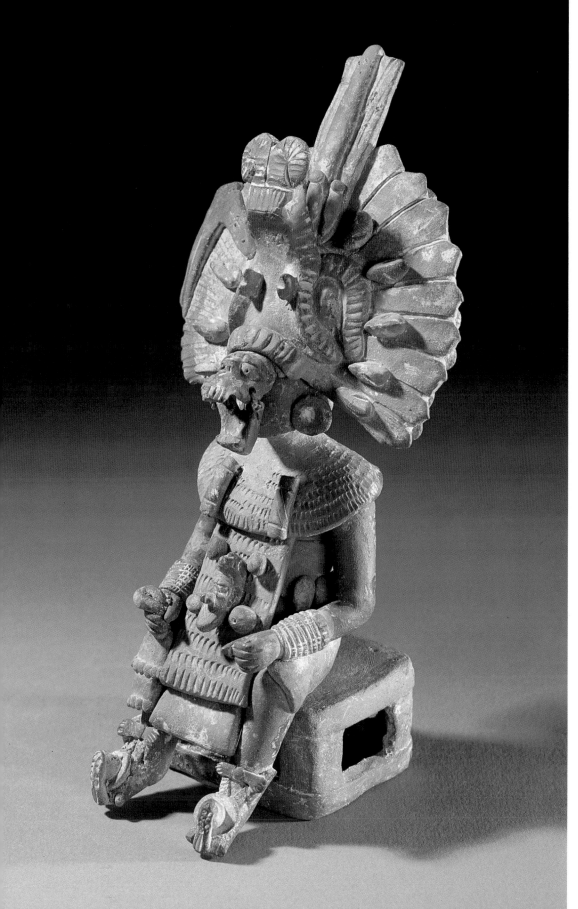

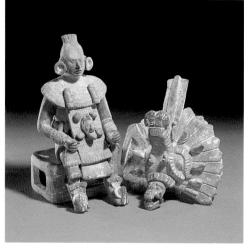

PLATE 3A. Figurine with headdress removed

PLATE 3. Figurine of a seated lord

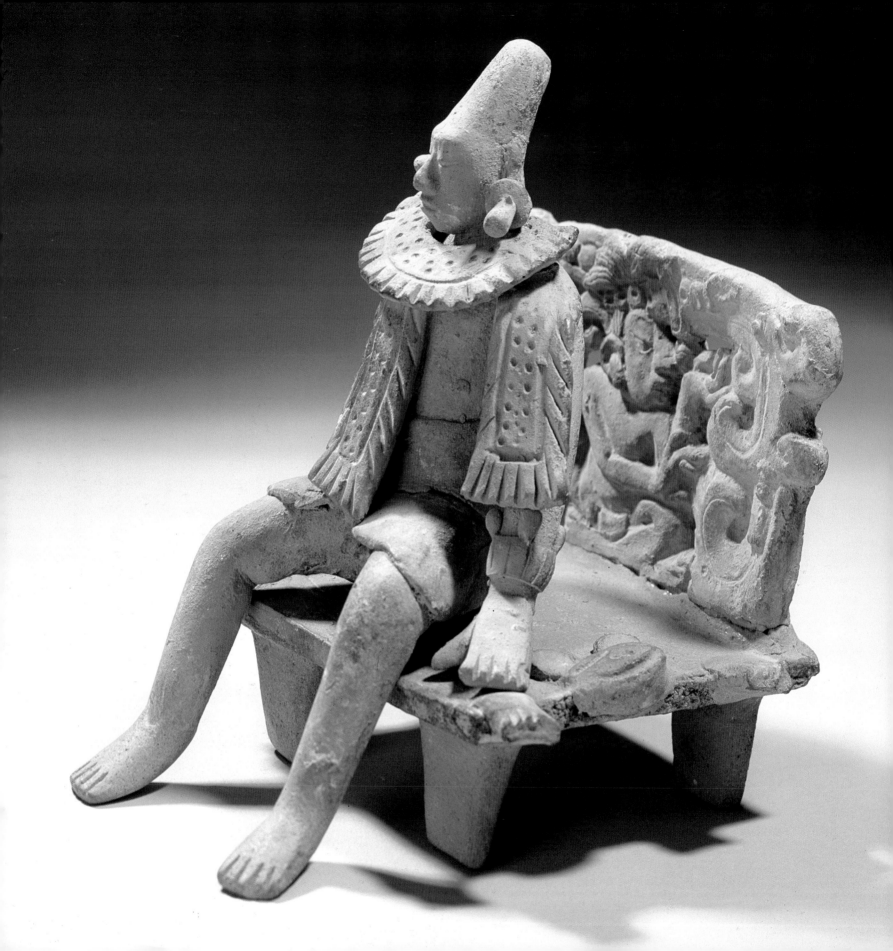

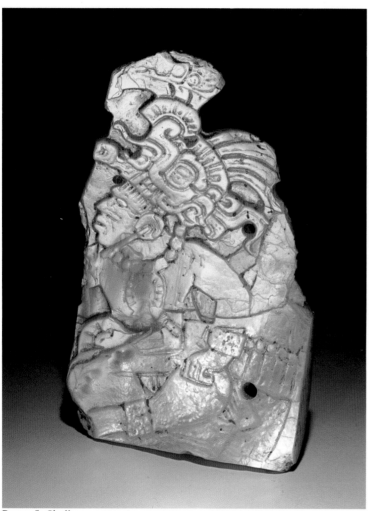

PLATE 5. Shell ornament

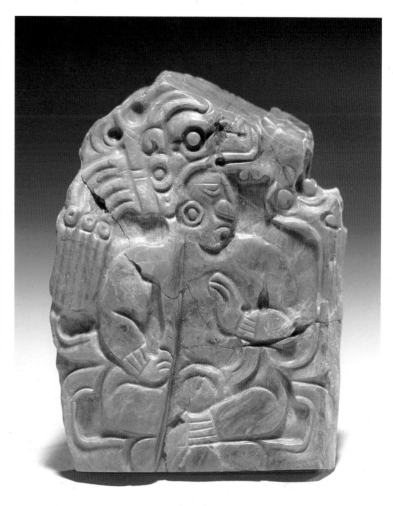

PLATE 6. Jade plaque

PLATE 4. Figurine of enthroned ruler

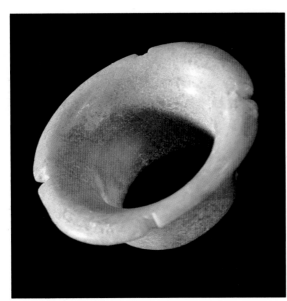

Plate 7. Hair ornament

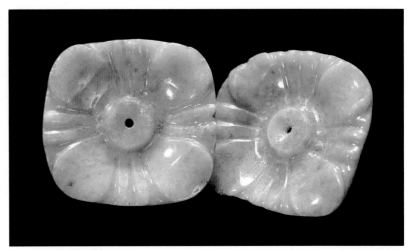

Plate 8. Headband ornaments

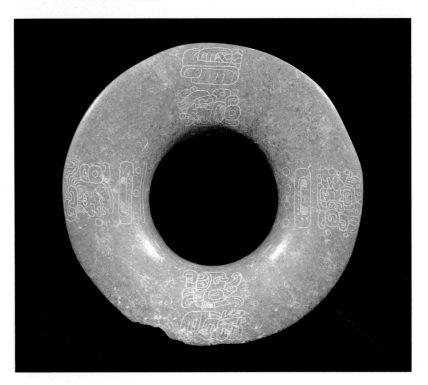

Plate 9. Earflare

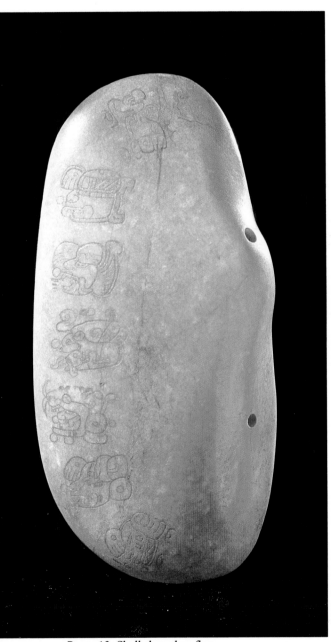

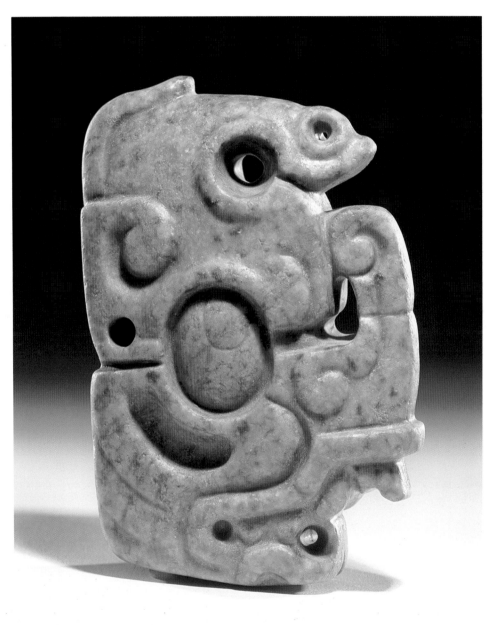

PLATE 10. Shell-shaped earflare   PLATE 11. A Jester God

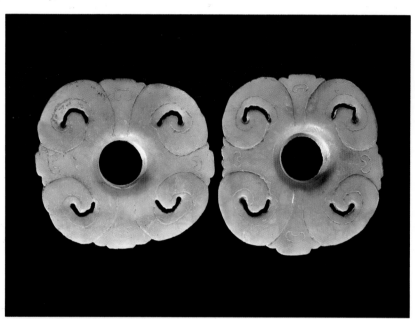

PLATE 12. Flower-shaped earflares

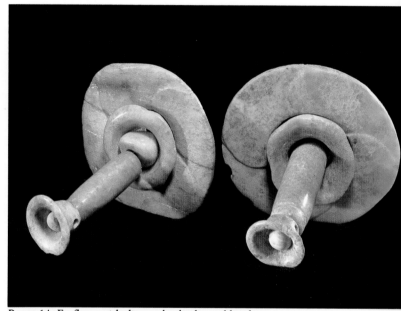

PLATE 14. Earflares with diagonal cylinder and bead

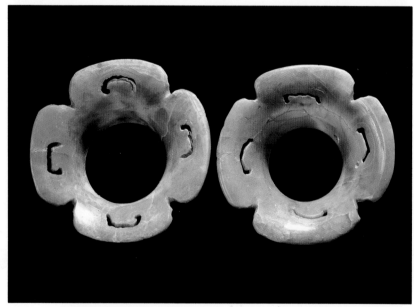

PLATE 13. Earflares carved with scroll patterns

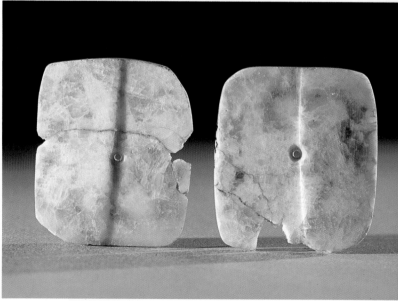

PLATE 16. Rectangular plaques

PLATE 15. Deity mask

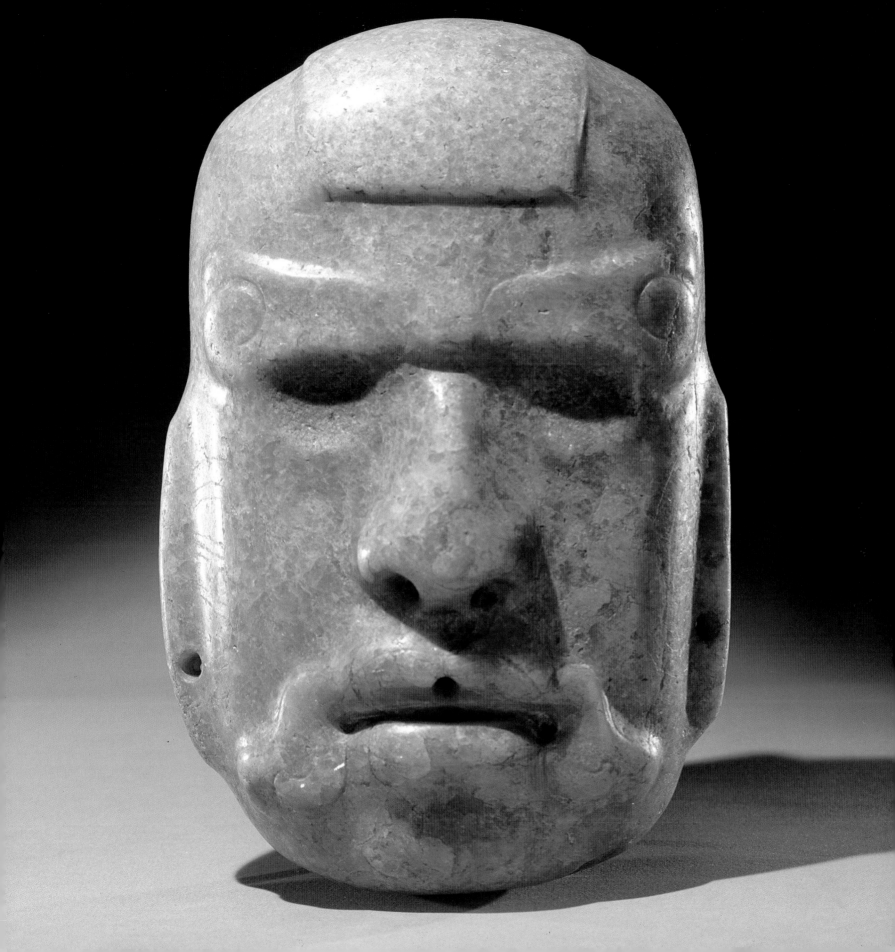

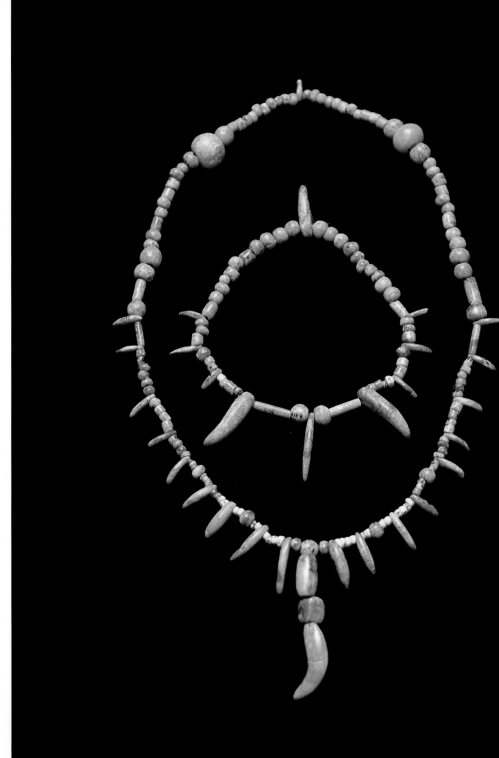

Plate 17. Bead and claw necklaces

Plate 18. (opposite) Profile of face

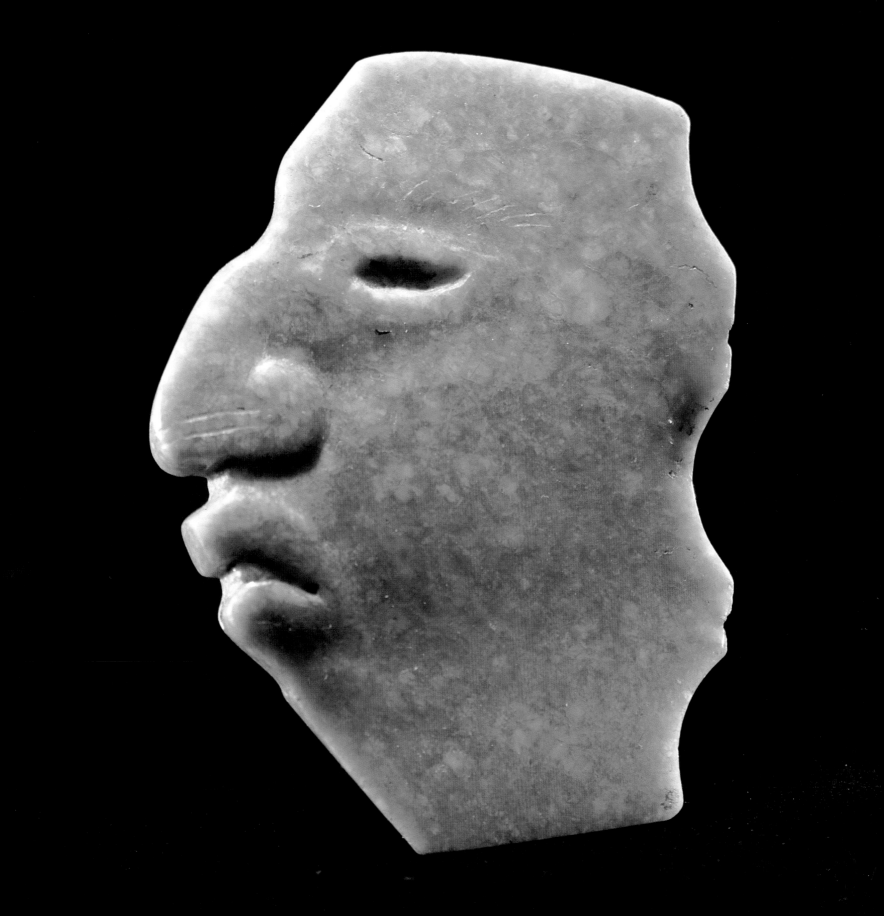

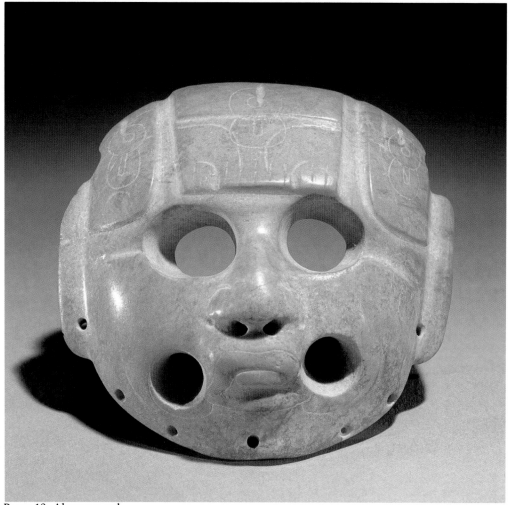

PLATE 19. Ahau pectoral

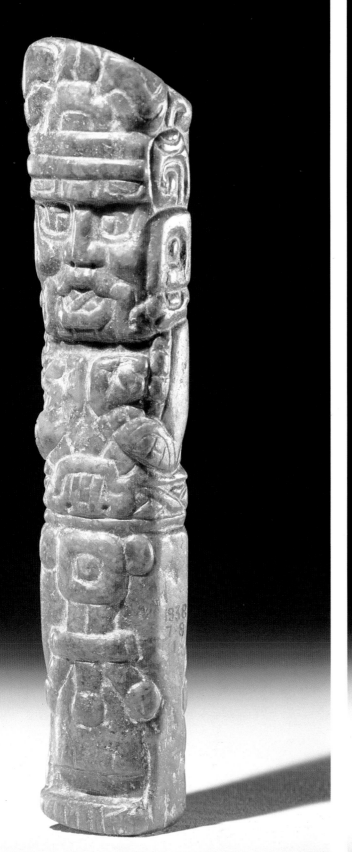 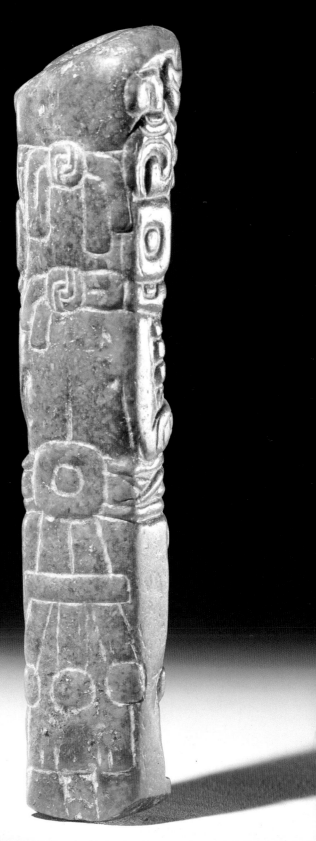

PLATE 20. Jester God bar pectoral (front)　　　　　　　　　PLATE 20A. Pectoral (rear)

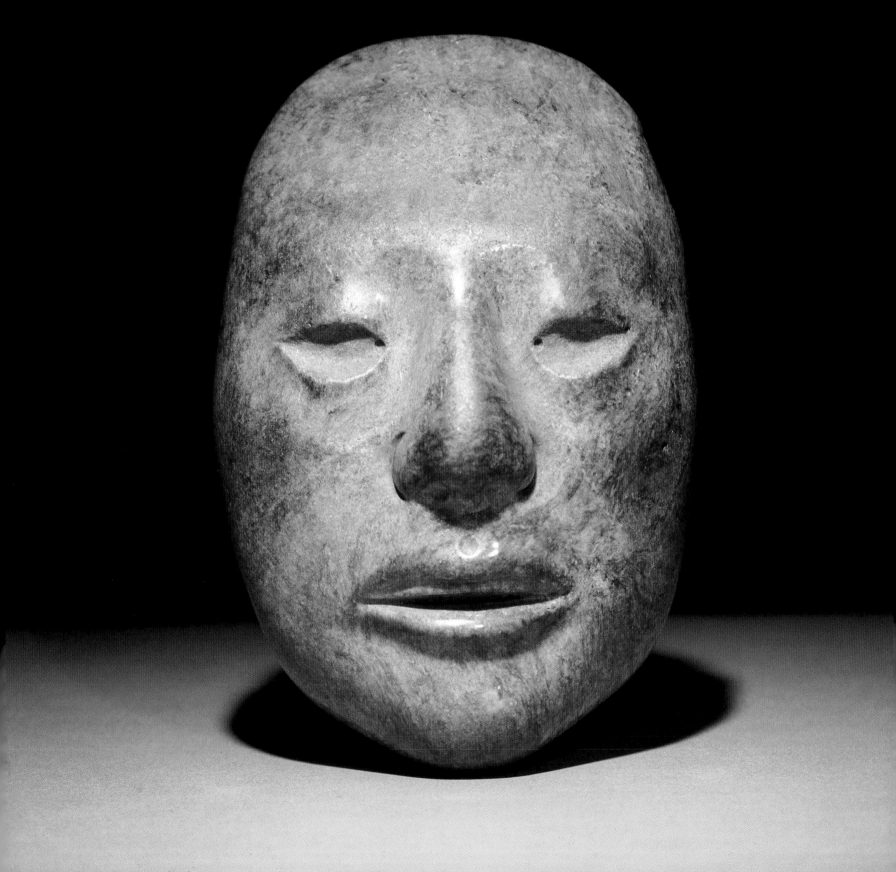

PLATE 21. Portrait head

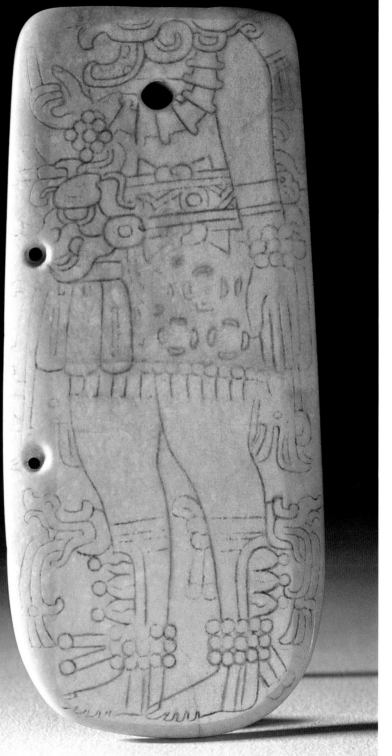

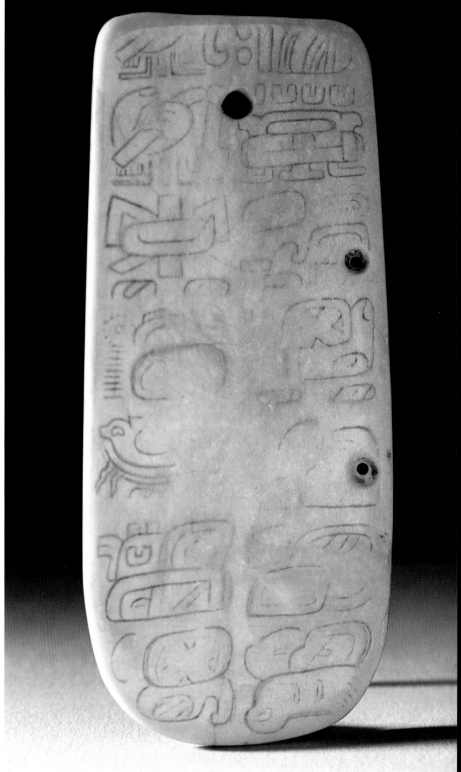

PLATE 22. Celt fragment (front)

PLATE 22A. Celt (rear)

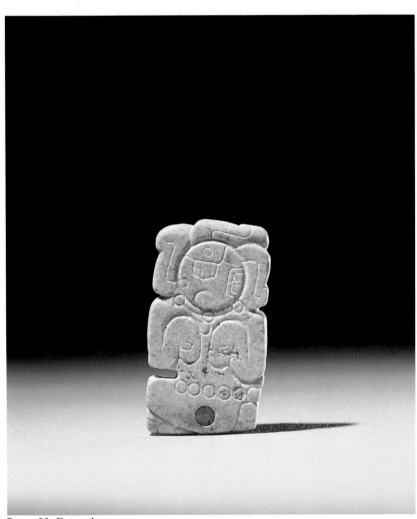

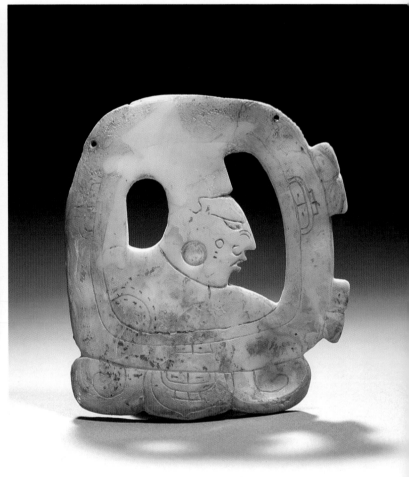

Plate 23. Deity plaque

Plate 24. Costume ornament

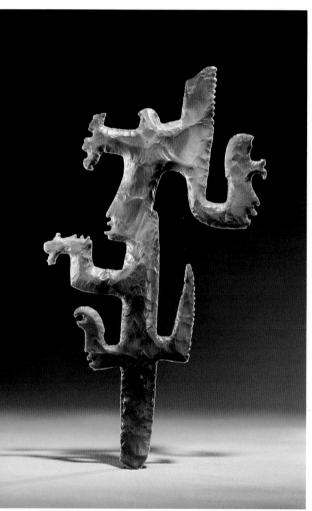

Plate 25. Eccentric flint

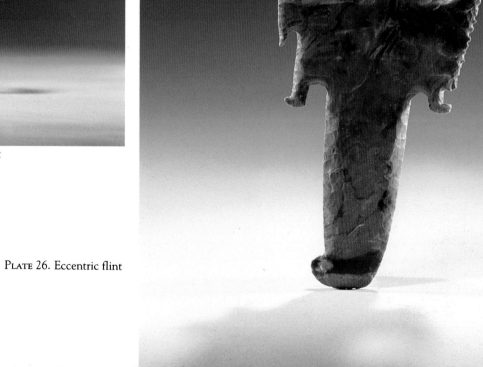

Plate 26. Eccentric flint

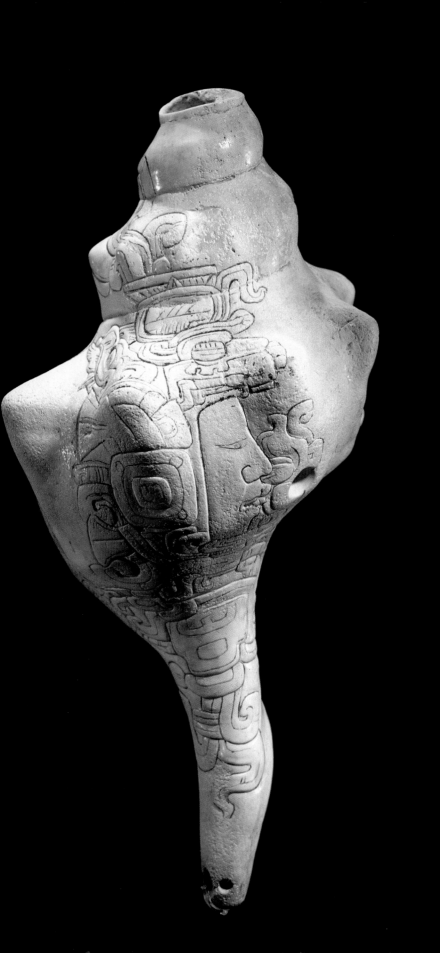

PLATE 27.
Incised conch shell

II

MAYA KINGSHIP AND RITES OF ACCESSION

For the ancient Maya and many other Mesoamerican peoples, the function of public art and architecture was to define the nature of political power and its role as a causal force in the universe. Maya imagery explains the source and necessity of kingly authority, by which the ancient Maya defined social order and expressed their perception of how the universe worked. Narrative images of accession rituals describe the transformation of a human being into a king, the wielder of sacred authority. Since Maya kings used art as propaganda to explain publicly the social order that supported them, they chose imagery that addressed social problems and communicated their standards of proper conduct and legitimate power. The information contained on the objects used by kings—the particular way history was recorded, the specific rituals depicted time and again, the procedures followed to assure legitimate accession—show the values that Maya rulers thought required support through symbolic display. As symbolic display, Maya art and architecture reveals the minds of the Maya and characterizes their view of the world.

The deep separation between the religious and civil that characterizes the contemporary western world view was an alien concept to the Maya for whom the king was not only a religious authority, but also the manifestation of the divine in human space. He not only asserted supernatural sanction to justify his actions and support his rule, but he also personified the supernatural. Through his ritual actions, gods were born and nourished, the fruits of the earth grew, mankind on earth could contact and speak with gods and the ancestral dead. The existence of the king demonstrated the supernatural order of all things within the Universe.

The information most consistently recorded in glyphs about individual kings concerns genealogical descent within the royal line, presumably because their legitimacy depended on birth in a correct lineage group. The Maya were preoccupied with demonstrating publicly that the king was a member of the proper lineage, which was often traced to the gods themselves, or to the Olmec, who were to the Classic Maya an ancient civilization of legendary character. Parents are shown delivering the symbols of authority to their child at accession or observing a king's activities from heaven. Narrative records of accession were often placed in public buildings that were configured as gigantic diagrams of the cosmos, so that accession was perceived as an act of supernatural import that expressed a universal law. The durable nature of records in stone asserts the central importance in the Maya world of genealogical information and public investiture of authority.

In the early history of the Maya region, the type of political symbolism that characterizes the Classic period is rarely found. Although the archaeological record suggests that the Middle Preclassic Maya led a rich and complex ritual life, they did not create public art as a major form of cultural expression. Sophisticated visual symbolism on pottery and architecture of Middle Preclassic period is conspicuously lacking, but a Middle Preclassic grave of about 900 B.C., recently found at Copan under a residential compound of the Classic period,[1] contained exceptional pieces. The contents suggest that the deceased was a man of unusual wealth. There were one large and seven smaller jade celts and enough jade beads to reconstruct four necklaces, including strands of jade jaguar claws alternated with spherical beads (Pl. 17) Most importantly, the grave also included four pots, two of which are marked with orthodox Olmec symbols (Pl. 28, 29, 30). The occurrence of similar pots with Olmec designs in many other less richly furnished graves at Copan from the same period suggests that they were produced and used locally. Thus, this use of Olmec symbolism must be viewed as a general phenomenon in the Valley of Copan during the Middle Preclassic period and not the isolated occurrence of foreign prestige items imported for a special burial.

The evidence of such wealth and the use of Olmec symbols in these burials suggests that Copan was one site in the network that spread Olmec symbolism through many parts of Mesoamerica. We do not know how the Copanecs came to know Olmec symbolism, but archaeologists have speculated that the Olmec came into the Maya highlands and western Honduras to procure jade, probably from the nearby Motagua valley. The people of the Copan Valley may have had direct contact with Olmec groups through trade, or they may simply have become aware of the Olmec symbols from those used by other groups in the Guatemala and Chiapas Highlands who were themselves influenced by the Olmec. The discovery of Olmec-style pottery in those graves that show the earliest evidence of stratified society in the Copan Valley indicates that the Copanec Maya quickly adopted Olmec imagery as the most effective expression of their newly emerging social structure. Mesoamerican trade networks exchanged ideas and symbols as well as material goods. More importantly, these recent finds show that Maya political symbolism did not evolve in a vacuum. It arose within a complex network of cultural systems spread across all of Mesoamerica. As early as 1100 B.C., the Olmec of the Gulf Coast had built large centers with massive programs of art and architecture designed to support their political system. This was the symbol system that spread throughout Mesoamerica and by 900 B.C. was utilized by many different ethnic and language groups, including the people of the Copan Valley. The Maya took systems of cultural symbols that the Olmec had already tried, and adapted them to their situation. They neither invented the idea of state art, nor did they have to experiment with different approaches to political art. At least in the Highlands, the Maya participated in the first international, cross-cultural symbol system in Mesoamerica.

Archaeological evidence suggests a different pattern of development during the Middle Preclassic in the central Lowland areas of the Peten and Belize. At this time, the Lowland Maya groups seem to have gained access to long distance trade while simultaneously developing intensive agricultural techniques. As a result, a de facto elite was created during the Middle Preclassic that had not figured previously in Maya world view. The social structure of the Lowland groups prior to the Late Preclassic transformation is not known with certainty, but settlement patterns and other archaeological evidence suggests that Lowlanders lived in fairly egalitarian communities. Most of their pottery is plain or simply decorated; burials and grave goods indicate that most people had about equal access to prestige goods, such as jade, obsidian and pottery; public propaganda through art and architecture was not utilized. The absence of public art was not accidental, nor is it possible that the Lowland Maya, who were surrounded by public art, had not yet thought of using it as a social tool.

The Lowland Maya dramatically and suddenly (in the sense of archaeological time) reversed their attitudes toward public art in the second half of the Late Preclassic period. Sometime between 200 and 50 B.C., the Lowland Maya exploded with a massive building program that altered forever their landscape. Remains of this construction have been found at Tikal, Uaxactun and El Mirador in Guatemala, and at Cerros and Lamanai in northern Belize. In each of these locations, village populations that had been stable for hundreds of years moved to establish new residential areas nearby. Over the remains of their villages, huge structures, composed of millions of cubic meters of building materials, were erected in single phase constructions. Two of the buildings erected during this explosive period, the Tigre and Danta pyramids at El Mirador, are among the largest monuments ever built in Precolumbian America, measuring in height 178 feet and 136 feet respectively.

Not only was the overwhelming size of these constructions new, but imagery appears in Lowland Maya architecture during the Late Preclassic period. Buildings became huge stage fronts, marked by symbolic displays that elucidate the order of the universe and explain the social experience that had become the norm for the Lowland Maya. Such public works were not undertaken to entertain the populace, but rather serve vital social functions in tying disparate groups together into a coherent whole. These huge architectural projects and the strategies of political control they embody must have been created to defend an elite class in a ranked, complex social structure.

Why did such a transformation occur? Why was it so sudden, if not in its cause, unquestionably in its effect? The Maya must have been responding to a profound social crisis, the nature of which we can only infer. We can assume that their strategy was to transform the ideology underlying the social structure, so that the existence of a ranked elite would be seen as the natural order of the Maya world. Second, the scale of the material efforts engaged to explain that ideology, and the fact that this system endured for over a thousand years, suggest that the ideological transformation was immensely

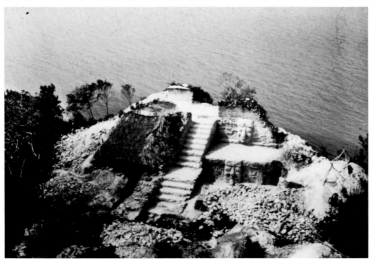
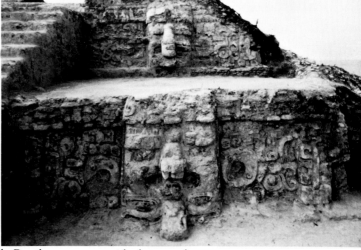

a. A distant view of Structure 5C-2nd

b. Detail, east terraces with plaster masks

FIGURE II.1
Structure 5C-2nd
Cerros, Belize
Late Preclassic period, 50 B.C.
Photographs by David Freidel

Built on the northern tip of a peninsula extending into the bay around it, Structure 5C-2nd of Cerros is a two-terraced pyramid, built around 50 B.C. The south facade is mounted by a stairway that once led to a thatch building on the summit. The terraces on either side of the stairs displayed huge plaster masks built on stone armatures. The upper masks on both sides have long snouts and probably symbolize Venus as Morning and Evening Star. The lower masks are blunt-snouted and are marked by *kin* signs on their cheeks. All four masks wear large earflare assemblages like those found at Pomona and are surrounded by a Double-headed Serpent frame symbolizing the sky.

successful. The social problem that precipitated this transformation, and its successful resolution are recorded in the symbolic system of public art.

Symbolism identifying the ruler with the forces ordering the cosmos informs the sculptural program on Structure 5C-2nd at Cerros, Belize, dated ceramically to about 50 B.C. This was the first major public construction project undertaken at Cerros, a small provincial center throughout its existence, and its program is typical of similar constructions at all other sites where this Late Preclassic transformation has been detected.

Structure 5C-2nd was placed on the north end of a peninsula with a public plaza to the south. As seen from the court, the facade terraces were set with huge masks symbolically representing the rising sun in the east preceded by the Morning Star, and the setting sun in the west followed by the Evening Star (Fig. II.1). Venus and the Sun are the Hero Twins central to Maya mythology. The building is oriented so that the sun actually rises from the sea on the east and sinks in the sea on the west. The Maya farmer, standing below this building for some ritual occasion, saw his ruler standing at the pivot of this symbolic program that represented the movement of heavenly bodies as they rose and set. Behind his ruler, he saw the sun and its twin, Venus, actually rise in the east and sink in the west duplicating the symbols on the monument that defined social and cosmic order. By taking his place at the apex of the symbolic program, the king declared himself to be the causal force that perpetuated this order.

For the Maya, the purpose of state art was to construct symbolic arrays and thus to define models of social reality whose purpose was generating social cohesion. The Maya solution to social crisis was not to manipulate economics or intensify agricultural technology; instead, they adjusted ideology. The crisis appears to have been caused by a disjunction between social experience in the real world and popular expectations about that world. While growing up, children learn through mythology and other processes the definitions of reality and social correctness which adults retain as reified models of reality or world view. When this shared mental system of beliefs and expectations no longer matches the reality of life experience, disjunction occurs and social crisis results.[2] The Maya responded to crisis by adapting an ideology to fit actual social experience. They asserted through myth and symbol that differential social ranking and a ruling elite are the natural order of existence ordained by the gods. The massive construction projects and intensive use of symbolic displays communicated this new ideology to the public. The architectural sculpture was enormous in scale and set above public space; the pyramids were constructed with terraces that served as platforms for dance and ritual. This architecture was intended to effect a mass transformation of society, so large numbers of people had to see the sculpture and believe its definition of social experience. Cerros is neither the sole example of this phenomenon, nor the largest. Variations on this basic program have been found at every Lowland site that has remnants of this transformation. The basic metaphor of the ruler as a pivotal force of nature, which was expressed in Structure 5C-2nd at Cerros, remained at the heart of Maya ideology and its definitions of social reality for the next thousand years.

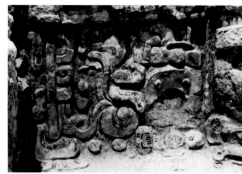

c. Detail, lower west mask and earflare assemblage

Although the institution of kingship was not fully elaborated until the Early Classic period three hundred years later, material from the Late Preclassic period hints at other, less public approaches to sanctifying elite rule that were developing at the time. A few caches of objects of Olmec manufacture, such as figurines and pottery, are known from the Middle Classic period in the Lowlands, but their number and distribution is quite limited. In the Late Preclassic period, however, Maya kings who needed a symbol system to support their rule valued Olmec objects because they established precedent for royal authority.

One such object, from the British Museum, is a stunning rendition of an Olmec face and an individualized portrait (Pl. 31). The style of this jade mask is clearly Olmec and would have been recognized as such by the Maya. It is possible that the identity of the portrait was still remembered in Maya times, but more likely the person portrayed was perceived to be from a legendary time, much as Postclassic peoples regarded the Toltec or the ruins of Teotihuacan. A Maya lord, drawn perhaps to the immediacy and lifelike quality of the portrait, used this mask. Two glyphs, probably his own name,[3] were carved on each flange, but only the left pair now survives. The way these two glyphs are drawn—backward so that they face toward the Olmec portrait— reveals the attitude of the Maya toward this object. By setting his name upon this heirloom, he claimed the Olmec portrait as his own, perhaps as a declaration of his identity with the kings of antiquity and as a means of controlling the sacred power stored in this extraordinary object.

Another Olmec object, a quartzite pectoral from Dumbarton Oaks that depicts a god rather than a human, features a central image carved in relief, with flat flanges projecting to the sides (Pl. 32). Because of its occurrence on major Olmec monuments and with the portraits of Olmec rulers, this god is associated with the Olmec system of royal sanctification.[4] This jadeite pectoral, transported by unknown means to the Maya region[5] by Late Preclassic times[6], was transformed by a Maya ruler into an instrument sanctifying his own power. The Late Preclassic Maya used antiquity to sanction changing political systems, as many other societies around the world have done. The Dumbarton Oaks pectoral demonstrates that the Maya rulers based their ideas of kingship not only on cosmic symbols and myth, but on an image of themselves as the natural inheritors of the Olmec, who were to the Maya as the Toltec were to the Aztec, or as the Greeks and the Romans are to modern Western peoples. The Late Preclassic

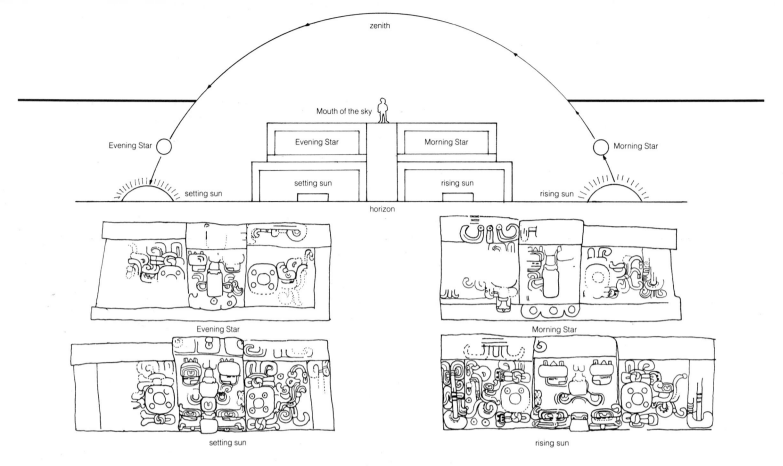

FIGURE II.1
Structure 5C-2nd
Cerros, Belize
Late Preclassic period, 50 B.C.
d. Schematic drawing of pyramid and mask program, showing its relationship to the movement of the sun and Venus.

Maya were not the only group who used antiquity to establish their power.

One critical sentence of the four column inscription on the back of the Dumbarton Oaks pectoral (Plate 32b) has been deciphered: it records that a person "was seated as lord," and it names the person as the lord pictured adjacent to the text. This pectoral is the earliest royal accession portrait known, and a vital source of information about the institution of Maya kingship at its earliest stages.

The symbols of kingship worn by the Maya lord are drawn directly from the cosmic program used on architecture in the Late Preclassic period. His Jester God headband is used on the upper heads at Cerros, and it is worn by contemporary kings from Tikal and Uaxactun.[7] It is shared by all Late Preclassic sites that use the same cosmic program as Cerros, and it remained the sign of kings and kingship until the Collapse about A.D. 900. The earflare worn by all four masks at Cerros is the model of this king's earflare assemblage. It consists of a wide jade flare mounted with cloth knots above and below it. The king wears exactly the same headgear as the gods, replacing only the face of the god with his own portrait, because for the Maya the king was the earthly incarnation of these gods. He literally takes their place as the focus of the symbolic array and becomes the incarnation of divinity.

Although the earflare assemblage in Highland costume also designated the status of kings and gods, the Highland religion focused on different gods. The most important of these gods is the Celestial Bird, which first appears in Lowland art during the Early Classic period. On Kaminaljuyu Stela 11 (Fig. II.2), this bird floats above the head of the Highland king who wears it as a mask. The Highland ruler also wears atop his head the personified tree almost identical to the one worn by the Lowland ruler on the Olmec pectoral from Dumbarton Oaks. This image is an early form of the World

Tree at the center of the Maya cosmos. Both rulers, then, declare themselves to be this tree, the *axis mundi* of the Maya world.

Before coherent data about the Lowland cultural development was available, dates associated with the Highland sites were consistently earlier than Lowland dates, and this sharing of traits was taken as evidence that Maya civilization was developed first in the Highlands and lent to the Lowlands. With new evidence from Cerros, Copan, El Mirador and Lamanai, joined to that from Tikal and Uaxactun, it is now certain that the Lowlanders developed indigenous forms simultaneously with the Highlanders. The symbol systems of the two groups share many components, but their methods of using art as propaganda were fundamentally different. The Lowlanders relied on massive public architecture to bear the ideology of social order. The rituals conducted on these facades must have been impressive, but they were unrecorded and ephemeral. Moreover, their rulers were self-effacing in the public record; names and actions were recorded on private ritual objects, but not on public monuments. Finally, the stela format was rarely used in the Lowlands during the Late Preclassic period. The Highlanders, on the other hand, did not use much architectural sculpture. It was not used at Kaminaljuyu until the Early Classic period, and then it clearly emulated Lowland forms. However, the Highlanders carved stone stelae to record historical events, fixed in time by the Long Count calendar and as a public record of kingship. Rulers were recorded in narrative portrayals of ritual action, and their historical identity was treated as important public information.

The Maya Lowlands and Highlands were interlocked in a dynamic, mutually stimulating relationship. Possibly the interchange of ideology, as well as material goods, between these regions led to the florescence of both. The Highland groups did not survive as a monument-making society beyond 400 A.D., while the Lowlanders continued to produce accomplished public and private art for another 500 years. When the Lowlanders achieved their full symbolic elaboration of kingship in the Early Classic period, it combined both Lowland and Highland systems. Once ephemeral rituals were recorded on stelae showing rulers enacting public rites, identified by name, time, event and ancestry in written inscriptions. The Celestial Bird and the stela format originated in the Highlands, but they are incorporated in a symbol and ritual system directly reflecting Lowland traditions. More importantly, those stelae were placed in front of the same kind of architectural facades produced long before at Cerros, where programs of sculpture symbolically replicated the cosmic source of human power.

By the Early Classic period, the transformation of humans into kings had been formalized into a precise ritual consisting of several stages that seems to have been used at most sites. Different sites and their rulers chose to emphasize different points in this ritual sequence. One of the most important actions depicted donning the attire and symbolic array of kingship. The Leiden Plaque[8] not only shows a ruler after he had donned this costume in his accession ritual, but it was itself part of a royal belt, one of the most important elements of this costume. The inscription on the rear of the Leiden Plaque (Pl. 33a) records that on September 17, A.D. 320 a ruler named Balam-Ahau-Chaan was seated as king[9]. On the front, he stands fully dressed as king (Pls. 33, 33b) and he holds the Double-headed Serpent Bar, a symbol derived from the serpent frames used to represent the sky on the Cerros facade executed 400 years earlier. At Cerros, the king stood at the pivot of the sky; here the king holds the sky in his arms and the gods who sanctify his rule emerge from the mouth of the snake that represents heaven. To his

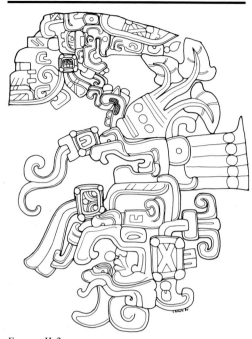

Figure II.2
Stela 11, detail of ruler's head and diving bird
Kaminaljuyu, Guatemala
Late Preclassic period, 100 B.C.–A.D. 100

right, the serpent belches God K, the deity of bloodletting, sacrifice and kingship; to his left, the Sun God emerges.

On his head, he wears the flanged headdress worn by the gods at Cerros, but here the king's face replaces the god masks implying that he manifests those same cosmic forces. Throughout Classic Maya history, this flanged headdress was one of the most important and sacred marks of kings. This headdress is more complex than the forms used on the Cerros masks and on the Dumbarton Oaks pectoral, but its main components come from the Late Preclassic period virtually unchanged. Maya rulers not only wore this headdress, they displayed it before them to prove in a ritual context that they had possession of it. On Tikal Stela 31, for example, Stormy Sky holds it aloft in the instant before it is placed on his head (Fig. II.3).

On the Leiden Plaque, the earflare assemblages, mounted on side flanges hanging from the headdress, frame the king's face, which is held in the mouth of the Jaguar Sun, echoing the emergence of God K from the Serpent Bar below. The jaguar wears the flower headband of the Celestial Bird and God D, reasserting that the authority of this king is cosmic. Atop the symbolic stack sits the anthropomorphic version of the Jester God, declaring that Balam-Ahau-Chaan is king.

Balam-Ahau-Chaan wears a royal belt with head-celt assemblages like those from which the Leiden Plaque came. This royal belt is known from earlier imagery, but on the Leiden Plaque it has a new component—a chain dropping from both sides of the belt to a zoomorph hung behind his legs. In this example, the zoomorph is simply a personification head but, in later examples, it is the Jaguar God of the Underworld and, most frequently, Chac-Xib-Chac. The intended meaning of this chain device is not entirely understood, but by the Late Classic the image of the god on the chain became an important title that in some of its forms contained a direct reference to the genitals of the king. The early date of the Leiden Plaque confirms that the concept of the king as a well-endowed giver of blood was an important and ancient characterization of Maya rulers.

The image on the Leiden Plaque refers to a second event that is vital to the process of accession. A captive, who is to be sacrificed as a blood offering sanctifying the transformation of the new king, lies bound and prostrate at his feet. The captive, marked as a noble by an *ahau* glyph on his head, was taken in battle specifically to serve in this ritual. Unhappy with his fate, he lifts his bound wrists and kicks his feet, twisting his body to look back across his shoulder, perhaps hoping for a reprieve. Other representations of accession ceremonies confirm that ritual sacrifice was a regular and necessary part of the process sanctifying the new ruler. At Piedras Negras, victims are shown stretched across an altar, their hearts excised. The heir designation rites recorded in the Bonampak murals were followed by sacrificial rituals that lasted for over a year. The battle to take the victims, their torture, and eventually their sacrifice are all depicted graphically. In these murals, the father of the heir mutilates his own tongue in the last of these sacrificial rites. Yaxchilan Lintel 25 shows that the accession rite involved a vision resulting from auto-sacrifice (Pl. 63). To the Maya, human beings were created to nourish and sustain the gods through sacrifice. The ruler was both human and god and, thus, the vehicle through which the sacred and the profane interacted. The transformation of an heir into the king required sanctification of the most sacred kind — human blood. The moment depicted on the Leiden Plaque is both completive — the king has donned the sacred costume of kingship — and inceptive — sanctification through blood sacrifice is about to begin.

In the traditions of artistic use, the components of kingly imagery described above became emblems, or short hand symbols, that implied the entire symbolic complex of a king's accession. These symbols were used in scenes of other events and rituals to identify the actor as a king, or to mark objects as the possessions of kings by recalling the accession rituals and their symbolism. A jade plaque in the collection of the British Museum (Pl. 34)[10] demonstrates this kind of emblematic usage. The plaque depicts a lord seated on a stone throne with a court dwarf before him. With this information alone, the person depicted could be any noble, but the rank of king is specified by the Double-headed Serpent Bar behind the figure. The bar alludes to accession rituals in which the right to hold the bar and the powers of the king are transferred. The position of the Serpent Bar, floating behind and above the king inverted from its normal orientation, emphasizes its emblematic function. This position connotes the original function of the serpent in the Late Preclassic period as the sky frame around the Venus and sun masks. Here, the history and significance of this royal symbol reinforce the identity of the seated figure as king.

Kingly imagery is the subject of a large waterworn jade pebble that was found in a cache under Stela 7 at Copan.[11] This jade pebble (Pl. 35), carved during the Early Classic with the portrait of a ruler, appears to have been a focus of sacred power that made it valuable as a cache offering. The ruler, who sits cross-legged, holds his arms to his chest—the position usually reserved for the Double-headed Serpent Bar—but he holds unidentified objects unique to this image. The position of the arms suggests that the objects are functionally equivalent to the Serpent Bar, and signifies this man is a king. This hands-to-chest gesture is so profoundly associated with accession and the symbolic definition of kingship that the secondary symbol, the Serpent Bar, can be replaced without losing the meaning of the gesture.

Throughout the Late Classic period, narrative accounts of accession continued to be a major theme in Maya art. At Piedras Negras, each Late Classic ruler recorded the important events of his reign on a monument series that begins with a depiction of the king mounting a scaffold to assume the throne.[12] The ritual depicted is the culmination of the sacrificial rites shown at their beginning on the Leiden Plaque and at an intermediate stage on a pot from the Chicago Institute of Art (Pl. 92). There, the new king is stepping from a palanquin in which he has been carried to the place of sacrifice. A victim, like the one seen behind the legs of the king on the Leiden Plaque, is tied to a scaffold. On Piedras Negras Stela 11 (Fig. II.4), the victim, who has already been killed by heart excision, lies dead stretched across an altar on the ground below the scaffolding.[13] The upper niche has been identified as a cosmic realm by the Celestial Monster that arcs around the niche. The king, bloody-footed from the sacrifice of the victim, has climbed to the niche leaving his tracks on a narrow cloth that covers the ladder. He sits comfortably upon a pillow inside the niche that had recently held the struggling victim.

At Palenque, the kings were depicted at the moment before they received the sacred costume and objects of kingship from their parents. This kind of documentation is also shown on at Tikal where on Stelae 29 and 31 the father floats in the air above the king. At Yaxchilan, parents often sit in a heavenly register above the king. Around A.D. 550, the artists of Tikal Stelae 24 and 25 used a new composition placing the king on the front plane of the monument and his mother and father on the sides. At about the same time, the rulers of Caracol depicted themselves seated with their parents in small scenes inserted into larger figurative compositions. This last composition, showing the

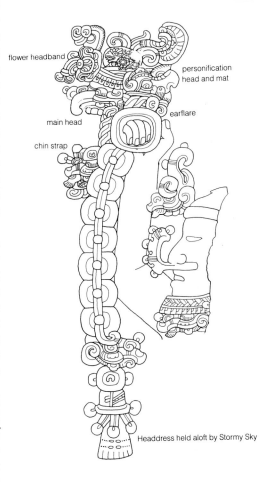

FIGURE II.3
Stela 31, detail of headdress
Tikal, Guatemala
Early Classic period, A.D. 445

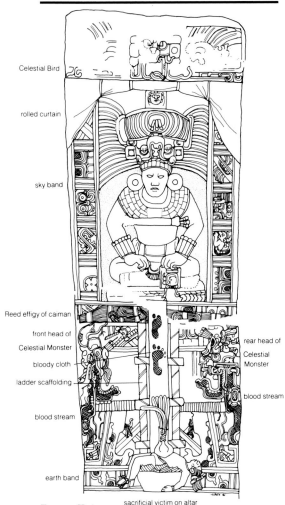

Celestial Bird

rolled curtain

sky band

Reed effigy of caiman

front head of
Celestial Monster

bloody cloth

ladder scaffolding

blood stream

blood stream

rear head of
Celestial
Monster

earth band

sacrificial victim on altar

Figure II.4
Stela 11
Piedras Negras, Guatemala
Late Classic period, A.D. 731

Stela 11, dedicated at the end of the fifteenth katun on August 22, A.D. 731, shows the accession of Ruler 4 of Piedras Negras on 9.14.18.3.3 7 Ben 16 Kankin, or November 13, A.D. 729. The king is shown seated on the top of a bamboo scaffold framed by a skyband. A Celestial Bird sitting atop a Celestial Monster, whose body is the same enframing skyband, surmounts the king. Huge blood scrolls falling from the front and rear heads of the Celestial Monster define the outside edges of the lower scaffolding. A dead sacrificial victim sprawls across an altar in the lower register of the stela. The blood shed by this unfortunate victim sanctifies the rituals of accession.

king with his parents seated beside him, was exploited at Palenque beginning around A.D. 650.

The Oval Palace Tablet, Pacal's accession monument at Palenque (Fig. II.5), shows him dressed in a sparsely decorated kilt. He sits on a double-headed jaguar bench waiting to take a Drum-major headdress from his mother. This transfer of objects is the critical action. The accession of Chan-Bahlum, Pacal's oldest son, records the same action in a far more elaborate narrative which is divided into three sections, depicted on three tablets mounted on a miniature house inside each of the temples in the Group of the Cross. The main tablet was mounted on the inner wall of the miniature house, with two smaller tablets mounted on either side of its entry door. The act of accession begins on the inner tablet and concludes on the outer ones, and the transformation of the heir to king is symbolized by this movement from interior to exterior (Fig. II.6). Inside, Chan-Bahlum, who is dressed only in underclothing with minimal markings of rank, stands opposite his father, who is acting after his death 132 days earlier. The transformation of Chan-Bahlum into the king is shown on the outside of the sanctuary where the living son replaces his dead father. More important to this record of transformation, Chan-Bahlum holds his father's scepter and he is dressed in the sacred costume of kings—the same that Balam-Ahau-Chaan wore 363 years earlier on the Leiden Plaque.

The accession monument of Kan-Xul, the second of Pacal's sons to become king, repeats the composition of the Oval Palace Tablet, but it depicts both parents (Fig. II.7). More importantly, Kan-Xul is seated on a throne immediately in front of an oval whose shape must refer to the Oval Palace Tablet. A throne with an inscription recording Kan-Xul's accession date once rested in front of the Oval Palace Tablet[14] to emphasize that he had acceded at exactly the same place as his father before him. His mother and father, Pacal and Lady Ahpo-Hel, are shown in the act of giving him the symbols of his new status—the Drum-major headdress that was Palenque's crown and a flayed-face shield and personified eccentric flint, the symbols of his rank as war leader and giver of sacrifices.

At Palenque, the transfer of royal authority was seen as a supernatural act, for the parents[15] are dead at the time of the accession. Pacal, Chan-Bahlum and Kan-Xul felt it essential to record their genealogies, to show the transformation in progress, but above all, to document forever that their legitimate right to office came from their parents. Kings at Bonampak also chose to depict the same moment of becoming king seen at Palenque, but the participation of noble lords in accession is emphasized more than the role of parents. Parentage is recorded in inscriptions, but pictorial records focus on scenes with nobles legitimizing kingly status. For example, a noble presents a Jester God headband already knotted and ready to be tightened to the acceding king on Sculptural Panel 1 (Fig. II.8). Other nobles appear as witnesses to the heir designation rites in the Bonampak murals, and as aides to the Yaxchilan rulers undergoing the scattering rite. In Room 1 at of the mural cycle, these nobles are called *ahau* ("lord"), a title reserved for the highest level of the nobility.

Temple 11 at Copan emphasizes the central role of accession in a ruler's life, in the life of the community and the workings of the universe. Completed in A.D. 775, twelve years after the accession of Yax-Pac, the temple dominates the plazas north of the acropolis where the stelae of 18-Rabbit and Smoke Jaguar, earlier kings of Copan, stand (Fig. II.9). Next to Temple 11 are Temple 26 and the Hieroglyphic Stairs erected by Yax-Pac's father as a summary record of the dynastic history of Copan up to its construction. A huge stairway mounts the acropolis to the front door of Temple 11. A reviewing stand projects outward from the front door, providing a place where rituals, such as bloodletting, could be viewed by people in the plaza below. Reliefs surrounding the front door of the temple are no longer extant, but their imagery probably replicated the mouth of a huge monster's head, so that the king was seen emerging from sacred space. On the north corners stood Pauahtuns (God N) figures, carved in remarkably volumetric and naturalistic form, which are so large that the heads alone measure about three feet. The roof of the temple is now missing, but the Pauahtuns placed at the corners of the building suggest that the roof was sculpted as a symbolic representation of the sky, probably as the Cosmic Monster. Thus, the very heavens, held aloft by the Pauahtuns, arched above the head of the king. The south facade and the court fronting it were symbolically defined as the Underworld and as a place of sacrifice. Temple 11, therefore, replicated the Universe itself: the roof was the sky supported by Pauahtuns; the temple proper was the middle world of kings; the lower terraces and the court to the south were the Underworld to which messengers were dispatched through sacrifice.

The inner sanctum within the temple is reached by four corridors penetrating the building, one each from the cardinal directions (Fig. II.10). Each entrance is flanked by texts that recorded the events of Yax-Pac's life as they relate to the larger cosmic intent of the building. These events are major observed movements of Venus and the sun that must have engendered fearful anticipation and intense ritual response. In the north is Yax-Pac's accession in A.D. 763, and in the east, the first appearance of Venus as Evening Star,[16] forty-six days after Yax-Pac's father had acceded to the throne in A.D. 747. The Evening Star was a death god whose first appearance often coincided with war between Maya cities throughout Late Classic history. The south door text records the end of the seventeenth katun in A.D. 771, a day that coincided with a partial eclipse of the sun visible at Copan. The west door records the next appearance of the Evening Star that occurred just sixteen days after the eclipse.

The Maya believed the universe to be a place filled with beings and forces that were dangerous and volatile if not contained by the proper rituals. They did not explain the movements of stars and planets through the heavens with the cool mathematics of orbital mechanics, but as living beings moving against the backdrop of a living cosmos. Celestial bodies were the visible manifestations of the Hero Twins and gods of all sorts. The darkening of the sun in an eclipse was perceived as a form of dying from which the sun might not recover, and the first appearance of the Evening Star was taken as signal of war. The Maya had tables for predicting eclipses and the cycle of Venus, and Yax-Pac made it appear as though he controlled these dangerous events. He recorded celestial movements on the entry doorways of Temple 11 to reinforce the cosmic symbolism of the building. As the ruler, he increased his prestige and power by using those predictions as instruments of statecraft, confirming that the king was vital to the maintenance of cosmic order.

More importantly, the interior of Temple 11 appears to recreate the vision Yax-Pac experienced through bloodletting on the day of his accession. The four corridors of the temple converge on a raised platform in the center of the structure that was the most sacred spot in the building. Located just south of the point where the corridors meet, the platform is enclosed by extraordinary sculptures of skeletal heads doubled to form an open maw of the Underworld. The north side of the platform, which also

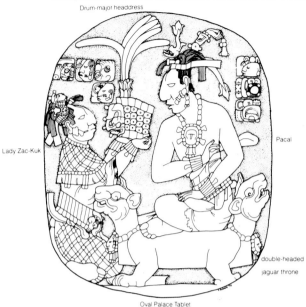

Drum-major headdress

Lady Zac-Kuk

Pacal

double-headed
jaguar throne

Oval Palace Tablet

Figure II.5
Oval Palace Tablet
Palenque, Chiapas, Mexico
Late Classic period, ca. A.D. 652

Pacal, who is about to become king of Palenque,
sits on a double-headed jaguar throne that is turned
toward the viewer so that both heads can be seen.
He wears only a cloth skirt, pectoral, and simple
headband. His mother, Lady Zac-Kuk, sits on the
floor in front of him. She wears a net overskirt and
cape over her *huipil* and is marked as a ruler by her
Jester God headband. She extends a Drum-major
headdress, the crown used by Palenque kings,
toward her son, giving him the first part of the regalia that will transform him into the king.

Figure II.6
Tablet from the Temple of the Cross
Palenque, Chiapas, Mexico
Late Classic period, A.D. 692

Chan-Bahlum and his dead father face each other
across the World Tree whose central position in this
composition reiterates that it is the central axis of
the world. At the base of the tree is the Quadripartite Sun Monster frozen partly above and partly
below the ground as it enters the Underworld in its
daily journey through the cosmos. Chan-Bahlum,
dressed in a simple kilt and barefoot, is as yet
unmarked as king. Streams of blood flow from the
Quadripartite Sun Monster that Pacal, the smaller
figure, holds as a scepter. Pacal's clothing is unique
to these tablets, but since he has been dead for 132
days by the time this accession occurred, this costume may signal that he is dead.

On the outer tablets, Chan-Bahlum,
having become the new king through the rituals of
accession, stands in the place of his father. To signal his new status, he wears the ancient and sacred
costume of kings with its flanged headdress, royal
belt and chain, and ornate backrack. The main
zoomorph in his headdress, a serpent with a stingray
spine attached to its muzzle, may manifest the name
U-Kix-Chan, the legendary first human in
Palenque's dynasty. The royal belt has a jaguar head
and a mat sign mounted above the three celts in a
reference to his status as the *balam pop*, "holder of
the Jaguar Throne," and the rear chain supports an
effigy of Chac-Xib-Chac hung from a chain. In his
right hand, he holds the Quadripartite Monster
that he received from his father; he lifts his left
hand toward God L who stands on the opposite
panel as a Lord of the Underworld, the next destination of the Sun Monster on the inner tablet.
This interaction between God L and Chan-Bahlum
reiterates the active role required of kings in the
maintenance of cosmic order.

Figure II.7
Detail, Palace Tablet
Palenque, Chiapas, Mexico
Late Classic period, ca. A.D. 721

In his accession scene on the Palace Tablet, Kan-
Xul deliberately echoes the composition his father
Pacal had used earlier on the Oval Palace Tablet by
showing his parents seated beside him in the act of
giving him the emblems of the office he is assuming. In an even more direct reference to the earlier
tablet, Kan-Xul is shown acceding on a throne directly in front of the Oval Palace Tablet, shown as
the outline behind him.

As in his father's and his older brother's
compositions, Kan-Xul has not yet become king for
he is still dressed in simple clothing. The transferral
of the emblems is caught mid-action; both parents
hold their objects away from their bodies as they are
extended toward Kan-Xul, and in anticipation, he
leans slightly toward his father. Both parents are
dead at the time of the action, Pacal for eighteen
years and Lady Ahpo-Hel for twenty-eight years, a
fact signaled by the water-lilies both wear in their
hair. In recognition of their rank, they sit on
thrones like their son.

The father gives his son the Drum-major
headdress with a large Jester God, the sign of kings,
mounted on the front. The mother holds a flat-bottomed bowl in which sits a personified eccentric
flint and a shield made of a flayed human face.
Cloth, from the opened bundle that held the flint
shield emblem until it was opened for this ritual,
falls over the rim of the plate. The plate itself is one
used in bloodletting and sacrificial rites, while the
eccentric flint and shield are signs used throughout
the Maya inscriptions in association with war. In
gaining possession of these emblems, Kan-Xul
becomes the king; by showing his parents resurrected from the Afterlife to give them to him, he
documents his legitimate claim to the throne as
their child.

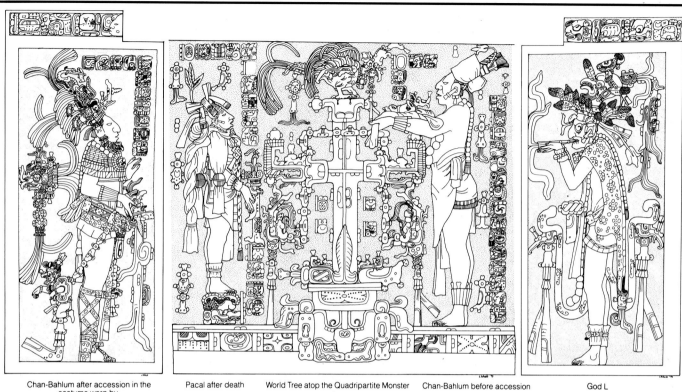

Chan-Bahlum after accession in the costume worn by Balam-Ahau-Chaan on the Leiden Plaque

Pacal after death

World Tree atop the Quadripartite Monster

Chan-Bahlum before accession

God L

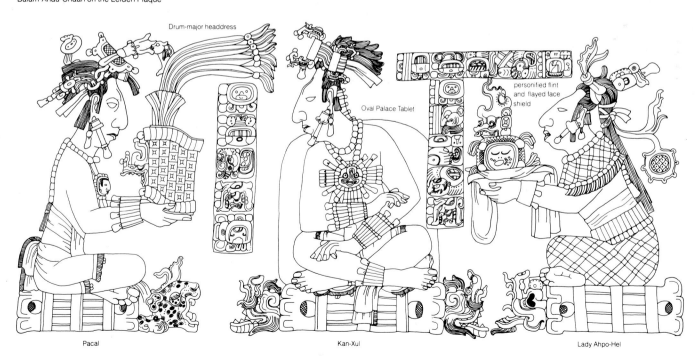

Drum-major headdress

Oval Palace Tablet

personified flint and flayed face shield

Pacal

Kan-Xul

Lady Ahpo-Hel

FIGURE II.8
Sculptural panel 1
Bonampak, Chiapas, Mexico
Late Classic period, A.D. 692

The text reads "On 4 Muluc 2 Zac he was seated on the jaguar throne as *ahau*." The scene shows the action recorded, the newly installed ruler seated on an architectural bench before three nobles of high rank who wear cloth skirts and headdresses. Two have their hands folded across their chests, while the third holds out a Jester God headband, already knotted and ready to be tied on the king's head.

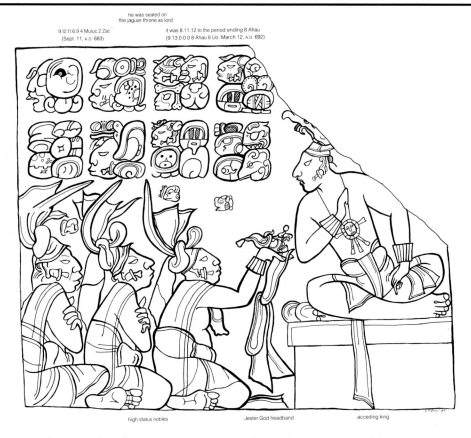

he was seated on
the jaguar throne as lord

9.12.11.6.9 4 Muluc 2 Zac
(Sept. 11, A.D. 683)

it was 8.11.12 to the period ending 8 Ahau
(9.13.0.0.0 8 Ahau 8 Uo; March 12, A.D. 692)

high status nobles   Jester God headband   acceding king

forms the monster's lower jaws, was fronted by a long horizontal bench panel sculpted with twenty seated figures, including Yax-Pac and nineteen ancestors (Pl. 36), as replacements for the teeth of the skeletal monster. On the lintel above the door, Yax-Pac sits with a sacrificial bowl in his hand (Pl. 37), flanking a now-lost full-figured inscription (Pl. 36a).

This sculpted bench panel is the critical focus of the building because it expresses the relationship of the king to the Maya cosmos. It is symbolically defined as the point of entry into the Underworld. These figures form the lower jaw of the maw of the Underworld because this is the portal from which they, and other visions, rise. On the Temple 11 bench panel, Yax-Pac is shown on the day of his accession as having resurrected his ancestors into physical existence to participate in the rites that made him king. Temple 11 is a powerful locus of energy; its symbolism focused upon the king as the conduit through which the natural and the supernatural interact.

The process of transformation that created a Maya king can be analyzed as a series of stages within a single accession ritual. Never before have the different representations of accession been considered to be parts of one ritual, perhaps because these scenes appear to record entirely different activities. However, recognizing that a scaffold sacrifice depicted on a pot from the Chicago Institute of Art is the beginning of the same rite shown on stelae at Piedras Negras, in which the king mounts a scaffolding to his throne, suggests that these represent different stages in a long ritual sequence, rather than entirely different and unrelated actions. Thus far, the following stages in accession have been identified, although the order in which they occurred is not known.

a. The designated heir, dressed only in a fringed kilt and minimal jewelry was given the elements of costume that marked him as king. The most important single items were a cloth headband with a Jester God mounted at the front and the flanged headdress. Tikal Stela 31 suggests that the king held this headdress aloft for people to see before he put it on.

b. The king, dressed in the full costume of office and carrying the ritual accouterments of kings, displayed himself to the people attending the rite. The ritual dressing and the display rituals seem to have had different audiences: for example, the king may have dressed with the court in attendance, then walked out to the edge of a pyramid to show himself to a larger audience.

c. The wife or mother of the king brought forth a bundle with bloodletting instruments and both drew blood from their bodies, the woman from her tongue and the male from his penis (see Chapter IV).

d. Either before or after the rites described above, the king went to war to take captives for use in sacrificial rituals.

e. The captive was displayed bound to a special scaffolding, then he was sacrificed by heart excision.

f. The king mounted the scaffold, now defined symbolically as a World Throne, where the ritual cycle was completed.

For the Maya, accession to office was a process critical to the political well-being of the state. Thus, in 50 B.C. at Cerros and in the late eighth century at Copan, it was portrayed in public art as central to the order of the universe as well as to the community of man. The earliest Classic period record of accession, on the Leiden Plaque, shows the ruler wearing regalia that referred to the earliest and most important gods of Maya state religion, the Sun and Venus as Twins. The Late Classic king of Copan, Yax-Pac, literally set himself in their place at the center of the cosmos through which they moved.

NOTES

1. An excavation undertaken by William Fash, Jr., in Plaza A of Group 9N-8, Copan, has yielded the longest occupation sequence in western Honduras. An Early Preclassic house lying at the bottom of the site contains ceramics (Rayo Complex) that are very similar to the Quadros Phase material at La Victoria and to the Tok Phase pottery at Chalchuhuapa. This and the subsequent Middle Preclassic ceramics are clearly of southern Maya origin, although not derived from or closely affliated with the Swasey, Xe or Mamom ceramics, which typify the Maya Lowlands. The Middle Preclassic component in Copan Group 9N-8, Plaza A, comprises two rectangular cobble-faced earthen platforms, aligned north to south on their long axes, with numerous burials placed beneath the floor of each. The north platform is stratigraphically higher and in all likelihood more recent than the south platform, and it contains more burials with jade offerings. Among these was Burial XVIII-27, the richest interment of its time thus far documented in the Maya Lowlands. There were four ceramic vessels (two of which are included here [Pls. 28, 29]), eight polished celts and over three hundred pieces of jade or greenstone, which had been placed with this young adult, of whom only the skull and two long bones were left undisturbed by subsequent interments. The other vessel in Plate 30 derives from Burial XX-7, the burial of the highest-status individual found in the south platform. This adult male was interred with four ceramic vessels but with no jade or greenstone. The other vessels include two red-rimmed tecomates and one necked globular jar (William L. Fash, Jr., "A Middle Formative Cemetary from Copan, Honduras" [paper delivered at the annual meeting of the American Anthropological Institution, Washington, D.C., 1982], and personal communication, 1985).

2. Freidel (in David Freidel and Linda Schele, "Symbol and Power: A History of the Lowland Maya Cosmogram," *The Beginnings of Maya Classic Iconography* [Princeton, New Jersey: Princeton University Press, forthcoming]) describes the response to these disjunctions as "thresholds, [which are] characterized by *structural impasse*, a situation in which the content of reified models of reality must be revised to accommodate actual social conditions. This revision requires manipulation of the structural arrangement of axiomatic propositions about the world such that novel propositions become both rational and necessary." He describes three responses to threshold: "First, there is *bounce* in which the society consciously identifies the major deviations between the actual and the ideal but is unable to change the structure of the model of reality and instead attempts to rectify the actual social condition to bring them back into concert with the ideal." For the Maya, this response would have entailed the elimination of the social situation that caused the crisis, such as by killing or otherwise getting rid of an elite that was not accounted for in the world view. "Second, there is *collapse*, in which the society addresses the cultural model but fails to solve for the impasse and instead generates unsuccessful rationales ushering in the disintegration of society into more stable lower-order fragments. The collapse of civilization is well attested in the archaeological record. [The Maya Collapse is one such example.] Finally, there is *transformation*, in which the society succeeds in changing the model of reality through the manipulation of existing axiomatic propositions about the world to allow the assertion of novel propositions which accommodate actual social conditions precipitating the crisis." We believe the Lowland Maya successfully passed the Late Preclassic threshold by transforming the propositions underlying their definitions of cosmic and social order so that the elite became rational and necessary.

3. The upper glyph seems to be a very early version of T1008 *xib*, a glyph that could also be used to read *ahau*, "lord," suggesting that these glyphs record a name phrase. The diagonal line between the eye and the earflare is characteristic of both the *xib* glyph and of its zoomorphic variant, the God C glyph, from as early as A.D. 200 until after A.D. 450. The drawing style seems to belong to the earlier half of this period.

4. The crossbands on the flanges, the cleft head and the fanged, upturned mouth suggest God I, the supernatural identified by Joralemon as the "protector and legitimator of Olmec kings." (Peter David Joralemon, "The Olmec Dragon: A Study in Pre-Columbian Iconography," in *Origins of Religious Art and Iconography in Preclassic Mesoamerica*, edited by H. B. Nicholson [Los Angeles: UCLA Latin American Center Publications, 1976], p. 46).

5. Michael D. Coe reports that it "can be traced to the collection of an American missionary in Mérida, Yucatan, who is said to have acquired it from a native of a village located 'about two days' journey' from Mérida" ("An Early Stone Pectoral from Southeastern Mexico," *Studies in Pre-Columbian Art and Archaeology* 1, [Washington, D.C.: Dumbarton Oaks, 1966], p. 6).

6. The earflare assemblage and headband worn by this ruler are identical to those of the Cerros masks, dating the Maya engraving to the Late Preclassic period.

7. The fuchsite figurine from Uaxactun Group A wears the bifurcated shapes that flank the Jester God on the Dumbarton Oaks pectoral; in addition, however, the Uaxactun king has the eyebrows and kin signs of the lower masks at Cerros (Fig. II.1). The fuchsite mask found on top of a bundle in Tikal Burial 85 is the portrait of a ruler wearing the same headband.

8. In 1864 J. A. Von Braem, a Dutch engineer, found the Leiden Plaque in a cache while cutting a canal northeast of Puerto Barrios, Guatemala. Morley tried, but failed, to relocate the mound from which the cache came; he believed, however, that a raised area near the eastern end of the canal was the most likely source. See Frances R. Morley and Sylvanus G. Morley, "The Age and Provenance of the Leyden Plate," in *Contributions to American Anthropology and History*, No. 24; *Carnegie Institution of Washington*, Pub. 509 (Washington, D.C.: Carnegie Institution of Washington, 1938), pp. 1-17. On October 3, 1879, Van Braem presented the celt and other material from the cache to the National Museum of Antiquity in Leiden, which in 1903 transferred all its Asian and American material to another institution in the city, the Rijksmuseum voor Volkenkunde, to which it now belongs. The Leiden Plaque was found with the following material: (1) a whole shell (50 x 27 mm) modeled to resemble a human head, (2) a dark greenstone cylinder (11 x 9 mm) drilled from both ends, (3) a light green, triangular bead (10 mm) with a drilled center hole, (4) a plain dark greenstone celt (219 x 67 mm) drilled with one small hole at the narrow end, and (5) a metal (copper?) bell (31 x 11 mm) with a hanging loop at the top and a sounding slit at the bottom. The presence of a metal bell in the cached material surely identifies the deposition as Postclassic. The Leiden Plaque was removed from its original location, presumably in an Early Classic tomb, and deposited as an heirloom in a Postclassic cache or tomb. If the plain celt is part of the original belt assemblage, then the Leiden Plaque was the center celt, flanked by two plain celts. The plain celt is somewhat smaller, however, and it has a concave cross section, unlike the planar cross section of the Leiden Plaque; it may well have been obtained from an entirely different source.

9. See pp. 319-320 for a full discussion of the text on the Leiden Plaque.

10. Adrian Digby in *Maya Jades* (London: The British Museum, 1964), p. 30, reports that this jade was found at Teotihuacan. Apparently, the superb carving and fine color of the jade made it a prestigious item that was valued outside of the Maya region. We do not know the means by which it was transported but since it is Late Classic in style we can assume it was not involved with the early interaction between Lowland Maya and the Teotihuacanos. Trade, tribute, or the giving of prestigious gifts seem likely possibilities. We do not know whether or not the Teotihuacanos would have understood the iconography enough to value the plaque for the message it encoded as well as its inherent value as worked jade.

11. Offerings were regularly cached under or in front of stelae during their dedication rights. At Copan, these caches were placed in special cruciform vaults built under the shaft of stelae before they were erected. This jade pebble was found in a cruciform vault under Stela 7, which was erected in the older center, now under the modern Copan Valley. Dated at 9.9.0.0.0 (A.D. 613), this stela has the first royal portrait to be carved at Copan in the Late Classic period. Morley's description of the cache did not include this jade, although Gann's did. He eventually gave it to the Museum of the American Indian, where it resides today. See Sylvanus G. Morley, *Inscriptions of Copan*, Carnegie Institution of Washington, Pub. 219 (Washington, D.C.: Carnegie Institution of Washington, 1920), p. 105; Thomas Gann, *Ancient Cities and Modern Tribes: Exploration and Adventure in Maya Land* (London: Duckworth, 1926), pp. 182-185.

12. Tatiana Proskouriakoff (1960) used this "ascension" motif and the arrangement of these stelae in discrete series to develop her historical interpretations of the Maya inscriptions ("Historical Implications of a Pattern of Dates at Piedras Negras, Guatemala," *American Antiquity* 25 [1960], pp. 454-475).

13. Karl Taube was the first to recognize that the Chicago pot and the Piedras Negras niched stelae represent the same sacrificial ritual ("A Study of Classic Maya Scaffold Sacrifice," *Studies of Maya Iconography* [Princeton, New Jersey: Princeton University Press, forthcoming]).

14. Linda Schele and Peter Mathews, *The Bodega of Palenque, Chiapas, Mexico* (Washington, D.C.: Dumbarton Oaks, 1979), Cat. #140.

15. Only the Oval Palace Tablet shows a living parent in an accession rite. Lady Zac-Kuk was alive at the time her son acceded, but since he was only twelve years old at the time, she probably served as regent for many years after his accession.

16. Floyd G. Lounsbury, "Astronomical Knowledge and its Uses at Bonampak, Mexico," in *Archaeoastronomy in the New World*, edited by A. F. Aveni (Cambridge: Cambridge University Press, 1982), pp. 143-165.

Plate 28
Cylindrical vessel, Olmec flame design
Burial VIII-27, Copan, Honduras
Middle Preclassic period, 800–600 B.C.
Incised ceramic (red clay)
Diam. 11.5 x H. 6 cm
Instituto Hondureño de Antropología e Historia,
Tegucigalpa, Honduras

Plate 29
Cylindrical vessel, meander design
Burial VIII-27, Copan, Honduras
Middle Preclassic period, 800–600 B.C.
Incised ceramic (white clay)
Diam. 10.3 x H. 8.1 cm
Instituto Hondureño de Antropología e Historia,
Tegucigalpa, Honduras

Plate 30
Cylindrical vessel, fish design
Group 85, Copan, Honduras
Middle Preclassic period, 800–600 B.C.
Incised ceramic
Diam. 14 x H. 8.2 cm
Instituto Hondureño de Antropología e Historia,
Tegucigalpa, Honduras

These three cylindrical vessels were found at Copan, Honduras in the burials of a cemetery under Group 9N-8 dating to 900 B.C. The vessels in Plates 28 and 29 were found in the richest Middle Preclassic grave yet discovered in the Maya region. The third vessel (Plate 30) is from a tomb in the south part of the cemetery where tombs rarely yield jade among the uncovered funerary offerings. Plate 28 has an Olmec flame eyebrow motif on one side and an X-shape with diamond designs on the other. Its companion vase has a meander pattern. The third vessel from the south building has an odd design terminating in a bifurcated shape scored with parallel lines. This motif and a smaller version to its left seem to be fish tails, but the remainder of the design does not correspond to a known naturalistic form.

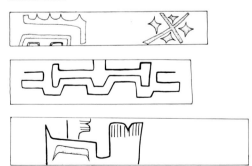

Plate 31
Portrait pectoral
Olmec, Middle Preclassic period, 1000–600 B.C.
Maya inscription, Protoclassic period, A.D. 50–250
Jade
10.5 x 10.9 cm
The Trustees of The British Museum, London

This large gray-green jade was carved into the portrait of an Olmec noble, probably a ruler. The subtle control of the surface modulation and the extraordinary treatment of the highly polished surface is typical of the finest Olmec lapidary art. Perhaps the Maya who reused this jade also valued this quality. Probably designed as a pectoral, the portrait was flanked by now-broken flanges. The iris of the eyes were depressed and the nose pierced, perhaps for an ornament made from another material, such as shell. Round ear ornaments hang from the earlobes, and the sensitively modeled mouth is downturned and toothless in the expression characteristic of Olmec portraiture. The hair is skillfully carved in informal, flowing locks, emphasizing the historical reality of the person shown and contrasting the geometrically precise facial expression that identifies supernaturals. It was subsequently valued both for its extraordinary presence and artistic quality and as a focus of sacred power of a legendary people.

Plate 32
Flanged pectoral
Olmec, Middle Preclassic period, 1000–600 B.C.
Maya inscription, Late Preclassic period, 100 B.C.–
A.D. 100
Quartzite
9 x 26.7 x 2.8 cm
Dumbarton Oaks, Washington, D.C.

The front surface of this quartzite pectoral is carved with the image of an important Olmec deity. The curved flanges are incised with crossed-bands and drilled, perhaps for an inlay that is now missing. The central face is carved in deeper relief in the geometric style used by the Olmec to emphasize the supernatural quality of their divine beings. The cleft-headed god has a human nose and eyes, but his mouth is rendered in the square, downturned shape usually associated with jaguars. This combination of features from different beings of the natural world is another signal of the supernatural. This particular god is often associated with historical portraits of Olmec rulers, apparently to declare divine sanction for the civil authority of the ruler.

The rear surface (Pl. 32a, c) was incised with the portrait of a Late Preclassic Maya ruler and the four column text that recorded his accession.

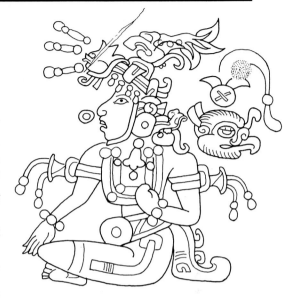

Dumbarton Oaks jade, rear

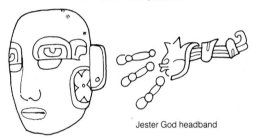

Uaxactun, fuchsite figurine

Jester God headband

Dumbarton Oaks jade earflare

Cerros earflare assemblage

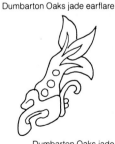

Dumbarton Oaks jade

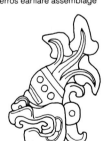

Kaminaljuyu Stela 11

Personified trees

Plate 32a

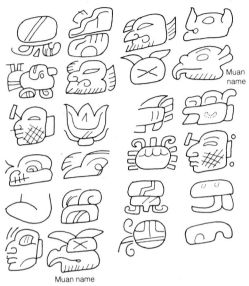

Muan name

Dumbarton Oaks jade, the rear text

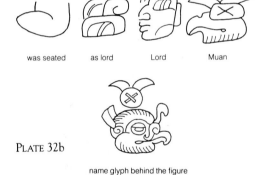

was seated | as lord | Lord | Muan

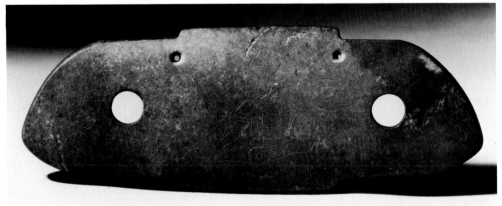

PLATE 32b

name glyph behind the figure

PLATE 32c

He sits in cross-legged position with his shoulder turned toward the viewer. He wears an ornate belt over a knee length cloth skirt. His loincloth is draped to his rear along the ground. Jade ornaments are tied around his upper arms and wrists, and he wears a heavy jade necklace of cylinders and beads. His headdress, critical to the iconography, resembles those worn by the god masks in Late Preclassic architectural sculpture. In wearing the headdress, his face replaces the supernatural face of the masks, making him the incarnation of the god. The Jester God is attached to the headband and a personified tree, the *axis mundi*, sits atop his head. The same headband appears in a fuchsite portrait of a contemporary king from Uaxactun and the personified tree is worn by another king from Kaminaljuyu. Much of the symbolism marking the rank of king and sanctifying kingly authority was shared by both Highland and Lowland Maya.

THE INSCRIPTION

The owl head with the cross-banded disk seen behind the shoulder of the king is his name. The same two signs are recorded twice in the text, at B6 and C2-D2. Although many of the other glyphs appear to be prototypes of deciphered signs in the Classic script, we have not been able to decipher this early text, with the exception of one very important sentence. A5 is clearly the lower half of a body seated in cross-legged position, exactly the posture of the king. Since his name is written in the two glyphs below, he is the one seated, and "to be seated" is one of the Maya expressions for accession. The next glyph appears to be a very early variant of the *ahau* title, recording that "he was seated as king." This text is the earliest historical event and the first royal accession to have been deciphered in Maya inscriptions.

PLATE 33
Jade celt, the Leiden Plaque
Early Classic period, A.D. 320
Incised jade
21.7 x 1 x 8.6 cm
Rijksmuseum voor Volkenkunde, Leiden, Holland

Carved from a light green, translucent jade, the Leiden Plaque was a celt from a royal belt-head assemblage. The front surface is polished to a smooth finish and incised with the portrait of a Maya king in the act of acceding to office. He stands dressed in the regalia of kings, holding a Double-headed Serpent Bar as the sign of his rank. Behind him, a victim who will be sacrificed in rites that sanctify the accession, struggles on his belly looking back across his shoulder.

The carving is an excellent example of Early Classic style and the highest craftsmanship of Maya art. The image is tightly packed with an array of symbols that define kingly rank. He is posed stiffly with the head in profile, the shoulder front view, and the legs in profile but separated, so that the detail of both cuffs are clearly visible. In Early Classic art, the clear transfer of symbolic information took precedent over the natural presentation of the human figure. An inscription on the rear surface (Pl. 33a, c) records the date, action and actor of the scene.

The clothing worn by Balam-Ahau-Chaan (Pl. 33b) became the most sacred costume of kings; to put it on for the first time was to become king. Because of its central importance to the symbolism of Maya kingship, we present a detailed examination of the Leiden figure isolating the parts to view each component unimpeded.

The king stands in side view with his shoulders turned toward the viewer so that the objects he wears and holds can be easily seen. He wears a backrack which emerges from behind his shoulder. A thick collar with a human head attached to the front is tied around his neck. He wears a cloth skirt with a beaded and fringed edge surmounted by a belt with the Jaguar God of the Underworld, crossed-bands and disks, and a belt and celt assemblage on the right front side. An elaborate loin ornament dangles to his knees. He wears cuffs on his wrists and anklets constructed of leather bands tied through jade disks into bows. He wears sandals of the Early Classic style.

The royal belt overlays the cloth skirt and the Jaguar God of the Underworld at his front waist. The side head appears to be mounted on the rear of the belt, but its position was shifted so that it would appear fully in profile view, rather than foreshortened. A chain drops from the belt to a personification head with a jade ornament hanging from its mouth.

The headdress, like the belt, is a critical part of the costume. It was constructed on a cap lined with jade cylinders and beads. A side flange was built on either side of the head so that the weight of the heavy jade flares would be supported by the headdress, rather than the earlobes. The main head is a naturalistic jaguar with nose ornaments extending in front of his muzzle. He wears a jade headband culminating in a flower design, perhaps a morning glory.

The king holds his arms against his chest in a position that naturally occurs when an object is held in the crook of the arms and against the chest. This position became the standardized way to hold the Double-headed Serpent Bar, the most important scepter of Maya kings. Sometimes shown with a rigid bar or a naturalistic serpent body between the two heads, the scepter terminates with gaping serpent mouths from which emerge the gods who sanctify the king's position. Balam-Ahau-Chaan shows God K on his right and the Sun God on his left.

Positioned on his stomach behind the ruler's feet, a bound captive struggles, anticipating his sacrifice in the accession ritual. A decorated *ahau* on his head marks the noble captive as a lord. He wears a large earflare and his head, turned to look back, is tied vertically by a cloth.

The Inscription
The Leiden Plaque date, 8.14.3.1.12 1 Eb O Yaxkin, or September 17 A.D. 320, occupies the first ten glyph blocks of the text; the action and actor occupy the last five. The verb is "he was seated," identifying the scene on the other side as accession. The second glyph is either the office into which this person was seated or it is part of his name. The next pair of glyphs name the new king with an *ahau* glyph half-covered by jaguar pelt and an unknown head variant followed by the "sky" *chaan* sign. Using the readable parts of the name, we can tentatively call him Balam-Ahau-Chaan.

The last glyph also occurs on Tikal Stela 4, dated 59 years later, in the position usually occupied by Emblem Glyphs. Since the provenance of Stela 4 is clear, the presence of the same glyph on the Leiden Plaque has been taken as evidence that it was manufactured at Tikal. However, the inscriptions of Tikal record that a ruler named Jaguar Paw was ruling that city both three years earlier and 56 years later than the Leiden date. If these two royal names refer to the same person, then Tikal was ruled by someone else when this accession took place, and the Leiden Plaque comes from another city.

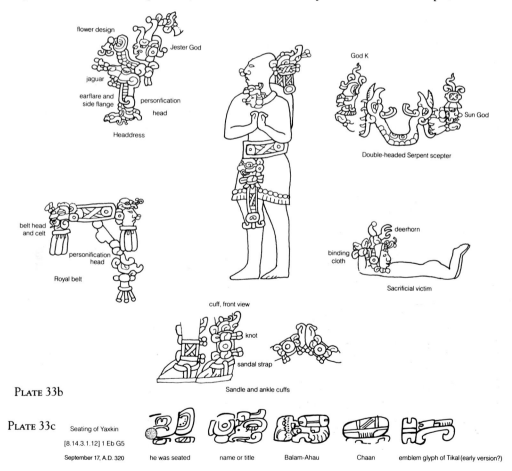

flower design
Jester God
jaguar
earflare and side flange
personification head
Headdress

God K
Sun God
Double-headed Serpent scepter

belt head and celt
personification head
Royal belt

deerhorn
binding cloth
Sacrificial victim

cuff, front view
knot
sandal strap
Sandle and ankle cuffs

Plate 33b

Plate 33c   Seating of Yaxkin
[8.14.3.1.12] 1 Eb G5

September 17, A.D. 320   he was seated   name or title   Balam-Ahau   Chaan   emblem glyph of Tikal (early version?)

Plate 33b

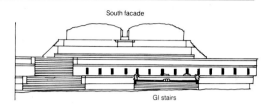
South facade

GI stairs

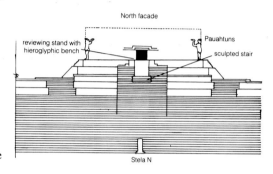
North facade

reviewing stand with hieroglyphic bench

Pauahtuns

sculpted stair

Stela N

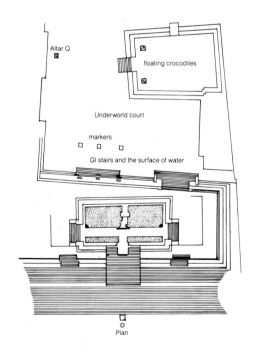
Altar Q

floating crocodiles

Underworld court

markers

GI stairs and the surface of water

Plan

PLATE 34
Jade plaque
Teotihuacan, Mexico
Late Classic period, A.D. 600–800
Carved jade
14 x 14 cm
The Trustees of The British Museum, London

This mottled green jade plaque was apparently transported to Teotihuacan from the Maya area as a prestige item. It appears to have been broken and repolished at least once. The composition seems to present a view of palace activities: a regally dressed king sits cross-legged on a stone throne. He wears a zoomorphic headdress, a half-mask, jade ear ornaments, a bar pectoral and the royal belt. He holds his right arm across his lap and wears a war shield with the Jaguar God of the Underworld on his left wrist. A court dwarf standing below the king is carved from the brown areas of the stone; the purest colors were reserved for the portrait of the king.

The Double-headed Serpent Bar floating behind him becomes an architectural frame in this composition. Its presence marks the main figure as a king; its inverted position floating behind the king is a reference to its original function as the skyframe in the Late Preclassic program at Cerros and elsewhere.

PLATE 35
Carved pebble
Stela 7 cache, Copan, Honduras
Early Classic period, A.D. 400–600
Jade
20 x 12 x 4 cm
Courtesy of the Museum of the American Indian, Heye Foundation, New York

The carving style of this jade does not rank with the best examples of Early Classic art, but the image is a powerful representation of a Maya king. Leaving the waterworn stone untouched on the rear, the artist teased the front view figure from the natural curves of the jade pebble. The king's earflares are suspended from his ears, rather than from headdress flanges, and above his square-cut bangs, he wears a headband marked by the glyph *cab* "earth." Double scrolls, perhaps referring to smoke, blood, or foliation, emerge from the *cab* sign, and a knot with side ribbons sits atop it. His ankles, wrists and waist are decorated by simple bead strands. A disk and cylinder pendants hang from the waist strand, and he wears a shell pectoral on a bead necklace. He holds his hands in the regal pose usually reserved for holding the Serpent Bar, but instead he holds an odd crosshatched object with four pointed shapes suspended below and flame-like scrolls rising above, that is presumed to be a scepter.

FIGURE II.9
Temple 11
Copan, Honduras
Late Classic period, A.D. 775

Temple 11 was built over earlier structures during the reign of the Copan king Yax-Pac ("First Dawn") and completed in A.D. 775. It stands at the north edge of the acropolis, overlooking the Ballcourt and the Great Plaza. Designed as a diagram of the cosmos, it also contains a record of the king's accession and significant events during his reign. The north facade sits above a huge stairway mounting the acropolis, then rising to the temple front. The entry door may have been rendered as the mouth of a monster. At the north corners of this double-storied building stood huge Pauahtuns no longer extant. The two heads, four hands and one pair of feet that have been found in the surrounding rubble, confirm that this god was represented in three-quarter round images. Since the Pauahtuns and their young counterparts, the Bacabs, are often shown holding up the arch of the sky (as on Temple 22), the now-destroyed entablature sculpture must have been a symbolic representation of the sky, perhaps depicting the Cosmic Monster.

The floor immediately in front of the north door was extended outward to a reviewing stand. Below the vertical face of this reviewing stand are three steps sculpted with full-figure glyphs recording the date of Yax-Pac's accession, that served as a throne for Yax-Pac while he observed ceremonies in the court below. Directly below this throne on the plaza floor stands Stela N, a period ending monument dedicated by Yax-Pac's father, Smoke Squirrel. Seated on the throne steps high above this stela, Yax-Pac was seen as the natural successor to his father who had ruled before him.

The south facade of the temple faces an interior court, which is built on a higher level of the acropolis. One off-center stairway leads from the temple platform down to this interior court, but the temple sanctuary above is not directly connected to it. A second stairway leads from the court to a low terrace that is marked by three stone conch shells to symbolize the surface of water. The head of GI is carved on the top step as if the god were standing shoulder high in water. Two grotesque monkey gods holding rattles and poised in the posture of a dance flank him as he rises from the water. On the platform opposite these GI stairs, the water symbolism is completed by two sculptures of crocodiles that are set to appear as if they are floating on the same level as the stone conch shells. Below the GI stairs are three rectangular stones, defining the stair as a symbolic ballcourt. Victims were dispatched on the terrace above the stairs and thrown down into the watery Underworld of the south court.

Temple 11 incorporates imagery symbolic of all parts of the cosmos. The north facade represents the arc of heaven held up by the Pauahtuns at the four world directions; it functioned as a place of audience and ceremony with stela portraying the father of the king centered below Yax-Pac's throne. The south facade is defined as the Underworld and a place of sacrificial death, especially death associated with the ballgame. The Middleworld is the interior of the temple itself, sandwiched between the roof, which represents the Heavens, and the south court, or Underworld. The king's accession is recorded in the interior. Yax-Pac conducted the rituals that preserved world order at the four doors of the Temple and the reviewing stand in front of the north door.

FIGURE II.10
Plan of the interior, Temple 11
Copan, Honduras
Late Classic period, A.D. 775

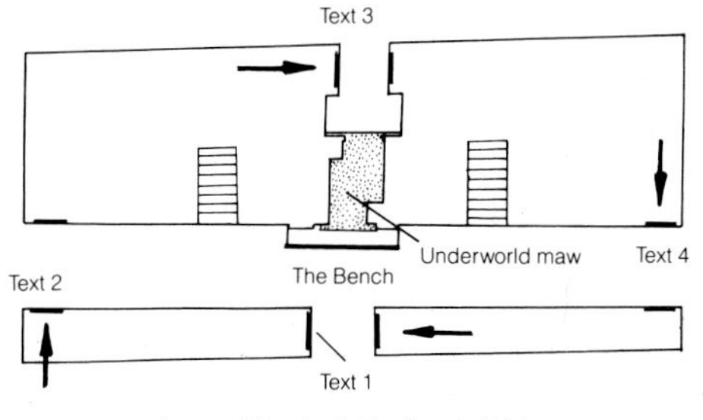

The upper temple is penetrated by four corridors that enter from each of the cardinal directions converging in a cruciform plan. Carved into the corridor walls on either side of the four entry points are two texts of twenty-four glyphs each. Each pair of texts is drawn so that one half of the pair reads in normal left to right orientation, and the other in mirror image, or right to left. Both texts of a pair are intended to be read from one exterior point, which cannot be done because the walls of the structure intervene. Clearly, since only gods can see through a wall, the inscriptions of Temple 11 are addressed more to a supernatural audience rather than to a human one.

The inscriptions record the important historical and astronomical events of Yax-Pac's reign and place his actions in the larger framework of the cosmos. Beginning at the north door, the inscriptions record Yax-Pac's accession, then it continues on to the east door to a first appearance of Evening Star that occurred shortly after his father acceded; to the south with a katun ending and a visible eclipse; and finally to the west with a first appearance of Evening Star sixteen days after the eclipse and the dedication of the building. Eclipses, especially when they occurred on dates of other significance, were perceived as times of great danger and fear. This eclipse, on the first katun ending of Yax-Pac's reign, must have been impressive indeed. The Evening Star was a death and war god of

Text 1: The inscription on the north door begins with the accession of Yax-Pac on 9.16.12.6.16 6 Caban 10 Mol, or July 2, A.D. 763. The opposite side has a date from 18 Rabbit's reign, perhaps because this king was famous for having been captured by Two-legged Sky of Quirigua.

Text 2: The inscriptional program on the east door features an event in Yax-Pac's reign which we do not yet understand. However, one of the dates, 9.15.15.12.16 5 Cib 9 Pop, or February 15, A.D. 747, is recorded with the sentence, "it shined, the Great Star," a known epithet for Venus. This first appearance of Venus as the Evening Star happened only forty-six days after the accession of Smoke Squirrel, Yax-Pac's father, and was the first important astronomical event in his reign.

Text 3: The inscription on the south door records 9.17.0.0.0 13 Ahau 18 Cumku, the first katun ending in Yax-Pac's reign and the occasion of intensive period-ending rites. However, this day, January 24, A.D. 771, was also significant as the day of an eclipse visible across the Maya region, recorded not

Layout of Temple 11: The Cosmic Clock

only at Copan but also at Quirigua and in the Dresden Codex.

Text 4: The reverse text of the west door records the date 9.17.0.0.16 3 Cib 9 Pop, or February 9, A.D. 771, only sixteen days after the eclipse date on the south door. Like the east door, the event recorded is the first appearance of Venus as the Evening Star. The opposite door records the latest date on the building, 9.17.5.0.0, or December 29, A.D. 775, which we take to be its dedication.

terrible power; the first appearance of this god after superior conjunction, when Venus passes behind the sun and disappears from view, was often the occasion of war between Maya cities. No direct evidence suggests that Copan actually went to war on either of these first appearances of Venus, but sacrificial rites of major public significance surely did occur.

The four corridors meet at a raised platform set south of their crossing point. Relief sculptures on the walls at the south and north ends of this platform define this raised platform as the portal into the Underworld where the dead reside before rebirth. The Vision Serpent that manifests both the ancestral dead and the gods of the Maya cosmos come into the human world through this portal. The sculpted panel now at the British Museum (Plate 36) that fronted the north end of the bench depicts Yax-Pac's accession attended by the ancestral kings of Copan. This bench is the heart of the temple and the pivot of the cosmic program displayed in both the sculptures and the astrological dates recorded in its inscriptions.

Venus can first be detected as Evening Star after its long disappearance behind the sun between twenty-three and thirty-five days after superior conjunction, depending on the particular orbital timing of Venus, the height of the horizon at the observation site and, of course, the weather. The first appearance of Venus recorded on the west

door in Temple 11 took place thirty-five days after superior conjunction. Since Copan sits in a valley surrounded by a high horizon, this unusually long period suggests that an observed sighting is recorded in this inscription rather than an average taken from a constructed table of means, such as that in the Dresden Codex. The earlier first appearance recorded in the east door was also long after the superior conjunction (thirty days), so it may also have been an observed event.

Yax-Pac chose to record the earlier event in his building for political reasons as well as astronomical ones. It was the first appearance of the Evening Star after his father's accession, and it had significance in the particular system that the Maya used to predict the stations in the Venus cycle. The lapse between the two appearances is 15 x 584 days, but, more importantly, it is exactly three runs of the Venus table recorded in the Dresden Codex, which was designed to correlate the Maya 365-day calendar (the *haab*) with the 584-day Venus cycle (584 x 5 = 365 x 8 = 2,920). The Evening Star appearance in the father's reign took place on February 15, while that recorded in Yax-Pac's reign occurred on February 9, but both events occurred on 9 Pop in the Maya calendar. Yax-Pac used this symmetry to reinforce his claim of genealogical descendent from his father, by declaring that the heavens behaved in a similar way for both of them.

PLATE 36
Sculpted bench panel
Temple 11, Copan, Honduras
Late Classic period, A.D. 775
Stone
Right panel: 51.5 x 263.7 x 17.8 cm
End piece: 50.2 x 48.9 x 12.7 cm
Left panel: 50.8 x 262.5 x 13.3 cm
End piece: 48.2 x 52.7 x 17.8 cm
The Trustees of The British Museum, London

Maudslay found this bench panel mounted on the north end of the raised platform base in Temple 11. It displays twenty seated persons, divided into two groups of ten who face a center text. The bench projected into the corridor and was wider than the entry door. Small sculpted panels finished the ends of the ledge which was used both as a step and a bench. The imagery of skulls and water lilies on the end pieces mark the context of the scene on the long horizontal panel as the Underworld.

Yax-Pac, the only person alive at the time of this event, is depicted to the right of the center text seated on a high throne. The other figures, who are his ancestors called back from the Afterlife to participate in his accession, sit on glyphs that constitute a continuous text. However, the ten glyphs on the left are drawn in mirror-image, while the nine on the right are in the standard orientation. This contrast establishes the reading order of both the figures and the text; both left and right texts read from the center outward. The vertical text in the center and the two flanking figures are the focus of the composition, which reads out from the center axis.

The central text records the focal event as Yax-Pac's accession; the running text under the figures appears to be a record of a ritual that other texts associate with both Yax-Pac's accession and the first appearance of Evening Star recorded in the west corridor. The nineteen figures surrounding Yax-Pac are the past kings of Copan from whom he derives his historic and genealogical right to the throne.

The figures sit in various positions— most are frontal, some are in profile—designed to enhance the immediacy of an ongoing event. The spontaneity imparts the idea that these deceased kings were physically present at the accession rite, thus permanently demonstrating in stone that all the past kings of Copan participated in Yax-Pac's accession.

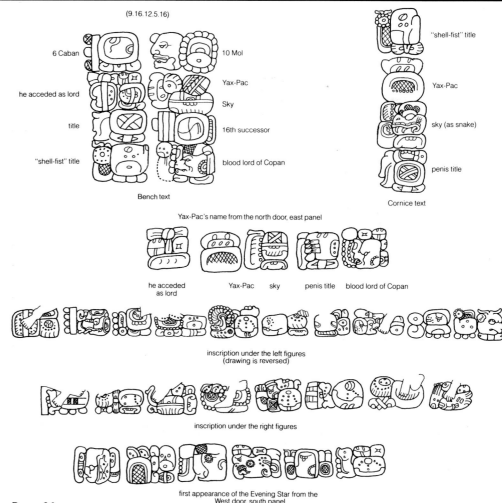

PLATE 36a

THE INSCRIPTION
The central text (Pl. 36a) begins with the date 6 Caban 10 Mol, 9.16.12.5.16, or July 2, A.D. 763. Accession is recorded at A2, with a sign for the bundle, now known to have held the instruments of bloodletting and statues of the gods, upon which the sanction of kingship was built. The office taken is the second part of this glyph; it reads *ahau* "lord." Yax-Pac's name is written at B2 in an unusual form consisting of *Yax* "first," the rear view of a fist and the sign for "house" (*otot*) set at an angle. Below these two signs is "sky," which is to be read with the next glyph, the phonetic spelling of the title that stands for the god hanging from the chain on royal belts, as on the Leiden Plaque. This title can also be written with a sign representing male genitals, which, in the text at the north door, is shown to be tied with bloodletting knots. The title also refers to the ruler's role as one who has the god from the belt and as the giver of blood through self-sacrifice.

Yax-Pac is named the "16th successor" at B3. The text closes with a title and the Emblem Glyph, naming him "Blood Lord of Copan."

The text under the figures has not yet been deciphered, but it also appears on other monuments. A similar text is used with Yax-Pac's accession date on the Temple 21a bench and on

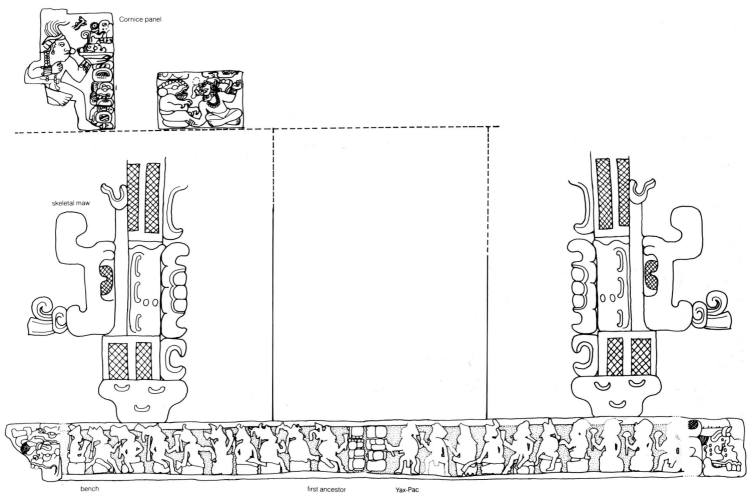

Cornice panel

skeletal maw

bench   first ancestor   Yax-Pac

PLATE 36b

Altar T, and part of it occurs on the bench of Temple 22, but without a date. The most important occurrence of this ritual expression, however, is on the west door of this temple, where it records the action on 3 Cib 9 Pop, which was a first appearance of the Evening Star (Fig. II.10,4). Here, it may refer both to the accession shown and to the first appearance as a means of establishing the ceremonial and sacred context of the accession event portrayed in the picture.

The figures on this bench (Pl. 36b) form a scene that is explained by text centered on the panel; its environment is defined by the Water-lily Death Gods whose portraits sit at right angles to the portrait row.

The special status of the protagonist, Yax-Pac, who sits to the right of this text on a high pillow throne, is marked by his posture; he is the only figure with both feet on the groundline. Because he is shown frontally, his legs are rendered in an awkward position. The nineteen flanking figures are identified by their clothing as his predecessors in office. The figures wear four kinds of pectorals: a zoomorphic head; a T-shaped monster's mouth; an Ik spirit pectoral; single or double bars (Pl. 36c). All but the bar pectorals have tied rattlesnakes draped over the top and bead strings hanging below. The figures of Altar Q at Copan, which archeologists now generally agree displays Yax-Pac and his fifteen predecessors, wear this same set of pectorals.

Most of the figures are barechested, barefooted, and hold a scepter. A few wear capes, and all wear simple loincloths. Three kinds of headdresses are shown. The headgear of the last three figures on the right has zoomorphic heads and personified wings. The others wear either a wrapped turban or a round balloon-shaped headdress. Some turbans are plain, but most bear symbols, perhaps a reference to their names, added to the crown. A shell diadem is attached to the round headdresses worn in one example with the shell earplugs of Chac-Xib-Chac and in the other with disk and cylinder earflares. One bearded and turbaned figure may refer to another bearded person found on the west side of Stela C.

Details of the Temple 11 Bench figures

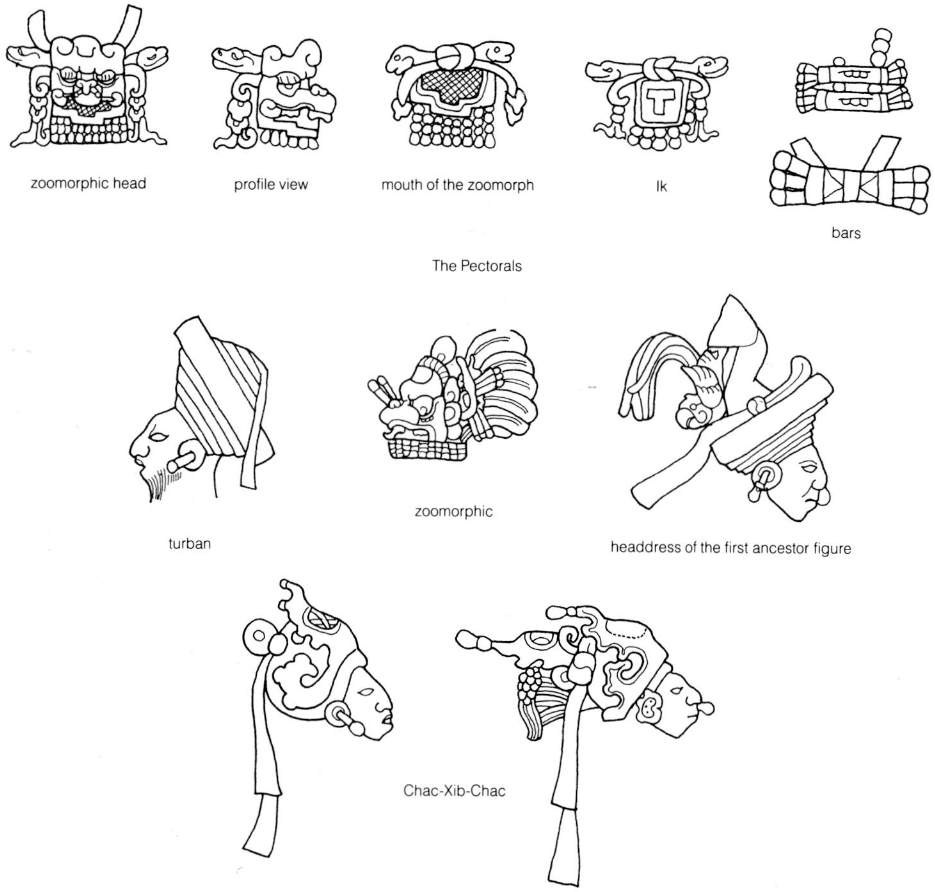

zoomorphic head   profile view   mouth of the zoomorph   Ik   bars

The Pectorals

turban   zoomorphic   headdress of the first ancestor figure

Chac-Xib-Chac

The Headdresses

PLATE 36c

The key to the meaning of the Temple 11 bench is found on Altar Q, which sits in the court south of Temple 11. Around its four sides sit sixteen figures dressed in the same costumes as the Temple 11 figures, holding the same kinds of scepter, and arranged around the same 6 Caban 10 Mol date. The text on top of Altar Q starts with a date early in the 9th baktun and an event from the reign of a very early ruler named Yax-Kuk-Mo' ("Blue Quetzal-Macaw"), whose accession on 9.0.0.0.0, or December 11, A.D. 435, is recorded on Stela J. The figure who faces Yax-Pac on Altar Q has a quetzal in his headdress. Since names are frequently placed in Maya headdresses, this figure may be the Yax-Kuk-Mo' referred to in the text, and the king

from whom Yax-Pac's lineage descended. On the Temple 11 bench, the figure facing Yax-Pac across the center text also has a quetzal on its turban, and may very well depict the same person.

The similarity of the Temple 11 bench to Altar Q in composition and iconographic detail is not coincidental; both have a dedication date of 9.17.5.0.0 and certain costume elements, especially the zoomorphic pectorals, appear only in these two sculptures. If Altar Q is interpreted as a portrait gallery of the sixteen successors of the Copan line, then the Temple 11 bench panel should likewise represent the Copan kings. However, twenty figures are included here, rather than the sixteen identified by numbered succession titles

found with the names of Late Classic Copan kings. Perhaps the Altar Q portraits refer to a lineage succession and thus include only people directly related to each other, while the Temple 11 bench panel records the historical succession, including every king who ruled Copan.

PLATE 37
Cornice panel
Temple 11, Copan, Honduras
Late Classic period, A.D. 775
Stone
104.1 x 76.2 x 15.2 cm
The Trustees of The British Museum, London

Mounted above the north door, this panel was one of several which recorded full-figure inscriptions as well as portraits of Yax-Pac. Yax-Pac sits on a now-missing throne with one leg drawn up and the other dropping to the floor. One arm is bent against his chest and the other extends away from his body holding a shallow offering plate on which rests the head of God K. His name is written in a column of glyphs placed around the plate.

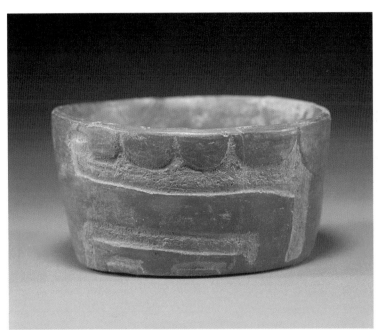

PLATE 28. Cylindrical vessel, Olmec flame design

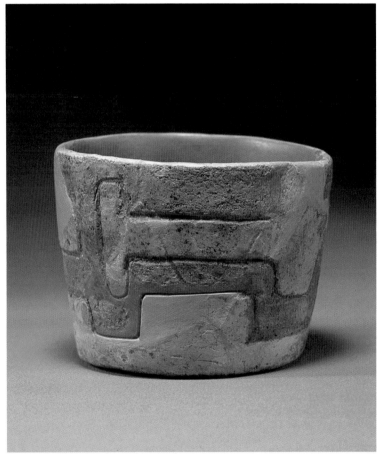

PLATE 29. Cylindrical vessel, meander design

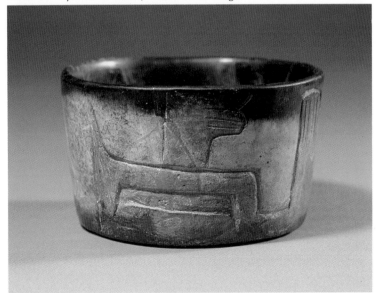

PLATE 30. Cylindrical vessel, fish design

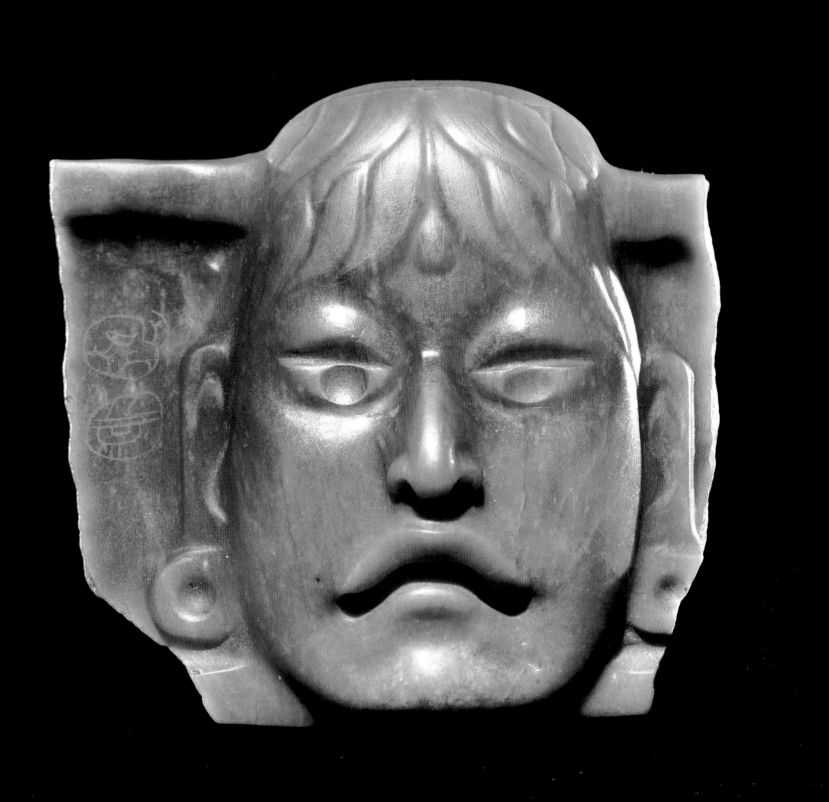

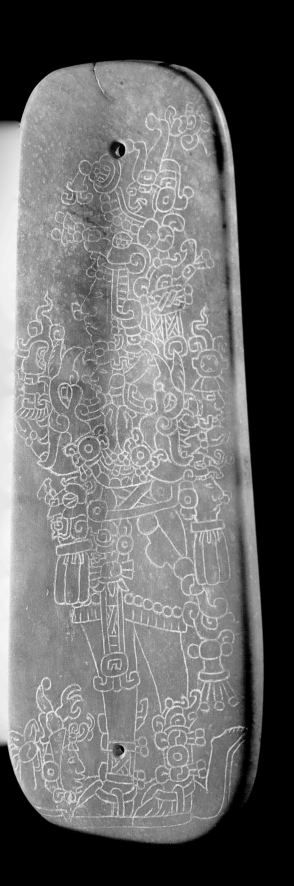

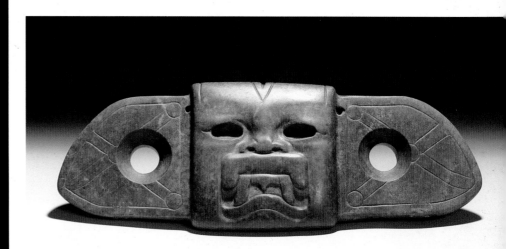

PLATE 32. Flanged pectoral

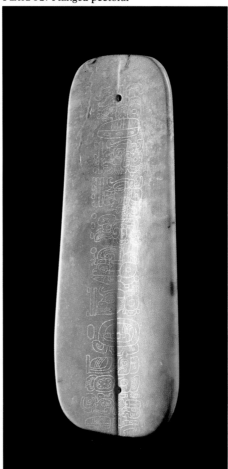

PLATE 33A. The Leiden Plaque (rear)
PLATE 33. Jade celt, the Leiden Plaque (front)

PLATE 31. Portrait pectoral (opposite)

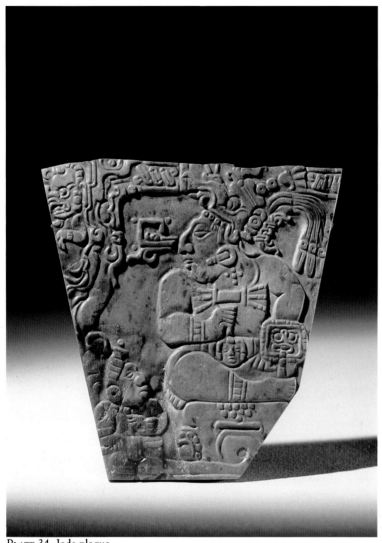

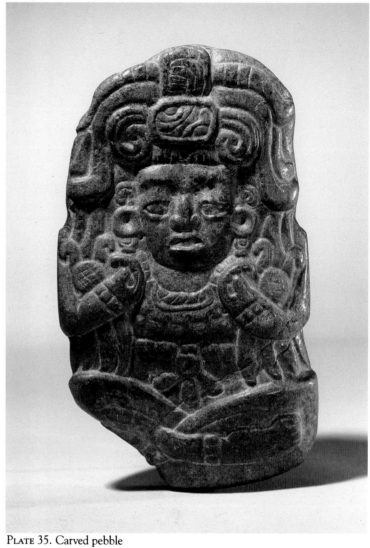

Plate 34. Jade plaque

Plate 35. Carved pebble

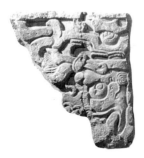

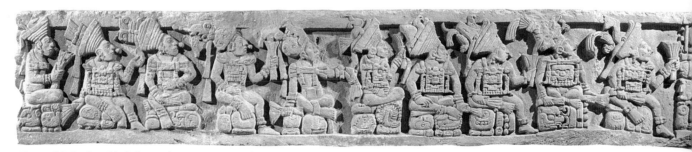

Plate 36. Sculpted bench panel

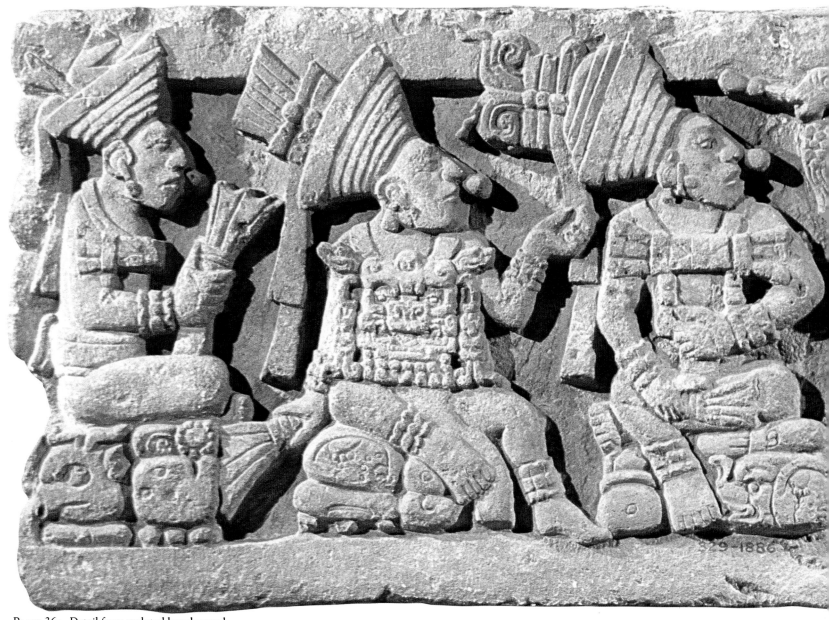

PLATE 36A. Detail from sculpted bench panel

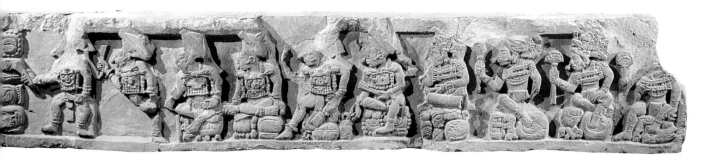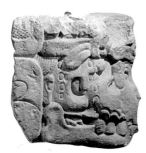

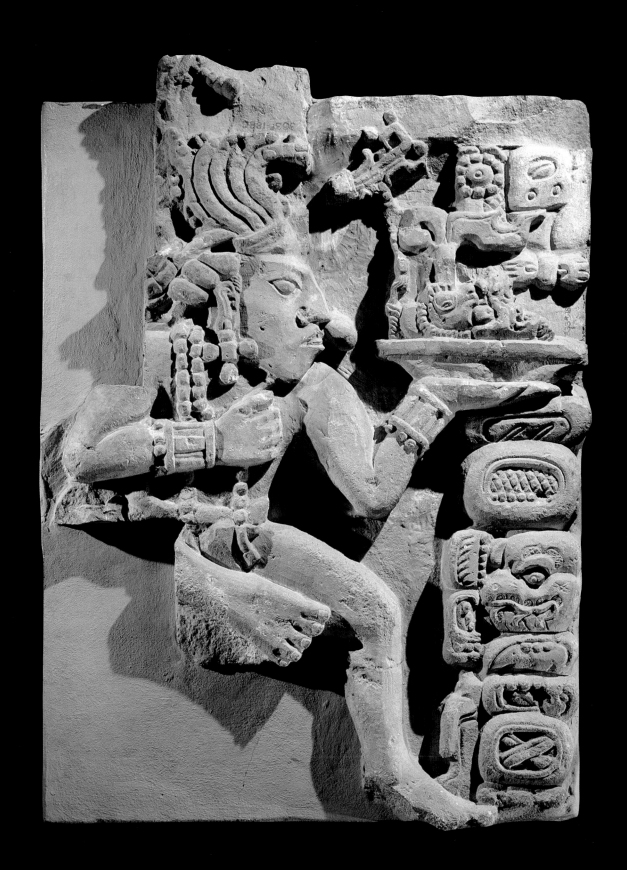

III

COURTLY LIFE

THE PALACE LIFE OF THE CLASSIC MAYA WAS SOPHISTICATED. THE SCALE and complexity of architectural remains, and a few surviving pieces of palace furniture such as thrones and benches, suggest that their great palatial compounds were the setting for dramatic rituals. Palace structures, which were the administrative center for Maya cities, are found at virtually every Maya site. Unlike temples, palaces were comprised of groups of buildings—featuring long multi-chambered interior galleries—organized around small plazas.

The Palenque palace, largely completed by A.D. 715, was the setting for many official functions of the ruling family (Fig. III.1). From the throne set within House E, the most private gallery, the royal family could preside over ritual events. Ruler A of Tikal, who died in A.D. 727, is thought to be responsible for most of the buildings that compose the Central Acropolis which was both an official palace and an elite residence (Fig. III.2).[1] Hearths found in the Central Acropolis suggest that some meals may have been prepared there.

At Piedras Negras, the palace compound is the West Acropolis, built by Ruler 3 and his successors between A.D. 680 and 750 (Fig. III.3). Worked into the natural rise of the Usumacinta River, the galleries become increasingly private and inaccessible as one moves away from the plaza level. An elaborate throne set into a gallery at the lowest level of the court suggests that this may have been the setting for official receptions; sweat baths, places for ritual cleansing, also adjoin the structure.

PLATE 37. Cornice panel

133

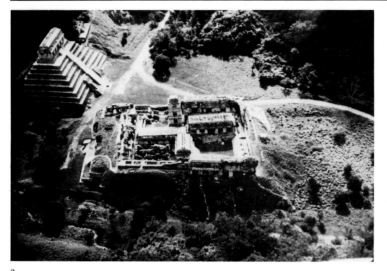

a

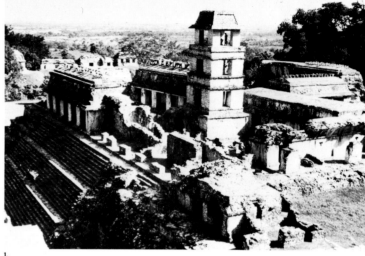

b

FIGURE III.1a,b
Views of the palace
Palenque, Mexico
Late Classic period, before A.D. 715
Photos by Linda Schele

These palaces are the settings for the rituals of court life, which included receiving visiting nobles, installing rulers, presenting tribute, displaying captives and ritual bloodletting. Adjacent to great multi-level funerary pyramids and ballcourts, the palaces were often joined by what we now know only as "house" mounds, which were probably palace structures made of more perishable materials. Some living spaces did exist in the large stone palaces, but these neighboring houses may have been the true center of domestic life for an extended royal family. The stone palaces were the settings for ritual pomp and administration and there the dynastic rituals—including heir designation, auto-sacrifice and accession—were carried out.

Representations of royal chambers on painted ceramics also picture perishable materials that furnished the palace—baskets, curtains, pillows, among them. Regrettably, most evidence on the nature of the daily life at the court has vanished. Textiles have decomposed, tribute records have rotted, and most paintings have flaked from the walls. Its record survives largely on small objects, such as painted vessels and small sculptures. This evidence, buttressed by some dramatic remains, such as the murals at Bonampak, allows us to infer the nature of courtly life and the hierarchy of society. These glimpses of the courtly world reveal the wealth and complexity of Classic Maya life.

The murals at Bonampak, painted just at the end of the eighth century, illustrate many events that took place in Maya palaces. In these scenes, the palace depicted resembles the existing structures at Palenque.[2] Bonampak today is limited to a few ceremonial buildings that frame a plaza. Structure 1 of Bonampak was painted with elaborate murals (Pl. 38) that cover the walls of all three small chambers with illustrations of great rituals and celebrations, an important battle, the presentation of captives, captive sacrifice and self-sacrifice. The three painted rooms of Structure 1 record activities that engage nearly 200 individuals. Produced in registers that wrap around the rooms, the figure paintings incorporate hieroglyphic titles and personal names that provide a guide to the sort of people who participated in the life of the Maya court toward

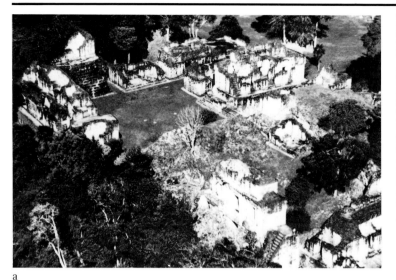

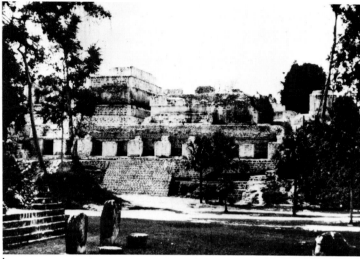

a

b

the end of the Classic period. The fact that only a few individuals appear in more than a single scene in Room 1 suggests that different events required different *dramatis personae*.

In Room 1, the paintings begin with a scene that shows the gathering of the royal family and lords who witness the presentation of a young heir seated on a throne (Pls. 38 b,c,d). This presentation apparently motivates all the festivities that follow. In the next scenes, the king and two companions dress in ritual garb for a celebration that takes place 336 days after the child was presented to the court Pl. 38e); the elaborate celebration is recorded on the lower register of all four walls of the room (Pls. 38 b,c,d). The fourteen witnesses in white mantles at the presentation of the child heir are identified in glyphs with the title *ahau* or "lord." *Ahau* is also a title carried by kings, and it is one of the highest titles recorded in Maya inscriptions. Some of the substantial lords, who display a girth that may also suggest a life of physical ease and epicurean habits, may have the right to rule city-states independently. Nevertheless, they have come to Bonampak to confirm the legitimacy of the heir of their peer, King Chaan-muan. This group also includes ranking males of the Bonampak lineage, who attend rites legitimatizing the little heir.

The great celebration that took place some 336 days after the installation of the Bonampak child was presumably held in honor of the heir. Like squires of the court, sixteen young men, simply clad, assist the principal lords, including Chaan-muan, in donning their ceremonial dress (Pl. 38e). Those who bear legible titles are named as *ah na:ab*. Masked entertainers to the left of the principal lords perform and play musical instruments in the festival, shown below (Pl. 38 b,c). Although most of the musicians bear no title, a few are named *ah na:ab*, and the compound, *ba-po*, is used as a title for two masked figures. At the right of the Bonampak king and his two companions stand another group of nobles whose costumes are characterised by an orange color and an odd "bowler" hat suspended in their headdresses (Pl. 38d). They are identified by the common title of *cahal*, a governor or subordinate lord. The role they play in the celebra-

Figure III.2a,b
Central Acropolis
Tikal, Guatemala
Late Classic period, before A.D. 760
Photo a by Nicholas Hellmuth
Photo b by Mary Miller

FIGURE III.3
Reconstruction of the West Acropolis
Piedras Negras, Guatemala
Late Classic period, A.D. 680–750
Drawing by Tatiana Proskouriakoff

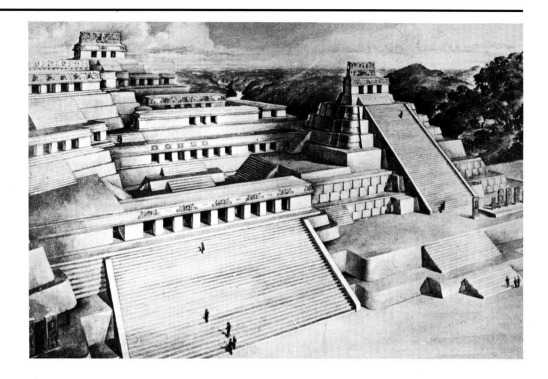

tion is not clear. Like the *ahaus* noted above, they may witness the rituals carried out by the three lords of greatest rank. *Cahals* may have been members of the royal family sent to administer foreign territory. Although they never bear personal names or Emblem Glyphs that identify them as such, they may also be members of lineages that once reigned independently, but who now pay the required allegiance to a larger, more important city that dominates them.[3]

Royal families were linked through marriage, and women left their homes to marry into other noble lineages. Women of rank, doubtless free of domestic chores, also presided at court. In Room 1 at Bonampak, one of the women seated beside the king on the throne is his wife, who is named in Room 2 as Lady Rabbit, Lady of Yaxchilan, Lady *Bacab*. Lady Rabbit was born into the Yaxchilan ruling family, and she attained high rank at Bonampak since she is called *bacab*, a title of many kings. Room 2 bears the names of another wife of Chaan-muan who has an equally prestigious title of Lady *Cahal*. These royal women held high office, and their rank may have been recognized both in their place of origin and their adopted site. Like the royal women of Europe in the age of monarchy, Maya women were the means by which the royal lineages became intertwined, but as in Europe, familial connections were not enough to prevent inter-necine conflict.

These paintings give us an overview of Maya social hierarchy. Kings are visited by *ahaus*, attended by *ah na:abs*, and watched by *cahals*. The records from other sites confirm this social structure and elaborate on other roles that these persons assume. On Piedras Negras Lintel 2 (Pl. 40), for example, Ruler 2 and seven youths celebrate what is probably an initiation ritual for young men on 9.11.6.2.1, October 24, A.D. 658. A son of Ruler 2, depicted behind the king, is named as an *ahau* of Piedras Negras in the accompanying caption. His smaller size indicates that he is a child.[4] Since the youths who kneel would be only as tall as the boy were they to stand, they are perhaps 12 or 13 years old. Each boy is named in a six-glyph caption, and each bears the title *ahau* and an emblem glyph indicating that they are members of the Bonampak and Yaxchilan royal families. Since five boys are named as Bonampak *ahaus*, it is clear that many members of the ruling family could hold the title at once.[5] The recorded event, "ahau-in-hand," generally refers to the display of God K; here, a helmet follows the verb. The celebration of the helmet display may have been an initiation ritual in which royal youths donned battle attire for the first time. When the son of the Piedras Negras king participated in the ritual, all eligible young men of the region may have joined in the ceremony.[6]

The frequent occurrence of royal titles in inscriptions suggests that a Maya royal family extended beyond the boundaries of the nuclear family to include many descendants of previous kings. To grasp the number of members in a royal family of a Late Classic eighth-century Maya city, imagine that a dynasty began with a founding couple about A.D. 600. If the first couple have four children who survive to produce their own four children, then their grandchildren will number 16. Even if all first cousins mate with other first cousins, the third generation of great-grandchildren would number 32. Since some rulers had multiple wives, we would expect those kings to have produced more than four children each. However, following a simple pattern of cross-cousin marriage and a family size limited to four children, within 200 years, or by A.D. 800, the direct descendants of the original couple would number, very conservatively, at least 500 people.[7] Many of these individuals must have borne noble titles as a birthright and carried out courtly functions. It should come as no surprise, then, that five lords from Bonampak would all be named *ahau* simultaneously, as they are on Lintel 2.

Some titles were not limited to royal lineage but also indicate political allegiance. The Leiden Panel, Lintel 2 of La Pasadita (Fig. III.4), names the Yaxchilan king Bird Jaguar, who is on the left, facing one of his *cahals* who ruled La Pasadita, a town located about 25 kilometers from Yaxchilan where the panel was found. The inscriptions indicate that La Pasadita was under the control of Yaxchilan after A.D. 750. If the town fell within the Yaxchilan sphere of influence through warfare, tribute and loyalty were probably demanded of its residents. The final glyph of the caption placed near the figure at right names him as *cahal*; the three preceding glyphs record his personal name. *Cahals* were regional governors, subject to a king, and this *cahal* first pledged fealty to Bird Jaguar, and lived to serve his son Shield Jaguar II in the same manner. On the brightly polychromed panel from La Pasadita that belongs to the Metropolitan Museum of Art, the same *cahal* is shown delivering tribute to Shield Jaguar II.

The enthroned lord on the Kimbell panel (Fig. III.5) is also a *cahal*, but he was only installed in that office three years after the event depicted on the panel occurred. Although the name of Shield Jaguar II is inscribed on this panel, the king is not pictured in the scene. Instead his *cahal*, or governor, presides and receives three captives delivered by an *ah k'in*.

Cahal, then, may be a birthright or include an office into which one may accede by the grace of a king. That eight persons to the right of the three principal lords in the Bonampak celebration can be identified as *cahals* indicates the great number of

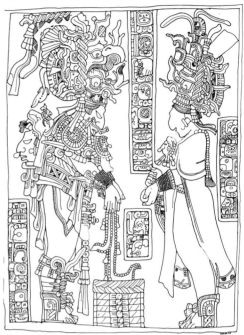

FIGURE III.4
Lintel 2
La Pasadita, Guatemala
Late Classic period, A.D. 761
See also Pl. 76

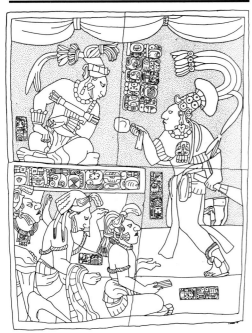

FIGURE III.5
The Kimbell panel
Panel showing presentation of captives
Laxtunich, Usumacinta river valley
Late Classic period, A.D. 783
See also pl. 86

subsidiary lords on whom kings depended. The *cahal* title designated not only governors and war chiefs, but one of Chaan-muan's wives bears the title Lady *Cahal*, and here it also denotes the plump individual blowing the conch shell in Room 2, whose simple dress suggests that he is a servant.

The title *ah na:ab* attached to several of the musicians, attendants, and performers in the Bonampak murals is occasionally carried by kings and is common among lesser nobility. The title may mean "young prince," based on a reading of the glyph that means "he, the first." In the dressing scene, the attendants who are called *ah na:ab* look like young squires, perhaps sons of the *ahaus* depicted who are of greater age, status, and girth. Reading the components of the glyph literally, *ah na:ab* also means "he of the water-lily." The water-lily headdresses worn by some of the musicians and performers may be a costume element that indicates their title. The relatively greater numbers of the *ah na:ab* title may indicate that it held lower status. This title also refers to practitioners of the courtly arts. The ubiquitous dwarfs and hunchbacks of the Maya court (Plates 41, 42, 43),[8] are frequently shown as attendants dressed for courtly life, and may also belong to *ah na:ab* group, since they occasionally wear the water-lily headdress.

The Maya court was extensive, including a royal family of perhaps 100 people, surrounded by a larger circle of persons engaged in courtly endeavors, such as musicians, reciters of poetry, entertainers, lords and ladies-in-waiting. One large group of the royal retinue who do not appear in the Bonampak paintings are the scribes and artisans. Nevertheless, their names, numerous depictions of them on objects such as painted vases and, most importantly, their work, reveal that they were central to the activities of the Maya court. Judging from the sheer volume of art and writing produced for the Maya city, the role of these individuals must have been significant. The architectural ornament of a residential compound recently excavated at Copan shows an elaborate architectural program that featured scribes and courtly arts.[9] In addition, David Stuart has recently demonstrated that the title *ah tz'ib*, or "he of the writing," frequently identifies the artist on painted pottery where it is used in a name-phrase or combined with a signature, and sometimes it accompanies an illustration of someone writing or carving.[10] A particularly interesting use of this title occurs on a carved door frame at Xcalumkin—a site that survived well into the ninth century in Campeche— where God D, or Itzamna, is named in glyph block 19; the name is followed first by *ah k'in*, which is frequently a priestly title, and then by *ah tz'ib*. This association is appropriate, since according to an early Colonial source, it was Itzamna who invented writing and books,[11] and on Maya pots, he as God D is occasionally shown writing or reading.[12] Reading and writing were, therefore, important activities for the Maya elite as well as for Maya gods. The titles designating scribes and artisans differ from other hierarchies, since gods and supernaturals, as well as nobles, are included as members.

The Maya may have thought that the ability to manipulate images, writing and numbers required skills beyond normal human capabilities. The Popol Vuh, which recorded the Maya creation myth at the time of the Conquest, accounts for the association of monkeys with this special class of noble artisans. Hun Chuen and Hun Batz were twin half brothers of Hunahpu and Xbalanque, the Hero Twins.[13] They were born to 1 Hunahpu and his wife in the Middleworld before he vanished into the Underworld. Until the Underworld princess, Xquic, arrived in the Middleworld and gave birth to the Hero Twins, they were the only children around and the light of their grandmother's life. Like real human half brothers, Hun Chuen and Hun Batz resented the birth of the Hero Twins. They tormented their younger brothers, placing them on anthills when they were still babies. After they grew up, Hun Chuen and Hun Batz took their food, forced them to do the hunting for the family, and denied them entry into the house. Unlike their more rugged brothers, Hun Batz and Hun Chuen preferred the courtly arts, and they dominated the interior world. There, they did everything well: they painted, they carved, they played the flute. To the Hero Twins, this interior world was forbidden. One day, when the Hero Twins returned home without any wild game, the old grandmother angrily demanded to know why. When the Twins explained that they needed the help of their older brothers, off the four brothers went. Hunahpu and Xbalanque took their blowguns and began to shoot their prey, but the birds did not fall. Each one became lodged in a tree, and the older twins had to scale the tree to retrieve them. As they did so, the tree magically began to grow, lifting Hun Chuen and Hun Batz high into the sky. Anxious at the height at which they found themselves, they implored the younger brothers to help them. "Undo your pants... with the long end trailing like a tail behind you, and then you'll be better able to move," Hunahpu and Xbalanque advised.[14] When the older twins complied, they grew the tails of spider monkeys, and they began to behave just like monkeys, making funny faces and scratching themselves.

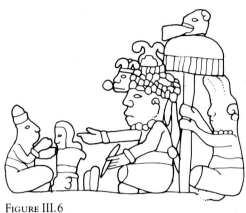

FIGURE III.6
Stela 5, detail
Izapa, Mexico
Late Formative period, 250 B.C.–A.D. 150
Drawing by Mary Miller

When the Hero Twins returned home alone, the old grandmother begged for the return of her favorite grandsons. The Twins told her that they would call them, but she must not laugh at the appearance of Hun Batz and Hun Chuen. Then Hunahpu took his flute and began to play a tune, and the monkey twins came out of the forest. Try as she might, the grandmother could not keep herself from laughing when she saw the tails and the silly behavior of her favorites, who then fled back to the forest. Twice more, Hunahpu called them with the flute, enticing them to appear, and twice more, the grandmother could not restrain her laughter. One last time, Hunahpu called his older brothers, but this time they did not appear. Monkeys now, cast away from their family, Hun Batz and Hun Chuen remained in the forest. They became the supernatural patrons of musicians, singers, painters, and sculptors, and they are frequently shown on polychrome ceramics, painting, carving and drawing in these roles.[15]

Usually shown with ugly monkey faces, but sometimes depicted with the faces of beautiful young men, these Monkey Scribes wear spangled turbans, hold paint pots made from conch shells, and write with pens or brushes. Frequently growing from the rear of their headdress or loincloth is a stylized tree on which columns of numbers may appear. One scholar has likened this symbol to a computer printout, but it is probably a reference to the tree that assisted the Hero Twins in transforming the scribes from humans to monkeys. Sometimes one scribe appears with the "printout" while the other has none, perhaps to differentiate the twins. On a Copan vase showing scribes (Pl. 44a), the fellow with the "printout," who also wears a deer ear characteristic of monkey scribes, carves a human head, suggesting that one of the endeavors of these supernatural patrons of artists was to fashion human masks, and perhaps even humans themselves.

The Maya apparently viewed the ability to make works of art with a certain awe. In the Popol Vuh, it was said of the Monkey Scribes that "they did everything well. They simply knew it when they were born, they simply had genius."[16] Even during the formative stages of Maya civilization, they had great respect for making works of

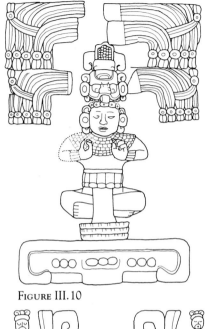

FIGURE III.10

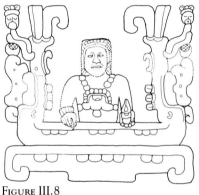

FIGURE III.8

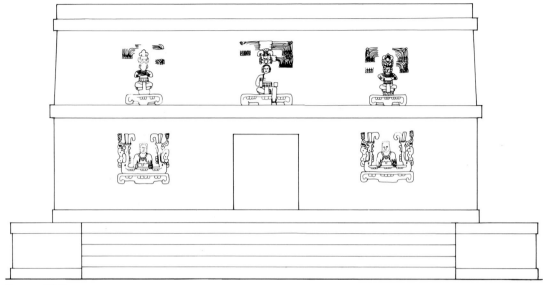

FIGURE III.7

FIGURE III.7
Reconstruction of Structure 9N-82
Copan, Honduras
Late Classic period, A.D. 780–800
Drawings by Barbara Fash

FIGURE III.8
Pauahtun
Structure 9N-82, lower level, Copan, Honduras
Late Classic period, A.D. 780–800

FIGURE III.10
Scribe
Structure 9N-82, upper level, Copan, Honduras
Late Classic period, A.D. 780–800

art and writing. Several extant works, notably carved jade, demonstrate that the Maya collected ancient Olmec works (Plate 45), which they then inscribed with their own texts, as if to claim the precious jades as well as the genius behind their creation.[17]

The notion that one could fashion a human body with genius or divine supervision was first recorded on Stela 5 at Izapa, a monument dating to the Late Formative period. The main face of the stela depicts the emergence of man at the dawn of time. A central figure drills a hole in a cosmic tree from which barely-formed humans flow. An old couple, possibly ancestors, conduct a divination over an incensario at the lower left; behind them, another seated figure holds out a spiny bloodletter. At the lower right, a small figure wearing a spangled turban, the characteristic attire of the scribes, shapes a human body, shown at a stage when it still lacks arms and legs (Fig. III.6). The suggestion is clear: scribes were present at creation, and they were instrumental in giving form to humans.

Copan, the Classic Maya site in northern Honduras, has been known for its great ceremonial plaza ever since John Lloyd Stephens and Frederick Catherwood visited it in 1839. From 1980 until 1982, the Proyecto Arqueologico de Copan (P.A.C.) excavated a palace complex located a kilometer northwest of the main plaza, in part of the city known as Sepulturas Compound. The main building, Structure 9N-82, has life-sized scribe figures in full three-dimensional relief on the facade. A carved hieroglyphic bench supported by *pauahtuns* was discovered inside the structure. The text on the bench features elaborate glyphs that are a tribute to the artistic skills of the scribes. The wittiness and sophistication of the text makes it difficult to decipher fully, but it can be dated to the late eighth century and the people named in the text were related to Yax-Pac, the last king of Copan.

A most remarkable, fully three-dimensional sculpture of a scribe (Plate 46) recovered from Structure 9N-82 permits greater understanding of the monkey scribe

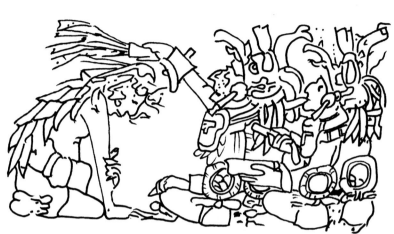

FIGURE III.11

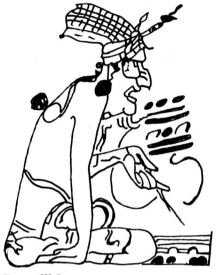

FIGURE III.9

imagery.[18] The seated, limestone figure holds a paint pot in right hand and a pen in left. Around his neck he wears a stylized water-lily pendant frequently seen on scribes; the face is rendered essentially as human, but it has the simian features of the Monkey Scribe. This monkey face was intentionally made ugly, but like a Renaissance grotesque by Leonardo, it is rendered with precision and aesthetic control.

FIGURE III.9
Scribe from a codex-style pot
Late Classic period, A.D. 600–800
Drawing by Mary Miller

FIGURE III.11
Detail from a polychromed vessel
Late Classic period, A.D. 600–800
Drawing by Mary Miller

    The discovery of the Copan Monkey Scribe aids in the interpretation of another Maya divinity, God N. The headdress of the Monkey Scribe is a net bag, or *pauah*, in Maya; his upper arms bear markings that look like a cluster of grapes, indicating the word *tun*, or "stone." Together these elements suggest that the figure represents Pauahtun, or the Maya God N, as well as a Monkey Scribe. Since this dual association is supported elsewhere in painted images of Pauahtun who appears as a scribe or as a teacher of scribes, he can be added to the circle of gods who paint, write or carve.[19]

    Pauahtuns also figure on the facade of the first story of Structure 9N-82. Figure III.7 is a reconstruction of the two-tiered building. Here, half-figure stone busts holding pens and paint pots emerge from open-mouthed serpent frames placed over the glyph *na* (Fig. III.8). Like the three-dimensional sculpture excavated from the site, they have the faces of Monkey Scribes, such as we also see on the New Orleans pot (Plate 47). On another painted Maya vessel, a God N is a chief scribe and he seems to instruct his subordinates (Fig. III.9). In this instance, the God N speaks numbers configured as if a computer printout, and he points at a codex. All three figures sit on *na* glyphs which may refer to *na:ab*, or water-lily.

    On the upper story of the Structure 9N-82 facade, three fully-sculptured figures also sit cross-legged tenoned to the wall (Fig. III.10). The two flanking figures sprout maize from their headdresses while the central one wears a great water-lily headdress, probably to represent the personification of the number thirteen and the word *na:ab*. *Na:ab* or *nab* not only means "water-lily", but it also means "to daub," as with paint, or

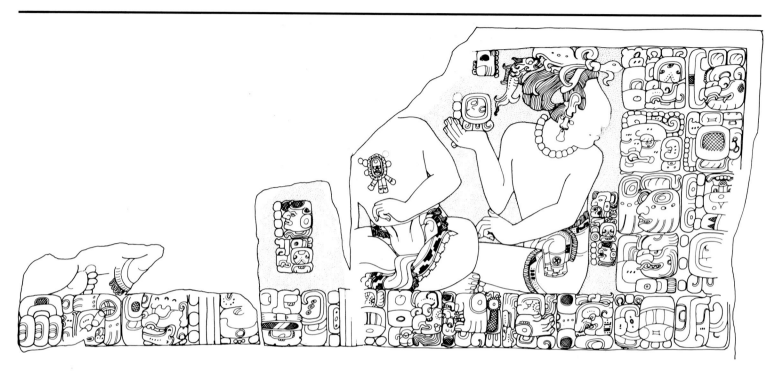

FIGURE III.12
Panel of lords and scribes
Pomona, Tabasco, Mexico
Late Classic period, ca. A.D. 771

"to varnish," or "to anoint."[20] The *na* glyphs on which the lord sits, then, indicate what the scribes do; some wear water-lilies as headdresses that also indicate title. This headdress is also worn by two old gods who asperse and daub a young man on a painted vessel in the November collection (Fig. III.11).[21] These *na:ab* figures, like the Pauahtuns on Structure 9N-82 at Copan, may also refer to the painters or artisans honored in the compound.

Four courtly lords, perhaps masters of courtly and scribal arts, on the Late Classic panel from Pomona (Fig. III.12), wear water-lily headdresses and bear the title 4 Pauahtun.[22] The text is elaborate in form with columns of "printout" numbers added to glyphs like a flourish suggesting the art of scribes. A few years after the panel was made, Piedras Negras was successful in a war campaign against Pomona, where these four Pauahtuns may have been taken captive. Stela 12 (Fig. V.8), the most beautiful and elaborate stela at Piedras Negras, records the victory. It is, however, worked in the style of Pomona and may have been executed by artisans acquired through tribute.

Various gods can be associated with the scribal arts. Itzamna, or God D, supposedly invented writing, and he is sometimes depicted writing or painting. God N, or *pauahtun*, is a title often borne by scribes or masters of arithmetic; other God N figures, who are associated with the personification of the number 13, paint or draw. The Monkey Scribes, who wear soft spangled headdresses and deer ears, appear to do much of the writing and carving depicted in Maya art. At both Pomona and Copan, persons who bear the title of scribe are nobles; their names and sometimes their portraits are recorded for posterity. Palaces that honor their work and their rank, such as Structure 9N-82, may have been residences and formal meeting places for these noble writers and painters.

Although depictions of men predominate in Maya art, the presence of women on major monuments—stone lintels, stelae and mural paintings—as well as their representations as figurines, suggests that they played an important role in Maya courtly life. Not only were women the wives, sisters, and mothers to kings, at times they actually ruled. Among several references to Late Classic period female rulers, the best documented are Lady Ahpo-Katun of Piedras Negras, Lady Ahpo-Hel of Palenque, and the Lady of Dos Pilas at Naranjo. Inscriptions indicate that kings had more than one wife. Shield Jaguar of Yaxchilan, for example, had two important wives whose names and portraits appeared with his. Yet a third wife's name appeared when his son Bird Jaguar became king and recorded his own parentage. Bird Jaguar, then, may not have been the son of the most important wife, but after his own installation as king he honored his mother. Royal women frequently left one important city to marry the king of a neighboring city. Yax-Pac, the last king of Copan, recorded that his mother, the previous king's wife, had come from Palenque.

The imagery on Maya vessels that show women richly attired is sometimes revealing of emotional and intimate relationships with men. A scene on a polychrome vessel shows a king who prepares to dance with two different women, who may be his wives (Plate 48). The upper body garment, or *huipil*, each woman wears over an underskirt, is made of fabric decorated in a complex batik design. The woman at left casts her eyes demurely downward, while the one at right, who directs her eyes at the king, appears to speak aggressively to him. Women are frequently depicted holding an object that looks like an aspergillum, a bloodletter, or feather fan. A bone handle for this kind of object (Plate 49) is incised with a portrait of a woman, clad in elaborate gauzy garb, who may have been its owner. A second bone, a carved deer tibia from Copan, may have belonged to the woman depicted on it who helps Yax Pac fasten his most intimate attire (Plate 50).[23]

Among the pantheon of Maya gods, two females are particularly associated with the activities of daily life; although these women are divinities, their behavior resembles that of human women. The most important female divinity is Ixchel, the moon goddess, known from the codices and the widespread devotion to her at the time of the Conquest. She has two aspects in Classic Maya depictions, both associated with making cloth. At times she appears as a demure, young weaver; at other times, she is a sexy, comely courtesan associated with spinning. The elegantly dressed figurine of a woman working on a backstrap loom (Plate 51) is typical of the depictions of Ixchel as a weaver. Frequently, a bird is perched on her loom, recalling illustrations of the Central Mexican goddess Xochiquetzal, who is also associated with the moon and weaving.[24] This Maya woman occurs commonly among Jaina figurines in a completely standardized form: she always wears the same costume that includes a *huipil*, an upperbody garment, and is frequently shown sitting at rest, hands on her knees or in her lap. Although they lack overt supernatural qualities, her characteristics are as codified as those of God K or the Water-lily Jaguar.

A second female type is the courtesan who wears unspun cotton in her headdress (Plate 52). In spite of the association with spinning, we never see this woman at work, in contrast to the industrious weaver. She sometimes wears a cape, but generally she is depicted wearing no garment over her breasts, which is the custom of many Maya women today when they are at home. Like the erratic moon, this woman is not a model of constancy. In paintings and clay sculptures she is paired with old men, deities, and even large rabbits, as if she wandered from one to the other. In one notable example from the Detroit Institute of Arts (Plate 53), she embraces a leering old man, who lifts her skirt to feel her thigh.[25] In similar figurines, her companions hug her or fondle her breasts. These figurines, produced with a keen eye for human behavior, comprise much of the erotic art known for the Maya. It is not known if these figurines had a particular function. They may have been treasured bedroom objects or funerary offerings for either men or women.

Although specific accounts of tribute no longer exist, scenes painted on extant objects show that in Maya culture the services of skilled individuals as well as goods were rendered as tribute. The scene on the Fenton vase (Plate 54) shows one lord who seems to deliver, or account for, a great pile of bundled textiles topped by a full basket set in front of the enthroned ruler.[26] A smaller lord seated behind the royal cushion may reach for a codex and his accounting tools. On another painted vessel at the New Orleans Museum of Art (Plate 55) an enthroned lord in a palace chamber is presented with ceramic vessels, which may again indicate the rich tribute received by the Maya court.

According to Maya mythology, man was formed by the gods from maize. Maize and blood were identified as the most potent substances by the Maya. Man's flesh was maize, transformed by the blood offerings of deities into human substance. Maize was the essence of the Maya, and also the staff of their lives. Although other foods contributed substantially to the Maya diet, then as now, maize was the staple, formed into tamales and steamed, or patted into tortillas and cooked directly over the fire on a *comal*, or griddle.

Prominent among the Maya deities is a Maize God, generally represented as a beautiful young man growing from corn foliage (Plate 56).[27] A particularly beautiful Maize God was recovered from the rubble of Structure 22, Copan. Along the corners and cornices of this building were matching series of two-dimensional Cauac Monsters with three-dimensional, half-figure sculptures of Maize Gods placed in the craggy clefts of their heads (Plate 57). The facade of the structure once featured a great reptilian monster mouth at its entrance. The lords stepped onto his lower jaw and then passed through the mouth of a great Bicephalic Monster to enter the inner sanctum, a room probably designated for ritual bloodletting. While the nobility let blood in the inner sanctum, maize flourished on the exterior of the building, suggesting that the king's most potent substance, his blood, flowed to fertilize and regenerate nature itself.

It is unlikely that the king and his retinue were involved in tending maize, but they undoubtedly monitored the progress of maize crops in the raised fields within their provinces. The king probably performed many rituals tied to the development of a crop; he may, for example, have sown the first kernels ot led the reapers to the fields. Some evidence suggests that royal women may have also performed rituals based on the labor of ordinary women. *Manos* and *metates*, grindstones for maize, are frequently recovered from palace debris by archaeologists not, we assume, because elite women were grinding corn day in and day out, but because maize was ground ritually for certain celebrations. Harvest festivities, for example, were probably celebrated with the royal persons directing the populace in gathering and preparing the first fruits.

Many rituals were celebrated in the courts of the Classic Maya. Although many formal representations of ritual convey solemn behavior, other objects indicate that the behavior of the Maya was not always staid and controlled. Painted pottery shows scenes of revelry that have passed beyond a dignified state, and intoxicated individuals sometimes appear deep in debauchery. A memorable Jaina figurine in the Heye Foundation collection depicts an old man who has drunk just enough (Plate 58). He grips his double-chambered jug in one hand and holds his chin with the other. His loincloth has slipped below his chubby belly and the befuddled expression on his noble face suggests that the motive for this celebration no longer matters.

Intoxicating brews were frequently the cause of drunkenness, and when the besotted Maya nobility could drink no more, they sometimes took such liquids as enemas. Intoxicating plants were also consumed, sometimes by direct ingestion, but also in the form of mind-altering snuffs and tobaccos.[28] On a carved piece of conch shell, a seated male puffs on a thin rolled cigar, probably made of native wild tobacco, which was a strong drug. Rendered in delicate incision, he epitomizes Maya courtiers (Plate 59). He is seated on a throne or step with an elaborate cushion, and simply dressed with the upper body garment suggested only by a crosshatch pattern across his chest. His headdress is a full deer head with the long, floppy ears typical of the small deer native to the jungle. Dots of blood, or possibly face paint, mark the man's nose and chin. While smoking, he beckons a serpent who emerges from the conch shell in front of him. Both the image and the text of this shell are unique in Maya art, but it reveals one of the many rituals that are now entirely lost to us. The refined dress, graceful hands and well-shaped fingernails of this figure belong to a courtier. The remarkable pictorial quality of this shell suggests that even in ritual the Maya were able to evoke a mood of relaxed elegance.

The principal subject of Maya arts is ritual but, almost in passing, their artists observed details of daily life. Judging from extant works, the Maya lived well. Their textiles were beautifully woven, their garments elaborate, their jewelry crafted of precious materials. They had ample food and enjoyed intoxicating substances. The complexity of their society is revealed in the elaborate titles borne by the extensive nobility, who were carefully differentiated from one another. Although we do not see all the elements of Maya culture, the treasures they left indicate what things were regarded as important, such as writing, carving, textile and ceramic arts. Their small scale arts, in particular, reveal a sophisticated view of human behavior. The foibles of an old man can be viewed with gentle humor, the sexuality of young women with keen interest. In no other works of Maya art do we come so close to a view of the world that we identify with ourselves.

NOTES

1. Based on the limited archaeological materials available to him, Peter Harrison decided that residence was one of the possible functions of the Central Acropolis at Tikal. The unexplored structures south of the Central Acropolis—like the great number of platforms on the Piedras Negras map that directly adjoin the West Acropolis stone palace, or like the mound just south of the Main Acropolis at Copan—were more likely the hearths of domestic life for the royal family, particularly during the Late Classic period. Neither in the West Acropolis nor at the Central Acropolis was sufficient refuse of ordinary, domestic life from Late Classic contexts recovered to argue for a large domestic population (Peter Darcy Harrison, *The Central Acropolis, Tikal, Guatemala: A Preliminary Study of the Functions of Its Structural Components During the Late Classic Period* [Ph.D diss., University of Pennsylvania, 1970]). Complexes like Groups 2, 3 and 4 at Palenque or like the Sepulturas Group at Copan, however, may have been palaces in which domestic and ritual life transpired.

2. Oddly enough, the map of Bonampak itself includes no such palace, but that may be a function of the extremely limited portion of the site that has been documented. Early observers of Maya ruins, among

them John Lloyd Stephens, termed such configurations *palaces*. The validity of the name has been questioned in recent years, and writers have sometimes substituted the ungainly term *range-type structure* for *palace* in order to avoid implying meaning. The word *palace* is used here, and the implications it carries for meaning are accepted.

3. Tatiana Proskouriakoff first noted the glyph now identified as *cahal*, and she called persons with this title members of the "moon-sign family" ("Historical Data in the Inscriptions of Yaxchilan, Part 1," in *Estudios de Cultura Maya*, vol. 3 [Mexico City: Universidad Nacional Autónoma de México, 1963], pp. 149–167). David Stuart has now worked out the phonetic value of this title and some of its sociological implications, and we are indebted to him for his work on the subject ("Epigraphic Evidence of Political Organization in the Usumacinta Drainage" [unpublished manuscript of 1983, provided by the author]). See also Peter Mathews and John S. Justeson, "Patterns of Sign Substitution in Mayan Hieroglyphic Writing: 'The Affix Cluster,' " in *Phoneticism in Mayan Hieroglyphic Writing*, edited by John S. Justeson and Lyle Campbell, Institute for Mesoamerican Studies, Pub. 9 (Albany: State University of New York at Albany, 1984), pp. 212–213.

4. Ruler 3 of Piedras Negras is recorded elsewhere as having been born on 9.11.12.7.2, six years after this event, although the glyphs of the caption resemble his name. The period ending of the monument is 9.11.15.0.0; by that time, Ruler 3 would have been nearly three years of age. He could not, therefore, even have *attended* the earlier events of the lintel. His representation here may indicate that the intended caption, perhaps for a boy who died, was not carved, and that Ruler 3's name was substituted—or it may indicate that whoever was to become Ruler 3 would have a certain name within the family, regardless of which son eventually took the throne.

5. This is also the case with the title called "rodent bone" and the title read *bacab*, both of which are widely used.

6. Morley came to different conclusions regarding the meaning of Lintel 2: "What is the meaning of this scene? Is it to be interpreted objectively as a conqueror receiving the submission of vanquished rulers, or is it to be interpreted allegorically, as representing the conflict of certain heavenly bodies, some myth of their astrologic pantheon? It is difficult to say. Judging from the general subject matter of the Maya inscriptions, which have been found to deal almost exclusively, in so far as they have been deciphered, with time in some of its various manifestations, this picture would represent some astronomic phenomenon, the triumph of one celestial body over a group of others." Morley noticed the helmet glyph in the text and correctly identified its use at Palenque as well, but he determined that it referred to the moon (Sylvanus G. Morley, *Inscriptions of Peten*, vol. 3, Carnegie Institution of Washington, Pub. 437 [Washington, D.C.: Carnegie Institution of Washington, 1937–1938], pp. 96–97).

7. For comparison, the numbers of the ninth-century Japanese royal family might be considered. In A.D. 870, 429 men and 262 women of the royal family were issued official court clothing; 5,000 other bureaucrats were also granted garments. Unlike the Maya, of course, there was only one royal family in Japan, and its members all lived in Heian-kyo (Kyoto); given the many royal families of the Maya, we might expect their size to be much smaller (Murai Yasuhiko, *Heian kizoku no sekai* [*The World of the Heian Nobility*] [Tokyo: Tokuma shoten, 1968], p. 31).

8. It is even possible that inbreeding in the royal families led to occasional dwarves in the royal house. For a fuller consideration, see Virginia E. Miller, "The Dwarf in Classic Maya Art," in *Fourth Palenque Round Table*, gen. ed. Merle Greene Robertson, vol. ed. Virginia Fields (San Francisco: Pre-Columbian Art Research Institute, forthcoming).

9. William L. Fash, Jr., "The Sculpture Facade of Structure 9N-82: Content, Form and Meaning," in *The House of the Bacabs*, edited by David Webster (Washington, D.C.: Dumbarton Oaks, forthcoming).

10. Identification made by David Stuart in a letter to Stephen Houston, July 29, 1985. Stuart determined the reading *ah tz'ib* and identified its use in the Primary Standard Sequence and as a scribal title, as well as an epithet for God D, Itzamna.

11. Alfred M. Tozzer, ed. and trans., "Landa's Relación de las cosas de Yucatan: A Translation," *Papers of the Peabody Museum of Archaeology and Ethnology, Harvard University* 18 (New York: Kraus Reprint Corp., 1966), n. 146.

12. He reads a codex on a carved Highland Guatemala pot (E. P. Dieseldorff, *Kunst und Religion der Mayavölker* [Berlin: Verlag von Julius Springer, 1926], pl. 32). This pot is reproduced and its meaning identified in Michael D. Coe, "Supernatural Patrons of Maya Scribes and Artists," in *Social Process in Maya Prehistory: Studies in Honour of Sir Eric Thompson*, edited by Norman Hammond (New York: Aca-

demic Press, 1977), p. 332. On vessel no. 7 in Michael D. Coe, *Lords of the Underworld* (Princeton, N.J.: The Art Museum, 1978), God D wears the attire of the scribe. In Nicholas M. Hellmuth, *Tzakol and Tepeu Maya Pottery Paintings* (Guatemala City: Foundation for Latin American Anthropological Research, 1976), fig. 29, an enthroned God D receives a quetzal and a parrot from a child; he wears the pectoral of many scribes, and his name, Itzamna, is prefaced by the name of God N, who, as we shall see below, is also often a scribe. In Landa's *Relación de las cosas de Yucatan*, it is also recorded that during festivities for the month of Mac, celebrants daubed and painted architecture, invoking Itzamna.

13. For summary of the Popol Vuh account of the Hero Twins, see Chap. 6.

14. Dennis Tedlock, *Popol Vuh: The Definitive Edition of the Mayan Book of the Dawn of Life and the Glories of Gods and Kings* (New York: Simon and Schuster, 1985), p. 121. The summary of the Monkey Scribe tale given here also depends upon Tedlock's translation (pp. 120–124).

15. For this identification, see the thorough argument in Michael D. Coe, "Supernatural Patrons of Maya Scribes and Artists," pp. 327–347.

16. Dennis Tedlock, *Popol Vuh*, p. 120.

17. In the paintings at both Cacaxtla and Bonampak, the defeated wear Olmec jades, as if in reference to antiquity.

18. For archaeological context and interpretation, see William L. Fash, Jr., "The Sculpture Facade of Structure 9N-82: Content, Form and Meaning."

19. God N, speaking numbers and reading from a codex, appears to chew out two inferiors on Vessel 56, in Francis Robicsek and Donald M. Hales, *The Maya Book of the Dead: The Ceramic Codex* (Charlottesville: University of Virginia Art Museum, 1981).

20. Alfredo Barrera Vasquez, *Diccionario Maya Cordemex* (Mérida: Ediciones Cordemex, 1980), p. 546.

21. See No. 11, Francis Robicsek and Donald M. Hales, *Maya Ceramic Vases from the Late Classic Period: The November Collection of Maya Ceramics* (Charlottesville: University of Virginia Art Museum, 1982). We are indebted to Karl Taube for drawing our attention to the association between the personification of the number 13 and the courtly arts.

22. Or so we imagine—the panel is fragmentary, and only two figures named "4 Pauahtun" survive. To their left, two more individuals (only fragments of whom survive today) were once seated; nothing remains of additional captions.

23. John M. Longyear, *Copan Ceramics: A Study of Southeast Maya Pottery*, Carnegie Institution of Washington, Pub. 597 (Washington, D.C.: Carnegie Institution of Washington, 1952), p. 111. Longyear also noted the resemblance of the male figure on the bone to one on Copan Stela 11. We might also note here that we use the Nahuatl terms *huipil* and *xicolli* to name Maya garments, even though these words are not native Mayan.

24. See, for example, the illustration of the Atamaqualiztli festival, held every eight years, in *Primeros Memoriales de Fray Bernardino de Sahagun*, translated by Wigberto Jimenez Moreno (Mexico City: Instituto Nacional de Antropología e Historia, 1974), pl. 6.

25. Elizabeth P. Benson ("From the Island of Jaina: A Maya Figurine," *Bulletin of the Detroit Institute of Arts* 57, no. 3 [1979], pp. 93–103) also suggested that the moon goddess's mate might be God N. Supporting evidence for this interpretation comes from a ceramic fragment from Uaxactun, where a God N looks on while a monkey fondles a naked, reclining woman (Robert Smith, *Ceramic Sequence at Uaxactun, Guatemala*, Middle American Research Institute, pub. 20, vol. 2 [New Orleans: Middle American Research Institute, Tulane University, 1955], fig. 2r).

26. The other known vessels by the painter of the Fenton vase are to be found in the following publications: Michael D. Coe, *The Maya Scribe and His World* (New York: Grolier Club, 1973), no. 26 (battle scene); ibid., *Lords of the Underworld*, no. 19 (tribute scene); Kerr photo files, #1392 (tribute scene); and Kerr photo files, #2206 (battle scene). See also A. Ledyard Smith and Alfred V. Kidder, *Excavations at Nebaj, Guatemala*, Carnegie Institution of Washington, Pub. 594 (Washington, D.C.: Carnegie Institution of Washington, 1951).

27. After years of oblivion, the Maize God was rejuvenated by Karl Taube in "The Maya Maize God: A Reappraisal," in *Fifth Palenque Round Table, Vol. 7*, gen. ed. Merle Greene Robertson, vol. ed. Virginia Fields (San Francisco: Pre-Columbian Art Research Institute, 1985), pp. 171–181.

28. See the comments of Peter A. G. M. de Smet, *Ritual Enemas and Snuffs in the Americas* (Dordrecht, Holland: Foris Publications, 1985), pp. 92–93.

PLATE 38
Wall paintings
Room 1, Bonampak, Mexico
Late Classic period, A.D. 800
Polychromed stucco

Discovered in 1946, the paintings at Bonampak reveal the rich court life enjoyed by the Maya during the eighth century. Even at the small site of Bonampak, hundreds of individuals were involved in the rituals associated with heir designation. The celebrations continued for at least two years and included events such as warfare and human sacrifice. In this copy of the paintings of Room 1, made by Felipe Davalos and Kees Grootenberg, damaged portions of the painting have been reconstructed. The hard, flat colors used in this reconstruction are probably characteristic of Maya painting.

In the first scene, upper register, of Room 1 Bonampak, a small child is presented to a court of *ahaus* on 9.18.0.3.4, or December 14, A.D. 790. From a chamber in a multi-galleried palace, King Chaan-muan, attended by his wife and some children, directs the proceedings while portly *ahaus* in white robes give their sanction to the child, ensuring his status as a legitimate member of the lineage. This scene is underscored by the text and framed by the parasols that reach from the lower register.

In the second scene, the principal lords of Bonampak, including Chaan-muan, dress for a celebration held 336 days after the first scene. Individuals labeled *ah na:ab* attend them, straightening a loincloth here, tying a wristlet there. The lords are nearly costumed, lacking only their feather backframes, which are being set in place in this scene. The lords are fully attired on the lower register, where they dance at the center of a great procession. Musicians and men in exotic costume, also titled *ah na:ab*, flank the right side of Chaan-muan and his two companions. A procession of *cahals* forms to the left of the lords. This great celebration was probably offered in honor of the new heir. It was set on a date of astronomical interest, 9.18.1.2.0, or November 15, A.D. 791, a day when Venus rose as Evening Star, and a date that may have been chosen to assure that the young dynast would be a great warrior. A broad cross-section of the Maya hierarchy attends his celebration at court.

This turtle-shell drummer is from the procession of musicians in Room 1 at Bonampak who play percussion and trumpet music for a dance ritual. The drummer, wearing a white headdress, is shown against an intense blue ground that represents an exterior setting. His profile with its sloping

forehead is distinctively Maya: the result of skull deformation practiced on infants. The distinctive forehead slope was an important ethnic feature of Lowland Maya peoples during the Classic period civilization that, here, enhances the curvature of this man's large nose. The open, relaxed mouth completes the characteristic visage of the Classic Maya nobles. These features were apparently admired as the most refined and elegant; conversely, humiliated captives are often depicted with blunt noses and domed foreheads. The rich red skin tone and dark eyes are quite realistic and consistent with features of contemporary Maya.

PLATE 39
Effigy vessel
Central Peten, Guatemala
Early Classic period, A.D. 400–550
Polychromed ceramic
University of East Anglia, Norwich, England

This finely dressed fellow wears jaguar skin as a painted pelt wrapped around his body and adorning his helmet. He sits with his body twisted as if he were looking over his shoulder. The color, painted in pure pigment suspended in a slip medium, sometimes follows the three-dimensional form but in other places, such as the armbands or earflares, it is added without regard for the contour of the clay.

PLATE 40
Lintel 2
Piedras Negras, Guatemala
Late Classic period, A.D. 667
Limestone
91.5 x 122 cm
Peabody Museum of Archaeology and Ethnology, Harvard University
Photo by Hillel Burger

Teobert Maler discovered Lintel 2 in the debris of Structure 0-13 at Piedras Negras and moved it to the Peabody Museum at Harvard University (which had sponsored his explorations), where the stone has been since. Although this monument is called a lintel, it was probably not used as such in Structure 0-13 at Piedras Negras, but rather as an exterior wall panel. Morley noted long ago that, since Lintel 2 records a seventh century ruler, it appears to have been taken from an earlier construction and reused in Structure 0-13. Structure 0-13, a nine-level funerary monument, is stylistically related to monuments dating to the second half of the eighth century (when this building was probably constructed) and may house the tombs of the late eighth-century Rulers 5 and 6. The use of earlier

sculptures of Piedras Negras lords indicates that Structure 0-13 was undoubtedly the focus of ancestor worship at the site, and the king who built it assembled and reused images of power and antiquity. Lintel 2 may have come from an earlier building on the same site and was reset as the centerpiece of an exterior sculptural program.

This impressive carved stone panel features eight persons dressed in nearly identical costume; they wear domed and plated caps topped by the so-called Mexican year, or trapeze-and-ray, sign. The six kneeling individuals at left are clearly subordinate to the two standing lords at right. Each figure carries a square shield; the Central Mexican owl and Tlaloc adorning the two at the right reinforce the similarity in costume between the two different regions of Mesoamerica, central Mexico and the Maya region. They all wear capes composed of individual broad strips (sometimes mistaken for sleeves), which are often worn by warriors and lords both at Teotihuacan and in the Maya area. This male attire may symbolize the warrior that each of the youths on Lintel 2 hopes to become.

A Late Classic king, Ruler 2 of Piedras Negras, is named as the protagonist of this monument. The subject of the scene can be understood through an examination of the text, which frames the sides and upper margin of this relief.

A1-B1 : 9.11.6.2.1 (October 24, A.D. 658)
C1 : 3 Imix
D1 : G5
C2 : F
D2 : 19 days since the beginning of lunation
E1 : D
F1 : Five months of lunar half year completed
E2 : Glyph X
F2 : 29-day month
G1 : 19 Ceh
H1 : ahau-in-hand event
G2 : helmet
H2–11 : name, Ruler 2
J1 : agency
I2 : his blood
J2 : *Yax na:ab*
K1 : Chac-Xib-Chac
L1–K2 : 8 Imix-compound; 1 Imix-compound
L2 : GIII (Jaguar God of the Underworld)
M1–N1 : he let blood (fish-in-hand)
M2–N2 : the Piedras Negras *ahau*

The first statement after the dates is "ahau-in-hand," a display event that usually refers to the display of God K. Since a helmet immediately follows the verb "ahau-in-hand" and all the figures wear

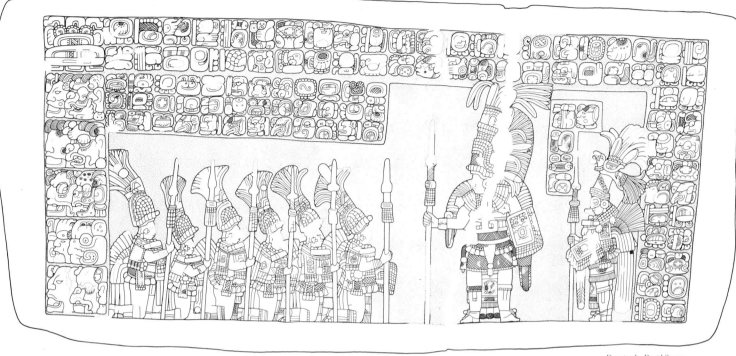

PLATE 40a

Drawing by David Stuart

helmets, it appears that this lintel commemorates the display of this attire; the person who celebrates the event is Ruler 2 of Piedras Negras. The *Yax na:ab* glyph at J2 generally indicates some sort of agency, and it might be paraphrased "under the auspices of." The agents here include Chac-Xib-Chac and the Jaguar God of the Underworld from the Palenque Triad. The statement is written as a dyadic couplet, and the "fish-in-hand" glyph indicates that a bloodletting event was also performed on the same day by Ruler 2.

O1–P1 : 8 Chicchan 3 Ceh (9.3.16.0.5, November 13, A.D. 510)
O2 : ahau-in-hand
P2–Q2 : name
R2 : ahau k'in, a priestly title
S1 : agency
T1–S2 : deity names?
T2 : fist title
U1–V2 : titles: *Na:ab tun, chik'in* (west) batab
W1 : count forward
X1–W3 : 16 k'in, 1 Uinal, 5 tuns, 7 katuns
X3 : from 9.3.16.0.6 to reach the date 9.11.6.2.1.

These calculations required there to be an error in the distance number: it should be 7.*10*.1.16 rather than 7.5.1.16 as written, in order to connect the two dates. This number unites two like events, one illustrated on the panel, and the other as it was performed by an ancestor 150 years before.

W4 : ahau-in-hand (event; same as H1 and O2)
X4–X6 : names and titles of Ruler 2
W7–X7 : Piedras Negras *ahau*
W8–W9 : 11 k'in, 12 uinals, 8 tuns, 1 katun
X9–W10 : after he had been seated as king
X10 : Ruler 2
W10–X11 : and then it came to pass, the day 4 Ahau 13 Mol, 5 tuns lacking to the katun, 9.11.15.0.0, July 28, A.D. 667

Glyph captions of individuals depicted:
YZ : a Bonampak *ahau*
A'B' : a Yaxchilan *ahau*
C'D' : a Bonampak *ahau*
E'F' : a Bonampak *ahau*
G'H' : a Bonampak *ahau*
I'J' : a Bonampak *ahau*

K'L' : Xul, Ah cauac (names associated with Ruler 3 of Piedras), Rodent Bone title, Piedras Negras emblem, *ahau*

Since the Initial Series date celebrates the "ahau-in-hand" and bloodletting ritual, this event is probably the subject of the scene. With the exception of the standing ruler, the individuals depicted on the lintel are all boys, not men; were the kneeling figures to stand, they would be the same height as the child behind the ruler, apparently youths about twelve years of age. The celebration displaying the helmet may have been an initiation ritual in which royal youths for the first time donned battle dress or engaged in bloodletting.

Lintel 2 was originally flanked by Lintel 1, of which only a fragment survives today in Harvard's Peabody Museum, and Lintel 3, which was discovered in the debris of Piedras Negras in 1936 and taken to the National Museum in Guatemala City. The composition of Lintel 2 (Pl. 40a) resembles that of yet another stone, Lintel 12, dated to A.D. 514, now in the National Museum, Guatemala City. At the time of the construction of Structure 0-13, Lintel 12 was cut in half and used as two building blocks, perhaps like cornerstones, in the superstructure. On that monument, three of the four warriors who attend the Piedras Negras ruler have their hands bound. The text on this lintel names Knot-eye Jaguar of Yaxchilan, who, like the *ahaus* of Lintel 2, had reason to be represented at Piedras Negras, either as a victorious or defeated warrior.

PLATE 41
Dwarf with flayed skin
Late Classic period, A.D. 700–900
Ceramic
12 x 6 cm
Department of Anthropology, American Museum of Natural History, New York

PLATE 42
Dwarf with moustache and shield
Late Classic period, A.D. 700–900
Ceramic
H. 12.5 cm.
The Art Museum, Princeton University. Gift of J. Lionberger Davis

PLATE 43
Dwarf with spangled turban
Late Classic period, A.D. 700–900
Ceramic
H. 12.9 cm
The Art Museum, Princeton University. Gift of J. Lionberger Davis

At the Maya court, just as at the court of the Aztec ruler Motecuhzoma, dwarfs were special courtiers who entertained the royal family. In monumental stone carvings, Maya dwarfs are usually shown dressed in the same costumes as the lords they attend. These three small terracotta dwarfs are all dressed differently, perhaps reflecting different costumes of lords that they attended in the grave. All three are figurines of the type generally associated with Jaina, a burial island off the Campeche coast, where hundreds of small, mold-made and hand modeled figurines have been recovered from both primary graves that originally contained fleshed corpses and secondary burials of desiccated bones. The figurines vary widely in quality, from small sculptural masterpieces to poorly made, mass-produced examples. Some of the images commonly produced as figurines are rare in other media. For example, females depicting the moon goddess (Plates 51, 52, 53) and dwarfs occur more frequently in terracotta sculpture than as subjects on painted ceramics. These less formal figures may

have been regarded as appropriate for burial offerings in the Campeche region.

The dwarf from the American Museum of Natural History wears a turban strapped to his head; face patches, probably painted or tattooed, or perhaps some kind of pelt, mark his cheeks (Plate 41). Another figure, nicknamed Yosemite Sam because of his resemblance to the Warner Brothers cartoon character, is dressed as a warrior who carries an elaborate headdress and shield (Plate 42). The paper strips shown running through his earlobes are those used by warriors, captives and those undergoing bloodletting. A figurine of especially regal bearing (Plate 43), wears the large spangled turban characteristic of scribes and resembles figures on the Fenton vase (Plate 54). His simple, elegant attire and visible paunch suggest that he lives a life of ease.

PLATE 44
Cylindrical vessel with lords and scribes
Tomb 27–42, Copan, Honduras
Late Classic period, A.D. 600–700
Incised ceramic
Diam. 14.5 x H. 16.5 cm
Instituto Hondureño de Antropología e Historia, Tegucigalpa, Honduras

This fine piece of burnished brownware was made during the seventh century. The design was incised and cut into the surface after the clay had dried to the hardness of leather. The background was daubed with a thin white wash or slip, and the glyphs added in the same medium, before the vessel was fired. The pot shows little wear; probably, shortly after its manufacture, it was deposited in Tomb 27-42, dated by context to the seventh century.

The text appears only below the rim and records a Primary Standard Sequence. The second

glyph, which can be read *ah tz'ib*, or, "he of the writing," suggests that the four figures shown engage in the scribal arts. But, unlike the scribe excavated from Structure 9N-82, these figures have beautiful, youthful human faces, and their courtly gestures reveal them to be cultivated young men.

The first individual is a monkey scribe who is shown working as an artisan, not as a writer, carving a mask or, perhaps, a human face. He bears characteristic markings of the monkey scribes such as the "printout" marked on the stylized tree, the deer ear tucked over his own, as well as maize foliage. Behind him, a second seated person gestures; he is not identified clearly as a scribe. Like Person 1, god markings on his body indicate his supernatural quality. Person 3 has the deer ear of scribes, although he is idle. Person 4 is the only member of the quartet who lacks god markings. He alone sits with his torso presented frontally, his hands raised in an active gesture, finger pressed to the thumb. Like other scribes, he wears a deer ear.

In 1952, John Longyear wrote that this was "surely the finest ceramic object ever found at Copan," a judgment that still holds true. Its clean, strong lines and calligraphic quality raise the possibility that codex-style pots, long thought to come from the Peten, might have a different origin.

PLATE 45
Jade pendant
Olmec Early or Middle Preclassic period, 1000–600 B.C.
Maya inscription, Late Preclassic or Protoclassic period, 150 B.C.–A.D. 150
Jade
8.4 x 12.1 x 2.9 cm
Anonymous loan to The Brooklyn Museum

This large flat plaque of light bluish-green jade was carved by an Olmec artist before 600 B.C. from stone that had been imported from the region that

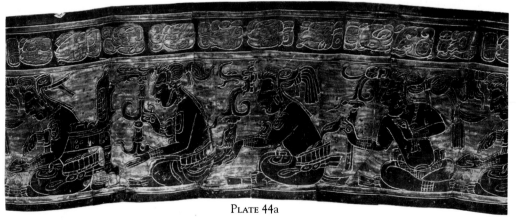

PLATE 44a

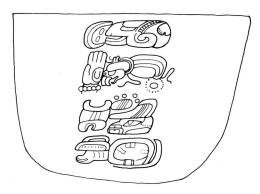

PLATE 45a

is now Costa Rica to the Olmec heartland along the Gulf of Mexico. With its fleshy, downturned lips and slanted eyes, it conforms to Olmec canons of beauty.

Five or six hundred years later, this Olmec jade was acquired by an early Maya lord, who inscribed his own name on its back. From the beginning of Maya civilization, writing was of primary importance, and among its first uses was labeling an object as one's own. The Maya text on this jade (Pl. 45a) may have been inscribed during the Late Preclassic period: the rounded, unusual form of the glyphs suggests an early date. The first glyph is the earliest known example of an auxiliary verb, which functions to introduce names or additional verbal statements. Here it is followed by either a name or another verb. The third glyph begins with a bone, followed by the glyph for God C, or blood. The juxtaposition of this symbol with the second glyph suggests that it is a verb related to bloodletting. The final glyph, a title suggesting "the well-endowed man," probably refers to the protagonist of the event.

Perhaps when it was recarved, this plaque was cut down at the sides and holes were drilled so that it could be worn. Olmec jades of human faces that were used and reworked by Maya artists are rare, but the Olmec jade tradition was widely known.

PLATE 46
God N Monkey Scribe
Structure 9N-82, Copan, Honduras
Late Classic period, A.D. 600–800
Stone
H. 55.6 cm
Instituto Hondureño de Antropología e Historia, Tegucigalpa, Honduras

From 1980 to 1982, the Proyecto Arqueologico de Copan excavated Structure 9N-82 in the Sepulturas compound, which stood on the site of an earlier structure. In separate trenches made nine meters apart, archaeologists fortuitously recovered the pieces of this three-dimensional sculpture. The body was in halves and the head had been removed and burned prior to the interment of the entire sculpture and the construction of the new building.

This monkey scribe, about half the size of an average human, may once have been set in a niche or simply kept inside a structure. He sits cross-legged, hunched slightly forward, wearing only a loincloth. In his right hand he holds a writing or daubing instrument, and in his left a section of a conch shell, cut to serve as a paint or ink pot. Like many monkey scribes, he has an ugly face—one rendered as hideous as the Maya ever conceived a face to be—but executed with loving care. This face avoids Maya standards of beauty: wide and flat with a flat pug nose, it is a striking contrast to the faces, and particularly the noses, of kings. His eyes are small and asymmetrically placed and the lines around his mouth are not quite even. The Maya artist also recognized that these monkey artisans were inherently human; except for the face, the anatomy is that of a human male, right down to the slight paunch of the belly. The most common attribute of the monkey scribes, a deer ear, is tucked over his own.

The net headdress, or *pauah*, that he wears characterizes God N, and the cluster of round markings, like a bunch of grapes, on his upper arm indicate the reading *tun*, suggests that his name is a composite of these reading *Pauahtun*, the name of God N. The Maya pantheon had a number of supernaturals who write, paint, and carve, including Gods N and D, whose characteristics can combine with those of the monkey scribes to form a new hybrid.

During the reign of Yax-Pac at Copan, Structure 9N-82 was rebuilt, but it retained the emphasis of the scribal arts in its sculptural program. Three dimensional sculptures of scribes set on the facade may have paid tribute to scribes who contributed to the flowering of the arts during the entire eighth century.

PLATE 47
Cylindrical pot with monkey scribes
Late Classic period, A.D. 600–800
Polychromed ceramic
H. 12.2 cm
New Orleans Museum of Art, Women's Volunteer Committee Fund

Hun Batz and Hun Chuen, whose names are sometimes translated One Monkey and One Artisan, were turned into monkeys by the Hero Twins, their twin half-brothers. The Popol Vuh describes Hun Batz and Hun Chuen as geniuses born with a supernatural talent for the arts, who were also subject to human foibles. They hated and mistreated their younger half-brothers who were demigods and who eventually maneuvered their transformation into monkeys.

Although these brothers were removed from the sphere of humans, Hun Batz and Hun Chuen remained the supernatural patrons of the arts, particularly writing, drawing and carving. On this vessel, they are depicted as scribes writing in open codices. These open-mouthed monkey scribes write furiously, their hands turning like whirlwinds. The frantic movement of their work is characterized by an active, energetic line. Deer ears ornament their soft, tied turbans, from the back of which grow stylized trees, referring to the trees that reduced them from man to monkey.

This pot is worked in white and black slip in the codex style, so called because of a projected similarity between these works and the style of long-lost Maya books. Several codex-style painters are recognized: this artist's work is characterized by an energetic, almost hasty line, which differs from the more careful work seen on other codex-style vessels.

PLATE 48
Cylindrical vessel
Late Classic period, A.D. 600–800
Polychromed ceramic
Diam. 15.8 x H. 25.8 cm
Kimbell Art Museum, Fort Worth

On each side of this handsome painted cylinder, a noble lord prepares to dance with a lady. The texts are not helpful in interpreting this vessel; the rim records a Primary Standard Sequence and the captions, one for each figure, are all monotonous repetitions of single glyphs. Since the rim text appears to be painted by a hand different from the painter of the figural scene, it is possible that the latter was not able to inscribe meaningful text.

Persons 2 and 5 appear to be the same individual, shown with two different women. The profile is identical in both depictions, and in both the figure wears a small goatee. This lord's head-dress is characterized by the band of jaguar pelt that binds it together and the small animal head at its front. He wears a hipcloth of cloth strips, and his loincloth appears to have flapped, cutout holes. In both scenes, he extends his right hand to the lady (although it is drawn as a left on Person 5), as if to take her hand in his.

Persons 1 and 4, the two ladies, are clearly different individuals, although each lifts her left foot off the ground as though in motion. Person 1 casts her eyes demurely at the lord, while Person 4 looks directly at him, opening her mouth wide, as if speaking angrily to him. Both women wear similar upper body *huipils* that just wrap around their chests with the ends of the cloth knotted between the breasts. The designs of the *huipils* might have been painted directly onto the cotton cloth. Their skirts differ; that of Person 4 has a simple diagonal design, while clustered circular motifs mark that of Person 1. Such designs could have been made by tie-dying, probably the technique indicated here.

Person 3 may be an attendant. He holds upright a baton that secondary figures in war scenes also bear, which may simply indicate his status. His position here, at the juncture between the two scenes, is also to guide the viewer. The nature of the action that is about to commence cannot be determined. It may be a simple dance; it may acknowledge the two wives of a given lord. In scenes that depict enema rituals, women frequently wear garments similar to those worn by the ladies on the Kimbell pot, and it is possible that this encounter between lord and ladies is the prelude to such an event.

PLATE 49
Carved jaguar bone
Late Classic period, A.D. 600–800
Bone
Diam. 2.0 x H. 13.0 x W. 2.9
The Art Museum, Princeton University. Gift of Frances Pratt in honor of Gillett G. Griffin

How this handle functioned in antiquity is not known. It may have held a great swatch of feathers or a fan, or it could have been the support for a perforator. The woman depicted in the delicate carving on this bone (Pl. 49a) may have been its owner, and she holds a similar object in her hand. On the basis of her costume, a long draping *huipil* that resembles one worn by a woman on the lintel of Temple II, Tikal, this bone can be dated to the Late Classic period, probably to the eighth century.

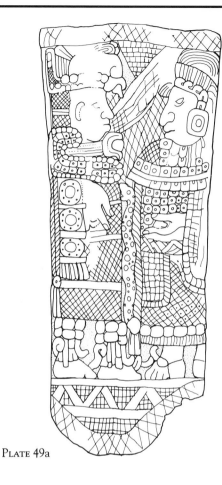

PLATE 49a

PLATE 50
Carved deer tibia
Copan, Honduras
Late Classic period, A.D. 750–800
Bone
24.6 x 5 cm
Instituto Hondureño de Antropología e Historia, Tegucigalpa, Honduras

The image of King Yax-Pac, the last ruler of Copan, is clearly inscribed on this bone (Pl. 50a), which was found sealed in a deep shaft in the floor of the central chamber of Structure 11, along with obsidian blades, bird bones and human teeth. Since Structure 11 at Copan commemorates the reign of Yax-Pac, this bone indicates that his reconstruction of the structure may have been completed before the end of his reign. It was undoubtedly a valued possession of Yax-Pac, which he may have personally deposited in the shaft when Temple 11 was under construction, or the entire offering may have been an ancient sacred bundle.

This inscribed deer tibia is one of the largest carved bones known. The text is simple: an eroded introductory verb is followed by Yax-Pac's name at B1; at B2–A3, he is named as a three-katun *ahau*; a *batab* title completes the inscription. An unnamed woman at the left, dressed simply in a jaguar pelt skirt, helps the king adjust his most intimate apparel, dressing or undressing him. This representation of Yax-Pac, with a beard and domed haircut, is very similar to his portrait on Stela 11, which is a posthumous monument set in front of Structure 18, his funerary pyramid. He and his female companion both stand on skyband symbols, but he is supported and elevated by a large Venus symbol.

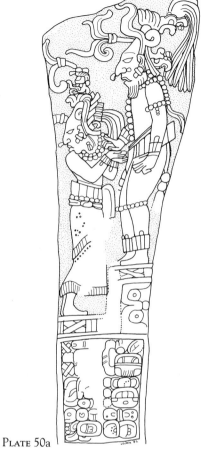

PLATE 50a

PLATE 51
Figurine of woman weaving
Late Classic period, A.D. 700–900
Ceramic
9.2 x 15.9 x 15 cm
Courtesy of the Museum of the American Indian, Heye
Foundation, New York

PLATE 52
Figurine of a voluptuous lady
Late Classic period, A.D. 700–900
Ceramic with traces of pigment
H. 22.5 cm
The Art Museum, Princeton University. Gift of
Gillett G. Griffin

PLATE 53
Figurine of couple embracing
Late Classic period, A.D. 700–900
Ceramic with traces of pigment
H. 24.7 cm
Detroit Institute of Arts, Founders Society Purchase,
Katherine Margaret Kay Bequest Fund and New Endowment Fund

Representations of Maya women occur more commonly as Jaina figurines than in any other medium. These Jaina figurines represent two kinds of women, both archetypes of female behavior. One is a stately, courtly woman who is sometimes shown weaving; the second is a courtesan who appears with all sorts of mates, from Underworld deities to oversized rabbits. The imagery of both derives from Maya concepts of the moon, perceived as an erratic, inconsistent heavenly body, whose constantly changing character follows the monthly cycle of female menses.

Weaving is usually an attribute of moon goddesses in Mesoamerica, and several Jaina figurines, including one at the Heye Foundation (Pl. 51), show this woman hard at work on her backstrap loom. Engaged in this industry, she resembles Xochiquetzal, the Central Mexican goddess associated with the moon and weaving who often appears at a loom. This same archetype also appears as a simple seated figure, her legs crossed and her hands extended to her knees. Her bearing is noble and her jewelry elegant. Her long hair is bound up in back and she has a characteristic narrow band of short, almost shingled, hair framing her face. The heads are often notched directly above the hairline, perhaps to support a perishable head ornament, but no such headdresses survive. The Heye weaver differs most dramatically from her counterparts in that her upper body is covered with a *huipil*.

The second female type is far more active, and she projects her sexuality. Like the woman portrayed in the Princeton and Detroit figurines, she is usually bare-breasted, and she gestures, as if offering herself to others (Plate 52). The demure woman may be painted in various colors, but this one is generally painted blue. Unspun cotton is twisted into her hair, a gesture retained even today by women who spin by hand. The cotton suggests that our blue moon goddess spins, but unlike her more reserved counterpart, this pretty woman is never seen working. Instead, she frequently appears paired with another figure: here (Plate 53), an ugly old man leers at her as he lifts her skirt and feels her thigh; she presses her knee to his groin, offering herself, and embraces him with her left hand as she reaches for his face with her right. His soft headdress could be a terracotta representation of God N's netted bag, and he may represent that deity. Like the erratic moon, this woman shifts, from one partner to another. The human ones are consistently aged, recalling the prevalence of unequal lovers in early sixteenth-century Northern Renaissance art, but the Maya woman also attaches herself to other beasts. She receives the affections, for example, of an oversized rabbit in one example at Princeton University. Nothing else in Maya art conveys sexuality more convincingly than these figures. Although they may be conceived as the moon goddess and her consorts, they also reflect human behavior. As companions for the dead—perhaps particularly for old men—they seem to promise renewed sexual activity. For the living, such Jaina figurines may have been titillating objects for private observation.

PLATE 54
Cylindrical vessel, The Fenton vase
Nebaj, Guatemala
Late Classic period, A.D. 600–800
Polychromed ceramic
Diam. 17.2 cm
The Trustees of The British Museum, London

This pot was excavated in Nebaj in Highland Guatemala in 1904, whence it came into the hands of the English collector C. L. Fenton, for whom it is named. In the past ten years, at least four other closely related cylinders have come to light, suggesting that a strong tradition, or perhaps a single artist, was responsible. Some of the *dramatis personae* that decorate the Fenton vase also appear on similar pieces. Thus, all supposedly come from Nebaj, but since limited excavations carried out at the site have not revealed a sherd painted in this style, they might very well have originated elsewhere.

Like the works by the Master of the Pink Glyphs, whose oeuvre commemorates the accession of the Fat Cacique, the pots by the Fenton Painter and his circle may have been commissioned by a single lord, perhaps to acknowledge a series of important, related events in his life. The examples known so far all depict scenes of warfare and the delivery of tribute, perhaps the latter a requisite of the former. These pots may record a sequential narrative, but our understanding of them is not sufficient to determine an order. The British Museum pot is the finest of the tribute scenes. It has, for example, more adventurous hand gestures than any other member of the group, so perhaps the Fenton Painter instructed the other painters. The themes and the loop that defines the ankle bone may be signatures of the style of the group, but the master himself drew unusual hands and feet. On this pot, the Fenton Painter draws graceful, nervous hands, the fingers configured in a U-shape by raised index and little fingers. Fingers broaden at the tip, and nails extend beyond the finger itself.

The Fenton vase records a scene of tribute that is delivered and tallied in a palace throne room. An enthroned lord (Person 3) points at the pile of cloth and food placed in front of him, as if to acknowledge its presentation from Lord 2, who kneels and gestures with an unusual object, perhaps a miniature fan or an oddly configured spondylus shell. Behind the lord on the throne, a smaller seated individual holds what appears to be a codex covered in a basket-weave pattern. If so, the long-skirted fellow who bends over it may be entering accounts. Two lords at either side of the scene form a visual frame, and a column of four glyphs of the Primary Standard Sequence divides the imagery.

The tribute deliverer is certainly not the abject captive of the enthroned lord, rather he might be his *cahal*. All figures on the pot wear the same basic headdress, but the enthroned lord wears the largest, most splendid version of it. The evidence of costume indicates that no individual on this vessel is of the inferior status of captive. The border of the kneeling attendant's loincloth is the same woven textile that is worn, carried or offered by all secondary lords on this group of vessels. This kneeling lord has an oddly drawn foot, perhaps intended to indicate a sandal or foreshortening, but the result is peculiar and no similar representation is known. All the figures on the vessel are drawn with expressive fingers (Person 5 has reversed right and left hands) that point with vigor at the objects around them. The basket set on the pile of tribute is trimmed with a chevron border, made perhaps of feathers, that recalls the Chama-style pots made in the Highlands, which also have chevron borders.

Each person is named by an individual hieroglyphic text placed near him. These five texts form frames that vaguely suggest palace architecture. The enthroned lord is named as a *bacab*; the *ah'*, "upended frog," glyph that follows is normally a birth verb, but since the syntax does not require a verb here, it may be another title. This glyph also accompanies the enthroned lord on a similar vessel and it may refer to him specifically. Other names and titles are shared among the five pots in this style. Longer Primary Standard Sequences are painted on the rim of the two battle pots and one other tribute scene. At the end of it, this same protagonist is apparently named as a 3-katun lord and the captor of prominent captives.

Most Maya ceramics retrieved intact come from tombs, where they have been preserved. This context may indicate that pots were primarily funerary vessels, but they may have had another meaning and function before the tomb. Nebaj pots, which record explicitly historical scenes, are usually recovered from burials, indicating that these Maya lords were buried with the pomp of their Lowland counterparts. But, to our knowledge, no stelae and wall panels were made at Nebaj or at other Highland sites, so perhaps ceramic vessels became the medium at Nebaj on which history as well as mythology was recorded.

PLATE 55
Cylindrical black ground vessel
Late Classic period, A.D. 600–800
Polychromed ceramic
H. 17.5 cm
New Orleans Museum of Art, Ella West Freeman Foundation Matching Fund

Like Greek red-figure vases, the black backgrounds of pots such as this example were painted first, leaving outlined spaces for figures in reserve. The figures were painted against the reserved lighter ground in the difficult medium of clay slip. Black-background pots were never very common among Maya ceramics, but those that survive have been recovered from Late Classic, and generally eighth-century, contexts.

Many Maya vases show two scenes of enthroned rulers. Frequently the same principal lord is repeated, but in this example, the lords are different, and each is identified by a hieroglyphic caption. In the rollout photograph of this vessel, the lord at the left sits on a simple throne and he is attended by a woman, who has apparently begun to feel his foot. We do not know the significance of this gesture, but her own foot is described by large ovoid toes that also characterize the foot of the attendant in the second scene. Both male and female are labeled by captions that end with the syllable, *chi*, whose meaning is not clear.

The second enthroned ruler sits on an elaborate throne whose legs bear glyphs like those on the thrones that have been recovered from Piedras Negras and Yaxchilan. The glyph on the leg at the right may read *ahau chaan*. The architectural support that frames this scene suggests the interior of a palace. The enthroned lord receives an offering of painted ceramics from a seated male attendant, who proffers a fine-quality ceramic vase with a cream ground and a double rim band text. A lidded pot already sits before the lord who prepares to accept this vessel. Both attendants and lords of this vessel have been rendered with either face or body paint, or possibly god markings, which may indicate that this scene transpires in a supernatural world.

PLATE 56
Head of a Maize God
Palenque, Chiapas, Mexico
Late Classic period, A.D. 600–750
Jade
3.6 x 5.2 x .4 cm
Courtesy of the Museum of the American Indian, Heye Foundation, New York

This beautiful jade head collected at Palenque many years ago represents the Maize God. The youthful head of this Maize God is carved into bright green stone that undoubtedly represents green corn, young but certain to reach maturity. The face is surrounded by cropped hair, symbolizing the corn silk, and surmounted by maize foliage. Unlike most Maya jades, this one has no holes for suspension, so it may have been designed to be held, warm and sensuous in the hand, rather than worn.

PLATE 57
Maize God
Temple 22, Copan, Honduras
Late Classic period, *ca.* A.D. 775
Stone
89.7 x 54.2 cm
The Trustees of The British Museum, London

Structure 22 at Copan was a palace of Yax-Pac, the last king. It is the most private structure on the Main Acropolis, reached only after passing through both the West and East Courts. The exterior facade of the structure was once a great monster mouth; his lower teeth are still *in situ* at the doorway and in entering one walks into his gullet. A Bicephalic Monster frames the interior doorway which leads to an elevated bench. According to the texts of such benches, this was a place reserved for the most private kingly rituals, including auto-sacrifice and perhaps yearly rites for the earth's fertility.

Two-dimensional Cauac-Monster faces once ornamented the exterior cornice level. From the clefts in their heads sprouted three-dimensional maize gods, including this example from the British Museum, the finest maize god known. The king's blood offerings made within the structure, where the monster mouth symbolized the heart of the earth, fertilized the maize that flourished on the exterior. The program not only acknowledges the importance of maize, the staff of life and the very composition of Maya mankind, but it also sets the king as its progenitor, giving bounty to all. The Maya conceived the beautiful face of this young man to be the cob of corn, his hair its silk. Undoubtedly they knew that each kernel of corn supported one single strand of cornsilk. The head is surrounded by foliage to indicate this is young, green maize, fully developed but not dried. Like a corn plant in the breeze, this maize god waves his hands, yet his closed eyes indicate that he is dead to this world.

This three-dimensional Maize God was once tenoned to the cornice of Structure 22. When Copan was abandoned and the building fell into ruin, the Maize Gods fell across the East Court like a ripened crop that was not harvested. This piece was excavated under the direction of Alfred P. Maudslay at the turn of this century.

PLATE 58
Figurine of a drunkard
Jaina Island, Mexico
Late Classic period, A.D. 700–900
Ceramic
36.4 x 14 x 9.5 cm
Courtesy of the Museum of the American Indian, Heye Foundation, New York

This large, solid Jaina figurine is a wonderful study of an older fellow, slightly in his cups, who raises his right hand to his beard as if wondering just where he is going. Carefully tucked under his left arm is a double-chambered pot that suggests the source of his befuddlement. The artist has carefully rendered the face to show the furrowed brow, beard and look of self-absorption. Elements of a mask decorate the false cheek pieces that reach from nose to ear. His loincloth droops below his slight paunch suggesting that he is not preoccupied with his appearance. Intoxication among the Maya may have been sanctioned during certain ritual celebrations, but this fellow may have ceased to care which occasion he is celebrating.

PLATE 59
Conch shell with scene of a smoking lord
Late Classic period, A.D. 600–800
Incised shell
H. 26.5 cm
The Cleveland Museum of Art, The Norweb Collection

Puffing away on a thin cigar of native American tobacco, *nicotiana rustica*, a drug stronger than modern, domesticated tobacco, this elegant lord reaches for the serpent whose head just emerges from the conch shell in front of him. The smoke from his cigar floats on the air, gently curving itself around the glyphs of his name. Although few of the glyphs are decipherable, the four of this caption appear to include a verb in the first two, then a jaguar name, and finally, "he of the blood," an expression that often accompanies royal names.

The scene is as unusual as the glyphs (Pl. 59a). The lord gestures gracefully, extending his hands in a mannered fashion, allowing us to see the long fingernails of an individual who never engaged in rough physical labor. He sits on a throne or step, and the glyphs underneath him form a pedestal support. His loincloth is worked in a woven, almost checkered, design, and his cushion is worked in what almost appears to be a jacquard weave, its border trimmed by a step-fret design. Across his chest are broadly incised designs that are intended to suggest either body paint or a garment. He wears a simple long bead around his neck, turned to one side. The dots on his face may indicate blood or body paint. The sharp, drilled eye is not common in Maya art, but it appears on monumental art most consistently at Bonampak. The lord's headdress is a full deer head helmet.

This finely incised, almost calligraphic, carving was made on a piece of conch (*Strombus gigas*, or Queen conch) and the pearly lustre of the nacre has survived intact. The line is sure and strong and may once have been filled with cinnabar, although no evidence of the substance remains. The incision of the body outline is deep and clean, while it is delicate and light for the textiles. The shell fits in the hand; it was a private object, made to be held and admired. The absence of drill holes suggests that it was not to be worn, but it may have been buried with its owner.

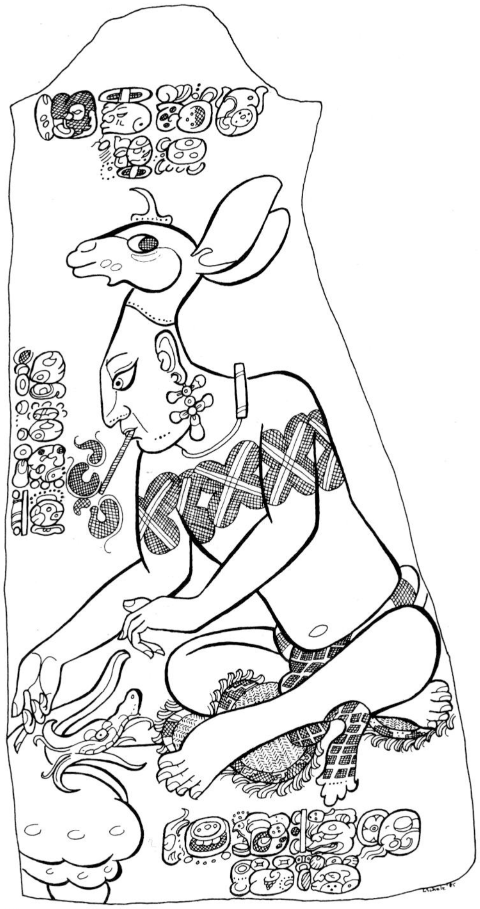
PLATE 59a

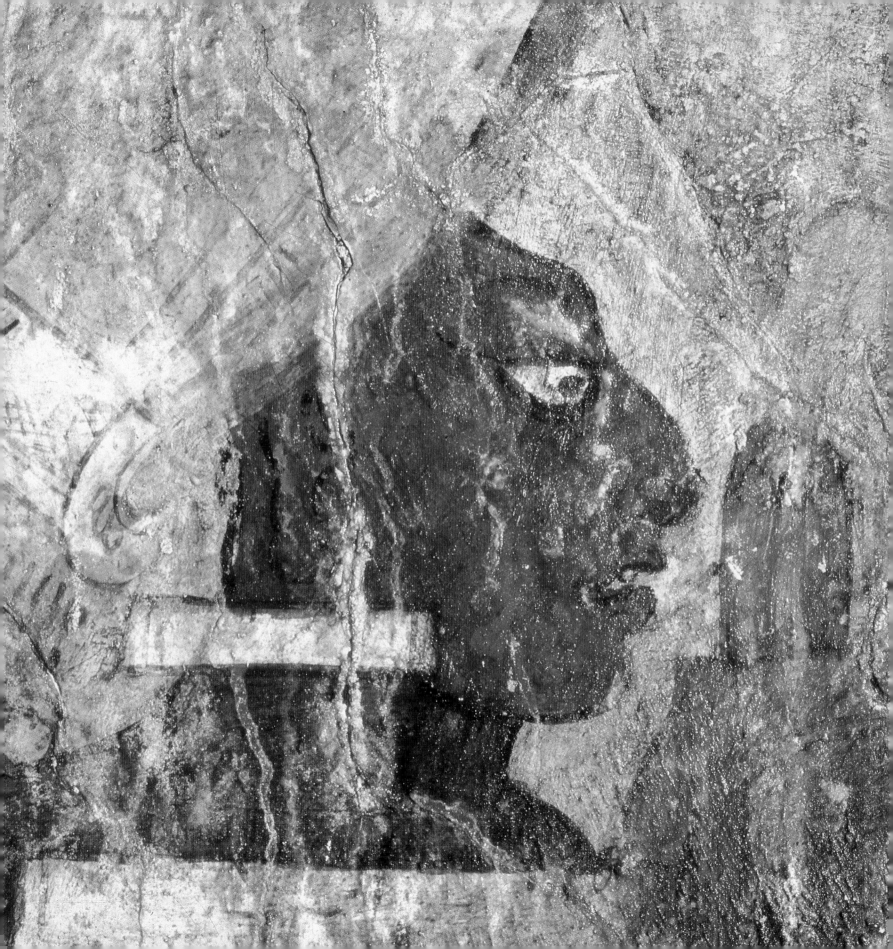

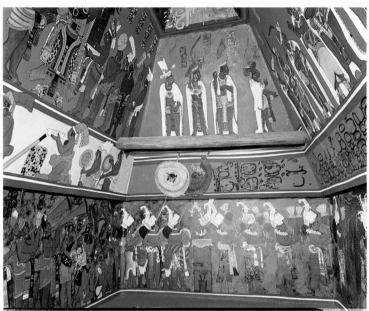

Plate 38b. East wall

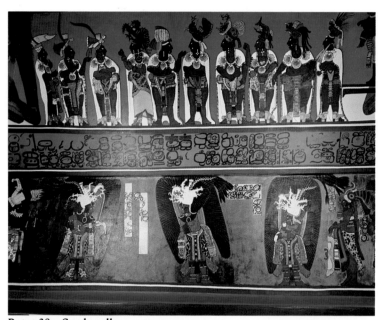

Plate 38c. South wall

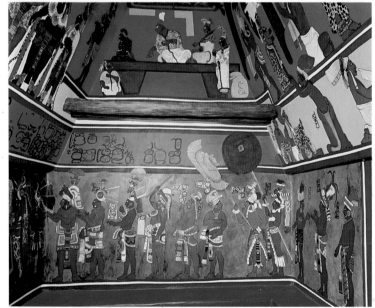

Plate 38d. West wall

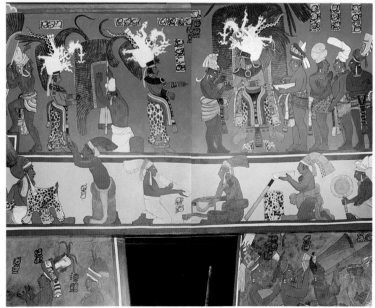

Plate 38e. North wall

Plate 40. Lintel 2

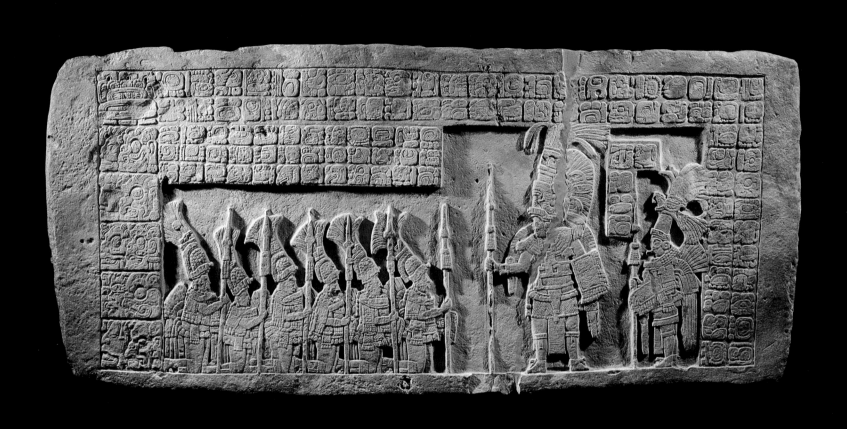

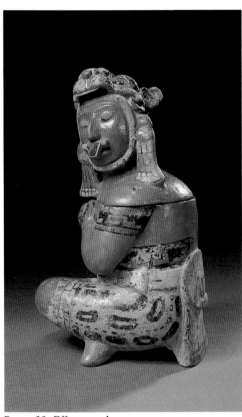

PLATE 39. Effigy vessel

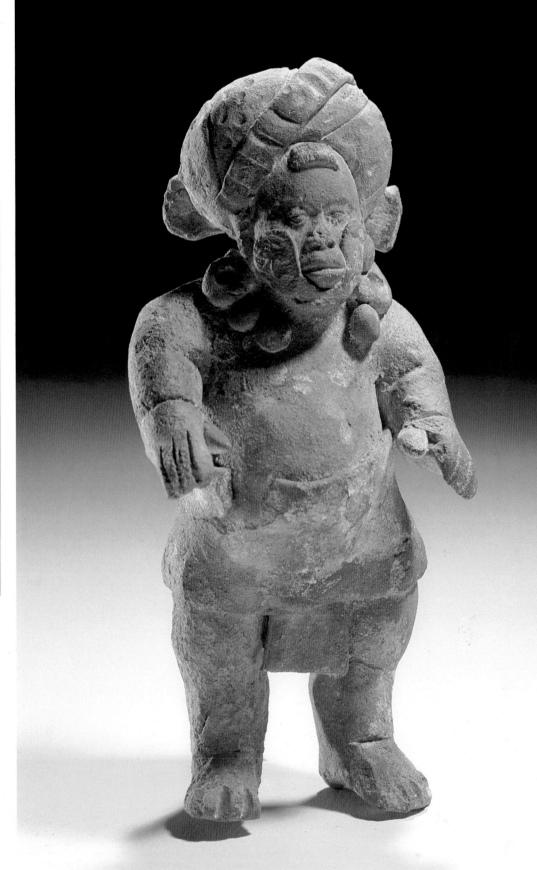

PLATE 41. Dwarf with flayed skin

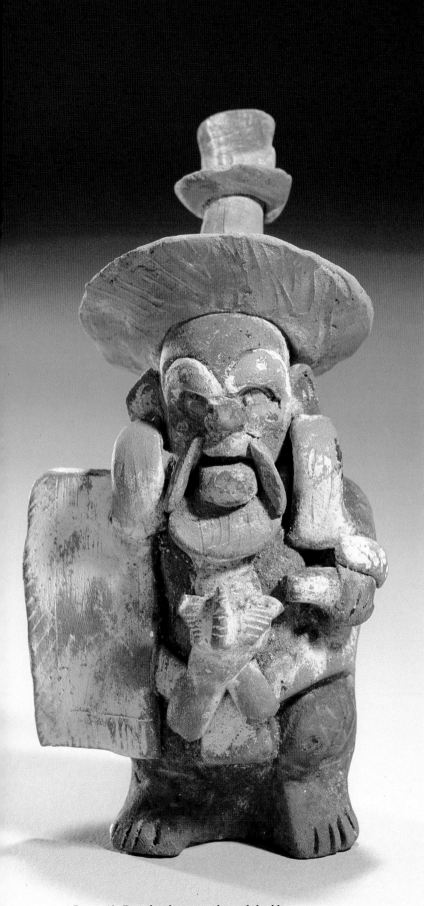

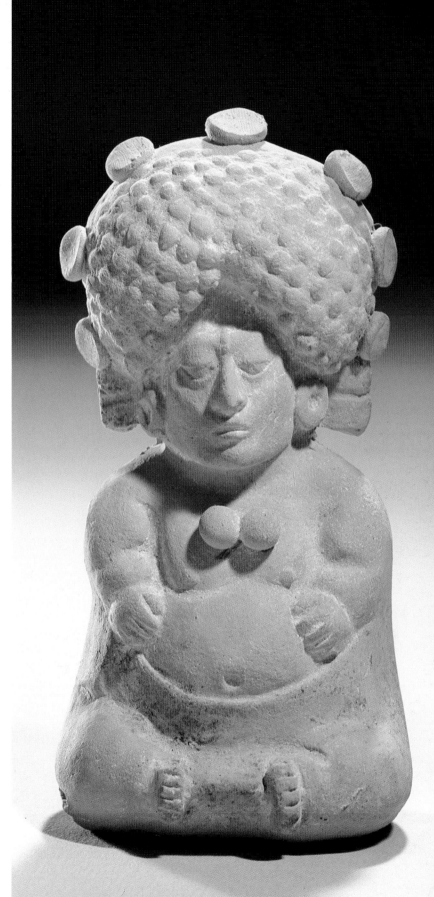

PLATE 42. Dwarf with moustache and shield

PLATE 43. Dwarf with spangled turban

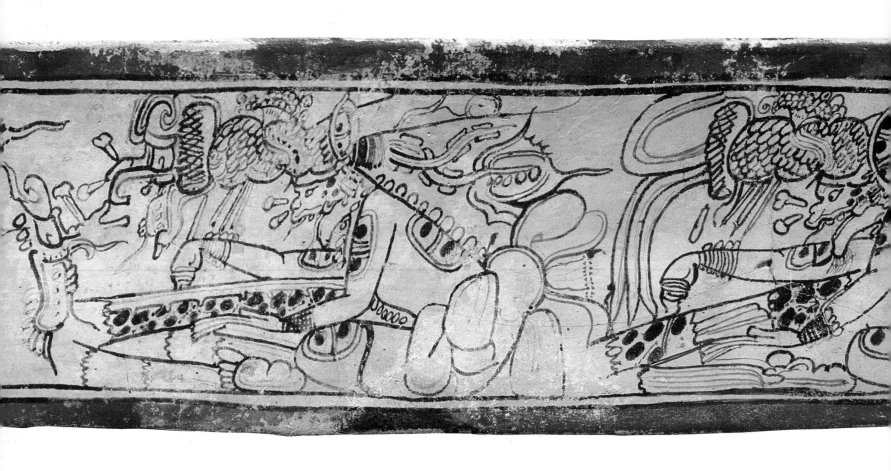

PLATE 44. Cylindrical vessel with lords and scribes

PLATE 45. Jade pendant

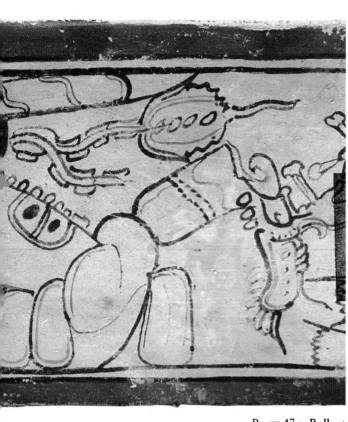

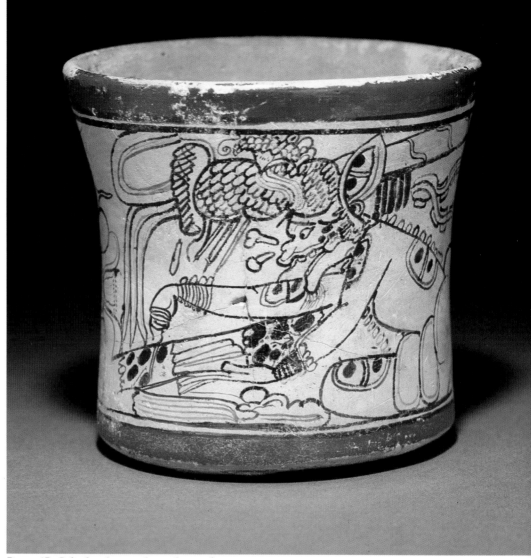

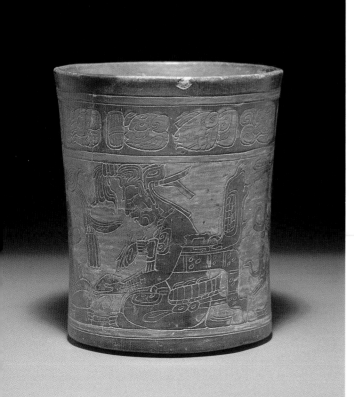

Plate 47a. Rollout

Plate 47. Cylindrical pot with monkey scribes

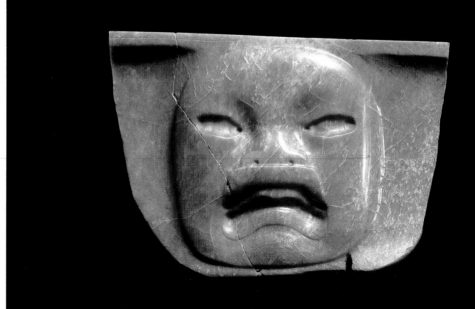

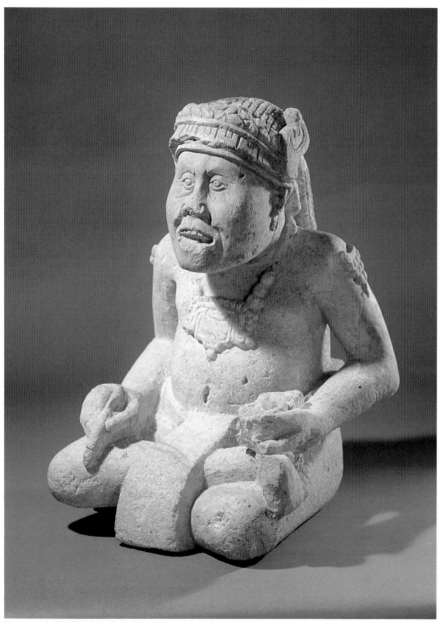

PLATE 46. God N Monkey Scribe

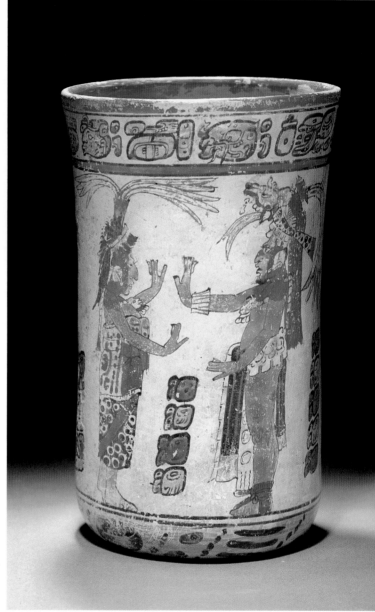

PLATE 48. Cylindrical vessel

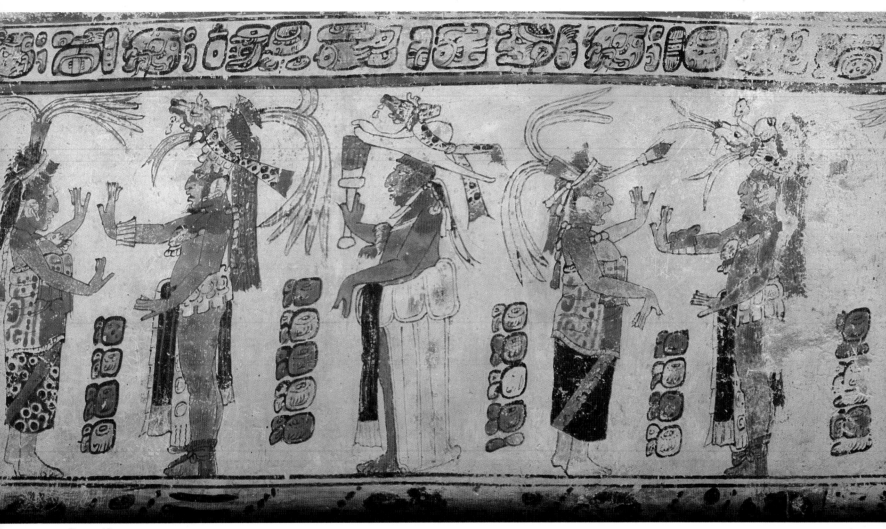

PLATE 48

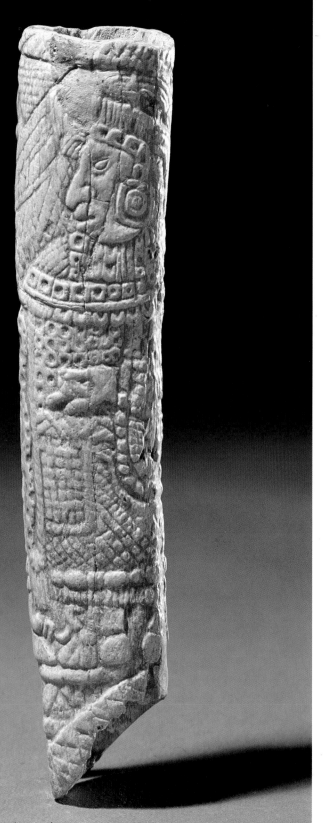

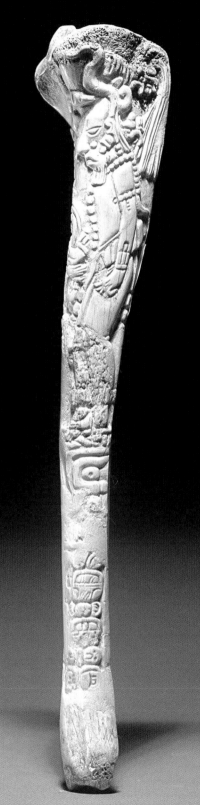

PLATE 49. Carved jaguar bone

PLATE 50. Carved deer tibia

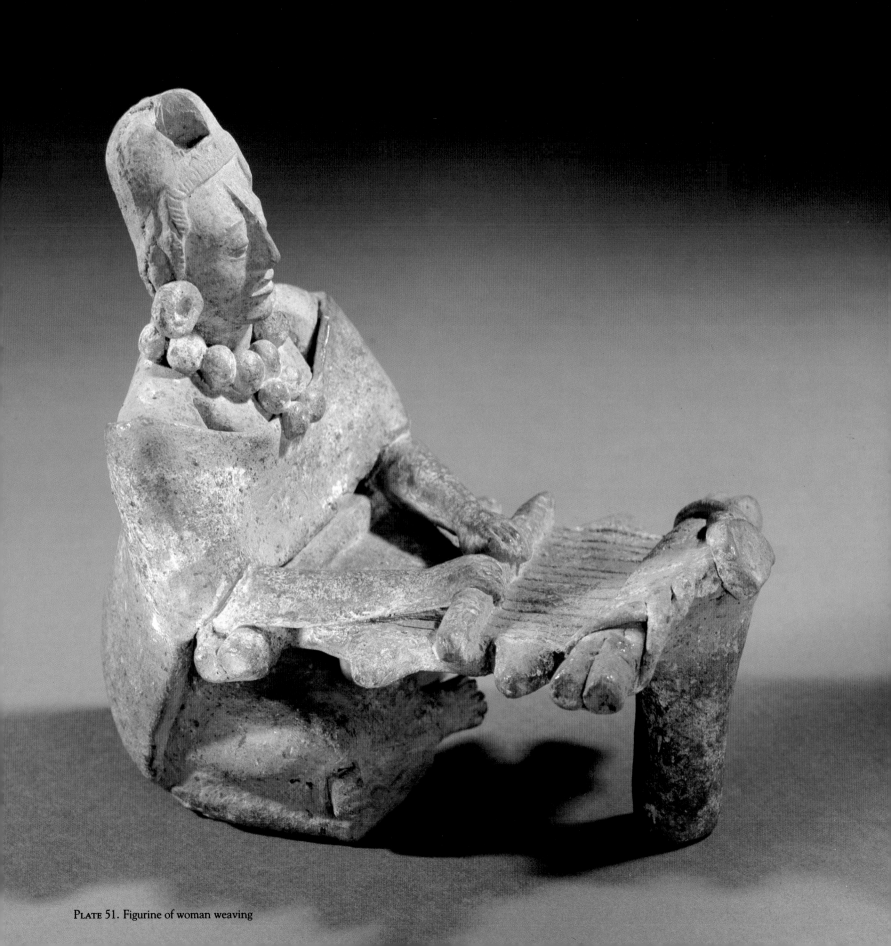

PLATE 51. Figurine of woman weaving

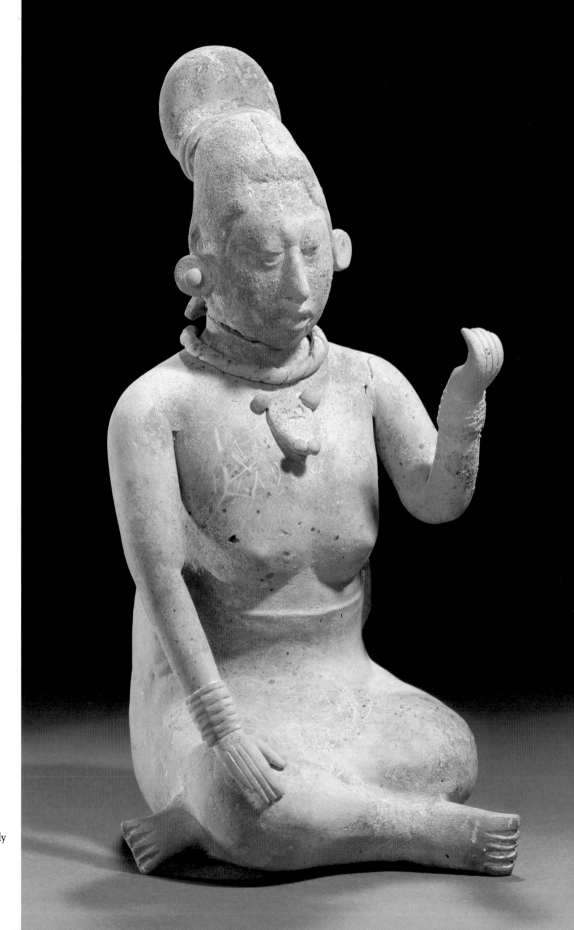

PLATE 52. Figurine of a voluptuous lady

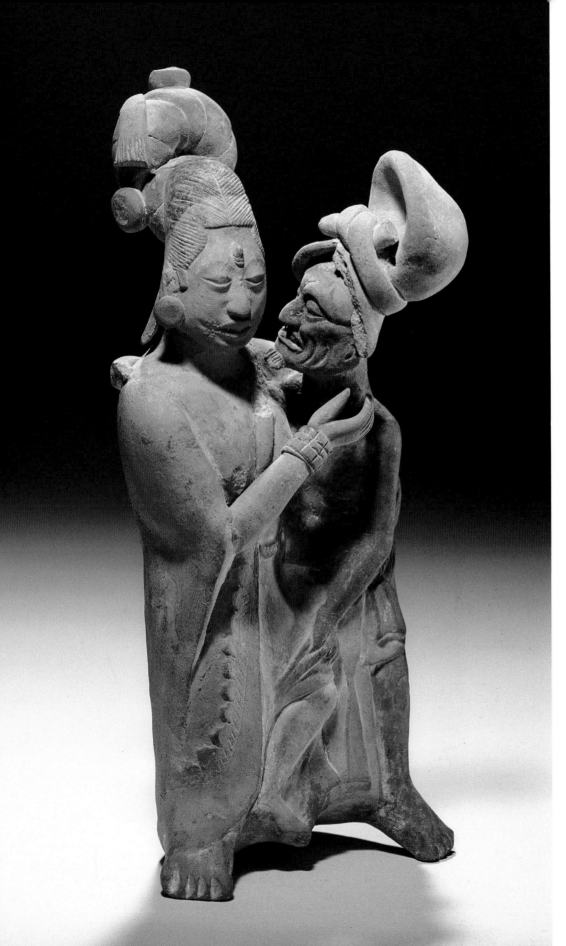

PLATE 53. Figurine of couple embracing

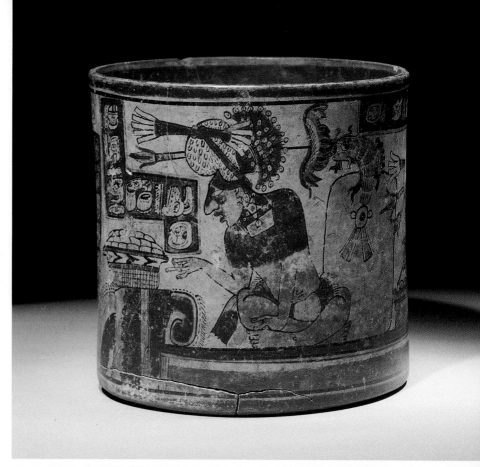

Plate 54. Cylindrical vessel, The Fenton vase

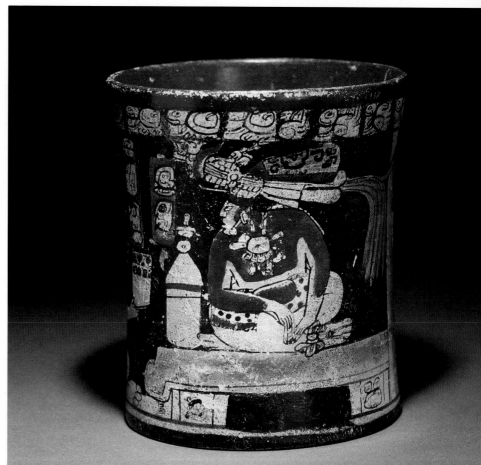

Plate 55. Cylindrical black ground vessel

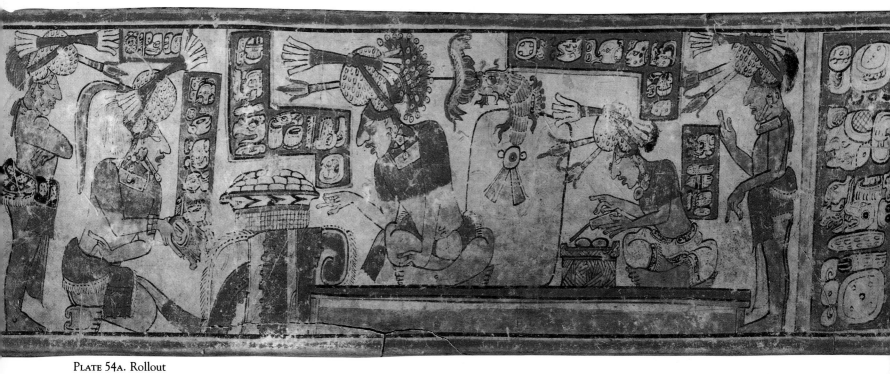

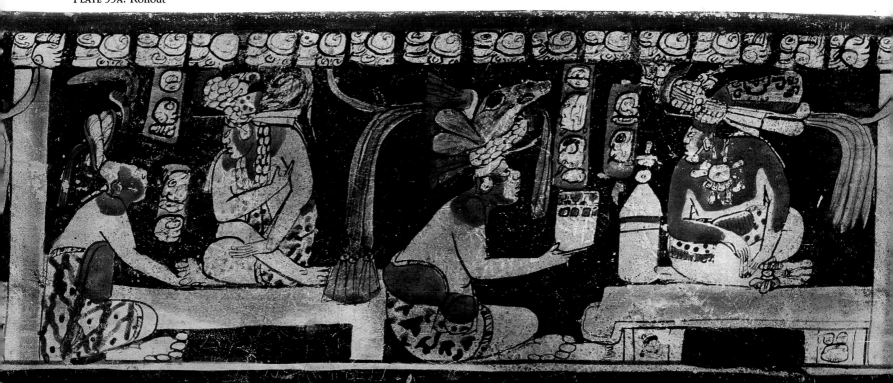

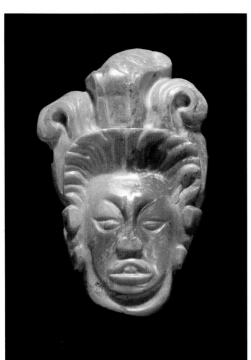

PLATE 56. Head of a Maize God

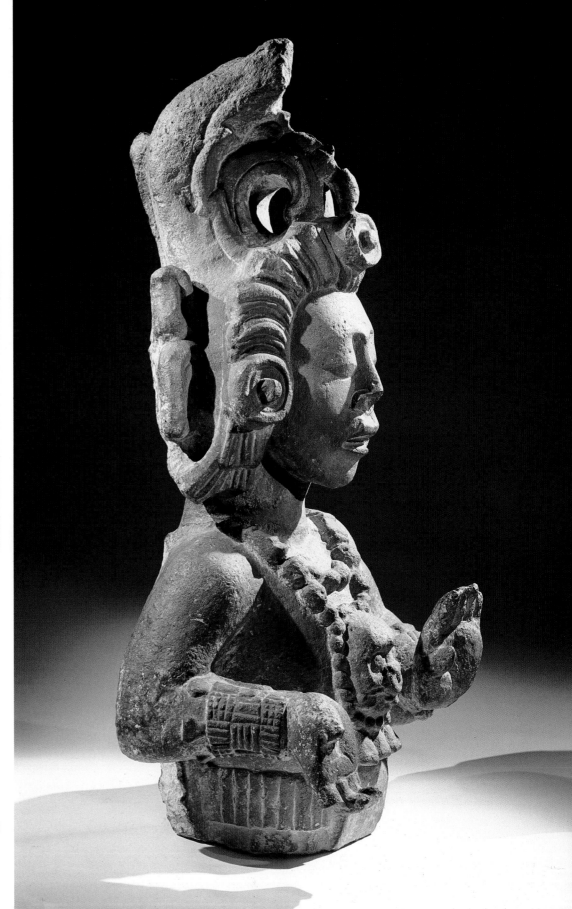

PLATE 57. Maize God

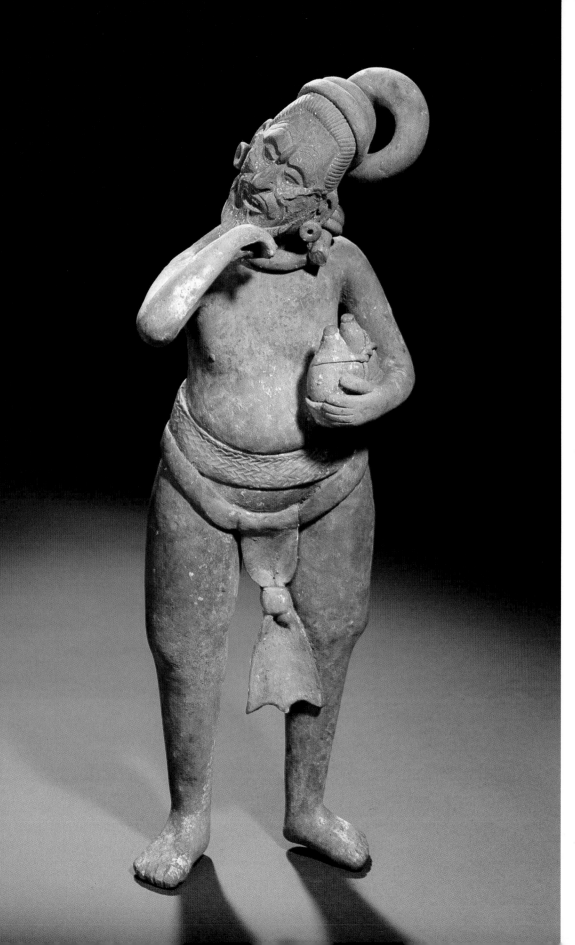

Plate 58. Figurine of a drunkard

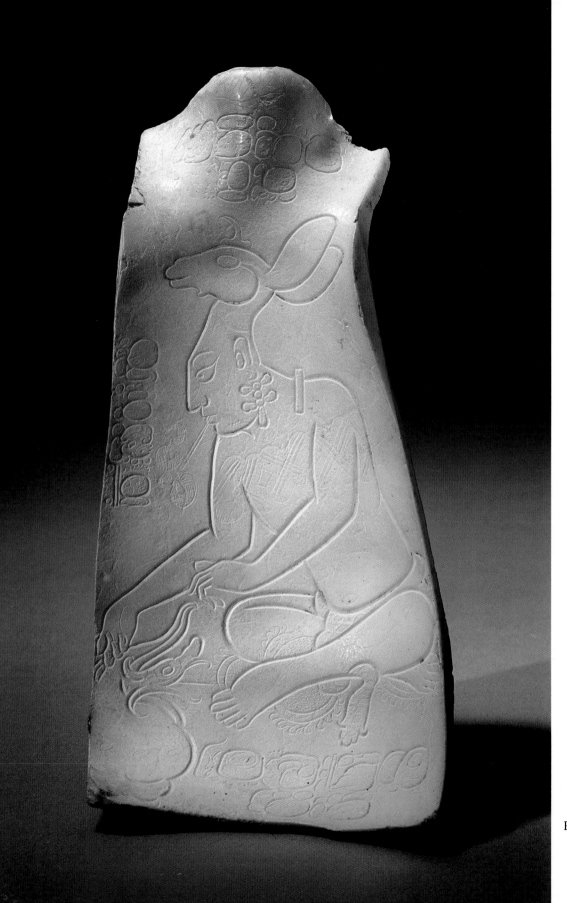

PLATE 59. Conch shell with scene of a smoking lord

IV

BLOODLETTING AND THE VISION QUEST

They offered sacrifices of their own blood, sometimes cutting themselves around in pieces and they left them in this way as a sign. Other times they pierced their cheeks, at others their lower lips. Sometimes they scarify certain parts of their bodies, at others they pierced their tongues in a slanting direction from side to side and passed bits of straw through the holes with horrible suffering; others slit the superfluous part of the virile member leaving it as they did their ears.[1]

THUS DID DIEGO DE LANDA, THE FIRST BISHOP OF YUCATAN, DESCRIBE THE bloodletting of the Yucatec Mayas. During the early years after the Conquest, similar ritual practices were reported from all the regions occupied by Mayan-speaking peoples. Bloodletting imagery pervades Classic Maya art as well. Archaeological evidence for it is abundant, although much of the regalia made of perishable materials is lost. Beginning in the Late Preclassic period, lancets made of stingray spines, obsidian and flint are regularly found in burials and caches. Stingray spines, for example, are often found in the pelvic regions of the dead and were perhaps originally contained in bags hung from belts. It is clear that bloodletting was basic to the institution of rulership, to the mythology of world order, and to public rituals of all sorts. Through bloodletting the Maya sought a vision they believed to be the manifestation of an ancestor or a god. Thus the Maya expressed piety by letting blood from all parts of the body. Blood was the mortar of ritual life from Late Preclassic times until the arrival of the Spanish, who were shocked by the practice and discouraged it as idolatrous worship.

While the importance of blood sacrifice in Mesoamerican societies has long been recognized, the practice was considered to be Mexican rather than fundamentally Maya. The recognition of event glyphs and the deciphering of iconography associated with bloodletting in the last twenty years has changed this view radically.[2] The Spanish reaction was not exaggerated: bloodletting did permeate Maya life. For kings, every

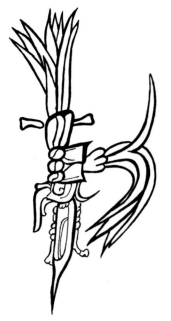

FIGURE IV.1
The Perforator God

The power and sacred nature of the lancet is symbolized by the Perforator God. Its most important feature is the double or triple knot—a symbol of bloodletting—mounted on the forehead of a zoomorphic head. Long feathers emerge from the top of the knots. The lancets, which can be depicted as obsidian or as stingray spines, emerge from the mouth of the jawless zoomorph.

stage in life, every event of political or religious importance, every significant period ending required sanctification through bloodletting. When buildings were dedicated, crops planted, children born, couples married or the dead buried, blood was given to express piety and call the gods into attendance.

Consequently, the lancet—the instrument for drawing blood—became a sacred object infused with power. Models of stingray spines were manufactured from precious stone (Pl. 60), not for use as lancets but rather as symbols of the power inherent in the spine. The Maya carved bone awls with bloodletting imagery to declare their function as lancets and to use in the costuming that signaled the rite (Pl. 61). The concept of the lancet itself was personified in the form of the Perforator God (Fig. IV.1), although this personified lancet is perhaps more accurately considered a sacred power object rather than a deity. The triple and double cloth knots tied around the forehead of the Perforator God became the most pervasive symbol of the bloodletting rite. The Maya wore cloth strips and knotted bows on their arms and legs, through pierced earlobes, in the hair and in clothing. Sacrificial paper made from the felted bark of the fig tree was used as cloth; unlike all other kinds of cloth, both this paper cloth and cotton cloth were cut and torn when used in the bloodletting rite. After the paper cloth became saturated with blood, it was burned in a brazier, for the gods apparently required that blood be transformed into smoke in order to consume it. Thus the icons of smoke and blood came to be indistinguishable in visual form; both are rendered as a bifurcated scroll, the specific reference for which is determined by context or by the addition of modifying signs.[3] In order to make this scroll understood indisputably as blood, the Maya added precious signs, such as bone beads or shells, to its basic configuration. Maya cosmological symbolism suggests that the building element of the Middleworld was blood; it was certainly the most precious and sacred substance of this world.

The creation story of the Popol Vuh provides a context for the rite of bloodletting. At the beginning of all things, when the creator gods finished their work, they wanted to be recognized by their living creations. The birds and beasts of the fields answered them with only a meaningless cacophony of sound, and for that they were forever destined to be the food of man and of one another. The gods tried several times to create special creatures who would know them, but nothing worked. Finally, using maize for flesh and water for blood, they created human beings who could recognize them and understand their relationship to the creator gods. The gods' prolonged efforts are central to the understanding of bloodletting: they wanted creatures to "name [their] names, to praise them" and to be their providers and nurturers.[4] The gods wanted creatures who could worship them, but—more important—they also needed men to give them sustenance.

Permeating this creation myth as well as many parallel myths from other Mesoamerican peoples is the concept of a reciprocal relationship between humans and the gods. The earth and its creatures were created through a sacrificial act of the gods, and human beings, in turn, were required to strengthen and nourish the gods. Gods and humans cannot exist without each other. It is clear from Classic Maya art and inscriptions, as well as from the Popol Vuh, that blood drawn from all parts of the body—especially from the tongue, earlobes, and genitals—was sustenance for the gods.

Some of the most dramatic representations of the Maya act of ritual bloodletting occur on two series of lintels found in buildings at Yaxchilan. The three lintels in each series are designed as a single program encoding one level of information into the imagery and another into the inscriptions. The scenes portray different points in the same ritual that compose a narrative whole, much like sequential frames in a comic strip. The inscriptions, however, record widely separated dates, implying that the same ritual occurred on several different occasions. This approach to narrative programming was attempted first by the artist called the Cookie Cutter Master during Shield Jaguar's reign, then repeated thirty years later, in the reign of his son, Bird Jaguar.[5]

The sequence of lintels featuring Shield Jaguar (numbered 24, 25 and 26) begins over the left doorway of Structure 23 with a scene of bloodletting (Pl. 62).[6] Elegantly dressed, Shield Jaguar wears the shrunken head of a past victim tied to the top of his head, signaling his sacrificial role. His principal wife, Lady Xoc, kneels before him in a *huipil* of finely woven, complex design. Her headdress, with its tassels, bar, trapeze and Tlaloc signs,[7] signals that she is engaged in a very special bloodletting rite that will eventually include captive sacrifice. She pulls a thorn-lined rope through the wound in her perforated tongue, letting the rope fall into a woven basket full of blood-spotted paper strips. Lady Xoc's lips and cheeks are covered with the dotted scrolls that signify the blood streaming from her wounded mouth.

Lintel 25, the second in the series, shows the consequence and purpose of the bloodletting rite (Pl. 63). The same woman, still kneeling, gazes upward at an apparition, a Tlaloc warrior, emerging from the gaping mouth of a Vision Serpent. In her left hand she holds a bloodletting bowl with the bloody paper, a stingray spine and an obsidian lancet; in the right hand, a skull and serpent symbol. The Vision Serpent rises from a separate bowl placed on the ground in front of her. The serpent is double headed, perhaps as a reminder of the royal scepter and the fact that the occasion of the rite is Shield Jaguar's accession. The serpent's writhing body surges upward through a blood scroll, declaring that the vision materializes from blood itself. The Tlaloc god and warrior brought forth refer to a special sacrificial complex that the Maya associated with the god of the evening star and with war. During the accession rites of the king, his wife underwent bloodletting so that she could communicate with this warrior, who may have been a dead ancestor or a symbol of the king's role as warrior in this cult. The warrior is not named, but it is clear that the purpose of the bloodletting rite was to cause this vision to materialize.

Today, scientists acknowledge that endorphins — chemically related to the opiates and produced by the brain in response to massive blood loss — can induce hallucinogenic experiences. But the Maya also knew that drawing large amounts of blood would, without the help of other drugs, produce visions that were the raison d'etre of their rituals. Through such visions, the Maya came directly into contact with their gods and ancestors. The great rearing serpent — the physical manifestation of visions arising from blood loss and shock — was the contact between the supernatural realm and the world of human beings. The precise supernatural being contacted by the rite is manifested by the image in the mouth of the Vision Serpent.

The Vision Serpent may have been more than a symbolic manifestation of hallucination. Information from Room 3 at Bonampak as well as from other pictorial records makes it possible to reconstruct some parts of the rituals that took place in the great open plazas of Maya cities. Against a backdrop of terraced architecture, elaborately costumed dancers, musicians, warriors and nobles entered the courts in long processions. Dancers whirled across the plaza floors and terrace platforms to music made on rattles, whistles, wooden trumpets and drums of all sizes. A crowd of participants wearing bloodletting paper or cloth tied in triple knots sat on platforms and terraces around the plaza. According to Bishop Landa, these people would have prepared themselves with days of fasting, abstinence and ritual steam baths. Well into the ceremony, the ruler and his wife would emerge from within a building high above the court, and in full public view, he would lacerate his penis, she her tongue. Ropes drawn through their wounds carried the flowing blood to paper strips. The saturated paper—perhaps along with other offerings, such as rubber (the chicle resin from which chewing gum is made)—were placed in large plates, then carried to braziers and burned, creating columns of black smoke. The participants, already dazed through deprivation, public hysteria and massive blood loss, were culturally conditioned to expect a hallucinatory experience. The rising clouds of swirling smoke provided the perfect field in which to see the Vision Serpent; gazing into the smoke, the celebrants may have actually seen it.

At Yaxchilan, the final act in Shield Jaguar's sequence is recorded on Lintel 26. Shield Jaguar, already dressed in cotton armor, carries a short stabbing knife (Fig. V.2). Lady Xoc stands silently beside him with blood still oozing from her wounded mouth. In her hands she holds her husband's jaguar helmet and flexible shield. She is helping him prepare for battle, perhaps to take captives for the final sacrificial act.

Bird Jaguar, Shield Jaguar's son, came to the throne in A.D. 752, ten years after his father's death. He constructed a building to house lintels showing the same three scenes commissioned by his father; however, he ordered the scenes differently by centering the war scene on Lintel 16, then flanking it on the left with the vision scene (Lintel 15) and on the right with the bloodletting scene (Lintel 17). The capture recorded in Lintel 16 occurred only eight days before the bloodletting depicted on Lintel 17, which was, according to its inscription, conducted in celebration of the birth of Bird Jaguar's heir, on 9.16.0.14.5, or February 18, A.D. 752.

Lady Balam-Ix, the woman who lets blood on Lintel 17 (Pl. 64), is not the mother of the newborn but apparently a second wife of Bird Jaguar who publicly lets blood in celebration of the birth of her husband's heir. She wears the same costume Lady Xoc wears in the earlier narrative sequence, which suggests that these rituals were closely regulated by tradition. The rope she uses to draw blood from her tongue, however, is not lined with thorns, perhaps because the artist neglected to represent them or because the thorn-lined rope was used only by Lady Xoc as a special gesture of piety. Bird Jaguar is shown preparing for his self-mutilation, thus confirming that the king and his wife both performed the mutilation rite and offered blood. Interestingly, by wearing a skull and snake headdress identical to those used by Lady Xoc on Lintel 25, Bird Jaguar seems to be emphasizing a special association with his father's principal wife, even though she was not his own mother.

On Lintel 15, Lady 6-Tun, yet another of Bird Jaguar's wives, stares at the vision she has brought forth through bloodletting (Pl. 65). Her *huipil* repeats the one Lady Xoc wore in this rite a generation before, although she contacts a different, unidentified person. He may embody the idea of sacrifice, just as the Tlaloc warrior on Lintel 25 personifies sacrifice and the Tlaloc war complex.

Both of these series of lintels are associated with accession. The vision scene on Lintel 25 took place on the day of Shield Jaguar's accession, and the bloodletting and capture scenes of Bird Jaguar's series occurred only seventy-five days before his accession. The Maya had long practiced bloodletting rituals as a required preparation for, or conclusion to, accession rites. The Hauberg Stela of A.D. 199, the earliest dated monument from the Lowlands, portrays the same bloodletting ritual exactly (Pl. 66). An early king, Bac-T'ul, stands with his right hand extended in the scattering gesture. A Vision Serpent writhing over his left shoulder poises above his head. A symbolic tree arches from his right shoulder toward the ground and identifies the king as the *axis mundi*, the central axis of the world. Sacrificial victims, their bodies cut in half, fall down the tree toward the Underworld. The Serpent is identified as a sacrificial being by the flint blade that forms its tail. The gods called forth by the rite—among them Chac-Xib-Chac—climb the Serpent's body and emerge from its mouth.

The image on the Hauberg Stela, considered in light of information from its text, yields important insights into the early definition of bloodletting (Pl. 66b). The featured event is written simply as "he let blood," but the image goes a step further by showing the vision produced. Moreover, since this rite occurred only fifty-two days before his accession, Bac-T'ul could have illustrated his accession and recorded in the text that fifty-two days earlier he had let blood; it might be expected, after all, that he would consider the act of becoming king to be the most important event. Nevertheless, he chose to represent the bloodletting as the more important act, which had to be verified in a permanent and public record. Furthermore, he depicts himself not drawing the blood but making physical contact with supernaturals. Bac-T'ul is shown in the midst of his vision, frozen between the natural and supernatural worlds. This early stela demonstrates that the gods portrayed sanctioned his accession and were the manifestation of his power.

Bloodletting, then, was the earliest kingly action to be documented in a public forum. The accession record on the plaque from Dumbarton Oaks (Pl. 32) is probably earlier, but the tiny text and image are scaled for private communication: it must be held to be read. The Hauberg Stela, although small compared to later stelae, is a public monument and thus reflects a significant shift in the strategy of the Maya toward public art. During the Late Preclassic period, architecture was the principal artistic medium. Buildings bearing huge sculpted plaster masks on their sides provided a symbolic context, setting the stage for the rituals of kingship. Yet the rituals themselves were ephemeral, surviving only in the memories of the participants, and for the Maya, memory was apparently not enough. Their social system required public confirmation that an individual enacted a rite at a certain time and place. The Hauberg Stela demonstrates the dual purpose of writing joined with imagery in public propaganda. The image portrays the ritual and the king's contact with the supernatural; the text records to whom, where and when this event occurred, then links this information to a chain of facts that constitute written history.

The quest for a vision through bloodletting has not yet been found on public monuments in the Late Preclassic period, but the imagery shows up just as forcefully in other ways. Throughout Maya history, the tools used in ritual were encoded with symbols to define their purpose and function and to transform an object of utility, such as a cup or a plate, into a focus of power. Such power is revealed in two ways: in the personification of these objects into animate forms (having either zoomorphic or anthropomorphic features) and in the ritual "killing" of such objects when their use was at an end. For example, the Maya would drill holes in the bottom of pottery vessels to release the power accumulated in them.

As early as the Late Preclassic period, ritual objects were defined by symbolic marking. One of the most refined examples, a carved stone vessel (Pl. 67), has long been in the collection of Dumbarton Oaks, its importance and meaning unrecognized.[8] This vessel, shaped as a drinking cup, is transformed into an instrument of the vision rite by the relief carving of Vision Serpents on its outer surface. While in later art, Vision Serpents are drawn on a vertical axis, on this cup they are placed horizontally, so that their bodies seem to undulate across the vessel's surface. This vessel may have been used to dispense drugs that stimulated the vision or to collect blood from the blood-letting rite. In either case, its ritual function is proclaimed dramatically by the imagery carved into its walls. The artist's choice of stone instead of the more fragile medium of clay reveals that the vessel was conceived as a valued object intended for long-term use. This cup further documents the extreme antiquity of the vision quest in Maya ritual, as well as confirming the conservative regulation of vision symbolism throughout Maya history.

The association of bloodletting with accession was carried into a variety of media. A Late Classic cylindrical pot from the Dumbarton Oaks collection (Pl. 68) shows an episodic narrative of accession. In the primary scene, Balam-Pauahtun, the new king, is seated on a bench in his palace surrounded by members of his court. In the smaller and more important scene, the king, standing outside the palace, aims a lancet at his penis, while one of his nobles pulls a rope through his own tongue. The noble takes on the role performed by the king's wife at Yaxchilan. Furthermore, the noble-man participant on this pot wears the same type of headdress as the wives at Yaxchilan. Thus, the ritual role rather than the gender or rank of the practitioner determines the headdress.

In his seventeenth-century account of the ceremony, Fray Delgado, a Spanish priest, vividly described the method of drawing blood from the penis, as practiced among the Manche Chol Maya:

> In Vicente Pach's ranch I saw the sacrifice. They took a chisel and wooden mallet, placed the one who had to sacrifice himself on a smooth stone slab, took out his penis, and cut it in three parts two finger breadths [up], the largest in the center, saying at the same time incantations and words I did not understand. The one who was undergoing the operation did not seem to suffer, and did not lose a drop of blood.[9]

An extant figurine (Pl. 69) displays the exact procedure. A seated lord, who is cutting his penis with a sharp blade held in his right hand, sheds drops of blood onto blue paper. The rope collar he wears symbolizes his acceptance of the role of penitent; he is a lord, but for this rite he has taken on the symbolic trappings of the lowliest of humans, the captive whose destiny is to die in sacrifice. His face, like that of the seventeenth-century Manche Chol practitioner, does not reveal pain, although other figurines show victims screaming in agony. Perhaps the ability to bear pain stoically was admired as both courageous and pious.

Another figurine (Pl. 70) shows a practitioner at the moment before the rite begins. Stoic and solemn, he sits in a scaffold chair with a large bowl between his feet. He is covered with the two signals of the rite, rope and cut paper. He does not seem to be a king, which suggests that in Classic Maya society, people other than the king also participated in the bloodletting rite.

Some bloodletting rituals included a dramatic dancing phase, shown in detail in the murals of Room 3 at Bonampak. The form of the dance and its costuming were apparently prescribed and used at other sites: a polychrome pot in the collection of the Kimbell Art Museum shows exactly the same dance (Pl. 71). A plump ruler, known among Mayanists as the Fat Cacique, sits inside his palace watching three dancers perform in a court outside. Their elaborate costumes feature large panels tied under their loincloths. In the Bonampak paintings, these side panels are decorated with abstract designs or figurative imagery, as are the ones worn by the left figure on the Kimbell pot. The panels of the other two, however, are red—but not because the material is red. These men have perforated their penises and tied long panels of what is probably painted paper around their wounded members. Their long white loincloths are splattered with blood as well, and as the dancers whirl, the centrifugal force of their spin pulls the blood into the paper of the wing panels. The panels worn by the right figure, the only one to have his heels raised in the dance position, have already become fully saturated.[10] To the Maya this dance was an act of piety; the very existence of the universe depended upon the willingness of human beings to sustain the gods with their blood offerings.

Furthermore, bloodletting was not practiced only by humans; the gods themselves gave their blood to maintain the order of the cosmos. The actors letting blood from their penises on the Huehuetenango vase, for example, are divine (Pl. 72). The Perforator God is floating in a red field defined as supernatural space by the presence of gods above and cartouches below the glyph band. Six gods squat over bowls using the same Perforator God as a lancet to draw blood from their genitals. This squatting position is so characteristic that it became a glyph for bloodletting itself.[11] Glyphs on this vase specify that the time and place of the action are supernatural. Even though the mythological context for this action is not yet clear, evidently the gods, like men, were required to let blood.

The result of divine bloodletting is shown on the magnificently carved Acasaguastlan pot (Pl. 73). The Sun God, the deity having the vision, sits in the center of the scene holding in each arm a Vision Serpent; they fold out from him as mirrored opposites, meeting head to head on the other side of the pot. The serpent in the god's right arm spits out the sun; its tail is night. Sitting just behind its head is a human, perhaps representing the king who commissioned the pot or all humans, creatures of the world of night and day. The turtle monster and crocodile (perhaps the front head of the Celestial Monster) move among the folds of the serpent's body. The bird at the corner of the serpent's mouth is a sky creature; the realized vision emerging from its mouth, the Sun God. The serpent on the left belches forth his realized vision—the watery deep of the Underworld, which is peopled with Death Gods, a deer-eared Celestial Monster, the personified flint of sacrifice and personified water. The world of the day is contrasted to the watery Underworld; they are the two opposite halves that make up the universe. The actor is a god; his sacrifice of blood creates a mirrored vision, and from that vision are created day and night, birds of the sky, the waters of the primordial sea in which the world floats, the plants of the earth, death and sacrifice. The god's bloodletting vision is thus the whole cosmos.

Two plates that were used as sacrificial vessels reinforce the message of the Acasaguastlan pot. One of these plates (Pl. 74), which was used to hold the bloody paper, lancets and rope for the bloodletting rite, has as its central image the Quadripartite Monster, the divinity that usually forms the rear head of the Celestial Monster. Together these two elements form a cosmic symbol representing the passage of Venus

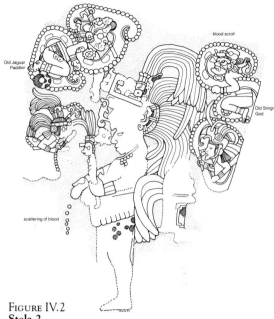

FIGURE IV.2
Stela 2
Ixlu, Guatemala
Late Classic period, ca. A.D. 850

This stela shows imagery of the scattering rite typical of central Peten at the end of the Classic period. The ruler holds the God K scepter and is scattering drops of blood. He wears a jaguar-pelt skirt and an ornate backrack and headdress. Around his head float four gods in the beaded scrolls identified at Yaxchilan as blood. The two upper gods are the Paddlers—the Old Jaguar God and the Old Stingray God, who paddle the canoe of life. The king has brought them into the human realm through the ritual of bloodletting.

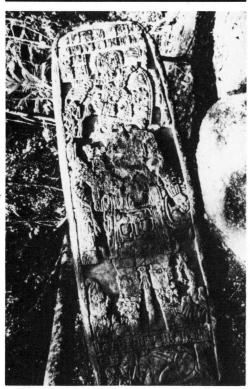

Figure IV.3a
Stela 25
Dos Pilas, Guatemala
Late Classic period, A.D. 711
Photo by Otis Imboden

and the Sun across the heavens. Normally the bloodletting bowl marked with the *kin* sun sign that composes the forehead of the Quadripartite Monster identifies it as the sun in its daily passage through all levels of the Maya universe. Here the Vision Serpent rearing out of the bowl, who is belching forth the head of a handsome young male, associates the Monster with bloodletting and its resulting vision. Since the Quadripartite Monster is part of the symbol that represents the whole cosmos, the image conveys a message to the supplicant who drops his bloody papers and rope in this plate that bloodletting and the vision quest are inherent to the fabric of the universe itself.

Moreover, nature's bounty was ensured through bloodletting rituals. An incised plate at the University Art Museum, Princeton (Pl. 75), once the top of a lip-to-lip cache vessel, again has the *kin* bowl of sacrifice as the central icon, but here it floats on a field of blood. The decapitated head of a young Maize God that lies in the plate, together with the three most common blades of sacrifice—a flint knife, a stingray spine, and an obsidian blade—associate bloodletting with maize.

The sacrificial image on this plate relates directly to the iconography of the Temple of the Foliated Cross at Palenque (Fig. IV.4), which clearly shows bloodletting to be vital to the production of maize and all other agricultural products. There, on a tablet that celebrates the accession of Chan-Bahlum, the World Tree icon is altered to represent the social world of man and the tamed world of domesticated agriculture. The tree, rising from the head of a Water-lily Monster, floats on a band of water. Its trunk is marked with God C, the sign of blood and sacredness, and its branches are ears of maize, complete with outer leaves and long silks. The ears of corn, however, are replaced by human heads, recalling the myth that man was created from maize and water. Perched on the tree is the Celestial Bird, also subtly changed. Instead of having the usual zoomorphic head, he wears a mask that nonetheless reveals a protruding beak, giving away his identity. He is a water bird and holds a clump of water plants in his beak. This imagery symbolizes the controlled agricultural world, the waters of the canal system and the water lilies that grew in them; the maize rising from the fields; and the water birds that searched for fish and food in the canals. Because domesticated maize seeds cannot escape the folds of the ear, the plant must be cultivated. It cannot exist without the intervention of man and thus is the ultimate symbol of the social world.

The scene at the center of the Palenque tablet encodes a powerful message about rulership and the blood sacrifice of kings. Here, Chan-Bahlum, who accedes to the throne, receives the Perforator God from his dead father as a symbol of the bloodletting that maintains the domesticated world of man, represented by the World Tree. Since maize is the substance of man's flesh and blood is necessary to ensure its survival, the cache vessel in Plate 75 represents a reciprocal act acknowledging that man cannot exist without gods, nor gods without man. There the Maize God submits to sacrifice—just as the grain provides food—to ensure the continued survival of humankind.

Bloodletting had one final function for the Maya: to bring the gods into man's presence. This aspect is best conveyed by the imagery of the scattering rite. Long thought to symbolize either the beneficent distribution of bounty to the people or the casting of maize seeds in augury, the scattering rite is named simply for the action shown—the scattering of what looks like pellets or streams, which are now recognized as blood. This rite was performed to celebrate the period endings in the Long Count calendar, especially the katun, the hotun (five years) and the lahuntun (ten years).

La Pasadita Lintel 2 (Pl. 76) is a particularly good illustration of the scattering rite. Bird Jaguar, the king of Yaxchilan, is marking a period ending (9.16.10.0.0) with the *cahal*, or underlord, who ruled La Pasadita for him. Dressed in the symbolic array of Chac-Xib-Chac and wearing his father's name on his belt to declare his line of descent, Bird Jaguar drops a dotted stream of blood into a knot-shrouded brazier. His groin is covered with the Perforator God, marking the source of the blood offering he drops. The *cahal* stands nearby, ready to assist him in performing the rite.

During both the Early and the Late Classic periods, this rite is recorded either in images or inscriptions at most sites; around A.D. 780, however, the Maya of the central Peten began depicting it in a new way (Fig. IV.2). Although, as before, the king wears an elaborate costume and drops blood from his hands, new elements—gods wrapped in blood scrolls—float around his head. Some of these floating gods are presently unidentified, although the principal ones are the two Paddler Gods. That the scrolls surrounding the gods are blood seems certain, since they are identical in form to the material through which the Vision Serpents of Yaxchilan rise and identical to the substance scattered by Bird Jaguar. One aspect of the scattering rite, then, is that gods are found to float in blood scrolls—much as the Vision Serpent rises through blood in other rituals.

The presence of the Paddler Gods in these depictions of period ending rituals is not coincidental. Their names—either written with their portrait glyphs or as *kin* and *akbal* ("night" and "day")—appear in period ending statements at many sites throughout the Late Classic period. At Dos Pilas it is possible to learn why and how this association became so widespread.[12] There, as at other Peten sites, scattering was the principal rite recorded for period endings, and, as expected, the Paddlers were frequently named. Yet Stela 25 (Fig. IV.3) does not mention scattering, even though it clearly records the end of the fourteenth katun as the featured event. Instead, a small secondary text records a birth with the statement, "They were born, his lords, the Paddlers, under the auspices of Shield God K." This is a baffling statement, since we expect the Paddler Gods to have been born in mythological time, and they are certainly recorded as actors on much earlier dates.

The declaration of these births is explained by the symbolism of the period ending rites that the monument commemorates. Scattering was the principal period ending rite throughout Late Classic Maya history; scattering was a bloodletting rite; the Paddlers are the gods in the blood scrolls above the king's head; and the Paddlers are the gods born. The conclusion is inescapable—the act of bloodletting literally gave birth to the gods. The Maya believed that bloodletting brought the gods as well as their ancestors into physical existence in human space and time. Thus the Vision Serpents were more than symbolic representations of hallucinations; they were the bodily fulfillment of those visions. The god or ancestor contacted in ritual actually appeared, and when the ritual ended, he was gone.

The power of ritual to incarnate the supernatural may also explain why the king could appear in so many different guises. It appears that the king was conceived to be a vessel of sorts and that through ritual, a god was brought into his body. At the end of a ritual, the god would depart, but in the next ritual, another god would come to reside within the vessel. This ability to host the supernatural may have been shared by all Maya, for masks and body suits are worn by many participants of public ritual. For the duration of a ritual, they would become the gods they impersonated.

Inscriptions associated with bloodletting rites imply other birthing symbolism:

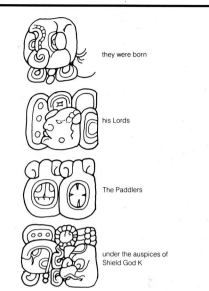

they were born

his Lords

The Paddlers

under the auspices of Shield God K

FIGURE IV.3b
Inscription of Dos Pilas Stela 25

The main text records the date 9.14.0.0.0 6 Ahau 13 Muan, or December 5, A.D. 711, and the ritual conducted to celebrate the end of a katun. The actor is the local Dos Pilas king, Shield God K. The small secondary text tells us the results of these period-endings rites; restated in a simpler form, the inscription reads, "The Paddlers were born under the auspices of Shield God K."

the king became "the mother of the gods" by giving them birth through ritual. This relationship is explicitly stated at Palenque, where the gods of the Palenque Triad are called "the children of Pacal and Chan-Bahlum." The glyph that records this relationship is one that stands between a mother and her child in all other contexts. The king is the mother of the gods because he gives them birth and nourishes them through his gift of blood. The blood scrolls and Paddler figures that float above the scattering king are pictorial representations of the result of bloodletting—the physical manifestation of the gods.

The ability to give birth to the gods through ritual is an awe-inspiring concept, for it means that ritual was far more than role playing. As the bearer of the most potent blood among humankind, the king was the focus of tremendous power—thus the pervasiveness of scenes showing his bloodletting in Maya art. Through his gift of blood, the king brought the gods to life and drew the power of the supernatural into the daily lives of the Maya.[13]

NOTES

1. Alfred M. Tozzer, ed. and trans., "Landa's Relación de las cosas de Yucatan: A Translation," *Papers of the Peabody Museum of American Archaeology and Ethnology, Harvard University* 18 (New York: Kraus Reprint Corp., 1966), pp. 113–114.

2. J. Eric S. Thompson first identified ritual bloodletting in Classic-period Maya iconography in "A Blood-drawing Ceremony Painted on a Maya Vase," in *Estudios de Cultura Maya*, vol. 1 (Mexico City: Universidad National Autónoma de México, 1961), pp. 13–20. David Joralemon focused attention on the iconography of bloodletting by identifying indisputable scenes of the act, the Perforator God and other regalia in his article "Ritual Blood-Sacrifice among the Ancient Maya, Part 1," in the *Primera Mesa Redonda de Palenque, Part 2*, edited by Merle Greene Robertson (Pebble Beach, Calif.: Robert Louis Stevenson School, 1974), pp. 59–77. Using this iconography as a base, epigraphers were able to identify verbs, titles and other written expressions recording the rite, which in turn led to the recognition of related pictorial representations.

3. In his study of the meaning of color in Late Preclassic architectural sculpture, David Freidel first suggested that scroll symbols for blood and smoke were identical, and he correlated an interrelationship between these two symbols and those of water and mist or clouds ("Polychrome Facades of the Lowland Maya Preclassic," in *Painted Architecture and Polychrome Monumental Sculpture in Mesoamerica* [Washington, D.C.: Dumbarton Oaks, 1985], pp. 5–30).

4. Dennis Tedlock, *Popol Vuh: The Definitive Edition of the Mayan Book of the Dawn of Life and the Glories of Gods and Kings* (New York: Simon and Schuster, 1985), pp. 77–80.

5. J. Alfred Maudslay, *Biologia Centrali-Americana: Archaeology* (London: Dulau & Co., 1889–1902).

6. Shield Jaguar's lintels were placed in Structure 23, a double-galleried, north-facing building on the lower level of the city. Lintels 24 and 25 were taken to The British Museum by Maudslay in 1882, and Lintel 26 was removed to Mexico City's Museo Nacional de Antropología in 1964. Originally the top member of a door, each lintel was carved with a text on the outer surface and with a scene on the underside, facing the floor.

7. Archaeological evidence suggests a strong interaction between Teotihuacan and the Lowland Maya, beginning about A.D. 400 and lasting for some two hundred years. During that period the Maya absorbed a complex of symbols, including this headdress and the so-called Tlaloc imagery, but it is increasingly clear that the Maya redefined this symbol complex for their own purposes, thereafter associating it with bloodletting rites, both self-inflicted and involving captives. Lady Xoc's usage of this Teotihuacanoid symbol does not mean that Teotihuacanos dominated Yaxchilan or that she was from that city; rather, it signals that this particular bloodletting ritual is being enacted.

8. David Freidel (personal communication, 1982) first pointed out the iconography of this vessel to the authors.

9. Alfred M. Tozzer, "Landa's Relación," p. 114.

10. An equally valid interpretation is that the three dancing figures represent the same person at three stages in the same rite, rather than three different people. This possibility is supported by the identical costumes of the figures and by the use of this compositional device in Bonampak Room 2, where in the war scene, Muan-Chaan and his opponent are shown at different points in the same ritual without a change of scene (Mary Ellen Miller, *The Murals of Bonampak* [Princeton, N.J.: Princeton University Press, 1986]).

11. Peter Mathews, "Maya Early Classic Monuments and Inscriptions" (unpublished manuscript of 1984, provided by the author).

12. David Stuart was the first epigrapher to recognize the pattern of the Paddler names in Maya inscriptions and to realize their great import to the scattering rite. He was also the first to propose the interpretation of the Dos Pilas inscriptions presented here. See David Stuart, "Blood Symbolism in Maya Iconography," *RES* 7/8 (1984), pp. 6–20.

13. In "Fertility, Vision Quest and Auto-Sacrifice: Some Thoughts on Ritual Blood-Letting Among the Maya," (in *Art, Iconography, and Dynastic History of Palenque, Part III, Proceedings of the Segunda Mesa Redonda de Palenque*, ed. Merle Greene Robertson [Pebble Beach, Calif.: Robert Louis Stevenson School], pp. 181-193), Peter Furst first suggested the interpretation of Maya bloodletting as a "vision quest: like the young Indian in the ordeals associated with the Sun Dance on the Great Plains, under certain specific circumstances the Maya may have sought to obtain divine guidance from deified ancestors or guardian spirits in an alternate state of consciousness or ecstatic trance triggered not by psychoactive plants but rather by a massive physical jolt to the system" (p. 184). He also discusses "non-hurtful pain" and its documentation in rituals and other experience around the world.

PLATE 60

Lancet shaped as a stingray spine
Late Classic period, A.D. 600–800
Jade
9.5 x 1.5 cm
Lent courtesy of The Art Museum, Princeton University

The stingray spine was most widely used as a lancet in Maya bloodletting rituals. It is frequently found in graves, near the pelvic area of skeletons. Perhaps because its source is the sea, the stingray spine epitomized all lancets and symbolized the substance and ritual characteristic of the Middleworld—blood and bloodletting. This sacred stingray spine, carved with three bloodletting knots above the handle, is made of jade to emphasize its symbolic status.

PLATE 61
Carved bone
Late Classic period, A.D. 600–800
Bone
34.2 x 7.5 x 2 cm
Courtesy of the Museum of the American Indian, Heye Foundation, New York

Givers of blood wore special costumes for the rite. Hair was bound up in the style usually shown on captives, and a long bone was often passed through the hair. Some such bone objects appear to have been sharpened for use as lancets, while others simply signaled the wearer's participation in the bloodletting rite.

This is one of these unsharpened hair ornaments. The size suggests it is a human femur, perhaps recovered from a sacrificial victim. The wider end of the bone is carved with the portrait of a seated lord wearing the regalia of bloodletting (Pl. 61a). The headdress zoomorph sits atop a stack of bloodletting knots, its lower jaw extending to become the chin strap. Emerging from the top of its head is a snaggletooth dragon with a huge blood scroll emerging from its mouth and falling to the floor. This bone, used in part of the bloodletting costume, depicts its owner performing the ritual.

PLATE 62
Lintel 24
Yaxchilan, Chiapas, Mexico
Late Classic period, A.D. 725
Limestone
110.5 x 80.6 x 10.1 cm
The Trustees of The British Museum, London

This lintel, considered one of the great masterpieces of Maya art, was removed from the left door of Structure 23 at Yaxchilan by Alfred Maudslay, who shipped it to Britain at the end of the nineteenth century. The sharp-edged, deep separation of the figures from the ground contributed to the identification of this artist as the Cookie Cutter Master. The precise and extraordinarily detailed surface depicts the richness of Classic Maya weaving, examples of which have not survived.

The scene depicts a bloodletting rite (Pl. 62a) that took place on 9.13.17.15.12 5 Eb 15 Mac, or October 28, A.D. 709. The king, Shield Jaguar, holds a huge torch, which suggests that the rite took place in a dark interior space or at night. In front of him, his kneeling wife, Lady Xoc, pulls a thorn-lined rope through her mutilated tongue. The rope falls to a woven basket, which holds blood-spotted paper and a stingray spine. Her lips and cheeks are smeared with dotted scrolls, symbolic of the blood she sheds to sustain the gods. Lady Xoc's face has a curiously blank look, considering that she is engaged in an act of self-mutilation. Perhaps she is in a trance induced by massive blood loss.

Shield Jaguar wears his hair in the style of penitents, for he, too, will draw blood as the rite continues. Feathers fall from the rear of his head, one twisting in the wind. The shrunken head of a past sacrificial victim is tied to the top of his head by a headband, marking Shield Jaguar's largesse in providing sustenance to the gods. He wears a finely woven pleated cape tied at his throat by a beautifully detailed knot; worn point down, the square cape covers his back to knee level. Around his neck

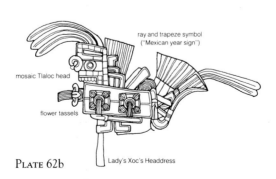

ray and trapeze symbol
("Mexican year sign")

mosaic Tlaloc head

flower tassels

PLATE 62b   Lady's Xoc's Headdress

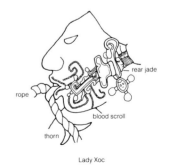

rear jade

rope

blood scroll

thorn

Lady Xoc

PLATE 61a

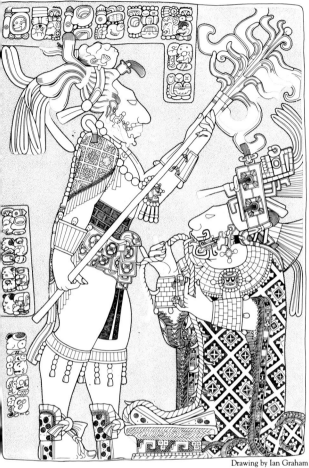

PLATE 62a

Drawing by Ian Graham

he wears a beaded necklace with its Sun God pectoral counterbalanced by a long strand falling down his back. In addition, he wears a rope collar, a signal of his participation in the bloodletting rite. A narrow belt with a herringbone design is wound repeatedly around his body and is overlaid by a second belt with cartouche and mat designs. His highback sandals are made from jaguar pelt, and jade ornaments encircle his knees and wrists.

His elegantly dressed wife, Lady Xoc, wears a *huipil* that piles up around her knees as she kneels in the ritual. It is woven in a complex diamond pattern with a skyband and fringe marking the edges of the cloth. Her shoulders and wrists are covered by a cape and cuffs made of a rectangular mosaic, perhaps assembled from thin jade or shell pieces. Her headdress has a flat drum shape mounted on a cloth cap. Adorning the main body are tassels, a Tlaloc head, a ray and trapeze symbol and cut feathers. This tasseled headdress is a signal of bloodletting and sacrificial rites.

THE INSCRIPTION

The text consists of two sentences (Pl. 62c), one relating to Shield Jaguar, the other to his wife. The first three glyphs record the date and the event, "he is letting blood," with additional glyphs apparently specifying the particular ritual context. Shield Jaguar's name begins at E2b, with a title telling us he was a "4-Katun *ahpo*"—that he had lived into his fourth katun (he was between sixty and eighty years old) at the time of the event. His personal name consists of a shield sitting atop a jaguar head. The name phrase concludes by naming him "the captor of Ah Ahaual" and "a blood lord of Yaxchilan." The actions of the woman are recorded in the smaller frame behind Shield Jaguar. The date is not repeated, since she performs the action at the same time as her husband. The last three glyphs record her name phrase.

PLATE 63
Lintel 25
Yaxchilan, Chiapas, Mexico
Late Classic period, A.D. 725
Limestone
130.1 x 86.3 x 10.1 cm
The Trustees of The British Museum, London

Lintel 25 shows a ritually induced hallucinatory vision manifested as a huge rearing serpent. The day of this event is Shield Jaguar's accession, 9.12.9.8.1 5 Imix 4 Mac, or October 23, A.D. 681. Although Shield Jaguar is named as the protagonist, he is not pictured in the scene. There is a clue why he is missing. The text is written in mirror image, as if it should be read from the other side of the stone; we believe this mirroring to be an ingenious device to signal that this activity takes place inside an architectural space. The kneeling woman, Lady Xoc, experiences the vision alone; Shield Jaguar has, perhaps, remained outside for this portion of the accession ritual.

Gazing upward at the apparition she has brought forth, Lady Xoc kneels with her elaborate *huipil* folded around her knees. It is gathered at the waist by a thick belt marked by the same cartouche and mat signs as Shield Jaguar's belt on Lintel 24 (Pl. 62). She wears a cape, a bar pectoral and a long strand of jade beads. In her right hand she holds a plate containing bloody paper and lancets; in her left hand, a plate containing bloodied paper, a stingray spine and an obsidian lancet (Pl. 63a). On her right wrist, she balances a skull with a skeletal serpent attached. The same device is used on her headband.

Another plate sits on the floor in front of her; it holds lancets, bloodied paper and a rope. From this plate rears a huge, double-headed Vision Serpent suspended in a lazy-S blood scroll. A warrior holding a spear and shield emerges from the mouth of the front head of the serpent. He has a cape, disk earflares and, before his face, the mask of Tlaloc, an image associated by the Maya with bloodletting, war and sacrifice. His headdress is balloon shaped, marked both by the bead and bone signs of blood and the hairs of a jaguar pelt. Bloodletting knots are tied to its front, where the cropped feathers and ray and trapeze sign of this Tlaloc complex are mounted. A fully zoomorphic Tlaloc image emerges from the lower mouth of the serpent. It has large goggle eyes and the same headdress assemblage; scrolls of blood emerge from its mouth.

The Vision Serpent twists as it rears upward, showing sometimes the patterns on its sides, at other times, its belly plates. Jade disks dot its body, and feather and blood fans are attached to its

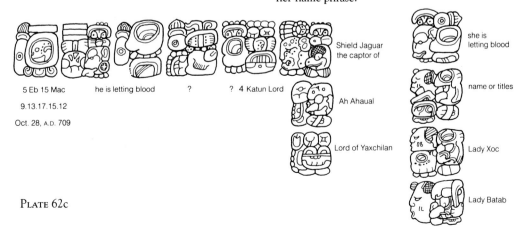

5 Eb 15 Mac
9.13.17.15.12
Oct. 28, A.D. 709

he is letting blood

?

? 4 Katun Lord

Shield Jaguar the captor of

Ah Ahaual

Lord of Yaxchilan

she is letting blood

name or titles

Lady Xoc

Lady Batab

PLATE 62c

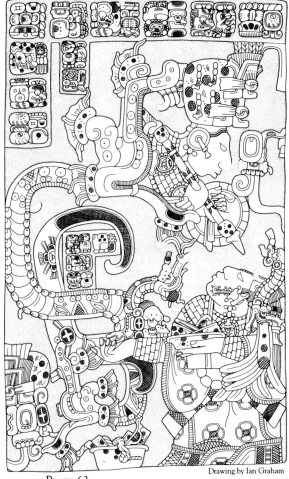

PLATE 63a

Drawing by Ian Graham

nostrils, eyebrows and cheeks. These designs are characteristic of Vision Serpents and can be used on pottery to signal the entire complex without the presence of the serpent itself.

THE INSCRIPTION

The text on the front (Pl. 63b) opens with the date 5 Imix 4 Mac and the verb "fish-in-hand," which can be used both for the bloodletting itself and for the resulting vision. The next three glyphs are not fully understood but give additional ritual information about the action; the glyph at C signifies the eccentric flint-flayed face shield emblem given to Palenque rulers on their accession (see Fig. II.7). The king's name reads, "4-katun lord, Shield Jaguar, captor of Ah Ahaual, blood lord of Yaxchilan, Bacab."

Lady Xoc is recorded only with a general verb (something like "she is") and her name phrase. The text from the front (not reproduced) records a house event—which was perhaps the dedication of this building or another ancestral event recalled through bloodletting—that took place forty-two tuns later, on August 5, A.D. 723. This text faced those approaching the door and was the first information encountered upon entering the building.

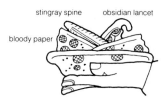

stingray spine   obsidian lancet

bloody paper

The Bloodletting Bowl

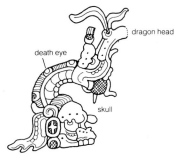

dragon head

death eye

skull

Skeletal Dragon and Skull

5 Imix 4 Mac   he let blood   his flint-shield   he of fire   chac   ??   4 katun lord

9.12.9.8.1

(Oct. 23, A.D. 681)

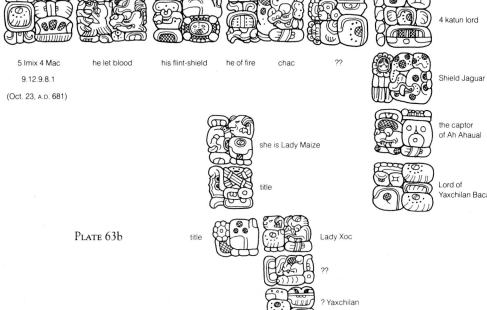

she is Lady Maize

title

PLATE 63b   title

Shield Jaguar

the captor of Ah Ahaual

Lord of Yaxchilan Bacab

Lady Xoc

??

? Yaxchilan

jaguar pelt helmet

bead and bone signs

bar and trapeze signs

knots

Tlaloc

blood scrolls

shield

spear

Tlaloc

The Warrior

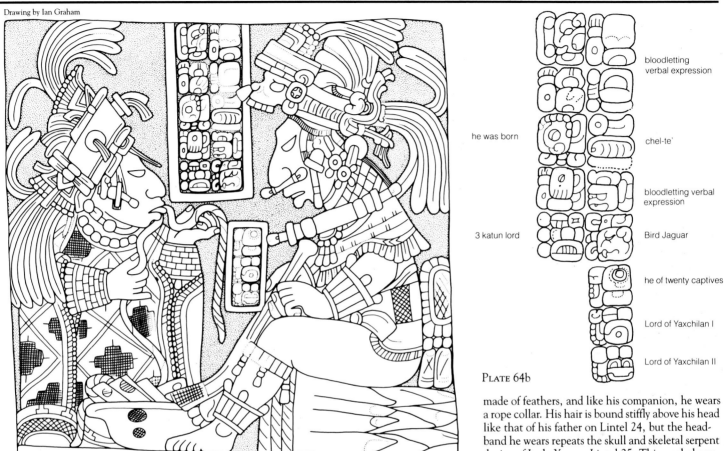

Drawing by Ian Graham

bloodletting
verbal expression

he was born   chel-te'

bloodletting verbal
expression

3 katun lord   Bird Jaguar

he of twenty captives

Lord of Yaxchilan I

Lord of Yaxchilan II

PLATE 64b

PLATE 64a   she is   title   Lady Balan   Balam   Lady Ix   maize title   Lady   Bacab

PLATE 64
Lintel 17
Yaxchilan, Chiapas, Mexico
Late Classic period, A.D. 770
Limestone
69.2 x 76.2 x 5 cm
The Trustees of The British Museum, London

The three lintels of Yaxchilan Structure 21, also removed by Maudslay, record Bird Jaguar's enactment of the ritual depicted in Lintels 24, 25 and 26 (Pls. 62, 63 and Fig. V.2). Although no date is given for the bloodletting depicted on Lintel 17 (Pl. 64a), the inscription records the occasion as the birth of Bird Jaguar's son and heir, which is elsewhere dated 9.16.0.14.5, or February 18, A.D. 752.

The woman depicted is Lady Balam-Ix—not the child's mother but another of Bird Jaguar's wives. She kneels, pulling the rope through her tongue. Although she doesn't have to suffer added damage from thorns, as did Lady Xoc a generation earlier, she wears the same tasseled headdress as that lady does on Lintel 24. The plate holding bloodied paper rests on the ground in front of her.

    The father of the newborn sits across from Lady Balam-Ix on a bundle of leaflike objects, imagery seen only in this scene. Bird Jaguar wears a cloth kilt with a shield mounted on the rear of a wide belt. He is bedecked with ornate earplugs, nosepieces, a bar pectoral and jade cylinder cuffs on wrists, knees and ankles. His cape appears to be

made of feathers, and like his companion, he wears a rope collar. His hair is bound stiffly above his head like that of his father on Lintel 24, but the headband he wears repeats the skull and skeletal serpent device of Lady Xoc on Lintel 25. This symbol suggests that he, too, is about to let blood, and the bone awl is handily placed for him to pierce his penis. The artist has drawn the sole of his right foot just above his left foot, showing that his legs are spread in preparation for the painful ritual.

THE INSCRIPTION
The inscription (Pl. 64b) is more difficult than most others because the structure of the sentence is unusual. The bloodletting ritual is recorded in a long expression composed of six glyphs, but in the middle of this expression, the scribe inserted an additional two-glyph phrase explaining why the bloodletting was required. The added phrase records the birth of Shield Jaguar II, so that the birth record is embedded within the expression for the ritual that celebrated it. The protagonist is named as a "3-katun lord, Bird Jaguar, he who took 20 captives, blood lord of Yaxchilan." In the horizontal text below the scene, his companion is named as Lady Balam-Ix.

Plate 65
Lintel 15
Yaxchilan, Chiapas, Mexico
Late Classic period, A.D. 770
Limestone
87.6 x 82.6 x 10.7 cm
The Trustees of The British Museum, London

Lintel 15 depicts the vision stage of the bloodletting rite (Pl. 65a). The kneeling woman—neither the mother of Shield Jaguar II nor Lady Balam-Ix—is yet another of Bird Jaguar's wives. She wears a *huipil* woven in the same pattern as that of Lady Xoc on Lintel 24. Jade jewelry decorates her wrists, ears, hair and neck. The collar characteristic of this rite binds her throat. It is curious that she does not wear a headdress; instead, her hair is tied back with bloody bark paper cloth. Her basket is made from woven reed, and the rope she has used falls casually across her forearm. Her Vision Serpent rears through a beaded blood scroll out of a clay bowl lined with bloody paper that is set on the floor before her. The Serpent is the most naturalistic of all known examples; it is bearded, and from its mouth emerges the ancestor the lady has contacted in the rite.

The Inscription
The best reconstruction of the partially eroded date is 9.16.3.16.19 4 Cauac 12 Zip, or March 28, A.D. 755, almost three years after Bird Jaguar's accession. The remainder of the main text (Pl. 65b) simply records the bloodletting rite in a couplet form, the same information being written twice in slightly varied forms. The smaller text simply names the woman in the scene as Lady 6-Tun. Since her Emblem Glyph is not that of Yaxchilan, we assume she came from another site to marry Bird Jaguar.

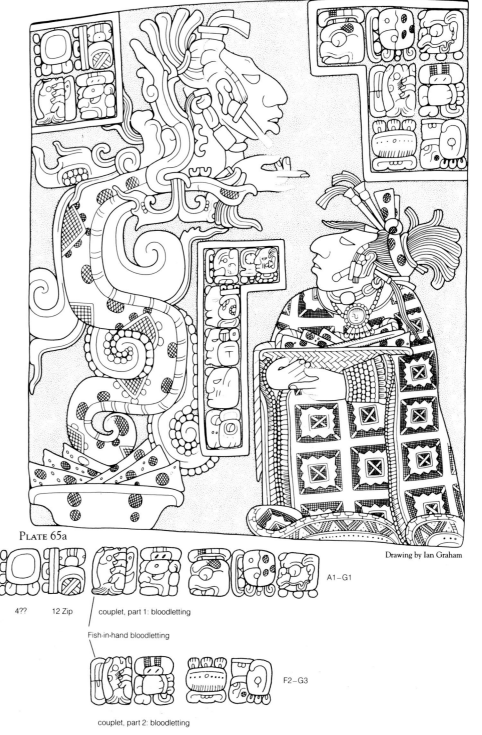

Plate 65a

Drawing by Ian Graham

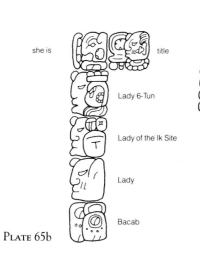

she is — title

Lady 6-Tun

Lady of the Ik Site

Lady

Bacab

Plate 65b

4??   12 Zip   couplet, part 1: bloodletting   A1–G1

Fish-in-hand bloodletting

F2–G3

couplet, part 2: bloodletting

Plate 66
Stela with a ruler having a vision
Protoclassic period, A.D. 199
Limestone
H. 83.8 cm
John H. Hauberg Collection, Seattle
Photo by Paul Macapia

This stela has the earliest deciphered date known from the Maya, 8.8.0.7.0 3 Ahau 13 Xul, or October 9, A.D. 199. The scene (Pl. 66b) records the vision experience of Bac-T'ul, an early ruler, who has let blood in preparation for his accession fifty-two days later. Wearing the mask of a god, he holds the manifested vision over his arms. By a most extraordinary coincidence, a mask with almost identical features was given to the British Museum in the late nineteenth century (Pl. 15). Since it is unlikely that the Hauberg artist ever saw the British Museum mask, we may assume that this particular god mask was a popular ritual item during early Maya history.

      The ruler wears a headdress with a Jester God headband, a large earflare and a quilted or net chin strap. His chest is bare and his skirt richly decorated with woven designs. He wears the crossbands and disk belt with a jaguar zoomorph hanging from the front, as well as jade cuffs on wrists and ankles. With his left hand he holds the Vision Serpent against his chest, while his right hand extends outward in the scattering gesture. From his back falls a scalloped tree design, down which three bodies are falling; they are severed at the waist, and scrolls signal blood emerging from the wounds.

      The Vision Serpent rears upward through the ruler's arms, twisting to stand above his head. The being who is contacted, symbolized by an anthropomorphic head, emerges from the Serpent's mouth. Four miniature gods climb the body of the Vision Serpent, whose identity as a sacrificial being is confirmed by the flint blade forming its tail. The head of the uppermost god has the Venus sign; the lowermost god is Chac-Xib-Chac.

The Inscription
The text (Pl. 66a) begins with an Initial Series Introductory Glyph warning that a date is coming, but the date is written without a Long Count and in reverse order from the expected format of a Calendar Round date: The *haab* precedes the Lord of the Night, the moon age and the Tzolkin. This peculiar order is not unique, being known from monuments at Quirigua and Copan, which appear to emulate the very early format deliberately. The order may have been used experimentally before a

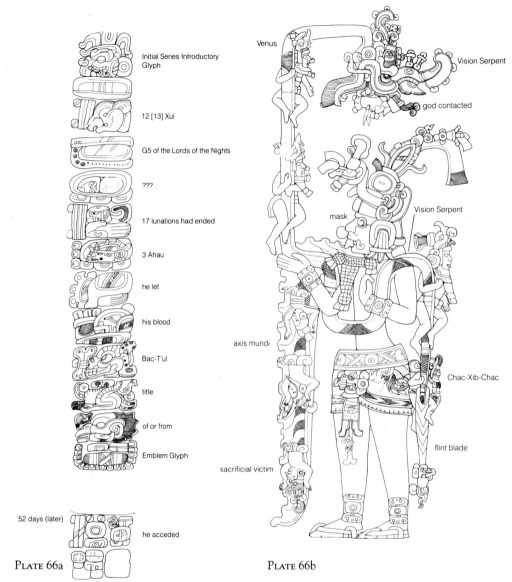

	Initial Series Introductory Glyph
	12 [13] Xul
	G5 of the Lords of the Nights
	???
	17 lunations had ended
	3 Ahau
	he let
	his blood
	Bac-T'ul
	title
	of or from
	Emblem Glyph

Plate 66a

52 days (later) — he acceded

Venus · Vision Serpent · god contacted · mask · Vision Serpent · axis mundi · Chac-Xib-Chac · sacrificial victim · flint blade

Plate 66b

convention for writing dates had been agreed upon.

      The date is in error, recording a 12 instead of a 13; nevertheless, it may be reconstructed as follows: 12 Xul, the 5th Lord of the Night, 17 lunations had ended, 3 Ahau, or October 9, A.D. 199. The verbal sign is the picture of an obsidian lancet, used to mean "bleed" or "let," much in the same manner we use the word *fish* to mean both the animal and the act of catching it. The lancet is followed by the glyph for blood and the name of the

ruler Bac-T'ul, Bone Rabbit. His name may end with an Emblem Glyph, but as yet, the place is not identified.

      The smaller glyphs below make up a second sentence that has not been successfully deciphered. It does, however, begin with a Distance Number of 52 days and a glyph for accession. The bloodletting depicted in the scene and recorded in the previous sentence was apparently a rite conducted in ritual preparation for Bac-T'ul's accession.

PLATE 67
Carved vessel with a vision serpent
Late Preclassic period, 200 B.C.–A.D. 100
Stone
Diam. 12 x H. 14.2 cm,
Dumbarton Oaks, Washington, D.C.

This extraordinary stone drinking vessel was carved by an early master adept at subtle relief modeling and precise linear drawing. From its style, it has always been assumed to be from the Highlands (where the use of stone was more common), but its iconography is purely Lowland. It represents the earliest known example of the Vision Serpent.

The vessel is heavy but perfectly proportioned for a two-handed grip. It was probably used either to gather blood from the bloodletting rite or to hold hallucinogenic beverages used in addition to, or instead of, bloodletting to induce visions (the Maya are also known to have used tobacco and intoxicating enemas for this purpose).

The relief is executed at different depths, so that the shapes merge from one to another in subtle modulation. Incised line delineating fine detail within individual shapes was perhaps once enhanced by a thin coating of cinnabar or specular hematite in the grooved areas.

Two Vision Serpents (Pl. 67A) wrap tail to nose around the vessel. Each blunt-snouted front head gapes open, emitting a thick stream of blood. The eyes have round irises, a feature found only in boa constrictors. Attached to the upper side of the curl of each serpent's tail is a second blunt-snouted head, possibly a personification of blood. As seen in later versions, the tail of the Late Preclassic Vision Serpent is anatomically complete—the second head is attached to the body rather than being an extension of it.

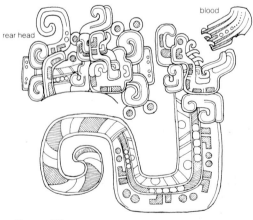

PLATE 67b
the serpent

PLATE 68
Cylinder vase
Late Classic period, A.D. 650–800
Polychromed ceramic
Diam. 19.6 x H. 25.3 cm
Dumbarton Oaks, Washington, D.C.

The painter of this large cylinder used a nervous and vigorous black line overlapping subtle slips of white and tans. The composition is episodic, recording two rites in an accession sequence. The order in which the two scenes are meant to be read is not known, but the palace scene gives the occasion for the events shown.

Three-quarters of the surface is occupied by the palace scene, which is demarcated by a rolled-up white curtain just below the rim text. The action takes place within a building consisting of a bench area and a blank wall. The protagonist sits at the highest level, leaning against a white pillow. One attendant sits on a step below him; the other five participants stand or sit on the floor. Everyone wears an elaborate cloth headdress and skirt of light-colored cloth. All the attendants wear dark capes, yet the protagonist wears what looks like a striped T-shirt. His headdress is also unique: it is white and features a long-necked monster that rears above his head. Beside him is a stand holding a large, deep bowl. Below him on the floor sit two or three bundles—one round with a head or mask on top; one composed of horizontal lines (perhaps folded cloth); and a third, large one with a covered perforator laid atop it.

The text immediately in front of the protagonist's face is the key to the scene. It begins with an auxiliary verb, followed by the glyph for seating; he is being seated in office as king, and these are the rituals required to confirm his office. The last two glyphs are his names—a jaguar head and the net-covered portrait head of God N, or Pauahtun, so he can be called Balam-Pauahtun.

The other scene is much smaller, having only two figures, at least one clearly identified. The right figure wears the same long-neck monster headdress as worn by the protagonist; the Balam-Pauahtun names are located above and behind his head. This extraordinary scene shows him practicing the ritual of bloodletting. He faces forward wearing a white loincloth and a string cape with white designs sewn to it. Holding a lancet in his right hand, he takes aim at his penis.

This man's companion is already well into the rite. Bending forward at the waist, he stands so that the rope he pulls through his perforated tongue will fall freely into the large receiving bowl below. He wears the rope collar and the same tasseled headdress as the women in the bloodletting scenes from Yaxchilan Lintels 24 and 17 (Pls. 62 and 64). A parrot, perhaps stuffed, perches on top of the headdress. This scene records the bloodletting rite necessary for the seating of Balam-Pauahtun as king.

PLATE 69
Figurine of a noble letting blood
Late Classic period, A.D. 600–800
Ceramic
19 x 8.5 cm
Department of Anthropology, American Museum of Natural History, New York

The high rank of this figure is revealed by his expensive earflares and the finely woven hipcloth. His headdress, composed either of stiff cloth or bark paper, is wound around his head, then bent forward by the segmented band that holds it in place. The rope collar—which would normally mark the wearer as a captive—reveals that this man is engaged in the bloodletting rite. He sits cross-legged, laying his exposed penis across a stack of blue paper as he makes the cuts to draw blood.

PLATE 70
Figurine of a seated man
Late Classic period, A.D. 700–900
Ceramic
25.4 x 12.7 cm
Department of Anthropology, Denver Museum of Natural History

This figurine shows a person just before a bloodletting rite. He sits on a scaffold platform before a deep bowl. His head is bound by bloodletting knots, and cloth strips are pulled through his earlobes. His status as a penitent is marked by the rope tied around his elbows, wrists, knees and ankles; the jagged pattern of his skirt is cut as the mark of sacrifice. His face is covered with raised lines forming the pattern of a skull, perhaps representing face painting assumed for the rite. The facial markings may indicate that he is a priest who paints on his face the role he assumes in the rite; or he may be a warrior who has painted his face in the imagery of death as he prepares for battle.

Plate 71
Cylindrical vessel
Late Classic period, A.D. 600–800
Polychromed ceramic
Diam. 11.1 x H. 22.3 cm
Kimbell Art Museum, Fort Worth

Painted by one of the finest Maya painters, this pot is one of a series depicting events in the life of a lord nicknamed the Fat Cacique. While one of the colors has disappeared because of chemical instability, considerable detail remains. This artist is particularly accomplished and innovative in the way he renders architecture. The action of the scene is divided between the interior and exterior of a palace building raised on a low platform with two steps. Three dancers stand on the lowest level in front of the blank outer wall of the building. The painter used the rim text as if it were painted on a band that encircled the Maya building just under the eaves. Inside the building, the Fat Cacique is comfortably seated on a bench with a huge pillow behind him. Both the bench and the pillow are covered by a jaguar pelt. The door that frames the Fat Cacique is indicated by vertical lines; the artist emphasized its shape by placing an attendant behind each door jamb. Their partial shapes, cut off by the building walls, reinforce the suggestion that another room extends beyond the door. The dancers, who are to be understood as standing in front of the Fat Cacique, overlap the doors from both directions, setting up a spatial ambiguity that helps to circulate the viewer around the pot.

The Fat Cacique is simply dressed, in a hipcloth, jade necklace and headdress. In front of him, a kneeling attendant lifts up another jade necklace for his inspection, while the attendant behind him appears to hold a now-eroded object toward him. A deformed dwarf with a marvelously carved pendant sits on the first step below him.

The lords who perform before the Fat Cacique are dressed like the dancers in the extraordinary ritual scene in the paintings of Room 3 at Bonampak. Each dancer wears a high, complex headdress with a stuffed iguana emerging from the front; the first two have ear ornaments made from bird's legs. Their faces are painted in a two-tone pattern, and their bodies are painted black. Their capes are light colored, and they wear jade necklaces and wrist cuffs. Their waists are thickly bound by cloth belts, and they wear fringed bands on the knees and ankles. All three dancers hold woven reed fans in one hand. The right figure has his heels raised as he steps to the dance, an activity confirmed by the Bonampak scene. Their white loincloths are spattered with blood because the dancers have perforated their penises. As they whirl, blood is drawn into the paper panels extending from their groins.

Plate 72
Cylindrical vessel with bloodletting scene
Huehuetenango, Guatemala
Late Classic period, A.D. 600–800
Polychromed ceramic
University Museum, The University of Pennsylvania, Philadelphia
Photo by Otis Imboden

The Perforator God and the Classic-period ritual of penis mutilation were first recognized on this red-background pot. The scene is broken into two registers by a central band of glyphs recording the Primary Standard Sequence. Below, the red field is broken by the upper halves of quadrifoil cartouches, each containing an Imix Monster sitting in a bowl. Perforator Gods float between the cartouches. These cartouches appear to symbolize penetrations (such as cave openings), the monsters inside to personify glyphs that record supernatural locations in the Dresden Codex. While the environment these symbols define is not yet fully understood, it does not seem to be of this world.

The upper register is divided into two scenes by vertical bands, one with an Initial Series Introductory Glyph and nine baktuns, the other with an Initial Series Introductory Glyph and four baktuns—neither of which can be fully interpreted at present. The dates do, however, signal that the upper register occurs in mythological time. In each scene, three figures squat over the ground or over bowls filled with paper strips. They aim the Perforator God at their genitals as they draw blood in the supernatural version of bloodletting. Most important, they are not men—they are gods, many of whom are recognizable. The first three are the Headband Twins and the Sun God; the third figure in the second group is known to be Hun-Ahau, one of the Headband Twins again. The Huehuetenango Vase demonstrates that in Maya cosmology, gods as well as humans gave sacrificial blood.

Plate 73
Redware jar with vision rite image
San Agustin Acasaguastlan, Guatemala
Early Classic period, A.D. 400–600
Carved and appliqued ceramic
Circum. 76.2 x H. 17 cm
Courtesy of the Museum of the American Indian, Heye Foundation, New York

Found in San Agustin Acasaguastlan in the Guatemala Highlands in the early twentieth century, this vase—long thought to be a fake—is one of the most extraordinary and beautiful examples of sculpted pottery now known. The vessel wall was built up by a combination of additive and subtractive techniques. Each layer was carefully cut in silhouette, then affixed to the surface below it, so that a relief of varying depths was gradually built up. Subtle modulation of the final surface and detailing with incised line produced a complex and richly detailed deep relief.

At the center of the composition (Pl. 73b) sits the Sun God, depicted in front view with his legs crossed and his hands held to his chest, in the regal position of historical kings. He holds two feathered Vision Serpents, the body of each running through an arm and curling up to a rear head near his elbow. Each Serpent rises above his shoulder, falls to the groundline, then runs around the pot to terminate in a head on the opposite side.

The Serpent in the Sun God's right arm has several distinctive signs: its muzzle is marked by a mirror-shell sign, and its rear forehead has the sign for night or darkness. Huge blood scrolls emerge from the top of the rear head. Water (or cloud) scrolls are attached to the last curl of its body, and cross-hatched shapes line the underside of its muzzle. The T-shape in this row of muzzle liners is a rare motif that also appears on the rear heads of the Late Preclassic Vision Serpents on the Dumbarton Oaks stone vase (Pl. 67). The head and neck of a bird emerge from the corner of the Serpent's mouth.

The Serpent in the Sun God's left arm has no special symbols attached to its body, and its muzzle infix is *akbal*, "darkness." The head at the rear of the monster has a half scroll, representing water, over the forehead, with a second water scroll and feathers attached to the top. The muzzle of the front head is lined with feathers, and a leaf and stem emerge from the corner of its mouth.

The Vision Serpents mirror each other and are meant to be understood as paired opposites. The mirror and blood scrolls of the right serpent signal brightness and blood, in contrast to the dark-

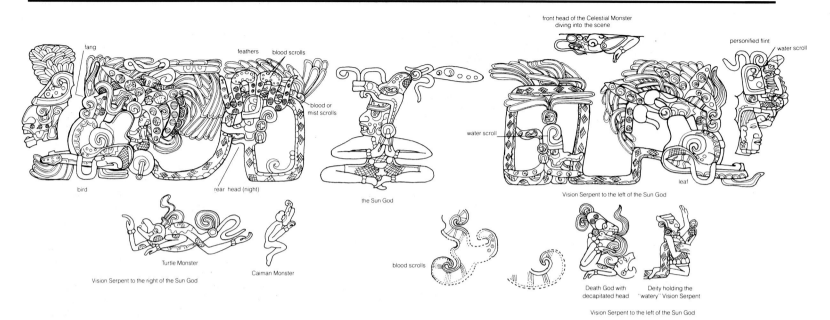

fang

feathers   blood scrolls

blood or
mist scrolls

front head of the Celestial Monster
diving into the scene

personified flint   water scroll

water scroll

bird   rear head (night)   the Sun God   Vision Serpent to the left of the Sun God   leaf

Turtle Monster

Caiman Monster

blood scrolls

Vision Serpent to the right of the Sun God

Death God with
decapitated head

Deity holding the
"watery" Vision Serpent

Vision Serpent to the left of the Sun God

PLATE 73b

ness and water scroll signs that mark the left serpent. The visions that emerge from the serpents are also contrasted: from the right comes the Sun God and from the left comes a human head wearing a reptilian monster as its headdress. The reptile in turn has the same water scroll as the rear head. A personified flint, the instrument of sacrifice, sits on the muzzle of the headdress. The small creatures that cavort among the twisting bodies of the Vision Serpents are also contrasted. A small human figure (perhaps representing the man who commissioned the pot) sits on the earflare of the bright, blood serpent; its correlate on the other side is an anthropomorphic god who holds up the body of the dark, water serpent. A turtle monster and a curl-snouted crocodile rest along the body of the bright serpent; they are replaced on the opposite side by a skeletal death god and a decapitated head. On the "dark" side, a deer-eared crocodile drops from the rim border into the feathers of the Vision Serpent; it is the front half of the Celestial Monster diving below the surface of the earth (symbolized by the rim of the pot) into the watery Underworld.

PLATE 74
Tripod plate with rattle feet
Late Classic period, A.D. 600–800
Polychromed ceramic
Diam. 32.5 cm
Edwin Pearlman, M.D., Norfolk, Virginia

This flat-bottomed plate with its slanting sides and three rattle feet is the type of bloodletting bowl used to hold the torn paper and receive the bloody rope. Most Late Classic depictions of these plates do not show feet, but footed plates are typically shown with offerings in the Dresden Codex, and the iconography is unmistakable. Painted in red, orange and black paint on a tan ground, the image is that of a Vision Serpent—complete with its disk body pattern and feather fan—rearing upward from the forehead of the Quadripartite Monster (which is also the rear head of the Celestial Monster). The face of a young male emerges from the mouth of the serpent.

This image is a multileveled visual play on the linguistic and symbolic identity of the Quadripartite Monster. The forehead shape is a bowl derived originally from a rebus usage of a bowl in the glyphic spelling of east (*lakin*). The sign for bowl (pronounced *lac*) stood for *lak*, meaning "next" in the word *lakin*, "next sun." Here, the artist plays on this word by treating the forehead of the

Quadripartite Monster as a bloodletting bowl. Furthermore, the top of the Quadripartite Monster would normally have a three-part symbol consisting of a shell, symbolizing the Underworld; a stingray spine, symbolizing the Middleworld; and crossed bands, symbolizing the Heavens. This complete symbol, which includes a blood letter, is replaced in this work by the vision that comes from the stingray spine. Finally, the Celestial Monster is often depicted with huge streams of blood pouring from the mouth of each of its heads; here, however, the blood is manifested as the vision itself. Thus, the symbolic message declares bloodletting and the resultant visions to be inherent to cosmic order. The bowl used in the rite conveyed this message to the penitent who placed his blood offering within its walls.

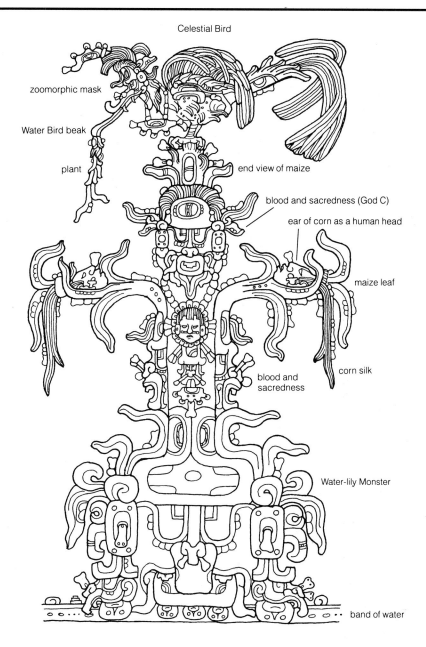

Celestial Bird

zoomorphic mask

Water Bird beak

plant

end view of maize

blood and sacredness (God C)

ear of corn as a human head

maize leaf

corn silk

blood and
sacredness

Water-lily Monster

band of water

FIGURE IV.4
Maize Cross
Temple of the Foliated Cross, Palenque, Chiapas, Mexico
Late Classic period, A.D. 672

PLATE 75
Cache vessel lid
Early Classic period, A.D. 350–500
Incised ceramic
Diam. 35.9 x H. 5.7 cm
Lent courtesy of The Art Museum, Princeton University

This plate was the lid of a special cache vessel consisting of two large plates set lip to lip. Known in particular from Late Preclassic and Early Classic buildings, these caches were placed under floors during dedication rites and contained offerings, such as decapitated heads, flint blades, stingray spines, thorns of various types and sea fans, coral, sponges and other material from the sea.

Many of these plates were plain, but a number are carved with finely incised drawings, which may have indicated the god being propitiated. On this plate, the central icon is the *kin* bowl seen previously as the forehead of the Quadripartite Monster. Here it has a square-nosed dragon drawn across the *kin* sign, and it rests atop the head of Bolon-Mayel, a little-understood god who appears mostly in glyphic form. The decapitated head of the Maize God lies in the plate with the three primary bloodletting lancets—an obsidian blade, a stingray spine and a flint knife. Kan-cross and bone-bead signs qualify the water pattern in the background as blood, indicating that the entire image floats in blood.

A single glyph is carved into the four opposite sides of the plate wall. At least two of these name gods. Below the central image is Chac-Xib-Chac; above is Tah-Balam-Ahau (a torch in front of an *ahau* sign half covered with jaguar skin), one of the names of GIII from his birth passage on the Tablet of the Sun at Palenque. The remaining two glyphs are more difficult; they may modify the two identified god names or, more likely, name two additional gods. One is Ahpo-Caban, Lord Earth; the other is Ahpo-Ix, Lord Jaguar.

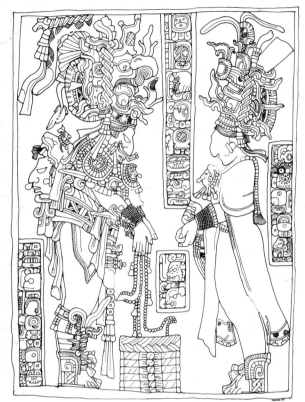

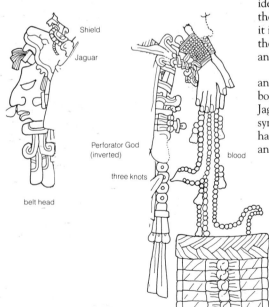

Shield

Jaguar

belt head

Perforator God
(inverted)

three knots

blood

censer

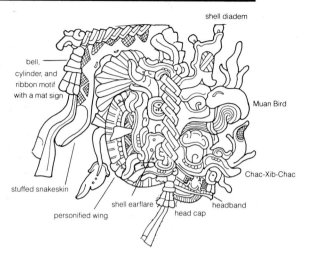

shell diadem

bell,
cylinder, and
ribbon motif
with a mat sign

Muan Bird

Chac-Xib-Chac

stuffed snakeskin

shell earflare

personified wing

head cap

headband

Bird Jaguar's Headdress

Plate 76
Lintel 2

La Pasadita, El Peten, Guatemala
Late Classic period, A.D. 766
Limestone
117 x 90 cm
Rijksmuseum voor Volkenkunde, Leiden, Holland

The text on this lintel identifies the two actors as
Bird Jaguar of Yaxchilan, who had crossed the
Usumacinta River in order to celebrate the end of a
ten-tun period (half of a katun), and his *cahal*, or
territorial administrator, at La Pasadita. Bird Jaguar
performs the scattering rite.

    The king on the left is dressed in the more
elaborate costume; he wears a heavy cape and pectoral, high-backed sandals, ornate cuffs on wrists
and ankles and jade jewelry on his ear, nose and
knees. Several elements are particularly important
to his role in this ritual and as king of Yaxchilan: his
headdress features Chac-Xib-Chac and the Muan
Bird, and the head he wears on the back of his belt
is a portrait of his dead father, Shield Jaguar. Its
headdress has a shield headband on a jaguar head.

    Bird Jaguar's genitals are covered by an
inverted Perforator God, identifying the material
he scatters as blood and the place from which he
takes it as his penis. He leans forward, dropping a
stream of blood into a large container shrouded in
bloodletting knots. Exactly this kind of container,
carved in stone, is known at Copan. There it can be
identified as a brazier, most probably used to burn
the blood offering, so that the gods could consume
it in the form of smoke. To consecrate the end of
the period, the king draws his most potent blood as
an offering to the gods.

    The *cahal* opposite him wears a long cape
and loincloth, each with finely woven decorated
borders. His headdress is as elaborate as that of Bird
Jaguar, although it bears a different assemblage of
symbols. He holds an unidentified object in one
hand, apparently in his role as noble assistant, host
and subordinate to the king.

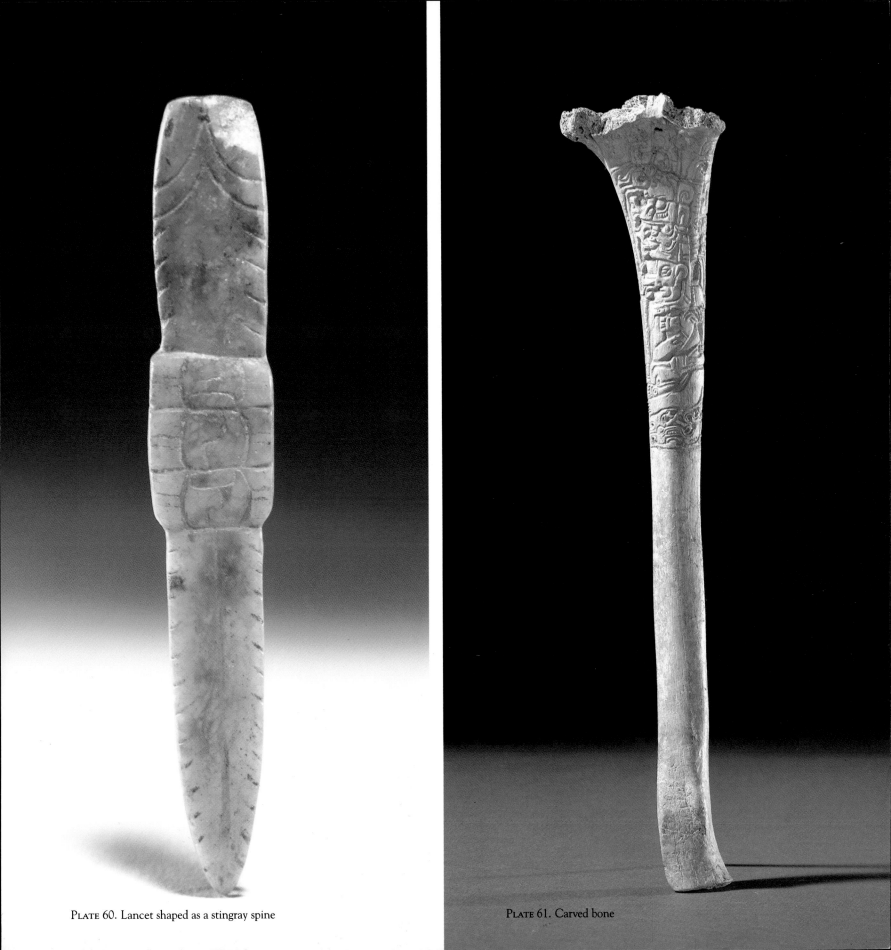

PLATE 60. Lancet shaped as a stingray spine

PLATE 61. Carved bone

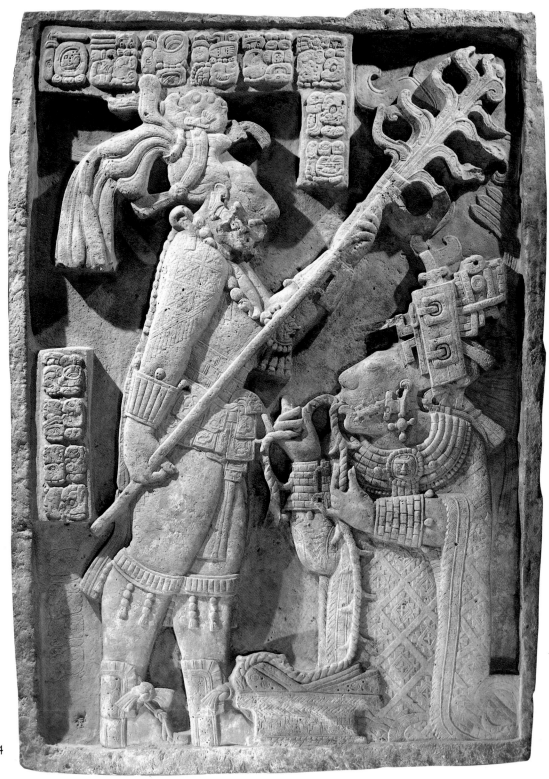

PLATE 62. Lintel 24

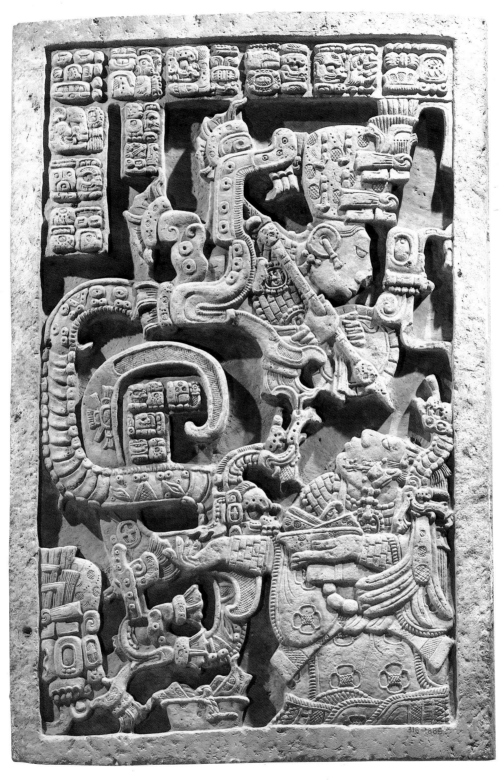

PLATE 63. Lintel 25

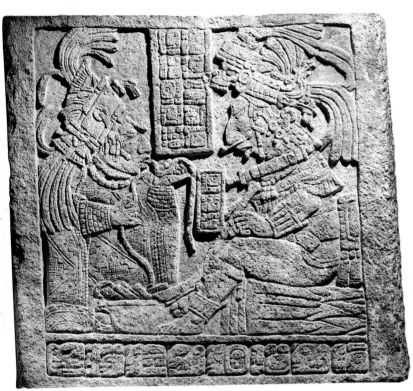

PLATE 64. Lintel 17

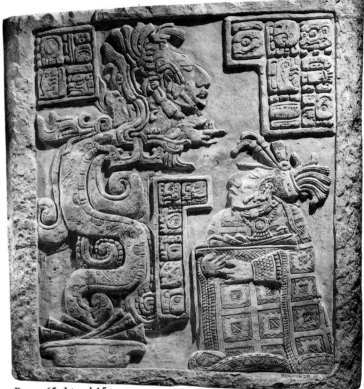

PLATE 65. Lintel 15

PLATE 66. Stela with a ruler having a vision

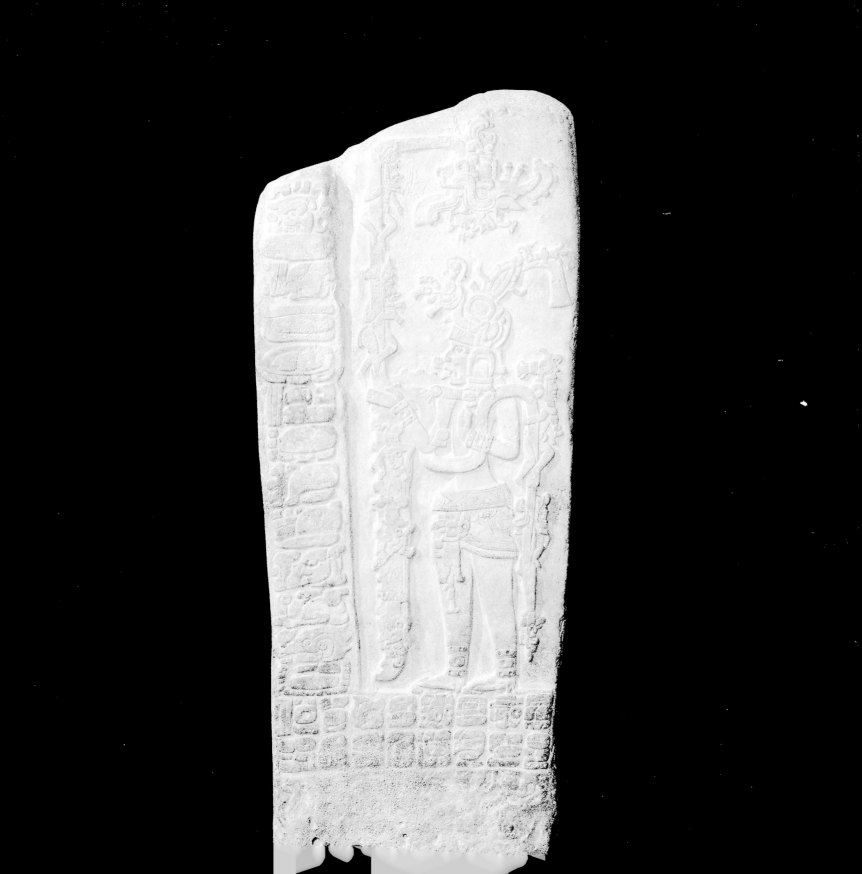

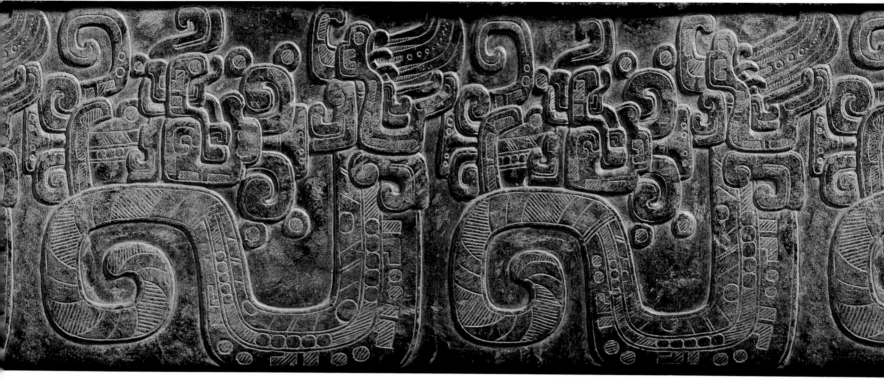

PLATE 67A. Rollout

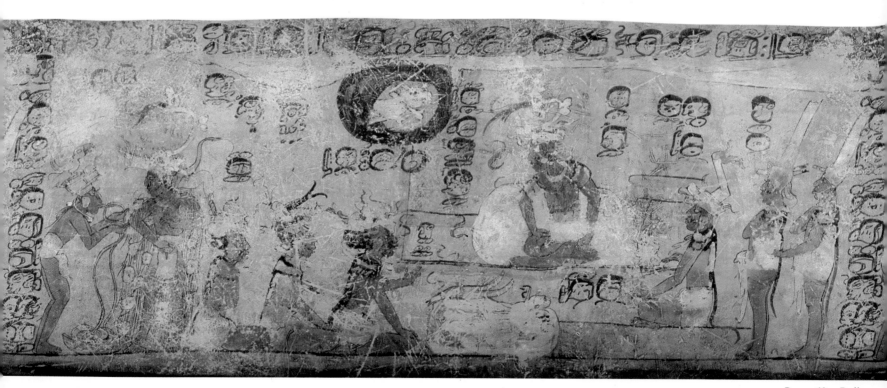

PLATE 68A. Rollout

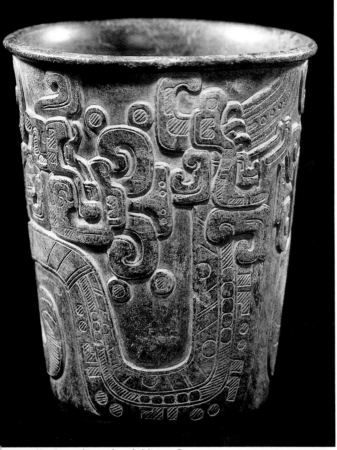

Plate 67. Carved vessel with Vision Serpent

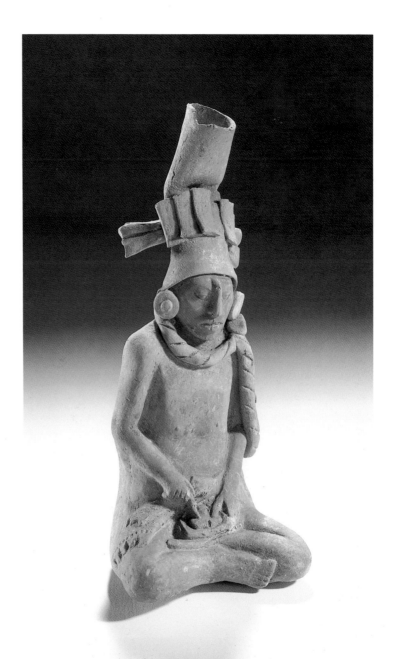

Plate 69. Figurine of a noble letting blood

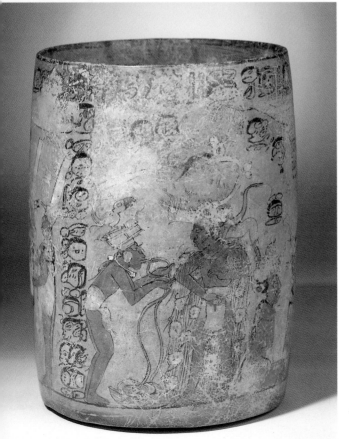

Plate 68. Cylindrical vessel with accession scene

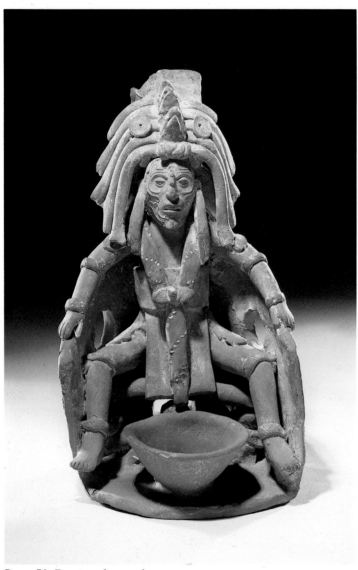

PLATE 70. Figurine of a seated man

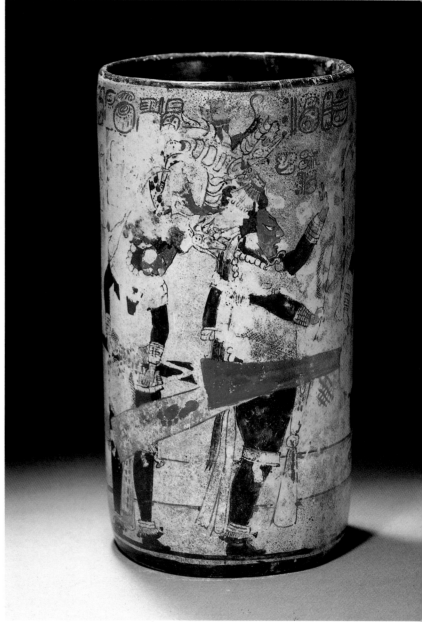

PLATE 71. Cylindrical vessel

PLATE 71A. Ro

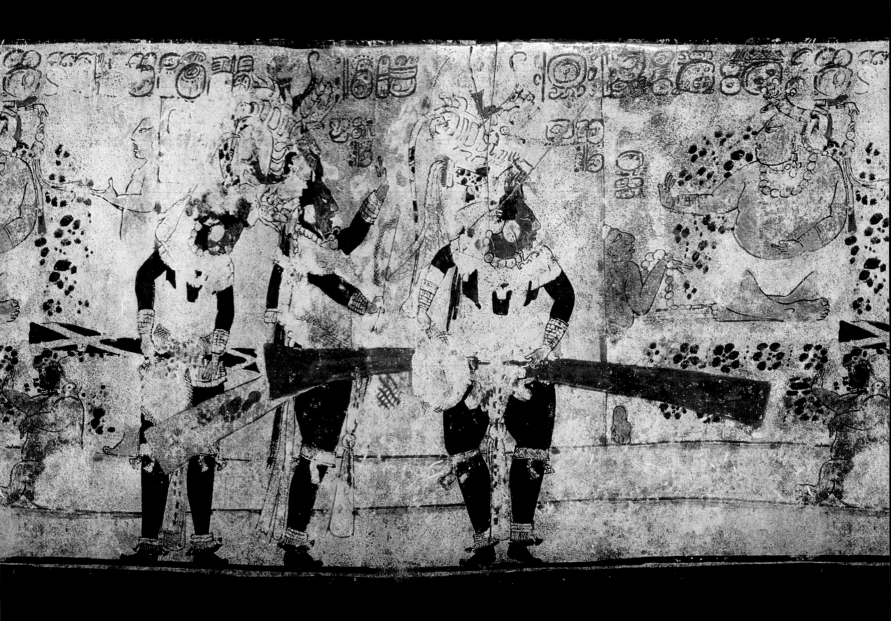

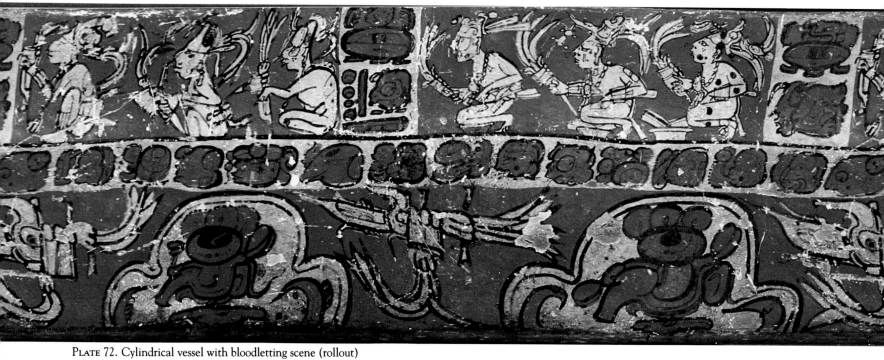

Plate 72. Cylindrical vessel with bloodletting scene (rollout)

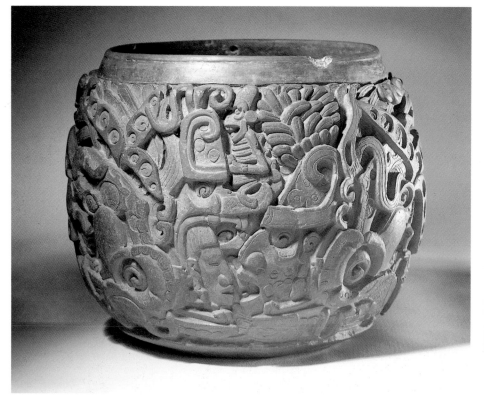

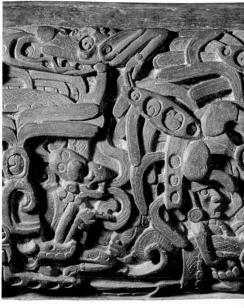

Plate 73. Redware jar with vision rite image
Plate 73a. Rollout

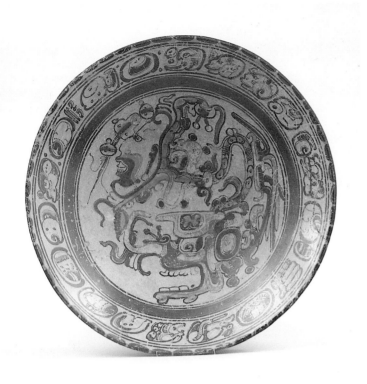

Plate 74. Tripod Plate with rattle feet

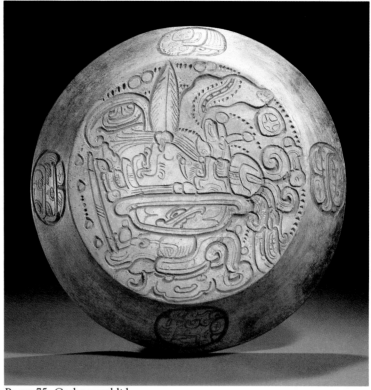

Plate 75. Cache vessel lid

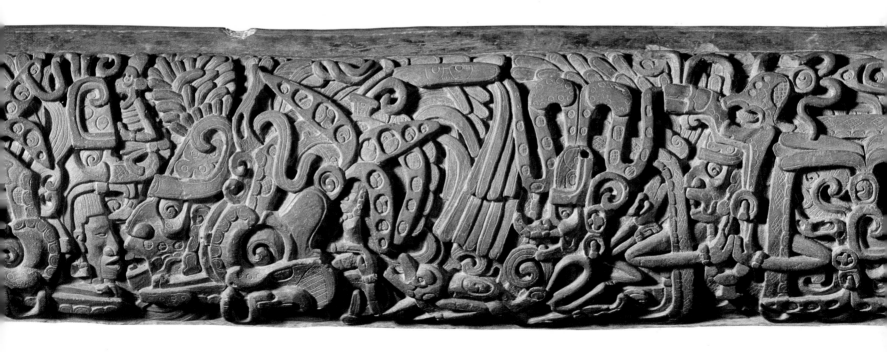

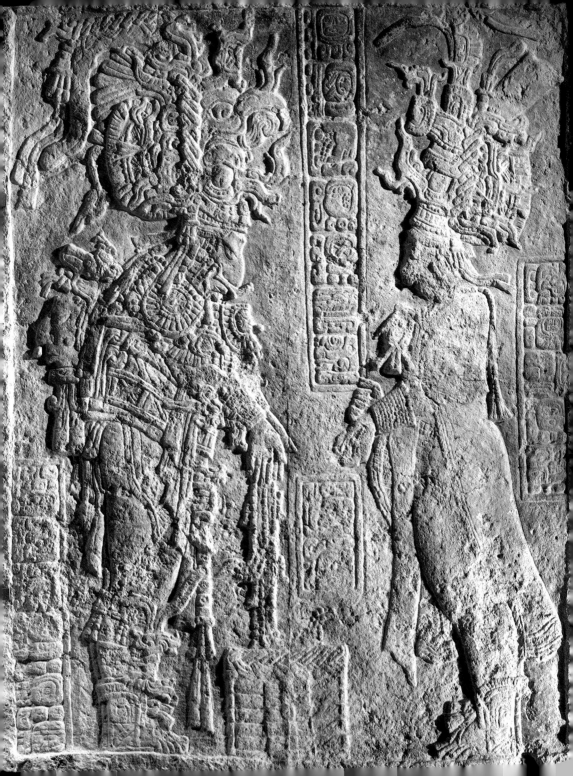

V

Warfare and Captive Sacrifice

ALL ACROSS THEIR REALM DURING THE EIGHTH CENTURY, MAYA KINGS commissioned monuments commemorating their success as warriors. From these monuments we have recovered dates of war events that—if they were recorded in the newspaper headlines of today—would read:

A.D. 695 Ruler A of Tikal Captures Smoking Jaguar Paw of Site Q
709 Ruler 3 of Tonina Captures Kan-Xul of Palenque
729 Shield Jaguar of Yaxchilan Captures Lord Ah-Chuen of Bonampak
735 Ruler 3 of Dos Pilas Captures Paw Jaguar of Seibal
737 Cauac Sky of Quirigua Captures 18-Rabbit of Copan
755 Bird Jaguar of Yaxchilan Captures Jeweled Skull
795 Ruler 7 of Piedras Negras Captures the Lords of Pomona

Even as early as the fourth century, evidence confirms that for the Maya, success in war had always been important; for example, the Leiden Plaque, dated A.D. 320 (Pl. 33), shows a captive lying at the feet of the hero king. Yet after the completion of katun 8 Ahau (9.13.0.0.0, A.D. 692), both the pace of warfare and the status of the captives increased. Everywhere, kings faced kings in battle, and so, inevitably, many fell in combat and were taken captive.

Maya glyphs record warfare and captive sacrifice by several means (Fig. V.1).[1]

PLATE 76. Lintel 2

FIGURE V.1
Warfare Glyphs

a. shell/star glyph, indicating war against a city or lineage

b. shell/star glyph combined with an emblem glyph: this combination means "war against Seibal"

c. verb glyph, phonetically read *chucah*, refers to the capture of a victim

d. ax glyph, indicates weaponry used in war

e. verbal construction with shield/flint glyph, indicating weaponry

f. glyph meaning "captor of," used as part of a lord's title

g. glyph, phonetically read *bak*, means "captive"

h. *nawa* means "to let blood"

    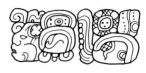

a. shell/star   b. star over Seibal   c. chucah ("capture")   d. ax event   e. shield/flint event

f. "the captor of"   g. "the captive of"   h. nawa

Just as pictorial representations show captives displayed in front of a ruler or show a particularly important captive under a ruler's feet, a Maya king might link his important captives to his own name all his life. Bird Jaguar, for instance, called himself Captor of Ah-Cauac until A.D. 755, when he captured Jeweled Skull. Thereafter, he was known as Bird Jaguar, Captor of Jeweled Skull. As if that were not enough, he also referred to himself as He of the Twenty *Bak* ("captives"), reiterating his strength and power.[2] Inscriptions record that captives are the protagonists of bloodletting events and ballgames, and since their names vanish after such sacrificial rituals, we can assume that the captives died.

The monuments the Maya used to commemorate warfare are diverse. Painted and carved scenes depicting war or related events tell much about the significance of warfare to the Maya. Their garments and other objects, such as weapons and figurines of warriors, contribute to an understanding of how the Maya fought. And characteristic Maya representations of war can begin to reveal the reasons the Maya fought and their attitudes toward war. The monuments that commemorate warfare and sacrifice record discrete stages of the ritual, from preparations to presentation of captives and their final sacrifice. Depictions of warfare show that warriors did not take their captives easily but, rather, through aggressive hand-to-hand combat, after which, captured warriors were stripped of their battle finery and led back to the city of the victors. In rituals that paralleled the auto-sacrifice of the reigning royal family, captives were bled and mutilated—their blood and flesh offered to the gods and ancestors—and eventually killed. The events depicted in Maya art are most frequently those rituals performed at home, not on the battlefield: it appears that moments that would be witnessed and sanctioned by the public were emphasized in art. The most frequently occurring scene (and thus possibly the most important stage in warfare celebrations) was the public display of captives, who are often shown being prepared for bloodletting rituals. While monuments that record the act of capturing opponents are not known beyond the Usumacinta drainage (and most of these are limited to Yaxchilan and Bonampak), almost every Maya site has monuments that display captives.

At Yaxchilan the various stages of warfare were elucidated in greater detail than at any other Maya city. Depictions on whole programs of carved stone lintels consist largely of ritual preparation for, and conclusions of, battle. Two Yaxchilan rulers in particular, Shield Jaguar, who died in A.D. 742, and his son, Bird Jaguar, who succeeded his father to the throne ten years later, erected temples with several series of lintels emphasizing points in the ritual of warfare.

Shield Jaguar constructed a building, called Structure 44, that enumerated his victories in battle and the humiliation of his foes. Structure 23, also constructed by Shield Jaguar, contains a series of three lintels, now numbered 24, 25 (Pls. 62 and 63) and 26, which were originally situated above the three doorways of the facade. These lintels, depicting bloodletting, vision quest and capture, constitute an iconographic program of three related ritual events. On Lintel 26 (Fig. V.2), one of his wives helps Shield Jaguar dress for battle on 9.14.12.6.12, or February 12, A.D. 724. Like a Maya Penelope dressing a departing Ulysses, she hands him a flexible shield of woven mat and a water-lily jaguar helmet. He already holds a knife like the one in Plate 77, and has donned a shawl-like wrap of cotton armor over a *xicolli*, or jerkin, with a woven mat design.[3] The Cookie Cutter Master (as we now refer to the artist who carved this series of lintels) was particularly adept at working architectural frames into his compositions. He carved the text of Lintel 26 into a T-shaped frame, probably to indicate the doorway of Structure 23, where these lintels were placed and in front of which the royal couple stands.[4] This event, then, probably took place outdoors, where all could witness it.

Bird Jaguar chose to depict essentially the same program of important events in his temples at Yaxchilan. Emulating his father, Bird Jaguar commissioned Structure 42 a few meters south of Structure 44, on the West Acropolis; like Shield Jaguar's monument, it records his own consolidation of power. While Shield Jaguar's building commemorates his battles, Bird Jaguar's celebrates not only his battles but other kinds of power consolidation as well. Bird Jaguar's building has three lintels, numbered 41, 42 and 43. On Lintel 41 (Pl. 78), which was placed over the left doorway, Bird Jaguar appears to be donning ritual attire before departure for battle, just as did Shield Jaguar on Lintel 26. Despite the damage to the lower half of the lintel, we can see that Bird Jaguar's wife presents him with the arms necessary for battle. Here, Bird Jaguar wears the same cotton armor his father wore on Lintel 26. And as a tribute to his predecessor or perhaps in reference to his family, he wears a round pectoral with a jaguar described within. Since it resembles the small shield in Shield Jaguar's name glyph, it may be a particular reference to him. Bird Jaguar's headdress and short cape of cloth strips are spattered with drops of blood, and his royal consort wears a headdress that characterizes secondary figures in battle, both winners and losers, such as the upper captive on Piedras Negras Stela 12 (Fig. V.8).

On the opposite side of the site, Bird Jaguar built another building, Structure 1, which is significant for having a series of lintels—numbered 5, 6, 7 and 8—that bear the same dates but illustrate different moments in the same course of events pictured in Structure 42. Lintel 8 (Fig. V.3) shows Bird Jaguar taking a captive—an event that occurred the same day he dressed for battle. Lintel 42 of Structure 42 shows Bird Jaguar exchanging God K staffs with a *cahal*, one of his governors; Lintel 5 shows him receiving a bundle from a woman on the same day, probably in preparation for bloodletting. On Lintel 43, he accepts a bowl with bloodletting instruments from Lady Balam, and on the same day, on Lintel 6, he exchanges jaguar paw clubs with a *cahal*. On Lintel 7 of Structure 1, which has no parallel image in Structure 42, Bird Jaguar again accompanies a woman with a bundle. All of these events took place within three years after the king's accession, and we may deduce from them that once having achieved the throne, Bird Jaguar consolidated his rule through marriage, oaths of allegiance from

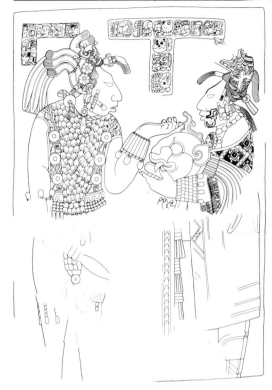

FIGURE V.2
Lintel 26
Yaxchilan, Chiapas, Mexico
Late Classic period, ca. A.D. 725
Drawing by Ian Graham

This handsome stone lintel from Structure 23 at Yaxchilan records that on 9.14.12.6.12, or February 12, A.D. 724, Shield Jaguar received his battle garb from his wife in preparation for battle. The armor he dons over his jerkin is a tufted garment that may have been made of feathers or unspun cotton. On his head Shield Jaguar wears only the Jester God headband with jade flower medallions, a simple crown of rulership, but the woman before him hands him a water-lily jaguar headdress. In his right hand he already holds a hafted knife, and he will also receive a flexible shield. Streams of blood still mark the face of Shield Jaguar's wife, indicating that she has just finished the bloodletting ritual that began on Lintel 24 (Pl. 62). An abstract frog design, made of a square with two sets of folded legs on opposite corners, was woven into her dress, which is trimmed with a skyband border, finished with tiny feathers and pearls or beads. The T-shaped architectural frame between the couple suggests that they stand in front of Structure 23.

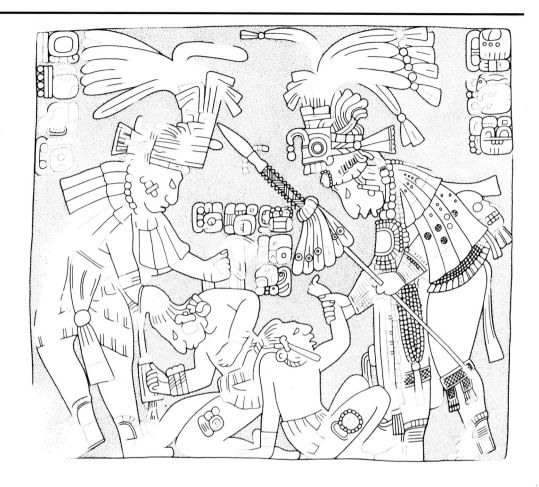

subservient lords and warfare, when necessary. Lintels 41 and 8, which depict warfare, bear the latest date in their respective structures, 9.16.4.1.1, or 1,101 days after accession.

Lintel 8 clearly portrays an act of capture. The figure on the right, Bird Jaguar, is dressed exactly as he was on Lintel 41. With the assistance of one of his *cahals*, he takes two captives, who are depicted with their names emblazoned on their thighs. The text informs us that on this day, 9.16.4.1.1, or May 9, A.D. 755, Bird Jaguar seized his most famous captive, Jeweled Skull. It was the most important war event of his reign, the act that conferred the greatest prestige. Bird Jaguar holds the tied, hafted spear that was presented to him on Lintel 41; his flexible shield hangs limply from his left hand. The two captives, stripped of battle dress, are forced into humiliating postures on the ground. Both kings and captives frequently wear cloth that has been cut into strips. On Lintel 8, these strips are fashioned into Bird Jaguar's short cape; his captive wears a hip cloth of the same materials. Throughout Mesoamerican art, the manner in which the captive at the left is held by the hair universally symbolizes capture and defeat. Lintel 8 reveals, then, that the immediate goal of Maya warfare was to capture, not to kill, the enemy, particularly an enemy of high status. These captured unfortunates were then taken back to the home of the victors for another series of rituals leading to their ultimate demise.

Like most images in Maya art, the representation of the climax of battle on Lintel 8 is a carefully reconstructed formal record of a successful event. On Lintel 6, dated two and a half years before the capture pictured on Lintel 8, Bird Jaguar exchanges jaguar clubs with the same *cahal* who assists in the capture. In what appears to be a contradiction, the text on Lintel 6 already describes the *cahal* as the conqueror of the very captive he is recorded as taking two and a half years later, on Lintel 8. These discrepancies suggest that Lintel 6 is either a retrospective monument—one carved well after the event itself (the *cahal* having meanwhile amplified his title)—or a reconstruction of historical fact. We should expect these scenes to involve some manipulation of fact, since these astute men clearly used art as propaganda. In the same manner, some images we accept as historical truths, such as *Washington Crossing the Delaware*, are reconstructions that may not accurately depict that historical event.

Ruler 3, depicted on Dos Pilas Stela 16, is the epitome of the splendidly attired successful ruler (Fig. V.4).[5] His balloon headdress, so named for the prominent round crown, is made of deer pelt, indicated by the cloven hoof over the ruler's forehead. Like an intertwined alpha and omega, trapezoidal forms link together into the trapeze-and-ray configuration known as the Mexican year sign, which apparently fixes the balloon in place. Two small circles of pelt on a stick extend from the top; this pattern is also seen on the headdress of the presiding female dynast on Naranjo Stela 24. The symbols in front of the ruler's face—a donut-shaped disk and three scrolls that look like the number 333—are the goggle eye, nose and mouth of a mask of Tlaloc, here presented in X-ray style, so that both the mask and the face are seen. The same mask appears on Ruler 3's hipcloth and on the long hanging apron. His bar pectoral decorated with a human skull is associated with Venus-sanctioned warfare. Also suspended around his neck are matching gauntlets with jaguar claws, which he would presumably wear during combat. Over his solar plexus the ruler wears a frontal jaguar head that has the mandible of a butterfly and a small owl covering the forehead. Beautiful jaguar boots and leggings that come to the knee round out his costume.

While the costume of the victorious warrior varied from site to site, at many sites the king wore Tlaloc imagery.[6] This deity of Teotihuacan from Central Mexico was adopted by the Maya, along with other fashionable ideas and goods, and turned to their own purposes during the Early Classic period. In the earliest Maya usages, Tlaloc faces characterized by goggle eyes, fanged mouth and tasseled headdress appear on shields and sacred bundles.[7] During the Late Classic period, Tlaloc and other Teotihuacan costumes are worn in battle and in bloodletting rituals. On Lintel 41 of Structure 42 and Lintel 8 of Structure 1, for example, Bird Jaguar wears what may be a skeletal Tlaloc mask in his headdress; on Lintel 8, the mask is set above the trapeze-and-ray symbol that accompanies the mask, forming part of the bloodletting costume. This combination is worn by men and women both when they let blood and when they make war (itself an act of ritual bloodletting), a fact that may account for the nearly identical costuming of these two events.

Frequently, jaguar pelt and jaguar imagery are added to the Tlaloc costume. At Piedras Negras, warriors wear a costume that bears elements derived from the Teotihuacan representation of jaguars, and, like those from Teotihuacan, the jaguar is

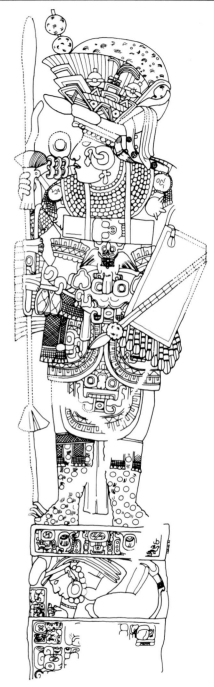

FIGURE V.4
Stela 16
Dos Pilas, Petexbatun, Guatemala
Late Classic period, ca. A.D. 735

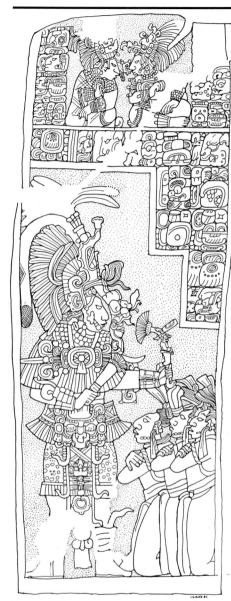

often shown as a mosaic plated beast. At Yaxchilan, the consistency of dress worn in images of several generations suggests that actual costumes were inherited.

Prior to the eighth century, Maya war costumes were not limited to the jaguar pelt and Tlaloc imagery. The greater diversity of these earlier costumes can be seen in Jaina figurines, the finely crafted terracotta works made for funerary offerings on Jaina Island. These figurines suggest that elaborate feathered costumes were once more common than those featuring jaguar pelt (Pl. 79). Yet during the eighth century, as well as in later Mesoamerican art, warriors in bird suits often fall prey to those in feline costume. In fact, the frequent occurrence of bird costumes worn by defeated warriors suggests that they symbolize defeat. The Aztecs believed that the current era had been initiated when Tezcatlipoca, a god frequently conceived as a jaguar, defeated Quetzalcoatl, a feathered serpent. Perhaps during the eighth century, the notions of cosmic cataclysm found to be prevalent among Aztecs at the time of the Conquest were formed.

Costumes on Jaina figurines show that for protection, the warrior frequently wore a garment covering the entire upper body, and he usually carried a flanged rectangular shield tufted with feathers and a weapon (Pls. 80–82). The *xicolli*, or sleeveless tunic, was generally limited to warriors. Elaborate patterns were woven into these garments, and in at least one example (Pl. 81), the design includes stylized Tlaloc faces, normally a part of the jaguar-pelt costume. Although described at the time of the Conquest and worn by the Yaxchilan lords, tufted cotton armor is only occasionally seen on Jaina warriors.

Victorious lords may have worn depictions of captives as costume elements, as, for example, on the carved shell earflares from the Denver Art Museum (Pl. 83). Paintings on ceramics show the design and decoration of weaponry and shields to be quite elaborate, in contrast to the simpler forms depicted on carved stone monuments, such as those at Yaxchilan. While all warriors probably entered the fray in full battle dress, the captives lost their finery in defeat. The pots attributed to the One Hand Painter (Pl. 84 and Fig. V.9a, b) show a sequence of one set of warriors falling prey to another and being stripped of their clothes as well as their weapons.

During the Classic period, powerful Maya kings considered the position of the planet Venus to be a guide to victory. The Maya believed that Venus played a tremendous role in war, and it appears that they invoked its assistance by wearing toothy skeletal masks, such as that worn by the king on Dos Pilas Stela 16. On this stela, the text proclaims the Dos Pilas lord to be the victor of a shell/star event against Seibal on 9.15.4.6.4 8 Kan 17 Muan, or December 3, A.D. 735, and like other events recorded by the shell/star glyph, this one took place on a day augured by Venus as appropriate for battle.[8] On most of the dates that record this verb, Venus made its first appearance as the Evening Star, visible after the superior conjunction, when Venus passes behind the sun.[9] On Lintel 8 in Structure 1 at Yaxchilan, Bird Jaguar wears a mask similar to that on Stela 16 at the rear of his belt; it is composed of jade plates. The toothy skeletal head at position B2 on the carved shell ornament from The British Museum (Pl. 85) is a substitute for the shell/star glyph. The lord who wore the shell, probably a king of Xcalumkin, in what is now the state of Campeche, did so to proclaim his success at an astrologically sanctioned war.[10]

According to the inscription on Stela 16, the battle between Dos Pilas and Seibal raged for a second day; then, six days later, after the victors led their captives back to Dos Pilas, the most important captive of their mission—Paw Jaguar, the king of Seibal—let blood and was doubtless tortured by his captors. He is depicted bound with ropes and deprived of his finery, cramped within the basal panel of the stela. The result of shell/star for the Dos Pilas campaign against Seibal is clear: the king of Seibal fell prey to the king of Dos Pilas.[11]

At one Maya site after another, king after king displayed his victims for others to observe and admire. Captives are shown on stairs, in front of thrones or simply at the feet of the victors. Most scenes appear to take place upon the return of the victorious to their home. There is, however, a painting in Room 2 at Bonampak that celebrates the display of prisoners immediately following their capture. Following a great battle, captives are bound and mutilated against a background of striated green vegetation.

The presentation of captives took various forms. On the wall panel belonging to the Kimbell Art Museum (Pl. 86), a lord who came to power under the auspices of Shield Jaguar II, a Yaxchilan king of the late eighth century, receives the offering of three captives from a subordinate, identified in the inscription as a war captain.[12] The text records a war event on 9.17.12.13.14 5 Ix 7 Zac, or August 23, A.D. 783, and a bloodletting ritual three days later, all performed under the aegis of the lord seated on the throne.[13] Like Dos Pilas Stela 16, this panel describes the fate of captives of war: just days after their capture, they were forced to let blood. The middle captive raises his left hand to his forehead in a gesture of woe, like that of the canoe-borne, Xibalba-bound lord of the Tikal bones (Fig. VII.1); like that lord, the middle figure is probably headed for the Underworld.[14]

On Yaxchilan Lintel 16, Bird Jaguar, wearing the same costume his father wore in Lintel 26, stands over a captive who has probably already suffered some bloodletting; beads of blood line his cheek and nose, and he bites his left hand as if in pain (Pl. 87). The artist has aligned the captive's eye with the warrior's spear, as if to reinforce the explicit defeat. Moreover, the captive holds a broken parasol in his right hand. This attribute of defeated warriors is held by most of the captives who form the treads of Hieroglyphic Stairs 3 at Yaxchilan, by other captives on stelae and lintels at that site, by captives about to be sacrificed in murals of Room 3 at Bonampak and by some figures on polychromed Maya pots (Pl. 88).[15]

Among the monuments that portray ceremonies of war and sacrifice directly preparatory to Bird Jaguar's accession is Stela 11, still at Yaxchilan. The secondary scene on the stela—facing away from public view—shows Bird Jaguar standing inside a corbeled arch frame (Fig. V.5a), his captives squeezed under the lintel in front of him and bound together like those of the Kimbell panel. Here, however, the king has chosen to manifest himself as a Maya deity, perhaps in deference to the divine sanction that allowed him to reign. In an unusual representation, Bird Jaguar's profile is shown within a cutaway, X-ray-style mask of the deity Chac-Xib-Chac, a supernatural closely related to GI of the Palenque Triad. The general role of this deity is to sacrifice others, usually menacing them first with an ax. Here, Bird Jaguar, dressed as Chac-Xib-Chac, holds out God K with his left hand, as if the god were his ax. No other deity is so well suited to carry out ritual sacrifice as the GI/Chac-Xib-Chac complex. He can appear as a miniature warrior, as on the figurine from the Heye Foundation (Pl. 89), as well as on ritual axes of precious materials, such as the jade ax from Liverpool (Pl. 90), which resembles the one Bird Jaguar holds in his right hand on Stela 11. Other axes were crafted into the form of a hafted ax (Pl. 91), such as the one GI wields.

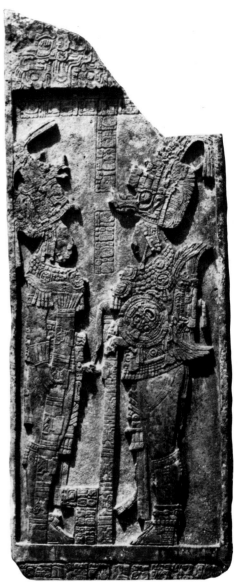

FIGURE V.5b
Stela 11
Yaxchilan, Chiapas, Mexico
Late Classic period, A.D. 755
b. Front face, photo courtesy of the Peabody Museum of Archaeology and Ethnology, Harvard University

The principal scene on Stela 11 (Fig. V.5b), which projects outward, commemorates an exchange of "holey banners," staffs wrapped with cloth that has flapped cutouts, between Bird Jaguar on the right and Shield Jaguar on the left. This event occurred some time prior to Bird Jaguar's installation. The inscribed date is 9.15.9.17.16, or June 26, A.D. 741, shortly before the time of Shield Jaguar's death, although Bird Jaguar did not succeed his father until A.D. 752. The Initial Series text under the ruler's feet records Bird Jaguar's accession on 9.16.1.0.0, or May 3, A.D. 752 (this text was carved by a hand distinct from the master who carved the scene above).

Stela 11 was commissioned by Bird Jaguar from the master responsible for Lintels 24, 25 and 26—the finest lintels made during the reign of his father, Shield Jaguar. It was placed at the front of Structure 40 at Yaxchilan, which in turn had been built by Shield Jaguar as a monument to his own accession. Glyphs arranged in a T-shape that frame the monument's front echo the shape of the doorways of Structure 40. The placement of the stela here must have been intended as an emphatic statement of lineage—emphasizing that at the shrine to his own accession, Shield Jaguar passed the torch on to his son. Taken together, the two sides of Stela 11 reveal that warfare supported kingship and was the power that upheld the throne.

The relationship between accession and the sacrifice of captives is made explicit on a painted ceramic cylinder that may have been produced to celebrate the inauguration of the character we call the Fat Cacique, who appears as the protagonist of at least five polychromed pots, including one now in Chicago (Pl. 92).[16] All painted in a style featuring pink hieroglyphs and masked figures, these vessels may form a set commissioned from a single master by the Fat Cacique himself. On the Chicago pot, a captive sits bound in a perishable structure atop a wooden scaffold with a lashed wickerwork lattice base. His expression suggests that he is probably also riveted in place by sheer terror. On the opposite side of the vessel, the Fat Cacique steps down from his sedan chair while his two bearers kneel. The moment is pregnant: the drama has just begun. A comparison of this scene with those of the various accession stelae of Piedras Negras (Fig. II.4), in which we see a similar scaffold inhabited by the new king rather than by a prisoner, permits reconstruction of this ritual's sequence of events. The captive bound to the scaffold was slain, his heart ripped out and his body placed at the foot of the scaffold. Attendants then draped the scaffold with cloth and jaguar skin, hung swag curtains over the front of the niche, and framed the whole structure with the Bicephalic Monster to give the event cosmic sanction. The new lord then stepped over the sacrificed captive and ascended to the niche, leaving bloody footprints on a cloth-draped ladder. Seated high in the niche, he received public recognition for his newly assumed office. On the Chicago pot, the sacrifice and its attendant festivities has just been set into motion; at Piedras Negras, these events have been completed. Perhaps the taking of a captive prior to accession rituals was a requirement, and his sacrifice sealed the accession ritual.

The scaffold scene on the Chicago pot and the beaded blood on the nose and cheek of the captive displayed by Bird Jaguar on Yaxchilan Lintel 16 (Pl. 87) suggest that captive sacrifice was rarely quick and immediate but involved protracted bloodletting. Although some kings were kept alive by their captors for years, monuments that record dates of capture and death indicate they may have had to participate in bloodletting rites many times before their deaths. The Bonampak paintings provide good examples of the ritual sacrifice of captives. In a battle staged on August 2, A.D.

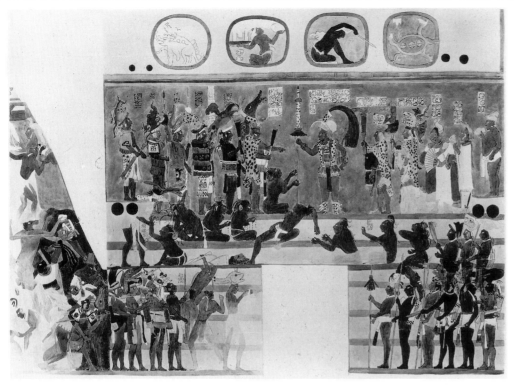

Figure V.6
Wall painting
Room 2, north wall, Bonampak, Mexico
Late Classic period, ca. A.D. 800
Watercolor copy of polychromed plaster original
Photo courtesy of the Peabody Museum of Archaeology
and Ethnology, Harvard University

The three rooms of Structure 1 at Bonampak were painted at the end of the eighth century to commemorate the installation of a young heir (Pl. 38). In Room 2 a battle is painted on the east, south and west walls. On the north wall, shown here in a copy by Antonio Tejeda, the captives taken in that battle were presented back at Bonampak. The battle itself was timed to coincide with the inferior conjunction of Venus on August 2, A.D. 792. A day or two later, when Venus rose as the Morning Star, the lords of Bonampak and their allies from Yaxchilan displayed their captives. Above the warriors, full-figure constellations present the layout of the sky at dawn on that day. Venus rose between Orion, at the far left, represented as two mating peccaries with three bright stars at the points of conjunction, and Gemini, at the far right, shown as a turtle with three bright stars on its body (rather than just the two stars that are perceived to be the feet of the Heavenly Twins). This entire scene, then, is like a tableau of the shell/star glyph (Fig. V.1a). Below the heavens, King Chaan-Muan, who wears a jerkin of jaguar pelt and a tasseled headdress, presides over the disposition of the captives.

792, during an inferior conjunction, when Venus passed in front of the sun, King Chaan-Muan of Bonampak led warriors, including Bonampak's allies from Yaxchilan, in a successful battle, defeated his enemies and took many captives. The north wall of Room 2 (Fig. V.6) depicts an event that took place a few days later, on the morning that Venus reappeared, or first rose, as the Morning Star. King Chaan-Muan displayed the nine captives and a decapitated head on a seven-level staircase at Bonampak. Although this representation is often characterized as the Arraignment, this is no reassuring scene from a familiar Anglo-Saxon courtroom but a vivid portrayal of how the Maya displayed their prey, celebrated the defeat of their enemies and drew their blood. The painting, partly truncated by the postholes of the decomposed crossbeams, shows a figure at the far left bending over a captive, lifting his arm and either pulling out his fingernails or cutting off the ends of his digits. Blood streams down the captive's arm. His sunken cheeks may signal that his teeth were pulled in this ritual, and black dots, which suggest dried blood or indicate intoxication, flow from his mouth. One step above, as blood streams from the fingers of other captives, they look at their hands in despair and howl pitiably. A captive facing Chaan-Muan on the upper step holds out his bleeding fingers and appears to plead for mercy. For the Maya, however, there was only the inevitability of sacrifice, as is emphasized by the beautifully delineated figure lying diagonally below the doomed supplicant. Heart sacrifice was the ultimate cause of this captive's death, but the cut marks across the body inform us that cat-and-mouse torture preceded it. In contrast, the quick, deliberate heart excision practiced by the Aztecs can be regarded a merciful act.

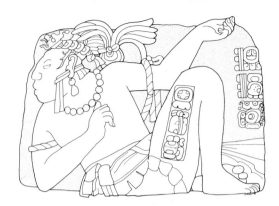

FIGURE V.7
Monument 122
Tonina, Mexico
Late Classic period, ca. A.D. 715

The Calendar Round date 13 Akbal 16 Yax is recorded at position A1–A2, and the war event, shell/star, follows at A3.

Isolated captives rarely occur in Maya art independent of their captors. When they do, they are typically carved on the risers or treads of stairs, which could be used for generations as sites of actual rituals commemorating the defeat of important captives. A scene such as that at Bonampak could be recreated if the stairs at Tamarindito, Dos Pilas or Yaxchilan (all of which are carved with captives and remain in place at those sites) were repopulated with victorious warriors. These captive figures are consistently worked into structures in basal panels of stelae, steps or altars, where their function or placement reinforces the humiliated posture of the captive. Thus, such architectural carvings symbolically reenact victory.

Jaina figurines of captives may have been produced for their captors, who used them as burial goods and reminders of their victories in life. These small objects, designed for private viewing, are sensitive portraits of pain and are among the most moving works of Maya art. The Jaina figurine at Princeton University shows that some captives faced their gruesome deaths with dignity (Pl. 93). This old man, bound and beaten, his nose swollen like a turnip, nevertheless holds his head high. His absent genitalia could represent mutilation in an ancient ritual, although they may be an accident of preservation. A figurine in the Baltimore Museum of Art (Pl. 94) is that of a tortured captive whose face strains in anguish as he emits a tremendous howl of pain. He has been scalped by his captors, as can be seen from the pate hanging from the nape of his neck. His hands and feet are contorted, as if they have been twisted out of joint, and his nose is swollen and bruised like that of the dignified old man. This captive, hollow from his sternum to his groin, is the victim of disembowelment, a torture also known from Maya painted ceramics and the remarkable battle scene at Cacaxtla, a site far from the Maya region, where wall paintings depict warfare between Maya and Central Mexican warriors.[17] As if this victim's disembowelment were not enough, small sticks of kindling have been tied to his lower back; his captors are about to set him on fire. This figurine is a reliquary whose receptacle was possibly created for holding yet other trophies of war.

A number of questions about Maya warfare remain. What, for example, were the goals of a Maya king, beyond the capture of the opposition's elite? Did victory bring material gain? Did individual kings expand their spheres of influence? Increasingly, emerging evidence suggests that the aims of Maya conflict did include material and territorial gains, even though the outcomes of particular conflicts are unknown. What might have happened at Palenque when King Kan-Xul was captured by the armies of Tonina in A.D. 711? Demands were doubtless made of the defeated, but it is not clear if the storehouses of Palenque were burned, if their contents were seized and carried away or if Tonina imposed levies of maize, cotton or cacao. Structured defensive precautions are only beginning to be understood as an element of Maya warfare. At some sites, at least during the Late Preclassic period, the Maya made efforts to protect people and property by constructing a large moat around the city.[18] Even the positioning of a site like Palenque, which has a commanding view of the plain to the north, suggests at least a minimal concern for the safety of persons, buildings and material goods.

Tribute has not yet been documented through excavation, but some extant scenes, such as the one on the Fenton vase from The British Museum, may show the presentation of such goods (Pl. 54). It is likely that commercial arrangements for goods or services were made, although the records have certainly perished. Nevertheless, one form of tribute resulting from war—the transfer of a new artistic style—can be documented. No record of Tonina's successful defeat of King Kan-Xul in A.D. 711 has been discovered at Palenque, but the result is clear at Tonina, where Kan-Xul is memorialized as a captive on a small panel that may have once formed part of a wall or frieze (Fig. V.7). The Calendar Round date 13 Akbal 16 Yax, or August 30, A.D. 711, recorded on the panel is followed by the shell/star war event.[19] The captive's name inscribed on the thigh—"Kan-Xul, Palenque Ahau"—reveals his famous origins. This image, then, declares the result of the shell/star event: the great Palenque king was taken captive. Although the panel shows him reclining, bound and helpless at the hands of his captors, he is nevertheless regal. Unlike any other Late Classic captive, Kan-Xul was depicted still wearing the emblem of kings, the Jester God headband. The Kan-Xul panel is most striking for its style, which is different from that of earlier stone monuments at Tonina. Typical Tonina carvings are generally worked in nearly three-dimensional relief, and faces are portrayed frontally. In contrast, the panel showing Kan-Xul as a prisoner was worked in very low relief, its effect much like a master drawing on stone. The fine line of the face in profile, the attention to elegant, simple costume and the figure's graceful gestures make it probable that the panel was carved by a Palenque artist. The limestone, however, is coarser and more porous than that used in Palenque. Thus, it is likely that artists from Palenque went to Tonina as required tribute.

Similarly, at Piedras Negras, a particular form of warrior monument was consistently carved for two hundred years. In these, a standing ruler was depicted frontally, his face worked in high, nearly three-dimensional, relief, while one or two captives, sometimes carved at a slightly smaller scale, knelt at his side. The ruler usually wore plated garments and a balloon headdress similar to that of the ancestral warrior on Yaxchilan Lintel 25 (Pl. 63) or the king on Dos Pilas Stela 16. However, in A.D. 795, when Piedras Negras proclaimed itself the victor of a shell/star event against Pomona, a smaller city downriver on the Usumacinta, Stela 12 (Fig. V.8)—a different kind of monument—was erected at Piedras Negras and worked in a very low relief characteristic of Pomona. On it, a ruler sitting atop a flight of stairs receives two war captains, who present him with a pile of captives depicted with great sensitivity. Eight captives are tied together on the lower register, and many show signs of having been tortured. Two captains deliver the well-dressed uppermost captive, seated on draped cloth, to the lord above, who triumphantly surveys his trophies. On his chest he wears what may be a shrunken human body or possibly an heirloom Olmec sculpture. The vivid description of the captives is particularly eloquent. The old man at the lower right, for example, studies his hands with an expression of pathos. By contrast, the artist has characterized the victors as coolly detached and without emotion.

Mastery of the arts may have been particularly emphasized in Pomona, the city conquered by Piedras Negras. Just a few years before, a monument erected at Pomona (Fig. III.12) illustrated four lords, at least two of whom were called Pauahtun, a title for scribes and masters of courtly arts. When Pomona was defeated by Piedras Negras, tribute was apparently demanded in the form of artists, who made Stela 12 as the official record of their own city's demise. In its emotive emphasis and the quality of the carving, Piedras Negras Stela 12 is a more deeply affecting monument to the captives than to the ruling lord.

In fact, the care and beauty with which captives are depicted in Maya art may be explained generally by the notion of artistic tribute. Many Maya sites exhibit sudden

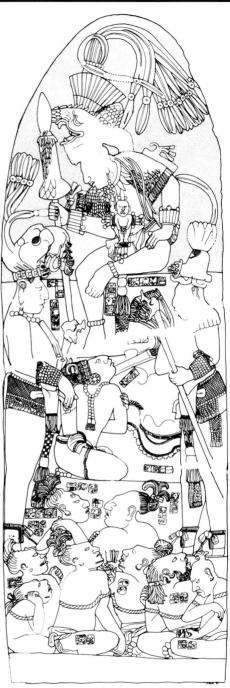

Figure V.8
Stela 12
Piedras Negras, Guatemala
Late Classic period, A.D. 795

changes in artistic style following warfare events. This is most evident at Cacaxtla, in the Central Mexican state of Tlaxcala, where the goring of Maya warriors by Mexican warriors is painted in a purely Maya style. Such records establish that Maya artists, either as captives or as tributary laborers, left home and made monuments to glorify their captors—monuments that also record their own demise with compelling beauty. This process, through which the art style of the conquered becomes that of their victors, subtly enabled the losers to endure.

Some extant Maya objects reveal that the goal of warfare was to expand the territorial control of a single city-state. The Leiden panel (Pl. 76), for example, probably comes from La Pasadita, a small site that by the eighth century had fallen completely within the sphere of Yaxchilan, whose dominance was probably established by warfare. The Kimbell panel (Pl. 86), too, was probably once from a small city neighboring Yaxchilan, known to archaeologists today as Laxtunich. Bird Jaguar may have allowed Jeweled Skull's heirs to accede to office as long as sovereignty was sworn to him, and such conquered territories may have been the domain of *cahals*, regional overlords.

The eighth-century ruler most successful in expanding his dominion was Ruler 3 of Dos Pilas, who reigned from A.D. 726 to 740. Records of conquest indicate that one after another, neighboring sites fell under his sway, their petty rulers kept hostage, which gave a single potentate control of the entire Petexbatun.[20] Thus, by means of warfare, Ruler 3 of Dos Pilas dominated the region until he managed to establish a sort of superstate with power and geographical extension beyond that of any other Classic Maya city-state. Under this state, the Maya Lowlands might have had the potential to become a political entity capable of surviving the troubles of the ninth century. Before that could happen, however, Ruler 3's successor was captured by an underlord whose dominion had been conquered by Dos Pilas. The last record of Dos Pilas occurs at Tamarindito, one of its tributaries, which apparently rebelled and presumably captured the king of Dos Pilas. The unified kingdom was shattered and the opportunity for a larger state lost.

Commemorations of war activity in Maya art show that because the capture of sacrificial victims was its fundamental goal, warriors avoided killing their enemy in battle. The subsequent elaborately recorded sacrifice of captives was a necessary component of many rituals in the cycle of dynastic life. Accession rituals, for example, required the offering of at least one human captive. Such offerings not only satisfied the constant demands by the gods for repayment of the blood debt incurred by man at his creation but tested the mettle of the new king as well. Perhaps the lineage even demanded proof of the physical prowess of the new lord before his installation in office could proceed. It is no surprise, then, that a king was frequently proclaimed the victor of a battle a few weeks before being formally seated on the throne. To be a king, he had to take captives in war. Once made king, he was in jeopardy of becoming the most valued booty of his enemy. To sustain his rule, a king would not only have to fight off his foe, he would also attempt to capture and humiliate his enemy.

It is striking that in the representation of warfare in their art, the Maya addressed no issues of material gain. Instead, they cast warfare and sacrifice in terms of ritual that upheld the cycle of kingship. Many of the questions we ask about warfare and its political and social repercussions may have been the sort that the Maya would have found irrelevant. Yet increasing evidence confirms that while the Maya made war as a ritual of intrinsic interest, and one that was necessary for the functioning of their world, they also fought to achieve the material ends that mankind has always sought in war.

NOTES

1. The first of these is the glyph that can be read *chucah*, "is captured," as determined by Tatiana Proskouriakoff ("Historical Data in the Inscriptions of Yaxchilan, Part 1,"in *Estudios de Cultura Maya*, vol. 3 [Mexico City: Universidad Nacional Autónoma de México, 1963], pp. 149–167). The others have been most systematically reported by Berthold Riese ("Kriegsberichte der klassichen Maya," *Baessler-Archiv, Beiträge zur Völkerkunde* 30, part 2 [1984], pp. 255–321). See also Stephen Houston, "A Reading for the Flint-Shield Glyph" (*Contributions to Maya Hieroglyphic Decipherment, I* [New Haven, Conn.: Human Relations Area Files, Inc., 1983]); David S. Stuart, "The 'Count of Captives' Epithet in Classic Maya Writing," in *Fifth Palenque Round Table, Vol. 7*, gen. ed. Merle Greene Robertson, vol. ed. Virginia Fields (San Francisco: Pre-Columbian Art Research Institute, 1985), pp. 97–101; and Floyd Lounsbury, "Astronomical Knowledge and Its Uses at Bonampak, Mexico," in *Archaeoastronomy in the New World*, edited by A. F. Aveni (Cambridge: Cambridge University Press, 1982), pp. 143–168.

2. David S. Stuart, "The 'Count of Captives' Epithet," pp. 97–101.

3. The garment Shield Jaguar wears may be similar to the *xicolli* worn by central Mexican warriors, but here and on Plate 87 it seems to be woven of a broad fiber rather than of cotton. The term *xicolli* is Nahuatl. These garments have great ritual importance: in the Madrid Codex, for example, three gods extend them as gifts received or offered (J. Antonio Villacorta and Carlos A. Villacorta, *Codices Mayas: Dresdensis, Peresianus, Tro-Cortesian* [Guatemala City: Tipografia Nacional, 1930], p. 846).

4. Mary Ellen Miller, "The Cookie Cutter Master of Yaxchilan," paper delivered at the College Art Association symposium The Uses of Methodology in Mesoamerican Art, Los Angeles, February 1985.

5. Stela 16 of Dos Pilas still remains at the site, as do most monuments in the Petexbatun. The representation on Stela 2 of nearby Aguateca is very similar, and the two monuments commemorate the same event. Stela 16 of Dos Pilas is the more complete and the better preserved.

6. Identified and discussed by Tatiana Proskouriakoff, "Historical Data in the Inscriptions of Yaxchilan, Part I," p. 150, and by Linda Schele, "Human Sacrifice among the Classic Maya," in *Ritual Sacrifice in Mesoamerica*, edited by Elizabeth Boone (Washington, D.C.: Dumbarton Oaks, 1984), pp. 7–48.

7. Karl Taube has pointed out that on the Early Classic Tikal Stela 4, the king named Curl Nose bears a small bundle with a Tlaloc headdress in the crook of his left arm.

8. About one-half of the known occurrences of the shell/star glyph occur during the month of Muan, and many occur on Ix days during the month of Muan. David H. Kelley first drew attention to this phenomenon in "Maya Astronomical Tables and Inscriptions" (in *Archaeoastronomy in Pre-Columbian America* [Austin: University of Texas Press, 1975], pp. 57–73). The patron of this month—shown within the comb affixes of the Initial Series Introductory Glyph—is deified blood. Perhaps so much warfare was waged during this month in order to satisfy its requirements. On Dos Pilas Stela 16, the bloodletting event takes place during the subsequent month, Pax, known at the time of the Conquest as an appropriate time for sacrifice (see Alfred M. Tozzer, ed. and trans., "Landa's Relación de las cosas de Yucatan: A Translation," *Papers of the Peabody Museum of American Archaeology and Ethnology, Harvard University* 18 [New York: Kraus Reprint Corp., 1966], p. 164). The patron of Pax is a relatively minor deity, but when he is depicted independent of the month sign, he is usually carrying out sacrifice (see Michael D. Coe, *Classic Maya Pottery at Dumbarton Oaks* [Washington, D.C.: Dumbarton Oaks, 1975], p. 20; see also Mary Ellen Miller, *The Murals of Bonampak* [Princeton, N.J.: Princeton University Press, 1986], p. 135).

9. Floyd Lounsbury, "Astronomical Knowledge and Its Uses," pp. 143–168.

10. Stephen D. Houston has drawn the authors' attention to the prominence of this lord from Xcalumkin on jades recovered from the Sacred Cenote at Chichen Itza. An important tomb from that site must have been looted in antiquity, its contents scattered and deposited in new contexts. This shell was collected in Belize. Compare Tatiana Proskouriakoff, *Jades from the Cenote of Sacrifice, Chichen Itza, Yucatan, Peabody Museum Memoirs*, vol. 10, part 1 (Cambridge, Mass.: Peabody Museum of American Archaeology and Ethnology, Harvard University, 1974), fig. 12 (especially 9, 11, 14, 15 and 17).

11. The text on Dos Pilas Stela 16 reads:

A1–B6   : On 9.15.4.6.4 8 Kan 17 Muan (December 3, A.D. 735)
C1   : a shell/star event against Seibal (war at Seibal)
D1   : one day later
C2   : 8 Chicchan 18 Muan (9.15.4.6.5, or December 4, A.D. 735)
D2–C3 : ax event and flint/shield glyph
D3–C6 : Ruler 3 of Dos Pilas (with epithets of a great warrior, including a shield glyph)
D6   : seven days later
C7–D7 : 2 Chuen 4 Pax (9.15.4.6.11)
A8   : *nawah* ("he was humiliated") Paw Jaguar
B8   : blood lord of Seibal
A9   : by
B9–A10 : Ruler 3

12. Stephen D. Houston, in a letter of September 24, 1985, has related the Kimbell panel to other monuments at the so-called Lamb site. Based on plates 203 and 204 in Karl Herbert Mayer's *Maya Monuments: Sculptures of Unknown Provenance in Middle America* (Berlin: Verlag Karl-Friedrich von Fleming, 1984), the accession of the Kimbell lord to the office of *cahal* can be fixed at 9.17.5.0.0, a period-ending date that can be likened to 9.16.1.0.0, the accession of Bird Jaguar.

13. See Linda Schele, "Human Sacrifice among the Classic Maya," p. 21.

14. See Virginia E. Miller, "A Reexamination of Maya Gestures of Submission," *Journal of Latin American Lore* 9, no. 1 (1983), pp. 17–38.

15. Many other such scenes, long thought to show fan bearers, can probably be linked to sacrificial rites.

16. Among the published examples of other pots by this artist, one is in the Kimbell Art Museum (Pl. 71). Another is in the November Collection; see Francis Robicsek and Donald M. Hales, *Maya Ceramic Vases from the Late Classic Period: The November Collection of Maya Ceramics* (Charlottesville: University of Virginia Art Museum, 1982), fig. 3. A third is illustrated in Michael D. Coe, *Lords of the Underworld* (Princeton, N.J.: The Art Museum, 1978), fig. 20. Two others, also in private collections, are published in Nicholas M. Hellmuth, *Tzakol and Tepeu Maya Pottery Paintings* (Guatemala City: Foundation for Latin American Anthropological Research, 1976), pls. 1, 2.

For previous discussion of the Chicago vessel, see Anne Paul, "History on a Maya Vase," *Archaeology* 29, no. 2 (1976), pp. 118–126; and Karl Taube, "A Study of Classic Maya Scaffold Sacrifice" (unpublished manuscript of 1982, provided by the author). Initial identification of this painter was made by Barbara and Justin Kerr, "The Painters of the Pink Glyphs" (paper presented at the Fine Arts Museum of Long Island, Hempstead, N.Y., October 1981). On another pot by the same master (vessel no. 2 in Nicholas M. Hellmuth, *Tzakol and Tepeu Maya Pottery Paintings*), the women also lack masks, even though men in the same scene are wearing them.

17. Compare Michael D. Coe, *The Maya Scribe and His World* (New York: Grolier Club, 1973), pl. 33.

18. David Webster, *Defensive Earthworks at Becan, Campeche, Mexico: Implications for Maya Warfare*, Middle American Research Institute, Pub. 41 (New Orleans: Tulane University, 1976).

19. See Pierre Becquelin and Claude Baudez, *Tonina: Une cité Maya du Chiapas (Mexique)*, vol. 2 (Paris: Mission Archéologique et Ethnologique Française au Mexique, 1982), pp. 844–846.

20. Stephen D. Houston and Peter Mathews, *The Dynastic Sequence at Dos Pilas, Guatemala* (San Francisco: Pre-Columbian Art Research Institute, 1985).

PLATE 77
Ceremonial knife
Chiapas, Mexico
Late Classic period, A.D. 600–900
Flint
40 x 10 cm
Courtesy of the Museum of the American Indian, Heye
Foundation, New York

This beautifully chipped blade and handle may
have been attached to a simple haft for easy handling. It closely resembles one that Shield Jaguar
wields on Lintel 26 at Yaxchilan (Fig. V.2).

PLATE 78
Lintel 41
Yaxchilan, Chiapas, Mexico
Late Classic period, ca. A.D. 760
Limestone
60.5 x 94.6 x 10.1 cm
The Trustees of The British Museum, London

Bird Jaguar dressed for battle on 9.16.4.1.1 7 Imix
14 Tzec (May 9, A.D. 755), then engaged in warfare
on the same day. On Lintel 41, which is from Structure 42 of the West Acropolis, Bird Jaguar finishes
his preparations for war in the company of the Lady
of Ik lineage, which is identified with the site of
San José de Motul in the Peten. Since only the top
half of the lintel remains, the full act depicted is
not clear, but she may be presenting him with costume elements, just as does the lady on Lintel 26
(Fig. V.2). Unlike her predecessor, however, this
woman is dressed as a warrior herself, as is indicated
by her warrior head ornament, a piece of spotted
jaguar pelt pulled through a cut section of spondylus
shell in her headdress.

It is useful to compare Lintel 41 with Lintel 8 (Fig. V.3), which is from Structure 1 at
Yaxchilan. These two different depictions of the
same war event provide insight into the sequential
nature of the event, from its preparation to completion. Lintel 8 shows the next step in warfare. Once
dressed for battle, Bird Jaguar and one of his *cahals*,
or underlords, engage in combat. They have
pressed the enemy to the ground and have stripped
them of their finery.

These two lintels were carved by two different hands and placed far apart from one another
at the site. Lintel 41 was worked by the same artist
who executed the program on Lintels 15 through 17
in Structure 21. He was a master working in the
tradition of the Cookie Cutter Master, who executed Lintels 24 through 26 for Shield Jaguar a
generation earlier. This artist worked on two distinct planes of stone. He cut the design away from a
clear background and frequently configured glyphic

texts into the shapes of architectural elements.
According to date and ritual attire, Lintel 8 shows
the capture during the same battle event, but the
style of workmanship lacks the deep "cookie cutter"
form of relief and thus belongs to a different hand.
Bird Jaguar's attire on Lintel 8 is identical to that on
Lintel 41, but it is worked in much less detail. He
wears the same cape, pectoral and headdress. The
feathers that sprout from the Tlaloc mask in his
headdress are bent just the same way, and his hair is
tied into an identical knot. The artist chose to represent the capture itself, the moment subsequent to
that shown on Lintel 41.

The record of the capture of Jeweled
Skull, Bird Jaguar's most famous captive, on Lintel
8, allowed Tatiana Proskouriakoff to determine the
presence of names in Maya hieroglyphic texts. Both
captives have glyphs on their thighs. Jeweled Skull,
as the glyph is nicknamed, is inscribed on the captive at the right, and the same glyph appears at the
bottom of the left-hand column of glyphs following
the Calendar Round date and the verb "is captured"
(Fig. V.1c). At the far right, the text continues
ubak, or "his captive" (Fig. V.1g), and the last two
glyphs name Bird Jaguar, king of Yaxchilan, as the
man who made him captive. The intermediate caption names the protagonist at the left as a *cahal* and
the captor of the second captive.

PLATE 79
Jaina warrior
Late Classic period, A.D. 700–900
Ceramic with blue pigment
H. 26 cm
The Cleveland Museum of Art, James Albert and Mary
Gardiner Ford Memorial Fund

This beautiful blue Jaina warrior was once a funerary offering, possibly placed in a tomb to bolster
the fighting spirit of the interred. In elaborate
paintings at Cacaxtla and Bonampak, warriors in
jaguar suits defeat warriors in bird suits. If bird costumes are to be interpreted as indicative of defeat,
this figurine may have been made to serve as a sacrificial victim for the interred. If he is a bird of prey,
he may also be a prototype of the later Eagle Knight
warriors of Aztec society, life-size clay examples
of which have been recently excavated in the
Great Temple.

This figure once held a shield and staff,
now lost, which may have been made of perishable
materials. Half of the figure's detachable bird helmet has been restored; its extended feathers make
the figure look like a bird that has just alighted.
The feather costume is worn close to the skin; a
fabric loincloth and hipcloth with woven selvages

are draped over the bird suit and knotted at the waist to the right. The warrior stands relaxed, thrusting his belly forward. The feathered ankle cuffs he wears over bare feet are similar to those that appear on many Yaxchilan lintels.

PLATE 80
Jaina warrior
Late Classic period, A.D. 700–900
Ceramic
H. 26 cm
Seattle Art Museum, Gift of John Hauberg

Dressed in the sleeveless *xicolli*, an elaborate feather headdress and a shoulder cape of thick strips, this Jaina warrior stands with his shield, ready to put on a skull mask that would give him the appearance of God A, the skeletal Death God. The round disks attached to the headdress are similar to those seen on secondary warriors, but the cluster of feathers makes the headdress similar to the war bonnet Bird Jaguar wears on Lintel 16 (Pl. 87). The short cape is worn on Lintel 41 (Pl. 78). The warrior holds the round shield in his left hand; his right forearm is bound with twisted cloth in a fashion identical to that of ballplayers (Pl. 96). These costume elements indicate that the warrior is also dressed for a ballgame, which he will play in the guise of a skeletal deity.

PLATE 81
Jaina warrior
Late Classic period, A.D. 700–900
Ceramic
H. 22 cm
Lent courtesy of The Art Museum, Princeton University

This finely crafted solid Jaina figurine was probably a secondary lord of the sort seen in Plate 86, because he wears the customary petal cap of subsidiary warriors. Like many other Jaina warriors, he wears what is probably elaborate face paint styled in intricate patterns on his brow. He has donned the warrior's sleeveless *xicolli*, whose design here would appear to be the conflation of a Tlaloc face and a year sign motif, which is so characteristic of costumes worn in battle. The warrior holds a flexible rectangular shield by a thong across his left palm, as do many other Jaina figurines. From their representations, it is clear that they are tufted with feathers. This warrior once carried a spear in his right hand. The figurine was burned at some point in its history, perhaps in rituals associated with its interment.

PLATE 82
Jaina warrior
Late Classic period, A.D. 700–900
Ceramic
H. 21.5 cm
The Denver Art Museum, Gift in honor of David Touff

This simply dressed warrior stands erect, lifting his chin in a posture of noble pride. The rectangular shield he holds in the left hand is the most common type carried by warriors during combat. Both Shield Jaguar and Bird Jaguar carry one, on Yaxchilan Lintel 26 (Fig. V.2) and Lintel 16 (Pl. 87), respectively. The artist treated the warrior's body in a simplified manner and styled the feet as little more than crude plugs to support the body. However, he labored over the detail of the face to reproduce a pattern executed in face paint or tattooing. On the right cheek, delicately worked in raised clay, is the Jester God, a symbol of rulership; its visual equivalent, the mat motif (equally symbolic of nobility), is worked like a dyadic couplet on the left cheek. The headdress, a simple wrapped cloth turban, is the type worn by figures on Temple 11 at Copan.

PLATE 83
Earflares
Early Classic period, A.D. 200–500
Carved shell
Diam. 8.9 cm
The Denver Art Museum Collection

The Maya warrior may have accumulated trophies and mementos of his exploits or may have commissioned ornaments to celebrate his prowess. These ear ornaments were carved in simple, clear lines, which form a flat, broad pattern suggestive of both very early Classic works and very late ones. The ground cut away from the main image has been colored with a bright red powder, probably cinnabar. Mirror images of two captives, kneeling and bound at the wrists, are worked within the round shell disks. Since the head-and-belt assemblages attached to the back of the captives' loincloths are a type generally worn by noble persons, they indicate that these are captives of high status. Their kneeling posture with one leg bent forward is not unusual for captives in Maya art; it is also seen later, in the art of the Toltecs and Aztecs. The Coyolxauhqui stone, recently excavated in the ancient Aztec capital and still in situ at the base of the Huitzilopochtli side of the Great Temple, depicts a defeated and dismembered goddess in this posture.

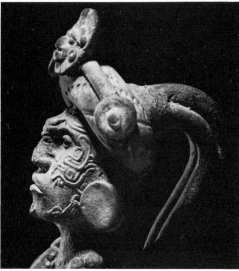

PLATE 82a

PLATE 84
Cylindrical vessel
Late Classic period, A.D. 700–800
Polychromed ceramic
Diam. 16 x H. 16 cm
Kimbell Art Museum, Fort Worth

Three pots painted by the same hand (Pl. 84, and Figs. V.9a,b) depict an elaborate battle, and the Kimbell pot shows the outcome that engaged these warriors. One figure, stripped naked, is the captive being marched home for sacrificial display; he is led off by the more elaborately dressed successful warriors. The captive's hair is highlighted with white dots, and the rope that binds his hands behind his back is rendered in the same bright white slip. The leader of this party of victorious warriors and their captive may be the third person, because he wears the Tlaloc-and-balloon headdress worn by the victorious Dos Pilas ruler on Stela 16 (Fig. V.4) and wields a bloody weapon. On his back, under the full jaguar pelt, it appears he has suspended the shield of the first person on the Pearlman pot, as if this warrior has fallen in battle. The other warriors on the Kimbell vessel shown here are also elaborately dressed. The first person wears a costume of cloth and paper strips studded with bloodied medallions; he has a spiny bloodletter in his headdress—he may be the one who carries out the bloodletting rituals. The fourth person wears a feathered cape and the petal cap characteristic of secondary figures.

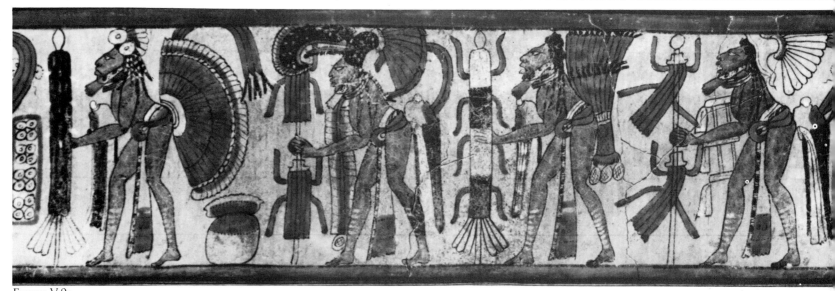

Figure V.9a
Warrior scene from a vessel
Late Classic period, A.D. 700–800
Museum of the American Indian, Heye Foundation, New York

Figure V.9b
Warrior scene from a vessel
Late Classic period, A.D. 700–800
Collection of Edwin Pearlman, M.D.

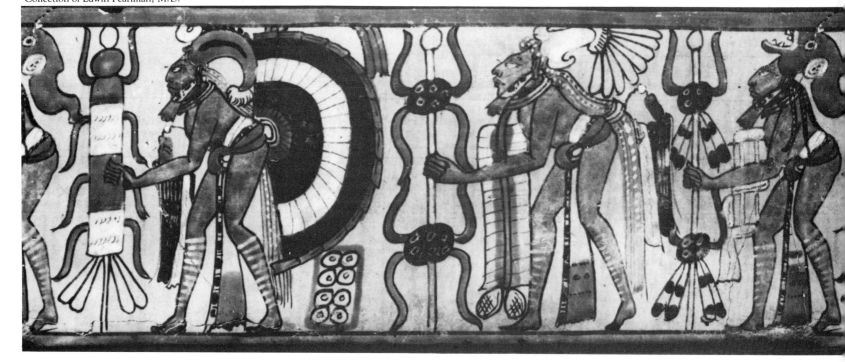

PLATE 85
Costume ornament
Late Classic period, A.D. 600–800
Incised shell
10.1 x 18.5 cm
The Trustees of The British Museum, London

Like a medal, this carved spondylus shell is a record
of success in battle. It may have been a costume element, worn either as a pectoral or sewn to a garment, or it may have been used in bloodletting rituals following warfare; compare, for example, those
worn by the *ahaus* in Room 1 at Bonampak (Pl.
38). The *ah k'in*, or subsidiary lord, in the Kimbell
Art Museum panel of captive presentation (Pl. 86)
holds just such an object when he presents his captives to his overlord. Suspended from its drilled
holes, the shell could not be read easily when
worn or used.

The interior of the spondylus has been
carved in very low relief. The artist prepared its surface by working the interior of the white shell until
its brilliant orange-pink inner stratum was revealed.
Glyphs and overall designs were then carved.

The second glyph is one that signals the
same Venus-sanctioned warfare normally indicated
by the shell/star sign. The glyphs that follow it may
refer either to the victim or to the victor of such
conflict; in this case, the name recorded is Zac-
Balam of Xcalumkin, who is also mentioned on a
number of jades dredged from the natural sinkhole
called the Sacred Cenote at Chichen Itza. The
agnathous head of a jaguar, which is the main
design of the shell, has the prefix *zac*, or "white" —
another reference to Zac-Balam. His tomb at
Xcalumkin was probably looted in antiquity, many
of its precious objects then thrown into the Sacred
Cenote. This shell was collected in what is now
Belize, where it may have been traded by the Maya.

PLATE 86
Carved panel
Usumacinta River Valley
Late Classic period, ca. A.D. 785
Limestone with traces of paint
115.3 x 88.9 cm
Kimbell Art Museum, Fort Worth

This limestone panel showing a seated lord, a
subsidiary lord and three captives has a glyphic text
that begins in front of the enthroned figure, with
the Calendar Round 5 Ix 7 Zac, a day most satisfac-
torily placed in the Long Count at 9.17.12.13.14,
or August 23, A.D. 783. On this day, a lord whose
title is Balam-Ahau was captured by "Ah Chac Ma

x." Three days later, blood was let, under the auspices of the enthroned lord at the left, an individual
here called the Kimbell Lord.

The figure at the right is kneeling with
one knee on a step, the left leg resting on the step
below. He is named by the title Ah K'in, which was
used as a priestly title at the time of the Conquest.
Here, dressed in warrior garb with captives in tow,
he clearly functions as a sort of war captain as he
presents the captives to his lord. He wears the same
scalloped petal hat commonly worn by secondary
warriors in other works, such as the Bonampak murals, and he holds a spondylus shell, bound by a
cloth tie, in his right hand. Each captive is bound
with cord and wears the cut cloth of bloodletting.

This official reception scene is set in a
palace throne room; swag curtains festoon the top
of the panel. The lord surveys the three captives,
who kneel and sit on the steps below him in a position characteristic of captives. The seat of his
throne is carved with the name and titles of the
reigning Yaxchilan king, Shield Jaguar II, but the
glyphs are inscribed in reverse order, from right to
left, perhaps to name him on the panel without emphasizing his authority.

Monuments that have recently come to
light in Europe reveal some of the historical circumstances of the scene on this panel. Two and a
half years after the seizure and bloodletting of these
captives, the enthroned lord was seated as *cahal*, or
underlord, under the auspices of the Yaxchilan king
Shield Jaguar II, who came to power after the death
of Bird Jaguar, around A.D. 771. The king, who
reigned over a large territory, had the power to
install others in subsidiary offices, perhaps to be
understood as governors or underlords. At
Yaxchilan, military achievements always preceded
official inaugurations, frequently with a significant
time lag between the two events. Judging from the
Kimbell panel, this was also true for provincial
administrators.

Like many monuments from the
Usumacinta region, this panel preserves much of its
original red, yellow and blue-green pigment. When
judged by the outline drawing on limestone, the
composition is of extraordinary quality. The sculptor who executed the relief, however, seems to have
relied on the paint to obscure his hasty work, and
the carving does not do justice to the quality of the
drawing.

PLATE 87
Lintel 16
Yaxchilan, Chiapas, Mexico
Late Classic period, ca. A.D. 755–770
Limestone
78.8 x 76.2 x 7 cm
The Trustees of The British Museum, London

This panel is one of a three-panel program of lintels, commissioned by Bird Jaguar and now numbered 15, 16 and 17, from Structure 21 at
Yaxchilan. In this series, Bird Jaguar emulated the
accomplishments — both in battle and in com-
memorative art — that his father Shield Jaguar had
achieved in Structure 23. On the day recorded on
Lintel 16, 9.16.0.13.17 6 Caban 5 Pop, February 10,
A.D. 752, Bird Jaguar captured a *cahal*, or prominent local lord. Eight days later, when Bird Jaguar's
heir, Shield Jaguar II, was born, he and one of his
other wives performed ritual bloodletting in celebration. Seventy-five days later, on May 3, A.D.
752, Bird Jaguar was officially installed as king,
something that appears to take place only after the
acquisition of noble captives, and — perhaps more
important in this case — after the birth of a male
heir.

On this lintel, Bird Jaguar displays his noble captive, who, judging from the beaded droplets
on his nose and cheek, has already let blood. In his
right hand he grasps the broken parasol that fallen
captives often hold; the ragged strips of cloth
draped over his left arm are also typical of captives.
The wrapped, dotted turban is the same as one
worn by the scattering figure on Piedras Negras
Stela 40 in the National Museum of Anthropology
in Guatemala City. The captive's hand-to-mouth
gesture seems a nervous one, although it may also
be the earth-eating gesture of the humiliated
captive.

PLATE 88
Cylindrical vessel
Late Classic period, A.D. 700–800
Polychromed ceramic
Diam. 11 x H. 21 cm
Department of Anthropology, American Museum of
Natural History, New York

Painted in a wide variety of colors, including a
lively purple, this Late Classic cylinder shows the
display of a captive, as does Yaxchilan Lintel 16 (Pl.
87); the event seems fresher and more fraught with
danger, however, when it is executed in the more
sketchy medium of slip painting. On Lintel 16, the
king, shown frontally, is featured; on this pot the
captive takes center stage. He is shown kneeling,
but he is so large that he would be the tallest figure

of the group if he stood up. Completely disarmed, he is bound with a white rope around his neck. With his right hand, he grasps a parasol with a broken handle, similar to those held by the captive of Lintel 16 and the captives of Yaxchilan Hieroglyphic Stairs 3. The right hand is drawn as though it were the left, a characteristic more common among captives; along with the parasol, it indicates that status. The prisoner wears a great mass of tattered loincloth and a water-lily jaguar headdress. He almost appears to speak the text of glyphs placed in front of his face, but it is too eroded to retrieve anything except the second-to-last glyph, a jaguar, which may be part of this fellow's name.

The first and second warriors on the left are apparently delivering the captive to their captain (the fourth person), who wears a great stuffed hide over his body. A "cruller" ornamenting the nose of his headdress indicates the Jaguar God of the Underworld, and the bloated hide below may form part of this costume. The two henchmen wear their hair short, perhaps indicating that they were once captives or that they are now slaves. The second man carries a threatening hafted flint; he wears a fan at the rear of his belt, as well as the stepped-fret loincloth occasionally seen elsewhere, as, for example, on Bonampak Stela 1. The bodies of all the figures are marked by daubs of darker slip—a technique opposite to chiaroscuro—which creates a suggestion of backlighting around the figures.

Plate 89
Jaina warrior
Late Classic period, A.D. 700–900
Ceramic with traces of pigment
7.4 x 21.8 x 9 cm
Courtesy of the Museum of the American Indian, Heye Foundation, New York

Seated in quiet meditation either before or after a battle, this Jaina warrior wears a mask of GI painted on his face. Although many GI attributes are lacking, such as the shell earflares and the quadripartite headdress, the fish fins and curled eyebrows here seem to point to this Maya supernatural.

Plate 90
Ceremonial ax
Kendal, Belize
Early Classic period, A.D. 250–400
Greenstone
22 x 3.5–6.4 x 3 cm
Merseyside County Museums, Liverpool

An image of GI or Chac-Xib-Chac is incised on the surface of this large jade axhead from Liverpool. It was found along with other very early finds, a GI shell earflare and a small mask (Pls. 10, 19), in a tomb at Kendal, Belize. The lord who was buried with these goods probably wielded this ax and entered the Underworld in the guise of the deity. The ax shows much wear near the base, probably from years of use. Because of the early style of the glyphs and the worn condition, the text eludes decipherment.

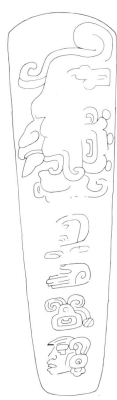

Plate 90a

Plate 91
Ceremonial ax
San José, Belize
Terminal Classic period, A.D. 900–1000
Obsidian
29.5 x 14.5 cm
Field Museum of Natural History, Chicago

Since obsidian was so precious to the Maya, this ax was probably reserved for ceremonial occasions. The Maya glyph (shown in Pl. 91a), sometimes thought to read *batab*, or "ax wielder," shows the Jester God with an ax of just this sort held close to his ear. The glyph seems to refer to noble warriors; it functions as a title.

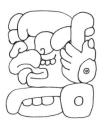

Plate 91a

Plate 92
Cylindrical vessel
Late Classic period, A.D. 600–800
Polychromed ceramic
Diam. 16.6 x H. 19.4 cm
Courtesy of The Art Institute of Chicago
The Ada Turnbull Hertle Fund

This intricate scene celebrating the accession of a king known to us as the Fat Cacique was painted by the Master of the Pink Glyphs, who earned this sobriquet because the texts on his pots are generally worked in gentle rose hues. The physiognomy of the Fat Cacique resembles that of the late eighth-century king represented on two wall panels at La Amelia, in the Petexbatun region. The Emblem Glyph inscribed on all these vessels, however, is that of San José de Motul, nicknamed the Ik site. Since San José de Motul seems to have few carved monuments, it may have resembled sites like Nebaj, in the Guatemalan Highlands, where the painting of pottery took priority, while stone carving languished.

On this pot, the Fat Cacique, the sixth person, steps down from a jaguar-covered sedan chair just as his two servants or slaves (the fourth and seventh persons), who do not have the red body paint or mask characteristic of the nobility in this scene, set the litter in place. The fifth figure, who also has a white-painted body and lacks a mask, moves forward to receive the king. The sharpened bone he wears in his simple headdress suggests he may be a priest or penitent.

The Fat Cacique, like the third, eighth, ninth and eleventh persons, wears a slim, cutaway mask shown in profile, but unlike most masks painted in the X-ray manner by this master, it is human rather than divine. The masks are attached to large headdresses with trailing veils, which are too eroded and pale to read clearly. These masks hide the refined profiles of their wearers, coarsening their appearance. The wearers have visible facial hair but do not have the artificially deformed nose characteristic of the Classic Maya. These individuals are all painted red and wear identical loincloths. The tenth person, a woman, also kneels. She wears no mask and holds a gourd rattle in her hand, as does the third person.

Facing the Fat Cacique and his luxurious sedan chair is the captive, who is bound to a spare scaffold. His captors have shaved his head, and the notch at the top of his head also shows that they have scalped him. In the drama that is poised to begin on this pot, the captive will be sacrificed and the scaffold refurbished with the jaguar pelt from the sedan chair. Then the Fat Cacique will step over the victim's body, ascend into the scaffold structure and receive the insignia of office.

Plate 93
Jaina captive
Late Classic period, A.D. 700–900
Ceramic
H. 19.3 cm
Lent courtesy of The Art Museum, Princeton University

Proud and noble, this Maya captive stands with his hands bound behind his back. Perishable hair was probably attached to his skull, knotted around the indentations that now remain. Bloodied and bruised and with swollen nose, the face nevertheless conveys the quality of a portrait. The slight paunch of the belly also suggests that this figurine represents a specific person, one who was made a captive.

Plate 94
Captive reliquary
Campeche, Mexico
Late Classic period, A.D. 700–900
Ceramic
H. 13.6 cm
The Baltimore Museum of Art
Gift of Alan Wurtzburger

This Jaina figurine, a living nightmare of torture, opens his mouth in a great howl of pain. His face is swollen and bloodied, and his scalp hangs down from his head, still attached to the nape of the neck. Evidence for this degree of torture among the Maya is not unknown. It appears, for example, that captives on the bench entablature in the Bonampak paintings have had their hands and fingers mangled out of joint. Although the hands and feet of this figure have been reattached, they, too, appear to have been twisted out of joint. Like many captives, this figure wears ragged strips of cloth for garments; tied over them at the lower back are pieces of firewood. Even though he is about to be set on fire, this captive will feel little pain, for he has already been killed through disembowelment. The gaping hole from his sternum to his groin has rendered him into a reliquary that was probably used to store some other trophy of war.

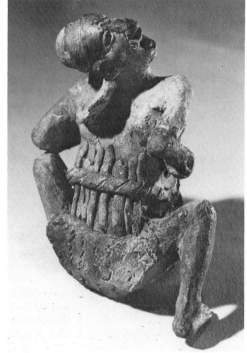

Plate 94a

Plate 78. Lintel 41

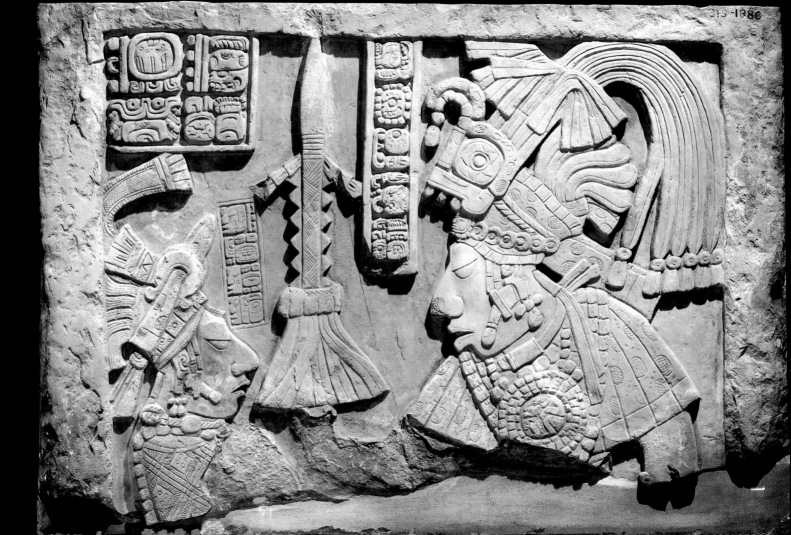

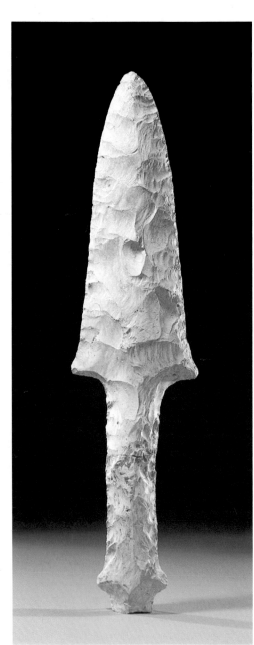

PLATE 77. Ceremonial knife

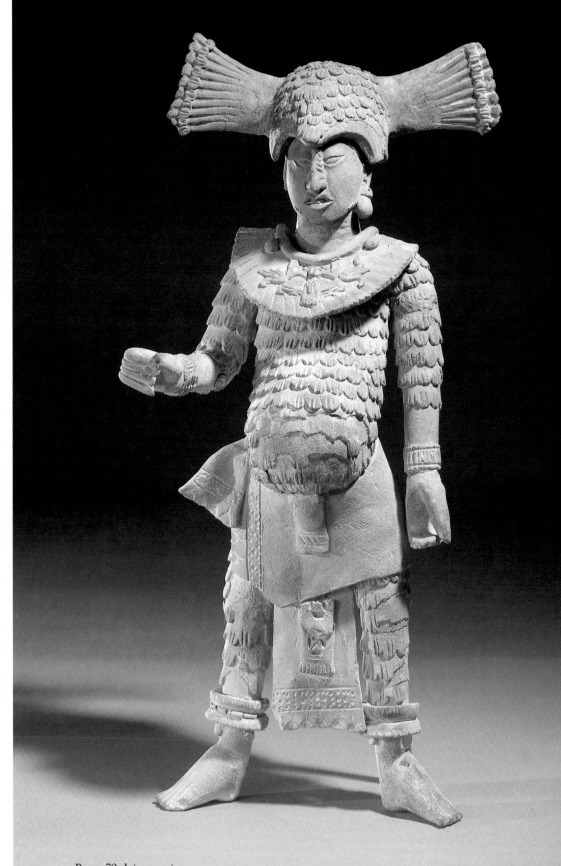

PLATE 79. Jaina warrior

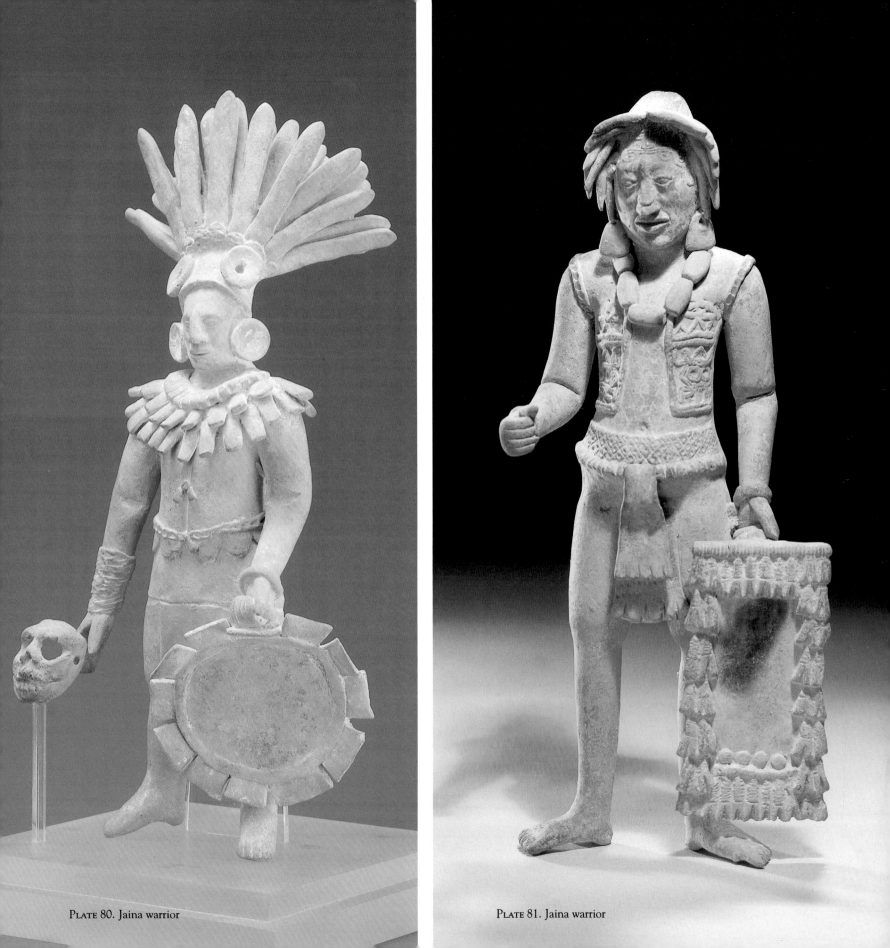

PLATE 80. Jaina warrior

PLATE 81. Jaina warrior

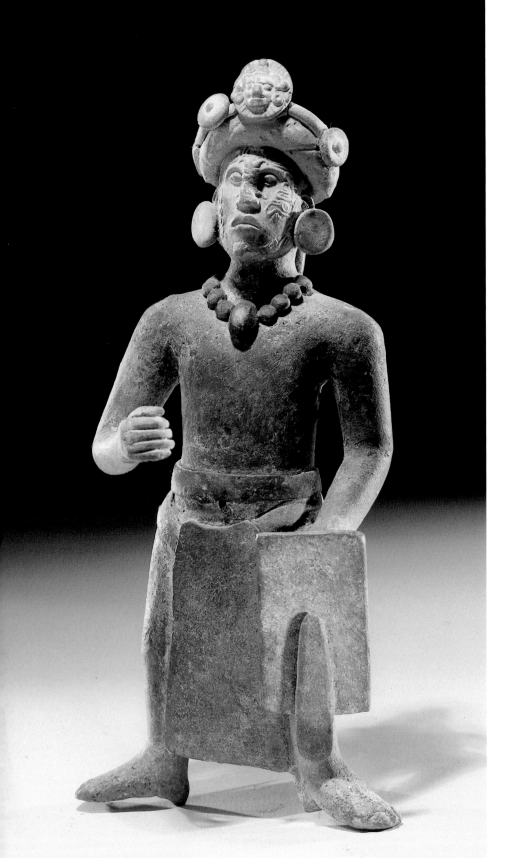

PLATE 82. Jaina warrior

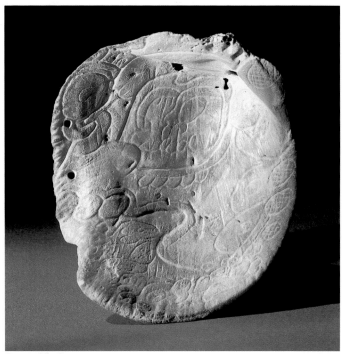

PLATE 85. Costume ornament

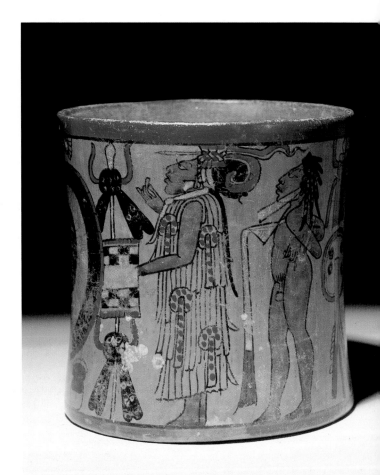

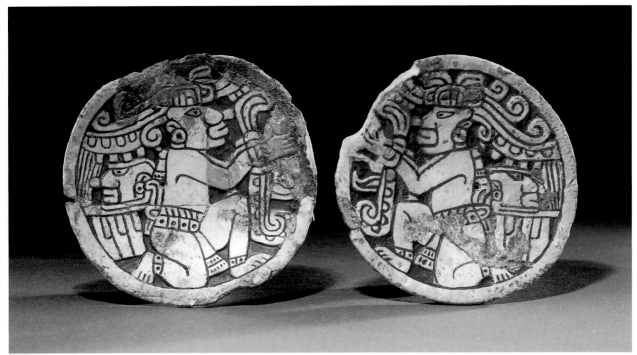

PLATE 83. Earflares

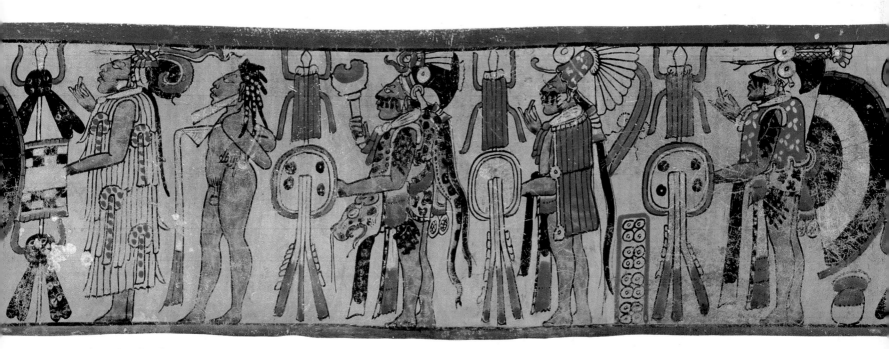

PLATE 84. Cylindrical vessel with warriors
PLATE 84a. Rollout

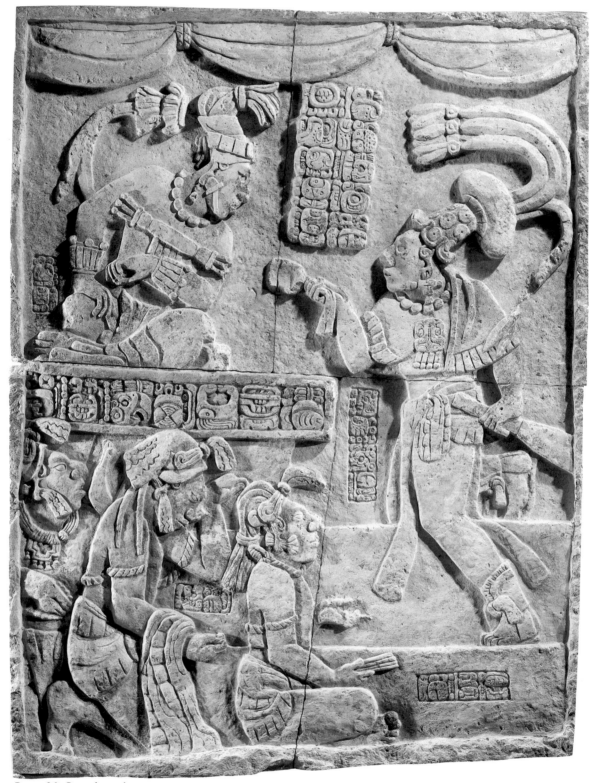

PLATE 86. Carved panel

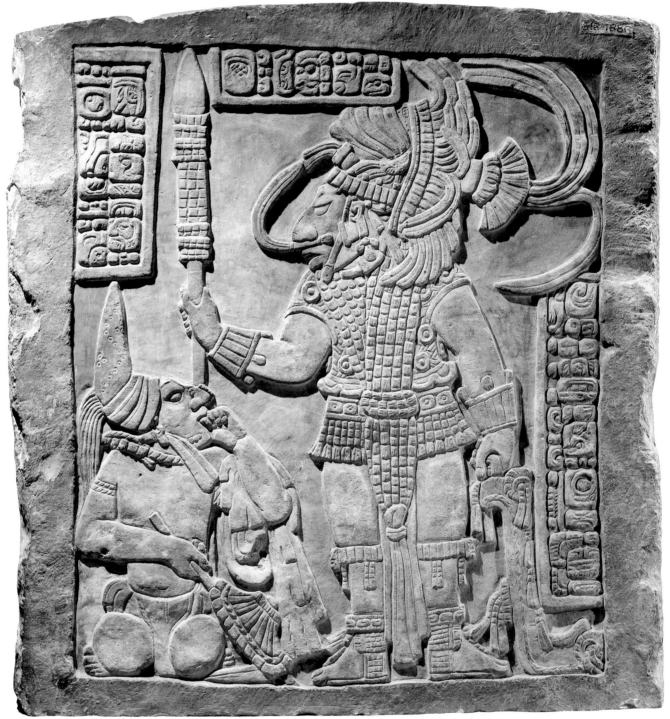

Plate 87. Lintel 16

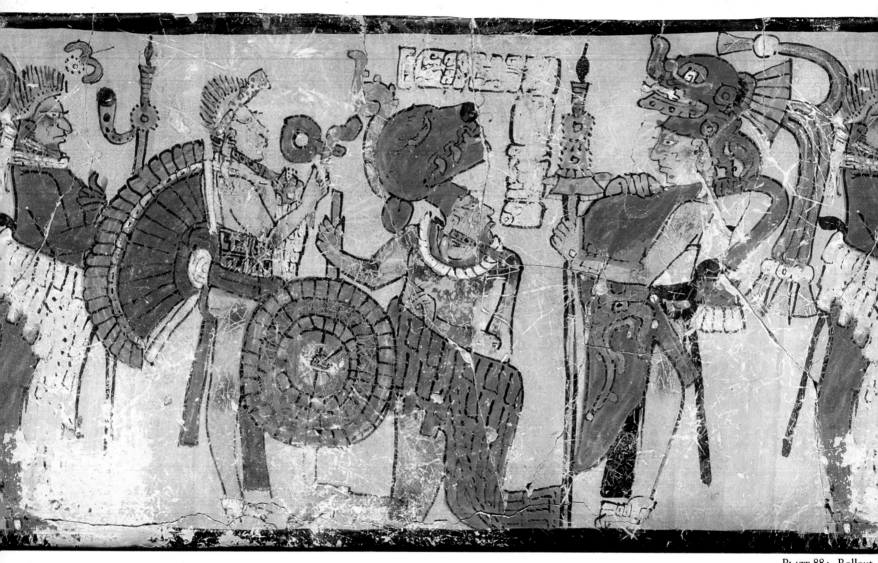

Plate 88a. Rollout

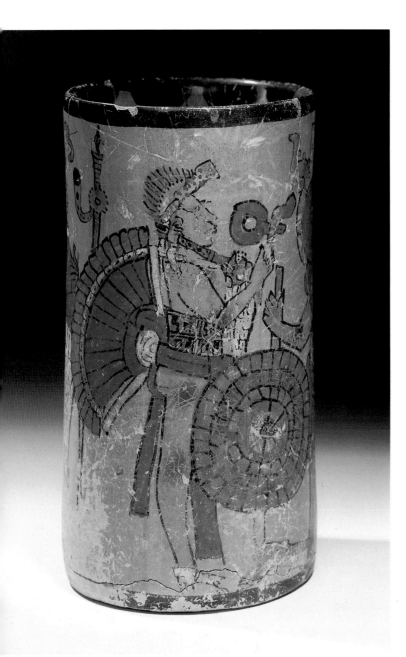

PLATE 88. Cylindrical vessel

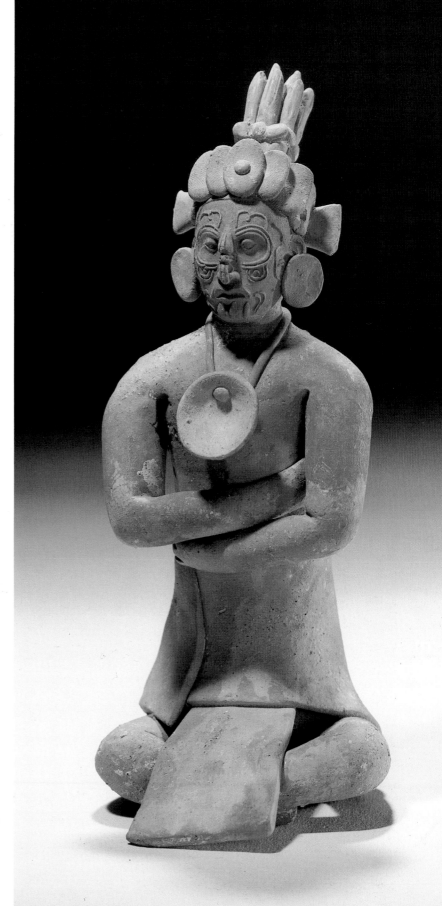

PLATE 89. Jaina warrior

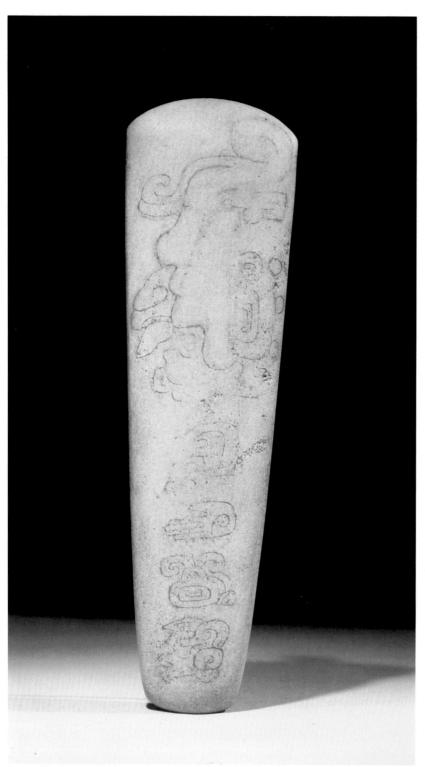

Plate 90. Ceremonial ax

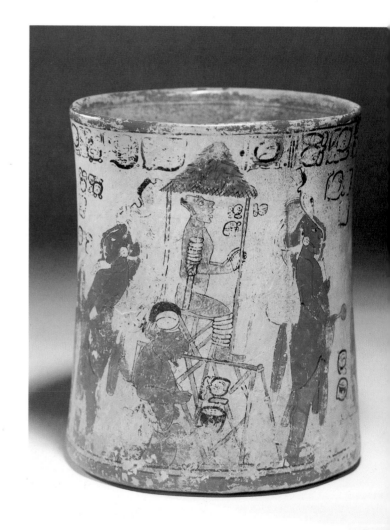

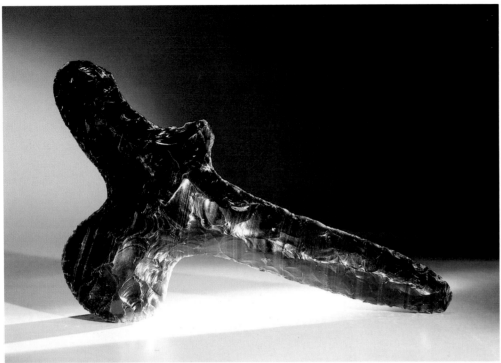

Plate 91. Ceremonial ax

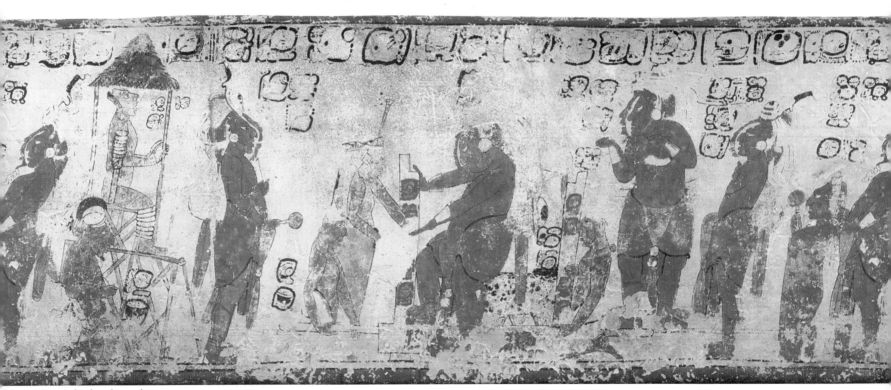

Plate 92. Cylindrical vessel
Plate 92a. Rollout

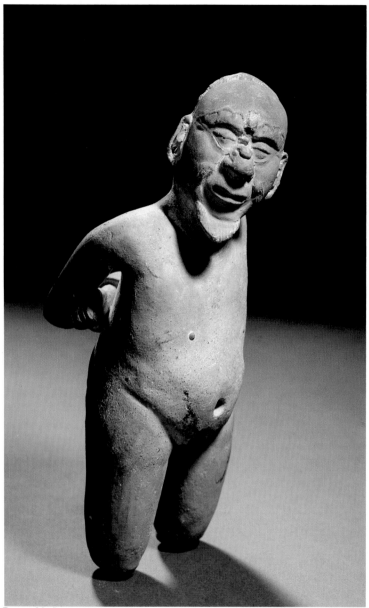

PLATE 93. Jaina captive

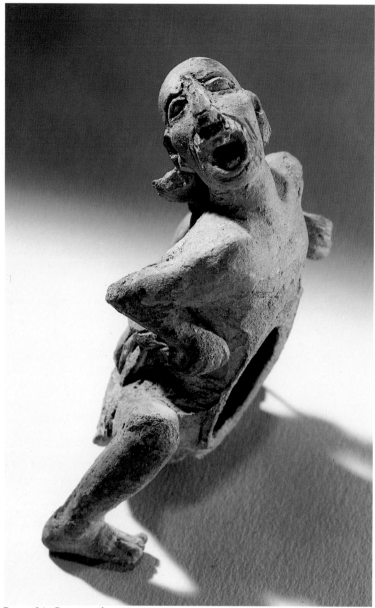

PLATE 94. Captive reliquary

VI

THE BALLGAME

THE MAYA BALLGAME IS A SUBJECT OF ENDLESS FASCINATION, PERHAPS because elements of the game are familiar yet shrouded in mystery. It was a dangerous sport that required the skillful manipulation of a heavy rubber ball and that frequently led to the sacrifice of the defeated. From the second millennium B.C. to the present, some sort of contest with a rubber ball has been played by Mesoamericans.[1] At the time of the Spanish Conquest of Mexico, a ballgame was played from the northern part of South America to the American Southwest. The ballgame so intrigued Europeans at the time of the Conquest that Cortés took a troupe of players to Europe in 1528, where they performed in royal courts (Fig. VI.1). Once the rubber ball was introduced to the Old World, it spawned the development of modern games that employed balls that bounce, rather than ones that used hard wooden or leather balls.

Probably because of our interest in modern ballgames, many of which have a potential for violence, contemporary Western societies have long been drawn to the Precolumbian ballgame. In it, human sacrifice was overt rather than suppressed. Just as in warfare, the Precolumbian ballgame makes death the final step in play, defining victory or defeat in stark terms.

No records explaining how to play the Classic Maya ballgame have been found, but from eyewitness accounts of a similar game described by European and native writers in the sixteenth century, we can infer much about how the Classic Maya may have played the game in earlier times.

FIGURE VI.1
Native American ballplayers
Sketch by Karl Weiditz, 1528

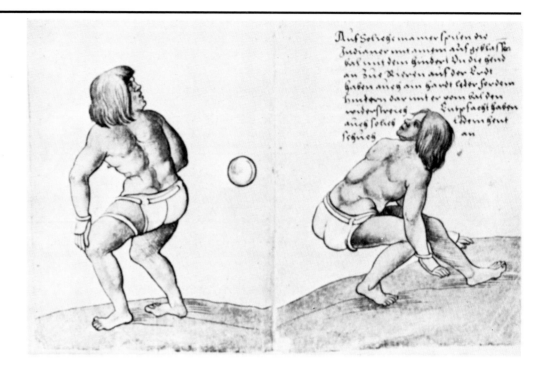

The Aztec game fulfilled various roles in society. It could be played for the sheer pleasure of demonstrating skill, and like sandlot baseball or urban stoopball, it could be practiced and played wherever two young men had enough space to bounce a ball. At other times, gambling motivated aggressive play and, sometimes, the game was played for the highest stakes of all: one's life. The play was fairly straightforward: teams of one to four players competed to control the ball without touching it with their hands and to make contact with markers or rings. The players took positions like modern soccer players when they controlled the ball with the lower leg or upper arm. To keep the ball from hitting the ground they lunged in front of it, intercepting it with arm, waist or thigh. Since thighs, torso and arms took the brunt of the blows, players wore small protective garments on their arms and legs. At midbody they wore thick, heavy deflectors called yokes that were also the player's most important instrument to control and direct the ball.

The markers to which players launched the ball took various forms in different cultures and eras. At the time of the Conquest, the markers were frequently small stone rings tenoned into walls of ballcourts at right angles to the ground so that the ball could only enter the ring on a strong horizontal trajectory. The angle of the ring, the weight of the ball and the rules for handling it made the game considerably more difficult than modern basketball. The ring tended to deflect the ball rather than guide its entry as a hoop parallel to the ground does; the weight of the ball makes gravity an important component of play; and the relative sizes of the ball and the goal—the goal only slightly larger than the ball—increased the difficulty of scoring. At the time of the Conquest, the ball was generally about eight inches in diameter; it was solid and heavy, rather like the modern medicine ball and unlike a hollow basketball, which is much lighter although of similar size. According to some Aztec accounts, even the most skilled and legendary players rarely managed to score direct points by passing the ball through the rings, but players could score points by making contact with the rings or by directing the ball into a goal area of the court.

Ballcourts are found throughout Mesoamerica. Ballcourts, consisting of two parallel structures (with either straight or sloping sides) flanking an earthen or paved stone alleyway that is the court, appear at almost every site from Olmec times to the Conquest. Often, ballcourts were located at the heart of the most sacred centers of ancient cities. At the Aztec capital Tenochtitlan, a ballcourt set within the walled Great Temple precinct was built in the fifteenth century beside important temples (Fig. VI.2). That a prominent rack for skulls, or *tzompantli*, was placed nearby was undoubtedly more than fortuitous. At El Tajin, a site contemporary with the Classic Maya but located at a distance from the Maya area in what is now Veracruz, at least eleven ballcourts were built, leading to speculation that it may have been a sort of Olympian center of the ancient New World. But whereas the Greek sculpture of ancient Olympia depicts sport as peaceable, the sculpture set into the ballcourts at El Tajin emphasizes only death and sacrifice.

At the time of the Conquest, gambling accompanied the game and created part of its excitement. According to some accounts, great wagers were laid, frequently of valuable textiles, which were the most measurable goods in a world without currency. When points were scored, the spectators would hastily throw their robes at the players in payment of their bets, and then flee to avoid paying higher losses. An Aztec ruler once wagered his kingdom against that of a neighboring sovereign on the outcome of a ballgame. His side lost and, faced with the demand to pay the debt, the lord had his adversary assassinated.[2] Perhaps because of their close association with this world of gambling, professional ballplayers were often regarded as unsavory types.

The potential for a disabling blow from the heavy rubber ball may have contributed to the excitement of the ballgame, but most of its drama undoubtedly derived from its role as a gladiatorial contest that tried the strength of a captive or slave and tested his desire to avoid death. Among the Aztecs, war captives weakened by deprivation frequently entered the ballcourt at a disadvantage and were pitted one against another until only one champion remained. Losers were sacrificed: their hearts were offered to the gods and, occasionally, their decapitated heads were placed in play. Time and again in depictions of the ballgame, images of human skulls are substituted for balls (Fig. VI.3). It was a gruesome game played for the highest stakes—the players' lives.

The Maya version of the ballgame at the time of the Conquest is described in the Popol Vuh, and its crucial role in the mythology of death and sacrifice is demonstrated. Just as ballcourts are set in pivotal locations at Mesoamerican sites, the ballgames played by the Hero Twins are the dramatic pivot of this epic narrative.

The stories relating to the ballgame in the Popol Vuh can be summarized as follows. The brothers 1 Hunahpu and 7 Hunahpu were the best ballplayers on earth.[3] They practiced tirelessly, bouncing the ball off their torso, hips and shoulders, learning skillfully to avoid contact between the hands and ball. But the noise of the relentless bouncing of the heavy, solid rubber ball disturbed the lords who lived in Xibalba, the Maya Underworld. Angry, the lords sent messenger owls to the Hunahpu brothers summoning them to a ballgame in the Underworld. The boys stored their equipment in the

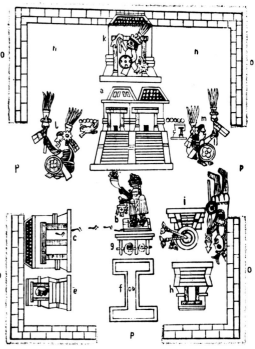

FIGURE VI.2
Plan of the Great Temple Precinct at Tenochtitlan, Mexico
From *Primeros Memoriales* of Sahagun's Codices Matritenses, Pl. XVI
Postconquest period, ca. 1560

The ballcourt is set within the ceremonial precinct, near the western entrance. The *tzompantli*, or skull rack, is directly over the ballcourt. Like most ballcourts of the Postclassic, it is I-shaped, and stone rings protruded from its side walls.

FIGURE VI.3
Great Ballcourt
Chichen Itza, Yucatan, Mexico
Postclassic period, A.D 900–1200

The sloping walls are carved at ground level with
elaborate scenes of the ballgame. Here, the
defeated ballplayers surrounded by blood scrolls are
being decapitated. The player to the left of the ball
holds the head of the figure to the right, whom he
has decapitated. Six snakes and an elaborate tree
sprout from the severed neck of the victim, showing
the fertility that such sacrifice will bring.

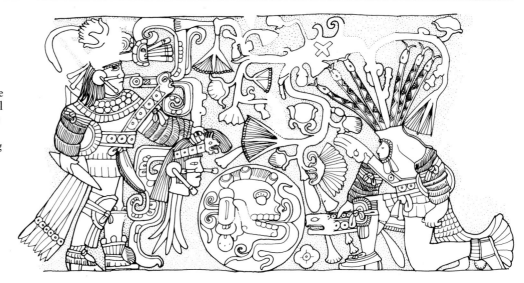

loft of their thatch house and followed the owls into the Underworld, to face the attempts of the lords to trap them and bring them to death. Not as wily as the gods, the brothers revealed their own weaknesses before they discovered those of their opponents. The gods won the ballgame easily, not through skill but by deception, and the two brothers were immediately sacrificed. The gods buried 7 Hunahpu's body in the ballcourt and hung 1 Hunahpu's head in a calabash tree to proclaim their victory.

One day the daughter of an Underworld lord walked past the calabash tree and spoke to the desiccated head, whereupon it spat into her hand, miraculously impregnating her. Her outraged father ordered her sacrificed, so she fled into the Middleworld where she sought refuge in the house of 1 Hunahpu and 7 Hunahpu, which was grudgingly granted by their mother. The old woman tested the younger woman, who proved her divinity and her worth by miraculously harvesting a full net of corn from a single plant. She then delivered twins, whom she named Hunahpu and Xbalanque.

Like Hercules, the Twins were demigods, capable of overcoming divine opponents. Years later, they discovered the ballgame equipment their father and uncle had left behind and soon they were playing the game, noisily bouncing the ball over the heads of the Underworld gods below. Once again angered at the racket, the gods issued an invitation to meet on their own court. The Twins accepted, but unlike their father and uncle, they penetrated the deception of the gods. Aided at every step by plants and animals, they learned to outwit the Xibalban lords at every encounter in the Underworld.

In their first ballgame, the lords of the Underworld tried to use a skull as a ball. The Hero Twins refused and forced the lords to play with a rubber ball. Although they could have won, the Twins deliberately lost the match to their opponents, 1 Death and 7 Death. Escorted to the "House of Darkness" for the night, the Hero Twins were ordered by the lords to pay off their wager on the game in flowers, or to forfeit their lives in the morning. Left in peace for the night, the Twins convinced cutter ants to steal flowers from the gardens of Xibalba. In the morning, the outsmarted lords found that the wager had not only been paid, but in their own flowers!

Day after day, play continued, usually to a tied score, and night after night, the Twins managed to frustrate the evil intentions of the Underworld lords. One night, however, when Hunahpu and Xbalanque found themselves in the "House of Bats," they slept inside their blowguns to hide from the bloodthirsty vampires. But Hunahpu, seeing a glimmer of light, stuck his head out to see if dawn had arrived and a killer bat decapitated him. Gloating, the evil lords hung Hunahpu's head over the ballcourt and announced that it would be used as the ball at the next match.

Xbalanque, seeking a way out of this new dilemma, sent the animals to bring their foodstuffs to him. He fashioned a temporary head for his brother's body from a pumpkin and devised a plan with a rabbit to retrieve the real head. When play began, he kicked the ball over the walls of the court into the underbrush, and the rabbit, impersonating the ball, bounced away, leading the lords of Xibalba on a merry chase. Xbalanque took advantage of the distraction to retrieve his brother's head and to replace it on his torso. Hunahpu, restored to whole, joined his brother in play, which continued until the substituted pumpkin head shattered. Once again, the Twins defeated the lords of Death by wit and quick thinking. Xbalanque and Hunahpu then let themselves be sacrificed, but their bones were ground up and cast into a river. Later they were able to reappear in the Underworld and present themselves as magicians who would entertain in the court of 1 Death and 7 Death. There, as part of their performance, they successfully dismembered their enemies. Having vanquished their enemies, Hunahpu and Xbalanque took their places as heavenly bodies, identified as the sun and the moon, or the sun and Venus.[4]

The Popol Vuh account contains many suggestions about the nature of the Maya ballgame. Ball was played only by males, but they might be humans, demigods or gods. Play took place in a court, probably of the sort known in Highland Guatemala at the time of the Conquest, which differ from those of the Classic period only in their I-shaped form. Court walls were not so high that an occasional wild ball could not escape its confines, and the ball itself may indeed have been about the size of a human head or a curled-up rabbit. Points were scored when a player drove the ball through a ring extended from the sides of the court. Each team was composed of two players; the hand could only contact the ball in throwing it into play. In the Popol Vuh, most contests ended in a score tied at one point apiece for the Hero Twins and the Underworld lords. After each match, the Twins were put in a house where, night after night, the Underworld lords attempted to kill them. The ballgame paraphernalia of the Twins—yokes, handstones, possibly the thin, flat stones generally called *hachas* today and, most importantly, the ball itself—was stored and used from one generation to the next.

For many years, because its violence did not accord with the prevailing view of the Classic Maya, the ballgame was considered only a very late phenomenon in Mesoamerica, attributed to Postclassic peoples like the Toltecs and Aztecs. Its importance to the narrative of the Popol Vuh was thought to be the result of Central Mexican influence in Guatemala rather than an indigenous phenomenon. Until fifty years ago, the presence of ballcourts at Chichen Itza was dismissed as an innovation of the Toltecs, who imposed their bloody rites on the Yucatan.[5] The imagery on sculptured walls of the Great Ballcourt at Chichen Itza (Fig. VI.3), which shows the ball as a belching skull and victorious ballplayers decapitating defeated ones, was implausible behavior for the peaceful Classic Maya that nineteenth century archaeologists had described.

Early in this century archaeologists discovered architecture, art and inscrip-

Three ballcourts are known at Tikal. The smallest but most important one is lodged between Temple I and the Central Acropolis, uniting the funerary pyramid of Ruler A with the royal compound. Ritual play in the small court may have been followed by sacrifice from the steep temple facade.

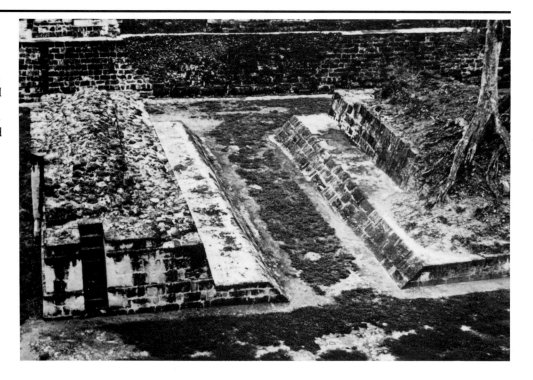

tions in Peten and Usumacinta sites that testified to the importance of the ballgame among the Classic Maya. During the 1920s mapping projects at several Classic Maya cities first demonstrated that the distinctive ballcourt layout was found among the Classic Maya and that the game was certainly played before the Toltec era. Ballcourts were found at almost every Classic Maya site and their absence, rather than their presence, is now considered an anomaly. Many pots and sculptures that show the ballgame in progress have been found and, although the action is often frozen in the pregnant moment preferred by Maya artists, the texts, paintings and carvings reveal much about the Classic game. This evidence, in conjunction with sixteenth century information, reveals the nature and at least some of the meaning of the Maya ballgame.

Once archaeologists had accepted that the Maya played a ballgame, they nevertheless assumed that the Maya game, unlike its successors, was played without the element of sacrifice. Maya art and inscriptions clearly indicate that the ballgame was the event in which war captives were sacrificed. However, it is becoming increasingly clear through studying texts and images that the Classic Maya ballgame had a role in kingship similar to the one held by the game in Aztec society. Most certainly the game could be played simply as a sport, and some Maya ballgame art can be interpreted to be illustrations of this sort of game. The protagonist of this play was the Maya king, at once sports hero and war captain. If the ballgame is considered a cosmic metaphor in which the ball replicates the trajectory of heavenly bodies, then the king was the agent who set their courses.

The largest and best constructed Maya ballcourts, like the one at Tenochtitlan, are found at the centers of ceremonial precincts. Unlike later examples known in other

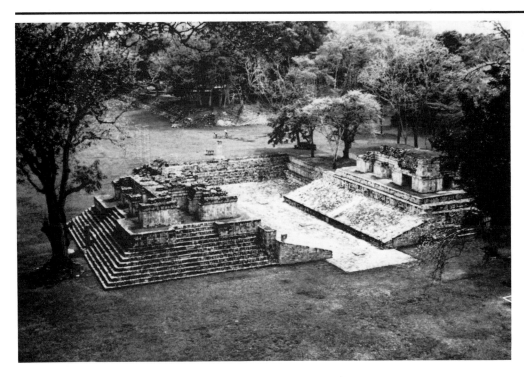

Figure VI.5
Ballcourt
Copan, Honduras
Late Classic period, A.D. 750–800
Photo by Linda Schele

The beautiful and thoughtfully designed ballcourt, located among the main ceremonial structures at Copan, visually unites the great open plaza with the Main Acropolis.

parts of Mexico, Maya courts are usually open-ended, and the facing walls of the long parallel structures that define the courts slope inward, providing surfaces on which the ball can roll or be deflected. With few exceptions, the courts have no rings; many have three round disks, often called markers, evenly spaced along the playing alley.[6] Generally, ballcourts flank palace compounds and temple groupings, the structures most important to the Maya rulers. Courts of a less permanent sort may have been constructed away from ceremonial precincts, but the location of permanent courts at the centers of many Maya cities suggests that the ballcourt rituals were an important activity in the lives of the elite. At Tikal, a small ballcourt (Fig. VI.4) is wedged between the Central Acropolis, the main palace, and Temple I, the most important funerary temple in the city. At Copan, the main ballcourt (Fig. VI.5) seems to reproduce the surrounding valley in its layout and orientation, and it unites the Main Acropolis— consisting of a palace and funerary complex—with the open plaza to the north. Most Maya courts are positioned to permit their activity to be observed by large crowds.

Although ballgame play is frequently depicted in courts of this sort, a ballgame played against stairs is recorded with even greater frequency. This second form of play seems to be distinct from the game conducted on the courts, in that humans are trussed and used as the ball, but it probably followed immediately after play in a ballcourt and took place on steps adjacent to the ballcourts. At Copan, a platform with stairs lies at the north end of the ballcourt; at Tikal, Temple I has the elements needed to play the game on stairs. In various works of art, players are shown framed against a section of a ballcourt structure recognizable by its gently sloping walls. The scene painted on a pot now in Leiden (Pl. 95) shows play against a stepped platform that could be a temple

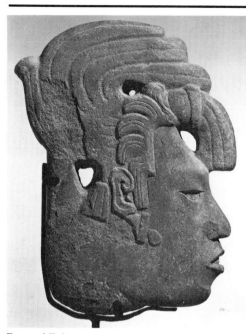

Hachas such as this were worn by Maya ballplayers as deflectors inserted in the yoke. They may also have functioned as markers of some sort, against which points could have been scored. This extremely beautiful example, carved in the form of a Maya head, is probably from Highland Guatemala, where most such objects have been recovered.

substructure. In the ballplaying scenes painted on the pot from Dallas (Pl. 96) and carved on the Hieroglyphic Stairs from Temple 33 at Yaxchilan (Fig. VI.7), the play is clearly carried out against a flight of stairs.

The Classic Maya may have played with the largest ball used in any indigenous American ballgame. Judging from the scale of the ball depicted in Maya art, its size ranged from one foot to eighteen inches in diameter. When shown in color, it is always black, the color of natural rubber after it has been cooked and solidified. A solid ball of this size probably weighed about eight pounds; the balls depicted at Chichen Itza or at El Tajin, which had hollow cores formed by human skulls, would have weighed less.[7]

To hit such a ball with their bodies, players wore heavy padding, and numerous extant works show the participants wearing extra cushions on arms, knees and waist. On the Dallas pot, only one knee, foot and wrist of each player is wrapped, but a long hide draped over the waist protector provides extra protection from the ball. In some cases, twisted, quilted cotton helps provide a cushion, as is seen on the players of the Chicago panel (Pl. 101).[8] Classic period Maya ballplayers wore an elaborate yoke at the waist that protected the body from groin to chest. Some objects like the Dallas pot (Pl. 96), the Chicago Art Institute stone (Pl. 101), and the Heye Foundation stone (Pl. 104), show the configuration of this yoke and how it was made. Unlike the stone yokes from Veracruz that are contemporary with the Late Classic period of the Maya, the horseshoe-shaped yoke was made of perishable materials such as wicker or other tough reed fibers. It was wrapped around the waist so that the open end came to the player's side where it was tied with cloth. Bulky cloth and other heavy fibrous materials were used under the yoke to protect the body and sometimes draped over the top of the yoke. A singular pot at the Metropolitan Museum (Pl. 97) also wears a yoke around its body, as if for protection.[9] This unusual vessel and its contents may have been a trophy carried away by a successful player, much like the prize amphorae granted to victorious Greeks in the ancient Olympics.

Stones of the shapes called either *palmas* or *hachas* today may have been inserted into the yokes, presumably to help control and deflect the ball (Fig. VI.6). Such an ensemble is shown in the Jaina figurine in the Seattle Art Museum (Pl. 98). Handstones may have been used to protect the hand in play, or perhaps when setting the heavy ball in motion, as appears to be the case on the Center Marker from the ballcourt at Copan (Pl. 102). A figurine in the Munson-Williams-Proctor collection (Pl. 99) shows a ballplayer seated in a stately posture as if posed for a formal portrait, who holds a handstone at his side. In depiction of play itself, Classic players assume postures much like those described at the time of the Conquest. Since the ball is usually deflected by upper arm, torso or thigh, a missile shown hurtling directly into an opponent's face indicates the imminent defeat—and probable death—of that player (Pl. 101).

According to the art and inscriptions, death and human sacrifice were frequently the outcome of the Maya ballgame. In some cases death is explicitly rendered; in others it is implied or cleverly suggested, as though death were an obstacle to be outwitted as it was in the Popol Vuh when the Hero Twins outsmarted the Underworld Death deities. In Postclassic images, such as the ballgame scenes at Chichen Itza, defeated ballplayers are decapitated. For many years, scholars refused to attribute this bloody finale to the Classic Maya ballgame, for they refused to think that the Maya, like other Mesoamericans, could have finished off their opponents in this violent fashion. Yet, the practice has been confirmed by evidence found at Yaxchilan where, in

1974, Mexican archaeologists uncovered an elaborate carved tier of steps near the top of Structure 33, a building that celebrates the accession and reign of Bird Jaguar, who acceded in A.D. 752. Of the thirteen carved blocks that make up the tier, eleven feature ballplaying scenes, and those that show active play record that the game was played on a flight of stairs, which may be understood as the front of Structure 33. Three of the central blocks repeat a single image: a Yaxchilan lord strikes a human whose neck is broken and snapped back; the body is bound and trussed into the form of a ball, then hurtled down a flight of stairs (Fig. VI.7). On Step VI, the king Bird Jaguar prepares to strike his victim who is identified in a caption within the ball as Jeweled Skull, an important noble taken captive in the most important battle of Bird Jaguar's life, and pictured on Lintel 8 (Fig. V.3) and Lintel 41 (Pl. 78).[10] At some point after his capture, he was compelled to face Bird Jaguar in the ballgame. It would not be surprising if the game were rigged so that the Yaxchilan king would win. Later, Jeweled Skull was taken to a long flight of stairs, probably Structure 33, where he played the ball in the sacrificial finale to the contest over which Bird Jaguar presided. This sacrifice of Jeweled Skull was integrated into rites celebrating Bird Jaguar's victory and rule.

On Step VII, the centerpiece of the carved riser near the summit of Structure 33, Bird Jaguar strikes another human bound into a ball, and two dwarfs with star signs on their bodies attend the king, as if to place the event in the cosmos. The text on the right of the Step VII scene records one of the greatest numbers in Classic Maya inscriptions. This huge number, carried to eight places above the *baktun*, is neither a distance number, nor a projection deep into the past or future. Rather, it is a number of enormous size that we would write as 20 to the ninth power and that the Maya have written as a fancy Long Count or Initial Series date which occurred in Bird Jaguar's lifetime. By writing the number in this special way, his action was set within the cyclical repetitions of cosmic time. In effect, by including this special Initial Series number, Bird Jaguar's action was removed from the realm of mundane behavior and treated as sacred behavior within a time frame that approached infinity. The date concludes in normal time with 9.15.13.6.9, or October 21, A.D. 744, when Bird Jaguar conducted his ballgame play.

The idea of the captive as sacrificial victim in ballgame play is also seen elsewhere. At Chichen Itza, the ball is shown with a human skull within (Fig. VI.8). Altar 8, Tikal (Fig. VI.9a,b), shows a bound, trussed human within the tied frame of a ball, nearly identical to the ball on Step VII. This Tikal captive, depicted within a ball, probably died in ballgame play. A ball tied in the same fashion hangs between the two players on the North and South Markers (Figs. VI.10, 11) of the Copan ballcourt. Although no figure is carved on the surface of that ball, it too may refer to a captive who faces death in ballgame. A figure of a ballplayer at New Orleans (Pl. 100) is dressed as a captive and for him the next step is to be bound as a ball.

In the Popol Vuh account of the ballgame contest, the Hero Twins were not sacrificed by the Underworld gods on the ballcourt. Their father and uncle had been defeated and sacrificed there, but Hunahpu and Xbalanque were taken each night to a house, where they had to survive trials to avoid death. Sacrifice was a deliberate sequel to play, an integral part of the ritual ballgame cycle, and it was attempted in a house. In Classic times, "house" in the context of the ballgame, probably meant the chamber located at the top of the stairway on a pyramidal platform. Many specific details of the Maya ballgame are still not known, but if the Popol Vuh reflects the reality of the Maya game, these events followed in sequence: captives were forced to play the ballgame in a

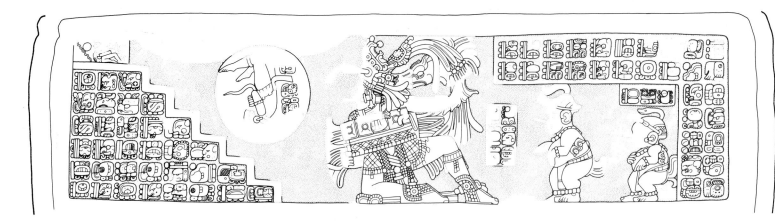

FIGURE VI.7
Step VII
Hieroglyphic Stairs, Structure 33, Yaxchilan
Late Classic period, ca. A.D. 750–760
Drawing by Ian Graham

court; the defeated captives were taken to a temple and bound into the form of a ball; in the finale, they were rolled down the stairway to their deaths.

The staircase ritual that concluded ballgame play is often the subject of Maya ballgame art. Glyphs associated with ballgame play are frequently carved on staircases and risers, in direct association with names of known captives and records of their deaths. In A.D. 735, the king of Seibal, a man named Paw Jaguar, was captured by the king of Dos Pilas, who had a stela carved to show the humbled king of Seibal at his feet. Twelve years later, on the day of the inferior conjunction of Venus—considered by the Classic Maya to be the most appropriate time for warfare and sacrifice—Paw Jaguar was the protagonist of a ballgame event.[11] Since the record of this event is the last mention of Paw Jaguar in the whole corpus of Maya inscriptions, he may well have met his demise in the ballgame on that day. Foreign kings were the most desirable trophies that other kings could garner in battle, and they were put to death conspicuously, probably in the ballgame.

In some cases, the relationship between battle and ballgame is made explicit, in both depictions and glyphs. In A.D. 631 Caracol successfully waged war on Naranjo, and a hieroglyphic staircase was erected at the latter site to record the victory of Caracol. At Naranjo, Step VI of the staircase records a war event ("shell/star" over Naranjo) followed by a ballgame verb, suggesting that the first event caused the second.[12] At Copan, in Temple 11, records of kingship are set at the summit;[13] on the south face, at the so-called Reviewing Stand, captives were sacrificed on stairs fronted by three square markers that symbolize a ballcourt.[14]

The ballplayer panel from the Art Institute of Chicago (Pl. 101) shows ballplayers dressed in the garb of warriors, as if the ballplaying paraphernalia were hastily put over other clothes. Although the upper portion of the panel is damaged and difficult to read, it is clear that the player at left is dressed in the garb of a victorious warrior. He probably had a jaguar pelt balloon headdress; he wears a human skull around his neck, and great Tlaloc faces at the waist and knee.[15] Frequently, the imagery of victory and defeat in Maya warfare scenes is cast as an opposition of a jaguar and a bird, perhaps to reflect the natural world where felines invariably win in contests with birds. This imagery is abundantly clear in Maya-style murals at the Central Mexican site of Cacaxtla, Tlaxcala, where men in jaguar costume disembowel their hapless victims, who all wear beautiful bird suits. The fallen ball player at the right on the Chicago panel, who is about to take a fatal ball on the chin, wears a feathered headdress composed of individual birds set like spikes from the central crown. His tangled legs immobilize him, like the bound captives frequently depicted on carved staircases.[16] And, like abject captives shown elsewhere, the defeated Chicago ballplayer wears torn cloth ties. His prominence on the panel, occupying more space than the victorious player at left, may indicate the importance of his capture and defeat. Unfortunately, his name glyph is gone, but a royal title in the caption over the ball suggests that he may have been a king. That he, like others, met his end in the ballgame, is expressed by the last glyph of the text at the right.[17]

The three carved ballcourt markers at Copan comprise a single narrative that appears to show the progression of play in a game between humans and divinities.[18] The markers were evenly spaced along the alley of the ballcourt and, shortly after their installation in the eighth century, covered by new sculptured panels (now hopelessly eroded) that protected the earlier program.[19] Each marker features two players with a ball separating them. On the North Marker (Fig. VI.10), two Underworld deities face one another across a large ball, poised but not in play, suspended by a rope from a support above. Although the condition of this South Marker (Fig. VI.11) is not as good as the North and Center Markers, enough remains to show that the scene depicted is nearly identical to that on the North Marker, but positions of the players are reversed. On the North Marker, a plant growing from a glyph is at the far left; on the South Marker, it is at the right. On the North Marker, the inclusion of a plant on the glyph may refer to a source of corn in the Underworld, but the reference is still elusive. Although the meaning of this glyph is not understood, it includes the number 9; on the South, it is marked with 7.

On both North and South Markers, the ball is shown suspended in the center, bound by a knotted rope, pending the start of play on the North Marker and following its conclusion on the South. Behind the knotted cord is a tiny I-shaped ballcourt seen in bird's-eye view. The juxtaposition and scale suggest that one stroke of a blade could set the ball tumbling into the court to initiate the contest. In the Popol Vuh, when the Hero Twins played ball in the Middleworld, the ball was suspended from a rope, and a rat chewed the fiber to set the ball in play.

On the Center Marker (Pl. 102), the ball has been freed from its hangings, and both players kneel to strike the ball. The player at the left is named by the first two glyphs as Hun-Ahau, the Classic equivalent of Hunahpu, one of the Hero Twins. The next glyph seems to name the contestant at right by his portrait glyph and the number 6, indicating that he is the death god of sacrifice and the God of Zero.[20] The figure personifies completion, or zero in the Maya counting system, and is characterized by the hand on the jaw. The last three glyphs refer to the king of Copan, 18 Rabbit, but, in what appears to be an error, his name is recorded as 13 Rabbit.[21] The imagery of the Center Marker, and the appearance of three names, including the incorrect rendering of 18 Rabbit, is puzzling. These stones might suggest that 18 Rabbit presided over the games or that he undertook refurbishing the ballcourt, but the facts emerging about the history of Copan at the end of his reign may support another interpretation. In A.D. 737, the king of Quirigua captured 18 Rabbit and thereafter prominently recorded his victory over the king of Copan on every monument built during his reign. Soon after 18

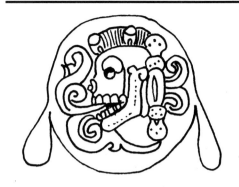

FIGURE VI.8
Detail of a human skull within a ball
Chichen Itza, Yucatan, Mexico
Late Classic period, A.D. 900–1200
Drawing by Mary Miller

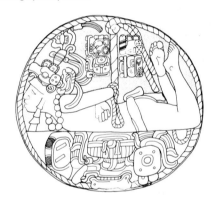

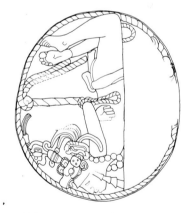

FIGURE VI.9
Detail of human bound up as a ball
Altar 8, Tikal, Guatemala
Late Classic period, A.D. 750–760
a) Figure horizontal
b) Figure vertical

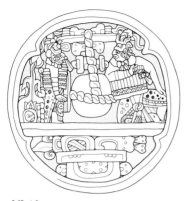

FIGURE VI.10
North Marker
Ballcourt II-B, Copan, Honduras
Late Classic period, A.D. 731–751
Drawings by Barbara Fash

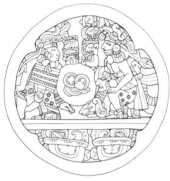

PLATE 102
Center Marker
Ballcourt II-B, Copan, Honduras

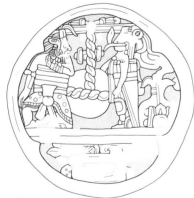

FIGURE VI.11
South Marker
Ballcourt II-B, Copan, Honduras

Rabbit was captured, a new king was installed at Copan. Quirigua kept 18 Rabbit hostage for many years and may have sacrificed him in a ballgame.

We hypothesize on the basis of imagery from the Popul Vuh that the Center Marker may record 18 Rabbit's demise at the hands of his Quirigua captors. In the tale, Hunahpu injudiciously loses his head to a killer bat. Xbalanque, thinking quickly, replaces it with a pumpkin, and then convinces a rabbit to curl up and imitate the ball during play so it can lead the lords of the Underworld away from the court and give Xbalanque time to put his brother's head back on his torso. The imagery of this clever substitution was evidently used by artists in Classic times. On a small mold-made bottle now at Leiden, for example, a ballplayer strikes a rabbit ball (Pl. 103). On Stela D, made during 18 Rabbit's reign at Copan, a ball of chert naturally occurring in the limestone was left in the carving and a coefficient of 18 was placed in front of it, to be read 18 Ball, instead of 18 Rabbit. The king probably enjoyed the pun: the rabbit was a ball, and the ball a rabbit.

On the Center Marker there were three names, two of which referred to the players, Hun-Ahau and the God of Zero. The third name, 18 Rabbit, appears to refer to nothing in the scene, unless to the ball itself. Could 18 Rabbit be depicted as the ball? Balls are commonly inscribed with the numbers 9, 12, 13, or 14 and a glyph to be read *na:b(a)*.[22] The apparent error in the coefficient of his name—13 instead of 18—may be a witty hint that the name glyph refers to the ball, which could bear no number higher than 14, as well as to the man.

In the Popol Vuh narrative, the substitution of the rabbit for the ball has an auspicious outcome. Hunahpu is restored; he and Xbalanque defeat the Underworld deities; and they ascend to the heavens where they reign as the Sun and Venus. For 18 Rabbit's subjects at Copan who lost their king, the imagery of the Center Marker may be analogous to a prayer, a wish that like a Hero Twin their king ultimately overcame the odds, bouncing like a rabbit, to defeat the Underworld gods.

In other examples of Maya art, the identification of ballplayers with Hero Twins is more direct. Two deities of the Palenque Triad, Chac-Xib-Chac and a Jaguar God—either the Jaguar God of the Underworld, the Baby Jaguar, or the Waterlily Jaguar—frequently appear together. These deities act like twins and their actions emulate the Hero Twins, Hunahpu and Xbalanque. In impersonating these paired deities, kings evoke the Hero Twins. On Stela 11 from Yaxchilan, Bird Jaguar, dressed as a Jaguar God, shows himself to be a warrior (Fig. V.5b); dressed as Chac-Xib-Chac, he presides over sacrifice (Fig. V.5a). Together, the two deities play the ballgame, and their adversaries appear to be old Underworld gods.

In a series of stone panels, now dispersed in various collections, which derive from an unidentified Maya site known only as Site Q, humans dressed as these two deities engage in the play of the ballgame.[23] The ball links one panel to another and sometimes is shown frozen between scenes, creating dramatic artistic tension (Fig. VI.12). On one small panel, a ruler wearing the head of Chac-Xib-Chac as a headdress launches the ball to a player on another panel. On another panel from this series he is a lord, dressed as the Jaguar God of the Underworld (Pl. 104), and properly poised to receive the ball on his yoke, not his exposed body. His opponent is dressed as God L, a principal Underworld lord and one of the evil ballplayers of the Popol Vuh. He is a formidable opponent, to be defeated not by the physical prowess but, following the model of the Hero Twins, by cunning.

Rulers may have dressed as the Hero Twins for the ballgame, enacting the roles of the demigods they emulated. The defeat of the opposition by victorious Maya kings, dressed as warriors or deities, was recast in stone as combat with death, darkness, and the Underworld. The actual capture during battle was a relatively private affair, but its celebration and ritual reenactment in the ballgame was designed as public spectacle. It allowed the king to reign as both athlete and warrior. Blood sacrifice, the mortar of Maya dynastic life, was offered at the same time that the enemies of the kingdom were extinguished.

NOTES

1. The most complete study ever made of the ballgame is Theodore Stern, *The Rubber-Ball Games of the Americas*, American Ethnological Society, Monograph 17 (New York: American Ethnological Society, 1948). An indigenous ballgame is still played today in Sinaloa, in northern Mexico: Ted J. J. Leyenaar, "Ulama, supervivencia de un juego de pelota precolombino," in *International Congress of the Americanists*, vol. 2 (1974), pp. 221–230; see also ibid., *Ulama: The Perpetuation in Mexico of the Pre-Spanish Ball Game Ullamaliztli*, translated by Inez Seeger (Leiden: E. J. Brill, 1978); and Eric Taladoire, *Les térrains de jeu de balle (Mésoamerique et Sud-ouest des Etats-Unis)* (Mexico City: Mission Archéologique et Ethnologique Française au Mexique, 1981).

2. Theodore Stern, *The Rubber-Ball Games of the Americas*, p. 62.

3. The names 1 Hunahpu and 7 Hunahpu refer to days in the 260-day calendar.

4. This summary of the details of the game from the Popol Vuh derives from Dennis Tedlock's translation (*Popol Vuh: The Definitive Edition of the Mayan Book of the Dawn of Life and the Glories of Gods and Kings* [New York: Simon and Schuster, 1985]).

5. Frans Blom, "The Maya Ball-Game Pok-ta-Pok," Middle American Research Series Pub. No. 4 (New Orleans: Department of Middle American Research, Tulane University, 1932), pp. 485–530.

6. Stone rings are known at both Naranjo and Uxmal. Other courts may possibly have held perishable rings. It has also been suggested that the *hachas* (see Fig. VI.6), or thin, carved stones, may have been portable markers for scoring, although the figure in Plate 98 is wearing one.

7. Ted J. J. Leyenaar, "Ulama," p. 225. The modern players of the ballgame use balls that they make by hand in molds; the diameter of the ball is 10 cm, and it weighs about 500 g. At the minimum, the ancient Maya ball would seem to have been about 30 cm in diameter and about seven times the volume of the modern ball described by Leyenaar. That a skull might serve as a ball with a hollow core is suggested only by depictions of balls with skulls inside.

8. Although deities and other ballplayers wear symbolic garments (see below), ballplayers do not seem to have worn "uniforms" that distinguished teams. In Plate 96, where teams of two face off, for example, all ballplayers wear athletic gear, but no distinctive headdress or hipcloth pattern distinguishes either side.

9. Julie Jones, "An Early Classic Maya Vessel: Some Questions of Style," in *Actas del XXIV Congreso Internacional de Historia del Arte* 1 (Granada: University of Granada, 1976), pp. 145–154.

10. Curiously, the text records Shield Jaguar as the protagonist of the ballgame event against Jeweled Skull, even though Shield Jaguar had been dead for about fifteen years when this important captive was taken. In the text, Shield Jaguar is referred to as the "5-katun lord," a title generally used after his death: It is likely, then, that he is the protagonist of this event in spirit only, and that his name occurs here as a memorial to the great king.

11. Floyd Lounsbury, "Astronomical Knowledge and Its Uses at Bonampak, Mexico," in *Archaeoastronomy in the New World*, edited by A. F. Aveni (Cambridge, Mass.: Cambridge University Press, 1982), p. 165.

12. Ian Graham, *Corpus of Maya Hieroglyphic Inscriptions* 2, no. 109 (Cambridge, Mass.: Peabody Museum of Archaeology and Ethnology, 1978), p. 109. The war event against Naranjo is recorded at N1; the ballgame verb appears at L3.

13. Including a Venus-sanctioned event that took place at the first appearance of the Evening Star (Floyd Lounsbury, "Astronomical Knowledge and Its Uses," pp. 154–155).

14. See Mary Ellen Miller, "The Meaning and Function of the Main Acropolis, Copan, Honduras" (paper delivered at the Dumbarton Oaks Conference on the Southeast Maya Zone, Washington, D.C., October 1984).

15. It is worth comparing this costume with the one worn by the victorious lord on Dos Pilas Stela 16 (Fig. V.4)—they are nearly identical. Our victorious warrior also wears the heavy *xicolli* of woven mat favored by Yaxchilan warriors (cf. Fig. V.3, Pl. 87).

16. Compare, for example, the bound captives depicted on the Hieroglyphic Stairs of either Tamarindito or Dos Pilas (Merle Greene Robertson, Robert L. Rands, and John A. Graham, *Maya Sculpture from the Southern Lowlands, the Highlands, and Pacific Piedmont* [Berkeley, Calif.: Lederer, Street, and Zeus, 1972], pl. 94).

17. The same ballgame glyph is recorded on the Naranjo panel, and the identical glyph occurs on other members of the Site Q series to which the Art Institute panel belongs (see n. 23, below).

18. As pointed out by many authors—among them, Marvin Cohodas ("The Symbolism and Ritual Function of the Middle Classic Ballgame in Mesoamerica," *American Indian Quarterly* 11, no. 2 [1975]), and Claude Baudez ("Le Roi, la balle, et le maïs: Images du jeu de balle Maya," *Journal de la Société des Américanistes* 62 [1984], pp. 139–152).

19. Stromsvik excavated the Copan ballcourt and reconstructed its phases. A third, seventh-century construction underlies the level under discussion here. It saw great use and was significantly eroded before being superseded by the 18-Rabbit phase (Gustav Stromsvik, *The Ball Courts at Copan, with Notes on the Courts at La Union, Quirigua, San Pedro Pinula, and Asuncion Mita*, Carnegie Institution of Washington, Pub. 596 [Washington, D.C.: Carnegie Institution of Washington, 1952]).

20. See Pl. 110.

21. His name is recorded by a rabbit glyph and a coefficient of 18, normally indicated by three bars and three dots, although a bar is omitted here.

22. *Na:ab* is generally understood to mean "water-lily" or "standing water," but no modern interpretation of the word makes sense—in terms of current research—in the context of the ballgame. It has been suggested that this is some sort of score, but a true score requires two numbers. Instead, it might possibly refer to the number of captives at stake in the game.

23. At least eighteen small panels of this series are known, and the site of their origin has been dubbed Site Q by Peter Mathews. Given its balanced composition, the Art Institute of Chicago panel (Pl. 101) was probably the centerpiece, even though it is the shortest of the group. Of the thirteen panels whose measurements are known, the variation in height is 19.5 cm, almost identical to that of the Yaxchilan ballplayer steps, and their average height is very close to that of the Yaxchilan steps as well (cf. Fig. VI.7). With a single exception, all these panels have been sawed so that they are now three to four centimeters thick—probably because they served as the risers to deep steps.

PLATE 95
Cylindrical vessel
Late Classic period, A.D. 600–800
Polychromed ceramic
Diam. 15.5 x H. 14.2 cm
Rijksmuseum voor Volkenkunde, Leiden, Holland

This Late Classic Maya pot is painted in codex style, so-named because the black line drawing on white ground is thought to resemble the draftsmanship of now-lost books. On it, two ballplayers are shown in front of a tiered structure, rather than in a ballcourt. Two secondary figures kneel behind the central ones, and from their yokes project their elaborate costumes in profile. The principal player to the left of the pyramid wears a hipcloth of cloth strips—often the garb of penitent or captive—that may indicate his imminent defeat. He strikes the ball with such energy that his entire body is lifted off the groundline, and his great hummingbird headdress arches over the pyramid and text in an amusing visual play. The attending figure at left wears a cap in petal shape characteristic of many secondary warriors, such as the captain at right on the Kimbell panel (Pl. 86). The large ball is inscribed with 14 na:ab, but this Maya word—generally thought to mean water-lily or still water—is not understood in this context. The rubber balls used by the Maya often appear inscribed with the numbers 9, 12, 13, or 14 na:ab. Their meaning is not known but the coefficient could refer to the number of human sacrifices at stake. Three Ik dates are inscribed on this pot—9 Ik, 11 Ik, and 6 Ik 5 Chen, a date that can be placed at 9.16.10.6.2, or July 17, A.D. 761—but the artist may have intended for the viewer to understand a supernatural date deep in the past or future. Calcified deposits obscure the seated figure on the rear of the pot, but unlike the other four, he is not dressed to play ball.

PLATE 96
Cylindrical vessel
Late Classic period, A.D. 600–800
Polychromed ceramic
Diam. 15.9 x H. 20.5 cm
Dallas Museum of Art
Gift of Mr. and Mrs. Raymond D. Nasher

This beautiful ceramic vessel depicts Maya ballplayers and architectural elements such as a flight of stairs and a temple riser. The painter of this vase was probably the master of other vessels that show interesting architecture, including a vessel at Dumbarton Oaks and the so-called hammock pot of the Regional Museum of Tabasco, which was reputedly found on Jaina Island. Thus, a source in Campeche is hypothesized for all the pots in this style, but many iconographic and stylistic elements also relate this artist's work to the Bonampak paintings in Chiapas.

The four players on this vessel wear black body paint and heavy padding for the competition. Only one knee, foot and wrist of each player was protected by padding. The natural, tapered shape of the long protective garments suggests that they are deer hides. The players' faces and hands are highlighted by a resist technique that prevents slip from adhering. Protecting the vital organs and providing a firm surface with which to strike the ball is a great yoke, perhaps made of wood or wicker, and tied at the side of the body under the arm. Additional padding and cloth protect the center of the body. The manner in which all of this is tied around the waist can be clearly seen on these figures. The text along the vessel rim records a Primary Standard Sequence, and the larger secondary text records a name and an Emblem Glyph. Stephen Houston has suggested the Emblem Glyph may be that of a ruler at Calakmul, in Campeche, where the vessel might have originated.

PLATE 97
Vessel with ballgame yoke
Early Classic period, A.D. 300–600
Carved and incised ceramic
H. 27.9 cm
Lent by The Metropolitan Museum of Art
Purchase, Mrs. Charles S. Payson, 1970

This unusual Early Classic ceramic tripod vessel is girded by a hollow, ceramic yoke, representing the ballgame yoke. The form of the vessel, the type of clay, the shape of lid and the method of carving are all characteristic of pots made by the Early Classic Maya in a style recalling vessels from Teotihuacan. Its glossy brown clay was carved before firing and later burnished to a high finish. In two similar scenes incised on opposite sides of the vessel, a pair of ballplayers are shown diving for the ball, which is wrapped and tied like a bundle. Similar images are repeated on the lid of the pot.

The yoke is carved, like many Gulf Coast stone yokes, with human faces at its two open ends. Just below the scenes of ballplayers, the yoke cinches the pot, creating a "waist," below which three feet supporting the pot emerge. These elements anthropomorphize the form, suggesting a cartoon-like walking vessel. Although there are many incised brownware vessels with imagery similar to this vessel, the yoked form of this pot is unique. Though it might have been a funerary vessel, the unusual shape suggests that this pot might have been made as a trophy and given to a victorious player and, like the amphorae granted to winners of ancient Greek Olympic contests, its contents, possibly an intoxicating beverage, would also have been prized.

Hundreds of stone ballgame yokes have been recovered from sites along the Gulf Coast. Stone yokes have been found at the Maya sites of Copan and Palenque, but the archaeological context—casual surface deposits—suggests that they were left by non-Maya individuals after the Classic Maya had abandoned these cities. Nevertheless, the stone yokes were known to the Maya in Classic times.

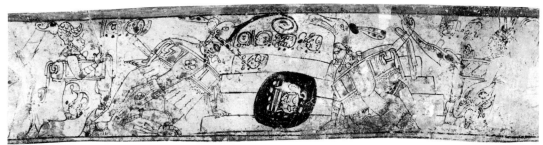

PLATE 95a

PLATE 98
Ballplayer figurine
Jaina Island, Campeche, Mexico
Late Classic period, A.D. 700–900
Molded ceramic with traces of pigment
H. 20.4 cm
Seattle Art Museum, Eugene Fuller Memorial Collection

Jaina figurines were often deposited in graves as funerary offerings, and this piece may represent a ballplayer defeated by the deceased. Although his body is clumsily formed, the face of this figurine reveals great dignity. With his left hand, he cradles the *hacha* inserted into his yoke; with his right, he makes a gesture that is sometimes thought to show subservience but that can also be used simply to indicate respect. A small circle on the surface of the *hacha* may indicate the glyph *ahau*, or "lord."

Care has been lavished on the costume and face of this figure, but his hands and feet were casually worked. A bird forms the headdress of this player, not unlike one worn by a player on the Dallas pot (Pl. 96). The cloth strips that hang from the bird, however, are marked with zig-zags and are of the type characteristically worn by captives or penitents.

This figurine is also a whistle.

PLATE 99
Seated ballplayer figurine
Late Classic period, A.D. 700–900
Ceramic with traces of pigment
14.3 x 12 cm
Munson-Williams-Proctor Institute, Utica, New York

Under their yokes, many ballplayers wore a draped garment that provided additional protection from the rough play and from the rough cement and stone surface of the court. On the Dallas ballgame pot (Pl. 96), this padding is shown as a reddish-brown material, probably deer hide. Padded for play, this seated Jaina figurine, like the player on the Copan marker (Pl. 102), wears a draped garment made from a full jaguar hide.

This ballplayer holds a small handstone, which, particularly in regions outside the Classic Maya domain, are frequently found with *hachas* and yokes. Just how such instruments were used in play remains obscure, but the Underworld deity on the central marker from Copan uses one to lift the ball, which may violate rules of fair play, or may be a legal way to set the ball in motion.

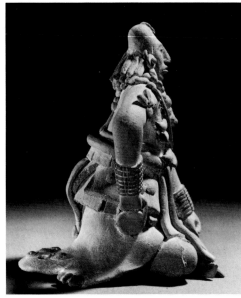

PLATE 99a

PLATE 100
Ballplayer as a penitent
Late Classic period, A.D. 700–900
Ceramic with traces of pigment
H. 23.7 cm
New Orleans Museum of Art
Women's Volunteer Committee Fund

Many elements of the ballgame costume—yoke, *hacha* and long, hide hipcloth—are peculiar to its players and rarely worn by other individuals. The non-standard elements of their costumes sometimes indicate the circumstances in which the ballgame is carried out. On the Chicago ballplayer panel (Pl. 101), for example, the game probably followed a battle since the players are dressed in costumes of war. In other depictions, the ballgame is indicated not by special costume but by a ball, whose presence indicates that the ballgame will ensue or already has occurred. This Jaina figurine grasps a small ball in his right hand, but he is not wearing the standard ballgame costume. He is not girded for rigorous play; instead, he wears the simple clothing of the penitent or captive. The beads of blood on his cheeks and chin show that he has undergone bloodletting rituals, and the cloth draped over the left arm characterizes both kings and captives who undergo bloodletting. The shorn hair and the bruised and swollen nose and forehead suggest that this figure is a royal captive, perhaps about to play the ballgame as the ball itself.

PLATE 101
Panel with a ballgame scene
Late Classic period, A.D. 700–800
Limestone
26.7 x 43.2 x 7.6 cm
Courtesy of The Art Institute of Chicago,
The Ada Turnbull Hertle Fund

This carved ballplayer panel may have been the central scene of the staircase to which the Heye panel (Pl. 104) also once belonged. The limestone is beautifully carved and has been sensuously worked giving a fluid, buttery surface to the hard material. On the panel, two players in lively competition are portrayed. The caption at left, in the subfix surviving at H2, names one of the players a *mah k'ina*, a title reserved exclusively for the ruler of a city-state. In this panel, then, at least one of the players is a Maya king. In a visual play most characteristic of the Usumacinta and Pasion regions, the text on the riser behind the player at left is truncated and blocked by the lord. It may once have included his full name and title, but all that remains clearly legible is the word *batab*, a title generally borne by kings. But the costume and posture of the two players, pitted as adversaries with the ball between them, also indicates who will win and who will lose this particular contest.

Both players on the panel are dressed in attire typical of Maya warriors. The left side of the panel has suffered more damage, leading the eye to perceive that figure as less prominent, but his costume is that of successful warriors. He wears the Tlaloc-jaguar costume of Petexbatun and Yaxchilan kings in warrior guise, and he may have had a jaguar balloon headdress, now lost. He wears the skull pectoral; Tlaloc faces are formed into a knee pad; and a *hacha* is worn at the waist. Unlike his opponent and most other ballplayers, he wears knee and forearm padding on both right and left sides; jaguar talons may be embedded in the padding he wears on the right forearm.

The costume of the reclining figure to the right has elements of those defeated in battle. He wears a feathered headdress composed of individual birds that, in Maya art at the end of the Late Classic, connotes the defeated, particularly when bird and jaguar are juxtaposed, as at Cacaxtla. Such costuming appears to have its roots in Classic Maya scenes of warfare, sacrifice and ballgame, but the symbolism persisted until the Spanish Conquest, when it was widely understood that the deity Tezcatlipoca, sometimes seen as a jaguar, was able

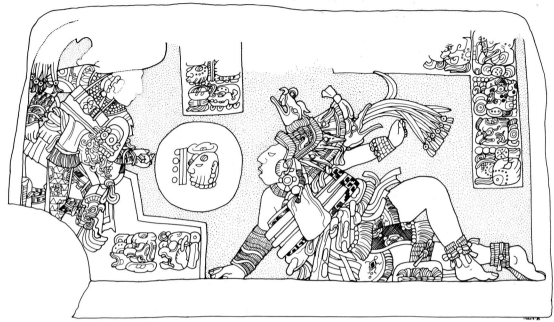

PLATE 101a

to best Quetzalcoatl, a feathered serpent, in repeated cosmic clashes. Three birds are set like spikes from the central crown of the fallen ballplayer, and feathers at the back fall from the open mouth of a fourth bird. Just over the brim of the headdress is set a shark or bird head, and it wears an early form of the Jester God, a standard mark of kings.

Along with the bird headdress, one other costume element indicates that the player at right is defeated. The cloth ties that hang from his yoke have holes, as if the cloth were punched, with the cutout pieces left suspended by a few threads. Flapped cutouts of this sort are unusual, particularly among the Maya who keep hand-loomed cloth whole and generally drape, rather than tailor, garments. Only captives and those carrying out penitential rites wear cloth with such cutouts. At Tonina (Fig. V.6), for example, ear ornaments and hip garments of strips with punched holes are worn by captives. Such strips on the yoke of the Chicago ballplayer indicate that he is a captive, destined to shed sacrificial blood. Both ballplayers are shown frozen in a single moment, engaged in the one-on-one public contest following the battle for which they are still dressed. The costumes and symbolism allow us to project the moment depicted to its conclusion.

PLATE 102
Center Marker
Ballcourt II-B, Copan, Honduras
Late Classic period, A.D. 731–751
Stone
Diam. 74 x 9.5 cm
Instituto Hondureño de Antropología e Historia, Tegucigalpa, Honduras

The Copan ballcourt, originally constructed between A.D. 500 and 600, was subsequently rebuilt twice: once during the reign of 18 Rabbit (early to mid-eighth century); and again, during the reign of the last king, Yax-Pac, at the end of the eighth century. When the court was excavated by the Carnegie Institution during the 1930s, Gustav Stromsvik found markers from the previous construction, including the piece illustrated here and those in Figs. VI.10 and VI.11, left in place under the later eighth-century stones. The absence of wear on these markers suggests that they were used for only a few years before they were covered by the subsequent court.

The location of the Great Ballcourt at the center of the ceremonial core of the site indicates that the ballgame was central to the kings of Copan. The scenes on these three markers reveal the drama of an Underworld confrontation in which 18 Rabbit plays a role. The quadrifoil outline

of each marker—an ancient shape used by the Olmec to specify the portal to the Underworld—may have the same meaning here. In the upper register of each marker are two figures flanking a very large ball. Below, cut off by double bands, is the image of the sun or *kin* sign, depicted within a closed cache vessel in a cutaway view, probably indicating that the scenes take place in the Underworld.

The Center Marker is the only one with a glyphic inscription that names three individuals: Hun-Ahau (the Classic equivalent of the Hero Twin Hunahpu), a death god, and 18 Rabbit, here written as 13 Rabbit who, at about this time, was defeated by the king of Quirigua. Only two individuals are depicted. Hun-Ahau is on the left, named in a glyph directly in front of him. His opponent, the Death God of Zero, is also known in a full-figure sculpture from Copan (Pl. 110). The appearance of 18 Rabbit's name could simply indicate that the game proceeds under his auspices, or, that this program was executed during his reign. However, given historical circumstances, it could also function as a caption. If 18 Rabbit is a caption, it may refer to the ball, which is understood to be the role played by the defeated king himself.

Hun-Ahau, at left, may not defeat the Underworld God of Zero, right, but he will outwit him. As a defeated king, 18 Rabbit could only hope to outsmart the Underworld lords, not overpower them and, like the clever rabbit, he may have planned to bound away from them at his first opportunity.

On the Center Marker both players kneel and prepare to strike the ball. The God of Zero wears a *hacha* and a yoke around his waist; he lifts the ball with a handstone attached to his right hand. Hun-Ahau tries to lift the ball in a similar fashion, but without a handstone. Since touching the ball with the hand was a foul in most forms of the Mesoamerican ballgame, it is possible that here the players are just setting the ball in play.

PLATE 102a   Drawing by Barbara Fash

PLATE 103
Small bottle
Late Classic period, A.D. 600–800
Molded ceramic
14.2 x 7.4 x 4.7 cm
Rijksmuseum voor Volkenkunde, Leiden, Holland

Small bottles with stamped designs have been recovered in the Highlands of Guatemala and at Copan. Paired deities are sometimes shown and multiple images are known, suggesting that the vessels were mass-produced.

On this bottle a ballplayer prepares to strike a large rodent, probably a rabbit. Although the image is at first a conundrum, it is a direct illustration of a scene from the ballgame contest in the Popol Vuh. In the final ballgame between the Hero Twins and Underworld deities, Hunahpu's head was severed and hung by the Underworld lords in the ballcourt as a trophy. Before the head was restored to Hunahpu's body, Xbalanque substituted a pumpkin for his brother's head, and then devised a plan with a rabbit to regain the real head. The scene illustrated on the bottle is the moment when Xbalanque prepares to strike the ball, which is really a curled-up rabbit who bounds out of the court. This ruse gave Xbalanque time to seize his brother's head and restore it to the body.

PLATE 104
Panel with a ballgame scene
Late Classic period, A.D. 600–800
Limestone
27.6 x 38.1 x 2 cm
Courtesy of the Museum of the American Indian, Heye Foundation, New York

This panel shows a ballplayer wearing the headdress of the Jaguar God of the Underworld preparing to receive a hurtling ball. It is from a group of at least eighteen extant panels from a yet-unidentified Maya site (called Site Q) that once formed either the riser of a staircase or a sloping *talus* of a ballcourt wall. The panels are now dispersed in collections around the world and many have not been published.

Some of these panels record only glyphic texts; others show ballplayers who actively engage in play. However, most of the panels have neither a continuous text nor enough continuous imagery to allow their reconstruction in sequence (Pl. 104a).

On the Heye Foundation panel only part of the ball is visible, on the lower right edge. Apparently the ball was depicted suspended between two panels to suggest movement and emphasize tension in the play. A second panel of this group, now in a private collection, which also has a

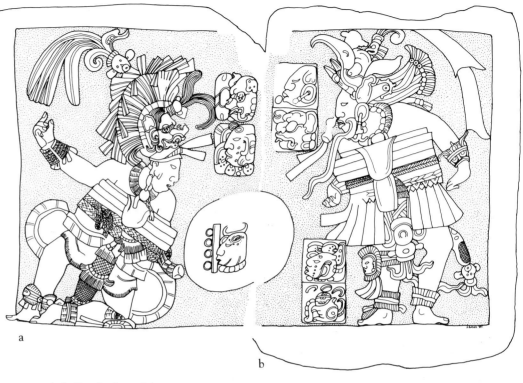

a

b

portion of a ball in the lower left corner, permits us to reconstruct tentatively the original order of these two panels (Fig. VI.12). Although the two panels no longer make a perfect fit, carved stone steps in situ today rarely fit better, but the juxtaposition suggests that the composition in this group of panels moved by launching the ball from one panel to another. The second glyph on the Heye panel is a ballgame verb; on the privately owned panel in Fig. VI.12, a ballgame verb is also visible directly in front of the player's knee.

On the Heye panel, the lord dressed as a Jaguar God is Xbalanque; his opponent on the privately owned panel is one of the Underworld lords, God L, identified by his jaguar pelt shirt and Muan Bird headdress. The dress of the two figures on this panel indicates that the two lords depicted re-enact the myth of the Hero Twins in the Underworld. The Heye panel is one of two from the group of eighteen panels that show ballplayers dressed as the Hero Twins. A third panel, also in a private collection, shows a lord wearing the headdress of Chac-Xib-Chac, who is the second twin, Hunahpu. Thus, these panels emphasize the importance of the Hero Twins in Classic period ballgame mythology.

FIGURE VI.12
Reconstruction of two ballgame panels
a. Panel from the Museum of the American Indian, Heye Foundation, Plate 104
b. Panel from a private collection

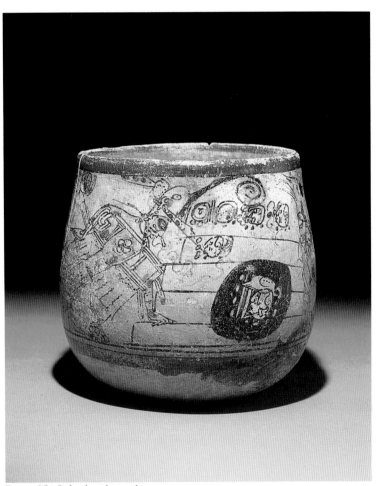

PLATE 95. Cylindrical vessel

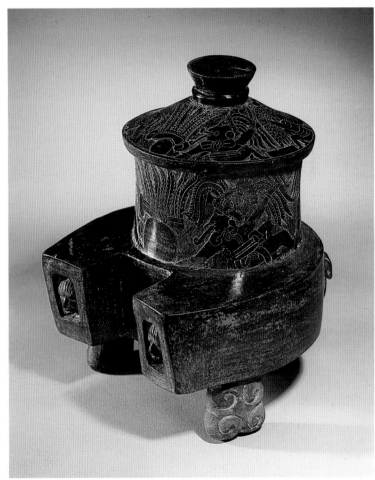

PLATE 97. Vessel with ballgame yoke

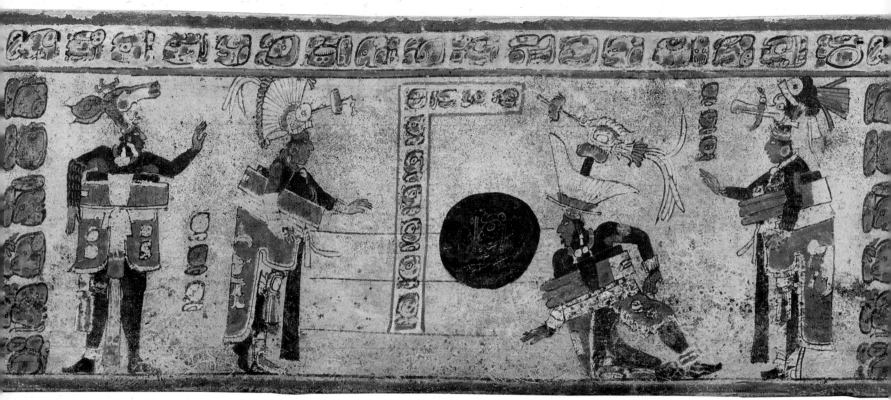

Plate 96a. Rollout

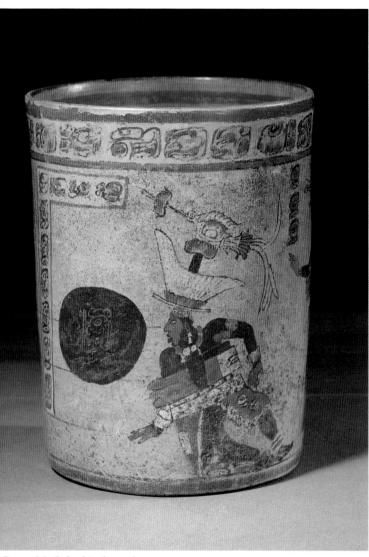

PLATE 96. Cylindrical vessel

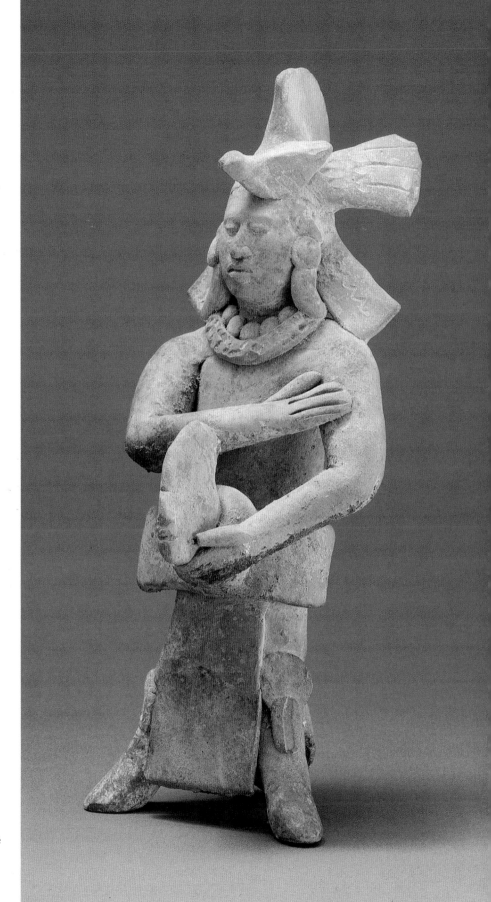

PLATE 98. Ballplayer figurine

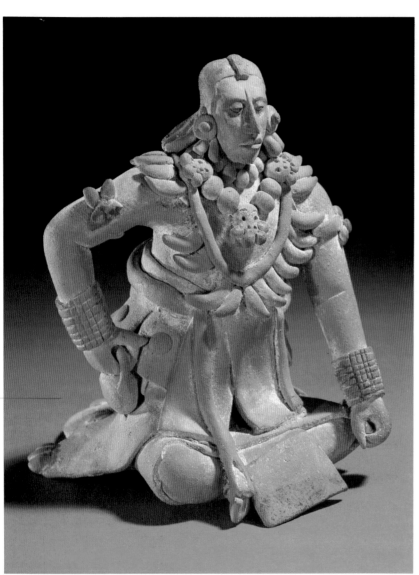

PLATE 99. Seated ballplayer figurine

Ballplayer as a penitent

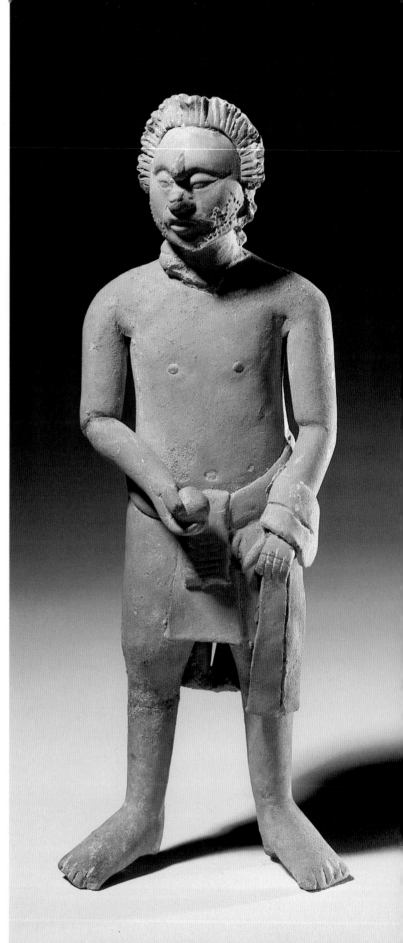

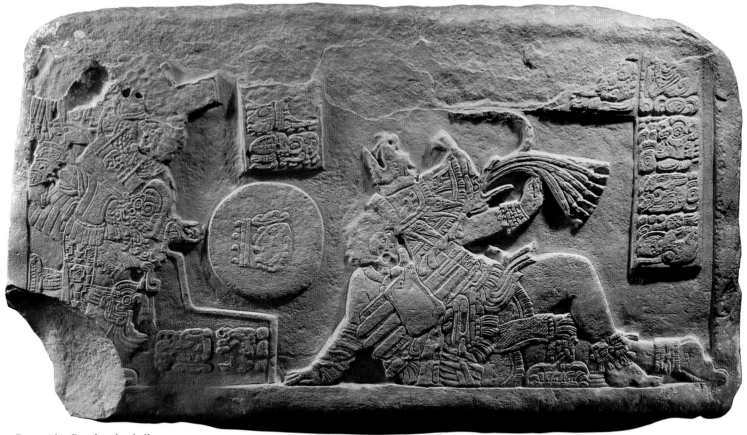

PLATE 101. Panel with a ballgame scene

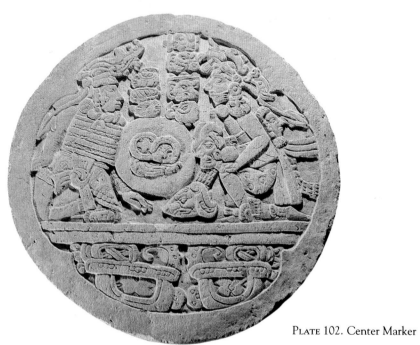

PLATE 102. Center Marker

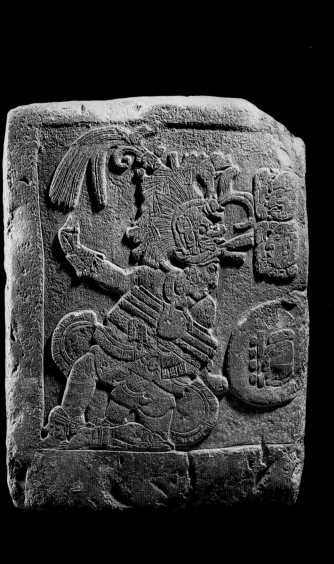

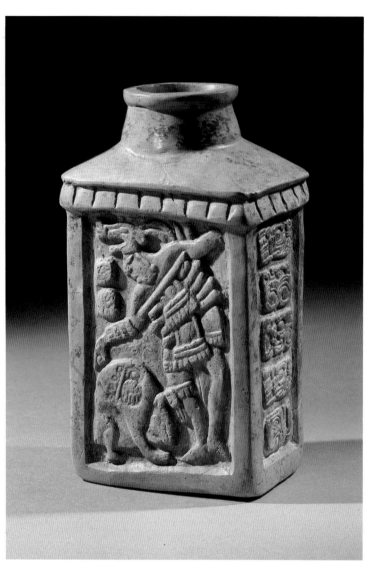

PLATE 103. Small bottle

PLATE 104. Panel with a ballgame scene

VII

DEATH AND THE JOURNEY THROUGH XIBALBA

For the Maya the anticipation of death must have been sharp. Life expectancy was shorter than it is today, infant mortality was higher, and everyone, elite as well as commoner, lived with warfare and sacrificial ritual as ever-present realities. The immediacy of death led the Maya to dedicate much of their ritual and art to the defeat of death's final grip on their lives. Depictions on objects of all types treat the whole process of death, from the soul's entrance into the Maya Hell, called Xibalba, to a final apotheosis or rebirth. We will see that much of mythology and funerary art describes death as a journey whose challenges were known. Death's special imagery is found on coffins, wall paintings, pottery, jades and other objects that accompanied the dead into their graves and guided them through their confrontation with the Lords of Death.

The journey after life was fraught with danger, both for the departed soul and for the disrupted society left behind. Funerary rituals and death mythology functioned as much to seal the rupture in the social fabric caused by the death of one of its members as they did to comfort the bereaved.[1] If a king died, the danger to society was a thousandfold greater than when a commoner or noble died. Since the king was the stabilizing instrument of both the natural and the supernatural worlds, his people were in terrible danger until another king filled the void. Furthermore, the ancient Maya (and their modern descendants) believed that the dead were not entirely gone and that they continued to influence the lives of their descendants, both for good and for ill. Children and grandchildren were called *kexol*, "replacements" of their ancestors, and kings were the *kexol* of the gods. The bloodletting rituals were designed, at least in part, for contacting the ancestral dead. Much of the pottery found in Maya tombs was made especially to accompany the soul on its journey. Funerary art represents many points in this journey. The scenes on some pots relate directly to Popol Vuh stories of the Hero Twins, while others refer to myths and legends now lost. In addition to these narrative scenes of Underworld activities, artists paraded the inhabitants of Xibalba in processions.

Michael Coe's recognition of the correspondence between scenes on funerary pottery from the Classic period and stories in the Popol Vuh has allowed penetration of the world of the dead.[2] The legends that describe the birth and adventures of the Hero Twins, Hunahpu and Xbalanque, are not post-Conquest inventions. They are instead the remnants of a Classic-period mythic cycle explaining the progress of life and the journey after death through Xibalba, a journey that each human being faced. The Hero Twins, greatly skilled as ballplayers, disturbed the Lords of Death with their play and so are summoned to Xibalba to take part in a series of trials. Unlike their father and uncle, who preceded them unsuccessfully to Xibalba a generation before, the clever Hero Twins detect each trick of the Xibalbans and thus are able to survive their trials.

The Hero Twins' adventures reveal the Maya concept of the progress of the soul after life and provide instructions for defeating death and achieving rebirth. One night after ballgame play, the Twins are placed in the Dark House and given a burning torch and one cigar apiece. Told that they must return the torch and cigar unconsumed in the morning, the Twins substitute the brightly colored tails of a macaw for the torch and place fireflies on the ends of their cigars to preserve the originals. They survive each test through cunning, leaving the Xibalbans in exasperated frustration. Despite their successes, the Twins foresee their own deaths and prepare for them by planning the disposition of their bodies to ensure revival. They arrange for local shamans to tell the Lords of Death how to kill them. Following those instructions, the Lords burn the Hero Twins in an oven and grind their bones into powder, which they throw into the river of Hell, in what they are confident is permanent and irrevocable death. Five days later, however, the Twins, now appearing with the facial features of channel catfish, emerge from the river alive and prepare to defeat the Lords of Death.

As wandering entertainers dressed in rags, they dance and perform sophisticated tricks. Their reputation spreads as they perform such miracles as setting fire to houses that are not consumed and sacrificing people and animals who do not die. Hearing of this magnificent entertainment, the Lords of Xibalba invite the Twins to court. The Lords first require the Twins to sacrifice a dog, then to burn a house. The dog revives, and the house is not consumed. Even so, the amazed Lords are still suspicious. "You have yet to kill a person!" they say; "make a sacrifice without death!" Seizing a bystander from the crowd, the Twins rip out his heart, yet he does not die. The Lords, beside themselves, push the Twins further, urging, "Sacrifice yet again; do it to yourselves." Obligingly, one of the Twins sacrifices and dismembers the other, then tells his dead brother to get up. As the brother rises and dances, the overwhelmed Lords beg to undergo themselves this miraculous sacrifice without death. Of course the Hero Twins oblige them; this time, however, they do not bring the Lords of Death back to life. After their victory, the Twins admonish the Xibalbans to cease their trickery against mankind, lest they suffer the fate of their lords. At last, Hunahpu and Xbalanque emerge from Xibalba and rise into the heavens, where the sun belongs to one twin and the moon to the other.[3]

Scenes from these myths were painted on funerary pottery that accompanied the dead to the grave. The Twins' adventures described the trials of the journey after life that each human soul must face in order to defeat death and finally exit Xibalba in the dance of rebirth. Again and again, dead souls, especially the soul of the king, had to confront the Xibalbans as the Twins did and emerge triumphant from treacherous trials in the Underworld. The ballgame was one way for the living to play out the myth of the Twins. More important, the king and other nobles (and perhaps all human beings) metaphorically assumed the identity of one of the Twins at death. Pots with scenes of the Twin myths gave the soul instruction on what to expect during the trials of the Afterlife and how a soul could triumph.

The word Xibalba is derived from *xib*, "fear, terror, trembling with fright." Representations of Xibalba in Classic-period art were consistent with its description in the Popol Vuh. Its primary characteristic was the stench of decaying corpses and rotting blood; it was the origin of diseases that entered the Middleworld, the world of man. Like the Middleworld, Xibalba had landscape and architecture, including temples and houses ruled by the Lords of Death. Since Emblem Glyphs of the great Maya cities appear in the names of Underworld creatures, we can assume either that those cities were thought to have correlates in Xibalba or that particular Xibalbans were regarded as residents or patrons of Maya cities. Jaguar creatures, for example, often occur with the Emblem Glyph of Tikal.

The Xibalba of the Classic period was different in one way from the Popol Vuh version of Hell. It was a watery world that could only be entered by sinking beneath water or by passing through a maw in the surface of the earth.[4] During the Early Classic period, funerary vessels often represented the watery surface of that Underworld. One of the newly discovered tombs at Rio Azul is painted with a band of water around the base of the vaulted chamber. The Water Bird, a cormorant-like fowl carrying a fish in its beak, came to symbolize the watery surface of the Underworld. One particularly interesting example of Water Bird imagery is a footed vessel in the collection of the New Orleans Museum (Pl. 105). The neck and head of the Water Bird emerge from the domed lid of the vessel in a three-dimensional realization of the cormorant rising to the water's surface after its hunting dive. On another pot from the Rio Hondo area of Mexico (Pl. 106), a human clinging to a water band is flanked by Vision Serpents that allow his living descendants to communicate with him after death.[5] Water was also signified by other symbols. On a basal-flanged bowl from the Denver Art Museum (Pl. 107), the handle of the domed lid is surrounded by a dot pattern that means water. The background is painted a brilliant red, as on the New Orleans pot discussed above; although this may simply have been a stylistic convention prominent in the Early Classic period, it may allude to Xibalban waters red with the blood of sacrifice. On a carved bowl executed in a different Early Classic style (Pl. 108), the lid handle is modeled to represent a water-lily. The water-lily and the Water Bird are the primary symbols of bodies of still water in the Maya landscape—the canals associated with raised-field agriculture, swamps and the primordial sea in which the land floats. Below the surface of these waters was Xibalba, the residence of the dead before their rebirth.

The inhabitants of Xibalba are numerous and varied: They include anthropomorphs, zoomorphs, animals and skeletal creatures of the most distasteful countenance. Many of the leading Xibalbans are shown with very old, toothless human visages, and some are transformational, combining male and female features. Xibalbans are named for the various causes of death, such as disease, old age, sacrifice and war, and are often depicted with black marks, representing decaying flesh, as well as bony bodies and distended bellies. Their jewelry consists of disembodied eyes that come complete with the hanging stalk of the optic nerve. Xibalbans are pictured emitting farts so pungent that they emerge in huge scrolls, and their breath is so foul it is visible (Pl. 109). *Cizin*, one word for "devil" still used today by Yucatec speakers, literally means "one who farts." Xibalbans can also personify different kinds of sacrifice. One particularly gruesome kind involved the removal of the jaw of a living victim; it is symbolized by the Death God of the Number Zero, who is shown with a hand gripping his lower jaw in preparation for this dismemberment (Pl. 110). The patron god of the month Pax is depicted with huge blood scrolls spurting from his mouth after his jaw has been removed.

The greatest funerary monument known from the Classic period, the stone lid of Pacal's sarcophagus in the Temple of Inscriptions at Palenque, is carved with a scene showing the moment of death as a fall into the Maw of the Underworld (Pl. 111). The sarcophagus, begun while Pacal was still alive, was never designed as public art. Instead, it was conceived of as a power object to instruct Pacal's soul during the journey through the Underworld and to represent his final destination among his ancestors. The huge stone lid, measuring over twelve by seven feet, rested on a limestone sarcophagus with a carved depression for the coffin. The ten portraits that surround the sarcophagus depict seven of Pacal's ancestors (his mother, father and great-grandmother are each repeated). The ancestors are shown rising, along with a fruit tree, from a cleft in the earth (Pl. 111e). They represent Pacal's ancestors of direct descent through six previous generations and culminate in the seventh—Pacal himself, whose body lies in the center of the sarcophagus. The edge of the lid was inscribed with the dates of Pacal's birth and death and with the death dates of each of these ancestors, as well as those of some of their siblings, who had also ruled Palenque.

On the top of the lid, Pacal himself is shown teetering at the beginning of his fall into the Maw of the Underworld, which is represented by two great dragon skulls set with their lower jaws joined below him (Pl. 111c and d). He poises, half sitting and half reclining, atop the head of the Quadripartite Monster, the symbol of the sun. In death, Pacal falls into Xibalba, along with the setting sun. Pacal and the Sun Monster have fallen down the *axis mundi*, the World Tree at the center of the world, represented by cross symbols rising above Pacal in the center of the sarcophagus lid. The branches of the tree terminate in bloodletting bowls and streams of blood, represented by square-nosed dragons with jade beads in their mouths. The trunk is marked by God C, another symbol of blood; in this instance God C also refers to the sap of the tree. Sacrificial blood, then, is likened to the sap of the tree[6] and is the medium through which the souls of the dead move from level to level in the Maya universe. The Double-headed Serpent Bar, which represents both the authority of the king and the larger human community, is wrapped around the branches of the tree. The serpent mouths belch out the two symbols of royal power, God K on the right and the Jester God on the left. The Celestial Bird, the symbol of the heavenly realm, sits on the upper branch, witnessing the event for the gods.

This image of death has cosmic implications. Pacal falling down the *axis mundi* is metaphorically equivalent to the sun at the instant of sunset. Like the sun, which rises after a period of darkness, he will rise after his triumph over the Lords of Death. Pacal carried this symbolic interpretation of his death over into the placement of the Temple of Inscriptions within the sacred precinct at Palenque. The temple was built just off the southwest corner of the Palace, a complex that formed the administrative heart of the city, where kings were seated in office and bloodletting rituals gave birth to the gods. The king sited the Temple of Inscriptions along the line connecting the center of the palace with one of the most important alignments of the sun in the tropical year. At the winter solstice, the sun reaches its southernmost point, setting exactly on the line that runs through the tomb. Thus, the sun falls into darkness, into the Maw of the Underworld, through Pacal's tomb, confirming the symbolic imagery of his death. As with the Preclassic temple at Cerros (Fig. II.1), the Maya manipulated architecture so that the movements of the universe confirmed the assertions of mythology. Just as the sun begins its move northward following the winter solstice, the dead, after the defeat of death, will rise from Xibalba to take up residence in the northern sky, around the fixed point of the North Star. Pacal, confident of defeating death, has made north his destination: His head was placed in the north end of the coffin, and the World Tree on the lid points north, although Pacal himself is depicted in his southward fall. Just as the sun returns from the Underworld at dawn, and as it begins its northward journey after the solstice, Pacal has prefigured his return from the southbound journey to Xibalba.

This symbolic representation of death as a fall into Xibalba was not limited to Palenque or to the Late Classic period. The same idea appears in a different form on a carved bone of Early Classic style now in The American Museum of Natural History (Pl. 112). The scalloped trunk of the World Tree on this bone is similar to the tree on the Hauberg Stela (Pl. 66). The second-century stela has sacrificial victims tumbling down its trunk on their way to Xibalba; on this bone, however, the tree rises from the ground to culminate in the head of the Vision Serpent—the means of communication along the path of the tree between the realms of the living and the dead. Most critically, the imagery on the bone reveals yet another element in the Maya concept of cosmic order: Next to the tree is a pyramid, personified by a zoomorphic head. Both the World Tree and the Vision Serpent enter the Middleworld through Maya temples. The buildings themselves are the portals between these levels of the cosmos. The knot with a Kan-cross at its base refers both to the bloodletting that generates the Vision Serpent and to the Kan-cross/Water-lily Monster on the base of the World Tree on the Tablet of the Foliated Cross at Palenque (Fig. IV.4). This combination of images confirms that the symbolism of death on Pacal's sarcophagus was both ancient and widespread. In the conceptual universe of the Maya, the trunk of the World Tree enters the Underworld through the Maya temple. Pyramidal temples, which housed the tombs of dead ancestors and recorded ancestral history in their inscriptions, were the sites of bloodletting. Since they were the gates between separate levels of the cosmos, every Maya temple had its own tree, brought forth by ritual. Thus, the Maya cosmic landscape was a forest of World Trees rising to the heavens from the hundreds of temples that dotted the earthly landscape.

A second metaphor of death was derived from the watery nature of the Underworld and from the major vehicle of water transportation, the canoe. By and large, the

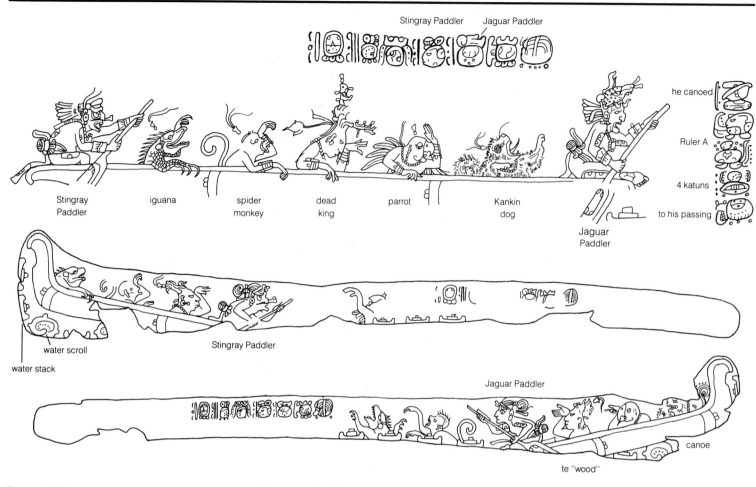

Stingray Paddler   Jaguar Paddler

he canoed

Ruler A

4 katuns

to his passing

Stingray
Paddler

iguana   spider
monkey   dead
king   parrot   Kankin
dog   Jaguar
Paddler

water scroll

water stack

Stingray Paddler

Jaguar Paddler

canoe

te "wood"

FIGURE VII.1
Incised bones
Burial 116, Tikal, Guatemala
Late Classic period, A.D. 735

Temple I at Tikal, a great mausoleum built after the death of Ruler A, celebrates the greatest events in his life and protects his tomb. The plaza-level chamber containing his body was sealed in by the massive fill of the pyramid. Ruler A was laid to rest with a treasure trove of jade, pottery and other objects, including eighty-nine carved bones. Four of the bones describe death through the metaphor of a canoe voyage. The scenes carved on the bones are among the most refined and elegant in Maya art. Their imagery suggests that the Maya at Tikal equated death with the sinking of a canoe into the watery Underworld.

Two of the bones depict a canoe guided by the Paddler Twins—the Old Jaguar God in front, the Aged Stingray Spine God behind. The canoes carry five passengers: the dog appearing as the day sign Kankin, a parrot, a human, a spider monkey and an iguana. The human wears a personified *ahau* atop his head and a Jester God tied around his head by a band that terminates in a leaf. He holds wrist to forehead in a gesture believed to signal impending death. He is thus the deceased Ruler A.

The second pair of bones show the canoe plunging under the surface of the water. On one, the Old Jaguar God holds the paddle; the human, the parrot and the dog are still in the canoe, while the iguana and monkey struggle in the water. On the other bone, the Stingray God is in the canoe with the iguana, the monkey and the man, while the parrot flounders in the water. (The dog was presumably also in the water, but he is now either eroded or has already sunk beneath the waves.) This sinking of the canoe metaphorically signifies death.

These bones carry two texts. The first is written in a horizontal band above the canoes on all four bones. It includes a date (11 Akbal 16 Zac, most likely September 16, A.D. 775), a verb ("Venus-over-earth") and the names of the two Paddlers. This text apparently records the supernatural aspect of the event. The second text, inscribed only on the bone depicting the level journey, is written in a vertical column immediately in front of the moving canoe. It has no date, but the verb is "he canoed," and the actor is Ruler A. The entire text reads, "Ruler A canoed 4 katuns to his passing," meaning that the king paddled through life for four katuns until he passed on in the sinking canoe.

Maya were a riverine people who transported goods and people in dugout canoes. On four carved bones from Ruler A's tomb at Tikal, life and death are symbolized as a canoe trip with the gods (Fig. VII.1). Two of the bones show the Paddler Twins, the gods given birth by the scattering rite, skimming across a surface filled with shell scroll and water stack motifs. Their passengers are a human, an iguana, a spider monkey, a parrot and a Kankin dog.[7] A Jester God tied by a vegetal headband on the forehead and a personified *ahau* on top of his head identify the man as a king. He holds his wrist against his forehead as a sign of impending death, which will come with the sinking of the canoe. The trip, a swift passage across the waters of this world under the guidance of the gods (here represented by the Paddlers), is a metaphor for life. When the canoe of life sinks, the passengers drop beneath the surface of the water to enter Xibalba. In the recently discovered Rio Azul tomb discussed above, the canoe is not depicted, but the lower walls are marked as water and the corpse was laid within this boundary. Although the canoe is absent, the king was nonetheless symbolically buried underwater.

The passengers conveyed by the Paddlers in the canoe of life were not limited to the dead king and his animal companions. A shell belonging to the Heye Foundation depicts the Old Stingray Paddler canoeing with a rabbit, the symbol of the moon (Pl. 113). Not only do the Paddlers convey the souls of humans through the journeys of life and death; they also carry the gods who represent the moon and the planets in their journeys across the heavens. Perhaps the most astonishing image of death in Maya art combines the canoe with the Palenque metaphor of the fall into Xibalba. Chipped and worked as a silhouette, this powerful eccentric flint personifies the canoe as the Celestial Monster arched in a downward plunge (Pl. 114). Pacal falls into the watery world of Xibalba atop the Quadripartite Monster, the usual rear head of the Celestial Monster. The scalloped bottom contour of the flint images wave-tossed water. The dead soul and its two companions, presumably Paddlers, lean back in response to the tremendous thrust of the dive. The energy concentrated through this powerful metaphor for death makes this eccentric flint one of the most extraordinary Maya objects now known.

Other funerary art shows activities in Xibalba following the fall of the soul into death. The codex-style painting on a large pot from the collection of the University Art Museum, Princeton, is one of the most beautiful Maya depictions of the Afterlife (Pl. 115). A familiar episode from the Popol Vuh takes place in a house in Xibalba, marked on the roofcomb with images of a Bleeding Jaguar and a Bleeding Xoc Monster. The house's owner, God L, sitting on a bench inside, is attended by five lovely bald-headed ladies, the Goddesses of the Number 2. The second scene's protagonists are the Hero Twins, disguised as dancers, who have returned from death to defeat the Lords of the Underworld. They are sacrificing a bound captive, the unwilling bystander of the court of Xibalba, whom they will bring back to life.[8] The Jaguar Twin wears a mask, while his brother, depicted with long, drooping lips, wears the headgear of the Headband Twins.

On a carved pot from the Kimbell Art Museum (Pl. 116), the Hero Twins prepare for the next stage in the myth, their own sacrifice. Chac-Xib-Chac and the Baby Jaguar, now in his guise of the Water-lily Jaguar, lean toward each other in deep conversation, undoubtedly discussing how to continue fooling the Lords of Death. Placed to one side, the head of a Cauac Monster serves as the sacrificial altar. Another vase, the codex-style pot in the Metropolitan Museum (Pl. 117), shows the Jaguar

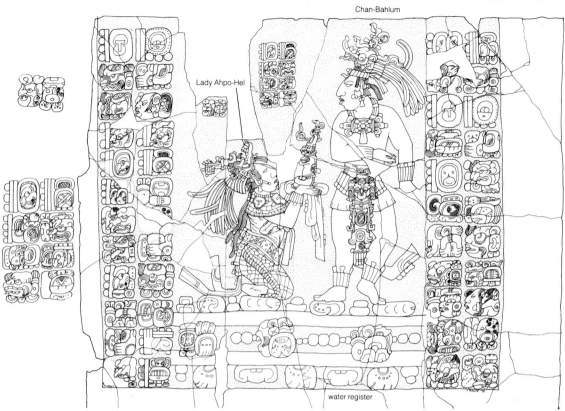

Chan-Bahlum

Lady Ahpo-Hel

water register

FIGURE VII.2
Limestone tablet
Temple 14, Palenque, Chiapas, Mexico
Late Classic period, A.D. 705

The tablet celebrates King Chan-Bahlum's triumphal dance out of Xibalba after his defeat of the Lords of Death. Found in the rear chamber of Temple 14, the tablet has a scene flanked on either side by two columns of glyphs. Two figures stand on a lower register marked by the shell and stacked rectangles that signify the surface of water. The center band has a row of water dots interspersed between three glyphs: the first includes *nicte* (the glyph for a sacred plant) and the Imix compound (which marked a supernatural location on the Huehuetenango bloodletting bowl [Pl. 72]); the second is a form of water-lily and the third is undeciphered. The lower band alternates syllabic signs spelling *ba, na, ba, na, ba. Naab* is the word for water-lily, as well as for large bodies of water, including the ocean. Thus, the lower register is the water of the Underworld.

With one heel raised, Chan-Bahlum dances in triumph, throwing his loincloth to one

side by his motion. He wears the skeletal Jaguar God of the Underworld on his belt and a *kin* "sun" sign and a personified tree in his headdress. His mother, Lady Ahpo-Hel, is rising from a seated position to greet him as he dances toward her. She wears a net overskirt, a belt and a richly decorated cape over her *huipil*. Her headdress is the Quadripartite Monster, although on it the square-nosed dragon replaces the usual stingray spine. She lifts God K toward her son, making sure to align its head toward her so that when Chan-Bahlum takes it, its staff will be in the proper position for ritual display. The tablet shows us the dead king after he has defeated the Lords of Xibalba. He is dancing out from the watery Underworld to be greeted by his mother, who welcomes him to the ranks of the triumphant ancestors.

THE INSCRIPTION
The inscription (Fig. VII.2a) equates the apotheosis of Chan-Bahlum with mythological events that occurred during a previous creation. The text begins on 9 Ik 10 Mol, more than 932,174 years before the event pictured, when God K was first dis-

played by the Moon Goddess. The ritual involved is not fully understood, but we do know that the kings received the God K scepter at their accessions, that heirs-designate were presented to their people in the guise of God K and that in death, kings fell into the Underworld dressed as God K. This text suggests that the gods and goddesses also carried out the same ritual. By replicating the Moon Goddess's display of the scepter, which occurred in mythological time, Chan-Bahlum's mother is likened to the Moon Goddess. A huge Distance Number, which recalls the event in mythological time, leads to a date, 9 Ahau 3 Kankin, exactly three years of 365 days apiece and one cycle of 260 days after the death of Chan-Bahlum. Therefore, his trials in Xibalba presumably required this period to complete. GI, GIII as the Jaguar God of the Underworld, the father of the Palenque Triad, and the Goddess of the Number 2 (who also appears on the Princeton Pot [Pl. 115]) are named as actors here. Their surrogate, or historical manifestation, is named as Chan-Bahlum. He had defeated the Lords of Death and danced out of Hell emulating the Hero Twins.

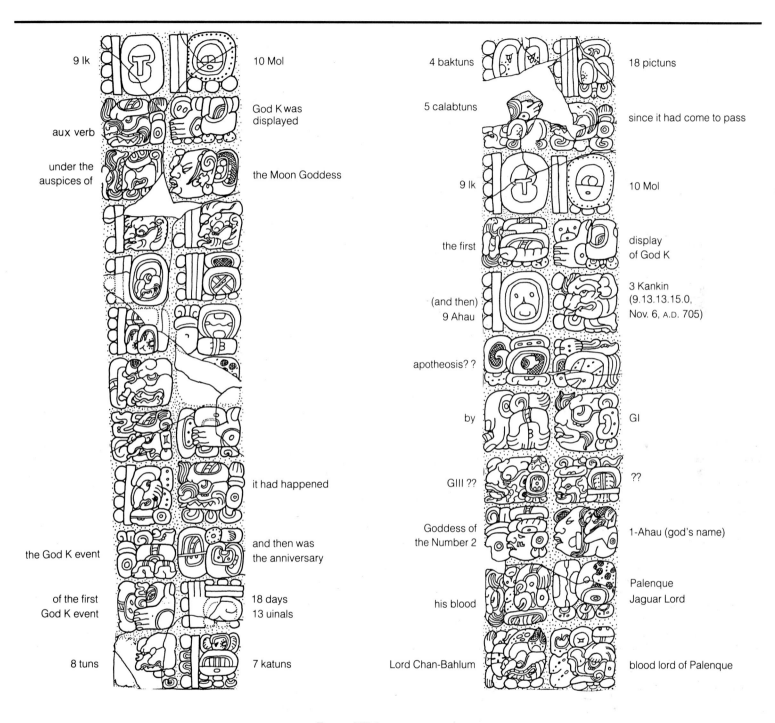

9 Ik

10 Mol

aux verb

God K was
displayed

under the
auspices of

the Moon Goddess

it had happened

the God K event

and then was
the anniversary

of the first
God K event

18 days
13 uinals

8 tuns

7 katuns

4 baktuns

18 pictuns

5 calabtuns

since it had come to pass

9 Ik

10 Mol

the first

display
of God K

(and then)
9 Ahau

3 Kankin
(9.13.13.15.0,
Nov. 6, A.D. 705)

apotheosis??

by

GI

GIII ??

??

Goddess of
the Number 2

1-Ahau (god's name)

his blood

Palenque
Jaguar Lord

Lord Chan-Bahlum

blood lord of Palenque

FIGURE VII.2a

Twin, now depicted as the Baby Jaguar, lying on the muzzle of the Cauac Monster altar, squirming as the ax wielded by his brother begins its fall. Here, the altar is turned muzzle up, as Chac-Xib-Chac dances toward his brother in the sacrificial dance that will lead to death's defeat.[9] One of the Lords of Death, in this case God A, has entered the scene with his dog, perhaps the very one the Twins had sacrificed earlier. The firefly, who saved the Twins in the House of Darkness, flutters behind the Lord of Death. The climactic episode of the mythic narrative is painted on yet another pot at Princeton (Pl. 118). This pot depicts one of the Hero Twins, now with fully human aspect, straining to pull God N from his shell, so that he may be dismembered in sacrifice. God N, like God L, is one of the principal lords of the Underworld; unlike the innocent bystander who was sacrificed and restored, he will not be revived and thus represents death defeated.

The finale of the journey after death, the soul's triumphal exit from Xibalba, was a clearly defined concept to the Maya; however, because most funerary objects were designed to accompany the dead into the tomb to aid in the struggle in the Underworld, this last episode in the journey was only rarely depicted. Of the two sculptural narratives on this theme that have been uncovered, the first is a stone tablet from Temple 14 at Palenque (Fig. VII.2), erected by King Kan-Xul, the younger son of Pacal, to obstruct the ceremonial entrance to the Group of the Cross as a way of "killing" it.[10] The tablet depicts Chan-Bahlum, Kan-Xul's older brother and predecessor, as he exits in triumph from Xibalba after his defeat of death. Executed in low relief, the scene shows Chan-Bahlum dancing across the water's surface toward his mother, Lady Ahpo-Hel. He is dressed in the guise of the Jaguar God of the Underworld, whose head adorns his belt. The *kin* "sun" sign he wears in his headdress, along with a personified tree, denotes the path he has followed in his journey into and out of Xibalba. Lady Ahpo-Hel rises from a seated, cross-legged position to hand her son God K. She holds the god so that its head faces her; thus, when Chan-Bahlum takes it, the god will be positioned for display.

The text provides important information about this dance of rebirth, for it likens Lady Ahpo-Hel's action to that of the Moon Goddess the first time she displayed God K, 932,174 years earlier. Chan-Bahlum left Xibalba and greeted his mother on November 6, A.D. 705, exactly three haabs and one tzolkin after his death on February 20, A.D. 702.[11] The action shown is supernatural, for the actors are dead on that date; even more important, however, is the fact that the actions of the dead king and his dead mother are likened to those of the Moon Goddess hundreds of thousands of years before: The scene not only records the fate of the king and his mother, it makes them equivalent to the gods.

A second important monument, the Palenque panel at Dumbarton Oaks, shows Kan-Xul at the moment of his apotheosis (Fig. VII.3). This work differs from the Chan-Bahlum panel in the presentation of the event and in the tactics of sanctification. The unfortunate Kan-Xul was captured in old age by the king of Tonina. We presume that he was sacrificed there, since there is no death date for him in the Palenque record. Nevertheless, he was respected enough to have been given an apotheosis tablet.[12] The text begins by recalling the ritual, on February 8, A.D. 657, in which Kan-Xul was named as the *kexol*, the "replacement," of a dead ancestor of the same name, who had died on February 10, A.D. 565, ninety-two years earlier. It ends with the rebirth of Kan-Xul on November 24, A.D. 722, after his sacrificial death at Tonina.

Figure VII.3
Carved limestone panel
Palenque, Chiapas, Mexico
Late Classic period, A.D. 722
Dumbarton Oaks, Washington, D.C.

With one foot raised, Kan-Xul dances out of Xibalba wearing the costume of Chac-Xib-Chac, which is identified by the string-knot belt, the shell diadem and the shell earflare. He also wields a serpent-handled ax and carries an *akbal* vase. His string pectoral is also associated with the gods of the Palenque Triad, the two Paddler Gods and Chac-Xib-Chac; when worn by a king, the pectoral signals the guise of one of those gods. His high-waisted undergarment is standard for high-ranking males, as are his jade wrist and ankle cuffs.

Lady Ahpo-Hel, seated on his right, is named by the small text above her head, as is Pacal, who sits on the opposite side. Lady Ahpo-Hel also wears a jade cape with Jester God medallions and a jade belt. Her headdress has an unidentified zoomorph, and she holds God K in her hands. Pacal holds a full-figure personification of a tree, perhaps the *axis mundi*. His headdress zoomorph, although unidentified, has a deer hoof as its muzzle. He wears a bead necklace and a bar pectoral hung on a leather strap. The leaf with three interior disks hung from his earflare identifies Pacal as a lineage ancestor of the deceased Kan-Xul.

When parents are shown with their offspring on other panels at Palenque, the father is always placed on the child's right, the mother on the left. In scenes of apotheosis, however, either the mother is shown without the father or she occupies the dominant position, to the right. The reversal of position signals that the mother is the more important parent at the moment of apotheosis, while the father dominates in contexts, such as the legitimate descent of the throne, where lineage is crucial.

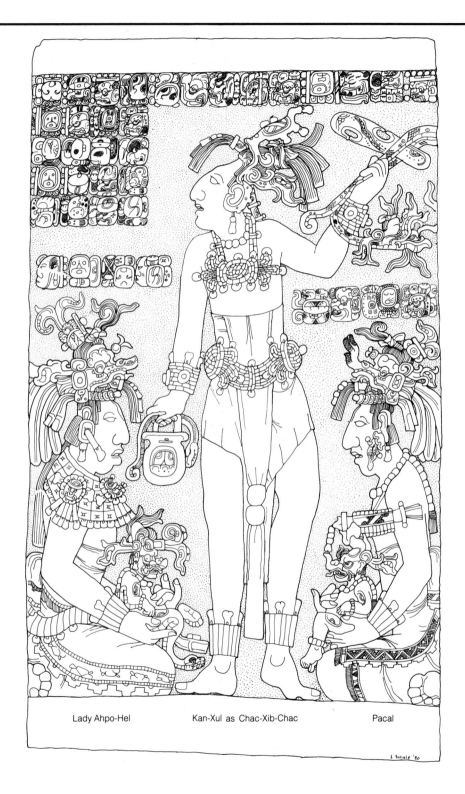

Lady Ahpo-Hel   Kan-Xul as Chac-Xib-Chac   Pacal

THE INSCRIPTION

The text (Fig. VII.3a) opens with a Distance Number that leads from the end of katun 11 to a date four years later, 9.11.4.7.0, or February 10, A.D. 657. The events that occurred on that day are twofold: Chac-Xib-Chac enacted a "house" event under the auspices of Pacal, and Pacal's twelve-year-old son, Kan-Xul, celebrated an unknown rite. The glyphs recording Kan-Xul's action have not yet been deciphered, but he is named as the "successor," or "replacement," of someone who is dead. The boy is apparently being named as the replacement of an earlier king in the Palenque dynasty list of the same name. The first Kan-Xul died on February 8, A.D. 565, exactly ninety-two years and two days before. Therefore, the replacement rite was planned to occur on the anniversary of the first ruler's death.

The second event occurred on the day 9 Manik 5 Muan. No Long Count is given, but the best placement would be on 9.14.11.2.7, or November 24, A.D. 722, a few years after Kan-Xul's death as a captive at Tonina. The event glyph is a variant of the apotheosis verb on Temple 14, and the actor is the god Chac-Xib-Chac. This is likely to be a reference to Kan-Xul's triumphant dance out of Xibalba in the persona of Chac-Xib-Chac, as shown here.

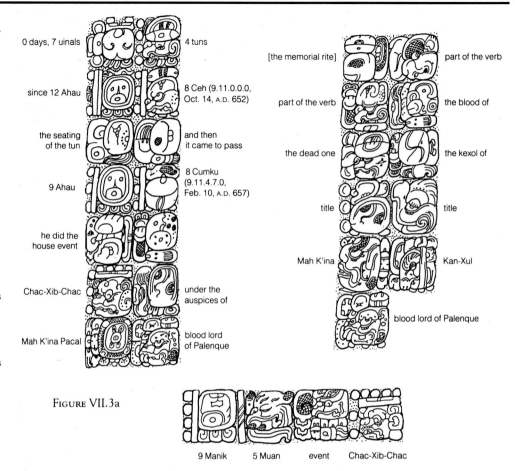

0 days, 7 uinals

since 12 Ahau

the seating of the tun

9 Ahau

he did the house event

Chac-Xib-Chac

Mah K'ina Pacal

4 tuns

8 Ceh (9.11.0.0.0, Oct. 14, A.D. 652)

and then it came to pass

8 Cumku (9.11.4.7.0, Feb. 10, A.D. 657)

under the auspices of

blood lord of Palenque

[the memorial rite]

part of the verb

the dead one

title

Mah K'ina

part of the verb

the blood of

the kexol of

title

Kan-Xul

blood lord of Palenque

FIGURE VII.3a

9 Manik   5 Muan   event   Chac-Xib-Chac

The scene on the panel has Kan-Xul, with one foot raised, dancing out of Xibalba in the guise of Chac-Xib-Chac, the god who engaged in the sacrificial dance with the Baby Jaguar on the Metropolitan vase (Pl. 117). Kan-Xul's mother, Lady Ahpo-Hel, awaits him on his right holding God K as she did for his older brother, Chan-Bahlum, on the panel in Temple 14. Their father, Pacal, is shown here also, although he is absent on Chan-Bahlum's panel. Pacal is seated on his son's left, waiting his arrival so that he can give Kan-Xul the personified World Tree—the same tree Chan-Bahlum wears in his triumphal dance on Tablet 14, as well as that which emerges from the earth along with the ancestors on Pacal's sarcophagus. The presence of this tree signifies that both kings have become ancestors and are now seated among the ancestral rulers of Palenque. The last concept is inscribed on the west tablet of the Temple of Inscriptions in a record of Pacal's death. There his death is recorded as "He was seated as *ahau* in death."

Evidence suggests that the Maya identified the north as the direction of the ancestral dead. In the Group of the Cross at Palenque, the north temple housed dynastic records of all the rulers, up to and including the ancestral king for whom Chan-

Bahlum was named, including their descent from the gods of the Palenque Triad and their birth and accession data. Moreover, the North Acropolis at Tikal, located on the north side of the Great Plaza, contained numerous royal tombs, the earliest dated to the first century B.C.;[13] it was literally the place of the ancestors at Tikal. The direction north was also significant at Palenque, where the head of the corpse was always placed to the north; the design on Pacal's sarcophagus lid also points north, as discussed above. It seems clear, then, that the Maya regarded the north sky as a logical place to house the dead. The north star is the pivot of the sky, around which the constellations revolve; the sea was also toward the north, and the rains came from the north. The Hero Twins rose into the sky to own the sun and moon, and the ancestral dead rose to occupy the north sky.

For the Maya, death called the soul to Xibalba, where it faced a series of trials and competitions with the Lords of Death. If defeated, the soul faced eternal extinction and burial in the evil-smelling world of Xibalba. The journey into the Underworld was couched in the mythology of the Hero Twins, whose cunning defeat of the Lords of Death gave the living hope for a final resurrection. The Hero Twins deceived the Lords of Death by posing as dancers and magicians. Like them, a soul triumphant after death can dance out of Xibalba to take his place among other reborn ancestors, to assist and guide his descendants.

NOTES

1. Michael D. Coe (*The Maya Scribe and His World* [New York: Grolier Club, 1973], p. 11) first discussed death and funerary practices in the larger context of Maya society. Following Robert Hertz (*Death and the Right Hand*, translated by Rodney Needham and Claudia Needham [Glencoe, Ill.: Free Press, 1960]), Coe proposed that funerary customs "follow not so much from the psychological fact of bereavement as from the necessity for society to reconstitute itself after the loss of one of its members." Funerary ceremonies are rites of passage, in which the deceased passes from one kind of being to another; this process of transformation is fraught with danger for both the individual and his disrupted society. The soul must cleanse itself of death, a process that is often symbolized as a journey in which obstacles and dangers must be overcome. The progress of this journey is often timed to the process of the body's decay and its reduction to incorruptible matter (such as bone) or, as among the Egyptians, to its mummification. There is good evidence that exactly this kind of journey was at the heart of Maya beliefs about death.

2. Michael D. Coe, *The Maya Scribe and His World*; idem, *Lords of the Underworld* (Princeton, N.J.: Princeton University Press, 1978).

3. Dennis Tedlock (*Popol Vuh: The Definitive Edition of the Mayan Book of the Dawn of Life and the Glories of Gods and Kings* [New York: Simon and Schuster, 1985], p. 296) interprets this passage of the Popol Vuh to mean that the Sun and the Moon belong to the Twins, rather than that the Twins become those celestial bodies.

4. Nicholas Hellmuth (personal communication, 1982) was among the first researchers to recognize the watery nature of the Maya Underworld and to organize visual evidence for this identification systematically.

5. Thomas Gann describes the location as on the north bank of the Rio Hondo in the territory of Quintana Roo. The mound was 35 feet high and 250 feet in circumference, and it had a flattened summit. This pot was found inside the fill, six or seven feet below the summit, along with several other pots, animal bones, earflares, shells and greenstone beads. Whether this was a burial or a dedication cache is unclear, although the absence of a chamber and human skeletal remains suggests that it was a cache. See Thomas Gann, *The Maya Indians of Southern Yucatan and Northern British Honduras*, Smithsonian Institution, Bureau of American Ethnology, Bulletin 64 (Washington, D.C.: U.S. Government Printing Office, 1918), pp. 105–109.

6. Linda Lybarger ("The Sarcophagus Lid of Pacal," a paper prepared for course credit at the University of Texas, December 1985) has observed that many of the attributes of the seiba tree account for the association of blood with the World Tree in Maya thought. One species, *Seiba pentandra*, grows to a height of 120

to 140 feet and has a trunk diameter of six to eight feet. This species is deciduous and has a yearly new growth of a rich reddish-brown color. The large size of the tree makes it particularly noticeable in the forest, and the red color of the new leaves provided an obvious basis for a blood association. More important, another species, *Seiba pochote*, is characterized by a conspicuously swollen lower trunk. A World Tree in the Dresden Codex (page 3) also has this distinctive shape. Furthermore, the sap of this tree is a deep red. Therefore, the use of blood symbols on the branches and trunk of the World Tree on the sarcophagus may be based on more than a generalized metaphor declaring that sap is to the tree as blood is to the human. The sap of the seiba is red, and the Maya reflected that fact by placing blood symbols on the World Tree.

7. David Kelley (*Deciphering the Maya Script* [Austin: University of Texas Press, 1976], p. 236) has associated these canoe scenes with the Popol Vuh story of the acquisition of maize and the creation of human beings. Reinforcing Kelley's ideas, Karl Taube has proposed that the human passenger is the Young Maize God. If these identifications are correct, then the death metaphor on the Tikal bones contains direct references to the Popol Vuh myths. See Karl Taube, "The Classic Maya Maize God: A Reappraisal," in *Fifth Palenque Round Table, Vol. 7*, gen. ed. Merle Greene Robertson, vol. ed. Virginia Fields (San Francisco: Pre-Columbian Art Research Institute, 1985), pp. 171–181.

8. Michael D. Coe, in *The Maya Scribe and His World* (p. 93), has proposed a slightly different, and perhaps an equally valid, interpretation of the iconography. Following a suggestion by Kelley, he identifies the Calendar Round date on this pot, 8 Caban 5 Ceh, as the day before 9 Etz'nab 6 Ceh, the station for the first appearance of the Evening Star in the 1 Ahau 9 Kayab run of the Venus Tables in the Dresden Codex. Using this calendric association as a basis, he suggested that the older set of Twins, Hun-Hunahpu and Vucub-Hunahpu, were the Morning Star and Evening Star, and that this pot represents the sacrificial death of Vucub Hunahpu on the day before the first appearance of the Evening Star.

9. Michael D. Coe, in *The Maya Scribe and His World* (p. 99), interpreted the date on this pot as 7 Muluc 7 Kayab and pointed out that it is one day after 6 Lamat 6 Kayab, a day registered in the 3 Ahau 13 Mac run of the Venus Tables of the Dresden Codex as the heliacal rising of the Morning Star.

10. See n. 3, Chap. 1.

11. The apotheosis of Chan-Bahlum was also associated with celestial activities. Floyd Lounsbury (personal communication, 1978) has noted that on November 6, A.D. 702, Jupiter was first seen to move after it had been frozen motionless against the star fields at its second stationary point. This association was not accidental, for Chan-Bahlum tied other important events to Jupiter during his lifetime. The day 9.12.18.5.16 2 Cib 14 Mol (July 23, A.D. 690) was the first of a four-day-long rite that celebrated the seventy-fifth tropical year anniversary of Pacal's accession; on that day Saturn and Jupiter were frozen at stationary points less than four degrees apart. On his accession date 9.12.11.12.10 8 Oc 3 Kayab (January 10, A.D. 684), Jupiter had just begun moving off its second stationary point. Chan-Bahlum keyed his ritual life to the movements of Jupiter in a very special way, but similar Jupiter stations are noted in the inscriptions of Tortuguero and Yaxchilan. Floyd Lounsbury ("Astronomical Knowledge and Its Uses at Bonampak, Mexico," in *Archaeoastronomy in the New World*, edited by A. F. Aveni [Cambridge: Cambridge University Press, 1982], pp. 143–168) has shown that the first appearances of the Evening Star and the Morning Star were also observed and recorded by the Maya in their inscriptions. The Evening Star was a death god of the most frightening kind, for its first appearance was the signal to take captives in war for use in bloody sacrificial rites. Lounsbury's work has shown us that the Classic Maya believed the heavens to be yet another environment populated by supernaturals of all sorts, whose actions were associated with the movements of the planets and the stars. Given the direct associations of Venus stations and Underworld scenes, the known use of Venus stations as the stimulus for war and other ritual behavior, and the use of Jupiter stations to correspond to apotheosis and other ancestral celebrations, it can also be speculated that the Maya conceived the night sky to be a map of Xibalba itself and that they conceived the movement of the heavens to be the interactions of the beings who populated it.

12. Since a probable location for this tablet within the archaeological zone at Palenque has not been identified, it may have been taken from a family compound located outside the present archaeological zone.

13. William Coe, in "Tikal: Ten Years of Study of a Maya Ruin in the Lowlands of Guatemala" (*Expedition* 8 [1965], pp. 15–21) documents three Late Preclassic tombs deep under the North Acropolis. He dates these three tombs—Burials 166, 167 and 85—in the order named and to the first century B.C. Paintings of extraordinary quality and complexity were found on the tomb walls of Burial 166 and on the outer walls of

the shrine built over Burial 167. Burial 85 contained a dismembered body with its skull and thighbones missing. The body was wrapped in a bundle, and a green fuchsite mask was sewn to the top of the bundle. The small mask is the portrait of a historical person who is wearing a very early version of the Jester God headband. The sumptuousness of the two earlier graves suggests that they were constructed for very highly ranked individuals (very probably rulers); the person buried in Burial 85 was clearly a ruler, for his portrait mask wears the headband "crown" of Maya kings. Other tombs, from the Early Classic period, were found throughout the North Acropolis. Clemency Coggins, in "Painting and Drawing Styles at Tikal: An Historical and Iconographic Reconstruction" (Ph.D. diss., Harvard University [Ann Arbor, Mich.: University Microfilms, 1976]) has suggested that two of these, Burials 10 and 48, were the tombs of Curl Snout and Stormy Sky, two Early Classic rulers known from the inscriptions at Tikal. At Tikal, many of the early rulers were buried in the North Acropolis.

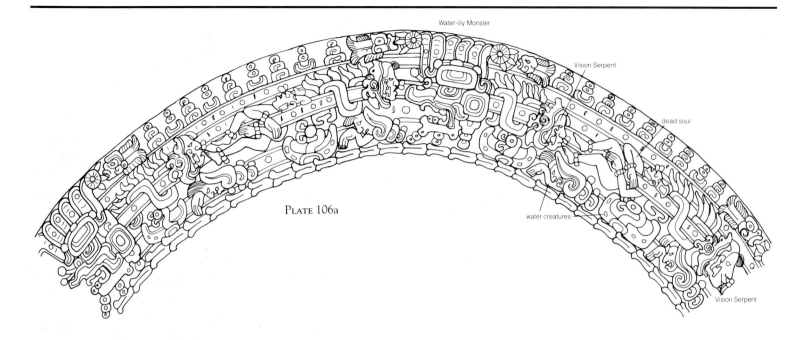

Water-lily Monster

Vision Serpent

dead soul

PLATE 106a

water creatures

Vision Serpent

PLATE 105
Tetrapod bowl
Early Classic period, A.D. 350–500
Polychromed ceramic
H. 22 cm
New Orleans Museum of Art
Ella West Freeman Foundation Matching Fund

This Early Classic basal-flanged bowl depicts the Water Bird fishing on the waters of the world. The neck and head of the Water Bird emerge from the domed lid of the vessel in a three-dimensional realization of the cormorant rising to the surface after its hunting dive. A small fish caught in its beak completes the three-dimensional arch of the lid handle, while its neck extends onto the surface as a color shape flanked by personified wings spreading across the dome of the lid.

The sides of the bowl are painted with an oddly arranged set of shapes that may be intended to represent a square-nosed dragon. The four hollow legs are painted and modeled to represent peccary heads, the firing slits serving as their mouths. Eyes are painted on either side of the legs, and the painted ears overlap the sides of the bowl walls. Several other Early Classic basal-flanged bowls, most of them also representing the watery world, have these peccary feet as well. They may represent the pillars of the world set in the four directions, for there are always four peccaries.

PLATE 106
Covered Bowl
Quintana Roo, Mexico
Early Classic period, A.D. 350–500
Molded ceramic
Diam. 20.3 x H. 17 cm
Merseyside County Museums, Liverpool

This mold-made bowl was found in a mound on the Rio Hondo, just north of the Belize border. Fragments of human bone had been deposited inside before the bowl was interred. Appropriately, the imagery on both the lid (Pl. 106b) and bowl sides depicts a dead soul in the watery Underworld. The scenes are divided into repeating halves by Water-lily Monsters set on opposite sides of the composition. Root formations emerging from their foreheads give rise to stems and blossoms, upon which fish are nibbling. The area between the Water-lily Monsters is filled with water bands that encircle the lid and the sides of the bowl. Water stacks line the upper band, and bifurcated shapes underline the lower one; they presumably represent the muddy bottom. Along the bottom are open bivalve shells whose resident creatures peek out; human heads emerge from conch shells nearby: These are the creatures of the primordial sea.

On each side of the composition, three creatures occupy the middle level. In the center, a nude human clinging to the water band flings his right arm and leg across it, while his body drops below. He wears beads on his wrists and ankles and double beads on his nose. Wrapped around the band on either side of these figures are feathered Vision Serpents whose mouths emit human heads. The souls of the dead and the Vision Serpent reside in the watery Underworld.

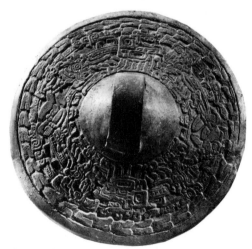

Plate 106b

PLATE 107
Basal-flanged vessel
Early Classic period, A.D. 350–500
Polychromed ceramic
Diam. 36.2 x H. 27.8 cm
The Denver Art Museum
Gift of Mr. and Mrs. Edward Luben

The Underworld is a common theme on Early Classic basal-flanged bowls of this type. Here, in keeping with the brilliant red ground, a chevron band encloses a circle of water dots alternating with large red blood spots marking the water as bloody. The top of the handle is carved with a Venus sign, which presumably fixes Venus above the surface of the Underworld. Two human profiles painted against the red ground look downward, as if they are diving through the surface of the water. The double line running from the eye to the earflare identifies these characters as God Q, an inhabitant of Xibalba. Scrolls and a shield are attached to the chin and forehead of each God Q. Quadrifoil shapes floating between the heads closely resemble similar emblems painted on the western outer wall of House E at Palenque.

On opposite sides of the bowl float dragons that are stylistically similar to the sky serpents seen on Late Preclassic architectural facades. By the Late Classic period, these dragons were substituted for stingray spines and flowing blood. Here the dragons surely signal the environment intended for this pot: Since Early Classic iconography primarily depicts the watery Underworld, square-nosed dragons probably serve to modify water imagery to blood, as does the band below the handle.

PLATE 108
Basal-flanged bowl
Early Classic period, A.D. 350–500
Carved, incised and burnished ceramic
Diam. 29.5 x H. 26 cm
The Museum of Fine Arts, Houston
Gift of Mr. and Mrs. George R. Brown

This basal-flanged bowl displays much the same imagery as the bowl from Denver, but it is executed in a different Early Classic style, one that used incision rather than painting. The lower bowl is marked with the same square-nosed dragon, and the lid (Pl. 108a) is divided into opposing panels, each filled with an anthropomorphic head and its headdress gear. The six-pointed handle represents a water-lily blossom, which signals the surface of water. Since this carved vessel style does not use pigment, blood signs behind the portrait heads—a *yax* sign on the left and a Kan-cross on the right—mark the water as bloody.

The portrait facing right has an elegantly painted eye, the line of the lashes extending beyond the contour of the nose. He wears a double-bead nose ornament, and his cheek is bordered by the beaded edge of the headdress flange. The earflare is a standard quincunx disk, flanked above by an inverted personification head and below by a personified scroll. The large zoomorphs suspended from his chin strap and sitting atop his face have downturned snouts. The upper one wears the cantilevered flower headband, a water scroll and a personified wing. Sitting on the water scroll is a Water-lily Jaguar with a large blood scroll at the corner of its mouth, a parrot or macaw atop it and an unidentified sign behind it. An *akbal* "darkness" sign is infixed into its forehead.

The opposing head on the left is significantly different in its detail. The eye is delineated as a single angled line with *caban*-like markings dropping from it. The earflare has a bell-shaped jade insert and is flanked by a scroll above and by a disk, crossbands and personification head below. The chin strap is woven; its suspended zoomorph is contained by a hanging strap attached to a bifurcated scroll. The beaded edge of the side flange of the headdress continues above the face to terminate in an open-mouthed personification head, beneath which are visible a second headband and a twisted rope. Crowning the headdress is the Water-lily Jaguar, who, however, lacks the *akbal* sign, the blood scroll and the macaw. Jaguars like these are often placed in headdresses to name the persons wearing them; this appears to be the case here, although it is not known if these faces represent supernaturals or dead souls shown at the moment they break the surface of the primordial sea during their fall into death.

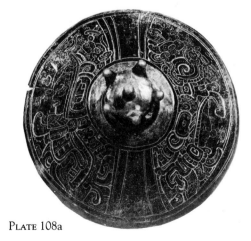

PLATE 108a

PLATE 109
Cylindrical vessel
Late Classic period, A.D. 600–800
Polychromed ceramic
Diam. 11.1 x H. 21.6 cm
The Museum of Fine Arts, Houston
Museum Purchase

This finely painted codex-style pot (so called because of its use of line and spatial conventions similar to those in the four known Maya books) depicts three Xibalbans receiving a sacrificial head on a drum altar. God A, his skeletal mouth smiling in glee, hovers over the sacrificial offering of a decapitated head. His fleshless skull has death eyes attached fore and rear, and paper ornaments hang from his human ears. The bony joints of his fleshed body give him the gaunt look of starvation, and the excrement streaming from his rear reinforces the impression of his awful smell and diseased condition. He wears a death collar with a hanging *akbal* "night" vase, and bloody red scrolls of gore squeeze out from under his striped shirt.

The next creature is distinguished from God A by the insect wings attached to his upper arms. His head is again skeletal and his body fleshed with the distended belly of parasitic disease. The bulbous scroll attached to his rear represents a foliated fart. The third Xibalban is feline, with white body and spots on paws and face; his mouth gapes open, emitting an effective visual representation of terrible bad breath.

PLATE 110
Head of the God of the Number Zero
Copan, Honduras
Late Classic period, A.D. 770–780
Stone
102.7 x 35.3 cm
The Cleveland Museum of Art
Purchase from the J. H. Wade Fund

This exquisite piece of architectural sculpture was found in the late nineteenth century in the first modern excavations of Copan. The life-size head depicts the God of the Number Zero as a handsome young male. He wears disk earflares flanked by a counterweight below and a scroll above; deer ears emerge from the top scroll, and a strip of mat is set behind the central disk. A scroll shield with a death-eye border is mounted on a headband of rattlesnake rattles. The god's status as a sacrificial victim is revealed by his bound hair and the indication of the method by which he is to die, the hand gripping his chin in preparation for removal of the jaw from its living owner. The hand gripping the chin identifies this supernatural as the God of the Number Zero.

Rendered in nearly three-dimensional form, this head was intended to emerge from the wall of a building. The stone shaft behind the head was set into the masonry of the bearing wall, along with other stones sculpted to complete the rest of the god's body. The body was probably fully detailed and seated cross-legged, as are most other figures from entablature sculpture at Copan.

PLATE 111
The sarcophagus lid
Temple of Inscriptions, Palenque, Chiapas, Mexico
Late Classic period, A.D. 684
Limestone
H. 372 x 217 cm
Photo by Merle Greene Robertson

This sarcophagus was found deep under the Temple of Inscriptions at Palenque by Alberto Ruz Lhullier in 1952. According to the inscription around the edge of the lid and in the temple above, it is the coffin of Pacal, who died on August 31, A.D. 683. Born on March 26, A.D. 603, Pacal acceded in A.D. 615, at the age of twelve, and ruled for sixty-eight years. During a long lifetime of accomplishment, he brought Palenque into its own as a leading city of the Late Classic period. As an old man feeling the approach of death, he began the construction of his funerary temple around A.D. 675.

The sarcophagus was carved from a solid piece of creamy white limestone. Since the enormous base is larger than the entrance to the chamber, it must have been in place before the pyramid above it was constructed. Pacal's corpse was placed into the body-shaped hole cut into the base, and the huge limestone lid was rolled in place to seal the coffin. After the burial rites were completed and the chamber sealed, five or six sacrificial victims were killed and laid in a small chamber in front of the plaster-covered door. The long stairwell leading down through the pyramid to the tomb chamber was filled with rubble in which cache offerings of jade, pottery and shell were deposited. A stone tube, called a psychoduct, which began at a notch in the sealing door and extended up the stairs to the floor of the temple, was also set in place; it gave the Vision Serpent a path to follow from Pacal's tomb to the space occupied by his living descendants.

The image on the sarcophagus lid (Pl. 111a) depicts the instant of Pacal's death and his fall into the Underworld. The entire image is framed by a skyband with *kin*, or "day" and "sun," in the upper right (northeast) corner and with *akbal*, or "night" and "darkness," in the upper left

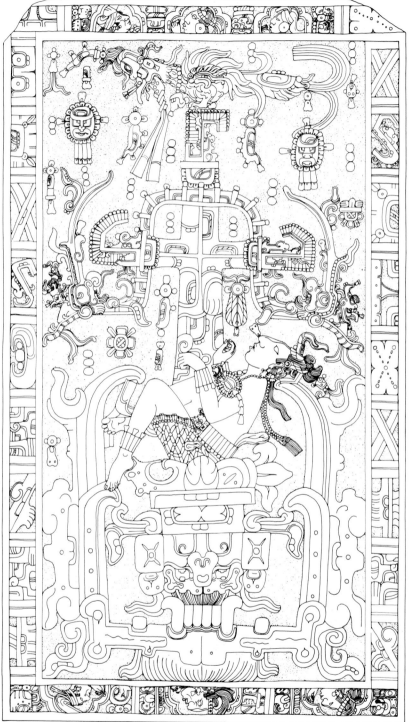

PLATE 111a

Drawings by Merle Greene Robertson

282   THE BLOOD OF KINGS

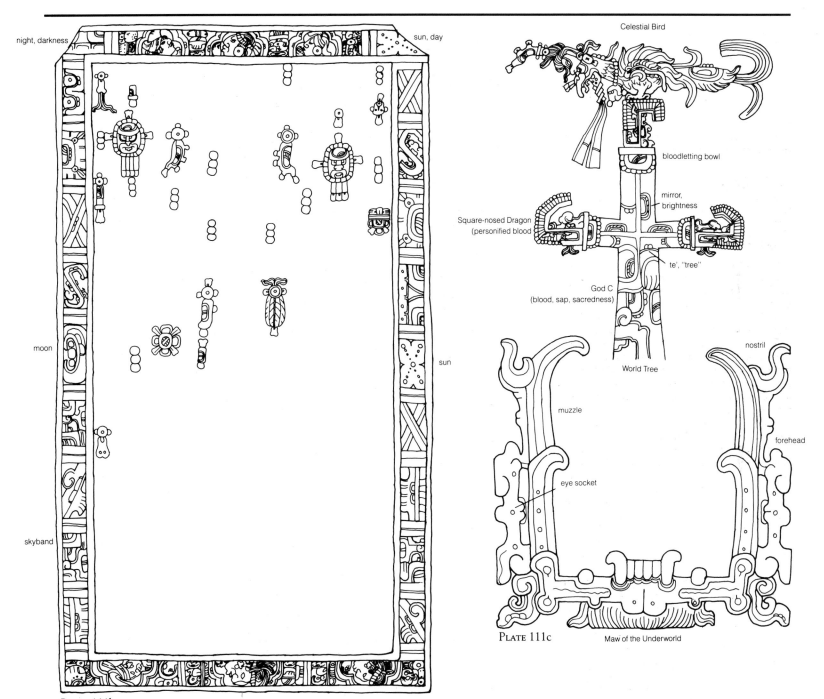

night, darkness

sun, day

Celestial Bird

bloodletting bowl

mirror, brightness

Square-nosed Dragon (personified blood)

te', "tree"

God C (blood, sap, sacredness)

moon

sun

World Tree

nostril

muzzle

forehead

eye socket

skyband

PLATE 111b

PLATE 111c

Maw of the Underworld

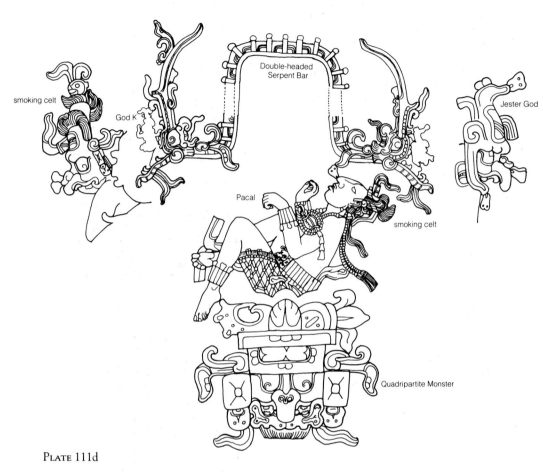

smoking celt

God K

Double-headed
Serpent Bar

Jester God

Pacal

smoking celt

Quadripartite Monster

PLATE 111d

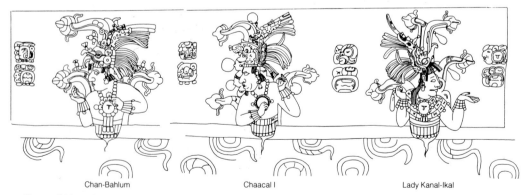

Chan-Bahlum

Chaacal I

Lady Kanal-Ikal

PLATE 111e

(northwest) corner (Pl. 111b). The cosmic event that forms the context for Pacal's passage into death is the movement of the sun from east to west. The background of the scene is filled with a set of signs—shells, God C, completion, jade beads and others—that occur on blood scrolls; thus, the medium of the action is blood.

The lower half of the main image is a split representation of the gaping Maw of the Underworld (Pl. 111c). Joined at the chin, two huge skeletal dragons form a U-shaped container representing the entrance to Xibalba. Their snouts curve inward, as if they are about to close over the falling body of Pacal. From the center of the cave rises the *axis mundi*, the World Tree at the center of the universe. A Celestial Bird, the symbol of the heavenly realm, sits atop the tree.

The World Tree is specially marked as a sacred being; *te'*, or "wood," signs tell us it is a wooden tree. *Nen*, or "mirror," signs mark it as a thing of brilliance and power. A huge image of God C, the symbol of blood and sacredness, is inscribed on the base of the trunk; it is partially overlapped by Pacal's body. The ends of the branches are shallow bowls with the reflection marks of a mirror on their sides. Outlined by beads of blood, they are the bloodletting bowls of sacrifice. The square-nosed dragons that emerge from these bowls have jade cylinders and beads lining their mouths, marking them as especially sacred. These bejeweled dragons are deliberately contrasted to the skeletal dragons below them. One represents the heavens, the highest and most sacred of the three levels of the Maya cosmos. The other represents the world of death, into which Pacal is falling.

The square-nosed serpents symbolize flowing blood. In other contexts, they emerge from stingray spines or replace them in the forehead emblem of the Quadripartite Monster. They often appear with other symbols of blood—shells, bone beads and *yax*, *chac*, *kan* or "zero" signs attached to them. Both the God C on the trunk of the World Tree and these Square-nosed Dragons are symbols with double meaning. The word for sap—in particular rubber and copal, a resin incense still prized by the Maya—simply means "the blood of the tree" in many Mayan languages. This use of blood symbols is, then, a play on words. On a deeper level, the sap of the tree is the medium through which the gods and the souls of the dead can pass. These blood symbols declare that the blood of sacrifice is to the world of kings and gods as the sap is to the tree.

A Double-headed Serpent Bar (Pl. 111d), the symbol of Maya kingship, lies wrapped around the branches of the World Tree in reference to the earthly Middleworld. In this manifestation of the bar, the body is made of jade segments, again signifying special value. The heads on either end of the bar correspond feature by feature to those of the skeletal dragons of the Underworld Maw. While the Underworld is skeletal, however, the Middleworld, represented by the Serpent Bar, is fleshed, and the Overworld, represented by the square-nosed serpent, is bejeweled. God K, the dark obsidian mirror and god of blood sacrifice, emerges from the western (left) head; it is balanced on the east by the Jester God, the bright mirror and god of kings.

As he falls down this World Tree, Pacal sits atop the Quadripartite Sun Monster. The crossed bands (usually depicted in its *kin* bowl) are replaced here by a *cimi*, the glyph for death. The Monster is skillfully depicted in a state of transition between life and death: He is skeletal from the muzzle down, but his eyes have the scroll pupils of living creatures. The sun enters into just such a transitional state at sunrise and sunset. Here, however, the Sun Monster's badge contains the *cimi* death sign, specifying that the image marks the "death of the sun," or sunset. The sun, poised at the horizon, is ready for its plunge into the Underworld. It will carry the dead king with it.

Pacal totters atop the Sun Monster's head in an impossibly awkward position. This awkwardness signals that he, too, is in transition from life to death. He falls away from his loincloth and the heavy beads of his counterweighted pectoral, which float up and away from his body. His knees are flexed, his hands relaxed, his face composed. He does not fall in terror, because he anticipates the defeat of death. A bone attached to his nose signifies that even in death he carries the seed of rebirth: In Mayan languages, the words for "bone" and "large seed" are homophonous; thus, the bone is the seed of Pacal's resurrection. Finally, Pacal falls as a god; his forehead is penetrated by the smoking celt of God K. Like the Hero Twins, he was a god during his life and a god as he fell in death.

On the sides of the sarcophagus, ten ancestral portraits depict each person emerging along with a fruit tree from a crack in the earth. On the east side (Pl. 111e), three ancestors are depicted with their fruit trees, marked from left to right as guanavana, chico zapote and avocado. Reading left to right, the first person is Chaacal I, the oldest of the ancestors and Pacal's grandfather, six generations removed. The middle figure is Chan-Bahlum I, the king for whom Pacal's son was

named and Pacal's great-great-grandfather. The third figure is Lady Kanal-Ikal, one of the few Maya women ever to have ruled in her own right. She was Pacal's great-grandmother. The two glyph columns interspersed between the figures name them. The left pair of glyphs records "Chaacal, blood lord of Palenque"; the two center columns record "Mah K'ina Chan-Bahlum, blood lord of Palenque"; and the right column reads, "Lady Kanal-Ikal, blood lord of Palenque."

Plate 112
Bone handle
Early Classic period, A.D. 100–400
Carved human bone
13 x 3 cm
Department of Anthropology, American Museum of Natural History, New York

This bone was probably once used as the handle of a ritual object, perhaps a fan or lancet. The figural style and imagery are similar to that of the Hauberg Stela (Pl. 66), which dates it to approximately the same period, from A.D. 200–400. A scalloped tree undulates upward from a groundline, terminating in a large Serpent head whose open mouth points upward, as if the object once mounted on this bone "emerged" from it. An upturned snout of a zoomorph marked with an *akbal* sign rests next to the base of the tree; it personifies the pyramid to which it is attached. Scrolls emerge from the pyramid, and a Kan-cross knot lies across its base. A jaguar-deer and another, unidentified zoomorph hover in the spaces between the tree and the pyramid. This image reveals that in Maya cosmology, the World Tree emerged from a pyramid to terminate in the head of the Vision Serpent. Visions would travel from the Underworld along this World Tree. Thus, Pacal's tomb does more than represent the Maw of the Underworld symbolically. The pyramid over his tomb was itself the portal to the lower world.

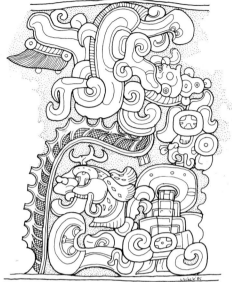

PLATE 112a

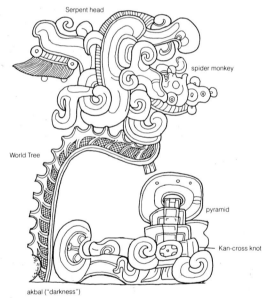

Serpent head

spider monkey

World Tree

pyramid

Kan-cross knot

akbal ("darkness")

personification head

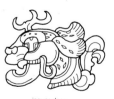

jaguar-deer

the zoomorph

PLATE 112b

Plate 113
Shell medallion
Late Classic period, A.D. 600–800
Diam. 6.4 cm
Carved and incised shell
Museum of the American Indian, Heye Foundation,
New York

This shell disk depicts the Old Stingray Spine God paddling a canoe. The image is cut as a silhouette; interior detail is rendered in incised lines. The Paddler sits in a short canoe, his paddle in his left hand and a thin shaft in his right; his passenger is a rabbit, whom the Maya saw on the face of the moon. This shell, carved as a costume element, was probably fashioned for attachment to a headdress or cape. While the Paddler Gods are shown or named in glyphs at many sites, the canoe scene is rare. The similarity of this canoe scene to those on the Tikal bones suggests that the canoe myth as well as the myth of the Paddler Twins were part of a widespread system of Maya religious mythology, not a phenomenon localized in Tikal.

Plate 114
Eccentric flint
Late Classic period, A.D. 600–800
Flint
25 x 41.1 x 2 cm
Dallas Museum of Art
The Eugene and Margaret McDermott Fund, in honor of Mrs. Alex Spence

Eccentric flints with this kind of complex, silhouetted imagery are too thin and fragile to have been used as cutting tools. They served instead as sacred power objects used in rituals, especially in the dedication and termination rites for Maya architecture and stelae, and as funerary objects to accompany the dead into the Afterlife. This flint fuses imagery of the diving Celestial Monster from Palenque with the sinking canoe of life from Tikal. The front, crocodilian end of the Celestial Monster is often shown with deer ears and hooves. In this example, a deer antler grows from the crocodile's forehead, confirming its identification as the front end of the Celestial Monster. The Quadripartite Monster, which would normally appear as the monster's rear head, is here replaced by a human profile with a God K smoking celt emerging from the forehead. The front leg of the Celestial Monster transforms into the same profile (these two profiles are identical to the flints of Pls. 25 and 26). If this type of human profile with its God K celt is reserved for representations of the souls of the dead, then the normal image of the Celestial Monster has been deliberately altered here to reinforce the particular association of this flint with the fall of the dead

soul, along with the Celestial Monster, into the Underworld. On the sarcophagus lid in Pacal's tomb in the Temple of Inscriptions, only the Quadripartite Monster is seen under the dead king, because the rest of the Celestial Monster is already inside the Maw of the Underworld.

This image of the fall at death is reinforced by the fusion of the Celestial Monster with the canoe, a fusion signaled by two visual components. The bottom edge of the Celestial Monster is cut to resemble the contour of wave-tossed water, and, more important, the three passengers on the monster's back are rendered as if they are seated in a canoe. The center head carries the forehead celt, although the flanking profiles do not. The central person is thus the soul of the deceased, and his companions are most likely the Paddler Gods, or they may be attendants to help him in the Underworld. Sacrificial victims were often placed inside or just outside Maya tombs. The flanking figures do not hold paddles because this canoe is self-propelled. Much of the dynamic sense of a downward plunge is accomplished through the arcing curve of the silhouette; even so, the most powerful signal is certainly the backward lean of the passengers as they respond to the force of the fall.

Plate 115
Cylindrical vessel
Late Classic period, A.D. 600–900
Painted ceramic
Diam. 16.6 x H. 21.5 cm
The Art Museum, Princeton University
Gift of the Hans and Dorothy Widenmann Foundation

This painted pot is one of the finest examples of the codex style of painting, a style characterized by images painted in fine linear brushwork on a ground of cream-colored slip, often finished with a red band around the rim. Fluently drawn dark lines define the figures on this vessel, and thin washes of brown separate the figural and architectural shapes from the background. The narrative is presented in two episodes, one on each side of the pot; they are connected by a subtle transition: As the rollout photo clearly shows, the female closest to the second scene (shown at center) turns her head toward the gory action behind her and taps the lady nearest her on the heel, as if to draw her attention to it.

One event takes place in a temple named on its roof by three creatures—two Water-lily Jaguars and one Xocfish Monster. Since this is an image of what is, of course, a three-dimensional building, the viewer is given to understand that there is a fourth head on the other side of the roof. Blood scrolls fall from the jawless mouths of the three visi-

ble monsters. Curtains are rolled up and tied at the top of the door opening, overlapping the flanking walls. The entire house is raised on a substructural platform, and the interior is occupied by a cloth-draped bench.

God L, one of the Lords of Xibalba, sits inside the temple enjoying the good life with five lovely, bald-headed goddesses who look after his needs. One leans over his back pillow, a second pours liquid into a cylindrical vessel; a third sits cross-legged talking to the second. God L is tying on the wrist cuff of a fourth lady kneeling at his feet, and the fifth woman twists to look toward the second episode, taking place behind her. Adjacent to three of these five ladies are names identifying them as the Goddesses of the Number 2. The scene is completed by a fuzzy, jowled rabbit writing in an open codex. The rigid front flap of the codex was evidently made of some stiff material, such as wood; spots on its surface apparently indicate that the entire codex was bound in jaguar pelt.

The second episode occupies a slightly smaller proportion of the picture plane and contains only three figures. A sacrificial victim with his arms bound behind his back and an ax at his neck struggles with his captors. The *akbal* "darkness" signs on his back and leg mark him as a supernatural victim. An ax wielder dressed in a jaguar skirt hovers over him, forcing his head down for the stroke of the weapon. A long serpent body emerges from the groin of the victim, to strike at the second masked attacker. While this image is not yet understood, it may be related to the Vision Serpent, so intimately associated with sacrificial iconography.

The identities of the two aggressors are problematic. Both wear jaguar-pelt skirts, cloth undergarments and thick belts. The left figure is marked with *akbal* signs on his body; the other carries them on his belt. The left figure wears the Jester God headband, and his bound hair emerges from his headband along with a deer ear. He has square eyes, a roman nose and long lips. The only other Maya image like him is the crouching figure on the Tablet of the Slaves at Palenque, which has an additional diagnostic feature, the fishfin cheek characteristic of GI of the Palenque Triad. Thus, while the ax wielder would seem to be GI, he also wears the headgear of the Headband Twins and wields the ax of Chac-Xib-Chac. He is apparently one of the Hero Twins coming back to Xibalba in disguise.

The second masked ax wielder has hair bound in a tall column on top of his head by sacrificial cloth knots, and he wears a cloth tied loosely around his neck. The mask of a zoomorphic monster whose muzzle transforms into a jaguar paw completely covers his face. This mask is unique, although a monster with a jaguar-paw nose appears in the names of two Early Classic rulers at Tikal and occurs as a loincloth in the royal costume of Early Classic kings at Tikal, Uolantun and Uxbenka (a newly discovered site in Belize). While very little can be said about the second figure, aside from the observation that he is dressed as a sacrificer and is marked by jaguar features, it is most important here that he is disguised by a mask. He must, then, be the other Hero Twin. The episode depicted is therefore the sacrifice of the unwilling bystander, whose subsequent revival overcame the suspicions of the Lords of Death.

THE INCRIPTION

The vessel's rim text, an abbreviated version of the Primary Standard Sequence, does not supply information directly related to the scene. The two columns next to the house are apparently spoken by God L, since cursive speech lines run from his mouth to this text; unfortunately, it eludes decipherment. Neither is the small text above the sacrificial scene deciphered, but the date is of interest, because it may be associated with a station in the cycle of Venus. The day 8 Caban 5 Ceh immediately precedes 9 Etz'nab 6 Ceh, the station for the first appearance of the Evening Star in the 1 Ahau 9 Kayab run of the Venus Tables in the Dresden Codex.

Inscriptions at several sites reveal that the Maya paid careful attention to the movements of the planets, Venus in particular. The first appearance of the Evening Star is repeatedly associated with historical episodes of war and with subsequent sacrificial rites. The god of the Evening Star is recorded both on Classic-period monuments and in the Grolier Codex as a skeletal Death God. This pot apparently does not record a historical first appearance of the Evening Star. Rather, the Calendar Round date is one day before a conventional station for the first appearance in the table that predicted the behavior of Venus. Thus, the text is not the historical response to an observed first appearance. Instead, it relates to the mythology that explained the meaning of Venus and its movements through the heavens. This kind of calendric reference and the mythology presented on the pot are the religious explanation for historical war and its resulting sacrificial rituals.

PLATE 116
Cylindrical vessel
Late Classic period, A.D. 600–800
Carved ceramic with traces of pigment
Diam. 17.5 x H. 16.8 cm
Kimbell Art Museum, Fort Worth

This cylindrical vase, perhaps the outstanding example of narrative relief in Maya pottery, is carved in a buff clay and depicts subtly modeled images of Chac-Xib-Chac and the Water-lily Jaguar. The Cauac Monster, who forms the altar, stands to the side, elegantly rendered with reptilian scales on its face and Cauac signs on its half-closed, window-shade eyelids. Its huge tongue drops to the ground from the roof of its gaping mouth.

The Water-lily Jaguar and Chac-Xib-Chac twist toward one another, each with one arm on the ground and the other extended from the shoulder. Chac-Xib-Chac, who holds his characteristic ax nonchalantly in his left hand, leans back, resting on his right hand and on a bifurcated scroll. The Water-lily Jaguar leans back on his left hand; one of his knees is raised, and his tail flicks upward between his legs. He is fully zoomorphic, complete with a rosette pattern of spots on his body, death-eye cuffs and collar and a smoking *ahau* sign on his head marking him as a lord. Chac-Xib-Chac wears the knot-string belt characteristic of this pair of gods and of the Paddlers, as well as a bar pectoral and an ornate head decoration, which is attached to his hair behind his shell diadem. The Twins have turned away from the Cauac Altar to lean toward each other, for their legs are pointed toward it. They appear to either be consulting before they continue their performances or congratulating themselves on their success in deceiving Xibalba's Lords of Death.

PLATE 117
Cylindrical vessel
Late Classic period, A.D. 600–800
Painted ceramic
H. 14 cm
Lent by The Metropolitan Museum of Art
The Michael C. Rockefeller Collection
Purchase, Nelson A. Rockefeller Gift, 1968

The master of codex-style painting who decorated this vase was particularly adept at using a vigorous line to produce energetic figural representation. His figures move with such energy, they leap off the groundline. Two of the three figures dance across the scene, kicking up a cloud of dust, which is represented by a thin wash in the lower half of the scene. A huge sacrificial altar, rendered as the reclining head of a Cauac Monster, is centered amid

the action. To its right, Chac-Xib-Chac dances, one foot raised high. He wears a death collar with an *akbal* vase and swings his ax in his right hand. In the other hand, he holds a flat oval object marked with a God C blood sign.

The Baby Jaguar lies on the Cauac Monster, flinging his arms and legs in the air as if to avoid the swing of Chac-Xib-Chac's ax. Behind him, God A cavorts with glee, one leg lifted and his hands extended in front of his body. He wears a death collar, and a long hank of black hair bound in cloth and knots hangs from his cracked skull. His swollen belly contrasts to the emaciated state of the rest of his body, whose ribs and vertebrae show through the skin. A huge backrack composed of a bone, death eyes, sacrificial cloth and a death-eye shield is tied to the rear of his loincloth. Most interesting, one leg simply emerges out of the double-line boundary around the forehead of the Cauac Altar.

A panting Kankin dog with spots marking his long ear, paws and tail sits behind the Baby Jaguar. As though he were waiting for his master's next order, he raises his forepaw. A grotesque insect flies above him. Its head is a skeletal *akbal* sign with a death eye attached, and its back has a carapace like that of a beetle. A large bulbous tail hangs below his belly and behind his hooked rear feet. The smoking cigar in his front hands reveals his identity as the firefly who helped the Hero Twins in the House of Darkness.

The text on this vessel commonly appears on codex-style vases, especially those that feature Chac-Xib-Chac and the Baby Jaguar. The Tzolkin day sign is unusual, but only the days Cauac, Kan, Muluc and Ix may occur on the seventh day of the month; Kan seems the most likely reading, but Muluc is also a possibility. The verb has one meaning, "to hold (or display)" God K. While the last three glyphs should name the subject, they do not correspond to any of the pictured actors. Furthermore, the same text appears with many different kinds of narrative scenes and thus apparently does not refer directly to the action pictured. Like the Primary Standard Sequence, this text must fulfill some other ritual function.

PLATE 118
Cylindrical vessel
Late Classic period, A.D. 600–900
Polychromed ceramic
Diam. 17.9 x H. 15.9 cm
Lent courtesy of The Art Museum, Princeton University

This cylindrical pot depicts the final defeat of the Lords of Xibalba by the Hero Twins. One of the Twins strains to pull God N from his shell. In his other hand, he holds the flint knife ready for the sacrificial cut. God N wears sectioned shell ornaments on his ears and a folded napkin headdress. His function as one of the patrons of writing is marked by the paintbrush that is thrust into his headband. A huge red blood-marked scroll, spurting from a wound already inflicted by the avenging Twin, emerges from the end of his shell. The Hero Twin wears a shell necklace and a segmented headband with cantilevered flowers. His body is painted a solid color with a light line left at the edges. His navel, rendered as a long flat shape above his loincloth, is placed off-center, which emphasizes the twisting of his body as he strains to pull God N within reach of his knife.

PLATE 119
West side of the sarcophagus (detail)
Temple of Inscriptions, Palenque, Chiapas, Mexico
Late Classic period, A.D. 684
Limestone
Photo by Merle Greene Robertson

This detail shows Lady Kanal-Ikal, Pacal's great-grandmother.

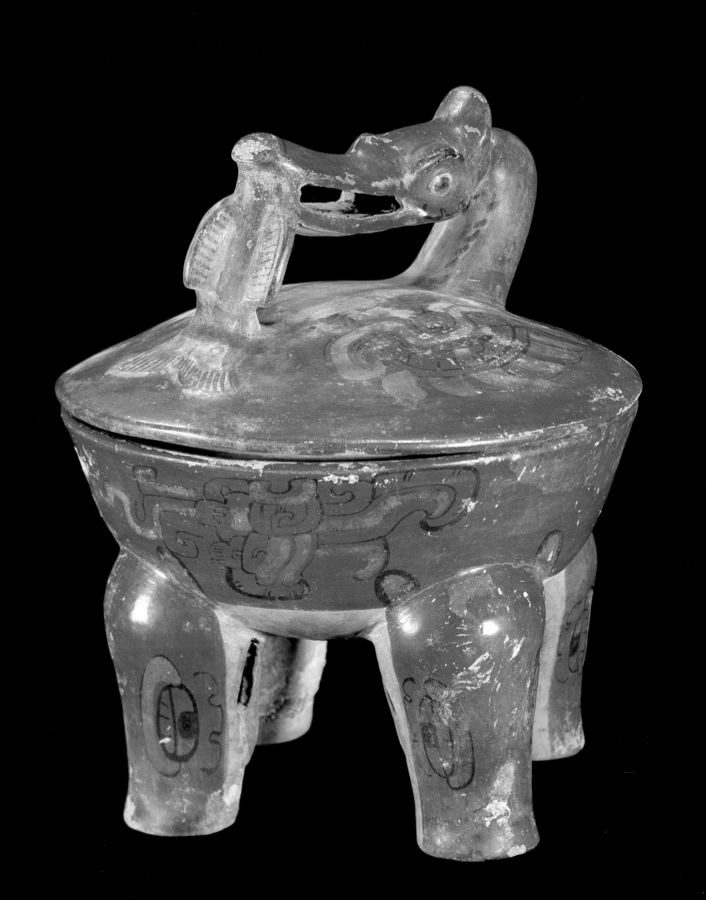

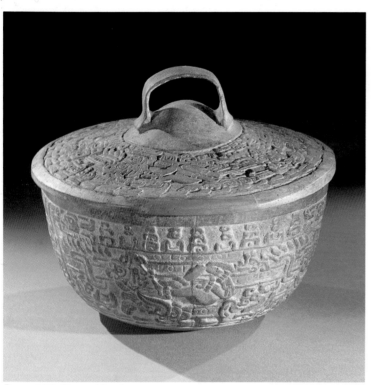

PLATE 106. Covered bowl

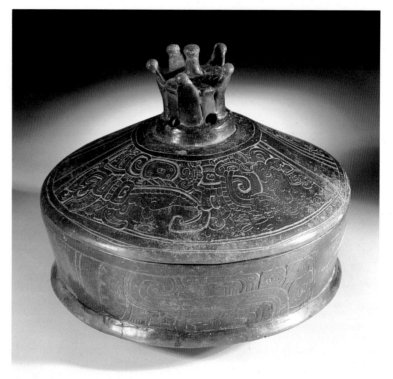

PLATE 108. Basal-flanged bowl

PLATE 107. Basal-flanged vessel

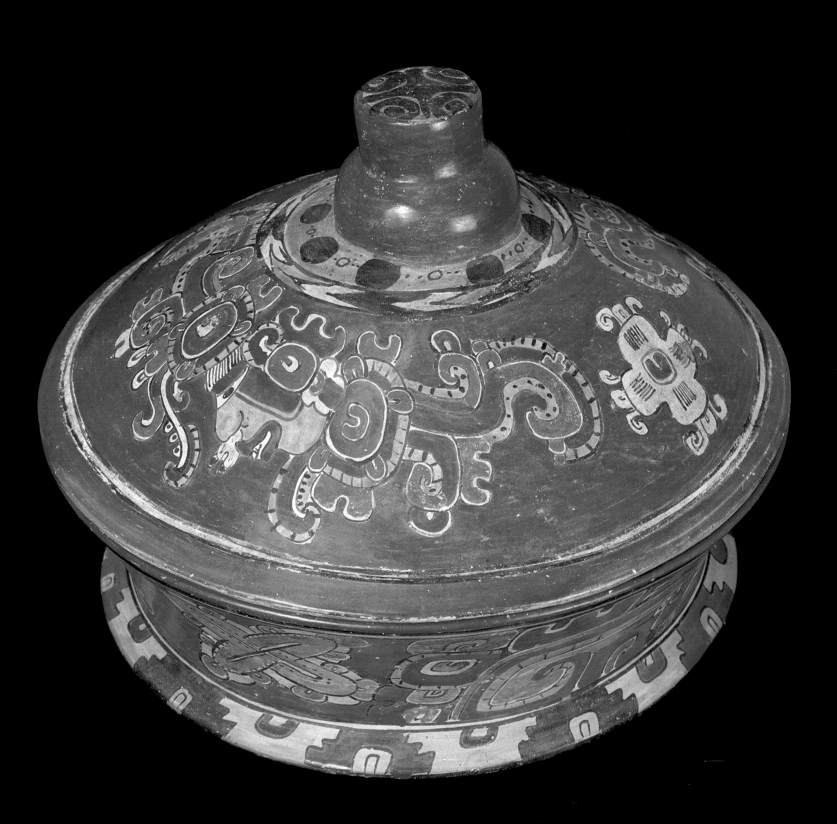

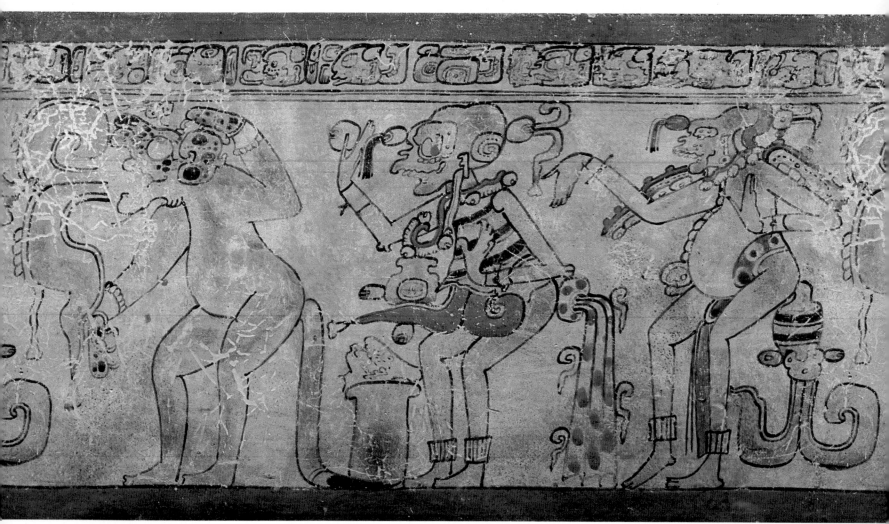

PLATE 109A. Rollout

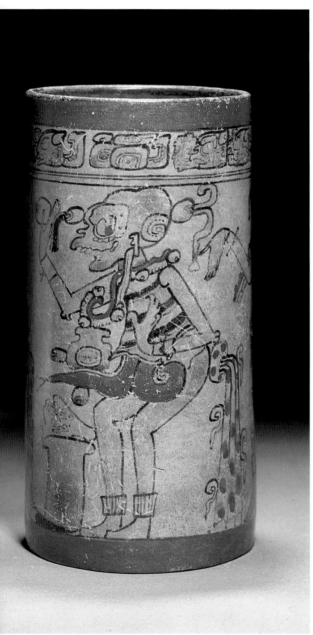

PLATE 109. Cylindrical vessel

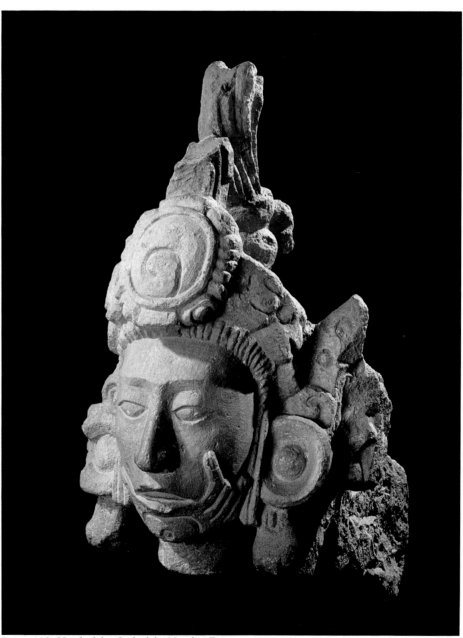

PLATE 110. Head of the God of the Number Zero

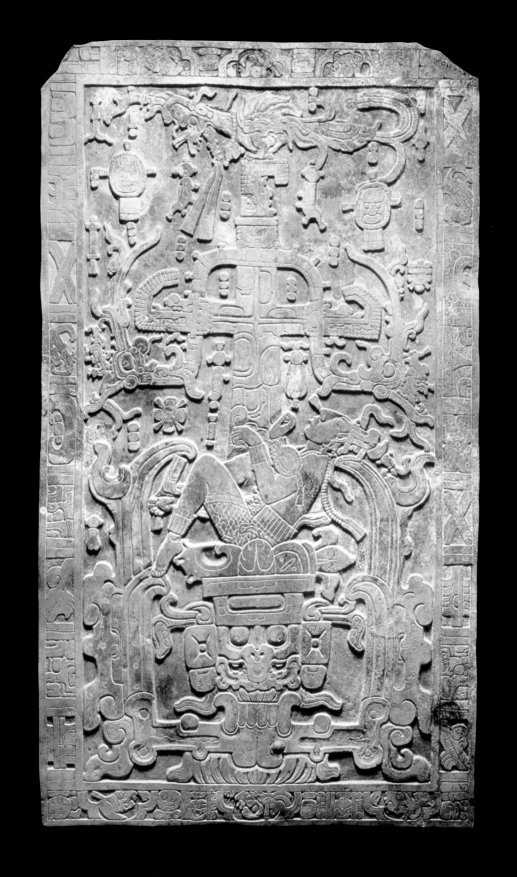

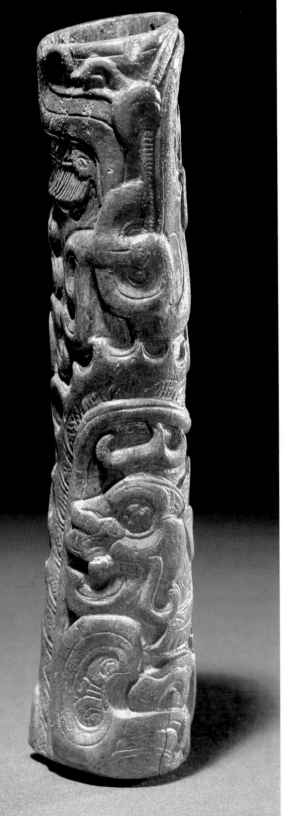

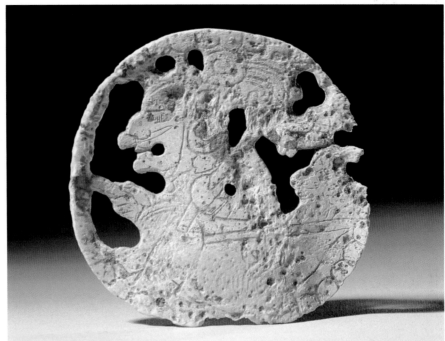

Plate 113. Shell medallion

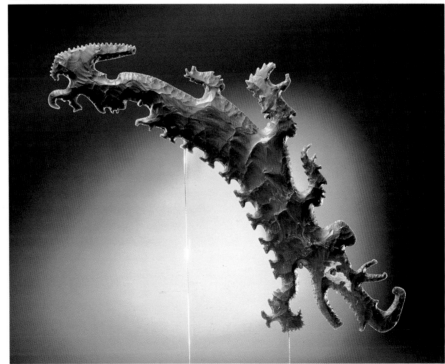

Plate 114. Eccentric flint

Plate 112. Bone handle

Plate 111. The Sarcophagus Lid (opposite)   DEATH AND THE JOURNEY THROUGH XIBALBA   295

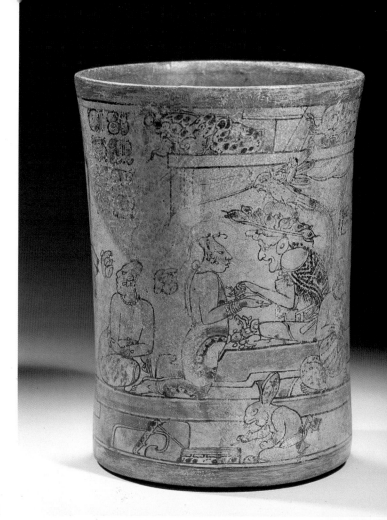

Plate 115. Cylindrical vessel

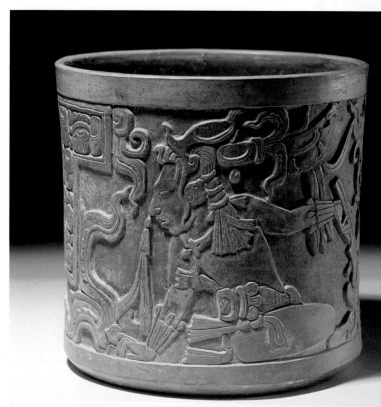

Plate 116. Cylindrical vessel

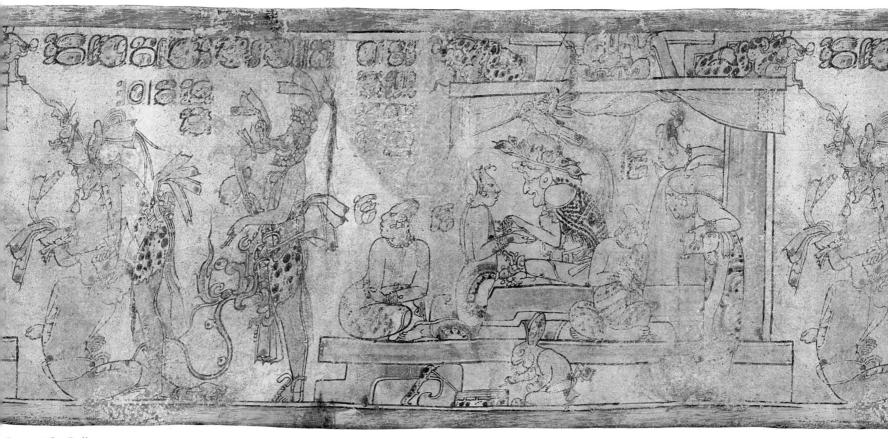

Plate 115a. Rollout

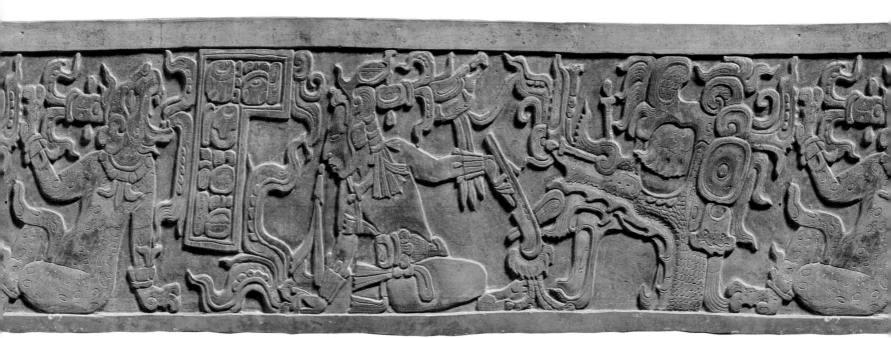

Plate 116a. Rollout

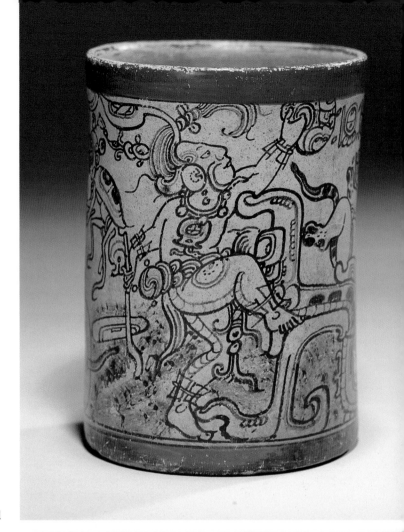

PLATE 117. Cylindrical vessel

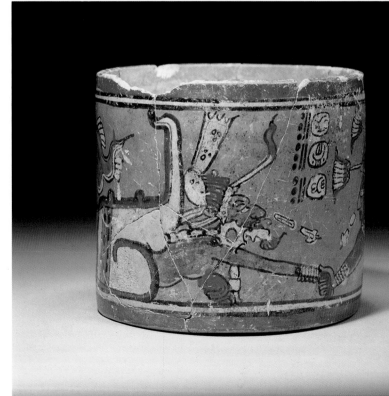

PLATE 118. Cylindrical vessel

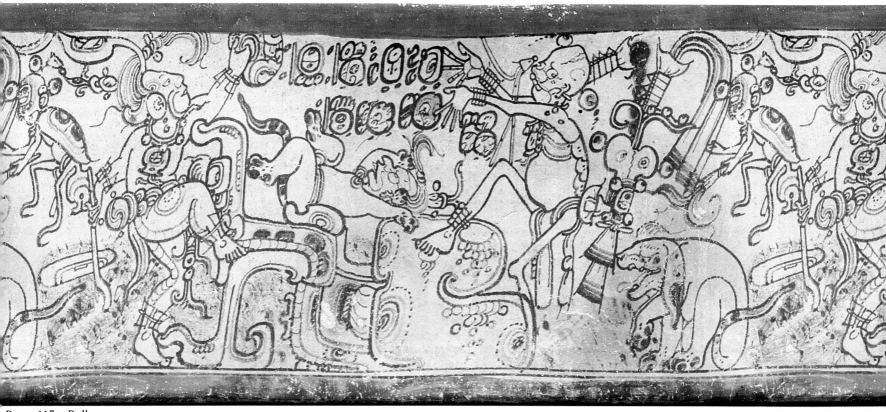

Plate 117a. Rollout

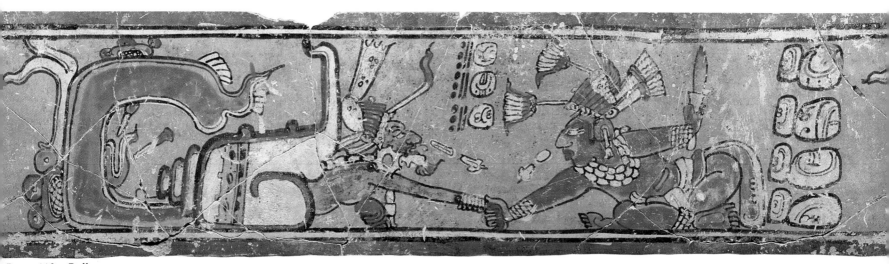

Plate 118a. Rollout

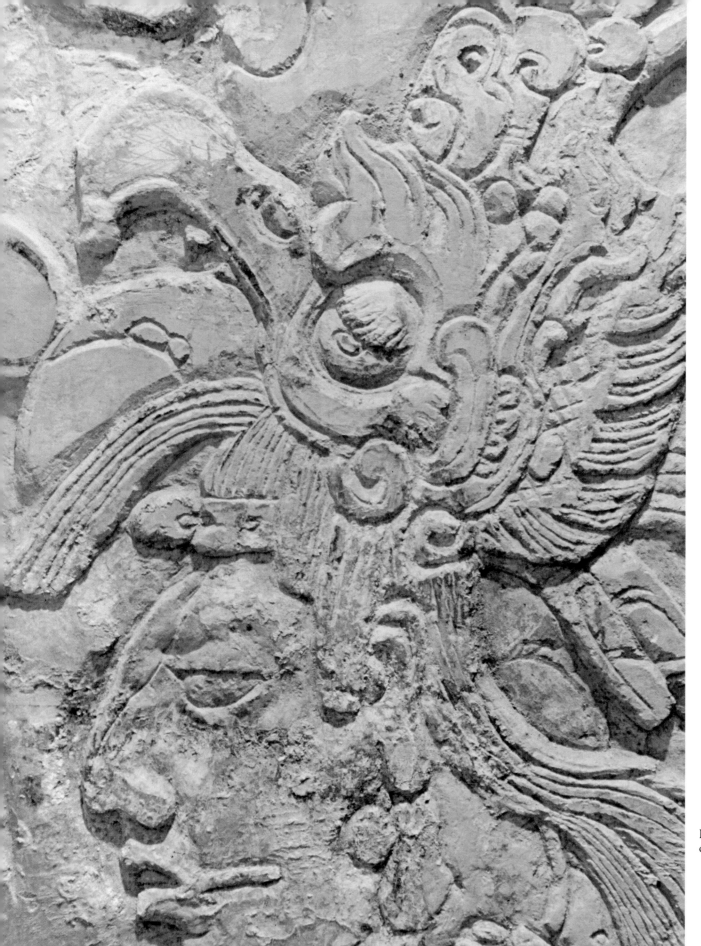

PLATE 119. Detail, west side
of the sarcophagus, Palenque

VIII

Kingship and the Maya Cosmos

For the Maya, the world was a complex and awesome place, alive with sacred power. This power was part of the landscape, of the fabric of space and time, of things both living and inanimate, and of the forces of nature—storms, wind, mist, smoke, rain, earth, sky and water. Sacred beings moved between the three levels of the cosmos: the Overworld which is the heavens, the Middleworld where humans live, and the Underworld or Xibalba, the source of disease and death. The king acted as a transformer through whom, in ritual acts, the unspeakable power of the supernatural passed into the lives of mortal men and their works. The person of the king was also sacred. His clothing reflected more than wealth and prestige: it was a symbolic array identifying rank, ritual context and the sacred person he manifested. Furthermore, supernatural power was focused in the objects manipulated by the king, which seemed to accrue sacred energy through their use in ritual.

The institution of Maya kingship was expressed in the metaphor of the cosmic vision. In its earliest manifestations, the king stood at the apex of pyramids with symbols that defined the movement of the sun and Venus across the backdrop of the sky. The king ensured that the heavens would rotate in perpetuity through the rituals of sacrifice and bloodletting. The gifts of blood served both to nourish and sustain the gods and to communicate with them. In this role, the king was a nourisher of the gods, of maize and of his people.

Ritual was apparently more than sequenced activity or the symbol of sacred interaction. On Dos Pilas Stela 25 (Fig. IV.3) the Maya themselves tell us that ritual, especially bloodletting, gave birth to the gods, bringing them into corporeal existence in human time and space. When dressed in the costumes of different gods, the king was more than just their symbolic stand-in. He was a sacred conduit, a vessel that gave flesh to the god by ritual action. He was more than just one god; he was a sacred being who could, through ritual, become them all.

Our journey into the world of the Maya will close with three extraordinary images, on two ceramic vessels and a conch shell trumpet, that unite ritual and the vision of the world that characterizes Maya society. The first, an incised vase in the collection of the American Museum of Natural History (Pl. 120), went long unnoticed, possibly because its complex imagery is very difficult to unravel. This image is not a narrative picture of humans enacting ritual, but rather the realization of the supernatural side of ritual. That is, the image shows what the ritual caused to happen. By invoking that happening, it transforms a lump of modeled clay, a simple container, into a tool of ritual power. It matters little that most people cannot read the fine, incised drawing because the encoded message is addressed to the gods and the forces called forth by ritual.[1]

The scene begins in a stepped depression that usually occurs as the forehead of the Cauac Monster (Pl. 120b). Here, it is presented as an independent, architectonic symbol of the door between the natural and supernatural worlds, as if the Cauac Monster personifies this symbol. Although at Palenque, Bonampak and elsewhere, maize and vegetation grows from the forehead depression, the Cauac Monster is identified fundamentally with stone and things stony. He is both the cave and the architectural opening into the interior of the temple. When the World Tree grows up through the temple to penetrate cosmic levels, it moves either through this stepped depression or another form of the gate—the Skeletal Maw, such as the one seen on Pacal's sarcophagus. Temple doors were articulated as the mouth of the Cauac Monster to identify them as a sacred locus. The entry doors of Structures 11 and 22 at Copan were both surrounded by huge architectural sculptures that transformed the doors into the mouths of monsters. The door to the inner chamber of Temple 22 had a second sculpture depicting the Celestial Monster arching over the dome of heaven, its body made of bloodscrolls, its two heads supported by Pauahtuns squatting over the skulls of the Underworld. As discussed in Chapter 2 (Figs. II.9, II.10, and Pl. 36b), the inner sanctum of Temple 11 was defined as the portal to the Underworld by huge skeletal monsters on the walls around its entrance. These two buildings at Copan, as well as the monster doors used in Chenes and Puuc buildings, were architectural manifestations of the stepped portal on this pot. In this image, the stepped form indicates that the supernatural gate is architectural.

On the American Museum of Natural History vessel (Pl. 120), the World Tree that grows from the upper level of the stepped opening bears three anthropomorphic beings who may represent the Palenque Triad. The Celestial Monster struggling up from the lowest step represents the rise of Venus. This upward movement is identified with the eastern side of the cycles of Venus and the sun, rather than the west and their setting as shown on the sarcophagus at Palenque.[2] The gaping mouth of the Celestial Monster emits a huge feathered Vision Serpent who loops around the circumference of the pot to meet the Tree on the other side. The moon, complete with the Moon Goddess and her rabbit, rises with the vision. An anthropomorphic god with a deer ear stands below and behind the head of the Vision Serpent, leaning over to avoid its passage and blowing on a conch shell trumpet to announce its arrival.

This remarkable image links the iconography of bloodletting and the vision quest to that of the journey after death. The architectonic Maw of the Underworld is here combined with the three primary symbols of the cosmos that have repeatedly occurred in the rituals of accession, bloodletting, war and death. The World Tree grows from the open Maw; the Cosmic Monster climbs out of it; and the vision rises from it. The imagery on this pot incorporates the symbolism seen on the facade of Cerros in fully realized form. This is not the vision that appears in scenes of the human act of the bloodletting ritual, as represented on Yaxchilan Lintel 24 (Pl. 62) and Lintel 25 (Pl. 63) and the Hauberg Stela (Pl. 66): Instead, this is the vision in the process of becoming manifest, a realization of what the Maya conceived to have occurred in ritual. This process is also defined by the image: the vision comes from Xibalba through the Underworld portal with the movement of Venus and the sun, who are personified as the Hero Twins of the Popol Vuh myth. The vision arrives with the moon riding on its back, because the moon is a symbol of the fundamental causal relationship between the vision ritual and the king, who was the prime giver of blood and, thus, central to maintaining order in the universe.

The conch shell trumpet used to announce the vision was a real object and several are extant. The magnificent Early Classic example from the Pearlman Collection (Pl. 121) personifies a deer god like the one who blows the trumpet on the American Museum of Natural History vase. A spicule on the broad end of the conch is used as the nose on the god's face, which is completed by incised eyes, mouth and face markings; the shell itself is his headdress. The conch is both the god and the trumpet he blows to announce the vision. Again, the imagery does not simply decorate the shell; it transforms the shell into a focus of power generated by ritual.

Divine counterparts to the human seekers of the vision are incised on the sides of the trumpet and named in its texts (Pl. 121a). Here they are the Hero Twins in their manifestations of the sun and moon.[3] Sitting at right angles to each other, one Twin holds the Vision Serpent, while the other sits on a throne before a moon sign. The vision emerges from inside the trumpet, as if it were the sound itself, but the inscription suggests that the origin of the vision is the Underworld. Each text refers to one of the Twins: the left text to the Twin with the Vision Serpent and the right one to the Moon Twin. Uc-Zip, the god who announces the vision and who is personified by the shell, begins the left text,[4] while God N, the Lord of Xibalba killed by the Hero Twin on the Princeton pot (Pl. 118), is named in the right text. Both texts include the supernatural location shown on the Huehuetenango pot (Pl. 72), thus confirming that the action takes place in the supernatural realm. The text adjacent to the Moon Twin records two bloodletting rites: in one, God N (Pauahtun) enacts the scattering rite, which gave birth to the gods on Dos Pilas Stela 25 (Fig. IV.3); in the other, Balam-U-Ahau, the Moon Twin, enacts a fish-in-hand vision rite. The transmission of the vision requires the active participation of Uc-Zip and Pauahtun, both denizens of Xibalba, and it bridges one world level to another.

Many of the events recorded in the journey after life were tied to dates of the heliacal risings of Venus, to stationary points of Jupiter, or to other similar astronomical events. From these images, we can infer that the Maya not only timed their ritual lives by the movement of planets and stars, they conceived of the sky as a living place filled with the movements of supernaturals and the ancestral dead. This concept of the universe is given its most eloquent and stunning voice in an image painted in codex-style on a funerary tripod plate (Pl. 122) by the master of the famous pot from Altar de Sacrificios in Guatemala. The outside of this large plate is defined as the primordial sea by a water band with floating water-lily pads and shell scrolls (Pl. 122a). On the interior, the cosmos spreads out in a splendid and dramatic realization (Pl. 122b). The framing border painted along the angled walls joins together the two halves of existence: in the lower border, the skeletal Maw of the Underworld encloses bloody water; in the upper half of the border, the Celestial Monster arches around the rim of the plate forming the dome of heaven.

The central scene on the plate is described in the text as the heliacal rising of Venus as the Evening Star (Pl. 122c). The bloody water of Xibalba generates a stream that becomes the black waters of the Middleworld (Pl. 122b). Under the water, Xibalbans and the dead go about their business, some hanging upside down. The Evening Star, here personified as Chac-Xib-Chac,[5] stands waist deep in the black waters. Holding his ax in one hand, he gazes at the blood spurting from the stump of his severed left hand. Although we do not know the meaning of this image, he may have lost it in his struggle to exit Xibalba, or cut it away himself as an act of self-sacrifice.

When Chac-Xib-Chac pops up through the waters into the Middleworld, he does not come alone—the World Tree grows from the top of his head. The Tree, with God C signs on its trunk, bifurcates and its branches are transformed into the bloody body of the Vision Serpent. The right branch continues upward to culminate in a personification head and a large single leaf. On the sarcophagus lid at Palenque (Pl. 111), the branches of the World Tree terminate in bloodletting bowls and personified blood streams; here, they become the Vision Serpent itself. The Water-lily Jaguar, twin brother of Chac-Xib-Chac, crouches high in the Tree, his arms spread, roaring at the Celestial Bird, who has been frightened away from his usual perch atop the Tree. The poor Bird is dripping blood from a wound inflicted by the Jaguar.

This single image (Pl. 122) encompasses the entire Maya cosmos and synthesizes all of the imagery that was integral to the lives and functions of kings. It explains the rationale behind accession, the role of bloodletting, the nature of the vision produced, the necessity of sacrifice, the inevitability of death and the possibility of renewal. The Celestial Monster and its journey above the world represent the heavens and the movement of the stars and planets; the Afterlife and the deadly world of Xibalba lie below the world. The waters of the earth float up from the bloody waters of the Underworld where the dead reside before apotheosis. The temporal action depicted is simply an astronomical event—the first appearance of the Evening Star—but also, on a deeper symbolic level, the rise of this star represented kingly activity, the cycle of human life and a source of social cohesion.

Venus, as Chac-Xib-Chac the Ax-wielder, rises from the sea holding an ax, having lost one hand to sacrifice. A king can become Chac-Xib-Chac through scattering and other sacrificial rites. Kan-Xul exited Xibalba as Chac-Xib-Chac; his name appears in kingly titles, and he is worn on a chain in the accession costume of kings. The rise of Chac-Xib-Chac through the waters generates the World Tree, and both rise through a door located in the temple. During his life, the king wears the tree across his loins, and he falls down its trunk at death. The sap that flows through the tree is blood.

On this vessel, the Tree is transformed into the Vision Serpent brought forth through the bloodletting with which the king fertilizes the earth.

To the Maya, this plate held a symbolic depiction of the fundamental causal forces of the universe, exactly as the equation $E = mc^2$ symbolically represents our understanding of the physical forces that structure our universe.[6] Today, the appearance of Venus is a simple event explained by orbital mechanics and physical law. For the Maya, it was neither mechanical nor simple in meaning. Venus was personified as a living being, just as the sky, the earth and the gateway to Xibalba were alive. The workings of society, the actions of the king, the behavior of people of all ranks were irrevocably linked to the movements and activities of these living entities. The king and ritual action were the means by which humans interacted with nature to maintain and change this living world. The definition of the human community in all of its manifestations—from the role of the nobility to the maintenance of agricultural productions—were rationally explained in a living cosmos that is dramatically described in this single, powerful image.

At a recent conference in Jerusalem, Claude Lévi-Strauss spoke of the art produced by societies like the Maya as encoding their beliefs about the fundamental structure of reality and of the universe. He made the point that some of us may spend our lives trying to decipher such art, only to find when we are successful that their messages were not intended for us. His observations are true about the Maya. Indeed, we may feel a profound sense of relief that some of the messages we have examined are not directed at us. Nevertheless, those messages also speak eloquently of a world now lost, rich with an internal logic and a science of its own. The living Maya world was filled with sanctity, power and beauty. Blood was a fundamental substance and most valuable commodity in Maya life; sacrifice held society together as a cohesive whole and gave meaning to individual lives. Genealogy and descent were the basis of social order.

To the materialists who work with potsherds, subsistence practices, lithic technology and settlement patterns, the Maya can only be known through the remains left scattered through their landscape. To them, the Maya mental life and view of the world, the Maya conception of what man is and where he fits in the greater universe, are lost to the obscurity of prehistory. But the dead speak through their art and architecture: Their material culture was encoded with information about the nature of the world and the history of man. Although these messages were never intended for us, they speak across the centuries; once again we can utter the names of their kings and remember their actions. We do not share their beliefs, but we can perceive what they believed. And by doing so, we can add their accomplishments and their perceptions to the human inheritance that we pass on to our children and our children's children.

NOTES

1. Addressing messages to unseen and sacred audiences is still practiced today among those Maya who follow a traditional way of life. Gene Stuart, in *The Mysterious Maya* (Washington, D.C.: National Geographic Society, 1977), p. 177, reported a conversation with Chip Morris, who has spent many years studying modern Tzotzil weaving from the Highlands in the state of Chiapas, Mexico. The following description is of a twenty-year-old *huipil* from the village of Magdelanas:

Symbols on the front and back explain the weaver's position in her community and the cosmos. The sleeves show the relationship of such important figures as the rain god and the earth lord to the fertility of the land. [Morris said of the *huipil*:] "The weaver has created a *huipil* which describes the whole universe in a way so subtle that even fellow weavers won't notice, but so repetitious that the gods cannot help but see. She has described the complex relationship of time and space, and placed the gods of fertility in positions of power in order that all life may flourish. Wearing this *huipil* she becomes one of the daughters of the rain god; fearful of lightning, yet praying for rain."

The subtle complexity of the woven design of this modern weaver has the same purpose as the subtle complexity of the drawing on the pot from the American Museum of Natural History. Neither design was meant to be understood in one seeing: not only are the compositions complex, but only a part can ever be seen at one time. The message of the art is directed at the sacred realm and to gods who are not limited by the clouded vision of human beings. Both artworks effect ritual magic for the people who use them. The Tzotzil becomes a prayer for rain; the Classic Maya transformed a mundane pot into a vessel to hold a god or an ancestor whom he was calling in the vision quest.

2. Pacal falls atop the Quadripartite Monster in a metaphor associated with the setting of the sun. In its most typical form, however, the Quadripartite Monster is attached to the rear of the crocodilian Celestial Monster as it follows its daily path of movement across the sky (Fig. 28). The Palenque image can be understood, therefore, as a view of the rear of the Celestial Monster at the moment when the crocodilian head and body are already disappearing below ground. The image from this pot is the opposite: the front crocodilian head of the Celestial Monster is just coming out of the portal; the rest of its body and the Quadripartite God are still below ground.

3. The Popol Vuh associates the Hero Twins with the sun and the moon, but J. Eric S. Thompson (*Maya History and Religion* [Norman: University of Oklahoma Press, 1970], pp. 234, 368) argues that in Maya mythology the moon is overwhelmingly female. Floyd Lounsbury ("The Identities of the Mythological Figures in the 'Cross Group,' " in *Fourth Palenque Round Table*, gen. ed. Merle Greene Robertson, vol. ed. Virginia Fields [San Francisco: Pre-Columbian Art Research Institute, forthcoming]) postulates that the Hero Twins correspond to GI and GIII of the Palenque Triad and argues for a Classic identification of GI-Hunahpu with Venus and GIII-Xbalanque with the sun. Dennis Tedlock (*Popol Vuh: The Definitive Edition of the Mayan Book of the Dawn of Life and the Glories of Gods and Kings* [New York: Simon and Schuster, 1985], pp. 296–297) argues the unlikelihood that each celestial object was assigned to one god or that each god was associated with a single celestial phenomenon. He points out that among the modern Quiche, the full moon is male and the nocturnal equivalent of the sun, while all other phases are female. He suggests that Xbalanque may have been the Moon as the nighttime Sun and that he became visible on earth once a month as the full moon.

The Twin manifestations in Classic imagery are even more complicated: the GI/GIII, Chac-Xib-Chac/Jaguar and Headband pairs can all be associated with the Hero Twins, but they also appear with contradictory astronomical associations. GI is, for example, born on 9 Ik, the birthday associated with Venus throughout Mesoamerica, yet he appears at Quirigua as the number 4, normally personified by the Sun God. The Hun-Ahau Headband Twin appears as the god of the Morning Star on page 50 of the Dresden Codex, yet he can also appear as the number 4. The cruller-eyed Jaguar God of the Underworld often appears with *kin*, "sun," on his cheek, but he also appears as the face on the moon in Glyph C of the Lunar Series. A handsome young male with a jaguar ear can also appear in this slot. The Maya were not consistent in their presentation of the Twins, using a variety of distinct but interrelated manifestations that perhaps corresponded to celestial bodies or to different phases of the same planetary cycle. The pair on this conch trumpet (Pl. 121) are surely the Twins as the Sun and the Moon. The lower figure wears the Jester God head ornament expected of the Headband Twins, the most widely recognized manifestation of the Hero Twins. Here, he is named 7-Ahau, in contrast to his name 1-Ahau in the Headband Twins manifestion. The other figure sits in a moon sign, but he is anatomically male. His name is written Balam-U-Xib or Balam-U-Ahau, "Jaguar Moon Lord." He is the young jaguar-eared lord who appears in Glyph C of the Lunar Series and is the male manifestation of the Moon.

4. This trumpet god seems to be the Classic-period prototype of God Y, a rarely shown deity who appears on page 13, register c, figure 1, of the Dresden Codex. His characteristic features are half-moon-shaped facial markings and a deer antler attached to the top of his head. James Fox and John Justeson have recently deciphered the name of this god as Uc-Zip ("Polyvalence in Mayan Hieroglyphic Writing," in *Phoneticism in Mayan Hieroglyphic Writing*, edited by John S. Justeson and Lyle Campbell [Albany: Institute of Mesoamerican Studies, State University of New York at Albany, 1977], p. 39). A very similar god appears frequently on Maya pottery of the Classic period. This god has the same deer features and facial markings, but he always carries a conch shell trumpet and often is shown in the mouth of a Vision Serpent.

The god seen on the pot in Plate 120 clearly has deer features; the god on this conch trumpet has the facial half-moon shapes that denote Uc-Zip and the Classic deer-man god. All of these images appear to represent the same entity, the god Uc-Zip, who was the deity of the conch shell trumpet and the announcer of oncoming visions.

5. David Stuart (personal communication, 1984) was the first scholar to recognize that the god shown on this plate is named Chac-Xib-Chac and has name glyphs identical to those used in the Dresden Codex, that the event is the same as the one recording "heliacal rising" for 9.11.0.0.0 on the middle panel of the Temple of Inscriptions at Palenque and that the "black cenote" and "black water" glyphs refer to the black water image below.

6. For us, the formula $E = mc^2$ is a mental construction of symbols that allow us to manipulate the world. Using such constructs in what we call science, we build in our minds models of reality; we test them, push them, adapt them, alter them as we investigate our world and think about cosmic matters. Most of us do not understand what the symbols of that formula stand for, except for their equivalent words, another symbol system. If we had to manipulate the matter of the world actively by using that symbolic expression as our guide, we would be helpless; yet it is basic to our own mythology. The imagery on this plate served exactly the same function for the Maya; it is a symbolic model of reality, which they tested, adapted, altered as they experienced their world. Their mental constructs of reality served them efficiently and eloquently for a thousand years; may we survive so long with ours.

Plate 120
Cylindrical vessel
Late Classic period, A.D. 550–800
Incised ceramic
Diam. 15.2 x H. 15.5 cm
Department of Anthropology, American Museum of
Natural History, New York

This cylinder is finely incised with a complex
cosmic scene that was cut into the clay at the
leather-hard stage, and highlighted by a subtle
tonal contrast between the positive shapes and the
background field. This image was never designed to
be read, especially from any distance, since it is too
complex to understand in a single viewing. Neither
was it intended to be narrative or instructive;
rather, the image functions to transform an ordinary container into an object that focuses power
through ritual. It is addressed not to a human user,
but to the gods called forth in ritual.

This extraordinary image begins with a
stepped portal that terminates on both sides with a
personified *akbal* "darkness" glyph. It represents
both an architectural opening and the forehead
depression of the Cauac Monster; it is the cave
entrance to Xibalba, and the Maw of the Underworld. On the upper right step grows a tree, certainly
the World Tree at the center of the universe. Three
anthropomorphic beings climb up it into our world.
We are not sure of their identities, but their Roman
noses, square eyes, and body forms put them within
the complex of gods that includes GI, GIII, the Sun
God and the Headband Twins, whom they may
represent as generic types. Since the Twins are usually represented in pairs, the presence of three
climbers may refer to the gods of the Palenque
Triad.

The front head of the Celestial Monster,
complete with forearm but lacking his deer ear, is
climbing onto the bottom step. His mouth gapes
open to spit out a huge Vision Serpent. The Serpent undulates outward, its body looping back on
itself four times, entirely encircling the pot. Stop-
ping just behind the World Tree, it belches out its
vision in the form of a square-nosed dragon. The
body of the Serpent is marked with jade disks, mirror signs and personification heads. A personification wing is attached to its eyebrow; an *akbal* sign is
inscribed on its cheek; and a bird emerges from the
corner of its mouth, as on the Acasacuastlan Pot
(Pl. 73b). The three loops of the feathered body
contain god heads: two appear to be personification
heads and the third is a long-lipped zoomorph with
death collar and *akbal* glyph. Most interestingly, the
Serpent's beard is personified as though to emphasize that the Vision Serpent is an icon of power.

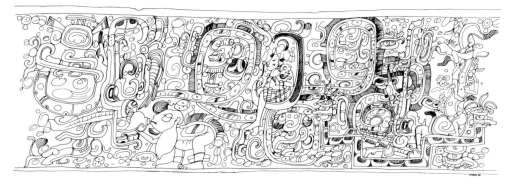

Plate 120a

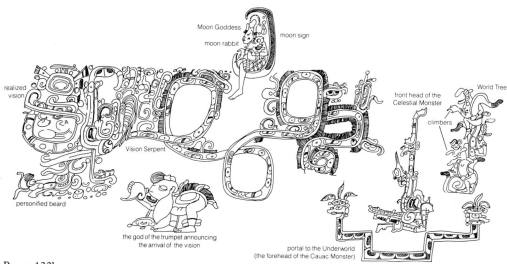

Plate 120b

Sandwiched between two of the body
loops is a moon sign. Inside sits the Moon Goddess
holding a rabbit, the one the Maya saw in the dark
areas of the moon. Under and behind the head of
the Vision Serpent is a deer-eared anthropomorph
who bends under the looping trajectory of the Serpent as it surges out of the Underworld. His back is
marked with a mirror sign and a feather fan runs
from shoulders to rump. He wears a trilobed shell
pectoral and blows mightily on a conch shell to
announce the arrival of the Vision Serpent.

Plate 121
Conch shell trumpet
Early Classic period, A.D. 300–500
Shell
H. 21.5 cm
Edwin Pearlman, M.D., Norfolk, Virginia

This conch shell, one of the masterpieces of Maya
art, is a trumpet like that blown by the deer god in
the vessel from the American Museum of Natural
History (Pl. 120) to announce the arrival of the Vision Serpent. The tip of the spire has been cut off to
form a mouthpiece and holes are drilled in the spire
portion to produce different notes. This trumpet,
marked with the imagery of its cosmic function,
communicates on two perceptual levels. The three-
dimensional form of the shell, when inverted with
the spire down, reveals the head and headdress of a

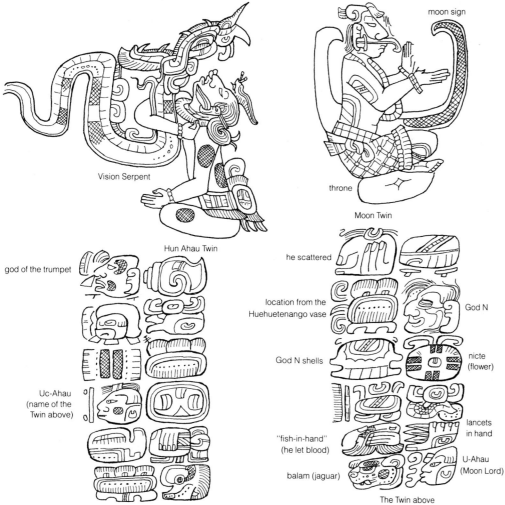

Vision Serpent

Hun Ahau Twin

god of the trumpet

Uc-Ahau
(name of the
Twin above)

moon sign

throne

Moon Twin

he scattered

location from the
Huehuetenango vase

God N shells

"fish-in-hand"
(he let blood)

balam (jaguar)

God N

nicte
(flower)

lancets
in hand

U-Ahau
(Moon Lord)

The Twin above

god whose features are defined with an incised line; oriented in the other direction, line drawings of two figures and texts wrap around the shell surface.

The face of the god was teased out of the spiral end of the conch with one spicule serving as the nose and a finger hole as an eye. Cinnabar-enhanced lines complete the remaining facial features. The distinguishing marks of this god are the half-moon shapes at the corners of his eyes and mouth, crosshatched to be understood as dark or black. His eyes are also surrounded by line circles and the incised one is human in form. The lower edge of his shell headdress is separated from his face by a wide, crosshatched line that runs from ear to ear. Triangles overlap this line and hang from the septum of his nose. His open mouth is filled with flat human teeth and his chin is bearded.

The glyphic names of this god—his portrait head and a conch shell—are the first two glyphs in the left text. He is not God N, whom we would expect to be associated with a shell; rather he appears to be a rare god, associated with the trumpet itself. Identified as God Y in the Codices, this god appears on Classic pottery with deer features and the same facial pattern. He is sometimes shown emerging from the mouth of the Chicchan Serpent Monster blowing his trumpet, and he appears in forms both young and aged. He is Uc-Zip, a god associated with hunting in the Postclassic period, and, perhaps, the god of the conch trumpet.

The incised drawings depict two figures, one adjacent to the text and the other below them. The lower figure is a young male wearing a Jester God attached directly to his forehead without using

a headband; his hair loops behind his head. He wears bloodletting paper in his ear, a woven collar around his neck, and a wide belt with an *akbal* sign attached to the rear. He sits on a throne and, in his arms, he holds a rearing Vision Serpent which emerges from the inside of the shell. His body markings are large crosshatched dots, identifying him as Hun-Ahau of the Headband Twins.

The upper figure also sits on a throne with his hands outstretched encircling a finger hole before the sweeping U-shape of the moon sign. His kilt is the net overskirt usually worn by women, but also worn by males undergoing the bloodletting rite. It is fringed and cut to a short length more often worn by men than women. His body is marked with mirror "brightness" signs and his hair is cut short. He wears a long beaded necklace, a bell-shaped ear plug, and a downturned half-mask that seems to be associated with moon imagery. Most importantly, the chest is bare and there are no signs of breasts. The presence of the moon sign would normally identify this figure as the Moon Goddess, but the anatomy and the adjacent inscription suggest the figure is male and one of the Hero Twins, since in the Popol Vuh one of the Hero Twins becomes the moon.

THE INSCRIPTION

The inscription on this conch shell has eluded decipherment for many years, but the identity of the actors can now be determined. The left text, the more difficult of the two, begins with the portrait glyphs of Uc-Zip, the god whose head is the trumpet itself. The next three glyphs are not understood, but the glyph at B3 is the supernatural location recorded in the cartouches on the Huehuetenango Pot. A4 appears to name the fellow who holds the Vision Serpent with the number 7 and his portrait head. He is apparently 7-Ahau. A6 is again the supernatural location.

The right text begins with "scattering" and a preposition (*ta* "in," "on," "from") followed again by the supernatural location. The actor is named as God N with an aged human head, a turtle shell and the *nicte* flower glyph. The next two glyphs are not deciphered, but C5 begins a new sentence with "fish-in-hand" bloodletting and a hand holding three lancets. The second actor is named in the last two glyphs which contain the signs for a jaguar head (*balam*), the sound *u*, and *xib* "young man." *U* is the word for "moon," thus giving the name *Balam-U-Xib* or *Balam-U-Ahau*, "Jaguar Moon Lord."

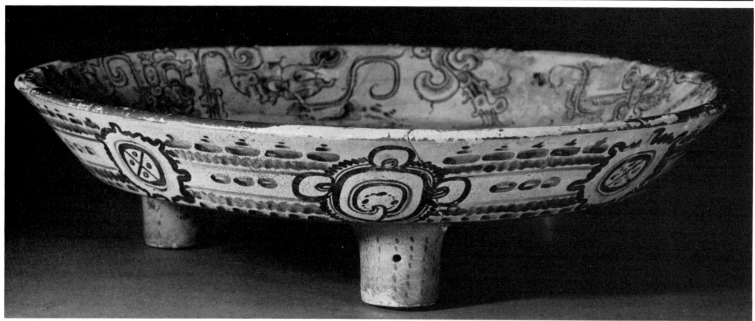

PLATE 122a

PLATE 122
Tripod plate
Late Classic period, A.D. 600–800
Polychromed ceramic
Diam. ca. 31 cm
Private collection

This shallow, tripod plate is a self-contained symbolic representation of all the imagery of Maya cosmos and ritual interaction. Painted in the codex-style, the outside of the plate is identified as the surface of the watery Underworld by a water band with water-lily pads and water shells floating along it. The interior surface is divided into two pictorial fields: the imagery on the walls establishes the framework of the narrative action that is shown on the bottom plane. This surrounding frame is itself divided into two opposing domains. Below, the rear head of the Vision Serpent sits in the center with personified water-lilies and blood streams growing from the top of his head. The water-lilies are contained on both sides by skeletal dragons like those on the sarcophagus lid at Palenque (Pl. 111c). The bottom of the frame is, then, the Maw of the Underworld in which the bloody water of Xibalba floats.

The top of the frame constitutes the other half of the circle: the heavens represented by the Celestial Monster. On the right, the front

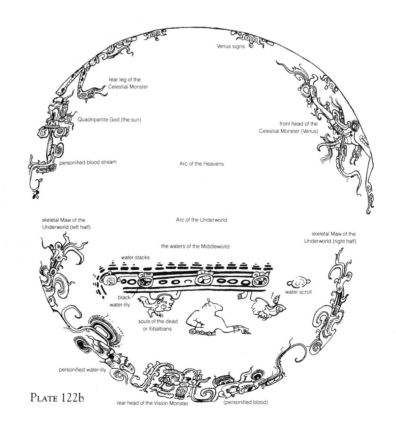

PLATE 122b

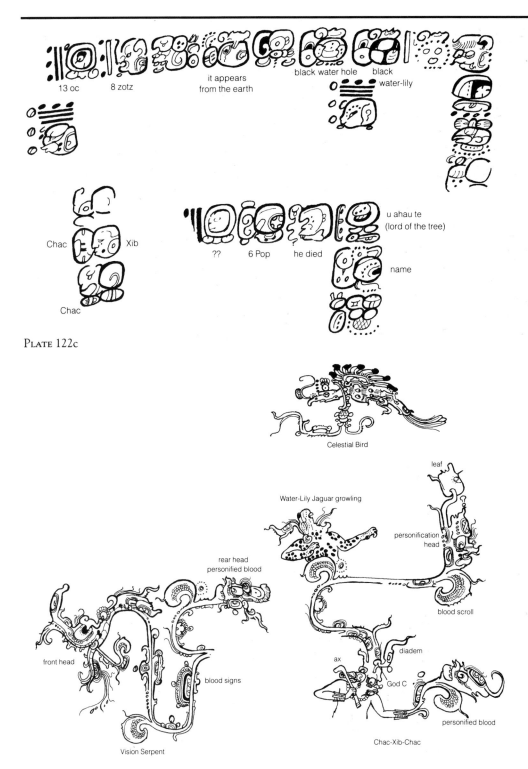

13 oc 8 zotz

it appears
from the earth

black water hole   black
water-lily

Chac   Xib

Chac

PLATE 122c

u ahau te
(lord of the tree)

??   6 Pop   he died

name

Celestial Bird

leaf

Water-Lily Jaguar growling

personification
head

rear head
personified blood

blood scroll

front head

blood signs

ax

diadem

God C

personified blood

Vision Serpent

Chac-Xib-Chac

crocodilian head falls into the scene from the red rim. His mouth is open and his tongue is personified with a serpent eye and teeth. His eyelid is a Venus sign and other additional Venus signs hang from his body defined by the red rim, which arcs around the plate to the rump of the Monster on the opposite side. The legs are in motion and crocodilian in form; a personified Imix-Water-lily glyph is attached to his elbow; the Quadripartite Monster hangs from his rump, head down and facing outward. A personified blood stream emerges from the stingray spine in the center of its *kin*-bowl forehead.

The scene encompasses the Celestial Monster and the domain of heaven in the upper arch, and the blood and water standing in the open Maw of the Underworld in the lower arch. The action occurs in the Middleworld in a lake of black water, complete with water stacks and scrolls, that rises from the Underworld water. It is marked by the same water-lily *uinal* sign that occurs in the water register on Tablet 14 (Fig. VII.2a). Under the water are three figures, two inverted and one right side up. A leaf sign, a reference to the World Tree, identifies the inverted figure on the right as an ancestor. The other two may also be ancestors or perhaps Xibalbans living under the waters of the earth.

Chac-Xib-Chac stands waist deep in the water holding an ax in one hand. Blood spurts from the stump of his amputated left hand. He wears the appropriate shell earflare and diadem, but the top of his head merges into the image of a fantastic tree. God C is on its base, marking it as the great World Tree on Pacal's sarcophagus (Pl. 111c). The trunk curves to the left, then forks into two branches. The right branch leads through two zoomorphic heads to culminate in a leaf at its summit, the same leaf worn by Chan-Bahlum on Tablet 14 (Fig. VII.2a) and held by Pacal on the Dumbarton Oaks Tablet (Fig. VII.3). The fork transforms into a Vision Serpent with the bulbous-nosed serpent head at the end of the left branch and the God C personified blood head at the midpoint of the right branch. Blood signs and blood scrolls are attached to the body at several points. As at Palenque, the trunk of the tree is God C and the branches of the tree are blood and the vision.

Normally the Celestial Bird sits in the Tree, but in this scene Chac-Xib-Chac's twin, the Water-lily Jaguar, has climbed the Tree after the Bird, who hovers above him in panicked flight. The Jaguar gazes up from his branch, roaring his frustrations. The Bird, apparently wounded by the Jaguar, bleeds from a gaping wound in his breast.

The Inscription

A long horizontal text in the upper center of the image is the central event shown. It begins with a date 13 Oc 8 Zotz', which is recorded as the day of the first appearance of the Evening Star in the 8 Ahau 13 Mac run of the Venus Tables in the Dresden Codex. The verb is an earth sign splitting open to emit scrolls from the cleft. A blood sign lies along the left edge of the glyph. This verb is used in the middle panel of the Temple of Inscriptions at Palenque to record the first appearance of the Evening Star on the katun ending 9.11.0.0.0, or October 14, A.D. 652. Since the date and the event correspond, the image records the Maya conception of what occurs when Venus as Evening Star rises from the Underworld at its first appearance.

A glyph consisting of the sign used in the Dresden Codex to record a cenote, or sinkhole, and other bodies of water follows the verb. Here it is preceded by a sign for the color black. In the scene, Chac-Xib-Chac rises from a body of water painted in a black line. The next glyph, "black water-lily uinal," is written on the black water band below. The text matches the action portrayed: Venus rises from black water. The remaining five glyphs of the text are not deciphered, but they may name the actors.

The small vertical text positioned near the head of the shell-eared ax-wielder names him as Chac-Xib-Chac, the name that is used for God B in the Dresden Codex and documented in colonial sources. In Postclassic cosmology, there were four Chacs assigned to the four directions. The chief among them was Chac-Xib-Chac, the Red Chac of the East. The other three Chacs have not yet been identified with specific Classic period images, but the shell-eared ax-wielder should be equated only with Chac-Xib-Chac, not with all Chacs. Most importantly, the date and event on this pot associate the Classic Chac-Xib-Chac with Venus as Evening Star, reinforcing his probable identification as GI of the Palenque Triad.

A third text is located near the right edge of the scene. It has an eroded date followed by a death glyph, a phonetic spelling *u ahau* "the lord of," a name, and possibly an Emblem Glyph. This text is not completely deciphered, but it appears to link the mythological event to an historical one, perhaps to the death of the lord for whom the plate was made.

PLATE 121. Conch shell trumpet

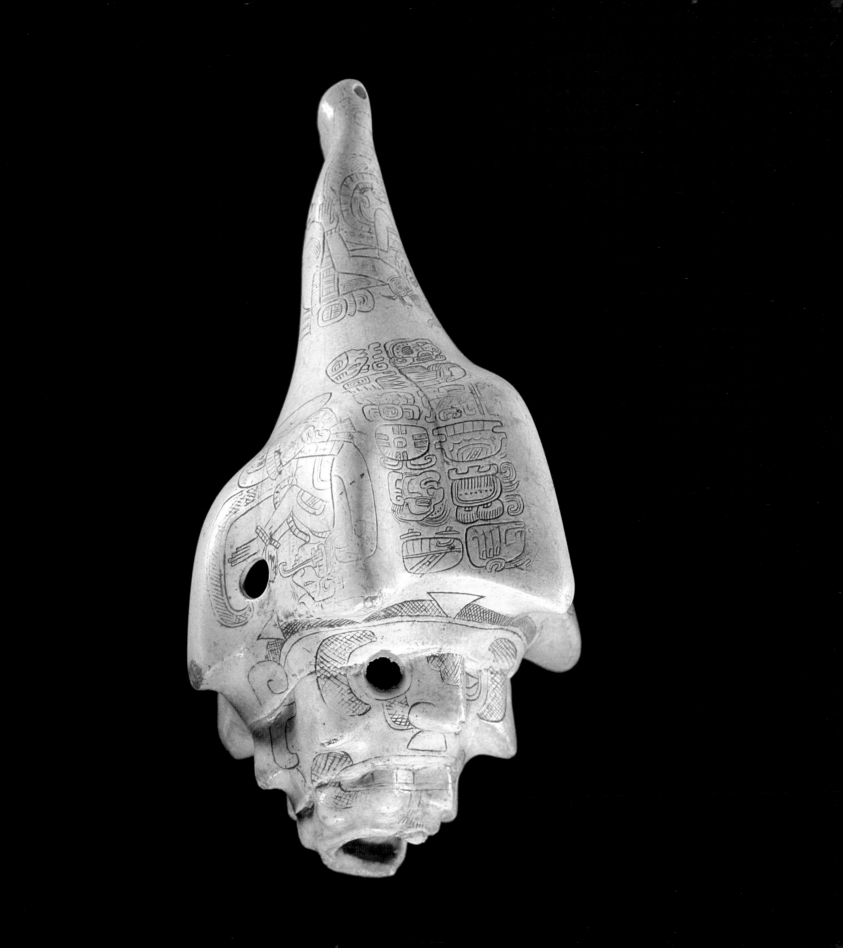

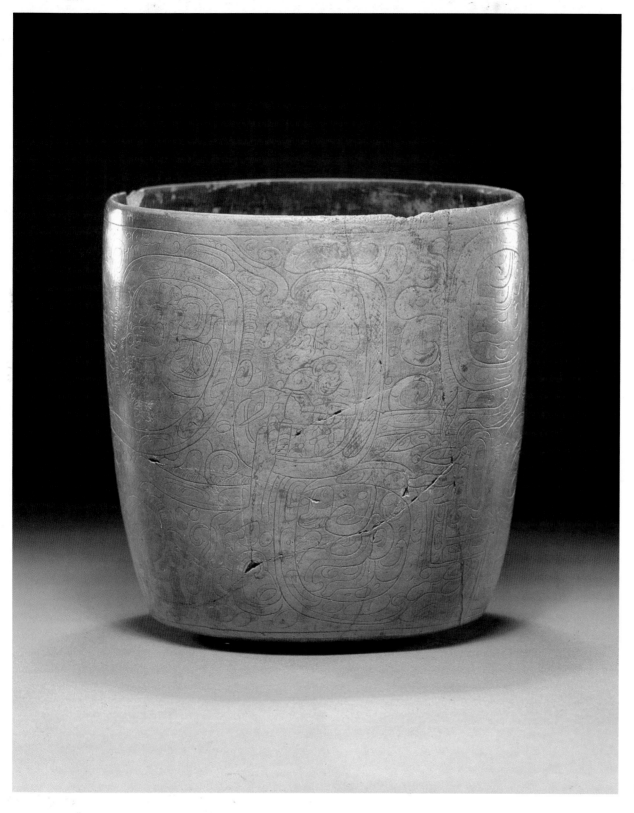

Plate 120. Cylindrical vessel

Plate 122. Tripod Plate

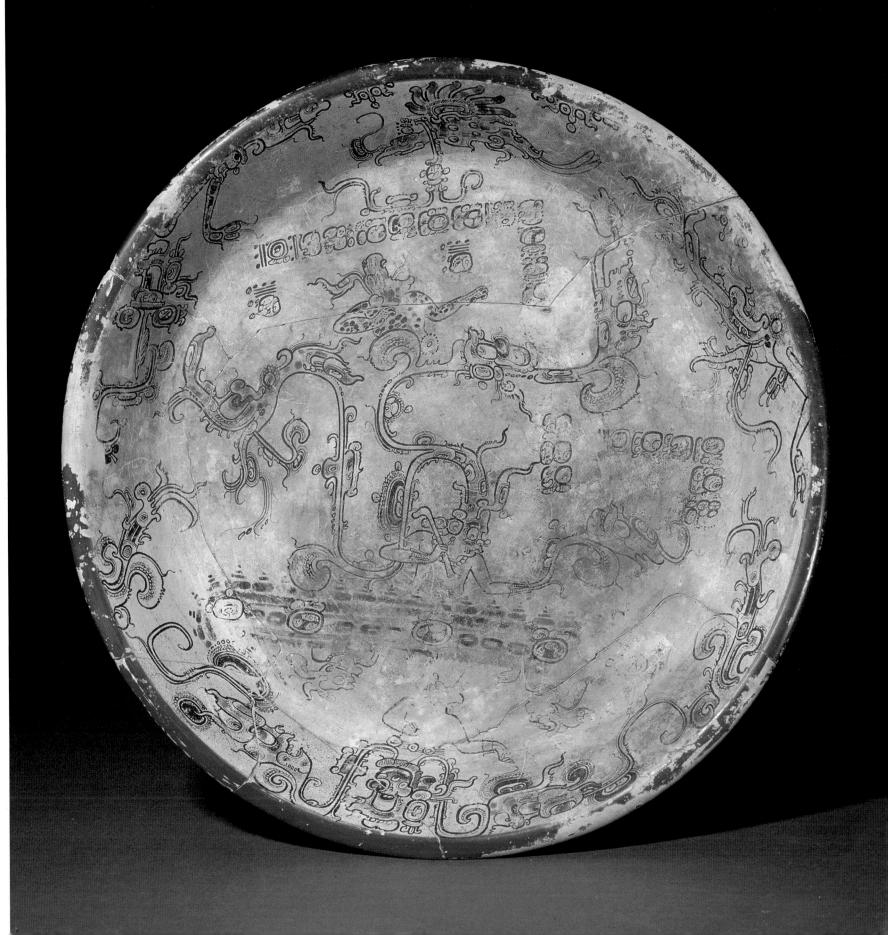

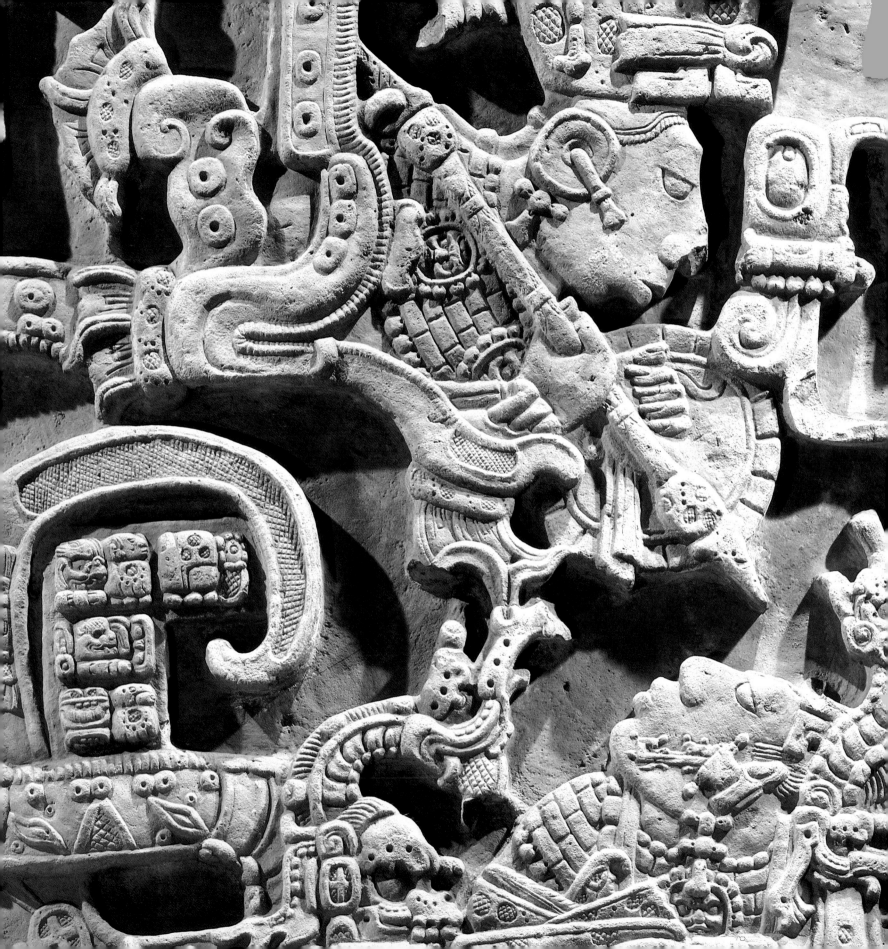

THE MAYA CALENDAR

THE CLASSIC MAYA EMBEDDED THEIR HISTORY IN A FRAMEWORK OF TIME THAT THEY DIVIDED into an overlapping set of cycles, each different in duration and reference. The prominence of calendric material in Maya inscriptions was initially taken as evidence of an obsessive fascination with time itself, but this assessment is no more true of the Maya than it is of contemporary man. Time pinpoints the sequence in which events unfold and memory takes form. The Maya developed their complex calendric system in order to locate the events of their lives precisely within this temporal framework. The information featured in their inscriptions—the reason for the existence of those monuments in the first place—is the history of human events. The calendric systems and the manner of recording points in time are the products of history itself.

The day on which I write this is Sunday, August 11, 1985. It is also the 223rd day of the year; the moon is in the fourth quarter; there are 135 shopping days until Christmas; it is a day in the second term of Reagan's presidency; it is a few days after the fortieth anniversary of the dropping of the atomic bomb on Hiroshima (which we perceive to have been the beginning of a new era); it is 142 days to the beginning of the 150th anniversary year of the state of Texas; and it is the year of the 300th anniversary of the births of Handel, Mozart and Bach. We have all experienced each of these ways of referring to a day in our calendar, and we accept them as the normal ways of acknowledging benchmarks in the passage of time. Although the Maya used a different system of benchmarks, their purpose was the same.

The Maya recognized the same kinds of benchmarks as those above, but because their number system was vigesimal, that is, base 20 rather than base 10, their benchmarks fall at different points in a sequence of time. Their way of writing numbers was also different. While we use ten marks in a place-notation system, they used only three signs, also in a place notation system, which was aligned vertically, with the higher values at the top. Their marks were a zero sign (which could be written several ways), a dot for one and a bar for five. Since their number system was vigesimal, the places in their vertical grids stood for 1, 20, 400, 8,000, 160,000, 3,200,000 and so forth. Abraham Lincoln's "four score and seven" is the Maya way of indicating numbers.

The calendar combined many different counts, each an independent cycle running without reference to any other cycle, much like our system of naming days. Sunday, August 11, 1985, is composed of a seven-unit cycle that runs independently of the "August 11"; not all days named August 11 will occur on a Sunday, nor in 1985. The Maya recorded some cycles that appear to have no naturalistic base and others that tracked the periods of various celestial bodies, especially the sun, moon and Venus. Not all cycles were regularly recorded on monuments; many were kept only in specialized books and never recorded publicly.

The counts kept by the Maya were not extraordinarily accurate, as the literature on the Maya often claims. Their calendar was not more accurate than our own, for example, and, in fact, was just about as accurate as the era-based calendar of comparable civilizations. You cannot go far wrong by counting whole days, and all Maya calendric cycles are whole-day counts. When the Maya tried to cope with short, fractional cycles, such as the 29.53-day lunar cycle, they were not particularly accurate, especially when they projected such cycles into the past.[1]

The cycles most often recorded on monuments are the Tzolkin, the Haab, the Long Count, the Calendar Round, the Lord of the Night and the age of the moon. All of these cycles were included in the records of elaborate, very important dates; even so, the scribe could elect to use only a few of them.

The Tzolkin, also called the Sacred Round, is a cycle of 260 days in which individual days are designated by a combination of a number (from 1 to 13) with one of twenty day names. Since the day names are arbitrary, we will use the first twenty letters of the English alphabet (A through T), combined with arabic numerals (1 to 13) to see how the system works.[2] The first day would be 1A; the second, 2B; the thirteenth, 13M—but on the fourteenth day the arabic number cycles back to 1, giving the day name 1N. The twentieth day will be 7T; the twenty-

PLATE 123. Vision Serpent,
detail from Yaxchilan Lintel 25

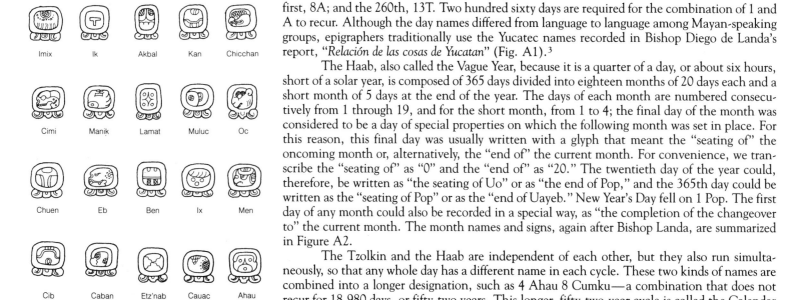

Imix	Ik	Akbal	Kan	Chicchan
Cimi	Manik	Lamat	Muluc	Oc
Chuen	Eb	Ben	Ix	Men
Cib	Caban	Etz'nab	Cauac	Ahau

FIGURE A1 Glyphs and names of the twenty days of the Tzolkin.

first, 8A; and the 260th, 13T. Two hundred sixty days are required for the combination of 1 and A to recur. Although the day names differed from language to language among Mayan-speaking groups, epigraphers traditionally use the Yucatec names recorded in Bishop Diego de Landa's report, *"Relación de las cosas de Yucatan"* (Fig. A1).[3]

The Haab, also called the Vague Year, because it is a quarter of a day, or about six hours, short of a solar year, is composed of 365 days divided into eighteen months of 20 days each and a short month of 5 days at the end of the year. The days of each month are numbered consecutively from 1 through 19, and for the short month, from 1 to 4; the final day of the month was considered to be a day of special properties on which the following month was set in place. For this reason, this final day was usually written with a glyph that meant the "seating of" the oncoming month or, alternatively, the "end of" the current month. For convenience, we transcribe the "seating of" as "0" and the "end of" as "20." The twentieth day of the year could, therefore, be written as "the seating of Uo" or as "the end of Pop," and the 365th day could be written as the "seating of Pop" or as the "end of Uayeb." New Year's Day fell on 1 Pop. The first day of any month could also be recorded in a special way, as "the completion of the changeover to" the current month. The month names and signs, again after Bishop Landa, are summarized in Figure A2.

The Tzolkin and the Haab are independent of each other, but they also run simultaneously, so that any whole day has a different name in each cycle. These two kinds of names are combined into a longer designation, such as 4 Ahau 8 Cumku—a combination that does not recur for 18,980 days, or fifty-two years. This longer, fifty-two-year cycle is called the Calendar Round. Among other groups in Mesoamerica, such as the Aztecs, the fifty-two-year cycle was of major importance and was perceived as a time of renewal, when tools, buildings, sculptures, even households, should be destroyed and made again. Such renewal behavior has often been attributed to the Classic Maya, but evidence from inscriptions does not support this view. The Classic Maya paid very little attention to the repetition of a Calendar Round date as the occasion for anniversary celebrations.

The Lords of the Night are a cycle of nine glyphs, believed to be the names of gods who held office on successive days. The cycle repeats every nine days, but since the combination of the Lord of the Night and a Calendar Round date will not repeat for 467 years, it was used to locate dates far more precisely in time than is possible using just a Calendar Round date. The age of the moon was also recorded, giving the number of days elapsed since the start of a lunation, its position in a lunar half-year of six moons, and its duration as a twenty-nine-day or thirty-day moon. Each of these calendric units is a cyclic count that, like a twelve-hour clock, repeats endlessly.

Linear time was recorded in yet another system, called the Long Count. The fundamental unit of the Long Count was a 360-day year composed of eighteen divisions of twenty days each. The year is called a *tun*, a term derived from the word for "stone," apparently from the practice of erecting a stone to mark the completion of each 360-day period.[4] The twenty-day subdivisions are called a *uinal*, and an individual day is a *kin*, which is also the word for the sun. Twenty tuns formed a *katun* (literally "twenty stones"), and twenty katuns composed a *baktun* (literally "400 stones"). Calculations in this system could be projected into the far distant past and future, if higher units—8,000, 160,000, 3,200,000 and more tuns—were employed.

Dates in the Long Count calendar are written in the place-notation system described above; in this case, however, the glyph for each unit in the calendar (kin, uinal, tun, katun and baktun) follows the number. The numbers are usually recorded in the bar-and-dot system, but, as with other glyphs, the signs of the numbers and the units of the Long Count also have personified variants in both head and full-figure forms. The personifications of these glyphs are often called "gods" because they appear in mythological scenes that decorate pottery.

The base date of the Long Count is written in the modern system of transcription as 13.0.0.0.0. In the Maya calendar system, this day corresponded to 4 Ahau in the Tzolkin, 8 Cumku in the Haab, and it was ruled by the ninth Lord of the Night. From this single alignment of repetitive cycles with the linear progression of the Long Count, the name of every day in history is set. The next day would be 13.0.0.0.1 5 Imix 9 Cumku, with the first Lord of the Night. For the highest number (13) in the Long Count to change, 144,000 days were required. The next position of the highest number is not 14, however, but 1 (1.0.0.0.0 3 Ahau 13 Ch'en). The Long Count on a monument, then, records the number of whole days that had elapsed since this zero day, as well as the name reached in each of the repetitive cycles. The "zero" day in the Maya calendar correlates to August 13, 3114 B.C. The day on which the exhibition, *The Blood of Kings*, opened was 12.18.13.0.3 11 Akbal 16 Uo, and it was ruled by the third Lord of the Night.

Maya birthdays and anniversaries were recorded in this calendar. The end of a katun and its quarter points every fifth year were the occasion of public rites that featured the bloodletting of the king. The shape of time, the symmetry of repeated events, and the connection between the supernatural and the mundane were all couched in the rhythm of the Long Count and set to the endless march of the katuns.

The date on the Leiden Plaque will serve to illustrate how such a date was written in the Maya system (Fig. A3). The first glyph, the Initial Series Introductory Glyph, simply announces that a Long Count date is coming. The main sign is a "drum," read *tun*, and the head above it is the Sun God, the patron of Yaxkin, the month into which this date falls. The next five glyphs are composed of numbers and the signs for the cycles that are being counted, but in this very rare format, the glyphs for the baktun (400 years) and the katun (20 years) are exchanged. Eight, the first number (A2), is followed by the katun "bird," recording "eight 400-year cycles." The next glyph includes the number 14 and the baktun "bird head," recording "fourteen 20-year cycles." The third component has the number 3 and the personification, or god, of the tun (the 360-day year), recording "three years." This tun glyph is particularly wonderful: it is a fish-dragon with a water scroll on its head and a fishfin on its spine; a fish is nibbling on the tail. In iconic form, this is the Water-lily Fish Monster. Together, the first three parts of this date record that eight groups of 400 years (3,200), fourteen groups of 20 years (280), plus three years—for a total of 3,483 years—have passed since the zero date of the Maya calendar. Remember that in the Maya system, the year, or tun, has only 360 days.

The next two glyphs (A5–A6) record the number of months and days that had elapsed in the next year. This is confusing to those accustomed to the Christian calendar, because for us the day after New Year's Day in the first year was January 2, A.D. 1. We have no zero year, but the Maya did. Their calendar works much like the way we record our ages: a child is not one year old until a year after birth. The Leiden Plaque records that the era was 3,483 tuns old. In the next year, one uinal (month) and twelve days had passed. The Leiden date occurred on the thirty-second (20+12) day of the 3,484th tun of the Maya era.

The glyphs recording the twenty-day month and the day are also worth noting. The uinal is personified by a toad monster with a water scroll atop his head, while the personification of the day is Hun-Chuen, the howler monkey god of writing.[5] A fully three-dimensional sculpture of this god is shown in Plate 46.

Thus, the first six glyphs on the Leiden Plaque record the day as the time elapsed since the zero year in a system. The next four glyphs tell us what this day is called in the repetitive cycles explained above. A7 records 8.14.3.1.12 after the zero date, the day 1 Eb is reached in the 260-day Tzolkin cycle. B8 records that on this day, the fifth of the nine Lords of the Night was in power. The date happens to fall on the 120th day of the Haab or the 20th day of Xul. In this instance, the scribe elected to call this day the "seating of Yaxkin," the next month: A8 is *chum*, "seating," and A9 is Yaxkin.

To summarize, the calendric information tells us that the patron of Yaxkin was in power; that eight baktuns, fourteen katuns, three tuns, one uinal and twelve days had ended since the zero date; that this day fell on 1 Eb in the Tzolkin; that the fifth Lord of the Night was in office; and that on this day, the month Yaxkin was seated in the 365-day Haab. In a more convenient system, using our own numbers, we write this day 8.14.3.1.12 5 Eb G5 0 Yaxkin; in our cal-

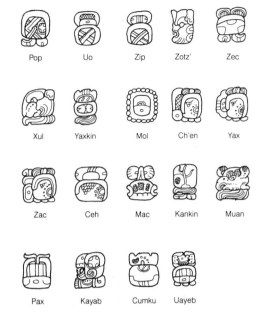

FIGURE A2 Glyphs and names of the nineteen months of the Haab.

Pop · Uo · Zip · Zotz' · Zec
Xul · Yaxkin · Mol · Ch'en · Yax
Zac · Ceh · Mac · Kankin · Muan
Pax · Kayab · Cumku · Uayeb

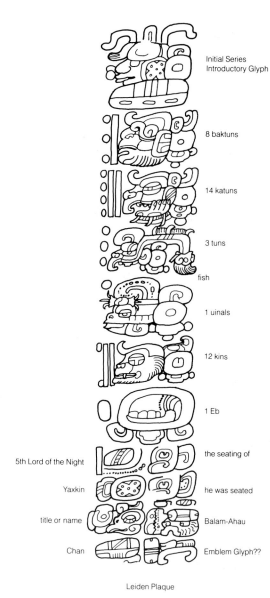

Initial Series
Introductory Glyph

8 baktuns

14 katuns

3 tuns

fish

1 uinals

12 kins

1 Eb

5th Lord of the Night

the seating of

Yaxkin

he was seated

title or name

Balam-Ahau

Chan

Emblem Glyph??

Leiden Plaque

FIGURE A3 Inscription on the rear
of the Leiden Plaque (see also Pl. 33).

endar, it was Friday in the cycle of seven weekdays, September 17 in the cycle of the tropical year, and in the 320th year of the present era—or Friday, September 17, A.D. 320.

Other texts record the date somewhat less elaborately, featuring the event and the actor. La Pasadita Lintel 2 is a good example of this kind of text, and it demonstrates a less orthodox reading order as well. The inscription includes two sentences, one referring to the left figure, the other to the right. The first sentence begins in the center of the panel with the date 7 Ahau 18 Pop; since this Calendar Round date recurs every fifty-two years, we normally could not determine its position accurately in the Long Count. In this case, however, history provides a control. The third glyph is a verb showing a human hand with drops falling from it. It represents the action of the left figure, who drops a long dotted stream from his hands. From the costume he is wearing and from comparing the image to related images from other sites, we know he is dropping blood. The rite is called scattering, and it took place primarily at the ends of katuns or at their quarter points.

The name phrase of the actor completes the sentence. The fourth through the seventh glyphs are called the skygod title, possibly in reference to the actor's affliation with a divinity. The text continues to the frame between the actor's hand with another title and the personal name of the protagonist. A small bird, perhaps a hummingbird, lays atop the head of a jaguar: Proskouriakoff called this name Bird Jaguar.

From other inscriptions at Yaxchilan, we know that Bird Jaguar was born on August 27, A.D. 709, and that the next ruler was in office by January 24, A.D. 779. Since the scattering rite was known to occur at period endings, the date above must fall on a period ending within the range of these two dates. There is only one candidate: 9.16.15.0.0 7 Ahau 18 Pop, or February 19, A.D. 766.

The first sentence continues to the left columns, giving a series of Bird Jaguar's titles. The first glyph says he was a "three-katun lord" (or that he was between forty and sixty tuns old at the time of the event). The next three mark his prowess as a warlord by celebrating him as the "captor of Uc" (B1–B2) and as "he of twenty captives." The last two are the Emblem Glyphs of Yaxchilan. The first sign in both glyphs is the blood he drops into the censer. The upper two signs in both (the round, biscuitlike shapes) read *ahpo*, or "lord." The largest signs in each glyph are the name designations of Yaxchilan—jade in the first, the split sky in the second.

The second person, who assists Bird Jaguar in this scattering rite, is named in the column at the right edge of the picture. The first two glyphs are an undeciphered verb; the third and fourth are his personal names; and the fifth records the title *cahal*, designating a governor.[6] The attendant figure is apparently the governor who ruled La Pasadita for Bird Jaguar. Bird Jaguar, then, crossed the river to celebrate the end of the fifteenth tun with his subordinate.

The Maya seem to have been uncomfortable with the linear nature of time as it is configured in the Long Count, because in their inscriptions they made a concerted effort to underscore the essential symmetry of time by emphasizing cyclic repetition of time and event. The actions of contemporary kings were declared to be the same as those of their near and remote ancestors and the same as those of gods tens of thousands—even millions of years—in the past. The Maya watched the heavens with committed concentration, not so that farmers knew when to plant (they already knew), but so as to detect the repetitive patterns against which history could take form. This symmetry and repetitive flow of events was such a forceful element in the Classic-period conception of history that when the conception was inherited by the Postclassic Yucatec Maya, it became the basis of the katun prophecies. People behaved as if the symmetry of time and thus the repetition of history were inescapable.[7]

Two kinds of dates open particularly meaningful windows into the extraordinary nature of the Maya conception of time: these are special records of the zero date and contrived numbers. On three stelae at Coba, the zero date is recorded with Long Counts that include twenty cycles above the katun, each prefixed by the number thirteen. We write this number in our transcription system:

13.13.13.13.13.13.13.13.13.13.13.13.13.13.13.13.13.13.13.0.0.0.0.

At Yaxchilan, there is another Long Count date corresponding to the day 9.15.13.6.9 3 Muluc 17 Mac, or October 21, A.D. 744. The date is a standard Long Count, one within Bird Jaguar's life, but it is written in a very special way, with eight cycles above the baktun, each prefixed by the number 13 as follows:

13.13.13.13.13.13.13.13.9.15.13.6.9 3 Muluc 17 Mac.

This number is not a Distance Number between two dates; it simply records that for this date, as for all dates in Maya history, the cycles above the baktun are set at thirteen. On this Yaxchilan date those higher cycles had not yet changed, because not enough days had accumulated to cause the odometer of time to click over to the next number. At Palenque, we learn one more fact. In the Temple of Inscriptions, Pacal tied his accession date by Distance Number to the end of the first pictun, the next higher unit after baktun, in the Long Count system. This calculation tells us two important facts: it takes twenty baktuns to make a pictun (or 8,000 years), and the number that follows thirteen in the system is one.

The first thirteen in the Coba dates turned to one after 400 years, on November 15, 2720 B.C. The baktun in which we live, the thirteenth, will end on December 23, A.D. 2012. The pictun unit will turn over to one after 8,000 years, on October 15, A.D. 4772: this is the date Pacal recorded. For the highest of the Coba cycles to change from thirteen to one will take slightly under 142 nonillion years or, in our number system, 142 followed by thirty-six zeros. In our world view, the Big Bang took place only fifteen billion years ago. The scale of the Maya vision of time is staggering by comparison.

The numbers in the Coba date do not mean that on 4 Ahau 8 Cumku, thirteen of each of the Long Count units had been completed. It is clear from the arithmetical operations in Maya inscriptions that the thirteens are functionally zero. They set the symmetry of this universe to replicate the Tzolkin; there are twenty cycles set at thirteen, just as there are twenty day names and thirteen numbers in the Tzolkin. We simply do not know how much time the Maya perceived to have been encompassed by the previous era.

The contrived numbers discovered by Floyd Lounsbury do, however, give another kind of information on how the Maya perceived the structure of time and space to exist.[8] Contrived numbers were used to set a prescribed distance between a date in historical time and one occurring in a previous era (or in the time before the Maya zero date). The distance between these dates was deliberately calculated so that both dates fell at exactly the same position in one or more of the repetitive cycles—including astronomical ones, such as the eclipse and Venus cycles, so important to Maya thought. Furthermore, they always chose the last day before 4 Ahau 8 Cumku in the previous era that could possibly have borne this symmetrical relationship to the historical date. By showing that the two dates had the same shape in time, the Maya declared that the actions and the actors associated with those dates—gods for the mythical dates, kings for the historical ones—were also the same.

The contrived numbers are thus a declaration of the divinity of kings and a demonstration of their sanctity, almost as if the zero date were conceived to be a membrane separating two kinds of space and time, having radically different symmetry and structure—much like matter and antimatter. The contrived numbers are points of sanctity so dense they pierce the membrane, bringing a part of the symmetry of the previous universe into historical space and time. The birth date of Pacal of Palenque was tied in this relationship to the birth date of the Mother of the Gods; the accession of Chaacal III of Palenque was set to echo the accession date of the same goddess. By indicating that these historical dates are made from the same symmetry as the mythological dates, the Maya declare the actors to be made of the same fabric: the human king was god, and his substance was intimately linked to the symmetrical order and matter of the previous creation.

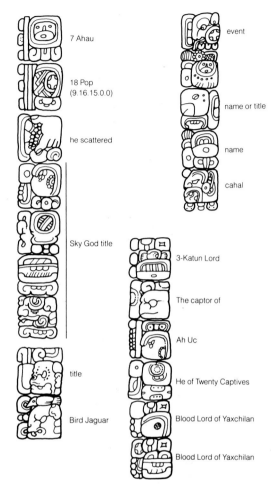

7 Ahau

18 Pop
(9.16.15.0.0)

he scattered

Sky God title

title

Bird Jaguar

event

name or title

name

cahal

3-Katun Lord

The captor of

Ah Uc

He of Twenty Captives

Blood Lord of Yaxchilan

Blood Lord of Yaxchilan

La Pasadita Lintel 2

FIGURE A4 Inscription from La Pasadita Lintel 2 (see also Pl. 76).

NOTES

1. The Maya alternated moon lengths of 29 and 30 days, giving an average moon of 29.5 days, as compared to the actual lunation of 29.530588 days. The fractional remainder was enough to produce a rapidly observable difference between the calculated age of the moon and its observed age. The Maya attempted to compensate by using longer groups of lunations (for example, eighty-one moons at Palenque) that began with two 30-day months, thus adding an extra day to compensate for the accumulating error. Various corrections were used at different times and at different sites, but none of the solutions was particularly accurate. As long as the scribes could check the calculated age against observations of the moon, the ages recorded were accurate; when they projected these calculations into the past, moon ages were always in error.

2. George Stuart developed this approach to explaining the Tzolkin in the Texas Workshops on Maya Hieroglyphic Writing, sponsored by the Institute of Latin American Studies, The University of Texas, 1980–1986.

3. Alfred M. Tozzer, ed. and trans., "Landa's Relación de las cosas de Yucatan: A Translation," *Papers of the Peabody Museum of American Archaeology and Ethnology, Harvard University* 18 (New York: Kraus Reprint Corp., 1966).

4. John S. Justeson and Peter Mathews, in "The Seating of the *Tun*: Further evidence concerning a Late Preclassic Lowland Maya Stela Cult" (*American Antiquity* 48 [1983], pp. 586–593), presented linguistic and glyphic evidence that the word for stone came to mean "year" because of the use of stelae to mark period endings, and that historically this development could have occurred only in a Yucatecan language.

5. Michael D. Coe, "Supernatural Patrons of Maya Scribes and Artists," in *Social Process in Maya Prehistory*, edited by Norman Hammond (New York: Academic Press, 1977), pp. 327–347.

6. This title accompanies secondary figures or the rulers of secondary sites but never occurs with the main king of major sites. Read phonetically as *cahal*, the title appears to designate a governor subordinate to a main king, as well as a member of his family. David Stuart, "Epigraphic Evidence of Political Organization in the Usumacinta Drainage" (unpublished paper) and Peter Mathews and John S. Justeson, "Patterns of Sign Substitution in Mayan Hieroglyphic Writing: The 'Affix Cluster,'" in *Phoneticism in Maya Hieroglyphic Writing*, edited by John S. Justeson and Lyle Campbell (Albany: Institute of Mesoamerican Studies, State University of New York at Albany, 1984), pp. 212–213.

7. Dennis Puleston, in "Epistomological Pathology and the Collapse, or Why the Maya Kept the Short Count" (*Maya Archaeology and Ethnohistory*, edited by Norman Hammond and Gordon R. Willey [Austin: University of Texas Press, 1979], pp. 63–71), has suggested that the katun histories were perceived as prophetic histories in which the patterns of the past were destined to be repeated as a kind of self-fulfilling prophecy. In Puleston's view, the Maya so couched their behavior in terms of this repeating pattern that they based their decisions on its inevitability, thus creating a "self-validating myth, and ultimately a positive feedback mechanism of awesome compass."

8. Floyd G. Lounsbury, "A Rationale for the Initial Date of the Temple of the Cross at Palenque," in *The Art, Iconography, and Dynastic History of Palenque, Part III: Proceedings of the Segunda Mesa Redonda de Palenque*, edited by Merle Greene Robertson (Pebble Beach, Calif.: Robert Louis Stevenson School, 1976), pp. 211–224, and "Maya Numeration, Computation, and Calendrical Astronomy," in *Dictionary of Scientific Biography*, vol. 15, edited by Charles Coulson Gillespie (New York: Charles Scribner's Sons, 1978), pp. 759–818.

The Maya Hieroglyphic Writing System

THE FORMAL STUDY OF THE MAYA WRITING SYSTEM BEGAN IN THE EARLY NINETEENTH
century with the work of an eccentric American naturalist, Constantine Rafinesque, who first
identified the writing system as Maya and correctly deciphered the bar-and-dot system of numeration. The publication of his work in the *Saturday Evening Post* in 1827 and 1828 initiated an
enduring public fascination with the Maya and the meaning of their hieroglyphic writings.
Rafinesque was the first of a long line of brilliant scholars who built the edifice of understanding
that we rely upon today in studying the writing system and the history it records.[1]

By 1950 glyph studies had yielded a working methodology for analyzing arithmetical and
calendrical data in Maya inscriptions. Names of deities and animals had been identified; tables
in the Dresden Codex, used by the Maya to follow the stations of Venus through five-year
periods and to predict eclipses, had been worked out; and other calendric portions of the three
Maya books then known—the Dresden, Madrid and Paris codices—had been analyzed.[2] The
general consensus, voiced by Thompson in 1950, was that the content of the writing system was
nonhistorical.[3] It was primarily ideographic and did not represent a spoken language; therefore,
decipherment was unlikely. This opinion was challenged in 1952 with the publication of a
controversial theory of phoneticism in Maya writing by the young Russian Yuri Knorosov.[4]
Although Knorosov's methods initially met with almost total rejection, they were subsequently
tested and found to be productive. Some of his individual decipherments were incorrect, but his
proposal that, like Egyptian and cuneiform scripts, Maya writing combines logographs, or word
signs, with signs that represent sound alone, was correct.

The second key to the decipherment of hieroglyphic writing was presented by two scholars who approached the writing system from an entirely different perspective. In 1958 Heinrich
Berlin published an analysis of the inscriptions on the sarcophagus from the Temple of Inscriptions at Palenque; he demonstrated that some of the glyphs named the ten figures pictured on its
sides. This was the first identification of names in Classic inscriptions and the first hard evidence
that the inscriptions concerned historical people. A year later he identified Emblem Glyphs,
which he proposed were special glyphs identifying each site, either by the name of its dominant
lineage or by its place name. His discovery assigned glyphic names to places in the Maya geogra-
phy and established a means of studying the political structure of Classic Maya society.[5]

The crucial, breakthrough study of Maya hieroglyphic writing, "Historical Implications
of a Pattern of Dates at Piedras Negras, Guatemala" by Tatiana Proskouriakoff, appeared in
1960. In the 1930s, when Proskouriakoff worked at Piedras Negras as an architectural artist, she
noticed that the stelae were arranged in discrete groups, each set on platforms in front of a
particular building. Later, in studying the inscriptions in each group of stelae, she noted that the
range of dates recorded never exceeded sixty-two years, a span well within human life expectancy. Furthermore, one particular glyph (the so-called upended frog) always accompanied the
earliest date, and a different one (the "toothache") accompanied a second date, which fell
twelve to thirty-one years after the first. Using the imagery represented on these stelae as evidence, she called the "upended frog" glyph with the earlier date the Initial Event, and "toothache," with the later date, the Inaugural Event, suggesting that they corresponded to the birth
of a ruler and his enthronement. From the inscriptions at other sites, she added "capture" and
two bloodletting events, summarizing her findings:

> It seems safe to say that glyphs which immediately follow dates and especially those that tend to
> combine with the "lunar" postfix make reference to actions, events or ceremonies, and are essen-
> tially predicate glyphs. Following them we can expect to find substantives referring to the protago-
> nists of the events, and if the representations are historical, some of these should be appellatives
> identifying the persons involved.[6]

The evidence she presented was so overwhelming and her arguments so elegant that she left no
room for equivocation: the Maya inscriptions are primarily historical. They relate the births,
accessions, wars, deaths and marriages of Maya kings.

day sign   cu in cuch "burden"   head variant

full-figure variant   tun "year"   tun "stone flint
spear blade"

FIGURE B1 Variations in the readings and
graphic representations of the *cauac* glyph.

In the decade following this seminal publication, Proskourikoff and Berlin led other
scholars in applying this new methodology to the Maya inscriptions, with the result that to date,
full or partial reconstructions of the dynastic histories of Yaxchilan, Bonampak, Palenque,
Tonina, Tortuguero, Copan, Quirigua, Naranjo, Caracol, Tikal and many other sites have been
produced. The list of deciphered events has expanded to include heir designation, war, sacrifice,
several other bloodletting rites, the ballgame, death and burial—to name a few—as well as
titles, not only of the kings but also of their wives and subordinate lords, who were part of the
nobility and government structure of the Classic period. The identification of parentage statements in the inscriptions, a most important breakthrough, has led to the establishment of the
descent lines of many sites. At Palenque, for example, it has been possible to reconstruct twelve
generations of kings.[7]

The discovery that inscriptions contain historical information proved an enormous
advantage in the work of decipherment, because it permitted the epigrapher to proceed on the
assumption that whatever was recorded concerned those things that human beings, especially
kings, are likely to do. Normal biological patterns could then be applied to test proposed readings and interpretations. Furthermore, Proskouriakoff and Berlin proved beyond doubt that the
images on Classic Maya sculpture relate to the information written on the same stelae. Ever
since the nineteenth century, this relationship between text and image has been a primary tool
in the decipherment of the codices; until recently, however, it had never been fully tested on the
monuments. The modern study of the pictorial and written systems of the Maya shows that
Maya inscriptions are to the study of Maya art as the *Iliad* and *Odyssey* are to the study of Greek
vase painting. They are the literature of the Classic Maya.

The advantages of the historical approach to decipherment notwithstanding, the final,
vital ingredient necessary to full and successful decipherment was still lacking—namely, a link
between the writing system and the spoken language. Maya hieroglyphs are not a set of abstract
ideographs or mnemonic cues such as the Aztec used to record conquests, place names and
tribute that were designed to be used by a professional reciter. The Maya writing system repro-
duces fully and without restriction the spoken form of language. Most epigraphers and linguists
agree that the Maya Lowlands, from Copan in the east to Palenque in the west, were occupied
by speakers of languages ancestral to the modern Yucatecan and Cholan languages, with
Yucatecan speakers concentrated toward the north and Cholan speakers toward the south. Both
language groups contributed to the development of the writing system, and speakers of both
language families used it. Understanding the linguistic base of the writing system added another
dimension to the process of decipherment.

In 1974 this process began to be explored systematically in a series of mini-conferences
organized by Dumbarton Oaks.[8] Building on the work of Proskouriakoff—in which she posited
an identification of her Event Glyphs as predicates and her Name Glyphs as subjects—a team of
epigraphers applied linguistic and structural methods in order to paraphrase the inscriptions of
Palenque in full sentence and clause structures. The method was productive in a number of
unforeseen ways. The preferred sentence construction in the inscriptions was quickly discovered
to consist of temporal statement/verb/subject, as Proskouriakoff's work had predicted. With this
structural pattern as a starting point, it was possible to identify glyphs as verbs, subjects or
objects, even when the signs occupying those structural positions were undeciphered. It was
found, for example, that the Maya combined two sentences into one, as in the English sentence
"Bird Jaguar captured and sacrificed Jeweled Skull." In the inscriptions, the same statement
would be arranged, "He captured him Jeweled Skull Bird Jaguar and he sacrificed him." To an
English speaker, it is obvious in the English sentence that Bird Jaguar was the agent who performed two actions, but without reference to the normal order of object and subject in the
language of the hieroglyphs, the Maya sentence would defy straightforward analysis. In the
absence of knowledge of the syntactical structure of Maya languages, the interaction between
image and text would be the only means of detecting actor, object and action. Texts not accompanied by an image directly related in content would not be decipherable.

Earlier forms of Mayan language have been reconstructed by historical linguists using comparative and structural methodology.[9] Proposals for deciphering individual glyphs can now be tested against known linguistic values. Linguists are also engaged in reconstructing the grammatical system used in the writing—identifying, for example, suffixes that denote past tense, the passive voice, plurals and possession.[10] Literary conventions, among them couplets and paired oppositions, have been documented. This rapid progress in deciphering the glyphs now permits epigraphers, linguists, archaeologists and art historians to use Maya inscriptions and pictorial records as a primary source of information on the identity of the Maya, their world view and social system. Maya history can now be understood from records describing the events of their lives, written from their own point of view.

The idea of writing was not developed first in Mesoamerica by the Maya. People of the valley of Oaxaca were using a very simple writing system by 600 B.C., and other, as-yet-undeciphered systems were widely used by many groups in southeastern Mesoamerica by the first century B.C. Early examples of writing in the Maya Lowlands are found on portable objects that have been dated stylistically to the Late Preclassic period. The Hauberg Stela (Pl. 66), the earliest dated stela known, carrying a date corresponding to October 9, A.D. 199, marks the appearance of a fully matured writing system. Writing was surely used by the Lowland Maya at a much earlier time, however.

Glyphic texts were inscribed into a grid of blocks set in horizontal and vertical rows. One or more glyphs was placed in each block. The normal reading order within a text is from left to right in pairs of columns; if a text has more than one pair of columns, the first pair is read to the bottom, followed by the second pair, the third pair and so on. Three-column texts sometimes read across all three columns, and texts could also be placed in L-shaped areas, single columns, circles or in other arrangements. Nevertheless, the left-to-right reading order in both texts and glyph blocks predominates, except in mirror-image formats, in which the entire image is reversed. Within a glyph block, signs are also read from left to right and from top to bottom, although sign order is subject to greater variability. Head variants, glyphs personified in the form of human or animal heads, usually face toward the direction of reading, and numbers are usually placed in front of or above other glyphs.

Individual glyphs are of three types: logographs, each representing a whole word; phonetic signs, representing the sound of a syllable (usually a consonant plus a vowel or, more rarely, either a vowel or a vowel plus consonant); and semantic signs, specifying one of many potential meanings. Words may be written with logographic signs, or as a logograph with a syllabary sign attached to it as a "helper sign," called a phonetic complement, to specify how the initial or final consonant should be pronounced. Words could also be spelled phonetically by use of these syllabic signs in combination. The spelling of a consonant-vowel-consonant word, such as *kuch* ("vulture"), will use two syllabary signs, *ku* and *chu*. The second vowel was not pronounced, and, where possible, it echoed the sound of the first vowel. Other helper signs, called semantic determinatives, help to specify particular meanings rather than particular sounds.

In Maya, signs that were derived from natural forms remained far closer to the original sources than did most other writing known from the ancient world. The glyph for house looks like a house; those for animals, objects of everyday use or gods were often simply portraits of the original models. Even so, these signs were not necessarily used only for representing the original object, nor were they always used with a consistent value. For example, the *cauac* sign has one value (*cauac* or *chauc*) as a day sign, another (*cu*) as a phonetic sign, another (*tun*, "year") as a logograph, and another (*tun*, "stone") as an icon (Fig. B1). The value intended was signaled by one of the "helper signs" discussed above (a phonetic complement and semantic determinative), or the reader was expected to ascertain the appropriate alternative from the context.

Furthermore, each value of a sign has several different forms, including a simple or geometric form and a personified form, which in turn could be animal or human and depicted as a head or as a full figure. Many personified forms can be easily recognized because they include the primary diagnostic features of the simple form; others, however, are graphically unrelated to the

day sign

human form

vulture form

rodent form

phonetic a-ah-wa ahaw

ahau

FIGURE B2 Various ways that *ahau*, "lord," can be written.

vulture as ahau

vulture as ti

FIGURE B3 The vulture sign written as *ahau*, "lord," and *ta*, "to, from, with."

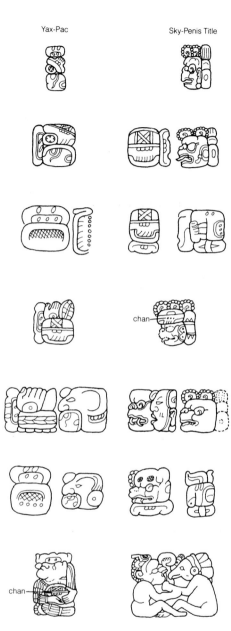

Yax-Pac   Sky-Penis Title

chan—

chan—

FIGURE B4 Comparative examples of the
glyphic name of Yax-Pac, a ruler of Copan.

simple forms and have been discovered only when patterns of substitution have clearly demonstrated equivalence. Many of these unlikely equivalences remain to be discovered. Syllabic values could also be written with many different signs, each having its own set of personified forms,
and some signs represent words that were pronounced differently in Yucatecan and Cholan
languages, so that more than one sound value could be attached to them. The use of the glyph
for vulture is a good example of how one sign can be used in different ways . In the codices, a
vulture head is often used simply as the glyph "vulture." However, in the Classic inscriptions, it
was used to write the day name and the title *ahau*, which could also be written in its simple form,
in anthropomorphic and zoomorphic personified forms or in various syllabic forms (Fig. B2).
When a vulture head was used as *ahau*, it always appears with the headband crown of Maya
kings to ensure that the vulture (or for that matter, the head of a human or any other creature)
was read with the meaning *ahau*, "lord" (Fig. B3). However, vulture glyphs could also refer to
the black-headed vulture, which was called *tahol* ("excrement head"). Using the vulture name
to represent the word *ta'*, "excrement," the scribes used the same vulture glyph without the *ahau*
scarf to stand for the word *ta*, which is a preposition meaning "to, on, with, from." This use of a
sign to represent a homonym is called a rebus. Notice that both as *ahau* and as the syllable *ta*,
the meaning "vulture" is not applied to the sign at all.

The placement of glyphs in the glyph block was another variable in the writing system.
Logographs could occupy a single glyph block; more often, however, a block also contained
affixes (small signs usually placed on the outer boundaries of the block) and larger glyphs, which
have traditionally been called "main signs," because of their prominence within the glyph
block. Two different glyphs could be compounded into a single glyph, or the diagnostic signs of
different glyphs could be placed within one contour in a form of writing called a conflation. The
most extreme variation occurs in the standard rim text used frequently on pottery, called the
Primary Standard Sequence.[11] This text consists of only a few standard glyphs, composed of one
or more signs. Each sign, whether a main sign, grammatical affix, syllabary sign or phonetic
complement, may be drawn in either simple or personified form, then combined with other
signs in one block. On the other hand, each of the signs can appear in its own individual block.
The same sequence may occupy as few as five or six blocks on one text, while it may require
fifteen or sixteen blocks on another, and yet both versions are equivalent. It is little wonder,
then, that this specialized inscription went unrecognized for so long, and that since its discovery,
it has eluded decipherment.

Finally, artistry and expertise in the art of writing seems to have been judged not only by
standards of calligraphy and the conventions of literature but by the measure of innovative and
humorous uses of substitution and word play, in both the lexicon and the visual identity of signs.
The Maya were magnificent visual punsters, a skill that is now only beginning to be appreciated.
The scribes at Copan during the Late Classic period seem to have been the most advanced in the
pursuit of this art. To the epigrapher struggling to unravel these complex inscriptions, it seems as
if the Copan scribes agreed among themselves never to write a king's name twice in exactly the
same way. Yax-Pac's name and titles, for example, are written in a plethora of different forms
(Fig. B4); while each appears different visually, the word or sound values of each variation are
exactly the same (Fig. B5).

A simple glyphic sentence is always composed of a statement specifying the time of the
action, a verb and its subject; transitive constructions take the form temporal-verb-object-sub-
ject. Phrases that simply name the actor often occur without a date or with a generalized verb
only, such as "he was." Texts may consist of one or more sentences. Time is usually specified by a
date, although dates may be omitted when a text occurs in the middle of the scene it describes.
When more than one action is recorded, the dates of the actions are linked by spans of time,
called Distance Numbers, that record the amount of time that elapsed between the two events.
When more than one action is recorded for a single actor, a compound sentence structure can be
used. Mayan sentence structure is different from that of English, but the principle is the same as
in the English sentence "John picked up the pen and wrote."

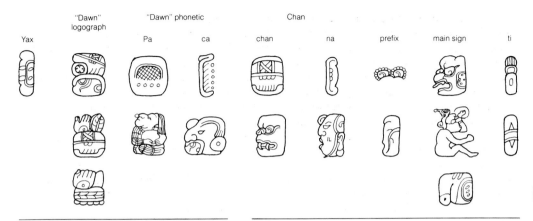

| Yax | "Dawn" logograph | "Dawn" phonetic | | Chan | | | | | |
| | | Pa | ca | chan | na | prefix | main sign | | ti |

FIGURE B5 The substitution pattern in Yax-Pac's name.

personal name   sky-penis title

Maya inscriptions usually refer directly to the pictorial scenes they accompany. The picture is like an illustration of the text and provides a type of information difficult to incorporate into a short text. The pictured event may also be placed in historical context by its being linked to related events that occurred earlier or later. The names of actors are given in simple or elaborate form. Titles record affiliation with gods, offices held, great actions of the past (such as the conquest of prestigious captives) or postures or responsibilities characteristic of the person, lineage affiliation and, most important, the parentage of the protagonist. Because the sanctification of authority was a divine prerogative, religious subject matter, in the form of named gods or narrative mythology, also occurs frequently. Maya inscriptions record the actions of kings, their captains and families and invoke the divine sources of legitimacy and social authority.

The literacy of ancient Maya society is still debated among researchers, with some assuming that literacy existed among a professional scribal class only; others argue for literacy among the entire elite class. We may never know with certainty who could read the inscriptions, but it seems certain that the Maya very probably had a low rate of literacy compared to modern society, with its emphasis on universal literacy. The authors believe it likely that most of the elite were educated to read and write and that calligraphic art was one of the skills expected of an accomplished noble. Merchants were probably literate as well, and any artisan who worked with glyphs certainly read and wrote. Most Maya of the lower classes (farmers, for example) were very probably illiterate, as has been the case with most societies like that of the Maya throughout history. It is likely, however, that every Maya would have been able to recognize some signs—perhaps the bar-and-dot numbers, the day and month signs and the names of their rulers; after all, if a modern tourist can recognize such signs, it is reasonable to suspect that a Maya peasant could have done the same. Literacy is not required to recognize the image of a jaguar head, nor to associate that picture with a king named Jaguar, especially if the "reader" knew the name of his king and expected to see it on a monument. In general, the texts on public monuments in public spaces tend to be short and directly related to the imagery. Since the information on public monuments was addressed to the general populace, it was in the interest of the scribe and the ruler to represent that information in a form that could be understood, at least on the simplest levels, such as the recognition of portrait signs. Texts recorded on relatively inaccessible parts of architecture, in specialized books or on private objects, such as pottery, tools and jewelry, are longer, and sentence structure and literary form are often more complex.

NOTES

1. For a more detailed history of hieroglyphic research, see George Stuart's historical study in *Ancient Maya Writing* (Austin: University of Texas Press, forthcoming) and David Kelley's *Deciphering the Maya Script* (Austin: University of Texas Press, 1976).

2. Three of the four Maya books were discovered in libraries or archives in Europe and were published in the late nineteenth century. These three—the Dresden, the Madrid and the Paris Codices—are named for the cities in which they now reside. The fourth codex was published by Michael D. Coe in *The Maya Scribe and His World* (New York: Grolier Club, 1973), after it had been first exhibited in a 1971 show, sponsored by the Grolier Club, that featured the art of Maya writing. Now in the National Museum of Anthropology in Mexico City, it is known as the Grolier Codex.

3. J. Eric S. Thompson, *Maya Hieroglyphic Writing: An Introduction*, 3rd edition (Norman: University of Oklahoma Press, 1971), pp. 15, 19, 35, 48–50, 63–65.

4. The first version of this paper was published in *Sovietskaya etnografiya* 3 (1952), pp. 100–118. An authorized Spanish translation was published as *La escritura de los antiguos mayas (ensaya de decrifrado)* (Moscow: Academy of Sciences, 1955), and an English translation was published in *The Current Digest of the Soviet Press* 4, no. 50, pp. 3–9.

5. Heinrich Berlin, "El glifo 'emblema' en las inscripciones mayas," *Journal de la Société des Américanistes*, 1958, pp. 119–121, and idem, "Glifos nominales in el sarcophago de Palenque," in *Humanidades* 2 (1959), pp. 1–8.

6. Tatiana Proskouriakoff, "Historical Implications of a Pattern of Dates at Piedras Negras, Guatemala," *American Antiquity* 25 (1960), p. 470.

7. Christopher Jones, "Inauguration Dates of Three Late Classic Rulers at Tikal, Guatemala," *American Antiquity* 42 (1977), pp. 28–60, and Linda Schele, Peter Mathews and Floyd Lounsbury, "Parentage Statements in Classic Maya Inscriptions" (paper presented at the International Conference on Maya Iconography and Hieroglyphic Writing, Guatemala City, 1977).

8. Following the first Mesa Redonda de Palenque, held in December 1973, Elizabeth Benson sponsored a series of mini-conferences, held at Dumbarton Oaks in Washington, D.C., concentrating on the inscriptions of Palenque. The participants were Linda Schele, Peter Mathews, Merle Robertson, Floyd Lounsbury and David Kelley. Called regularly between 1974 and 1979, these conferences were amazingly productive, with each one yielding new decipherments and pioneering new analytical approaches to decipherment. Perhaps the most important contribution was the forging of a team methodology in which the skills and experiences of different individuals were combined into an effective way of working that no single participant could have achieved an as individual. These conferences have in many ways been pivotal to the astonishing progress in decipherment that has been achieved since 1973.

9. Terrence Kaufman and William Norman have used these comparative methods to reconstruct proto-Cholan, the language believed to have been ancestral to one used in the hieroglyphic script. They have been able to reconstruct rules of grammar and syntax as well as an extensive lexicon. Terrence S. Kaufman and William M. Norman, "An Outline of Proto-Cholan Phonology, Morphology, and Vocabulary," in *Phoneticism in Maya Hieroglyphic Writing*, edited by John S. Justeson and Lyle Campbell (Albany: Institute of Mesoamerican Studies, State University of New York at Albany, 1984), pp. 77–167.

10. The most successful application of these linguistic approaches can be seen in *Phoneticism in Maya Hieroglyphic Writing*.

11. The Primary Standard Sequence is a standard text used on Classic-period pottery. Since it occurs with many different types of scenes and was used with many different styles of painting, we believe it to be some sort of ritual text. (Michael D. Coe, *The Maya Scribe and His World*, pp. 17–22 and 158–159).

Suggestions for Further Reading

Benson, Elizabeth P. *The Maya World*. Rev. ed. New York: Thomas Crowell, 1977.

Coe, Michael D. *The Maya*. 3rd ed. London: Thames and Hudson, 1984.

———. *The Maya Scribe and His World*. New York: The Grolier Club, 1973.

Corpus of Maya Hieroglyphic Inscriptions. Vols. 1-6. Cambridge, Mass.: Peabody Museum of Archaeology and Ethnology, Harvard University, 1977–present.

Hammond, Norman. *Ancient Maya Civilization*. New Brunswick, N.J.: Rutgers University Press, 1982.

Kubler, George. *Studies in Classic Maya Iconography*. *Memoirs of the Connecticut Academy of Arts and Sciences*, vol. 18. New Haven: Connecticut Academy of Arts and Sciences, 1969.

Miller, Mary Ellen. *The Art of Mesoamerica, from Olmec to Aztec*. London: Thames and Hudson, 1986.

———. *The Murals of Bonampak*. Princeton: Princeton University Press, 1986.

Morley, Sylvanus G. *The Ancient Maya*. 4th rev. and enlarged ed., edited by Robert L. Sharer. Palo Alto, Calif.: Stanford University Press, 1983.

———. *The Inscriptions of Peten*. Carnegie Institution of Washington Pub. 437. 5 vols. Washington, D.C.: Carnegie Institution of Washington, 1937–1938.

National Geographic Society. *People and Places of the Past: The Illustrated Cultural Atlas of the Ancient World*. Washington, D.C.: National Geographic Society, 1983.

Proskouriakoff, Tatiana. *An Album of Maya Architecture*. Carnegie Institution of Washington Pub. 558. Washington, D.C.: Carnegie Institution of Washington, 1946.

———. *A Study of Classic Maya Art*. Carnegie Institution of Washington Pub. 593. Washington, D.C.: Carnegie Institution of Washington, 1950.

Robertson, Merle Greene, gen. ed. *Palenque Round Table Series (Mesa Redonda de Palenque)*. Vols. 1-4, Pebble Beach, California: Robert Louis Stevenson School, 1974-79. Vol. 5, Austin: University of Texas Press, 1980. Vols. 6-7, San Francisco: Pre-Columbian Art Research Institute, 1985-86.

———. *The Sculpture of Palenque*. Vol. 1, *The Temple of Inscriptions*. Vol. 2, *The Early Buildings of the Palace and the Wall Paintings*. Vol. 3, *The Late Buildings of the Palace*. Princeton: Princeton University Press, 1983–1986.

Robicsek, Francis, and Donald M. Hales. *The Maya Book of the Dead: The Ceramic Codex*. Charlottesville: University of Virginia Art Museum, 1981.

Schele, Linda. *Maya Glyphs: The Verbs*. Austin: University of Texas Press, 1982.

———. *Notebook for the Maya Hieroglyphic Writing Workshop at Texas*. Austin: Institute of Latin American Studies, 1978—present.

Spinden, Herbert J. *A Study of Maya Art*. *Memoirs of the Peabody Museum of Archaeology and Ethnology*, vol. 6. Cambridge, Mass.: Peabody Museum of Archaeology and Ethnology, Harvard University, 1913.

Stuart, George E., and Gene S. Stuart. *The Mysterious Maya*. Washington, D.C.: National Geographic Society, 1977.

Tedlock, Dennis. *Popol Vuh: The Definitive Edition of the Mayan Book of the Dawn of Life and the Glories of Gods and Kings*. New York: Simon and Schuster, 1985.

Thompson, J. Eric S. *Maya Hieroglyphic Writing: An Introduction*. Carnegie Institution of Washington Pub. 589. Washington, D.C.: Carnegie Institution of Washington, 1950.

Weaver, Muriel Porter. *The Aztecs, Maya, and Their Predecessors: Archaeology of Mesoamerica*. 2nd ed. New York: Academic Press, 1981.

INDEX

U-Kix-Chaan of Palenque, 114

Woman from Palenque, 71, 82, 143

Yax-Pac of Copan, 14, 64, 71, 82, 112, 113, 116, 122, 124–126, 140, 143, 151, 152, 154, 257, 326–327

Yax-Kuk-Mo of Copan, 126

Zac-Balam of Xcalumkin, 226

General Index

Bold face numerals indicate objects shown in *Blood of Kings* exhibition.

Abaj Takalik, 26–27, 34

Acasaguastlan, San Agustin, pot, 134, 178, 179, 181, 191, 192, 193, 195, 207–208, 308, **Pl. 73**

Accession, 14, 17, 49, 59 n.47, 69, 108–117, 122–125, 143, 215–216, 220, 222 n.12, 226, 228, 277, 303–304, 321, 323; ascension motif, 118 n.11; rituals of, 109–110, 116, 120. *See also* Hieroglyphic texts, decipherment of

Afterlife, beliefs about, 73, 265–288. *See also* Death, Underworld

Agriculture, 10, 56 n.1, 105–106, 144, 305, 305 n.1; raised fields, 25–26, 55, 58 n.31, 182, 267; slash and burn, 10, 19, 23, 25; abundance in, 10, 46

Aguateca, 58 n.37; Stela 2, 221, n.5

Akbal (darkness, night), 41, 43, 54, 81, 183, 193, 244, 265, 282, 308

Altars, 46, 110, 271, 281, 287

American Museum of Natural History: Carved Bone, 269, 285, 295, **Pl. 112**; Figurine of Dwarf, 138, 150, 160, **Pl. 41**; Figurine of a Lord Letting Blood, 180, 192, 203, **Pl. 69**; Incised Vase with Vision Scene, 302–303, 307 n.7, 308, 314, **Pl. 120**; Warrior Vase, 215, 226–227, 236–237, **Pl. 88**

Ancestors, 14, 36, 43, 48, 72–73, 124–126, 149, 182, 266, 268–269, 275, 277, 285, 304, 306 n.1; recall of, 83, 113, 116, 123, 124, 175, 177; worship of, 42, 149

Animation of objects, 42–43, 73, 75 n.3, 76. *See also* Personification

Animals, 32, 42–43; ants, 244; butterfly, 213; caiman, crocodile 10–11, 27, 43, 122, 181, 306 n.2, 310; deer, 10, 43, 45, 143, 145, 151, 152, 155, 303; deer-jaguar, 285; dog, 266, 270, 271, 274, 287; firefly, 266, 287; fish, 43, 46, 119, 182, 266, 280; jaguar, 10, 26, 50–51, 55, 69, 79, 119, 213, 267, 281, 306 n.3, 320; monkeys, 10, 52, 138–139, 147 n.25, 270, 271, 319; iguanas, 193, 270, 271; peccary, 10, 217, 280; rabbit, 10, 32, 55, 153, 245, 252, 254 n.20, 258, 271, 286, 303, 308; rat, 250; shark, 10, 56 n.2; turtle, 54, 217

Anthropomorphs, 42–43, 51, 53, 268

Apotheosis, 78, 113, 265, 272. *See also* Afterlife; Death; Rebirth; Underworld

Archaeology, history and discovery, 18–25; history of objects, 75 n.5, n.6, n.13, n.16, 118 n.8, n.10, 151, 254 n.19; 277 n.1; settlement pattern and population, 20, 23, 74 n.21, n.28, 105, 305

Architecture, 9, 23, 26, 30, 32, 34–35, 109, 116, 137, 301, 305; acropolis compounds, 112, 122; ballcourts, 134, 243, 245, 247; corbel vault in, 35, 215; dedication and termination ritual for, 62 n.60, 75 n.3, 176, 195, 247, 270, 286; defensive, 218; funerary, 75 n.4, n.5,

n.6, n.11, n.13, 134, 148, 152, 221 n.10, 247, 268–269, 270, 271, 278 n.13, 282; exterior ornament, 34–35, 145 n.2, 105, 179, 281; masks on, 26–27, 75 n.3, 80, 106, 108, 110–111, 120, 281; monster mouth doors of, 113, 122, 144, 154, 302, 304; palaces, 142, 144, 145 n.2, n.35, 153, 154, 180, 247, 269; plazas and courtyards, 35, 177–178; residential, 35, 75 n.11, 80, 104, 134, 145 n.1; stairs in, 217–218, 246; symbolic function of, 15, 63, 105, 106–107, 110, 112, 113, 116, 122–124, 151, 269, 217, 269, 301, 302

Art, Maya, 220, 302, 305; addressed to the gods, 123, 302, 307 n.1; anatomical representations; architecture in, 37, 116, 187, 192, 211, 215, 255, 269, 285–286; canons in, 35, 111, 120; chiaroscuro in, 35, 59 n.44, 227; conventions (traditions) in, 32, 40, 41, 63, 66, 178, 180; episodic narrative in, 37–38, 180, 192, 274, 286; foreshortening in, 37, 121, 153; framing devices in, 37, 45, 47, 154, 282, 304, 310, Pl. 122; function of, 30, 32, 40, 42, 63, 73, 75 n.5, 103, 106, 113, 117, 124, 210, 211, 213, 306 n.1; funerary, 152, 266–271, 274, 280–288; groundlines and registers in, 36, 125, 134, 272; line in, 35–36, 38–39, 151, 155, 216; mass-production of, 40, 150; master artists, 39 (*see also* Artists); mistakes in, 39, 59 n.47; moments in narrative, 37, 38, 41, 124, 216, 246; narrative in, 41, 50, 103, 109, 111, 153, 178, 211, 215, 223, 257, 274, 286–287, 308, 310; oppositions in, 45, 51, 143; patronage of, 41, 153, 216; portraits in, 22, 40, 44, 64, 73, 75 n.3, n.4, 107, 110, 118 n.10, 143, 228, 268, 281, 285; private use of, 35, 155, 179; public art, 34, 39, 41, 104–105, 109, 211; eroticism in, 143–144, 147 n.25, 153; spatial devices in, 35–38, 193; style of, 32, 119, 154; techniques of, 40, 192–193, 223, 308; tension in, 15–16, 38, 252; text-image relationship, 15, 41, 119, 177, 324, 326; three-dimensional in, 32, 38, 43, 122, 140, 141, 150, 151, 154, 213, 267, 280, 282

Artisans, 40, 52, 59 n.47, 142

Artists, as tribute, 142–143; rank of, 40; Cookie Cutter Master at Yaxchilan, 37, 176, 186, 211, 216, 223; Master of the Pink Glyphs, 153, 216, 227, **Pl. 92**; Fenton Painter, 147 n.26, 153; One Hand Painter, 214, 224, **Pl. 84**

Astronomy, 16, 19, 42, 113, 123, 269, 278 n.6; North Star, 269, 277; uses of, 42, 106, 108, 278 n.8, n.11, 287, 303–304, 306 n.3, 320–321

Axis mundi. *See* World Tree

Aztecs, 15, 19, 20, 21, 23, 25, 150, 214, 218, 223, 224, 246; Eagle Knight, 223; Great Temple, 223, 224, 243; Aztec rituals, 147 n.24, 243; Aztec kings, 243; pochteca, 19; Tenochtitlan, 246

Ballgame, 17, 32, 37, 241–264, 253 n.7, 254 n.17, 255, 256; Aztec rules of, 242; ball of, 242, 244, 245, 249, 251, 252, 253 n.7, 255, 256; defeat in, 243, 248, 256; equipment of, 242, 248, 252, 253 n.6, 255, 256, 257; in Europe, 241; gambling in, 242, 243; rules of, 245, 247; sacrifice in, 58 n.37, 243–244, 245, 247, 248, 249, 251, 255, 256; scoring in, 243, 245, 253 n.6, 254 n.22; on stairs, 247, 249, 250. *See also* Architecture, ballcourts

Baltimore Museum of Art: Captive Figurine, 218, 228, 240, **Pl. 94**; Jade Pectoral, 35, Fig. 11

Beards, 45, 46, 49, 50, 52, 152, 154, 155, 228

Bench. *See* Throne

Birds, 38, 42–43, 54, 74 n.7, 139, 143, 175, 181, 257, 308, 319; cormorant, 10; hummingbird, 10, 63, 255, 320; macaw, 67, 266, 281; owl, 120, 148, 213, 243–244; parrots, 67, 147 n.12, 192, 270, 270, 281; quetzal, 10, 67, 126, 147 n.12; vulture, 325–326

Birth, rituals for, 50, 76, 178, 183; miraculous, 34, 244. *See also* Gods, birth of

Blood, 14, 43, 44, 47, 48, 60 n.56, 110–112, 122, 144, 145, 175, 180, 181, 183, 198, 195, 196, 211, 215, 216, 217, 220, 226, 267, 268, 281, 283, 301, 304, 311, 320; bloodscroll, 61 n.61, 112, 177, 183, 186, 190, 193, 221 n.8, 268, 284, 304, 310; meaning for Maya society, 14, 78, 220, 305; symbols of, 15, 48, 60 n.52, 176, 184 n.3, 278 n.6, 284

Bloodletting, 9, 17, 38, 49, 71–72, 84, 110, 117, 124, 148, 149, 150, 151, 175–209, 184 n.7, 210–211, 213, 215, 216, 224, 226, 253, 256, 278 n.11, 285, 301, 303–304, 309, 319–320, 323; bloodletting bowls, 45, 72, 114, 116, 126, 177–178, 180–181, 187, 190, 192, 194, 211, 268, 283–284, 304; by gods, 181, 193–194; endorphines in, 177; function of, 17, 124–126, 178, 179, 181, 193; pain in, 177; penis mutilation, 110, 117, 178, 180, 181, 192, 193, 196; rope in, 177, 178, 181, 186, 187, 189, 192, 194, 224; tongue mutilation, 175, 176, 177, 192. *See also* Cloth, cut; Paper; Stingray spines; Vision quest

Bonampak, Murals, 24, 29, 35–38, 40, 49, 68, 110, 112, 116, 138, 148, 145 n.2, 147 n.17, 155, 156–158, 184 n.10, 190, 193, 210, 215–217, 226, 302, Fig. V.6, Pl. 38; Sculpture Panel 1, 67, 112, 113, Fig. II.8; Stela 1, 45, 227

Bone, 60 n.52; 228, 271, 277, 280, 285; awls, 52, 176, 186, 228, **Pl. 61**; carved, 152, 215, **Pl. 60**, **Pl. 49**, Pl. 50b; as handles, 143, 152, 285

British Museum: Carved Spondylus Shell, 214, 226, 232, **Pl. 85**; Fenton Vase, 144, 147 n.26, 150, 153–154, 170–171, 218–219, **Pl. 54**; Jade Plaque from Teotihuacan, 111, 122, 130, **Pl. 34**; Lubaantun Jade Plaques, 70, 75 n.10, 80, Pl. 16; Mask from Laguna, 37, 69, 80, 93, 191, **Pl. 15**; Nohmul Bar Pectoral, 70, 81, 97, **Pl. 20**; Olmec Jade Pectoral, 107, 119, 128, **Pl. 31**; Pomona Earflare, 68, 75 n.5, 79, 90, Pl. 9; Pusilha Deity Plaque, 72, 83, 100, **Pl. 23**. *See also* Copan, Yaxchilan

Brooklyn Museum Reused Pendant, 140, 151, 163, Pl. 45

Bundles, 71, 72, 114, 117, 124, 144, 152, 192, 213, 221 n.10, 279, n.13

Burials, 12, 22, 39, 64, 70, 71, 75 n.10, n.11, n.13, 82, 104, 117 n.1, 150, 154, 175, 218, 221 n.10, 226, 256, 277 n.5, 280; rituals, 282, 286, 324

Cacaxtla, 147 n.17, 251, 256

Cache, 75 n.17, 118 n.8, 175, 277 n.5, 282; lip to lip, 48, 52, 61 n.60, 195

Calendar, explanation of, 15, 16–17, 31, 59 n.47, 317–321, 322 n.4, 326; anniversaries in, 319; arithmetic and numbers, 317, 319, 321, 323; Calendar Round, 16–17, 317–320; day and month names, 221 n.8, 253 n.3, 318–319; Haab, 317–318; katun prophecies, 17, 320, 322 n.7; Long Count, 19, 26, 46, 76, 109, 182, 191, 249, 317–318, 320–321; lunar

THE BLOOD OF KINGS
was produced for the
KIMBELL ART MUSEUM
by PERPETUA PRESS, Los Angeles
Edited by LETITIA O'CONNOR and SYLVIA TIDWELL
Designed by DANA LEVY
Typeset in GOUDY OLD STYLE typefaces by
CONTINENTAL TYPOGRAPHICS, Chatsworth, CA
Printed in Japan